CONTEMPOR
POLICING

CW00968859

Controversies, Challenges, and Solutions

An Anthology

Quint C. Thurman
Southwest Texas State University

Jihong Zhao
University of Nebraska at Omaha

Preface by
Samuel Walker
University of Nebraska at Omaha

Roxbury Publishing Company
Los Angeles, California

Library of Congress Cataloging-in-Publication Data

Contemporary policing: controversies, challenges, and solutions: an anthology / Quint C. Thurman, Jihong Zhao.
p. cm.
Includes bibliographical references.
ISBN 1-931719-11-X
1. Police—United States. 2. Police Administration—United States. 3. Law enforcement—United States. I. Zhao, Jihong. II. Title.

HV8141.T483 2004
363.2'068—dc21 2003043190

Copyright © 2004 by Roxbury Publishing Company. All rights reserved under International and Pan American Copyright Conventions. No part of this publication may be reproduced, stored in a retrieval system, or transmitted in any form or by any means, electronic, photocopying, recording, or otherwise, without prior permission of the publisher.

Publisher: Claude Teweles
Managing Editor: Dawn VanDercreek
Production Editor: Sacha A. Howells
Production Assistant: Renée Ergazos
Typography: SDS Design, info@sds-design.com
Cover Design: Marnie Kenney

Printed on acid-free paper in the United States of America. This book meets the standards for recycling of the Environmental Protection Agency.

ISBN 1-931719-11-X

ROXBURY PUBLISHING COMPANY
P. O. Box 491044
Los Angeles, California 90049-9044
Voice: (310) 473-3312 • Fax: (310) 473-4490
Email: roxbury@roxbury.net
Website: www.roxbury.net

Contents

Acknowledgments ix

Preface x

Introduction 1

Part I: New Policing Strategies

Introduction 7

1. Trust and Confidence in Criminal Justice 8

Lawrence W. Sherman

While public confidence in the criminal justice system is fairly low, support for the police is substantially higher. Sherman challenges the police and other component parts of the justice system to treat people fairly, keep local residents informed, and listen more carefully to public concerns in order to earn citizens' trust and enhance public safety.

2. Defining Police Strategies: Problem Solving, Problem-Oriented Policing and Community-Oriented Policing 18

Ronald V. Clarke

Clarke offers a review of the contribution of problem solving to policing based upon observations from several hundred applications submitted for PERF's Herman Goldstein Award for Excellence in Problem-Oriented Policing.

3. New Skyline. 25

Eli B. Silverman

Silverman offers insight into the development of CompStat in the New York City Police Department in the late 1990s, which led to a dramatic turnaround in public safety in the nation's largest city.

4. The Third Generation of Community Policing: Moving Through Innovation, Diffusion, and Institutionalization 39

Willard M. Oliver

This chapter traces the evolution of the community policing movement in the U.S. from its origins twenty years ago through its widespread acceptance by the end of the twentieth century. Oliver reasons that despite growing institutionalization, the future of the movement, now in its third stage, is unclear and difficult to predict.

Part II: Promising Approaches to Crime Reduction and Prevention

Part III: Challenging Issues in the Internal Police Environment

Part IV: Challenging Issues in the External Police Environment

Part V: Innovations, Boundary Spanning, and Capacity Building

Part VI: Police Deviance and Ethical Issues

Part VII: The Challenges Ahead

Acknowledgments

The authors of *Contemporary Policing: Controversies, Challenges, and Solutions* spent several months developing the outline for this work, several more months making adjustments in our selections based upon reviewers' comments and the availability of newer scholarship, and additional time tracking down permissions and making final preparations. Accordingly, there are many people we wish to acknowledge for their help during this lengthy process.

First, we wish to thank our wives, Caryn and Ping, and our children, Nathan, Nicholas, Sarah, and Evan for their support and patience during the entire process. Making the world a better place for those we love and care deeply about truly is an inspiration for pressing ahead at those times when we might otherwise begin to wonder if we could just leave it to others to produce textbooks for teaching the next generation of criminal justice scholars and practitioners.

Second, we would like to acknowledge two sets of reviewers who helped us shape this work into a useful and worthwhile product. Their wisdom is greatly appreciated for broadening our perspective and simultaneously encouraging us to think through our pedagogical goals concerning this text. The early set of readers included Mark Alley, Michigan State University; Ricky S. Gutierrez, California State University, Sacramento; Richard Holden, Central Missouri State University; Ronald Hunter, State University of West Georgia; James Lasley, California State University, Fullerton; Ken Peak, University of Nevada, Reno; Roy Roberg, San José State University; Joseph A. Schafer, Southern Illinois University at Carbondale; and Gerald Williams, University of Colorado. Round two reviewers included Rhonda Allen, California State University, Fullerton; Tom Barker, Eastern Kentucky University; Dean J. Champion, Jr., Laselle College; Dana DeWitt, Chadron State University; Brian Forst, American University; Jim Golden, University of Arkansas at Little Rock; Patricia Joffer, Mesa State College; Peter Kraska, Eastern Kentucky University; Kenneth Novak, University of Missouri–Kansas City; David Swim, California State University, Sacramento; and James Vardalis, Florida International University.

Finally, in the production trenches we want to thank Southwest Texas State University's Ryan Weichelt for his steadfast devotion to seeing this project through to the finish; to Jill Syron for helping out during initial development while the lead author was still working at Wichita State; to Kimberly Hassell, who helped from her position as a graduate assistant at the University of Nebraska; and to Sacha A. Howells for his much appreciated attention to detail during final production at Roxbury. ✦

Preface

Samuel Walker
University of Nebraska at Omaha

This anthology brings together an outstanding collection of articles on contemporary policing, written by some of the leading experts in the field. The first four selections examine the major new developments with respect to rethinking the role of the police in American society. Lawrence W. Sherman opens the collection with a discussion of the basic issue for the police in a democratic society: the trust and confidence of citizens in criminal justice institutions. Ronald V. Clarke discusses both problem-oriented policing and community policing. Eli B. Silverman examines CompStat, a new administrative tool that has emerged as the most important innovation for enhancing police response to crime and disorder and responsiveness to community needs. Williard M. Oliver, meanwhile, looks at the processes by which innovation such as community policing and CompStat are diffused (or fail to diffuse) through the law enforcement community and become institutionalized.

Part II covers specific programs for controlling crime and disorder. Lawrence W. Sherman opens the section with a discussion of the larger police goal of crime prevention. The common theme of the other selections in Part II is problem-oriented policing. David Weisburd and Lorraine Green Mazerolle examine the effectiveness of "hot spot" policing, a place-oriented approach that is widely regarded as the most promising police strategy. Glensor, Peak, and Correia examine another problem-oriented program that shifts the focus to crime victims and away from criminal offenders. Finally, Hochstein and Thurman look at another problem-oriented program that seeks to ensure safety in public housing units by screening out suspected offenders.

Part III examines a set of issues related to the internal management of police departments, including the role of middle management, job satisfaction among officers, early warning systems for identifying officers with performance problems, and the selection and training of new officers.

Part IV covers the external environment of policing. It examines the particularly controversial issues of the use of force, high-speed pursuits, policing gangs, and racial profiling. In each of these areas there are new public concerns, new data, and new administrative controls designed to reduce misconduct.

Part V is devoted to a variety of innovations in policing. It includes selections devoted to aspects of community policing and problem-oriented policing, and three selections cover new technologies and their applications to policing.

Part VI examines police misconduct and issues related to police ethics. Two selections cover traditional issues, corruption and drug-related misconduct, while two others look at new issues—at least, issues that have not been publicly examined—using citizen complaints as a management tool for identifying officers with problems and sexual misconduct by officers.

The final section offers three selections that discuss the future of policing from three different perspectives, drawing on the material in the previous articles. ✦

Introduction

A primary purpose of this anthology is to provide readers with an up-to-date perspective on contemporary policing and emergent issues. In part we focus on controversial topics, of which there is certainly no shortage; we also look at the components of policing that might be broken or antiquated, of which there are also more than a few, and which are in need of resolution or reform. Finally, in addition to controversies and challenges, we also seek to offer the reader some examples of solutions that appear promising, and surprisingly enough, we did find some of these.

In putting together this anthology we committed ourselves to looking at excellent scholarship that is also very recent—the oldest article in the bunch is from 1996, ten of the thirty featured articles were published in 2000 or later, and six articles are new. This anthology may indeed be the most contemporary collection of policing articles currently available to academicians, practitioners, and students.

A Theoretical Perspective for Understanding Our Selections

Contingency theory, which developed out of the 1960s school of management, views the external environment as the driving force behind reform and organizational change. Such a case can also be made for policing. If it weren't for changes in the surrounding world, there would be little motivation for policing to adapt or transform. Organizations must conform to the external environment in order to survive, or risk becoming obsolete or irrelevant.

The contingency perspective that provides an overarching scheme for understanding the controversies that challenge police organizations to change is based upon at least two cardinal assumptions. First, individual organizations must adapt when their goal or goals are affected by changes in the external environmental conditions under which they operate. That is, organizations must be responsive to a demanding external environment (Hage and Aiken, 1970). A second key assumption asserts that an adaptive organization must develop a good fit between the organization and its environment. A good fit is achieved when an organization attains optimal levels of performance and efficiency within the external environment in which it operates (Van de Van and Poole, 1995). Donaldson (1995:32) argues that in order to find an optimal fit, organizations must be able to alter both their goals and operations over the course of time.

But what does all this have to do with American policing? Simply this: Many practitioners and scholars have lamented the fact that traditional strategies of crime control developed under the professional model became increasingly ineffective in the late 1960s and 1970s (Kelling et al., 1974; Greenwood et al., 1977). When examined from a contingency theory perspective, the failure of traditional policing methods to control crime is suggestive of a poor fit between the external societal environment and the prevailing structural and strategic organization of policing (Brown and Wycoff, 1987; Skogan and Hartnett, 1997). Accordingly, in order to become more effective in protecting the public from crime, police agencies had to change their operations, their goals, or both. (Short of real change, the only other alternative was to manipulate public opinion to believe that police were effective when they actually were not—perhaps the most difficult feat of all.)

How did American police agencies react to the need to change in the latter decades of the twentieth century? The publication of Wilson and Kelling's "Broken Windows" thesis (1982) helped to re-establish order maintenance as an organizational goal that should supplant crime control as police work's top priority. In their widely read article, Wilson and Kelling argued persuasively that because social disorder provides a promising climate for criminal incidents to flourish, local police agencies should develop new strategies to resolve the problems underlying crime rather than just responding to the actual incidence of crime (Goldstein, 1990). Here was a new goal that policing could embrace, and effectively so!

In this anthology we examine several important factors that exert significant influence on police departments and their internal and external organizational environments. The external environment consists of the community, its residents, and the local political structure that might exert influence on local law enforcement agencies and their policies and practices. There are three attributes of the external environment. First, it cannot be controlled by police agencies.

While there is little doubt that controlling crime continues to be a top priority for any law enforcement agency, the influence that the police have on crime control is marginal at best. Criminologists have argued that crime is a social problem that reflects the demographic and socioeconomic composition of a community or neighborhood (e.g., Sampson and Groves, 1989). If a community has a large proportion of young people, for example, it is likely that crime rates will be higher than in a community inhabited by more senior citizens, because the offending rate among young people aged 14 to 24 is simply higher than for any other age group (Osgood and Chambers, 2000).

Some criminologists also note that the disintegration of neighborhood infrastructure is closely related to social disorder and crime. Social disorganization theory suggests that three dimensions of community characteristics are positively associated with crime and disorder (Shaw and Mckay, 1972; Bursik, 1988). The relationship between racial heterogeneity and juvenile delinquency is closely correlated, because heterogeneity implies lack of a dominant culture and shared beliefs that can be commonly accepted to regulate residents' behaviors. Similarly, single-headed households and poverty are considered to be signs of family disorganization. Children who grow up in single-headed households usually lack sufficient supervision. At the same time, a considerable percentage of single mothers live in poverty because they often do not have the means to simultaneously accomplish both roles as primary bread earners and caregivers. In addition, mobility is often considered to impede neighborhood integration and cohesion (Shaw and Mckay, 1972). If the mobility rate in a neighborhood is high, residents are less likely to have an opportunity to know each other and adequately build up mutual trust. Furthermore, they are less likely to help each other or watch out for others' property.

A second attribute of the external environment is that changes in its component parts (e.g., socioeconomic factors, public opinion, and politics) will likely result in corresponding changes in police agencies. A case in point is the most recent reform effort in American policing. Different from the reforms of several decades earlier, police administrators in place at the beginning of the community policing movement were better informed about the approaches most likely to be ineffective in preventing or controlling crime. At the time, the academic community was actively pursuing scholarship that showed that preventive patrol and detective work had little effect on crime reduction (Kelling et al., 1974; Greenwood et al., 1977). Soon thereafter, addressing social disorder and the fear of crime were added to the public's list of expectations for policing. The early community policing programs, for example, reflected this shift in focus to the fear of crime and social disorder (Brown and Wycoff, 1987). Changing public expectations raised two challenges for police administrators. Should a local police agency adapt a new program or alter its existing operations to meet public demand? What kind of new program should be adopted, and at what cost?

A third attribute of changes in the external environment is that the consequences of change are difficult to predict. Management theory suggests that adaptation of innovations is always accompanied by the implementation of a number of different programs on a "trial and error" basis. This occurs because individual organizations are typically unsure about how best to respond to a changing environment, often due to limited knowledge concerning the nature of change and its impact on the organization. Consequently, a key strategy is for individual organizations to adopt a number of programs that might prove themselves useful and/or cost effective. Those that work are retained and even institutionalized, while those that fail are discarded. In turn, the most successful boundary-spanning units can even impact the core mission of the organization should the external environment deem them essential.

Organization of the Book

The first section of this anthology, New Policing Strategies, features four chapters that set the stage for broad developments that have shown up relatively recently in the field of American policing. Lawrence Sherman's piece locates policing in the context of the other two major components of the criminal justice system: courts and corrections. Here we learn about the important emphasis that public trust and confidence play in setting expectations for the police. It is from these expectations that police executives and students of policing may derive a direction for policing in a post-9/11 world.

Problem-oriented policing, CompStat, and community-oriented policing are some of the main directions in which policing has been pulled over the past several years, as discussed in articles by Ronald Clarke, Eli Silverman, and Willard Oliver. It remains to be seen how international terrorist attacks on U.S. soil will impact the evolution of American policing, and which of these perspectives may prevail or be discarded in the future. While it may really be too soon to tell, we hope that our readers draw insight from these selections that will help them contribute to meaningful discussion about the future of American policing and its response to the external environment in which we find ourselves in the years ahead.

The next section, Promising Approaches to Crime Reduction and Prevention, highlights some of the methods that police organizations have tried to control or prevent crime. Once again we lead off with an article by Lawrence Sherman to set the stage for a snapshot of promising approaches. Then we turn to three articles that have dissimilar approaches to fighting crime, and yet all propose solutions that work "upstream" of the crime problem.

For example, David Weisburd and Lorraine Green Mazerolle examine the utility of policing drug hot spots as a specific tactic to defeat crime and disorder in a community, thus reducing the flow of criminogenic traffic into a neighborhood. By contrast, Ron Glensor, Ken Peak, and Mark Correia recommend a problem-solving approach to crime prevention that starts with an analysis of those who are most frequently victimized by crime. They argue that understanding the nature of habitual victimization might be a fruitful way to reduce crime by keeping unsafe swimmers out of dangerous waterways. In the section's final article, Lucy Hochstein and Quint Thurman discuss screening out criminal offenders from low-end apartment complexes. At the risk of using the "crime as a river" analogy once too often, keeping criminal predators out of streams where they are likely to encounter would-be victims is also a promising crime-prevention approach.

The next two sections of the anthology group contributions by their scholarship on the topic of internally and externally focused challenges to police organizations, respectively. In so doing, we selected articles that closely fit with a contingency perspective for examining American policing.

For example, in Part III, Challenging Issues in the Internal Police Environment, we first introduce a provocative article by Thomas Cowper on the myth of the military model as it has been applied (or misapplied, as Cowper contends) to American policing organizations. The implicit question is this: If policing adopted a military model to establish its initial organizational structure, will police agencies follow suit as the military changes?

Gennaro Vito and Julie Kunselman's article emphasizes the importance of the role of middle managers in the internal organization of the police. Following this, Jihong Zhao and his colleagues write about the link between police work conditions and job satisfaction. Next, Samuel Walker, Geoffrey Alpert, and Dennis Kenney discuss the need for early warning systems to help police organizations become proactive in preventing internal policing problems and enhancing police accountability. The final selection in this section concerns hiring the right people to serve as police officers in a complex and changing world.

Five articles on the challenges facing police organizations from the external environment comprise Part IV, Challenging Issues in the External Police Environment. We begin with a chapter written by a well-known (and sometimes controversial) advocate for policing reform. Former Minneapolis police chief and noted author Anthony Bouza writes about why he believes that crime fighting is an unwise goal for police organizations to embrace, and hence, why policing has to change. Two articles that follow (one by Kenneth Adams and the other by Dennis Kenney and Geoffrey Alpert) provide examples of external issues facing the police that cannot continue to be ignored: police use of force and police pursuit policies. As if these topics were not challenging enough, Charles Katz addresses the controversies surrounding police gang units, and David Carter and Andra Katz-Bannister examine racial profiling.

Part V, Innovations, Boundary Spanning, and Capacity Building, features articles on innovations in policing. Jihong Zhao and Quint Thurman consider how best to understand innovations such as boundary-spanning units, and whether or not innovative practices will be institutionalized. Next we introduce a piece by Brian Forst on the innovative use of problem-solving techniques in criminal investigations. The third article in this section, by D. Kim Rossmo, may well be the most sophisticated in the book. Here Rossmo introduces the concept of geoprofiling, a theoretical approach from environmental criminology that has considerable and impressive applications for managing information in serial crimes investigations.

The last two selections pertain primarily to capacity building in policing. Mark Correia and Craig Bowling predict that electronic disorder in the modern world poses a vexing challenge that police organizations will have to rise to meet. Their analysis suggests that current policing is poorly equipped to counter electronic crime. Similarly, Delores Craig-Moreland's article identifies some of the technology in use at larger U.S. police departments that will likely spread to the rest of the country. While efficiency does not necessarily translate into effectiveness, working smarter to control and prevent crime is preferable to working harder with the same or less impact.

Part VI, Police Deviance and Ethical Issues, includes four selections. Three of the four articles presented here were written at the invitation of the editors. Kim Lersch's piece on when badges get too big and Brian Withrow and Jeffrey Dailey's chapter on understanding the role of gratuities in police corruptibility are provocative new works that we expect to make a lasting contribution to the important study of police ethics. In addition, we are glad to have Tim Maher's examination of police officer sexual misconduct as well as a previously published article by David Carter on drug use and drug-related police corruption. Both contributions exemplify areas where there is little extant research.

Our final section, The Challenges Ahead, features three articles on the future of policing in the United States. Each represents a very different view, albeit addressing the same topic.

David Bayley and Clifford Shearing's article is the oldest, and hence should be afforded more leeway if the future proves their predictions off the mark—after all, they published their work five years earlier than the other two contributors. Jihong Zhao's work was previously published as the final chapter in another Roxbury publication, *Community Policing in a Community Era* (Thurman et al., 2001). Finally, Sheldon Greenberg's chapter is an excellent final selection given the breadth and nature of his scholarship. We wholeheartedly agree with him when he writes in his closing comments that "this is an exciting and challenging time in the history of police service." Indeed it is.

References

Brown, L. and M.A. Wycoff. 1987. "Policing Houston: Reducing Fear and Improving Service." *Crime and Delinquency* 33:71–89.

Bursik, Robert. 1988. "Social Disorganization and Theory of Crime and Delinquency: Problems and Prospects." *Criminology* 26:519–551.

Donaldson, L. 1995. *American Anti-Management Theories of Organization: A Critique of Paradigm Proliferation.* New York: Cambridge University Press.

Goldstein, H. 1990. *Problem-Oriented Policing.* Philadelphia: Temple University Press.

Greenwood, P., J. Chaiken, and J. Petersilia. 1977. *The Criminal Investigation Process.* Lexington, MA: D.C. Health.

Hage, J. and M. Aiken. 1970. *Social Change in Complex Organizations.* New York: Random House.

Kelling, G., A. Pate, D. Dieckman, and C. Brown. 1974. *The Kansas City Preventive Patrol Experiment: A Summary Report.* Washington, DC: Police Foundation.

Osgood, D. and J. Chambers. 2000. "Social Disorganization Outside the Metropolis: An Analysis of Rural Youth Violence." *Criminology* 38:81–115.

Sampson, R. and W. Groves. 1989. "Community Structure and Crime: Testing Social Disorganization Theory." *American Journal of Sociology* 94:774–802.

Shaw, C., and H. McKay. 1972. *Juvenile Delinquency and Urban Areas,* 3rd ed. Chicago: University of Chicago Press.

Skogan, W. and S. Hartnett. 1997. *Community Policing: Chicago Style.* New York: Oxford University Press.

Thurman, Q., J. Zhao, and A. Giacomazzi. 2001. *Community Policing in a Community Era: An Introduction and Exploration.* Los Angeles: Roxbury.

Van de Ven, A. and M. Poole. 1995. "Explaining Development and Change in Organizations." *Academy of Management Review* 20:510–540.

Wilson, J.Q. and G. Kelling. 1982. "Broken Windows: The Police and Neighborhood Safety." *Atlantic Monthly* (March):29–38. ✦

Part I

New Policing Strategies

Over the past twenty years, police agencies across the U.S. have embarked on a journey to search for new strategies to combat local crime problems. What they have discovered, however, is that crime problems are only the tip of the iceberg; communities face a myriad of social problems that feed into the issues of crime and disorder.

In many cases, new strategies have been developed to address a wide array of neighborhood problems with direct links to crime. Ordinarily, these innovative strategies can be grouped according to one of two foci. The first group is marked by changes in police practices; here the innovative strategies developed over the past two decades have focused not only on crime incidents per se, but also on social disorder problems like family disputes, drug markets, and school violence. The rationale behind the implementation of these new strategies is clear and straightforward: The police need to pay attention to incivilities and lesser criminal offenses before minor problems turn into major ones.

A second focus involves the use of technology. A growing number of police departments have adopted innovative strategies that are technology driven. This is particularly true in large police agencies with the financial and personnel resources to implement technological innovations such as computerized crime mapping. Crime mapping enables police agencies to more comprehensively review crime incidents in order to better understand the correlations between a variety of related factors. This section presents the benefits of new operational strategies and their impact on contemporary American policing. ✦

Chapter 1

Trust and Confidence in Criminal Justice

Lawrence W. Sherman

Lawrence Sherman examines the public's assessment of the criminal justice system. He observes that public confidence in the justice system is relatively low, while support for local police—a key component of the system—remains substantially higher. Additionally, Sherman points out a clear racial disparity with regard to public ratings of various components of the American criminal justice system. For example, African Americans consistently score the system (and the police) lower than do American citizens who are white.

Changes in American culture may be a primary source for explaining how citizens view the criminal justice system. Sherman suggests that "As the spread of equality has combined with growing freedom from want, political culture has shifted away from Puritan views of a hierarchical *communal democracy to Quaker views of a more* egalitarian *individualistic democracy. Indeed, the consistently greater support for police than for courts may result from a perception of police as egalitarian individualists (the new cultural ideal) while judges are seen as bossy conformists (the outdated ideal)." Sherman challenges the police and other criminal justice agencies to redouble their efforts to treat citizens fairly, inform local residents of new programming, and listen more carefully to the public to learn their concerns. Such an approach may be the best way to win back the "personal nature of citizen trust in criminal justice."*

Criminal justice in America today is a paradox of progress: While the fairness and effectiveness of criminal justice have improved, public trust and confidence apparently have not.

Criminal justice is far less corrupt, brutal, and racially unfair than it has been in the past. It is arguably more effective at preventing crime. It has far greater diversity in its staffing. Yet these objectively defined improvements seem to have had little impact on American attitudes toward criminal justice.

Understanding this paradox—better work but low marks—is central to improving public trust and confidence in the criminal justice system.

How Low Is Public Confidence?

Gallup polls over the last few years have consistently found that Americans have less confidence in the criminal justice system than in other institutions, such as banking, the medical system, public schools, television news, newspapers, big business, and organized labor.[1]

The most striking finding in the Gallup poll is the difference between the low evaluation of "criminal justice" and the high evaluation given to the police and the Supreme Court. Other sources of data show similar attitudes: Confidence in local courts and prisons is far lower than it is for the police.[2] These large differences suggest that Americans may not think of police in the same way as they do the criminal justice system.

The Racial Divide

A 1998 Gallup poll reports little overall demographic difference among the respondents saying they had confidence in the criminal justice system. But what is most clear is the difference in opinion between whites and blacks about the individual components of the criminal justice system and especially the police. Whites express considerably more confidence

Exhibit 1.1

Confidence Ratings for Criminal Justice System Agencies, by Race

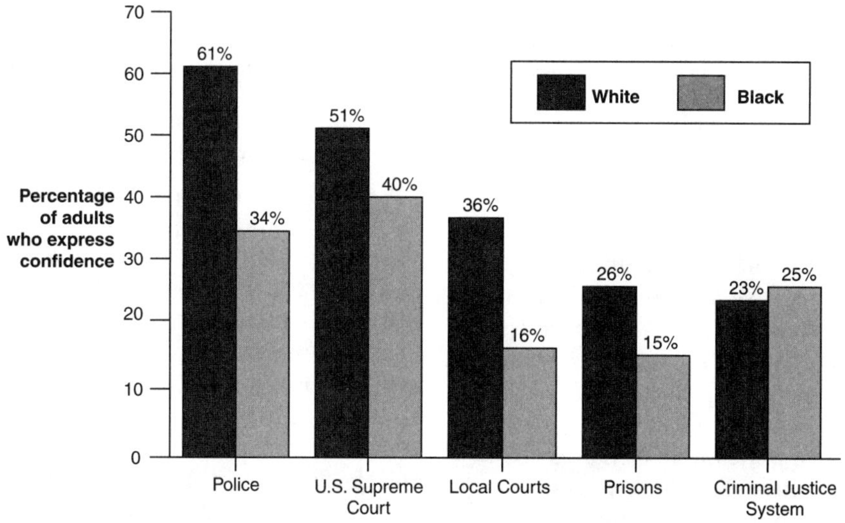

Source: The Gallup Organization, "Confidence in Institutions," retrieved from the World Wide Web site http://gallup.com, October 10, 2000.

in the police, local court system, and State prison system than blacks (see Exhibit 1.1).

Race, Victimization, and Punishment

Racial differences also appear in rates of victimization and punishment: Blacks are 31 percent more likely to be victimized by personal crime than whites and twice as likely as whites to suffer a completed violent crime.[3]

Young black males are historically 10 times more likely to be murdered than white males.[4]

Arrest rates for robbery are five times higher for blacks than for whites; four times higher for murder and rape; and three times higher for drug violations and weapons possession.[5]

Blacks are eight times more likely to be in a State or Federal prison than non-Hispanic whites (and three times more likely than Hispanic whites). Almost 2 percent of the black population, or 1 of every 63 blacks, was in prison in 1996.[6]

Race and Neighborhood

What these data fail to show, however, is the extent to which the racial differences in attitudes, victimization, and punishment may be largely related to more blacks being the residents of a small number of high-crime, high-poverty areas concentrated in a small fraction of urban neighborhoods. This is the case even though Harvard University sociologist Orlando Patterson has estimated that only 1 in every 30 black adults resides in these high-crime, high-poverty areas; the proportion is higher for children.

What we may understand as a problem of race in America may largely reflect conditions in those neighborhoods that are generalized by both blacks and whites to conditions of the larger society.

Due to limited national data, it is difficult to determine what precisely drives the lower levels of confidence in criminal justice among blacks, but insights from city-by-city analysis suggest two conclusions:

- ***There is no race-based subculture of violence.*** Blacks and whites who live in neighborhoods with similar conditions have similar views on the legitimacy of law. To the extent that race is associated with attitudes toward law, it may be a reflection of the greater likelihood that blacks reside in poverty areas.

- ***There is no race-based hostility to police in high-crime areas.*** High levels of dissatisfaction with police are endemic to high-crime areas. Whites residing in such areas express attitudes just as hostile as blacks toward police.[7] The distrust of police in high-crime areas may be related to the prevalence of crime rather than to police practice. If negative attitudes are driven by police practice, it may be because those practices fail to prevent crime rather than because police presence or behavior is excessive. Or it may be that the practice of policing in such areas offers less recognition and dignity to citizen consumers than is found in lower crime areas.

Strong Demands for Change

The findings and responses from a random digit-dialing telephone survey of 4,000 residents of 10 northeastern States in 1998 found that more than 80 percent—four out of five respondents—preferred the idea of "totally revamping the way the [criminal justice] system works" for violent crime; 75 percent said the same for all crime.[8] The responses varied little from State to State or from one demographic group to another. The majority of respondents believed that:

- Victims are not accorded sufficient rights in the criminal justice process.
- Victims are not informed enough about the status of their cases.
- Victims are not able to talk to prosecutors enough.
- Victims should be able to tell the court what impact the crime had on them, but most victims do not get that chance.
- Offenders, even if jailed, should reimburse victims for the cost of the crime.
- Offenders should acknowledge their responsibility for the crime.
- Victims should have the opportunity to meet with the offender to find out why the crime occurred and to learn whether the offender accepted responsibility.
- Ordinary citizens, not courts, should set penalties for nonviolent crimes.
- Drug treatment should be used more widely for drug using offenders.

The personal opinions of the survey respondents are consistent with a major theory about the declining public confidence in all government—not just criminal justice—in all modern nations, not just the United States. The concerns arise from the decline of hierarchy and the rise of equality in all walks of life. The rise in egalitarian culture increases the demand for government officials to show more respect to citizens.[9]

Egalitarianism in Modern Culture: Raised Expectations, Reduced Trust

Americans' trust in government has declined sharply in the last quarter century.[10] A similar loss of trust has been found in 18 other democracies. Citizens now expect higher levels of recognition, respect, and status from the government. Criminal justice serves as a flashpoint for this change in citizen attitudes because so many Americans have contact with the criminal justice system and because the hierarchical design of criminal justice institutions juxtaposes so starkly with the egalitarian demands of the public.

As the spread of equality has combined with growing freedom from want, political culture has shifted away from Puritan views of a *hierarchical* communal democracy to Quaker views of a more *egalitarian* individualistic democracy.

Indeed, the consistently greater support for police than for courts may result from a perception of police as egalitarian individualists (the new cultural ideal) while judges are seen as bossy conformists (the outdated ideal).

The massive three-decade decline of public trust in liberal democratic governments suggests a deeper paradox of success: As democracies become more materially successful and better educated, the perceived need for governance declines and expectations of government for appropriate conduct increase.[11] The crisis of government legitimacy has thus been prompted less by declining quality of government conduct than by increasing public dissatisfaction with institutions in general, driven by what Ronald F. Inglehart, Professor, University of Michigan, calls "postmaterialist values."[12]

Social changes taking place around the globe appear to be resulting in challenges to the legitimacy of virtually all forms of social hierarchy of authority (although not hierarchy of wealth)—of husbands over wives, doctors over patients, schoolteachers over students and parents, parents over children, and government officials over citizens. This evolution may have led to widespread preference for the recognition of individual dignity over the recognition of communal authority.[13]

Thus, what Robert J. Sampson, Professor of Sociology, University of Chicago, and other scholars refer to as "legal cynicism"—the extent to which people feel that laws are not binding—is not the product of a criminal subculture.[14] It is a 400-year-old Christian political theology that has become globally accepted across people of all religions in a more egalitarian and individualistic modern culture.

In such a world, people are less likely to obey the law out of a sense of communal obligation, and more likely to obey laws they support through a personal sense of what is moral.

Trust and Recognition

What changing culture may be creating is a world in which people trust *laws* but not *legal institutions.* This new world may be one in which trust in criminal justice is no longer automatic; it must be earned every day, with each encounter between legal agents and citizens.

The research of Tom R. Tyler, Department of Psychology, New York University, shows that Americans—especially members of minority groups—are extremely sensitive to the respect they perceive and the procedures employed when they come into contact with criminal justice.[15] Tyler's evidence suggests that in building citizen trust in the legal system, it may matter less whether you receive the speeding ticket than whether the police officer addresses you politely or rudely during the traffic stop. Similarly, sentencing guidelines that punish possession of crack more harshly than possession of powdered cocaine may discriminate against blacks. But dissatisfaction may be greater with some police officers engaged in drug enforcement who treat suspects and arrestees like people who are enemies rather than like people who are equal fellow citizens.

Tyler concludes that the procedural justice perceived in treatment by legal officials affects the level of trust citizens have in government.[16] That level of trust, in turn, affects the pride we have in our government and the degree to which we feel we are respected by other members of our democracy—including the government.

Tyler further concludes that the odds of citizens reaching the conclusion that the law is morally right are much higher when citizens feel that the law has given each of them adequate recognition and respect.

Rather than creating a willingness to *defer* to the power of the law, Tyler suggests that respectful treatment creates a stronger *consensus* about what is moral and what the law must be. The consensus model assumes more equality than the deference model on which our legal institutions were designed.[17]

Consensus thus appears to be a much better fit to the new political culture. Standing up when judges enter a room and obeying orders barked out by police, for example, are procedural forms that may imply officials are more important than citizens. Such forms may do more to undermine legal trust than to build respect for the law.

Alternative Community Justice Conferences

In the Canberra experiments, the police invite victims, offenders, and their respective supporters to a meeting in which the offenders must not—for these purposes—dispute their guilt. At the meetings, everyone sits in a circle to discuss the harm the crime has caused, acknowledge the pain and emotional impact of that harm, and deliberate democratically as to how the offenders should repair that harm.

The egalitarian proceedings begin with the police officer moderating the proceedings, offering only questions, not answers. For example, what did the offender do? How did it hurt the victim? How does the victim feel about that hurt? How do the victim's friends and family feel? How do the offender's family and friends feel about what has been said? What would be the right way for the offender to repay the debt to the victim and to society? Does everyone agree? Is there anything the offender wants to say to the victim (sometimes the offender says "I'm sorry")? Is there anything the victim wants to say to the offender (possibly "I forgive you")?

One of the most important parts of the proceedings is that everyone is allowed to talk, just as in a Quaker meeting, but no one person dominates speech, as might happen in a Calvinist church or in an Anglo-American courtroom. Emotions can be intense at the conferences—unlike the restraint valued by Puritan cultures and Western courts.

No Lawyers. Lawyers are not allowed to attend the conferences as legal advocates for either an offender or the State, although they may attend as personal supporters. They are always on call, ready to act to protect anyone whose rights may seem abused. But as long as the victim-offender consensus is under discussion, everyone in the circle has equal authority, regardless of age or education.

Extra Time Required. A community justice conference takes, on average, about 70 minutes to resolve. A similar case in traditional court may take 10 minutes spread across several different appearances, which have no emotional significance for victim or offender, and thus leave citizens feeling like cogs in a wheel. A community justice conference is about the people present rather than the legal formalities. People come only once, prepared to stay until the case is resolved.

Trust in Justice. Research shows that sentences imposed in the community justice conferences and the traditional court process were fairly similar despite the major differences in the decision making procedures employed.[1] But the conferences produced far better results in terms of citizen respect for legal institutions.

1. Sherman, L. W., H. Strang, and G. C. Barnes, "Stratification of Justice: Legitimacy of Hierarchical and Egalitarian Sentencing Procedures," unpublished manuscript, Fels Center of Government, University of Pennsylvania, 1999.

Fitting Legal Institutions to the Culture: The Canberra Experiments

For all Americans, regardless of race, the central cause of declining trust may be the misfit of hierarchical legal institutions in an egalitarian culture. In many ways, citizens may experience the conduct of judges, prosecutors, and police as being overly "bossy" and unnecessarily authoritarian.

Results of experiments in Canberra, Australia, suggest that an egalitarian, consensual procedure of stakeholder citizens deciding the sentence for a crime creates more legitimacy in the eyes of both offenders and victims than the hierarchical, deferential process of sentencing by a judge.[18]

The experiments compared traditional court sentencing of youthful violent and property offenders to an alternative community justice conference making the same decisions.

Offenders who were sent to conferences were far less likely than offenders who were sent to traditional court to say that they were pushed around; disadvantaged by their age, income, or education; treated as if they were untrustworthy; or not listened to. They also were more likely to report that their experience increased their respect for the justice system and the police, as well as their feeling that the crime they had committed was morally wrong.

Victims also were far more satisfied with community justice conferences than with court proceedings. Much of this difference may be because most victims of criminals sent to court were never informed of the offenders' court appearances, either before or after sentencing. The victims invited to community justice conferences with offenders, in sharp contrast, gained increased trust in police and justice, as well as decreased fear of and anger at the offender. (For more details, see box, "Alternative Community Justice Conferences.")

Building Trust One Case at a Time

The Canberra experiments suggest the highly personal nature of citizen trust in criminal justice. The *personal* legitimacy of legal agents may depend on a leveling of distinctions in rank between citizen and official.

As Albert J. Reiss, Jr., Professor Emeritus, Sociology Department, Yale University, observed, the legitimacy of police authority in the eyes of citizens varies widely from one situation to the next.[19] Thus, officials must earn the legitimacy of their authority one case at a time.

The most dramatic demonstration of this principle is the finding that *how* police make arrests for domestic violence affects the rate of repeat offending. Raymond Paternoster, Ph.D., University of Maryland, et al. demonstrated that offenders who were arrested for domestic violence and who perceived that the police officers' arresting procedures were fair were less likely to repeat the offense than offenders who perceived the arresting procedures as unfair.[20] Actions that constituted "procedural justice" included the police taking the time to listen to both the offender and the victim, not handcuffing the offender in front of the victim, and not using physical force.

As Exhibit 1.2 shows, the risk of repeat offending was 40 percent for offenders who had a low perception of police procedural fairness, but only 25 percent for those who perceived a

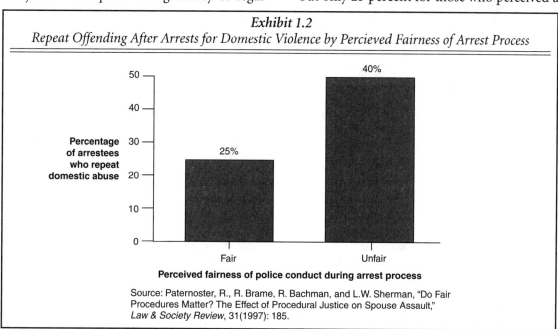

Exhibit 1.2

Repeat Offending After Arrests for Domestic Violence by Percieved Fairness of Arrest Process

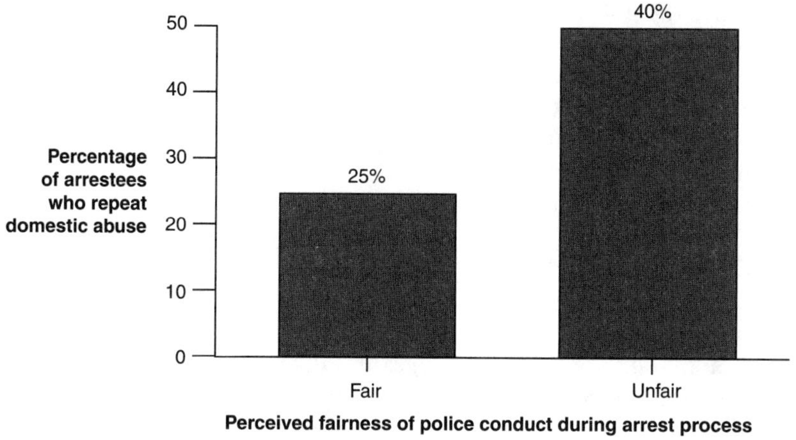

Source: Paternoster, R., R. Brame, R. Bachman, and L.W. Sherman, "Do Fair Procedures Matter? The Effect of Procedural Justice on Spouse Assault," *Law & Society Review*, 31(1997): 185.

high level of police fairness. The estimate of offending risk took prior levels of violence into account; hence the findings shown in Exhibit 1.2 increase our confidence that *how* the police make an arrest may affect the crime rate (much of which comes from repeat offending) through trust and confidence in the criminal justice system.

Reducing Complaints Against Police

Other tests of the hypothesis that trust in criminal justice comes from egalitarian procedures can be seen in actions that have been shown to reduce complaints against police.

In the 42nd and 44th precincts in the Bronx, complaints reached a 10-year high in 1996. But after the precinct commanders instituted a program to promote respectful policing and improve police relations with community residents, complaints dropped dramatically. Among the elements of the new program was vigorous training for officers on how to treat citizens respectfully, zealous monitoring of complaints, and followthrough with consequences for officers who received complaints.

In addition, the simple elimination of the precinct's high desk and bar in front of the desk in the reception area helped the precinct present a less hierarchical face to the community. Research on the effects of the strategy, conducted by the Vera Institute of Justice, found that citizens began to perceive the police as responsive to community concerns.[21]

The second test of the procedural equality theory comes from a community with a population of almost one million; 55 percent of the population is African American.

Complaints dropped in this department of 1,400 officers when a new procedure for traffic stops was initiated in 1997–99. The procedure, called "Take Away Guns" (TAG), was one part of a larger strategy to reduce gun violence. One of the first steps the department took was to increase traffic enforcement—a 400-some percent increase—so that police had an opportunity to explain the program at each traffic stop and distribute a letter from the district police captain explaining the program. The letter contained the captain's phone number and invited citizens to call the captain with complaints or questions. Officers were trained to be very polite in explaining the program to drivers and then asking permission to search the car for guns.

The program not only received a high rate of compliance with the requests, but also received praise from the drivers stopped who approved of the efforts to get guns off the street. Over the first 2 years of the program, both gun violence and citizen complaints of excessive force by police dropped substantially.

In sum, a growing body of theory and evidence suggests that it is not the fairness or effectiveness of decisions criminal justice officials make that determines the public's level of trust. Changes in modern culture have made the *procedures* and manners of criminal justice officials far more important to public trust and left officials out of step with modern culture.

This explanation gains further support from scholarship on the effect of television and other communications media on the nature of authority and trust in government. For despite Tyler's focus on personal contacts with criminal justice, most citizens have little if any personal contact with legal officials. For this majority of Americans, the level of trust in criminal justice may depend on what they hear about criminal justice encounters with other citizens, a little-studied area. But it also may depend on how legal agencies are portrayed in entertainment and news media.

Authority and Media Celebrity

The future authority of the criminal justice system may well depend on how the system appears not just to those directly involved in the system, but to all citizens. That, in turn, may depend heavily on how criminal justice manages its image in the electronic media. Legal historian Lawrence Friedman notes that modern culture has changed the very nature of authority from *vertical* (where people look up to leaders in high position) to *horizontal* (where people look in to the center of society to find leaders who are celebrities, defined by the number of people who recognize their names and faces). "Leaders are no longer distant, awesome, and unknown; they are familiar figures on TV. . . . The horizontal society is [one in which] the men and women who get and hold power become celebrities" and the public come to know them, or think they know them, through the media. "By contrast," Friedman writes, "traditional authority was vertical, and the higher up the authority, the more stern, distant, and remote it was."[22]

A celebrity culture creates still another paradox: Americans now feel more personal connections with celebrities living far away than they do with legal officials in their own hometown. Just as many people felt more emotional loss at the death of Princess Diana than at the death of a neighbor, the celebrity culture makes us feel personal connections to people we do not know.

Thus, for all the programs designed to foster community policing or community prosecution with legal officials in the neighborhood, Americans still are more likely to form their impressions of criminal justice from vicarious contact through friends or through television shows than from personal experience with their own legal system. The evidence is clear: On a Wednesday night when police convene a neighborhood meeting in a church basement, more local residents are home watching television than attending the meeting.

We may well ask if there are any celebrities of American criminal justice, and if so, who they are—the Chief Justice of the Supreme Court? The director of the FBI? Probably not. These positions appear to fit Friedman's characteristics of traditional authority: stern, distant, and remote. Television's Judge Judy, on the other hand, is an internationally recognized celebrity, with far greater name-face recognition than the traditional authority figures.

Unfortunately, the entertainment values of the television business conflict with the core values of legal institutions. What sells TV audiences is conflict and putdowns, tools Judge Judy uses to portray a rude, in-your-face (but perhaps egalitarian), power-control image of the bench. Audiences find this fun to watch, although judge Judy may confirm their worst fears, leaving them reluctant to have anything to do with the legal system.

The difficulty in using celebrity power to send messages about the trustworthiness of criminal justice is the clash of cultures between law and entertainment. The reticence of the legal culture conflicts with the chattiness of celebrity culture.

One can imagine a legal official appearing weekly on a talk show with a huge audience, saying things that could help shore up public faith in criminal justice as an egalitarian and fair system. One can equally imagine such a strategy being condemned by leaders of the American Bar Association, conservative journalists, and other defenders of traditional remoteness of authority.

The kind of public education programs that legal culture would approve of—such as tasteful PBS specials or public service announcements on radio and television—would seem unlikely to reach much of the public, let alone those citizens most distrustful of the system.

Portraying Values in the Media

The media often portray criminal justice through a morality play that explores themes of what Elijah Anderson, Charles and William L. Day Professor, Sociology Department, University of Pennsylvania, calls "street" and "decent" values. Based on years of field research in high-crime areas of Philadelphia, Anderson has observed people who exhibit "decent" values as patient, hopeful, respectful of authority, and with a belief in the predictability of punishment. Those who exhibit "street" values take on a bitter, impatient, antisystem outlook that is disrespectful of authority and demanding of deference.[23]

Television dramas that portray a hero's impatience with red tape may glorify the "street" enforcement of vengeance and personal respect. TV interviewers who ask officials provocative and insulting questions may reflect an effort to produce a "street" response.

The paradox of such media portrayals is that the more frequently legal officials are portrayed breaking the official rules out of distrust for "decent" government, the less reason the public has to believe the criminal justice system will treat citizens decently. By showing criminal justice agents pursuing street values, the media may create a self-fulfilling prophecy, defining conduct for legal officials and the public alike.

The research on respect for authority suggests that street sanctioning styles interact with different kinds of citizen personalities in ways that produce the following differences in repeat offending:

- Decent sanctioning of "decent" people produces the lowest repeat offending.
- Street sanctioning of "decent" people produces higher repeat offending.
- Decent sanctioning of "street" people may produce even higher repeat offending.
- Street sanctioning of "street" people produces the highest levels of repeat offending.[24]

The research on respect for authority consistently suggests that when people in positions of authority impose "street" attitudes or sanctions, the reaction is almost always negative. It is more productive for criminal justice officials to show more respect to, and take more time to listen to, citizens. To the extent that this message is portrayed in entertainment media and identified with celebrity authority, the criminal justice system might be able to increase its public trust and confidence. Yet to the extent that "decent" values are themselves communicated in an illegitimate way, it will be difficult to foster a more "decent" legal culture.

Half a century ago and half a world away, a French journalist observed during a 2-month tour of China in the early 1950's that police had become far more polite under Mao's early communism:

> In the olden days the Peking police were renowned for their brutality, and pedestrians frequently suffered at their hands, smacks in the face being the least form of violence offered them. Today they are formally forbidden to use any kind of force. Their instructions are to explain, to make people understand, to convince them.[25]

It may be easier to change official conduct in a dictatorship than in a democracy, but the power of electronic media may make the dynamics totally different today. Electronic communications comprise a highly democratized, free-market institution that cannot be manipulated easily for official purposes. But the media can be a venue in which celebrity power is built and put to use in fostering support for "decent" styles of criminal justice, both in the image and the reality of how criminal justice works.

The Domains of Public Trust

Three major domains appear to affect public trust and confidence in criminal justice:

- The conduct and practices of the criminal justice system.
- The changing values and expectations of the culture the system serves.
- The images of the system presented in electronic media.

Changes in each domain affect the others. Trust, as the product of all three combined, is likely to increase only when changes in all three domains can be aligned to create practices and values that are perceived to be fair, inclusive, and trustworthy.

Discovering how that can be made to happen is a daunting task. But the data suggest that fairness builds trust in criminal justice, and trust builds compliance with law. Thus what is fairer is more effective, and to be effective it is necessary to be fair.

Notes

1. Retrieved from the World Wide Web site http://www.gallup.com, October 10, 2000.
2. Maguire, K., and A. Pastore, eds., *Sourcebook of Criminal Justice Statistics, 1997,* Washington,

DC: U.S. Department of Justice, Bureau of Justice Statistics, 1998 (NCJ 171147).

3. Maguire and Pastore, *Sourcebook,* 182, see note 2.
4. Reiss, A.J., Jr., and J. Roth, *Understanding and Preventing Violence,* Washington, DC: National Academy of Sciences, 1993: 64 (NCJ 140290).
5. Hacker, A., *Two Nations: Black and White, Separate, Hostile, and Unequal,* New York: Free Press, 1992: 181.
6. Maguire and Pastore, *Sourcebook,* 494, see note 2.
7. Sampson, R., and D. Bartusch, "Legal Cynicism and Subcultural Tolerance of Deviance: The Neighborhood Context of Racial Differences," *Law & Society Review,* 32(4)(1999): 777–804.
8. Boyle, J.M., *Crime Issues in the Northeast: Statewide Surveys of the Public and Crime Victims in Connecticut, Delaware, Maine, Massachusetts, Vermont, New Hampshire, New Jersey, New York, and Rhode Island,* Silver Spring, MD: Schulman, Ronca, and Bucuvalas, Inc., 1999.
9. Fukuyama, F., *The End of History and the Last Man,* New York: Free Press, 1992.
10. Orren, G., "Fall From Grace: The Public's Loss of Faith in the Government," in *Why People Don't Trust Government,* eds. J.S. Nye, Jr., P.D. Zelikow, and D.C. King, Cambridge, MA: Harvard University Press, 1997: 83.
11. Fukuyama, F., *The End of History,* see note 9; Heclo, H., "The Sixties' False Dawn: Awakenings, Movements, and Postmodern Policy-making," *Journal of Policy History,* 8(1996): 50–58; Balogh, B., "Introduction," *Journal of Policy History,* 8(1996): 25.
12. Inglehart, R., "Postmaterialist Values and the Erosion of Institutional Authority," in *Why People Don't Trust Government,* eds. J.S. Nye, Jr., PD. Zelikow, and D.C. King, Cambridge, MA: Harvard University Press, 1997.
13. Baltzell, E.D., *Puritan Boston and Quaker Philadelphia: Two Protestant Ethics and the Spirit of Class Authority and Leadership,* New York: Free Press, 1979.
14. Sampson and Bartusch, "Legal Cynicism and Subcultural Tolerance of Deviance," see note 7.
15. Tyler, T., *Why People Obey the Law,* New Haven, CT: Yale University Press, 1990; Tyler, T., "Trust and Democratic Governance," in *Trust and Governance,* eds. V. Braithwaite and M. Levi, New York: Russell Sage Foundation, 1998.
16. Tyler, "Trust and Democratic Governance," see note 15.
17. Baltzell, *Puritan Boston,* 369, see note 13.
18. See details of the Reintegrative Shaming Experiments project at http://www.aic.gov.au/rjustice/rise.
19. Reiss and Roth, *Understanding and Preventing Violence,* 2, 3, 59–65, see note 4.
20. Paternoster, R., R. Brame, R. Bachman, and L.W. Sherman, "Do Fair Procedures Matter? The Effect of Procedural Justice on Spouse Assault," *Law & Society Review,* 1(1997): 185.
21. A more complete description of the Vera Institute of Justice study can be found in *NIJ Journal,* July 2000, p. 24, http://www.ncjrs. org/pdffilesl/jr000244f.pdf. The authors' presentation of findings also is available on videotape from NCJRS (NCJ 181106).
22. Friedman, L., *The Horizontal Society,* New Haven, CT: Yale University Press, 1999: 14–15.
23. Anderson, E., *Crime and Justice,* Chicago: Chicago University Press, 1999.
24. Just how much harmful impact "street" conduct by agents of criminal justice can have has been revealed by experimental and quasi-experimental research on diverse situations using different levels of analysis. See, for example, Nisbett, R.E., and D. Cohen, *Culture of Honor: The Psychology of Violence in the South,* Boulder, CO: Westview Press, 1996: 46–48; Raine, A., P Brennan, and S.A. Mednick, "Birth Complications Combined With Early Maternal Rejection at Age 1 Year Predispose to Violent Crime at Age 18 Years," *Archives of General Psychiatry,* 51(1994): 986; Greenberg, J., "Employee Theft as a Reaction to Underpayment Inequity: The Hidden Costs of Pay Cuts," *Journal of Applied Psychology,* 75(1990): 561–568; Makkai, T., and J. Braithwaite, "Reintegrative Shaming and Compliance With Regulatory Standards," *Criminology,* 32(1994): 361–385.
25. de Segonzac, A., *Visa for Peking,* London: Heinemann, 1956.

Lawrence W. Sherman, "Trust and Confidence in Criminal Justice." Reprinted from *National Institute of Justice Journal,* Issue No. 248, pp. 23–31. ✦

Chapter 2

Defining Police Strategies

Problem Solving, Problem-Oriented Policing and Community-Oriented Policing

Ronald V. Clarke

Clarke offers a review of the contribution of problem solving to police work based upon several hundred applications submitted for review to the Police Executive Research Forum's (PERF's) Herman Goldstein Award for Excellence in Problem-Oriented Policing (POP). POP encourages police officers to go beyond the isolated crime incidents they deal with on a daily basis. Instead, POP encourages police officers to use a standardized problem-solving approach to identify patterns among related crime incidents and then create ways to solve them.

In his review of POP applications from police agencies across the nation, Clarke found that a majority of police agencies did not fully use a POP approach. For example, "officers frequently fail to specify the problems they are addressing. They make this mistake in one of two ways: either they undertake a project that is too small to fit the definition of problem-oriented policing," or they select an issue that is too big of a problem for POP to tackle. Clarke concludes by discussing how such mistakes can be avoided when engaging in the problem-solving process.

Introduction

Problem-oriented policing represents the future of policing. Unfortunately, many recent examples of problem-oriented policing projects bear little resemblance to Herman Goldstein's original definition. This misrepresentation is dangerous because faulty implementation puts the concept at risk of being pronounced a failure before it has been properly tested.

This paper contains a laundry list of "lessons learned" derived from reading several hundred submissions for the Police Executive Research Forum's (PERF's) Herman Goldstein Award for Excellence in Problem-Oriented Policing. While many of the projects submitted for this award are well-written and creative examples of problem-oriented policing, the majority do not seem to fit the original definition. Rather, they simply represent efforts that individual departments feel are commendable. Whether they successfully deviate from the traditionally reactive approach to policing, however, is unclear.

The focus of this paper, however, is not on submissions that were either commendable or irrelevant. It addresses submissions that are recognizable as problem-oriented policing projects, but that fall significantly short of the ideal. Such projects lack rigor—in other words, precision and specificity. The following discussion will use the four stages of the SARA (scanning, analysis, response, assessment) model of problem solving to identify ways in which the current practice falls short, and make recommendations for how it might be used appropriately.

Deficiencies in Current Problem-Oriented Policing Practices

Scanning

During the scanning stage, officers frequently fail to specify the problems they are addressing. They make this mistake in one of two ways: either they undertake a project that is too small to fit the definition of problem-oriented policing, but that satisfies the criteria for problem solving; or they address a problem with a response that is too ambitious and broad in its objectives and that more closely satisfies the definition of community-oriented policing.

Small, beat-level projects in which an officer is able to solve a troublesome, recurring problem often fit the definition of problem solving more than that of problem-oriented policing. For example, imagine a situation in which a confused, lonely, old man has been making calls to the police department almost daily for a variety of concerns. In reality, he might be calling just to have someone to talk to. Imagine further that the officer assigned to the neighborhood in which the man lives persuades the man's family to find him professional care and that, as a result, the man stops calling the police department. In this situation, the beat officer's response fits the definition of problem solving and is the kind of initiative that should be encouraged and rewarded. However, it does not fit the definition of problem-oriented policing as it was originally intended. A problem-oriented approach to this example would have played itself out as follows: the experience of dealing with this particular old man led to an examination of calls for service in the department as a whole, and confirmed a hypothesis that older citizens who lived alone were generating a significant portion of the total number of calls for service and absorbing an even greater amount of police resources. In the latter scenario, the scanning revealed a problem in the aggregate that the police could first analyze before responding. This is a very different process from that of beat-level problem solving.

Both problem solving and problem-oriented policing are meritorious activities that should be encouraged through training and rewards. However, the police do not serve either activity well by confusing them or treating them as identical.

Examples of more ambitious projects that do not fit the definition of problem-oriented policing include those that address a "problem neighborhood," "problematic public housing project," or "gang delinquency." Each of these represents not a single problem, but a collection of many different problems that need to be separately analyzed and for which solutions need to be separately developed. In a public housing development, for example, the police may encounter such problems as drug markets, juvenile joyriding, auto theft by adult criminals, and vandalism in the elevators. These are all separate problems that require individual examinations, data collection methods and responses.

When an overambitious problem is identified as the focus of a problem-oriented project, there is a serious danger of confusing problem-oriented policing with the wider, more diffuse concept of community-oriented policing. This is the case for many of the projects submitted for the Goldstein Award. Failure to specify the nature of the problem destroys the discrete problem focus of the project, and leads to a lack of direction at the beginning of analysis.

Analysis

Officers who are working through the SARA model of a problem-oriented policing project often skip the analysis phase or conduct an analysis that is too rudimentary. During an investigation of calls for service or crime reports, they rarely identify patterns about how often or when a crime is occurring, or about where the problem is concentrated. They also make few attempts to disaggregate statistics to determine the precise nature of the problem. For example, juveniles may be stealing automobiles for any number of reasons, including joyriding, temporary transportation, selling for parts, etc. These are very different problems that involve different motivations, and therefore require tailor-made solutions. Frequently, however, officers combine all of these separate occurrences into one large "auto theft" category without examining in detail the nature of the particular problem being addressed.

Finally, officers undertaking a problem-oriented policing project do not always take full advantage of information collected by other agencies, including schools, hospitals and shopping malls. Even telephone companies regularly gather data concerning vandalism to public phones, thefts and graffiti. By failing to utilize such relevant information, officers forfeit the chance to learn all they can about a situation and permit a careful analysis of all possible responses.

Response

Too frequently, the responses in current problem-oriented policing projects are variations of conventional police practices (e.g., crackdowns, surveillance, arrests). There have been indications that officers are making greater use of CPTED (e.g, environmental changes in the layout of a city park or parking lot), abatements and other civil remedies. However, a large repertoire of other kinds of responses are being neglected. As will be discussed later, many of these have been developed in the field of situational crime prevention.

Assessment

Assessment is one of the most crucial yet most underutilized parts of problem-oriented policing projects. For busy police officers, this final step may seem a luxury; in actuality, however, it is the key to facilitating an active exchange of experiences among different departments. If law enforcement agencies do not have a mechanism to learn from others' mistakes and assist others to learn from their experiences, they will always be reinventing the wheel.

In some cases, especially for projects more appropriately defined as problem solving, evaluation may not be needed because it is obvious that matters have improved. Using the above example, if the lonely, old man is no longer making calls, the problem is solved. Evaluation in this case would be redundant. In situations where evaluation is appropriate, however, and some attempt has been made to move beyond a purely impressionistic assessment, it is rarely done properly. Common limitations among law enforcement agencies include the following:

- Police report reductions in calls for service or arrests without relating the results to specific actions taken. In other words, the police frequently fail to examine whether variations in "dosage levels" of the response correlate with variations in relevant crime statistics.
- Police consider assessment only as an afterthought, rather than building it into the original outline for the entire project.
- Police fail to present any control data. For example, if some action has been taken in one location that appears to have produced a decrease in the number of calls for service, the police do not generally document what, if anything, happened in a similar, nearby location where no action was taken.
- On the rare occasions when control data are presented, police fail to ensure that the control is adequate. For example, the control location may be so different from the original site that it is impossible to conclude anything from the comparison.
- Police fail to study displacement. Many agencies do not realize that their response may simply have pushed the problem elsewhere.

Improving the Situation

These deficiencies must be corrected if problem-oriented policing is to prosper. The most important requirement for police departments is to improve their research and analysis units. The key to effective problem-oriented policing, according to Goldstein, is to understand the who, what, when, where, why and how of the problem. However, adding more units or staff will not of itself solve the problem; agencies also need to assign these units a different role. At present, police managers often perceive research and analysis units only as a source of data. Crime analysis units could and should perform a much more active role in problem-oriented policing by being involved right from the start of a project. They can assist other project team members not only to conduct a proper analysis, but also to formulate a response that is appropriate to the analysis, and to design a complete assessment plan.

The second important requirement is that officers involved in problem-oriented policing become much more familiar with the field of environmental criminology, particularly the work on situational crime prevention. This concept is very similar to problem-oriented policing in that it uses exactly the same "action research" methodology. A situational crime prevention project begins by identifying a highly specific crime problem, analyzing it in detail, selecting a response, implementing that response and evaluating the outcome. The only difference is that situational crime prevention is not only available to law enforcement agencies; rather, it has been designed for use by any agency, public or private, that wishes to address a crime problem in its jurisdiction. For example, situational crime prevention projects have been implemented by managers of transportation systems, retail chains, town centers and entertainment districts, public housing projects, schools, hospitals, libraries, university campuses and many other organizations. A particularly good example concerns a project initiated by the management of the Port Authority Bus Terminal in Manhattan. Specifically, they introduced a wide-ranging situational crime prevention intervention that resulted in dramatic reductions in the number of robberies and instances of prostitution, drug dealing, baggage theft and phone scams. This experience holds many useful lessons for problem-oriented policing. The following section will track some of these recommendations through the four stages of the SARA model.

Scanning

Much research in environmental criminology has sought to break down larger categories of crime into more specific kinds of offenses and analyze these in detail. This ensures that problems are specified correctly—an essential requirement for any problem-oriented policing project.

The importance of correctly specifying the problem is illustrated by a recent study of residential burglary in a small British city, as undertaken by two environmental criminologists, Barry Poyner and Barry Webb (1991). In the scanning phase of the project, they determined that there were at least two separate problems. The first consisted of residential burglaries taking place in the inner core of the old city. The dwellings in this part of the city consisted mostly of row houses or duplexes—high-density housing on narrow streets with buildings immediately abutting each other. The problem at this location involved break-ins during the day, usually from the front. The items stolen were easily carried, such as cash and jewelry. The offenders seemed to be on foot and were probably juveniles.

The second, rather different problem occurred in the newer suburbs surrounding the city. The targets of theft were mostly electronic goods, such as VCRs, small televisions and audio equipment. In this case, the thieves used cars to transport the stolen goods. The researchers determined that the items being stolen at the suburban locations were more difficult to fence and that these burglaries required more planning and organization. Consequently, they theorized that the people committing these burglaries were probably more experienced and resourceful.

In this study, the broad problem of residential burglary turned out to encompass two quite separate problems, most likely committed by two different groups of offenders using different methods and seeking different goods. Combining the two problems into one would almost certainly result in a loss of focus and inefficient problem solving.

This is just one example of studies in which environmental criminologists have identified and studied highly specific types of crime. The methodologies they employ, as well as the results of their research, have considerable relevance for improving problem specification in problem-oriented policing. As mentioned earlier, this would help police practitioners to differentiate between problem-oriented policing and community-oriented policing. More important, however, the key to distinguishing between these concepts lies in the theory that underpins situational crime prevention—what criminologists call "opportunity theory." Opportunity theory specifically refers to the routine activity and rational choice theories, which consider opportunity to be a cause of crime. The main principles can be summarized as follows:

- Immediate situational factors are vital in determining the occurrence of crime, perhaps more important than distant "root causes."
- Opportunity does not merely determine the place and time of crime, but helps to determine its occurrence.
- An increase in opportunities will result in more crime.
- Human weaknesses are widespread, and nobody is exempt from the temptation to commit crime.
- Each offender makes a choice to commit a crime, which serves some purpose for him or her.
- It is as important to understand these *motives* as the background factors that provide the *motivation* for a crime.
- Targets and guardians are as much the proper subject matter for criminology study as are offenders.
- Crime can be reduced by reducing opportunities for crime.

Situational crime prevention is unambiguously focused on reducing opportunities for crime. This is also true for most problem-oriented policing projects, although the objectives for this approach are much less clear because of its common confusion with community-oriented policing. However, if opportunity reduction were more clearly and openly articulated as the objective of problem-oriented policing, the police would be able to distinguish it from community-oriented policing, which has a much broader (and vaguer) set of objectives, including mobilizing community support. It would also enable the police to defend themselves against criticism that they are only dealing with the symptoms, rather than the root causes, of crime. Opportunity is a cause of crime; therefore, the police are automatically addressing a root cause of a crime by reducing opportunity.

Analysis

The analysis step of the SARA model plays a key role in environmental criminology. Indeed, the field is defined as the analysis of crime patterns in time and space. Some of the concepts environmental criminologists have developed, such as "hot spots," are already well known to police. However, the police are not generally familiar with "crime generators" and "crime attractors," both of which are varieties of hot spots. The former are "hot" simply because they are places where large numbers of offenders and victims come together in the natural course of their daily activities, while the latter are "hot" because they attract offenders based on the opportunities they offer for crime. Each requires different types of responses.

Another environmental criminology concept with great relevance for problem oriented policing is that of repeat victimization. Most of the recent research on this subject has been conducted in Britain. The results have indicated that, for many different categories of crimes, the chances of falling victim are greater for those who have already been victimized. In addition, the more recent the victimization, the greater the probability of being victimized again. These facts are important for prevention because they suggest that if a preventive effort is focused on recent victims, there is a greater chance of achieving a successful outcome.

In addition to theoretical and conceptual tools, environmental criminology has developed various data-collection methods that could be of considerable assistance in the analysis phase of problem-oriented policing projects. These include:

- victimization surveys, which provide more detail about the impact of the problem on people's everyday lives;
- crime audits, where interviewers walk around a neighborhood with people who live there or around a park with regular users, and record where they report being afraid; and
- structured interviews with offenders to find out more about their motives and their methods of committing crimes.

The wider use of these and many other data-collection methods from environmental criminology would greatly enrich the understanding of problems being addressed in problem-oriented projects. An improved analysis would, in turn, result in the development of more effective responses.

Response

Environmental criminology can also help at the response stage by expanding the repertoire of methods used to reduce opportunities for crime. The following four methods for achieving this goal have been identified in the situational crime prevention literature:

- increase the perceived effort needed to commit a crime,
- increase the perceived risks of committing a crime,
- reduce the rewards of committing a crime, and
- remove the excuses for committing a crime.

A variety of means can be used to accomplish each of these objectives. Table 2.1 outlines 16 of the more common techniques applied to crime and disorder problems. Examples are provided to clarify each of these ways; the final column in particular focuses on ways to reduce

Table 2.1
Sixteen Opportunity-Reducing Techniques

Increasing Perceived Effort	**Increasing Perceived Risks**	**Reducing Anticipated Rewards**	**Removing Excuses**
1. Target Hardening Slug rejecter device Steering locks Bandit screens	*5. Entry/exit screening* Automatic ticket gates Baggage screening Merchandise tags	*9. Target removal* Removable car radio Women's refuges Phonecard	*13. Rule setting* Customs declaration Harassment codes Hotel registration
2. Access control Parking lot barriers Fenced yards Entry phones	*6. Formal surveillance* Red light cameras Burglar alarms Security guards	*10. Identifying property* Property marking Vehicle licensing Cattle branding	*14. Stimulating conscience* Roadside speedometers "Shoplifting is stealing" "Idiots drink and drive"
3. Deflecting offenders Bus stop placement Tavern location Street closures	*7. Surveillance by employees* Pay phone location Park attendants CCTV systems	*11. Reducing temptation* Gender-neutral listings Off-street parking Rapid repair	*15. Controlling disinhibitors* Drinking-age laws Ignition interlock V-chip
4. Controlling facilitators Credit card photo Gun controls Caller-ID	*8. Natural surveillance* Defensible space Street lighting Cab driver I.D.	*12. Denying benefits* Ink merchandise tags PIN for car radios Graffiti cleaning	*16. Facilitating compliance* Easy library checkout Public lavatories Trash bins

Source: Clarke, R. 1997. *Situational Crime Prevention: Successful Case Studies,* 2nd ed. Albany, NY: Harrow and Heston.

routine offenses, such as speeding, drunk driving and stealing small items from employers.

Assessment

Much of the work in situational crime prevention has been done by researchers, who routinely make provisions for assessment at the beginning of each project. The National Institute of Justice recently reviewed many of the 90 intervention studies conducted to date that have been carefully evaluated, and found that more than 90 percent of them showed substantial reductions in crime. Examples of such interventions include:

- baggage screening at airports,
- steering locks,
- security-coded car radios,
- improved street lighting,
- video cameras in city centers,
- video cameras in senior citizen apartment blocks,
- red light and speed cameras,
- shoplifting tags and inktags,
- road closures and street barriers,
- graffiti removal from New York City subway trains,
- a CPTED design on the Metropolitan Washington subway system,
- anti-bandit screens in a British post office,
- exact fare on buses, and
- cash reduction in convenience stores and betting shops.

In these and many other studies, the evaluation generally included an examination of displacement to determine whether the intervention achieved a real reduction in crime or simply pushed the problem elsewhere. Rene Hesseling, of the Dutch Ministry of Justice, recently reviewed 55 situational prevention studies that examined displacement. He found that in 22 of these studies, there was absolutely no evidence of displacement, even though the problem was greatly reduced. In the remaining 33 studies, there was some evidence of displacement, but in no case was the amount of crime displaced equal to the amount of crime prevented. In other words, in every one of these studies, there was some net gain. This finding is important because it shows that displacement does not always undermine the value of the approach.

In addition, researchers are now learning that focused interventions, such as those common in problem-oriented policing projects, sometimes reduce crime beyond the target intervention through a process called "diffusion of benefits." This is illustrated by a project undertaken at a university campus in Britain where CCTV cameras were installed to monitor the parking lots. Although the cameras provided surveillance to only three of the four campus parking lots, crimes involving automobiles dropped in all the lots. According to the displacement hypothesis, if the cameras reduced crime in the lots they surveyed, the number of crimes should have increased in the lot that was not covered. That crime did not increase in the fourth lot suggests that the thieves who had been coming to the university to prey on automobiles decided that this was no longer worthwhile. While they were aware that the cameras had been installed, they most likely did not know where the cameras were. This sort of reversed displacement frequently occurs and gives a metaphorical extra bang for the preventive buck.

Conclusion

An injection of environmental criminology into problem-oriented policing would help to improve the rigor of the projects being undertaken. It would also have the academic benefit of making this type of crime prevention more relevant to practice. Most important, however, it would help to demonstrate that problem oriented policing can achieve substantial reductions in crime and other troublesome behaviors.

Ronald V. Clarke, "Defining Police Strategies: Problem Solving, Problem-Oriented Policing and Community-Oriented Policing." Reprinted from T. Shelley and A. Grant (Eds.), *Problem-Oriented Policing,* pp. 315–326. Copyright © 1998 Police Executive Research Forum. Reproduced with permission. ✦

Chapter 3

New Skyline

Eli B. Silverman

E*li Silverman offers an insightful perspective on the direction of a major technological development in modern police departments based on his field study of a unique approach implemented in the New York City Police Department (NYPD). In the early 1990s, the city's crime rate had reached an unusually high level. Under the leadership of a new chief, William Bratton, a new strategy of fighting crime was created.*

CompStat makes use of modern computer technology to provide accurate and up-to-date crime information for administrators to use in analyzing and solving local crime incidents. Computerized crime mapping in a neighborhood, for example, is one of the major tools used in the CompStat approach. Consequently, crime incidents are not looked upon as isolated problems but instead are examined for their connection to patterns of problems that require coordinated efforts of various units, shifts, and administrators. As a result, CompStat has produced an impressive reduction in crime. For example, Silverman notes that from 1993 to 1998 the murder rate decreased 67 percent in New York City to a 30-year low.

According to Silverman, such "intelligence-led" policing reflects a new direction that allows departments to take advantage of technological improvements that can be used to help control crime. Such an approach emphasizes the crucial role of information in the decision-making process of police administrators and rank-and-file officers, and simultaneously demonstrates the potential benefit of information sharing among agencies and internal units.

> First Rule of Holes: When you are in one, you should stop digging.
>
> —Molly Ivins[1]

The reduction of crime in New York City continues to get good reviews. As important as New York's crime abatement is, it is not the main focus of this [chapter]. Rather, I have sought to answer the following question: If pre-1994 NYPD reform movements were short-lived and cyclical, what is it about today's NYPD that may keep it vibrant and one step ahead of crime? Decentralization, greater accountability, and a flattened hierarchy—issues that typically dominate the current bureaucratic reform agenda—are not new. What is new since 1994 is the setting in place of unusual engines of organizational change within the NYPD. This change has been sustained not just by strong leadership but through the dynamics of intelligence-led policing. And it is this informed decision making that is the focus of this [article].

The NYPD currently is breaking out of its old bunker mentality, which has been "when in doubt, dig deeper." Police departments have traditionally been shackled by outdated ideas, such as the belief that a rapid, beefed-up response to crime incidents reduces crime. When more cops and radio car runs did nothing to stop rising crime rates, the police sought refuge in social and economic explanations. The former high-ranking chief James Hannon noted, "There were blocks in the city so bad—where rocks were thrown off roofs at the cops—that the department simply did not send anyone into them; they stationed patrol cars at either end instead."[2] Such sections of the city with impoverished conditions, entrenched unemployment, and long-standing animosity toward the police were written off.

Since 1994, however, the NYPD has made structural changes in the ways it looks at and deals with crime. The current NYPD mind-set contrasts starkly with that of previous eras.

One police analyst remembered, "The department of 1982, despite its changes at the top, seemed to be working very much like the police department of 1976. . . . [I]t was a well-oiled machine and the chiefs were all more or less interchangeable . . . as long as they stayed honest and were committed to a clean and nonviolent department."[3]

"Well-oiled" and innovative can represent opposite ends of a spectrum. Today's young cast of precinct commanders and higher-echelon officers sharply differs from previous decades when "it was only after reaching retirement status, after putting in your twenty years, that you began climbing the appointive ranks. That was why the police department's 'young tigers' were well into middle age."[4] Risk takers in the old days received less organizational encouragement than they do today. To make matters worse, the crime workload far exceeded the current number of cases. Manhattan alone had 661 homicides in 1972, more than all of New York City in 1998. As recently as 1993, there were more than 600,000 felonies committed in the city; 1998 will see under 300,000 felonies—a very significant drop.

Yet . . . it was the police administrations of those high-crime years that prepared the ground for today's new structure. Increased decentralization, enhanced supervision, and greater command accountability and authority have been NYPD reform themes for more than a century. And although these ambitious aims have proven elusive or transitory, they have had a residual, if not a cumulative, effect.

Robert McGuire, commissioner for almost six years (1978–1983) and one of the longest-serving modern-day commissioners, could still observe five years after Commissioner Patrick Murphy departed, "We are trying to reverse a trend. We want the area commanders and the precinct captains to take more responsibility. We have to let them see they're not going to get hurt if they make their own decisions."[5]

In the 1990s, Commissioner Lee Brown's community policing program advocated mini–police chiefs within the department responsible for their particular communities. One observer heralded Brown's arrival with an optimistic forecast: He "has creative ideas about policing . . . [d]ecentralizing the police bureaucracy, reemphasizing the importance of the cop on the beat (as opposed to those in patrol cars and special units), reestablishing a sense of law and order in neighborhoods that have teetered on the brink of anarchy for decades."[6]

If many post-1993 reform impulses differ little from previous attempts, what accounts for their greater success? The answer is twofold. The first reason is firm external backing. The strong political support from Mayor Giuliani was a *sine qua non*. The mayor propelled many of the forces for change, and he stood by them. There were occasions when commanders complained to their community political leaders that they felt mistreated at CompStat meetings. When the politicos in turn complained to the mayor, he did not back off. Giuliani's close relationship with Commissioner Howard Safir has also been critical to NYPD success. The second essential factor is the successful convergence of information and decisions in CompStat meetings.

Intelligence-Led Policing

I have become an addict of sorts—a CompStat junkie, having attended well over 100 headquarters and borough CompStat meetings, as well as miniprecinct meetings and numerous precinct-related activities. And it seems the more you look, the more you find, the more you learn, the more you want to see, and the more there is to learn.

The lessons of CompStat are there for practitioners and researchers alike, as the old divisions between them erode and common areas of interest come together. The NYPD, assisted by the National Institute of Justice (NIJ) and others, has fostered an unprecedented sharing of information—both internally and among law enforcement organizations and students of policing.

Quickly bringing the right information to bear on police decisions, or on any decisions, for that matter, is not a novel notion. Over fifty years ago, a young social scientist and future Nobel Prize winner diagnosed the malfunctioning of large organizations. Long before Tom Peters, James Champy, and other modern-day management gurus unleashed the curative powers of down-sizing, flattening, empowerment, and reengineering, Herbert Simon examined the managerial elixirs of the 1940s.[7] The management approaches of that period were based on certain principles of administration that were considered universally applicable. Simon demonstrated how some of these principles—unity of command, task specialization, hierarchical arrangements, and increased numbers of people reporting to a supervisor—clash operationally and work at cross-purposes. He posited that all decisions are composite decisions, arising from "informational premises" and can be traced through formal and informal channels of communication.[8]

Particular administrative and managerial arrangements make sense only when they provide key decision makers with the appropriate and timely "premises" necessary for decisions. Therefore, every supervisory and managerial arrangement in the organization must be customized to support the decision makers' informational needs.

The NYPD has made enormous strides in feeding information to appropriate decision-making levels. Traditionally, NYPD headquarters was perceived as the nerve center of the department's decision-making apparatus. Changes in operational police tactics were conceived, formulated, and issued from headquarters, primarily on a citywide basis, and often with very little input from field commands. The post-1993 restructuring and crime-control strategies provided field commanders with far more leverage over their own troops. The changes also required the formation of teams designed to break down the informational barriers separating the generalists assigned to the patrol divisions from specialized units such as the Detective Bureau and Organized Crime Control Bureau. Citywide specialty units such as the Street Crime Unit and the School Program to Educate and Control Drug Abuse (SPECDA) were subdivided, and their personnel reassigned to boroughs.

The post-1993 NYPD leadership also realized that uniform, citywide crime-fighting decisions were not as effective as individualized strategies designed for particular communities. One precinct anticrime supervisor explained that a plainclothes unit in midtown Manhattan could easily follow a suspect on foot or by car without being detected, whereas the police unit would immediately be identified on the far less populated streets of Brooklyn.

By increasing the authority and responsibility of precinct commanders, the NYPD freed them from having to forward information along the chain of command simply to receive high-level confirmation or reassurance.

Information from headquarters is no longer released to units only on a "need-to-know" basis, or maintained solely by specialized units. Precincts have become not only sources of information but also centers for rapid decision making based on firsthand analyses of crime data.

Strategic Information

Post-1993 strategy documents publicly acknowledge the failure of previous crime-fighting initiatives that were introduced on an incremental basis in isolated units or geographic areas. New administrative positions have been created to facilitate the flow of information within the NYPD. For example, Strategy Number Four, "Breaking the Cycle of Domestic Violence," directed precincts to designate a "Domestic Violence Prevention Officer," charged with gathering and maintaining precinct domestic violence information. This officer was responsible for monitoring the status of cases through a review of departmental records and personal contacts (such as home visits, correspondence, phone calls, and station house interviews). One of the officer's major functions was to identify any locations requiring special attention. Domestic violence investigators were also named in each precinct detective squad to investigate open complaints and identify patterns of abuse.

In addition to creating entirely new information sources, the strategies transferred some units and positions, again for the purpose of coordination of information. One Narcotics Division unit, for example, was assigned to work with homicide detectives to make connections between murders and illegal drug activity. For the connections to be of help, information had to be accurate and timely. Strategy Number Four, for example, introduced the "Domestic Violence Incident Report," so that alerted patrol officers would record their responses to domestic incidents. Such data are fed into a "Domestic Incident Database" to supply critical information regarding past violent episodes, existing orders of protection, and outstanding warrants for household members. A new police database of "Chronic Emotionally Disturbed Persons" was put together to aid responders, the courts, and medical practitioners in identifying individuals with a history of violent encounters.

At the end of 1996, Commissioner Safir unveiled a detailed strategy to reduce the numbers of persons who avoid prosecution by failing to appear before the courts. The strategy, "Bringing Fugitives to Justice,"[9] creates and utilizes more systematic informational databases to apprehend those who jump bail, disobey the terms of their parole or probation, or ignore appearance tickets or summonses. The strategy calls for compiling and prioritizing lists of fugitives wanted for serious crimes or narcotics offenses and coordinates efforts to apprehend them.

The vital link between information and crime fighting as demonstrated by the NYPD is receiving worldwide attention. The University of Maryland criminologist Charles F. Wellford found that the most important factor leading to the solution of a murder case is the swift notification of a homicide detective by the officer at the crime scene. Other critical information comes from running checks on guns, interviewing witnesses, and performing computer checks on witnesses and suspects. Taken together, these factors accurately predict the disposition of 99 percent of homicide cases.[10]

A movement in the United Kingdom called "intelligence-led policing" recognizes information's key role. This approach involves more refined police tactics, deployments, and strategies geared toward ensuring that all members of the force are in the right place with the right information. One strategy encourages the lowest level, British street bobbies (constables), to become more involved in solving major crimes because they are often in possession of vital community information.[11] While teaching at the Police Staff College in Bramshill, Hampshire, England, I learned of a constable who, as part of this new emphasis on total involvement and the sharing of information, was able (through his intimate knowledge of local conditions) to provide the key to locating a missing child who had diabetes.

CompStat Intelligence

The NYPD and organizations emulating its successes are undergoing a revolutionary change—a new way of relating to their environment. As NIJ Director Jeremy Travis writes:

> The new forms of policing that have emerged in recent years view crime as problems to be solved, not simply as an event to which the police react. The community is viewed as a partner in this effort, not merely as a collection of witnesses to be canvassed after the event and a public to be informed about police issues.[12]

The ability of police to function in this new way depends on their having access to accurate information and a mechanism for the coordinated use of that information.

CompStat has been the informational cement of reform, the central mechanism that provides communication links to traditionally isolated specialized units. Fragmentation is not unique to the NYPD. It plagues all large police departments and most large organizations. The Harvard management expert Rosabeth Kanter calls it "segmentalism" and notes, "The failure of many organization-change efforts has more to do with the lack . . . of an integrating, institutionalizing mechanism than with inherent problems in an innovation itself."[13] Without CompStat, fragmentation would continue to rule supreme. CompStat's confrontation of informational splintering is indispensable to the NYPD's organizational well-being.

Sorting out CompStat

CompStat's multidimensional qualities have positioned it as the catalyst of change within the NYPD. CompStat's beauty lies in its diversity. Informational, "need-to-know" crime stats have expanded into a multifunctional vessel for management planning and coordination.

As a management tool, CompStat has extended beyond crime fighting. Commissioner Safir uses it to monitor and address civilian complaints of misconduct against members of the police department. CompStat now includes citywide, borough, and precinct data by hour and time of day for FADO (force, abuse, discourtesy, and obscene language) citizen complaints.

It is no secret that questions have been raised about whether the new policing, with its assertive pursuit of low-level crime, actually encourages incidents of FADO—most dramatically illustrated by the terrible incident involving a Haitian immigrant, Abner Louima. On August 9, 1997, Louima was allegedly tortured, sodomized, and brutalized by four NYPD officers inside a police precinct when a wooden stick was shoved in his rectum and then his mouth. Louima had to wait an hour before he was taken to a hospital, where physician records document severe internal damage to his intestines and bladder. Fortunately, the incident triggered the arrest of four officers, the suspension of several others, and the transfer of still more officers, including the commanding officer of the precinct, who was on vacation at the time. The incident also led to the creation of a special mayoral task force, an inquiry into the effectiveness of the existing civilian complaint review board, the involvement of federal prosecutors, and an examination of the extent to which this incident was indicative of a pattern of police brutality. Commissioner Safir's FADO mechanism, along with the other measures just described, strongly suggests that the new policing is a force against, not in favor of, police brutality.

Nevertheless, safeguarding the rights of all citizens requires constant vigilance and scrutiny. Controversy erupted after the February 1999 killing of an unarmed West African street peddler in the foyer of his Bronx apartment building. Four white members of the NYPD's elite Street Crime Unit (SCU) fired forty-one times. Amadou Diallo, who had arrived from Guinea almost three years earlier and had no criminal record, was struck by nineteen bullets. The critics have every right to complain, but they have it wrong. It is not racism; it is not insensitive white cops systematically singling out minorities because of their ethnicity and color. What the police are doing is more of what they've been doing, and that is the real problem.

The NYPD's dramatic and highly successful onslaught on crime is rooted in the department's eagerness to examine crime critically and mount innovative, targeted crime-fighting approaches. If citizen trust and intelligence are critical to crime fighting, then the department is in danger of losing vital sources of information if it increases enforcement activities without regard to the community. For example, the strong nexus that the department uncovered between drugs and crime in Brooklyn North . . . is now being targeted in other boroughs, requiring a substantial increase in narcotics officers throughout the city. Even though the force has grown, it is not yet large enough to support the rising number of undercover narcotics officers, many of whom are being drawn from street patrol and other units. Although crime has gone down throughout the city, the decreasing uniformed presence intensifies public anxiety.

Policing involves both negative and positive citizen contact. When the negative far outweighs the positive, public confidence declines. The SCU, involved in the tragic Diallo shooting, has been highly successful in harvesting guns from the street, no doubt thereby decreasing violent crime. But more intensified police action is necessary to recover the dwindling number of street guns. Ratcheting up the pressure leads to more searches at the margins and possible mistakes, which rob the public of its sense of security and trust. In addition, the recent rapid expansion of the undercover SCU inevitably affects quality control and further drains the visible police force. Similarly, many community police officers—key citizen connectors—are being shifted to narcotics and other specialized units, further diminishing police visibility and public confidence.

We expect a lot from our police: enforce the law, reduce crime, and honor the rights of all citizens. In the last several years, the NYPD has been quite innovative in navigating these often conflicting currents. New times require a new commitment to innovative policing. Fear of police should not replace fear of crime.

CompStat Myths

Exploring some CompStat myths and misleading assumptions helps to spotlight its multidimensional qualities.

MYTH NUMBER ONE: CompStat is nothing more than up-to-date information—knowing what the level of crime is and when and where it is happening.

Response: Yes, CompStat is up-to-date crime information, which for many years was absent in the department. But it took vision to see the value and potential in these crime statistics, and confidence and a "can-do" mentality to believe that the police could do something about crime. The need and ability to know about the extent of crime and the events related to it had to precede the ability to manage crime. And it took creativity and diligence to establish a system to capture crime complaints and arrest activities. Primitive by today's standards, the first CompStat book later evolved into more refined and sophisticated versions. CompStat insiders refer to their first year as "spring training," a period of "tryouts and team building before the season began in earnest."[14]

MYTH NUMBER TWO: The only major difference between CompStat and approaches taken by other police departments is the use of sophisticated computer technologies and software mapping capabilities that complement statistical analyses and deployment data.

Response: The transformation of pin-mapping to computer mapping and other technological advances were unquestionably important. However, their value would not have been so pervasive without the injection of CompStat into the department's bloodstream. CompStat coordinates operations through the consistent review of various strategies. In the past, for example, a drug operation such as Operation Pressure Point would not be systematically and simultaneously observed for its impact on adjoining precincts. The examination of maps by all relevant participants is extremely important in addressing the complexity of the city and its neighborhoods. CompStat facilitates both uniform crime strategies applicable to all areas and special approaches.

A good case in point was a creative approach to bicycles, which, beginning about 1996, were used in robberies, shootings, and drug transactions. A commanding officer identified laws regulating the operation of bicycles. Through lawful bicycle inspections, enforcement swept up nineteen guns within that one precinct by the end of the summer. This success was heralded at a CompStat meeting and resulted in a citywide adoption of this strategy. The approach has subsequently resulted in the confiscation of hundreds of guns and large quantities of narcotics from this previously "invisible" criminal element.

MYTH NUMBER THREE: CompStat is just a crime strategy meeting. What is so innovative about having police officials focus on reducing crime?

Response: CompStat meetings represent a pioneering assemblage of multiple sources of information before all key NYPD and criminal justice agencies. CompStat coordinates the activities of parole and probation officials, district attorneys, corrections personnel, and other law enforcement groups. In years past, other concerns were considered more pressing—minimizing scandals, maintaining community well-being, and preserving a low police profile.

MYTH NUMBER FOUR: There are some who argue that CompStat is irrelevant to the way the police reduce crime. "It's a matter of priorities," reported one columnist.[15] They argue that the attacks on quality-of-life crimes and the department's "zero tolerance" policy have had the greatest impact on crime.

Response: Of course, police priorities and practices count. But through CompStat they are continually reviewed so that they can be revised as needed. CompStat helps the department assess the rigor and effectiveness of its crime strategies regarding quality of life, reclaiming public spaces, the Civil Enforcement Initiative, the nature of detective debriefings of arrestees, and the search for accomplices involved in particular crime incidents.

MYTH NUMBER FIVE: CompStat, after all, is only the application of modern management approaches and techniques, which ensure that precinct commanders are held accountable for results and are given the tools and authority to achieve these results. What is new about this? We have been hearing about these concepts since the turn of the [twentieth] century.

Response: CompStat is certainly a modern management tool to ensure commander accountability. And it is true that since the early 1900s, public officials and academics have been stressing the need to give executives authority commensurate with responsibility.

What the naysayers of CompStat fail to take into account is that change is not on autopilot, especially in a large, hierarchically structured organization. As practitioners and students of complex organizations know, change requires constant application through systematic reinforcing mechanisms.

MYTH NUMBER SIX: CompStat generates disagreement and conflict among different units of the department. This effect is detrimental, since stories (some accurate, some not) of conflict spread quickly and can demoralize participants.

Response: CompStat does not generate disagreement and conflict within the police department as much as it *reveals* them. This is a functional, not dysfunctional, aspect of the organization. Conflict and disagreement within various units are inevitable and can provide the grist for change. The CompStat quest for integration never ends; it is constantly pursued. Change is not painless, however. Organizations need to be committed to and open to learning.

CompStat: Double-Loop Learning

As police scholar Herman Goldstein observed, organizational change is multidimensional.[16] As an agent of change, CompStat has generated key NYPD reform processes such as new strategies, reengineering, and reorganization. CompStat has also been, to a large extent, the organizational glue that has bonded many of the changes together. CompStat operates on three major levels. Like the tip of an iceberg, the top level—informational sources and analyses—is most visible to the observer. One must be fairly close to the policing process to view the second layer, management and planning. And the bottom layer, organizational learning, which constitutes the structural base for the other two layers, is the least visible. Yet this layer tends to generate the most change. As often is the case, the hidden may be the most profound.

Constant Experimentation

A great deal of CompStat's activity falls under the heading of what organizational theorists call "double-loop learning."[17] This contrasts with single-loop learning (the predominant mode in most organizations), which involves the detection and correction of error, enabling an organization to continue with or achieve its policies and objectives. Double-loop learning, on the other hand, is more rare and involves questioning basic operating assumptions, entertaining disparate approaches, and experimenting with different arrangements. This experimental approach is reflected in many CompStat efforts, such as SATCOM–Brooklyn North and the Manhattan North Initiative (MNI), which are competing organizational and managerial arrangements devoted to different major antidrug efforts.

Critical Thinking

CompStat meetings discover difficulties and obstacles, defend positions, debunk the past and discard existing practices, demand ownership or responsibility, diagnose problems, design alternative strategies, deploy resources, delegate and coordinate responsibilities, devolve authority, disseminate information, and, finally, define and deliver solutions.

Coterie of Dedicated Staff

The CompStat process includes an extremely committed and imaginative staff. The CompStat office not only prepares for and analyzes meetings and data but also develops new CompStat informational components and issues. Remove the CompStat office from the chief of department's office, and you remove a substantial portion of its influence on reform.

Creative Problem Solving

CompStat is the forum where new problem-solving approaches are often presented, reviewed, analyzed, reexamined, and circulated. Many of these solutions are first developed at the precinct level. Operation Close Out, which was first tested in the 77th Precinct, provides a classic example of CompStat's problem-solving approach in terms of origination, diagnosis, classification, and the presentation of alternative solutions.

Continuity and Consistency

On a number of levels, CompStat is the central mechanism for the articulation of its own four-part mantra—accurate and timely intelligence, effective tactics, rapid deployment, and relentless and consistent follow-up, with particular emphasis on follow-up and constant monitoring.

Rarely noted aspects of CompStat's continuity and consistency are the regularity of its meetings and the commitment of attendees. The adoption of a regular schedule was a conscious decision made at the outset. It was based on the belief that CompStat would not be taken seriously by the troops if it met only occasionally. When a police officer was shot the night before a meeting in 1995, the 7:00 A.M. meeting still took place the next day. Headquarters and top-level borough participants rarely miss meetings, sustaining CompStat's continuity and consistency. Events, incidents, and discussions raised at one CompStat meeting are recorded, remembered, and revisited by these participants at subsequent meetings.

Control

While CompStat and other departmental innovations have placed some responsibility, accountability, and decision making at the borough and precinct levels, where they are most appropriate, the top-level officers have not lost control. Authority is still exercised at the top, but it is now a more informed version of control based on results, not just activities. When subordinates are evaluated, more emphasis is placed on crime rate declines than on such activities as arrests and radio car responses. These statistics still count, but they count in terms of their relationship to results, a reversal of previous policies.

Central Nervous System

CompStat serves as a thermometer of organizational well-being. If things go wrong or information is not being shared, the problem probably will emerge at some point at a CompStat meeting. The flow of a meeting can be interrupted when it becomes apparent that previous department directives (for example, distributing equipment from headquarters units to the field) have not been carried out.

Center Stage

Whether or not a patrol officer has ever attended a CompStat meeting, he or she is likely to have an opinion about CompStat. At the precinct level, CompStat meetings are known as the place where precinct commanders are grilled on crime-reduction efforts. This impression reinforces the patrol officer's desire to combat crime. Precinct commanders occasionally bring precinct officers who have performed a heroic feat to a CompStat meeting, where they are applauded for their accomplishment. The fact that CompStat has been noted at least twice on the television show *NYPD Blue* illustrates how its reputation has reached into popular culture.

Reframing Reform

The future course of reform hinges on several factors. The first is the need for reform champions—strong and energetic advocates who control resources. Although reform has been substantially advanced, it is never securely anchored. The former commissioner William Bratton's claim of *turnaround*[18] in the NYPD is not the same as "stay around." Bratton's recent observation that the department is on some sort of autopilot for further crime reduction "as a direct result of the systems we put in place"[19] understates the dynamics of reform. Systems do not operate independently of people taking action; they must be periodically changed and upgraded.

Previous reform efforts disintegrated once their vigilant champions left the scene. There is no reason to believe that the present is any different. Regardless of the nature of structural reform, there is also a visceral quality to police leadership. Cops need leaders who connect with the job, who are really there. Commissioner Safir's advancement in rank of vigorous reform advocates shows an understanding of this principle—that to be a leader is to be a connector, an energizer.

Reform will also depend on continued CompStat creativity. Despite denials, serious consideration at the top echelons was given to decentralizing CompStat and replacing most headquarters meetings with borough CompStat meetings. In 1998, there was a seven-week headquarters CompStat experiment in which the borough leaders were substituted for the top brass as the lead questioners. The quality of questioning varied, depending on the borough leadership.

In addition to continuing to shift operational responsibility to lower levels, effective borough CompStats could help deal with a long-standing NYPD problem: inadequate middle-level supervision. Repeated corruption and other scandals have revealed middle-level supervision as the fragile link in the chain of command. Despite the flattening of its hierarchical pyramid, the NYPD is still a large, thick bureaucracy. Addressing supervisory issues at the borough level makes sense.

CompStat and Communities

Long-lasting reform requires reaching out. The NYPD is learning that police action taken to reduce crime means little without constructive citizen contact and cooperation. Commissioner Safir has made encouraging moves in this direction. If precincts have an excessive number of complaints about abuse or discourtesy, commanders are queried at CompStat about how they are handling problem officers. The more this practice is developed and made known to the community, the stronger community ties will become.

An NYPD strategy issued in August 1997 forthrightly acknowledges that "whatever gains we have achieved in fighting crime are minimized if the price is the trust and respect of the community we serve."[20] This strategy seeks to incorporate courtesy, professionalism, and respect (CPR) through updated recruitment processes, executive development, officer training, monitoring of street behavior, CompStat review, and strengthened citizen involvement.

Community outreach, however, means far more. Public alliances, as George Kelling and Catherine Coles persuasively demonstrate, can pay huge dividends.[21] Harvard Public Health Professor Felton Earls noted, "Police work may help troubled neighborhoods. This could be the leading edge of greater change because reduced crime brings neighborhood life under better control."[22] The department has been working more closely with communities, and there are several encouraging signs.

For years the Washington Heights section of Manhattan served as the center of wholesale drug traffic for New York and the entire East Coast. Lying at the foot of the George Washington Bridge, the area was easily accessed from Upper Manhattan and New Jersey. West 163rd Street, between Broadway and Saint Nicholas Avenue, was the hub of this drug distribution. Gang leaders presided over an apartment building on the block by terrorizing legitimate tenants, "sometimes firing weapons indiscriminately and sometimes earning $70,000 a week in high-volume sales of small packages of cocaine and marijuana."[23] They also controlled two storefronts in a building on 163rd Street. The dealers spray-painted hallways to mark where drugs could be purchased and left threatening messages. The vacant apartments in the tenement building had become "a maze of traps, meant to block out . . . rivals and the police. Electrified wires had been stretched across window frames and holes had been smashed in walls and floors to provide easy escape routes. Hallway floors had been smeared with Vaseline to trip up unwary intruders."[24] Drivers and pedestrians were solicited and harassed on the street.

The NYPD launched a major antinarcotics project, the Northern Manhattan Initiative (NMI), in the fall of 1996 to shut down this criminal activity and help residents take back their neighborhood—if necessary, piece-by-piece, a block at a time. Eleven months later, intelligence gathering and law enforcement on 163rd Street resulted in what the *Boston Globe* characterized as a "virtual invasion" by the police.[25] By arresting and removing gang members, padlocking two gang-affiliated storefronts (through a nuisance abatement procedure), sealing off vacant apartments, and securing the targeted block, the police effectively shut down drug dealing, though some civil-liberties advocates voiced their outrage.[26] One officer, remembering the intensity of the situation, said, "We had lists of suspected drug locations on the block, and every building on that list you went into, you were going to come out with somebody who was either buying or dealing drugs."[27]

What followed was a textbook case of community policing. The department realized that dismantling one major drug organization does not prevent its replacement by another, especially when there are affluent customer bases in adjoining suburban Westchester County and New Jersey. "We're not going to put a Band-Aid on the problem," said precinct commander Garry McCarthy.[28] For the next three months, the department maintained a twenty-four-hours-a-day, seven-days-a-week presence, with uniformed police and established checkpoints on both ends of the block. Motorists attempting to enter the area were questioned by officers who had been designated as "point men" to choke off drive-by drug purchases. Deputy Commissioner George Grasso, who is in charge of NYPD legal matters, said, "We have designed this in a way where everyone's rights are protected. Residents have a right to live in a safe environment."[29]

People living in the neighborhood enrolled in the Trespass Affidavit Program: Residents signed a document giving the police permission to question and search anyone who entered their premises. The NYPD enlisted the help of numerous city agencies, including Sanitation, Parks, Transportation, Fire, Public Health, and Consumer Affairs, plus the New York City Chapter of the American Society for the Prevention of Cruelty to Animals. Streets were cleaned, abandoned cars were towed, potholes were filled, graffiti on walls and street lamps was painted over, and trees were planted.

Community mobilization followed. A community meeting attracted a record 300 attendees. Residents expressed increased confidence in the area's safety and in the police. The police formed a block association, a tenant association in each building, and a youth council. Tenant groups began patrolling each building, and citizens volunteered as block watchers. Landlords granted the newly formed tenant associations first right of refusal to new renters who they believed might be involved in the drug trade. The community vigorously responded to the NYPD's invitation to participate actively.

Crime has plunged dramatically. Before the gang was removed, there were twenty-seven major crimes on the block in nine months. In the next nine months, only four crimes occurred there. As McCarthy described police strategy, "We're trying to effect a long-term solution to something that has plagued this neighborhood, and still does. If we have to do it block-by-block, so be it."[30] Perhaps even more telling is a comment by eighty-eight-year-old community activist John Matthews, Sr., regarding a Christmas tree that stood outside in the neighborhood, untouched for five weeks: "Nobody took a light or a bulb or anything."[31]

New York City's community policing, in the words of criminal justice expert Jerome McElroy, "has apparently served enough time in purgatory" and is reemerging. The NYPD highlighted the "Model Block Program," as it came to be known and replicated elsewhere in the city, in its second annual CompStat conference, which drew hundreds of people from around the world. It is instructive that this 1998 conference was called "CompStat and Community Policing." In addition to McCarthy, seven other commanding officers recounted their activities in a session called "Problem Solving and Community Oriented Policing in the NYPD."

Inspector Edward Cannon, for example, the 75th Precinct's respected, crime-fighting commanding officer, presides over one of the city's most populous and busiest precincts. With a population of more than 161,000 people in 5.5 square miles, police dispatchers at this East New York section of Brooklyn receive between 95,000 and 100,000 radio calls annually. For years, Cannon has worked closely with the community. "Prevention and deterrence of crime is the goal," said Cannon. "The premise is simple—a very small number of criminals are doing a very large number of crimes." Cannon's multipronged strategies, which involves constantly mobilizing community groups, paid off with a 43 percent reduction in robberies in 1997 compared to 1993; 175 fewer persons were shot, and 91 fewer people were murdered.

Missing Intelligence

Since 1993, old and new NYPD strategies have swiftly combined to produce an avalanche of change. The department, however, is not positioned to objectively determine the factors most critical to its successes. Using SATCOM Brooklyn North as an example, the following criteria could be factored into that command's success: effective leadership, additional resources, innovative organization and management groupings, and high-intensity tactics. Brooklyn North advocates assert that its unique geo-based organization and managerial arrangements are the main reasons for its exemplary record. Headquarters, patrol, narcotics, and detective leaders, on the other hand, assert that the infusion of additional narcotics and other officers is what fueled SATCOM's accomplishments.

The NYPD's systematic attempts to assess its own accomplishments have traditionally been scanty. In recent years, senior-level officials, who . . . attend the Columbia University Police Management Institute (PMI), are required to evaluate specialized projects and then to report to the commissioner and his senior executive staff. One PMI group analyzed SATCOM. The report cogently summarized and lauded the strengths of SATCOM and other major antidrug efforts, such as the Manhattan North Initiative, and also offered suggestions. But true to form, there were no objective comparative assessments.

Such sparse evaluation efforts should be no surprise. As social scientist James Q. Wilson has observed:

> No good idea will be seriously evaluated by anyone who has a patent on it. A test requires objectivity, technical skills, and a long time horizon. A practitioner is subjective (he or she must struggle to get the idea launched in an often hostile environment), is skilled at creating ideas but not necessarily at testing them, and has a time horizon shaped by tomorrow's newspaper story or next month's budget hearing, not by the two or three years that an adequate testing in the field involves.[32]

Headquarters' data monitoring scarcely makes its way into the department's operational mainstream. For several years, the Office of Management Analysis and Planning, under the enlightened leadership of Deputy Commissioner for Policy and Planning Michael J. Farrell, has tracked "certain key indicators of performance that reflect Department activity within the crime strategies." The report, *Action Indicators for Police Strategies,* for example, assesses the antigun strategy and provides comparative borough numbers on reports of shooting victims, shooting incidents, firearms search warrants, arrests for possession, and guns received. These figures compare current figures with last year's numbers and are distributed to all department chiefs. But many of the units are not acquainted with the report and its information.

Final Assessment

It has been said that criminologists aren't much better predictors than meteorologists.[33] That's a pity, because prediction is crucial. The NYPD asserts, "If you can predict it, you can prevent it."[34] This message reflects the department's post-1993 response to reducing crime. Following the department's lead, an assessment and a recommendation regarding the NYPD are in order.

CompStat reform has had a successful run. But no show runs forever. To forestall closing, CompStat requires constant rejuvenation. There are many possibilities: treating CompStat as a supervisory training mechanism; sending staff to CompStat college (described below); and using CompStat to improve CPR (courtesy, professionalism, and respect), citizen satisfaction, and community outreach. Without an aggressive drive to find new solutions and innovations to old problems, CompStat will become static, and reform will dwindle.

The NYPD can stay fresh and proactive through independent, objective analyses of its operation at different stages. If the NYPD sees itself as more than just a large police department, but instead as a laboratory for the benefit of police organizations everywhere—a testing ground in which innovations are successfully applied—it will help ensure CompStat's flourishing run.

This approach closely resembles what University of Maryland criminologist Lawrence Sherman labels "evidence-based policing." He proposes more "basic research on what works best when implemented properly under controlled conditions and ongoing outcomes research about the results each unit is actually achieving by applying or ignoring basic research in practice."[35] Sherman forcefully argues that closer linkages between research and practice will aid police strategies and problem solving.

Sherman praises CompStat for advancing "the results accountability principle farther than ever before," but he contends that CompStat "has not used the scientific method to assess cause and effect. Successful managers are rewarded, but successful methods are not pinpointed and codified."[36] Although . . . CompStat does pinpoint and codify successful methods quite well, it is true that assessments have not been done scientifically.

Of course, police departments do not exist in order to provide laboratories for social science research, but they can provide data for the benefit of both scholarship and practice. Missed evaluations are missed opportunities, especially when there are so many new initiatives. A practical benefit of objective evaluations of the NYPD would be sharpened resource allocation. There are numerous models of optimum manpower distribution. Usually, however, the department bestows additional personnel to precinct, subway, or public housing areas where crime is rising or where influential constituents live. To its credit, CompStat is not tolerant when precinct commanders automatically respond "we need more people" to questions about below-par crime fighting. Yet, in some cases, insufficient or poorly used personnel may be the true explanations for crime spikes.

CompStat is good at examining police deployment but rarely reviews staffing levels of comparable precincts. Consider the scenario where Precinct A is more productive than comparable precincts with similar staffing levels. Perhaps Precinct A deserves even more resources to multiply its effectiveness. These types of analyses rarely enter the resource-allocation process. They would enhance the impact of hard information and possibly decrease bureaucratic infighting.

Today's police departments share knowledge and information on a scale far broader than ever before; the NYPD has been the source of much of this organizational restructuring. CompStat embodies the spirit and actions of many reformers seeking to make their groups more manageable and accountable—to deliver what is promised. It is not surprising that correctional, educational, and other institutions have also explored CompStat.

Within the NYPD itself, there is a great deal of sharing. In spring 1998, the Police Academy launched a curriculum consisting of fifteen-week sessions of three hours a week in which savvy commanding officers (COs) share their crime-strategy experiences with new and soon-to-be COs. CompStat College, according to Dr. James O'Keefe, NYPD's director of training, is a way of "perpetuating the corporate culture" by featuring a specific crime strategy approach during each session. Instead of having new COs get "beat up" at CompStat meetings, observes O'Keefe, "we try to shorten their learning curve." CompStat College sessions are videotaped, and a Crime Control Strategies Reference Guide is provided to participants. The guide and seminar discussions also explore effective ways to organize, display, and present information at CompStat meetings. The goal is for the participants to arrive together at innovative crime strategies. CompStat is growing institutional offshoots.

In an age when societal forces seem inexorable and overwhelming and the collective action of professionals often seems inconsequential, the NYPD has by most accounts made an enormous contribution to the city's well-being. Reflected in the city's polished image is its newest commodity, policing strategies that transform the way organizations gather and use information. This revolution in "blue" may resonate for decades as a profound contribution from the city that has no bounds.

Notes

1. Quoted in William A. Geller, "Suppose We Were Really Serious About Police Departments Becoming Learning Organizations?" *National Institute of Justice Journal* (Dec. 1997), p. 2.
2. Barbara Gelb, *Varnished Brass: The Decade after Serpico* (New York: Putnam, 1983), 229.
3. Ibid., 277.
4. Ibid., 56.
5. Ibid., 248.
6. Joe Klein, *New York Magazine*, 2 Oct. 1990, p. 7.
7. Herbert A. Simon, *Administrative Behavior*, 3rd ed. New York: Free Press, 1967).
8. Ibid., 221.
9. New York City Police Department, *Bringing Fugitives to Justice* (New York, 1996).
10. Charles F. Wellford, "Factors Affecting the Clearance of Homicides: A Multi-City Study" (paper presented at the Annual Conference on Criminal Justice Research and Evaluation, Na-

tional Institute of Justice, Washington, D.C., July 26–29, 1998).

11. Her Majesty's Inspectorate of Constabulatory, "Policing with Intelligence, Criminal Intelligence, " *HMIC Thematic Inspection Report on Good Practice, 1997/1998* (London: Her Majesty's Stationery Office, 1997); U.K. Audit Commission, "Tackling Crime Effectively (I and II)" (London: Her Majesty's Stationery Office, 1994, 1996).
12. Jeremy Travis, "Foreword," *Justice Quarterly* 12 (1995): 623.
13. Rosabeth Moss Kanter, *The Change Masters* (New York: Simon and Schuster, 1983), 301.
14. Bill Gorta, "Zero Tolerance—The Real Story or the Hidden Lessons of New York," *Police Research and Management* 2 (1998): 20.
15. Leonard Levitt, "It's a Matter of Priorities," *Newsday,* 17 Feb. 1997, p. 21.
16. Herman Goldstein, *Problem-Oriented Policing* (New York: McGraw-Hill, 1990).
17. Chris Argyris, *Reasoning, Learning and Action* (San Francisco: Jossey-Bass, 1982), 159–183.
18. William Bratton with Peter Knobler, *Turnaround* (New York: Random House, 1998).
19. Craig Horowitz, "What Should Cops Do Now," *New York Magazine,* 20 July 1998, p. 32.
20. New York City Police Department, *Courtesy, Professionalism, Respect* (New York, 1997}, 1.
21. George Kelling and Catherine Coles, *Fixing Broken Windows* (New York: Free Press, 1997).
22. Fox Butterfield, "Crime Fighting's About Face," *New York Times,* 19 Jan. 1997, sec 4, p. 1.
23. John Sullivan, "Taking Back a Drug-Plagued Tenement, Step One," *New York Times,* 16 Aug. 1997, sec 1, p. 23.
24. Ibid.
25. Fred Kaplan, "A Blockbuster Effort vs. Drugs: NYC Police Barricade Neighborhood," *Boston Globe,* 2 Nov. 1997, sec. A, p. 10.
26. Ibid.
27. Jacob B. Clark, "Taking Back What's Theirs," *Law Enforcement News,* 15 Jan. 1998, p. 8.
28. Ibid.
29. Chrisena Coleman, "Manning Barricades in the War on Drugs," *New York Daily News,* 24 Oct. 1997, suburban sec., p. 1.
30. Clark, "Taking Back."
31. Ibid.
32. James Q. Wilson, "What, If Anything, Can the Federal Government Do About Crime?" in *Perspectives on Crime and Justice: 1996–1997* (Washington, D.C.: National Institute of Justice, 1997).
33. Edna Erez, "From the Editor," *Justice Quarterly* 12 (1995): 619.
34. New York City Police Department, *Chief of Department Training Memo,* vol. 1, no. 3 (New York, 1998), 1.
35. Lawrence W. Sherman, "Evidence-Based Policing," in *Ideas in American Policing* (Washington, D.C.: Police Foundation, 1998), 4.
36. Ibid., 6.

Eli B. Silverman, "New Skyline." Reprinted from Eli B. Silverman, *NYPD Battles Crime: Innovative Strategies in Policing*, pp. 179–204, 229–231. Copyright © 1999 by Eli B. Silverman. Reprinted with the permission of Northeastern University Press. ✦

Chapter 4

The Third Generation of Community Policing

Moving Through Innovation, Diffusion, and Institutionalization

Willard M. Oliver

Willard Oliver focuses on a recent development in American policing that has been pervasive both nationally and internationally—the implementation of community policing. He argues that three generations or stages of implementation can be identified in the history of the community-policing movement. Each stage identified by Oliver shows a marked progression throughout American police agencies over the past twenty years.

The first stage involves "moving through innovations." A primary characteristic of this stage was that change was initially met with heavy skepticism, until a few notable success stories attracted national attention (e.g., foot-patrol programs in Houston and Newark) and illustrated community policing's promise. A massive diffusion of information about community policing followed, beginning in 1987. In this second stage, the extent of widespread changes in police organizations around the country was evident and community policing began to attract a more serious commitment from police administrators.

The third and current stage of community policing began in 1995. Oliver argues that this stage could be conceptualized as one of growing institutionalization. After more than ten years of implementation, community policing has become a familiar way of doing police business. However, Oliver observes that, "The state of community-policing innovation during the third generation is now somewhat unclear." For this reason it is difficult to predict whether or not police agencies in the future will be able to achieve the complete institutionalization of community policing.

> History in illuminating the past illuminates the present and in illuminating the present illuminates the future.
>
> —Benjamin N. Cardozo

Community policing has become the primary formulation for police practices and the provision of police services in the United States and several other democratic nations as well, such as Australia, Canada, Great Britain, and Iceland. As a result, it has become a popular subject of commentary among the media, in government circles, for many citizen groups, and to an ever-increasing degree among both police practitioners and criminal justice academics as well. The various forms of the media, ranging from local newspapers to national television networks, have provided considerable coverage to community policing, nearly always highlighting the philosophy in a positive tone of commentary. It has become the primary means of police service provision among many local and state police agencies throughout the United States (Edwards & Hayeslip, 1997), and it has been the central focus of federal crime control policy since passage of the 1994 Crime Bill. Citizens have also come to view community policing as a positive development, and despite having a very broad and limited understanding of the concept, citizens are overwhelmingly in favor of its implementation as judged from many polls and surveys

(Gallup, 1996). In addition, police practitioners have become increasingly more actively engaged in community policing; a recent survey revealed that 80% of police chiefs and more than 50% of sheriffs surveyed indicated that their departments had adopted or desired to adopt community policing in the future (McEwen, 1995). Moreover, a majority of larger county and municipal police departments maintain a formal community-policing plan (63% and 61%, respectively), support full-time community-policing officers (80% and 79%, respectively), and have trained all of their new officers in this philosophy of policing (80% and 73%, respectively) (Reaves & Goldberg, 1999). It has also been considered by many police practitioners to be one of the primary reasons that overall crime rates in the United States have fallen since 1992 (Federal Bureau of Investigation, 1999), and it is seen as the hallmark for improved quality of life among policing jurisdictions (Goldstein, 1993; Kelling, 1988; Trojanowicz & Bucqueroux, 1990).

Finally, academicians have begun focusing a significant portion of their research time on community policing, a fact that is clearly witnessed by a growing number of journal articles and doctoral dissertations on the topic of community policing. Many of these academicians have called for community policing to "become the organizing paradigm of public policing" (Bayley & Shearing, 1996, p. 604); some scholars claim it already has (Oliver & Bartgis,1998; Pelfrey,1998; Turner & Wiatrowski,1995). The public sentiment and national agenda in regards to community policing can perhaps be best summed up by President Clinton (1998) in his 1997 State of the Union Address when he stated, "To prepare America for the 21st century, we must build stronger communities. We should start with safe streets. Serious crime has dropped five years in a row. The key has been Community Policing" (p. 1154). This level of attention has most assuredly confirmed the general impression that the advent of community policing has constituted a distinct era in the history of policing, and it will carry policing well into the 21st century as the proper foundation for the provision of public safety services.

Although there remains little debate that policing in the United States has entered the era of community policing (Kelling & Moore, 1988; Oliver, 1998; Sparrow, 1988), there is a continuing energetic disagreement over its appropriate definition (Seagrave, 1996) and some discussion as to its precise origins. Some contend that community policing commenced with the works of Germann (1969) and Angell (1971); others argue that it is truly a result of the works of Goldstein (1979) and Wilson and Kelling (1982); still others credit Robert Trojanowicz (see Trojanowicz & Bucqueroux, 1990) for his work in moving policing from the police/community relations perspective to community policing. Regardless of the debate over definition and origins, the terms *community policing* and *community-oriented policing* have emerged as the ubiquitous common terminology for describing the current era in policing.

Although community policing has been around as a concept since the late 1970s and early 1980s, community policing as a concrete philosophy in action has changed, evolved, and become increasingly mature in its many functional forms at the turn of the century. To say that community policing in the late 1970s was substantially the same as it is in the late 1990s would be similar to saying that the political era of policing (Kelling & Moore, 1988) featured unchanged practices from the late 1700s to the early 1900s. This would be a false statement, quite assuredly. Consequently, identifying the changes occurring across the era of community policing and conceptualizing them in a heuristic conceptual framework that denotes generational differences is an important element required for understanding the community-policing movement. As Cardozo alluded to in the opening quote, by illuminating and developing an understanding of community policing's past we are assisted in coming to a deeper understanding of where we currently stand in this new paradigm of policing and where policing is headed in the 21st century.

Accordingly, the purposes of this article are to (a) document that we are currently in the era of community policing; (b) document that changes have been made during the era of community policing and categorize them into three distinct generations of innovation, diffusion, and institutionalization; and finally, (c) use this information to comprehend current and speculate on future patterns of change in policing.

The Eras of Policing

It has been widely recognized that policing has moved through several paradigmatic shifts leading to distinctive eras of police practices in the United States (Kelling & Moore,1988; Pelfrey, 1998). Regardless of which categorization of eras one uses, the current paradigm of policing is definitively cited as that of community policing by most historically oriented scholars (Kelling & Moore, 1988; Oliver & Bartgis, 1998; Pelfrey, 1998; Sparrow, 1988; Turner & Wiatrowski, 1995; Zhao, 1996). Recognizing that eras of policing have come and gone or, more subtly, that policing itself has changed, it is important to understand how we came to be situated in an era of community policing.Two of the more simplistic conceptualizations of how policing has changed focus on police organization in the United States. Recognizing that there is a profound organizational change currently under way, Sparrow (1988) argued that we have moved from a "traditional" era to the community policing era. He explained that the police are no longer a government agency exclusively focused on the enforcement of laws, solving crimes, and responding in a reactive manner. Contemporary police agencies have become much more actively concerned with improving the quality of life in their communities; they have gone beyond enforcing laws to solving public safety problems, and they are increasingly proactive in their work (Sparrow, 1988). Zhao (1996) likewise focused on the way police have organized in the United States and delineated a distinction between the "bureaucratic model" and the "COP (Community-Oriented Policing) model." He ascribed the characteristics of centralization, standardization, and mechanistic behavior to the bureaucratic model (era) and democratic, proactive, and decentralized operations to the COP model (era) (Zhao,1996). Both Sparrow and Zhao acknowledged that we are currently in the community-policing era based on the way contemporary police agencies have organized their activities and utilized their resources.

Another means by which policing has been segregated into eras, and perhaps the most cited and recognized (although not without its critics: Strecher, 1991; Williams & Murphy, 1990), uses an organizational approach to policing by focusing on police strategies (Kelling & Moore, 1988). Analyzing the organizational strategies of the police such as where an agency receives its authority, how it functions, how it organizes, the level of demand for their services, the environments in which they work, the tactics they utilize, and the outcomes desired, Kelling and Moore (1988) identified the following three historical periods of policing: the political, reform, and community-policing eras. The political era of policing ran from the 1840s, when public policing–provided services were first beginning to develop in the United States, through the 1920s. It was marked by strong political ties to the local political machines, patronage, corruption, and was highly decentralized. In the 1930s, policing underwent a series of reforms from reform-minded chiefs such as August Vollmer and O. W. Wilson, whose work in due time brought about the widespread professionalization and centralization of the police featuring a narrow focus on enforcing laws and solving crimes (Kelling & Moore, 1988). Finally, Kelling and Moore argued that by the late 1970s and early 1980s there was a movement away from the reforms that marked the largest portion of the 20th century entailing a movement toward the decentralization of police operations to achieve a more intimate provision of services intended to improve the quality of life of communities, enhance citizen satisfaction with police services, and induce citizen coproduction of public safety. This era was denoted as the community-policing era by Kelling and Moore.

A final means by which to segregate the history of policing looks more toward the relationship between the police and the public over time. This viewpoint also recognizes that early policing in the United States was predicated on the political relationship between the police and the public and that police officer jobs were largely patronage positions. In moving away from these political ties, police management came to emphasize "public relations," understood as "doing a good, efficient job in a courteous manner and then letting the public know about the job" (Holcomb, 1954, p. 6). As a result of this new "above politics" understanding of the policing function, the police began to distance themselves from the public in an attempt to become more "professional" in demeanor and bearing, which, coupled with a number of social changes (e.g., Supreme Court decisions, racial tensions, research on the effectiveness of the police, etc.), resulted in a highly withdrawn cadre of officers working within a highly closed system of policing practice.

Events of the 1950s and 1960s, including the civil rights movement and protests against the war in Vietnam, exposed many of the drawbacks of the professional model of policing and resulted in a demand for attention to "police-community relations" (Radelet, 1973). The use of this concept reflected the belief that police needed to work on improved relations with the public and needed to have a much better understanding of the communities they police. During this period, many departments created specialized units to work with specific groups of people (e.g., elderly, youth, etc.) to achieve this better understanding of the public (Cohn & Viano, 1976; Johnson, Misner, & Brown, 1981; Radelet, 1973; Watson, 1966). This movement, however, failed to achieve any dramatic breakthroughs in police and community relations primarily due to the fact that the function of enhanced relations was relegated to special units (e.g., Team Policing, Community Relations units, etc.) while the rest of the agency continued practicing traditional forms of policing reflecting the professional model. Searching for answers throughout most of the 1970s yielded a recognition of the problems not only in police/community relations but also in the overall conceptualization of policing itself; this searching led in time to the concepts of community policing and the advent of the current era of American policing (Trojanowicz & Bucqueroux, 1990). The community-policing era acknowledges the need for enhanced police and community relations, but it attempts to achieve this end by sharing power with the community, moving the entire agency toward the community-policing philosophy, and developing ongoing partnerships between the police, their community, and other government agencies.

In sum, whether one takes the perspective of organizational strategies or the perspective of police and community relations, there is strong recognition by practitioners and academics alike that we currently find ourselves in the era of community policing and that we arrived at this era sometime in the early 1980s. In addition, there is broad acknowledgment that there have been significant advances in community policing over the course of the past 20 years that deserve notice. For example, the introduction of problem-oriented policing (Goldstein, 1979) contributed to community policing's development into a practical application method by line officers via the SARA (Scanning, Analysis, Response, Assessment) model in the mid-1980s (Eck & Spelman,1987). The model is in common usage in dealing with a variety of community issues such as drugs (Bureau of Justice Assistance, 1993) and domestic violence. Similarly, improving conditions for community policing can be seen in moving from the limited number of grants that went to a few specific agencies for conducting research and implementing community policing in the early 1980s (Rosenbaum, 1994) to the passage of the Violent Crime Control and Law Enforcement Act of 1994, which has provided more than $8 billion toward additional officers, equipment, and training on the concepts of community policing. We have most assuredly moved beyond where we were in the early 1980s, which is why two scholars in the field of community policing were able to ask, "Where Are We Now?" (Zhao & Thurman, 1997). It is certainly not where we were at the start of the era.

The Three Generations

To identify the three generations of community policing, it is important to state the criteria being used to assess when the evolution of this era of policing moved from one generation to the next. A general overview of each generation is pertinent to understanding the criteria being employed to formulate a heuristic device for understanding an evolving concept. In addition, using criteria in a fashion similar to that done by Kelling and Moore (1988), I have identified key variables that marked the critical points of the evolution of community policing; these points are organization, location, style, and evaluation techniques.

The first criterion is focused on how community policing is organized within a police agency. It is recognized that many agencies have changed to community policing in name only (Goldstein, 1987), others have adopted a "team policing" approach (Greene, 1987; Sherman, 1975), whereas still others have adopted a systemic community-policing approach throughout the entire agency. The methods by which departments in both rhetoric and reality have come to perceive community policing organizationally will be used to articulate changes over time in regards to this new era in policing. The second criterion looks at where community policing has been practiced during each generation. What type of agency practiced community policing? How large were the jurisdictions? Were they large metropolitan agencies or small-town and rural agencies? The third criterion to be used is based on the style of community policing adopted. This consists of the types of programs used by the agencies practicing community policing, how they incorporate citizens into their programs, and how police-citizen contact is defined. Finally, the fourth criterion to be used is based on the types of evaluations used by both the police and academicians to understand the implementation of community policing.

Finally, after analyzing the four criteria to assess the evolution of community policing, the theoretical construct of J. L. Walker (1969; also see Gray, 1973; Rogers, 1983) that policy innovations tend to diffuse across states and other political entities is used as a framework for categorizing the three eras of community policing. Public policies are said to be innovative when one or a few isolated cities or states develop a "new" policy such as hate crime legislation or the reduction of the blood alcohol content levels from the most common standard of .10 to .08. As other agencies begin to formulate these policies, the policy undergoes the process of diffusion. When the policy becomes normed, it is considered to be an institutionalized policy.

The innovation and diffusion literature is well accepted in the area of policy studies and has seen application in a number of fields (Savage, 1978, 1985a, 1985b). It essentially posits that most public policies are developed by specific political entities (e.g., states, counties, etc.) and that these policies then spread across other similar political entities. This process of diffusion moves public policy into a common state of being as accepted practice among a majority of political entities. In other words, the policy becomes institutionalized. Yin (1979) explained this as the *emergence* stage of policy, which is then followed by the process of *institutionalization*. Although his study uses the public policy theory of innovation, diffusion, and institutionalization, it does not empirically test the theory but rather posits his theory as a plausible heuristic to categorize the changing evolution of community policing.

Consequently, through these methods the three generations of community policing have been identified and dates have been attached to each generation to provide the heuristic device to distinguish each one of them as separate and distinct. The generations in question consist of the innovation generation ranging from 1979 though 1986, the diffusion generation ranging from 1987 through 1994, and the institutionalization generation, which has run from 1995 to the present.

First Generation: Innovation

The first generation of community policing spans the period 1979 through 1986 and is labeled the *innovation* generation. The specification of a precise starting date is indeed somewhat arbitrary, but attempting to demonstrate a year where policing moved from traditional to community policing is perhaps best shown by the seminal work of Goldstein (1979) in his review of "improving policing." Although the early works of Germann (1969), Angell (1971), and Radelet (1973) provided some groundwork for the community-policing movement, it was the realization in the 1970s that many commonly held police practices did not work and that an alternative approach was necessary that launched the search for alternative programs to the professional model (Goldstein, 1977, 1979). This succinct recognition by Goldstein in his problem-solving methods, coupled with the "broken windows" theory by Wilson and Kelling (1982), would become the primary theoretical catalysts for significant innovations in policing.

The early concepts of community policing were most often called *experiments, test sites,* and *demonstration projects* (Eck & Spelman, 1987; Trojanowicz, 1983, 1986). They were often restricted to large metropolitan cities such as Flint, MI, Newark, NJ, Newport News, VA, Baltimore County, MD, and Houston, TX. These experiments were typically funded through a combination of taxes and state grants and foundation support and had the support of progressive police chiefs (Brown & Wycoff, 1987; Greene & Mastrofski,1988; Police Foundation, 1981; Rosenbaum, 1986; Skolnick & Bayley, 1986; Taft, 1986; Trojanowicz & Bucqueroux, 1990; Williams & Pate, 1987). The style of policing that was employed was predominately narrow in focus and investigated a single method of community policing such as foot patrols (e.g., Flint, MI, and Newark, NJ), problem-solving methods (e.g., Baltimore County, MD, and Newport News, VA), or community substations (e.g., Boston, MA, and Houston, TX). Finally, the methods of evaluation under these community-policing test sites and projects included case studies, nonequivalent comparison pretest/posttest surveys, and one-group pretest/posttest designs (Greene & Taylor, 1988). Although these methods represented a substantial improvement over past studies of policing, it was recognized that there were many shortcomings (Greene & Taylor, 1988) and that both theoretical and empirical improvements were necessary in reconceptualizing the role of law enforcement agencies.

In sum, the innovation stage of community policing was primarily characterized by a few isolated experiments in a small number of major metropolitan areas across the United States that were testing specific methods of community policing, generally in a small number of urban neighborhoods. These small-scale test sites provided a source of innovative ideas for others to consider. The merging of provocative ideas and preliminary indicators of success spurred the development of a new era in policing (Kelling & Moore, 1988) and the diffusion of a new public policy through state and local government channels.

Second Generation: Diffusion

The second generation of community policing spans the period from 1987 through 1994, and it is properly considered the diffusion generation. The term *diffusion* used here to describe this generation is derived from the public policy diffusion literature (Gray, 1973; Rogers, 1983; J. L. Walker, 1969) and is based on the following definition: "the adoption of a communicable element, symbolic or artifactual, over time by decision-making entities linked to some originating source by channels of communication within some sociocultural system" (Savage, 1981, p. 102). In this case, it was the concepts and philosophy of community policing, whether a matter of rhetoric or actual reality (Greene & Mastrofski,1988), that began to spread rapidly among American police departments through a variety of communication means within the policing subculture. The spread of community-policing adoptions was fast becoming a reality during this generation, as is evidenced by the fact that in 1985, slightly more than 300 police departments had adopted some form of community policing (S. Walker, 1985), whereas by 1994, it is estimated that more than 8,000 agencies had moved toward community policing (McEwen, 1995).

Community policing during the diffusion generation was largely organized through various programs that consisted of newly created units or extensions of previously existing organizational units. Some examples of the newly created units include the COMPASS (Cartographic Oriented Management Program for the Abatement of Street Sales) program in Hartford, Connecticut (Tien & Rich, 1994), the COPPS (Community Oriented Policing and Problem Solving) project in Hayward, California (Sadd & Grinc, 1994), the CPOP (Community Police Officer Program) program in New York City (McElroy, Cosgrove, & Sadd, 1993), and the COPE (Citizen Oriented Police Enforcement) program in Baltimore County, Maryland (Cordner, 1986; Taft, 1986). In many cases, these programs were derived from federal and state grants that allowed the organizations the funding ability to adopt these types of programs, such as the INOP (Innovative Neighborhood Oriented Policing) initiatives funded through the Bureau of Justice Assistance (Sadd & Grinc, 1994).

In the case of community policing operating through previously existing organizational units, most were focused on the extension of community crime prevention programs already in place. Where agencies had previously focused on crime prevention concepts such as CPTED (Crime Prevention Through Environmental Design), collaborative police-citizen patrols, or neighborhood/apartment/block watch programs (Rosenbaum, 1986), it was found that with a little retooling these existing units could become community-policing units.

The practice of community policing during this second generation was still largely restricted to large- and medium-sized cities. The diffusion was faster in reaching these types of agencies because of the greater access to information, larger budgets to absorb any additional costs to community policing (with or without grant funding), and the preexisting structures in these agencies in which community policing was often placed. Although some small police agencies (defined as serving populations fewer than 50,000) adopted community policing, diffusion to small and rural jurisdictions was rare, and the discussion of small-town and rural community policing was nearly nonexistent. Community policing during this generation was primarily found in places such as Chicago, Houston, Ft. Worth, Las Vegas, Oakland, Portland, and San Diego (Kratcoski & Dukes, 1995; Police Executive Research Forum, 1996; Rosenbaum, 1994; Trojanowicz & Bucqueroux, 1990).

The style of community policing under the second generation was much broader than the first in that it was no longer fixated on one specific program (e.g., foot patrol, substations, etc.); instead, community policing was increasingly seen as being much more encompassing in how police need to deal with neighborhood crime and quality-of-life issues. The concepts typically entailed targeting the problem of drugs, reducing fear of crime, improving police/community relationships, and assisting in organizing and involving the community in the maintenance of order (Sadd & Grinc, 1994). The emphasis of community policing became one of extending the concepts of community policing throughout a community and throughout the police department. Community-policing agencies were seeking a "total community policing program" (Lasley, Vernon, & Dery, 1995), one that was more systemic in nature and holistic in approach than the early experiments had conceptualized.

In regards to evaluations conducted during this generation, many of the criticisms of the early innovative period had been met through a flourishing number of research studies conducted on community-policing programs throughout the United States. Research analysis during this generation focused on both the means and ends of policing (Moore, 1994); it dedicated an enormous amount of effort toward evaluating the community along with the police (Thurman & Reisig, 1996), and it became far more sophisticated in its use of appropriate research methodologies as evidenced by the reporting of many more longitudinal, comparative, and quantitative studies (Alpert & Piquero, 1998; Mastrofski, Worden, & Snipes, 1995; Zhao, 1996). In addition, several research institutes were created that have provided in-depth research studies on community policing that have most assuredly contributed to the quality of the evaluations being conducted during this diffusion generation (Community Policing Consortium, 1999; National Center for Community Policing, 1999; Washington State Institute for Community Oriented Policing, 1999).

Third Generation: Institutionalization

The third and current generation of community policing spans the period from 1995 to the present, and it is properly considered the institutionalization generation. This specific term is used to denote the fact that community policing has seen widespread implementation across the United States and has become the most common form of organizing police services. This is evidenced by the fact that around 13,000 police agencies had made some effort to move toward community policing by 1996 (Edwards & Hayeslip, 1997). In addition, it is used to denote the importance of intergovernmental relationships among federal, state, and local governments that have also contributed to this process. Since the 1994 Crime Bill, community policing has become deeply entrenched within the national political process, a strong sign that a public policy has become institutionalized. Although community policing had a pronounced grassroots quality about it in the early 1980s (Kelling, 1988), with the election of President Clinton in 1992 and the passage of the Violent Crime Control and Law Enforcement Act in 1994 (Department of Justice, 1994), it became a high-visibility national public policy.

In the presidential campaign of 1992, Arkansas Governor Bill Clinton spoke early in the race of the concepts of community policing and its benefits. Realizing that *community policing* was not an attractive media sound bite, his policy staff members created the concept of "adding 100,000 cops" to the streets of America (J. Brann, personal communication, December 20, 1996). He campaigned on this predominantly conservative slogan as the centerpiece of his crime policy (Marion, 1997; Poveda, 1996) and won the election in 1992. He failed, however, to carry his crime policy with him into the White House, and it was not until the fall of 1993 that Clinton began focusing heavily on the formation of a crime bill that would feature the funding for an additional 100,000 cops (Chernoff, Kelly, & Kroger, 1996; Poveda, 1996). By the beginning of 1994, he began campaigning for his anticrime legislation by appearing at criminal justice functions, giving speeches on crime to a variety of organizations, and giving more than a half dozen radio addresses on crime and his proposed crime legislation (Clinton,1995). Where he had failed to gather support for his health care legislation, he carefully crafted his crime bill to have overwhelming bipartisan support by conceding to many of the Republicans' demands. On September 13, 1994, Clinton signed into law the Violent Crime Control and Law Enforcement Act of 1994, allocating nearly $9 billion to be directed toward hiring, equipping, and training police officers under the community-policing philosophy.

The Office of Community Oriented Policing Services (COPS) was quickly created and given free reign to begin funneling the grant money to any state or local law enforcement agency applying for funding to hire an additional officer to do community policing. Agencies across the United States began filling out application forms to receive funding to support an officer's pay and benefits (at 75%) for 3 years and agreed to hire them with the intent of moving their agency toward community policing. The grants had names such as COPS Phase 1, COPS FAST (Funding Accelerated for Small Towns), and COPS AHEAD (Accelerated Hiring Education and Deployment), which would eventually become the UHP (Universal Hiring Program). Following quickly behind the grants to hire officers came the COPS MORE (Making Officer Redeployment Effective) grants that allowed departments to purchase computers, pay officers overtime, and hire support staff members to ease the agency's movement toward community policing. And finally, through the already existing Community Policing Consortium and the newly created Regional Community Policing Institutes (RCPIs), training on community policing became available to educate officers on the practices of community policing. Although the rhetoric to enact the crime bill and secure its $8.8 billion funding fell under the guise of adding 100,000 cops, its execution was most assuredly tied to the philosophy of community policing. This federal intervention, namely in terms of grant dollars, has dramatically changed the community-policing landscape; that is why it is possible to say that in 1995 we have entered a new generation of community policing.

The state of community-policing innovation during the third generation is now somewhat unclear. Many of the agencies that implemented community policing during the first and second generations had made the move to implement community policing organization-wide rather than leaving it as a demonstration project or as an add-on unit of the agency. However, many of the agencies coming to community policing during the third generation were simply seeking grant funding, and they would hire the officers as community-policing officers, or they would create a specialty unit to justify their community-policing grants (General Accounting Office, 1997; Oliver, 1999). Hence, the third generation has seen a number of new start-up community-policing programs as a result of the monetary incentives provided by the Office of Community Oriented Policing Services.

Whereas the first generation of community policing was mainly relegated to large metropolitan cities with innovative police departments and the second generation was focused primarily on large- and medium-sized jurisdictions, the third generation, featuring the federal grant money, allowed for almost any agency of any size to apply for community-policing grants. This inclusive program included agencies from the size of New York City Police Department and Los Angeles Police Department to Greenbrier County Sheriff's Department (West Virginia) and Window Rock Police Department (Arizona, Navajo Nation) (General Accounting Office, 1995, 1997; Office of Community Oriented Policing Services, 1999). Although the availability of federal grants did not lure all small-town and rural agencies into community policing (Thurman & McGarrell, 1997; Weisheit, Falcone, & Wells, 1996), their availability has increased the number of jurisdictions taking up community policing dramatically, especially under the COPS FAST program, which was dedicated to providing hiring grants to agencies serving populations fewer than 50,000.

The last two criteria of community-policing generations are wide open for reasons primarily resulting in the amount of grant money available to agencies and researchers through the COPS office. The style of community policing has consisted of a number of programs such as the Youth Firearms Violence Initiative, Anti-Gang Initiative, and Community Policing to Combat Domestic Violence programs (Community Policing Consortium, 1999; Office of Community Oriented Policing Services,

1999). In addition to these, more extensive use of the types of programs under the first and second generation have flourished in the third generation such as geo-mapping software and CPTED as well as the SARA model and Problem Oriented Policing.

Finally, in regards to the types of evaluations conducted during the third generation, there has been a wide proliferation of research projects funded by the COPS office, either attached to the various grant programs (e.g., Youth Firearms Violence Initiative, Regional Community Policing Institutes, etc.) or specifically focused on evaluating the success of community policing. They have ranged from further case studies of specific agencies and specific programs to quantified statistical analysis and meta-analysis (Kane, 2000; Mazzerolle, Ready, Terrill, & Waring, 2000; Zhao, 1996) of a variety of community-policing initiatives. Community-policing research has become prevalent in the academic journals and is seeing widespread dissemination. However, despite these advancements in the area of community-policing research, the majority of studies continue to use weak analytical techniques [and] fail to account for environmental influences, and the use of one-shot case studies without benefit of comparison or control groups is still the norm. Although community-policing research has progressed, it has not yet reached the highest level of sophistication possible.

The Future or the Next Generation?

What does all this mean, then, for the future of community policing? There are seemingly two alternatives: (a) Community policing can evolve to a fourth generation, or (b) policing moves beyond community policing to a new era in policing. These two scenarios are based on the progression of community policing through the three generations as it relates to the common cycle of most public policies that move from innovation through diffusion to institutionalization and eventually extinction. As it is clear that community policing has moved through these three generations and is now in the process of becoming institutionalized as the primary means of delivering police services nationwide, the question to ask at this point is what is next?

In regards to the former alternative, that community policing will evolve into a fourth generation, it was originally intended that the Office of Community Oriented Policing Services would sunset at the end of its 6-year tenure at the end of 2000 (Department of Justice, 1994), thus formally ending the third generation of community policing. However, as any good public bureau is most assuredly seeking its own survival, especially a start-up bureau (Downs, 1994), there is little belief that the COPS office will close its doors in 2001. Signs of this have already been actualized in that President Clinton successfully fought for the inclusion of enough funding in the budget negotiations of 1999 to hire an additional 50,000 cops under the community-policing program. It would appear the COPS office will not sunset anytime soon, leaving one to wonder again—just what does this mean for community policing?[1]

Although it is true that community policing represents a groundswell change in the philosophy of policing, the effect the availability of federal funding has had on community policing cannot be ignored. For many police agencies throughout the United States, federal grants have come to be equated with community policing (Oliver, in press); take away the grants and you take away community policing where this is the case. In addition, even if the grants survive, it has also been documented that the success of the COPS office in promulgating and promoting community policing is somewhat questionable in that they have maintained poor oversight of the grantee agencies, they have not funded 100,000 new officers (often counting equipment, overtime, and secretarial work as a new officer), and suspicions that much supplanting of preexisting programs and officers is occurring (General Accounting Office, 1995, 1997).

In addition, there are a number of instances where officers are being hired for the 3 years of the grant and then being terminated because the local jurisdiction cannot afford to pay the officer's full salary and benefits (Associated Press, 1996; Sharp, 1999). This situation raises the important question of future budgets for agencies such as Los Angeles, which plans to hire more than 700 new officers through COPS grants by the end of 2000 ("Community Policing," 1998). Finally, one also has to question whether the allocation of these officers will have any dramatic effect on crime or crime prevention in that the officers are being allocated largely on the basis of population (Leyden, Kilwein, & Oliver, 2000), and as Sherman (1997) pointed out quite appropriately, "in general, the evidence suggests that federal appropriations to prevent crime through additional policing [are] most effective when allocated on the basis of serious crime rather than on the basis of population size" (p. 37). In sum, the federal role in community policing is faulty at best, and if it is perceived as being community policing, then when the grants dry up so too will community policing. The next generation of community policing would then have to survive without the federal funding. This will result in, at a minimum, many agencies dropping the community policing rhetoric, whereas in the worst case, community policing will be considered a failure and agencies will then move onto something else. Perhaps a new era in policing will rise. Yin (1979) argued that once a public policy reaches the institutionalization phase, what often follows is the phenomenon of disappearance.

As community policing evolved out of a progression of eras in policing, it is probably safe to say that another era will follow community policing. In acknowledging Kuhn's (1962) model of scientific revolutions, Pelfrey (1998) argued that "the current paradigm, community policing, will be refined by this process and may eventually be replaced by a different paradigm" (p. 90). If this is in fact to be the case, and it likely is, then the next logical question is What will the new era of policing be? Although it is pure speculation at this point to say what will occur in the policing field over the next decade, the key is to look for developments that are occurring now to recognize what will be the paradigm of tomorrow. One possible scenario was provided in recent research by Kraska and Cubellis (1997), who identified a growth in the number, expansion of activities, and the movement toward normalizing small-locality police paramilitary units (PPU) (also see Weber, 1999). One only has to note the increased use of such units in the war on drugs, look at the response by local police to the massacre at Columbine High School, or watch the more recent footage of the riots in Seattle, Washington, during the World Trade Organization negotiations to understand the prevalence of this phenomenon. The militarization of policing may very well replace the current paradigm of community policing—for it can be justified in the name of countermeasures to "terrorism," "drugs," and "massacres"; it is a political policy that emphasizes "how military-type bureaucracy, discipline, technology, deployment and coercion" can be used to "fight criminal sources of insecurity" (Ericson & Carriere, 1994, p. 100); and it extends the power of the government (Lyons, 1999; Reed, 1999). Clearly, this represents a formula for a potential revolution in American policing. Although this development may appear to be a complete turnaround from current practices, if the "failure" of community policing is coupled with a more tactical anticrime orientation, the militarization of the police is not beyond comprehension.

Conclusion

It has been recognized that contemporary American law enforcement finds itself in the era of community policing. It should also be recognized, however, that community policing at the turn of the century only slightly resembles community policing in the late 1970s and early 1980s. Acknowledging this point, it can be argued that community policing has moved through three distinct generations—innovation (1979 through 1986), diffusion (1987 through 1994), and institutionalization (1995 to present). As policing finds itself in the current institutionalization generation of policing primarily as a result of the federal incentives of grant money, current assessments of actual community-policing implementation have demonstrated that current institutionalization is in many ways more rhetoric than reality (Oliver, 1999; Reed, 1999; Zhao & Thurman, 1997). Although community policing may have been more of an honest grassroots initiative in the innovation and diffusion generations, it has become highly equated with federal grants in the institutionalization generation and will most likely see a dramatic decline when the grant money is no longer available. In other words, community policing, similar to so many other innovative public policies that have arisen in American government, has gone through a series of phases moving from innovation, through diffusion, to institutionalization, and it will most likely continue into obsolescence, as have many previous innovations.

Yin (1979) argued that the process of organizational change also tends to occur in three phases—emergence, institutionalization, and disappearance (also see Zhao,1996). As community policing finds itself in the throes of the institutionalization phase, the next logical movement is into a state of disappearance (perhaps the fourth generation?) and ultimately replacement by another paradigm (Pelfrey, 1998). What that paradigm, or new era of policing, may be is sheer speculation at this point, but it would not be inexpedient to call for more research into the area of police militarization.

Editors' Note

1. The COPS office still exists today, although in recent years its funding has been dramatically reduced.

References

Alpert, G. P., & Piquero, A. (1998). *Community policing: Contemporary readings.* Prospect Heights, IL: Waveland.

Angell, J. (1971). Toward an alternative to the classic police organizational arrangement: A democratic model. *Criminology,* 8, 185–206.

Associated Press. (1996, October 29). Finding promised cops a tough task. *Parkersburg News,* p. 6B.

Bayley, D. H., & Shearing, C. D. (1996). The future of policing. *Law and Society Review,* 30, 585–606.

Brown, L. P., & Wycoff, M. A. (1987). Policing Houston: Reducing fear and improving services. *Crime and Delinquency,* 33, 71–89.

Bureau of Justice Assistance. (1993). *Problem-oriented drug enforcement: A community-based approach for effective policing.* Washington, DC: Author.

Chernoff, H. A., Kelly, C. M., & Kroger, J. R. (1996). The politics of crime. *Harvard Journal on Legislation,* 33, 527–579.

Clinton, W. J. (1995). *Public papers of the presidents of the United States.* Washington, DC: Government Printing Office.

Clinton, W. J. (1998). *Public papers of the presidents of the United States.* Washington, DC: Government Printing Office.

Cohn, A. W., & Viano, E. C. (1976). *Police community relations: Images, roles, realities.* Philadelphia: J. B. Lippincott.

Community policing. (1998, October 6). *All things considered.* Washington, DC: National Public Radio.

Community Policing Consortium [Online]. (1999). Available: http://www.community policing.org

Cordner, G. W. (1986). Fear of crime and the police: An evaluation of a fear-reduction strategy. *Journal of Police Science and Administration,* 14, 223–233.

Department of Justice. (1994). *The violent crime control and law enforcement act of 1994: Briefing book.* Washington, DC: Author.

Downs, A. (1994). *Inside bureaucracy.* Prospect Heights, IL: Waveland.

Eck, J. E., & Spelman, W. (1987). *Problem solving: Problem-oriented policing in Newport News.* Washington, DC: Police Executive Research Forum.

Edwards, S., & Hayeslip, D. (1997, March). *Community policing: Where are we now?* Paper presented at the annual meetings of the Academy of Criminal Justice Sciences, Louisville, KY.

Ericson, R., & Carriere, K. (1994). The fragmentation of criminology. In D. Nelken (Ed.), *The futures of criminology* (pp. 89–109). Thousand Oaks, CA: Sage.

Federal Bureau of Investigation. (1999). *Uniform crime reports—1998.* Washington, DC: Author.

Gallup, G. (1996). *Community policing survey.* Wilmington, NY: Scholarly Resources, Inc.

General Accounting Office. (1995). *Community policing: Information on the "cops on the beat" grant program.* Washington, DC: Author.

General Accounting Office. (1997). *Community policing: Issues related to the design, operation, and management of the grant program.* Washington, DC: Author.

Germann, A. C. (1969). Community policing: An assessment. *Journal of Criminal Law, Criminology, and Police Science,* 60, 89–96.

Goldstein, H. (1977). *Policing a free society.* Cambridge, MA: Ballinger.

Goldstein, H. (1979). Improving policing: A problem-oriented approach. *Crime and Delinquency,* 25, 236–258.

Goldstein, H. (1987). Toward community-oriented policing: Potential, basic requirements, and threshold questions. *Crime and Delinquency,* 33, 6–30.

Goldstein, H. (1993). *The new police: Confronting complexity* (National Institute of Justice, Research in Brief). Washington, DC: Department of Justice.

Gray, V. (1973). Innovation in the states: A diffusion study. *American Political Science Review,* 62, 1174–1185.

Greene, J. R. (1987). Foot patrol and community policing: Past practices and future prospects. *American Journal of Police,* 6, 1–15.

Greene, J. R., & Mastrofski, S. D. (1988). *Community policing: Rhetoric or reality.* New York: Praeger.

Greene, J. R., & Taylor, R. P. (1988). Community-based policing and foot patrol: Issues of theory and evaluation. In J. R. Greene & S. D. Mastrofski (Eds.), *Community policing: Rhetoric or reality* (pp. 195–224). New York: Praeger.

Holcomb, R. L. (1954). *The police and the public.* Springfield, IL: Charles C Thomas.

Johnson, T. A., Misner, G. E., & Brown, L. P. (1981). *The police and society: An environment for collaboration and confrontation.* Englewood Cliffs, NJ: Prentice Hall.

Kane, R. J. (2000). Permanent beat assignments in association with community policing: Assessing the impact on police officer's field activity. *Justice Quarterly,* 17, 259–280.

Kelling, G. L. (1988). *Police and communities: The quiet revolution* (Monograph). Washington, DC: National Institute of Justice.

Kelling, G. L., & Moore, M. H. (1988). From political to reform to community: The evolving strategy of police. In J. R. Greene & S. D. Mastrofski (Eds.), *Community policing: Rhetoric or reality* (pp. 3–25). New York: Praeger.

Kraska, P. B., & Cubellis, L. J. (1997). Militarizing Mayberry and beyond: Making sense of American paramilitary policing. *Justice Quarterly,* 14, 607–629.

Kratcoski, P. C., & Dukes, D. (1995). *Issues in community policing.* Cincinnati, OH: Anderson.

Kuhn, T. S. (1962). *The structure of scientific revolutions* (2nd ed.). Chicago: University of Chicago Press.

Lasley, J. R., Vernon, R. L., & Dery, G. M. (1995). Operation cul-de-sac: LAPD's "total community" policing program. In P. C. Kratcoski & D. Dukes (Eds.), *Issues in community policing* (pp. 51–67). Cincinnati, OH: Anderson.

Leyden, K., Kilwein, J., & Oliver, W. M. (2000, February). *Is crime control policy another form of pork barrel politics?* Paper presented at the Annual Meeting of the Western Political Science Association, Seattle, WA.

Lyons, W. (1999). *The politics of community policing: Rearranging the power to punish.* Ann Arbor: University of Michigan Press.

Marion, N. E. (1997). Symbolic policies in Clinton's crime control agenda. *Buffalo Criminal Law Review,* 1, 67–108.

Mastrofski, S. D., Worden, R. E., & Snipes, J. P. (1995). Law enforcement in a time of community policing. *Criminology, 33,* 539–563.

Mazzerolle, L. G., Ready, J., Terrill, W., & Waring, E. (2000). Problem-oriented policing in public housing: The Jersey City evaluation. *Justice Quarterly,* 17, 129–158.

McElroy, J. E., Cosgrove, C. A., & Sadd, S. (1993). *Community policing: The CPOP in New York.* Newbury Park, CA: Sage.

McEwen, T. (1995). *National assessment program: 1994 survey results.* Washington, DC: National Institute of Justice.

Moore, M. H. (1994). Research synthesis and policy implications. In D. P. Rosenbaum (Ed.), *The challenge of community policing: Testing the premises* (pp. 285–299). Thousand Oaks, CA: Sage.

National Center for Community Policing [Online]. (1999). Available: http://www.ssc.msu.edu/~/cj/cp/cptoc.html

Office of Community Oriented Policing Services [Online]. (1999). Available: http://www.usdoj.gov/cops/

Oliver, W. M. (1998). *Community-oriented policing: A systemic approach to policing.* Englewood Cliffs, NJ: Prentice Hall.

Oliver, W. M. (1999). *The West Virginia regional community policing institute (RCPI) West Virginia community policing organizational assessment.* Charleston: West Virginia Regional Community Policing Institute.

Oliver, W. M. (in press). Community policing in West Virginia: An organizational assessment survey. *Police Practice and Research: An International Journal.*

Oliver, W. M., & Bartgis, E. (1998). Community policing: A conceptual framework. *Policing: An International Journal of Police Strategies and Management, 21,* 490–509.

Pelfrey, W. V., Jr. (1998). Precipitating factors of paradigmatic shift in policing: The origin of the community policing era. In G. P. Alpert & A. Piquero (Eds.), *Community policing: Contemporary readings* (pp. 79–92). Prospect Heights, IL: Waveland.

Police Executive Research Forum. (1996). *Themes and variations in community policing: Case studies in community policing.* Washington, DC: Author.

Police Foundation. (1981). *The Newark foot patrol experiment.* Washington, DC: Author.

Poveda, T. G. (1996). Clinton, crime, and the justice department. *Social Justice, 21,* 73–84.

Radelet, L. A. (1973). *The police and the community.* Encino, CA: Glencoe.

Reaves, B. A., & Goldberg. A. L. (1999). *Law enforcement management and administrative statistics, 1997: Data for individual state and local agencies with 100 or more officers.* Washington, DC: Bureau of Justice Statistics.

Reed, W. E. (1999). *The politics of community policing: The case of Seattle.* New York: Garland.

Rogers, E. M. (1983). *The diffusion of innovations* (3rd ed.). New York: Free Press.

Rosenbaum, D. P. (1986). *Community crime prevention: Does it work?* Beverly Hills, CA: Sage.

Rosenbaum, D. P. (1994). *The challenge of community policing: Testing the promises.* Thousand Oaks, CA: Sage.

Sadd, S., & Grinc, R. (1994). Innovative neighborhood oriented policing. In D. P. Rosenbaum (Ed.), *The challenge of community policing: Testing the promises* (pp. 27–52). Thousand Oaks, CA: Sage.

Savage, R. L. (1978). Policy innovativeness in the states. *Journal of Politics, 40,* 212–224.

Savage, R. L. (1981). The diffusion of information approach. In D. D. Nimmo & K. R. Sanders (Eds.), *Handbook of political communication* (pp. 101–119). Beverly Hills, CA: Sage.

Savage, R. L. (1985a). Diffusion research traditions and the spread of policy innovations in a federal system. *Publius: The Journal of Federalism, 15,* 1–27.

Savage, R. L. (1985b). When a policy's time has come: Cases of rapid policy diffusion, 1983–1984. *Publius: The Journal of Federalism, 15,* 111–125.

Seagrave, J. (1996). Defining community policing. *American Journal of Police, 15,* 1–22.

Sharp, A. G. (1999). Special report: A report card on COPS. *Law and Order, 43,* 76–80.

Sherman, L. W. (1975). Middle management and democratization. *Criminology, 12,* 363–377.

Sherman, L. W. (1997). *Preventing crime: What works, what doesn't, what's promising.* Washington, DC: Office of Justice Programs.

Skolnick, J. H., & Bayley, D. H. (1986). *The new blue line: Innovation in six American cities.* New York: Free Press.

Sparrow, M. K. (1988). *Implementing community policing* (Monograph). Washington, DC: National Institute of Justice.

Strecher, V. (1991). Revising the histories and futures of policing. *Police Forum, 1,* 1–9.

Taft, P. B. (1986). *Fighting fear: The Baltimore County COPE. project.* Washington, DC: Police Executive Research Forum.

Thurman, Q., & Reisig, M. D. (1996). Community-oriented research in an era of community-oriented policing. *American Behavioral Scientist, 39,* 570–587.

Thurman, Q. C., & McGarrell, E. F. (1997). *Community policing in a rural setting.* Cincinnati, OH: Anderson.

Tien, J. M., & Rich, T. F. (1994). The Hartford COMPASS program. In D. P. Rosenbaum (Ed.), *The challenge of community policing: Testing the promises* (pp. 192–206). Thousand Oaks, CA: Sage.

Trojanowicz, R. (1983). *The neighborhood foot patrol program in Flint, Michigan.* East Lansing, MI: National Neighborhood Foot Patrol Center for Community Policing.

Trojanowicz, R. (1986). Evaluating a neighborhood foot patrol program: The Flint, Michigan project. In D. P. Rosenbaum (Ed.), *Community crime prevention: Does it work?* (pp. 157–178). Beverly Hills, CA: Sage.

Trojanowicz, R. C., & Bucqueroux, B. (1990). *Community policing: A contemporary perspective.* Cincinnati, OH: Anderson.

Turner, R., & Wiatrowski, M. D. (1995). Community policing and community innovation: The "new institutionalism" in American government. In P C. Kratcoski & D. Dukes (Eds.), *Issues in community policing* (pp. 261–270). Cincinnati, OH: Anderson.

Walker, J. L. (1969). The diffusion of innovations among the American states. *American Political Science Review, 63,* 880–889.

Walker, S. (1985). *The police in America: An introduction.* New York: McGraw-Hill.

Washington State Institute for Community Oriented Policing [Online]. (1999). Available: http://www.idi.wsu.edu/wsicop/default.htm

Watson, N. A. (1966). *Police-community relations.* Washington, DC: International Association of Chiefs of Police.

Weber, D. C. (1999). Warrior cops: The ominous growth of paramilitarism in American police departments. CATO *Institute: Briefing Papers, 50,* 1–14.

Weisheit, R. A., Falcone, D. N., & Wells, L. E. (1996). *Crime and policing in rural and small-town America.* Prospect Heights, IL: Waveland.

Williams, H., & Murphy, P. V. (1990). *The evolving strategy of policing: A minority view* (Monograph). Washington, DC: National Institute of Justice.

Williams, H., & Pate, A. M. (1987). Returning to first principles: Reducing the fear of crime in Newark. *Crime and Delinquency, 33,* 53–70.

Wilson, J. Q., & Kelling, G. L. (1982, March). Broken windows: The police and neighborhood safety. *Atlantic Monthly, 249,* 29–38.

Yin, R. (1979). *Changing in urban bureaucracies: How new practices become routinized.* Lexington, MA: Lexington Books.

Zhao, J. (1996). *Why police organizations change: A study of community-oriented policing.* Washington, DC: Police Executive Research Forum.

Zhao, J., & Thurman, Q. C. (1997). Community policing: Where are we now? *Crime and Delinquency, 43,* 345–357.

Willard M. Oliver, "The Third Generation of Community Policing: Moving Through Innovation, Diffusion, and Institutionalization." Reprinted from *Police Quarterly,* Vol. 3 No. 4, December 2000, pp. 367–388. Copyright © 2000 by Sage Publications, Inc. Reprinted by permission of Sage Publications, Inc. ✦

Part II

Promising Approaches to Crime Reduction and Prevention

Police departments have made some significant changes in their organizational structure and the operational approaches they have used throughout their history. Prior to the 1980s, police agencies across the nation exclusively depended on two primary units to control and prevent local crimes. The first was the patrol unit, which usually accounted for about 70 percent of police personnel. Random patrol strategies were believed to prevent criminal incidents by deterring potential criminals from openly engaging in street crime. For several decades (from the 1930s to early 1970s) the preventive nature of patrolling was assumed but not empirically proven. Rising crime rates during the 1960s and early 1970s made police administrators take a second look at their traditional operations. A well-cited study on randomized patrol in Kansas City found that patrolling had little impact on crime (Kelling et al., 1974).

A less well-known but equally significant study on the effectiveness of police detective units—the second unit relied upon most heavily to control crime—found that detectives actually contribute little to solving local crimes. Researchers from the Rand Corporation surveyed over 100 large police departments and made field trips to 25 of them (Chaiken et al., 1975) to determine that detectives were able to independently solve only a small percentage of active cases. The Rand study researchers concluded that detectives were not vital participants in the battle to control crime.

These two studies led to a call for significant changes in police operations and crime-control strategies. The chapters in this section depict key police strategies and operations implemented over the past three decades. In general, the innovative strategies and operations adopted in the past several years can be distinguished by an internal or external organizational focus.

Externally focused strategies are typically created to increase responsiveness to the needs of communities or neighborhoods. For example, storefront stations enable police officers to maintain close contacts with residents in neighborhoods and learn first-hand information about local crime and social disorder problems. Similarly, specialized units might be established to address specific community issues. For example, during the 1980s, most police departments established domestic violence units in order to control and prevent family violence.

Internally focused strategies are aimed at reforming the bureaucratic nature of police organizations. Over the past thirty years, calls for change in the organizational structure of police agencies concerning authority hierarchy and impersonal rules have resulted in some noticeable improvements. For example, police officers involved in community-policing activities have been given more discretion in making contact with local residents and conducting problem-solving projects. In addition, NYPD's CompStat approach, featured in the previous section, is widely considered as another alternative for breaking down barriers in an organizational hierarchy, thereby allowing top administrators to learn about and then establish new crime-fighting strategies at the precinct or beat level.

Since the 1980s, hundreds of innovative strategies have been adopted and implemented by police departments across the nation. Accordingly, we must look to researchers to answer concerns about the effectiveness of these strategies and programs. Do police innovations of the past several years have the intended effects on crime and social disorder? Does the effectiveness of a strategy differ by city size, region, or other factors?

References

Kelling, G., A. Pate, D. Dieckman, and C. Brown. 1974. *The Kansas City Preventive Patrol Experiment: A Summary Report.* Washington, DC: Police Foundation.

Chaiken, J., P. Greenwood, and J. Petersilia. 1977. "The Criminal Investigation Process: A Summary Report." *Police Analysis,* 3, 182–217. ✦

Chapter 5

Policing for Crime Prevention

Lawrence W. Sherman

Sherman reviews the existing literature on the relationship between the number of police officers employed by an agency and their impact on crime. Two opposing arguments are identified throughout the literature: On one hand is the view that "the more police we have, the less crime there will be." Alternatively, social scientists have claimed that the true effect of increased police population on crime is minimal, as crime largely results from social problems that police are not in a position to solve.

Over the years, both sides have debated the question without reaching a conclusive agreement about what the data show. For example, many studies on the relationship between drugs and crime or family disorganization and crime suggest that both drugs and family disorganization are significant contributors to local crime, even when controlling for other factors. While this research might seem to indicate that social problems lead to crime, Sherman disagrees that police activities are irrelevant in combating crime.

Sherman's assessment of existing research indicates that the extent of the police impact on crime reduction or control depends upon the nature of the strategies that the police use to solve a particular crime problem. Promising strategies, according to Sherman, include proactive arrests and problem-oriented policing. Furthermore, for policing to be effective in fighting crime, police strategies should have clear objectives and a well-planned approach.

Introduction

The more police we have, the less crime there will be. While citizens and public officials often espouse that view, social scientists often claim the opposite extreme: that police make only minimal contributions to crime prevention in the context of far more powerful social institutions, like the family and labor markets. The truth appears to lie in between. Whether additional police prevent crime may depend on how well they are focused on specific objectives, tasks, places, times and people. Most of all, it may depend upon putting police where serious crime is concentrated, at the times it is most likely to occur: policing focused on risk factors.

The connection of policing to risk factors is the most powerful conclusion reached from three decades of research. Hiring more police to provide rapid 911 responses, unfocused random patrol, and reactive arrests does not prevent serious crime. Community policing without a clear focus on crime risk factors generally shows no effect on crime. But directed patrols, proactive arrests and problem solving at high-crime "hot spots" has shown substantial evidence of crime prevention. Police can prevent robbery, disorder, gun violence, drunk driving and domestic violence, but only by using certain methods under certain conditions.

These conclusions are based largely on research supported by the National Institute of Justice, the research arm of the Office of Justice Programs in the U.S. Department of Justice. In recent years, increasing numbers of police executives have incorporated these findings into their crime prevention strategies. University of Wisconsin law professor Herman Goldstein's (1979) paradigm of "problem-oriented policing" directed research attention to the specific things police do, and how they can focus their resources to attack the proximate causes of public safety problems. The Justice Department's adoption of this perspective has yielded an increasingly complex but useful body of knowledge about how policing affects crime.

One of the most striking recent findings is the extent to which the police themselves create a risk factor for crime simply by using bad manners. Modest but consistent scientific evidence supports the hypothesis that the less respectful police are towards suspects and citizens generally, the less people will comply with the law. Changing police "style" may thus be as important as focusing police "substance." Making both the style and substance of police practices more "legitimate" in the eyes of the public, particularly high-risk juveniles, may be one of the most effective long-term police strategies for crime prevention.

This [article] begins with a review of the eight major hypotheses about how the police can prevent crime (Exhibit 5.1). It then describes the varying strength of the scientific evidence on those hypotheses, in relation to the "rigor" of the scientific methods used to test them. The available studies are summarized for both their conclusions and their scientific rigor. The [article] then attempts to simplify these results by answering the questions about what works, what doesn't, and what's promising. Major gaps in our knowledge are also examined. The [article] concludes with recommendations derived from these findings for future federal investment in both evaluation research and police methods to be developed for evaluation.

Testing the Hypotheses

All of these hypotheses pose formidable challenges to scientific testing. The measurement of crime is difficult under any circumstances, let alone in relation to experiments or natural variation in police practices. Control over police practices is difficult for police administrators under normal conditions, let alone under experimental protocols. Measuring the many dimensions of police activity, from effort to manners, is expensive and often inaccurate. Only a handful of studies have managed to produce strong scientific evidence about any of these hypotheses. But the accumulated evidence of the more numerous weaker studies can also provide some insights on policing for crime prevention.

Exhibit 5.1

Eight Major Hypotheses About Policing and Crime

Other things being equal,

1. **Numbers of Police.** The more police a city employs, the less crime it will have.
2. **Rapid Response to 911.** The shorter the police travel time from assignment to arrival at a crime scene, the less crime there will be.
3. **Random Patrols.** The more random patrol a city receives, the more a perceived "omnipresence" of the police will deter crime in public places.
4. **Directed Patrols.** The more precisely patrol presence is concentrated at the "hot spots" and "hot times" of criminal activity, the less crime there will be in those places and times.
5. **Reactive Arrests.** The more arrests police make in response to reported or observed offenses of any kind, the less crime there will be.
6. **Proactive Arrests.** The higher the police-initiated arrest rate for high-risk offenders and offenses, the lower the rates of serious violent crime.
7. **Community Policing.** The more quantity and better quality of contacts between police and citizens, the less crime.
8. **Problem-Oriented Policing.** The more police can identify and minimize proximate causes of specific patterns of crime, the less crime there will be.

This report employs a scale of 1 to 5 to summarize several different dimensions of scientific "rigor": the strength of scientific evidence. A score of 5 = strongest evidence for inferring cause and effect, while 1 = the weakest. These dimensions vary somewhat by institutional setting, with different issues inherent in the kinds of programs being evaluated. In the police evaluation literature, crime is almost always measured by either official crime reports (with all their flaws) or by victimization surveys of the public (with all their costs). Police practices are measured either not at all, through citizen perceptions of those practices, through police records, or (in one instance) through direct observation of police patrol activity. It is not clear that any of these methods except the last is superior to any others in drawing valid inferences about the actual practices of the police. Thus the greatest difference across police evaluations lies not in their methods of measurement, but in their basic research designs: the logical structure for drawing conclusions about cause and effect.

Evaluations of police crime prevention generally follow five basic research designs which can be ranked for overall strength of the inferences they can suggest about cause and effect. These designs are 1) correlations at the same point in time (e.g., in 1995 the cities with the most police had the least crime), 2) before-after differences in crime without a comparison group (e.g., doubling drunk driving arrests was followed by 50 percent reduction in fatal accidents), 3) before-after differences with comparison (e.g., the 50 percent reduction in fatal crashes compared to a 10 percent increase in fatal crashes in three cities of comparable size in the same state), 4) before-after large sample comparisons of treated and untreated groups (e.g., 30 neighborhoods organized for neighborhood watch compared to 30 that were not), and 5) randomized controlled experiments (300 offenders selected by a computerized equal probability program to be arrested had higher repeat offending rates than 300 offenders selected to be given warnings only).

Scientific Evaluations

This section reviews and interprets the reported tests of each of the hypotheses. The discussion attempts to integrate both the scientific score of the various studies and the number of studies converging on the same conclusion. More detailed discussion is offered for some of the major findings, in order to connect the evidence more clearly to the hypotheses. The main concern throughout this section is the cumulative success or failure of the studies in ruling out competing theories in the attempt to provide a conclusive test of each hypothesis.

Numbers of Police

[M]ost of the studies of the effects of police numbers on crime are scientifically weak. They consist of two basic research designs. One is evidence from police strikes[1] about a sudden and drastic reduction in police numbers. The other is evidence from correlational studies of police strength and crime rates.

The police strike evidence, while weak in both measurement and design, is fairly consistent in showing the effect of this natural experiment: crime rates skyrocket instantly. The strongest design is the Makinen and Takala (1980) study of crime in Helsinki before and during a police strike. The Helsinki measures included systematic observation counts of fights in public places, as well as emergency room admissions for assault-related injuries. Both measures rose substantially during the strike despite severe winter weather. The only purportedly negative evidence on this conclusion is the Pfuhl (1983) study of police-recorded crime in 11 American police strikes, in which 89 percent of the "strike" period in the analysis consisted of non-strike days. Both the measure and the definition of the strike period hopelessly confound cause and effect, rendering the study irrelevant to the conclusion reached from the stronger evidence.

None of the strike findings have comparison groups, so in theory it is possible that crimes would have risen dramatically during the strike period even without the strike. The substantial magnitudes of some of the increases, however, greatly exceed typical daily variations in crime in big cities. In the Montreal police strike of 1969, for example, there were 50 times more bank robberies and 14 times more commercial burglaries than average (Clark, 1969). Thus despite the weak research design, the large effect size suggests that abolishing a police force can cause crime to increase.

Whether adding more officers to an already large police force causes crime to decrease, however, is somewhat less clear. A recent review of 36 correlational studies, most of them weak in research design, found little evidence that more police reduce crime (Marvell and Moody, 1996). The same authors, however, offer a twenty-year analysis of 56 cities of over 250,000 people each and of 49 states. Using a complex technique called the Granger test, Marvell and Moody (1996) find consistent evidence that increases in the numbers of police cause reductions in crime in the following year. This study rates a level 4 because it employs multiple comparison groups and uses appropriate controls for well-specified differences across units. While it lacks random assignment, it is the best evidence available about the effect of modest increases in police numbers. While it runs against the conclusion of the preponderance of the other studies, the difference in scientific rigor tips the preponderance of the evidence in the direction of the conclusion that police numbers alone do help to reduce crime in a big city or a state. What the causal mechanism for that effect may be or how it may be enhanced, however, is not clear.

The Marvell and Moody (1996: 632) analysis also allows a test of the hypothesis that the prevention benefits of hiring more police officers are greater in higher-crime cities than across the country in general. The analysis estimates that for each additional officer added to a police force in a big city, 24 Part I crimes are prevented annually. For each officer hired anywhere in a state, only 4 Part I crimes are prevented. States, on average, have much lower crime rates than the big cities (over 250,000 population); in 1995 the rate of Part I crimes was 8,563 per 100,000 in the big cities, compared to 5,624 per 100,000 across all police agencies. Yet the ratio of crime prevention benefit is far greater than the ratio of reported crime risks. The Marvell and Moody estimate shows that six times as much crime is prevented for each officer added in cities than added in all places on average. Why the benefit ratio exceeds the risk ratio is unknown, but one likely candidate is the greater population density in cities which lets additional police officers have greater effects on patrol visibility per resident.

Rapid Response to 911

One major theory about the crime prevention benefits of hiring more officers is that it reduces police response time. The research on this theory is an excellent example of how different conclusions can result from research results with very different levels of scientific strength. The initial studies of the response time hypothesis produced strong support, suggesting that shaving minutes off response time could lead to the arrest of many more offenders. The extension of this hypothesis into a strategy of policing included the development of 911 systems to speed victim contact with police radio dispatchers, and the hiring of more police nationwide in the early 1970s in order to reduce average response times and deter crime through greater certainty of arrest. Only the 1977 NIJ response time analysis in [the] Kansas City study, and the NIJ replications in four other cities, were able to call that strategy into question, and open the door to more focused alternatives (Goldstein, 1979).

The original test of the hypothesis was based on a scientifically weak research design, a nonrandom sample of 265 police responses to citizen calls by the Los Angeles Police Department (Isaacs, 1967). Its results were confirmed by a later study in Seattle (Clawson and Chang, 1977): the probability of arrest per police response increased as police time in travel to the scene decreased. Two other studies (Brown,

1974; Holliday, 1974, as cited in Chaiken, 1978) failed to find that pattern, perhaps because, as Chaiken (1978: 130) observes, "the curves are essentially flat for response times larger than three minutes, and therefore a substantial amount of data for responses under three minutes is needed to observe any effect."

The Kansas City (1977) response time analysis took a far more systematic approach to the issue. Its first step was to divide crimes into victim-offender "involvement" (e.g., robbery, assault, rape) and after-the-crime "discovery" categories (e.g., burglary, car theft). It then focused response time analysis on involvement crimes, since the offender would not be present at the discovery crimes. The analysis then divided the involvement crime "response time" into three time periods: crime initiation to calling the police ("reporting time"), police receipt of call to dispatch ("dispatch time"), and "travel time" of police from receipt of dispatch to arrival at the scene. Using systematic observation methods and interviews of victims, the Kansas City study (1977, Vol. 2: 39) found that there was no correlation between response-related arrest probability and reporting time once the time exceeded 9 minutes. The average reporting time for involvement crimes is 41 minutes (K.C.P.D. 1977, Vol. 2: 23). Cutting police travel time for such crime from 5 to 2.5 minutes could require a doubling of the police force, but it would have almost no impact on the odds of making an arrest.

Police chiefs in the Police Executive Research Forum (PERF) told NIJ that they did not think citizens in their own communities would take so long to call the police. NIJ responded by commissioning PERF to replicate the citizen reporting component of the response time analysis in four other cities. Over 4,000 interviews about 3,300 "involvement" crimes produced unequivocal support for the findings of the Kansas City response time analysis (Spelman and Brown, 1981). The probability of arrest in those serious crimes was only 29 per 1,000 reports, with 75 percent of serious crimes being discovered by victims long after the crimes occurred. Of the 25 percent that directly involved the victims, almost half were reported five minutes or more after the crime was completed. The findings were consistent across cities, including one that had a 911 system and three that did not.

The conclusion that reduced response time will not reduce crime is based on strong but indirect evidence. The evidence is strong because it is based on large samples, careful measurement, and a replicated research design in five diverse cities showing little variation in arrest rates by police travel time, the main factor that tax dollars can affect. It is indirect because an experimental test of the effects of reduced police travel time on citywide arrest and crime rates has never been conducted. Yet there is neither empirical nor theoretical justification for such an expensive test. Given the strong evidence of citizen delays in reporting involvement crimes, and the small proportion of serious crimes that feature direct victim-offender involvement, further tests of this theory seem to be a waste of tax dollars. Those dollars might be better spent on communicating the findings to the general public, which still puts great priority on police travel time for public safety (Sherman, 1995).

Random Patrols

Another major theory about the benefits of more police is that they can conduct more random patrols. [Research efforts to date] show weak evidence of no effect of moderate variations in numbers or method of patrols. The most famous test of the random preventive patrol hypothesis, the Kansas City Preventive Patrol Experiment (Kelling et al., 1974), reveals some of the difficulty in testing this claim. This experiment claimed to have varied the dosage of patrol presence for one year across three groups of five randomly assigned beats each, preceded and followed by extensive measures of crime from both household surveys and official records. The results of the experiment showed no statistically significant differences in crime across the three groups.

Many criminologists conclude from this experiment that there is no crime prevention effect of adding patrol presence in a big city, where low density of crime makes the extra patrol a mere drop in the bucket (Felson, 1994). Yet the experiment has been criticized for its failure to measure the actual differences in patrol dosage and the possible lack of them (Larson, 1975), its inadequate statistical power to detect large percentage differences in crime as not due to chance (Fienberg et al., 1976), and its failure to assign patrol dosage at random (Farrington, 1982). Similar limitations are found in the Newark Foot Patrol Experiment (Police Foundation, 1981), where despite large victimization surveys no crime prevention effects were detected in association with adding or eliminating daytime and early evening foot patrols from selected patrol beats.

The weakness of the evidence is even greater for the one study claiming to find a crime prevention effect from random patrols not focused on crime risks (Trojanowicz, 1986). The design of this study was limited to recorded crime and calls for service, with no victimization surveys. After daytime foot patrols were added to 14 beats in Flint, Michigan for three years, the official crime counts in those beats were down by 9 percent in the foot patrol beats and up 10 percent in the other beats citywide. Large increases in burglary and robbery in the foot patrol areas were matched by reportedly greater increases in the rest of the city. No significance tests were reported, nor were there any controls for the demographic characteristics of the areas selected for foot patrol compared to the rest of the city. Since the foot patrol areas were not selected at random, it is possible that those areas might have experienced different crime trends even without the foot patrols. The fact that the increase in burglary and robbery occurred largely at night when the foot patrols were not working is perhaps the most interesting fact in the study, supporting the conclusion reached from evaluations of directed patrols focused on high crime-risk times and places.

Directed Patrols

The evidence from the directed preventive patrol hypothesis is more voluminous, scientifically stronger (in two tests), and consistently in the opposite direction from the weight of the (weak) evidence on the random patrol hypothesis. In order to be assigned to this category, the studies had to indicate that they were somehow focused on high-crime places, times or areas. In the New York City study (Press, 1971: 94), for example, the test precinct was known as a high robbery area, and had over three times as many robberies per week as each group of five areas in the Kansas City experiment. All eight of the reported tests of this hypothesis show crime reductions in response to increased patrol presence.

The crime prevention effects of extra uniformed patrol in marked police cars at high-crime "peaks" are especially evident in two very different research designs imposed on one large NIJ study designed to improve upon the Kansas City Preventive Patrol Experiment. Based on the NIJ-funded research showing extreme concentrations in spatial and temporal distributions of crime, the Minneapolis Police Department (MPD) reorganized its entire patrol force in 1988–89 to test a pattern of directed patrols at hot spots during hot times. With the unanimous consent of the City Council, the MPD substantially reduced patrols from low-crime areas in order to provide 2 to 3 hours of extra patrol each day during high-crime hours at 55 street corner hot spots. The corners were randomly selected for extra patrols from a carefully compiled list of 110 high-crime locations that were visually separate from each other (Buerger, Petrosino and Cohn, 1995). Under a million dollar NIJ grant, both the patrolled and unpatrolled hot spots were subjected to over 7,000 randomly selected hours of observations by independent researchers over the course of a year. The observers recorded every minute of 24,813 instances of police presence in the hot spots, and 4,014 observed acts of crime and disorder (Koper, 1995: 656).

Koper's (1995) analysis of the Minneapolis Hot Spots Patrol data found a very strong relationship between the length of each police patrol presence (which averaged 14 minutes) and the amount of time the hot spot was free of crime after the police left the scene. The longer the police stayed before they left, the longer the time until the first crime (or disorderly act) after they left. This relationship held for each additional minute of police presence from one to 15 minutes, after which the relationship began to reverse. Thus the "Koper curve" in the Minneapolis data suggests the optimum length of a police patrol visit to a hot spot for the purpose of deterring crime is about 15 minutes.

Koper's correlational analysis of all police presences observed in both the extra-patrol and no-extra-patrol hot spots combined is consistent with the results of Sherman and Weisburd's (1995) comparisons of the two groups. The experimental analysis found that there was an average of twice as much patrol presence and up to half as much crime in the extra-patrol hot spots as in the no-extra-patrol group. The observational data showed crime or disorder in 4 percent of all observed minutes in the control group compared to 2 percent in the experimental group (Sherman and Weisburd, 1995: 64). Most of the difference in the observed crime was found when police were not present in the hot spots. Crime-related calls for service increased for both groups of hot spots over the one-year experiment as well as citywide, but the average growth per hot spot was up to three times as great in the no-extra-patrol group (17 percent) as in the extra-patrol group (5 percent) (Sherman and Weisburd, 1995: 644).

These findings can be questioned, like most place-linked crime prevention effects, with the possible side effect that the crime simply moved elsewhere. So, too, can a reduction of crime in one city be questioned on the grounds that offenders may have focused on other jurisdictions. The theoretical perspective of "routine activities" (Cohen and Felson, 1979; Felson, 1994), under which crimes are only likely to happen in certain places and times, makes the displacement hypothesis less plausible. It suggests that if crime is displaced, it would have to be displaced to other hot spots. That argument is still consistent with the experimental-comparison group analysis, given the rising numbers of calls in the experimental year relative to the baseline year. But it does not explain away Koper's cross-sectional analysis of the effects of longer patrol presence on post-patrol crime rates.

Reactive Arrests

The evidence in support of the reactive arrest hypothesis is remarkably unencouraging at both the community and individual levels of analysis. As a matter of general deterrence, the tests are all fairly weak and generally negative. As a matter of individual deterrence, the results are consistently negative for juveniles, and contradictory for two different groups of domestic assailants, employed and unemployed. The scientific evidence for the latter is among the strongest available in the police literature, while the evidence about juveniles is much weaker. Taken as a whole, these results make a vivid demonstration of the complexity of police effects on crime.

The evidence on the general deterrent effects of reactive (Reiss, 1971) arrests is based on correlational analyses, with and without temporal order. There is some weak evidence that there is a threshold beyond which the effect of increased arrest rates becomes evident, while no such effect is apparent below the "tipping point" of minimum dosage level (Tittle and Rowe, 1974). This evidence is complicated by the suggestion that the arrest effects are only evident among cities of less than 10,000 people, even with the "tipping point." The finding by Greenberg and his colleagues (1979, 1982) of no arrest rate deterrent effects in a temporal sequence design in big cities throws great doubt on a simple claim of general deterrence. Here again, without focusing arrests on high-risk persons or places, the effects of higher arrest levels may get lost in the many factors causing crime.

The consistent individual level evidence of the criminogenic effects of arrests for juveniles is all longitudinal, but only one of the studies is a randomized experiment (Klein, 1986). The other studies are natural observations of the difference in self-reported offending before and after juvenile offenders were arrested. These studies cannot adequately control for the rival hypothesis that the same factors that led to the youth being arrested also caused a higher level of repeat offending. A pattern of "defiance" (Sherman, 1993), for example, would account for both variables and their correlation. The Klein (1986) experiment reported some difficulties in maintaining random assignment, but still managed to make the formal charging of juveniles in police custody a matter of equal likelihood across cases. Holding juvenile characteristics relatively constant, then, Klein found that the more legalistic the processing of a juvenile suspect, the higher the official recidivism rate.[2] In interpreting these results, it is necessary to recall that most juvenile [arrests] are for fairly minor offenses, and that most juveniles with one police contact never have another (Wolfgang, Figlio and Sellin, 1972). Thus to a certain degree, arresting some juveniles and not others for such offenses may be perceived as arbitrary or procedurally unfair.

The evidence on the effects of arrest for misdemeanor domestic violence is contradictory across cities but consistent within arrestee characteristics. While three experiments have found some evidence of deterrent effects of arrest (Sherman and Berk, 1984; Pate, Hamilton and Annan, 1991; Berk et al., 1992), three other experiments have found some evidence that arrest increases the frequency of officially detected offending (Sherman et al., 1991; Hirschel et al., 1992; Dunford, 1992). All four of these six experiments for which the data have been analyzed separately by employment status of the offender show consistent results. Arrest increases repeat offending among unemployed suspects while reducing it among employed suspects. Marciniak (1994) has shown that this difference operates even more powerfully at the census tract level than at the individual level, with arrest backfiring irrespective of individual employment status in neighborhoods of concentrated unemployment and single-parent households. There is a literature raising concerns about measurement issues in these data (Garner and Fagan, 1995; Fagan, 1996) that are not generally raised about other studies in the police literature. Yet there is no other example in the police literature of six similar randomized experiments all testing similar hypotheses with similar (though not identical) designs, and these studies feature a scientific rigor score that is twice the mean of all (reactive arrest) studies classified for this (evaluation). The consistency of the effects of arrest on crime for employed and unemployed offenders even extends to similarity in effect sizes.

Proactive Arrests

Like the evidence on focused patrol, the evidence on the focused proactive arrest hypothesis is generally supportive across a wide range of studies and research designs. While most of the studies are relatively modest in scientific strength, there are some randomized controlled experiments. With the exception of arrests targeted on drug problems, there appear to be substantial results from focusing scarce arrest resources on high-risk people, places, offenses and times.

The evidence on high-risk people comes from two strong (level 4) evaluations of police units aimed at repeat offenders. The Washington, D.C. unit employed pre-arrest investigations, designed to catch offenders in the act of crime to enhance the strength of evidence. The Phoenix police unit employed post-arrest investigations, designed to enhance the evidence in the offender's latest case based upon the length and nature of the offender's prior record. Both projects aimed at increasing the incarceration rate of the targeted offenders, and both succeeded. Just how serious or active the offenders were is an important issue in these studies, one which could illuminate future analyses of dollars invested per crime prevented.

Two weaker studies use national samples of cities to test the effects of police arrest rates for minor offenses on robbery. Both employ multivariate models to control for the effects of some of the other factors that could influence the city's robbery rate. Both find that the higher the per capita rates of traffic arrest, the lower the rates of robbery. One uncontrolled factor in these analyses is the number of pedestrian robbery opportunities. This may be much higher in cities where there is less use of automobiles, such as New York City, in which under 3 percent of the United States population suffers 12 percent of the reported robberies. Since that is the only crime type for which New York is so disproportionate, and since other dense, pedestrian cities like Baltimore and Boston also have high robbery rates, there may be a spurious relationship between traffic enforcement and robbery. That is, the more cars per capita, the fewer robbery opportunities and the more traffic enforcement opportunities.

That is just the kind of limitation in causal inference that experiments can address. Quasi-experimental evidence on this hypothesis was recently reported by the Hudson Institute study of the Indianapolis Police Department, in which substantial increases in traffic enforcement in a high robbery area were followed by a sharp reduction in robbery (Weiss and McGarrell, 1996).

The evidence on drug crackdowns shows no consistent reductions in violent crime during or after the crackdown is in effect. The strongest evidence is the randomized experiment in raids of crack houses (Sherman and Rogan, 1995), in which crime on the block dropped sharply after a raid. The rapid decay of the deterrent effect in only seven days, however, greatly reduces the cost-effectiveness of the labor-intensive raid strategy. Only the high yield of guns seized per officer-hour invested (Shaw, 1994) and its possible connection to community gun violence over a longer time period (Sherman, Shaw and Rogan, 1995) showed great cost-effectiveness. Other drug enforcement strategies in open-air markets have even less encouraging results, with the exception of the Jersey City experiment in which the principal outcome measure was disorder, not violence.

The evidence on drunk driving, in contrast, is one of the great success stories of world policing. Despite relatively low rigor scores, the sheer numbers of consistent results from quasi-experimental evaluations of proactive drunk driving arrest crackdowns suggest a clear cause and effect. The ability of the police to control drunk driving appears to be a direct and linear function of the amount of effort they put into it (Homel, 1990). Since more deaths are caused annually by drunk driving than by homicide, the cost effectiveness of saving lives through DUI enforcement may well be far greater than for homicide prevention. The evidence on drunk driving prevention seems far clearer than anything we know how to do to have police prevent murders.

The evidence for the broken windows-zero tolerance arrests hypothesis (Wilson and Kelling,1982) is also consistently supportive. The research designs are only moderately strong, but they all suggest that a police focus on street activity can help reduce serious crime. The specific tactics by which this is accomplished can be controversial, and some methods used in the 1982 Newark test have been described in the literature as "unconstitutional" (Skolnick and Bayley, 1985: 199), including the ordering of loitering teenage males off of street corners on the grounds of obstructing traffic. Field interrogations have often been a flash point of poor police-community relations, yet they have also been a favorite crime prevention tactic for police in both the US and Europe. The evidence from both the San Diego field interrogation experiment (Boydstun, 1975) and the NIJ Oakland city center study (Reiss, 1985) suggest that it is possible to regulate public behavior in a polite manner that fosters rather than hinders police legitimacy. That possibility, however, is by no means guaranteed, and generally takes substantial managerial investment in order to bring about.

The larger concern about zero tolerance is its long-term effect on people arrested for minor offenses. Even while massive arrest increases, such as those in New York City, may reduce violence in the short run—especially gun violence—they may also increase serious crime in the long run. The negative effects of an arrest record on labor market participation are substantial (Schwartz and Skolnick, 1962; Bushway, 1996). The effects of an arrest experience over a minor offense may permanently lower police legitimacy, both for the arrested person and their social network of family and friends. The criminogenic effect of arrest may make arrestees more defiant (Sherman, 1993) and more prone to anger in domestic violence and child abuse. The data suggest that zero tolerance programs should be evaluated in relation to long-term effects on those arrested, as well as short-term effects on community crime rates. Program development to foster greater legitimacy in the course of making the arrests is also advisable, based on findings from procedural justice research. This could include, for example, a program to give arrested minor offenders an opportunity to meet with a police supervisor who would explain the program to them, answer questions about why they are being arrested, and give them a chance to express their views about the program while listening respectfully to them. Such innovations would not be expensive, but would pose many testable hypotheses.

Community Policing

The results of available tests of the community policing hypotheses are mixed. The evidence against the effectiveness of police organizing communities into neighborhood watches is consistent and relatively strong. The evidence about the crime prevention benefits of more information flowing from citizens to police is at best only promising. The two tests of police sending more information to citizens are both very strong, but clearly falsify the hypothesis. The tests of increasing police legitimacy are the most promising, especially since they draw on a powerful theoretical perspective that is gaining growing empirical support.

One of the most consistent findings in the literature is also the least well-known to policymakers and the public. The oldest and best known community policing program, Neighborhood Watch, is ineffective at preventing crime. That conclusion is supported by moderately strong evidence, including a randomized experiment in Minneapolis that tried to organize block watch programs with and without police participation in areas that had not requested assistance (Pate et al., 1987). The primary problem found by the evaluations is that the areas with highest crime rates are the most reluctant to organize (Hope, 1995). Many people refuse to host or attend community meetings, in part because they distrust their neighbors. Middle class areas, in which trust is higher, generally have little crime to begin with, making measurable effects on crime almost impossible to achieve. The program cannot even be justified on the basis of reducing middle class fear of crime and flight from the city, since no such effects have been found. Rather, Skogan (1990) finds evidence that Neighborhood Watch increases fear of crime.

Another popular program for increasing contact between police and public is community meetings. The careful NIJ evaluation of the Madison, Wisconsin community policing project in which meetings played a central role found no reduction in crime (Wycoff and Skogan, 1993). A different approach to the meetings in Chicago shows more promise, with the meetings focused much more precisely on specific crime patterns in the area and ideas for what the police should do to attack those problems. While the crime reduction evidence for "community policing, Chicago style" is mixed, it is striking that Chicago has mobilized high-crime communities to participate in these meetings (Skogan, 1996). Unlike neighborhood watch meetings, the Chicago meetings are held in public places rather than local residences. The best attendance at these meetings for almost two years has been found in the police districts with the highest crime rates.

A less popular but often effective community policing practice is door-to-door visits by police to residences during the daytime. These visits may be used to seek information, such as who is carrying guns on the street (Sherman, Shaw and Rogan, 1995). The visits may be used to give out information, such as burglary reduction tips (Laycock, 1991). The visits may be used simply to introduce local police officers to local residents, to make policing more personal (Wycoff et al., 1985). Four out of six available tests of the door-to-door visits show modestly strong (rigor = 3) evidence of substantial crime prevention. In the NIJ-funded Houston test, for example, the overall prevalence of household victimization dropped in the target area substantially, with no reduction in the comparison area. The prevention effects were primarily for car break-ins and other minor property crime. Here again, however, there was a substantial "Matthew effect": the benefits of the program were highly concentrated among white middle-class homeowners, with virtually no benefit for the Asian, Hispanic and African-American minorities living in rental housing in the target area (Skogan, 1990).

A far more popular program is far less effective. Police storefronts are often requested by communities, often staffed during business hours by a mix of sworn police, paid civilians and unpaid volunteers. The evidence from tests of substations in Houston, Newark and Birmingham (AL) consistently shows no impact on crime. While there are some positive citizen evaluations associated with storefronts, the problems of staffing the offices once they are open may counterbalance any non-crime benefits.

Increasing the flow of information from police to public has been tested in the form of police newsletters. In two randomized NIJ-funded experiments, the Newark and Houston police departments found no effect of newsletters on the victimization rates of the households receiving them. The finding was true for both newsletters with and without specific data on recent crimes in the community.

The most promising approach to community policing is also the most theoretically coherent. Based on two decades of laboratory and field studies on the social psychology of "procedural justice," a growing body of research suggests that police legitimacy prevents crime. Tyler (1990) finds a strong correlation across a large sample of Chicago citizens between perceived legitimacy of police and willingness to obey the law. The legitimacy was measured by citizen evaluations of how police treated them in previous encounters. This finding is consistent with the Houston door-to-door experiment, in which citizen fear of police after a major scandal over police beating to death a Mexican immigrant was reduced by the door-to-door visits. Community policing Chicago style (Skogan et al., 1996) also [found] the greatest perceived reduction in serious crime in the districts where surveys showed police were "most responsive" to citizen concerns. The most powerful test of this hypothesis is the Paternoster et al. (1996) reanalysis of the Milwaukee Domestic Violence Experiment, which found that repeat domestic violence was lowest among arrestees who thought police had treated them respectfully; a powerful effect on recidivism was associated with police simply taking the time to listen to the offender's side of the story. The capacity of police legitimacy to prevent crime is something community policing may well be effective at creating; Skogan's (1994: 176) review of six community policing evaluations (SM scores = 2 or 3) found every one showed positive or improved perceptions of police in the treated areas.

Still in progress, but with encouraging preliminary results, is the Australian test of community accountability conferences. The Australian Federal Police in the Australian capital, Canberra, use this procedure as an alternative to prosecuting juveniles. Only cases in which the offender(s) admit(s) guilt and the victim(s) are willing to attend the conference are eligible. The conference of offenders and victims with their respective families and friends is led by a trained police officer, who focuses the discussion on what happened, what harm it caused, and how the harm can be repaired. The officer tries to insure that everyone, especially victims, is allowed to have their say. Sometimes offenders apologize, but always an agreement for repaying the cost of the crime to the victim is reached; failure to do so results in the case being prosecuted. Preliminary findings from subsequent interviews with victims and offenders in a randomized experiment show that the procedure greatly increases respect for police and a perception of justice, regardless of the outcomes (Strang, 1996; Barnes, 1996). The National Institute of Justice has funded a similar ongoing project in Bethlehem, Pennsylvania. This method may turn out to have long-term effects on police legitimacy in the eyes of both juvenile offenders and their families, which could in turn reduce crime.

The interesting point about the Australian model of community policing is that it builds on actual community ties rather than anonymous geographic areas. Moreover, the attendees form a community of concern about the criminal act bringing them together, holding the offender accountable for over an hour to a "village-like" community rather than for a few minutes to a distant and anonymous judge. Of all the approaches to community policing yet tried, this one may have the most focused empowerment of "community" to prevent future crimes.

Problem-Oriented Policing

The tests of this hypothesis are generally more positive than the tests of community policing. As Moore (1992) suggests, however, this may be due to a process of selective reporting, in which failures are not included. The most basic problem with testing this very rich and complex hypothesis is that it is essentially about insight, imagination and creativity. The essence of problem-oriented policing as Goldstein (1979) defined it is science itself (Sherman and Strang, 1996): classification, prediction, and causation. Evaluations of the scientific method, paradoxically, are not readily susceptible to the scientific method—except in gross comparison to unscientific methods. From this perspective, problem-oriented policing embraces all of the other strategies described in this chapter, with the problem to be solved that of crime prevention.

This section reviews some evidence on police efforts to prevent crime that do not fall into the preceding seven hypotheses, and that self-consciously adopted a scientific process that involved police officers in analyzing crime patterns, imagining and creating an intervention, and testing it in the field. The two basic categories of interventions reported in the literature to date are "removing criminogenic substances" and "separating potential victims and offenders." These two categories simply reflect a convergence of police and criminological thinking about the proximate causes of criminal events. There is nothing in the basic problem-oriented policing (POP) strategy (Goldstein, 1979) that requires the use of these two approaches. Many others are possible, and may even be more effective. If POP succeeds at making scientific research and development the core technology of police work (Reiss, 1992), we may expect that its approaches to crime prevention will evolve with the evolution of knowledge about crime causation.

Criminogenic Substances. The evidence on cash control is weak but suggestive. As part of a multiple intervention strategy to reduce crime in an English public housing project, the coin-operated gas heaters were removed from residences. Rather than having the cash in the house as an attraction to burglars, the gas charges were switched to monthly billing. Burglary went down substantially. It is uncertain, however, whether other efforts, such as the "cocoon" neighborhood watch around recently burglarized residences, might account for the crime reduction.

Gun Carrying. The evidence on gun carrying is stronger. In the NIJ Kansas City Gun Experiment, police focused traffic enforcement and field interrogations on gun crime hot spots during hot times (Sherman, Shaw and Rogan,

1995). With special training in the detection of carrying concealed weapons, police focused on seizing illegally carried weapons. Gun seizures in the target area rose by 60 percent, and gun crimes dropped by 49 percent. A similar area in a different part of town showed no change in either guns seized or gun crimes. In Boston, police have used a mix of strategies to discourage gun carrying in public places among juveniles, especially gang members and probationers. Qualitative evidence from an NIJ project suggests gun carrying by the high-risk groups has been substantially reduced, while early quantitative evidence shows an elimination of juvenile gun homicide (Kennedy et al., 1996).

Alcohol and Prostitution. The evidence on alcohol and prostitution is also encouraging. . . . In the Minneapolis RECAP (Repeat Call Address Policing) experiment, however, four police officers were unable to implement a broad mix of efforts to separate potential victims and offenders across a sample of 250 target addresses. The YMCA refused to limit access to its lobby during evening hours, the Public Library refused to bar intoxicated persons, public housing officials were unable to segregate young "disabled" but predatory alcoholics from elderly co-residents, and private landlords resisted efforts to evict drug dealers (Sherman, 1990; Buerger, 1994). While a randomized experimental design gave the test strong science, police inexperience at persuading property managers gave the strategy a weak technology. Given the theoretical power of the idea, further development of the methods of persuasion might be justified, and only then followed by further research.

Curfews. One of the most popular practices for separating victims and offenders is evening curfews for juveniles. While such curfews give police additional powers to search for guns, they have not been used consistently in that fashion. The primary objective is to get kids, not guns, off the streets. Some cities, such as San Antonio, have reported reductions in reported crimes against juveniles. But in preliminary results of an NIJ evaluation, Adams (1996) finds no consistent crime reduction effects across cities adopting curfews. The scientific rigor of these studies is quite low given their complete absence of control groups, and there may also be difficulties in police willingness to follow curfew policies. Thus the question of the effectiveness of curfews at preventing youth violence is still quite open to further research and development.

Conclusions

For all of its scientific limitations, the evidence shows substantial consistency on a number of the hypotheses, and some tentative conclusions on others. All science, of course, is provisional, with better research designs or theories revealing previously undiscovered patterns. It is no small achievement that police crime prevention research has developed to the point of having reached some conclusions to discard.

The available evidence supports two major conclusions about policing for crime prevention. One is that the effects of police on crime are complex, and often surprising. The other is that the more focused the police strategy, the more likely it is to prevent crime. The first conclusion follows from the findings that arrests can sometimes increase crime, that traffic enforcement may reduce robbery and gun crime, that the optimal deterrent effect of a police patrol may be produced by 15 minutes of presence in a hot spot, and that prevention effects generally fade over time without modification and renewal of police practices. The second conclusion follows from the likely failure to achieve crime prevention merely by adding more police or shortening response time across the board.

The substantial array of police strategies and tactics for crime prevention (Reiss, 1995) has a small but growing evaluation literature. Using the standard of at least two consistent findings from level 3 scientific methods score (well-measured, before-after studies with a comparison group) and a preponderance of the other evidence in support of the same conclusion, the research shows several practices to be supported by strong evidence of effectiveness, and several with strong evidence of ineffectiveness.

What works:

- increased directed patrols in street-corner hot spots of crime
- proactive arrests of serious repeat offenders
- proactive drunk driving arrests
- arrests of employed suspects for domestic assault

What doesn't:

- neighborhood block watch
- arrests of some juveniles for minor offenses
- arrests of unemployed suspects for domestic assault
- drug market arrests
- community policing with no clear crime-risk factor focus

Several other strategies fail to meet the test of strong evidence for generalizable effectiveness, but merit much more research and development because of encouraging findings in the initial research.

What's promising:

- police traffic enforcement patrols against illegally carried handguns
- community policing with community participation in priority setting
- community policing focused on improving police legitimacy
- zero tolerance of disorder, if legitimacy issues can be addressed
- problem-oriented policing generally
- adding extra police to cities, regardless of assignments
- warrants for arrest of suspect absent when police respond to domestic violence

What is notably absent from these findings, however, are many topics of great concern to police. Gang prevention, for example, is a matter about which we could not find a single impact evaluation of police practices. Police curfews and truancy programs lack rigorous tests. Police recreation activities with juveniles, such as Police Athletic Leagues, also remain unevaluated. Automated identification systems, in-car computer terminals, and a host of other new technologies costing billions of dollars remain unevaluated for their impact on crime prevention. There is clearly a great deal of room for further testing of hypotheses not listed here due to the absence of available scientific evidence.These conclusions suggest important implications for both DOJ crime prevention funding of police agencies, and improving that effectiveness through stronger evaluations.

Notes

1. And in one case, the arrest of the entire Copenhagen police force by the Nazis in 1944, which was equivalent to a strike because the occupying German army did nothing to en-force civilian criminal laws before or after arresting the police (Andenaes, 1974).
2. There was no difference in the self-reported offending data, but only 60 percent of the offenders gave followup interviews.

References

Abrahamse, Allan F., Patricia A. Ebener, Peter W. Greenwood, Nora Fitzgerald, and Thomas E. Kosin. 1991. "An Experimental Evaluation of the Phoenix Repeat Offender Program," *Justice Quarterly* 8: 141–168.

Adams, Kenneth. 1996. Paper Presented to the National Evaluation Conference, National Institute of Justice, Washington, D.C.

Andenaes, Johannes. 1974. *Punishment and Deterrence.* Ann Arbor, MI: University of Michigan Press.

Annan, Sampson and Wesley Skogan. 1993. *Drug Enforcement in Public Housing: Signs of Success in Denver.* Washington, DC: Police Foundation.

Barker, M., Geraghty, J., Webb, B. & Key, T. 1993. *The Prevention of Street Robbery.* Police Research Group Crime Prevention Series Paper No. 44. London: Police Department, Home Office.

Barnes, Geoffrey C. 1996. Paper presented to the American Society of Criminology, Chicago.

Bennett, Trevor. 1990. *Evaluating Neighborhood Watch.* Basingstoke: Gower.

Berk, Richard A., Alec Campbell, Ruth Klap, and Bruce Western. 1992a. "A Bayesian Analysis of the Colorado Spouse Abuse Experiment," *Journal of Criminal Law and Criminology* 83: 170–200.

——. 1992b. "The Deterrent Effect of Arrest in Incidents of Domestic Violence: A Bayesian Analysis of Four Field Experiments," *American Sociological Review* 57: 698–708.

Black, Donald. 1980. *The Manners and Customs of the Police.* NY: Academic Press.

Boydstun, John. 1975. *The San Diego Field Interrogation Experiment.* Washington, DC: Police Foundation.

Brown, W. 1974. *Evaluation of Police Patrol Operations.* Unpublished M.A. Thesis, University of Ottawa.

Brown, Don W. 1978. "Arrests and Crime Rates: When Does a Tipping Effect Occur?" *Social Forces* 57: 671–82.

Buerger, Michael E., Ed. 1994. *The Crime Prevention Casebook: Securing High Crime Locations.* Washington, DC: Crime Control Institute.

Buerger, Michael E., Anthony Petrosino and Ellen G. Cohn. 1995. In John Eck and David Weisburd, Eds., *Crime and Place.* Monsey, N.Y: Criminal Justice Press and Police Executive Research Forum.

Burney, E. 1990. *Putting Street Crime in Its Place: A Report to the Community/Police Consultative Group for Lambeth.* London: Goldsmith's College.

Bushway, Shawn. 1996. *The Impact of a Criminal History Record on Access to Legitimate Employment.* PhD Dissertation, H. John Heinz School of Public Policy and Management, Carnegie Mellon University.

Chaiken, Jan M. 1978. "What Is Known About Deterrent Effects of Police Activities," in James A. Cramer, Ed., *Preventing Crime.* Beverly Hills, CA: Sage Publications.

Chaiken, Jan M., M. Lawless and K. Stevenson. 1975. "The Impact of Police Activity on Crime: Robberies on the New York City Subway System," *Urban Analysis* 3: 173–205.

Chamlin, Mitchell. 1988. "Crimes and Arrest: An Autoregressive Integrated Moving Average (ARIMA) Approach," *Journal of Quantitative Criminology.*

——. 1991. "A Longitudinal Analysis of the Arrest-Crime Relationship: A Further Examination of the Tipping Effect," *Justice Quarterly* 8: 187–199.

Clark, Gerald. 1969. "What Happens When the Police Go on Strike," *New York Times Magazine,* Nov. 16, sec. 6, pp. 45, 176–85, 187, 194–95.

Clawson, C. and S.K. Chang. 1977. "The Relationship of Response Delays and Arrest Rates," *Journal of Police Science and Administration* 5: 53–68.

Cohen, Lawrence and Marcus Felson. 1979. "Social Change and Crime Rate Trends: A Routine Activities Approach," *American Sociological Review* 44: 588–607.

Crowell, Nancy A. and Ann W. Burgess. 1996. *Understanding Violence Against Women.* Washington, DC: National Academy of Sciences.

Dahmann, J.S. 1975. *Examination of Police Patrol Effectiveness.* McLean Va.: Mitre Corporation.

Dunford, Franklyn W. 1990. "System-Initiated Warrants for Suspects of Misdemeanor Domestic Assault: A Pilot Study," *Justice Quarterly* 7: 631–653;

——. 1992. "The Measurement of Recidivism in Cases of Spouse Assault," *Journal of Criminal Law and Criminology* 83: 120–136.

Dunford, Franklyn W., David Huizinga, and Delbert S. Elliott. 1990. "The Role of Arrest in Domestic Assault: The Omaha Police Experiment," *Criminology* 28: 183–206.

Dunworth, Terence, Peter Haynes, and Aaron J. Saiger. 1997. *National Assessment of the Byrne Formula Grant Program. National Institute of Justice Research in Brief.* Washington, DC: U.S. Department of Justice.

Eck, John E. and William Spelman. 1987. *Problem Solving: Problem-Oriented Policing in Newport News.* Washington, DC: Police Executive Research Forum.

Eck, John E. and Dennis Rosenbaum. 1994. "The New Police Order: Effectiveness, Equity and Efficiency in Community Policing," in Dennis Rosenbaum, Ed., *The Challenge of Community Policing: Testing the Promises.* Thousand Oaks, CA: Sage.

Epperlein, T. 1985. *The Use of Sobriety Checkpoints as a Deterrent: An Impact Assessment.* Phoenix: Arizona Department of Public Safety.

Fagan, Jeffrey. 1996. *The Criminalization of Domestic Violence: Promises and Limits. Research Report.* Washington, DC: National Institute of Justice.

Farrington, David P. 1977. "The Effects of Public Labeling," *British Journal of Criminology* 17: 112–25;

——. 1982. "Randomized Experiments on Crime and Justice," in Michael Tonry and Norval Morris, Eds., *Crime and Justice: An Annual Review of Research.* Chicago: University of Chicago Press.

Felson, Marcus. 1994. *Crime and Everyday Life.* Thousand Oaks, CA: Pine Forge Press.

Fienberg, Stephen E., Kinley Lamtz, and Albert J. Reiss, Jr. 1976. "Redesigning the Kansas City Preventive Patrol Experiment," *Evaluation* 3: 124–131.

Garner, Joel, Jeffrey Fagan, and Christopher D. Maxwell. 1995. "Published Findings From the NIJ Spouse Assault Replication Program: A Critical Review," *Journal of Quantitative Criminology* 8: 1–29.

Gibbs, Jack. 1975. *Crime, Punishment and Deterrence.* New York: Elsevier.

Gold, Martin and Jay Williams. 1970. "National Study of the Aftermath of Apprehension," *Prospectus* 3: 3–12.

Goldstein, Herman. 1979. "Improving Policing: A Problem-Oriented Approach," *Crime and Delinquency* 25: 236–258.

Gorer, Geoffrey. 1955. *Exploring English Character.* London: Cresset.

Gorer, Geoffrey, David F. Greenberg, Ronald C. Kessler, and Charles H. Logan. 1979. "A Panel Model of Crime Rates and Arrest Rates," *American Sociological Review* 44: 843–50.

Greenberg, David and Ronald C. Kessler. 1982. "The Effects of Arrests on Crime: A Multivariate Panel Analysis," *Social Forces* 60: 771–90.

Gurr, Ted Robert, Peter N. Grabosky, and Richard C. Hula. 1977. *The Politics of Crime and Conflict: A Comparative History of Four Cities.* Beverly Hills, CA: Sage.

Hayes, Gary. 1979. Personal Communication.

Hirschel, David, Ira W. Hutchison III, Charles W. Dean, Joseph J. Kelley, and Carolyn E. Pesackis. 1990. *Charlotte Spouse Assault Replication Project: Final Report.* Charlotte, NC: University of North Carolina at Charlotte.

Hirschi, Travis. 1986. "On the Compatibility of Rational Choice and Social Control Theories of Crime," in Derek B. Cornish and Ronald V Clarke, Eds., *The Reasoning Criminal.* NY: Springer-Verlag.

Holliday, L.P. 1974. *A Methodology For Radio Car Planning.* Unpublished Manuscript. New York City: RAND Institute.

Homel, Ross. 1990. "Random Breath Testing and Random Stopping Programs in Australia," in R.J. Wilson and R. Mann, Eds., *Drinking and Driving: Advances in Research and Prevention.* NY Guilford Press.

——. 1993. Reference supplied upon request.

Hope, Tim. 1995. "Community Crime Prevention," in Michael Tonry and David P. Farrington, Eds., *Building a Safer Society.* Crime and Justice, Vol 19. Chicago: University of Chicago Press.

Huizinga, David and Finn Esbensen. 1992. School Safety 15: 15–17.

Hurst, P. and P Wright. 1980. Deterrence at Last: The Ministry of Transport's Alcohol Blitzes. Paper Presented to the Eighth International Conference on Alcohol, Drugs and Traffic Safety, Stockholm.

Isaacs, H. 1967. *A Study of Communications, Crimes and Arrests in a Metropolitan Police Department. Task Force Report: Science and Technology, A Report to the President's Commission on Law Enforcement and Administration of Justice.* Washington, DC: USGPO.

Kansas City, MO, Missouri Police Department. 1977. *Response Time Analysis.* Kansas City, MO: Author.

Kelling, George L. 1988. Community Policing. Presentation to the Executive Sessions on the Police, Kennedy School of Government, Harvard University.

Kelling, George L., Antony M. Pate, Duane Dieckman, and Charles Brown. 1974. *The Kansas City Preventive Patrol Experiment: Technical Report.* Washington, DC: Police Foundation.

Kelling, George L. and Catherine M. Coles. 1996. *Fixing Broken Windows: Restoring Order and*

Reducing Crime in Our Communities. NY Free Press.

Kennedy, David M., Anne M. Piehl, and Anthony A. Braga. 1996. *Youth Gun Violence in Boston: Gun Markets, Serious Youth Offenders, and a Use Reduction Strategy.* Boston, MA: JFK School of Government, Harvard University.

Kleiman, Mark. 1988. "Crackdowns: The Effects of Intensive Enforcement on Retail Heroin Dealing," in Marcia Chaiken, Ed., *Street-Level Drug Enforcement: Examining the Issues.* Washington, DC: National Institute of Justice.

Klein, Malcolm. 1986. "Labeling Theory and Delinquency Policy: An Empirical Test," *Criminal Justice and Behavior* 13: 47–79.

Koper, Christopher. 1995. "Just Enough Police Presence: Reducing Crime and Disorderly Behavior by Optimizing Patrol Time in Crime Hot Spots," *Justice Quarterly* 12 (4): 649–672.

Larson, Richard. 1975. "What Happened to Patrol Operations in Kansas City," *Journal of Criminal Justice.* 3: 299–330.

Laycock, Gloria. 1991. "Operation Identification, or the Power of Publicity?" *Security Journal* 2: 67–72.

Lee, W.L. Melville. 1901 [1971]. *A History of Police in England.* Montclair, NJ: Patterson-Smith.

Lindsay, Betsy and Daniel McGillis. 1986. "Citywide Community Crime Prevention: An Assessment of the Seattle Program," in Dennis Rosenbaum, Ed., *Community Crime Prevention: Does It Work?* Beverly Hills, CA: Sage.

Logan, Charles H. 1975. "Arrest Rates and Deterrence," *Social Science Quarterly* 56: 376–89.

Makinen, Tuija and Hannu Takala. 1980. "The 1976 Police Strike in Finland," *Scandinavian Studies in Criminology* 7: 87–106.

Marciniak, Elizabeth. 1994. *Community Policing of Domestic Violence: Neighborhood Differences in the Effect of Arrest.* PhD Dissertation, University of Maryland.

Martin, Susan and Lawrence Sherman. 1986. "Selective Apprehension: A Police Strategy for Repeat Offenders," *Criminology* 24: 55–72.

Marvell, Thomas B. and Carlisle E. Moody. 1996. "Specification Problems, Police Levels and Crime Rates," *Criminology* 34: 609–646.

Moore, Mark. 1980. "The Police and Weapons Offenses," *Annals of the American Academy of Political and Social Sciences* 452: 22–32.

——. 1992. In Michael Tonry and Norval Morris, Eds., *Modern Policing: Crime and Justice,* Vol 15. Chicago: University of Chicago Press.

——. 1968. *National Advisory Commission on Civil Disorders Report.* NY. Bantam Books.

Pate, Tony, Amy Ferrara, Robert A. Bowers, and Jon Lorence. 1976. *Police Response Time: Its Determinants and Effects.* Washington, DC: Police Foundation.

Pate, Antony M. and Wesley Skogan. 1985. *Coordinated Community Policing: The Newark Experience.* Technical Report. Washington, DC: Police Foundation.

Pate, Antony M., Marlys McPherson, and Glenn Silloway. 1987. *The Minneapolis Community Crime Prevention Experiment. Draft Evaluation Report.* Washington, DC: Police Foundation.

Pate, Antony, Edwin E. Hamilton and Sampson Annan. 1991. *Metro-Dade Spouse Abuse Replication Project: Draft Final Report.* Washington, D.C.: Police Foundation.

Pate, Antony M. and Edwin E. Hamilton. 1992. "Formal and Informal Deterrents to Domestic Violence: The Dade County Spouse Assault Experiment," *American Sociological Review* 57: 691–698.

Paternoster, Raymond, Bobby Brame, Ronet Bachman and Lawrence W. Sherman. 1996. "Do Fair Procedures Matter? The Effect of Procedural Justice on Spouse Assault." Paper accepted for publication in *Law and Society Review.*

Pfuhl, Edwin H., Jr. 1983. "Police Strikes and Conventional Crime: A Look At the Data," *Criminology* 21: 489–503.

Pierce, Glenn, Susan A. Spaar, and LeBaron Briggs, IV. 1988. *The Character of Police Work: Strategic and Tactical Implications.* Unpublished Manuscript., Northeastern University, Center for Applied Social Research.

Police Foundation. 1981. *The Newark Foot Patrol Experiment.* Washington, D.C.: Police Foundation.

President's Commission on Law Enforcement and Administration of Justice. 1967. *The Challenge of Crime in a Free Society.* Washington, DC: USGPO.

Press, S.J. 1971. *Some Effects of an Increase in Police Manpower in the 20th Precinct of New York City.* NY New York City Rand Institute.

Pringle, Patrick. 1955. *Hue & Cry: The Birth of the British Police.* London: Museum Press.

Reiss, Albert J. Jr. 1971. *The Police and the Public.* New Haven: Yale University Press.

——. 1985. *Policing a City's Central District: The Oakland Story.* Washington, DC: National Institute of Justice.

——. 1992. "Police Organization in the Twentieth Century," in Michael Tonry and Norval Morris, Eds., *Modern Policing: Crime and Justice,* Vol 15. Chicago: University of Chicago Press.

——. 1995. "The Role of the Police in Crime Prevention," in Per-Olof Wikstrom, Ed., *Integrating Crime Prevention Strategies: Propensity and Opportunity.* Stockholm: National Council for Crime Prevention.

Reiss, Albert J. Jr. and Jeffrey A. Roth, Eds. 1993. *Understanding and Preventing Violence.* Washington, DC: National Academy of Sciences.

Reppetto, Thomas. 1996. *Reducing Gun Crime in New York City: A Research and Policy Report.* NY Citizens Crime Commission of New York City.

Rosenbaum, Dennis, Dan A. Lewis, and Jane A. Grant. 1986. "Neighborhood-Based Crime Prevention: Assessing the Efficacy of Community Organizing in Chicago," in Dennis Rosenbaum, Ed., *Community Crime Prevention: Does It Work?* Beverly Hills, CA: Sage.

Ross, H. Laurence. 1973. "Law, Science and Accidents: The British Road Safety Act of 1967," *Journal of Legal Studies* 2: 1–78.

——. 1975. "The Scandinavian Myth: The Effectiveness of Drinking-and-Driving Legislation in Sweden and Norway," *Journal of Legal Studies* 4: 285–310.

——. 1977. "Deterrence Regained: The Chesire Constabulary's 'Breathalyser Blitz,'" *Journal of Legal Studies* 6: 241–249.

——. 1981. *Deterring the Drinking Driver: Legal Policy and Social Control.* Lexington, Mass: Lexington Books.

——. 1992. *Confronting Drunk Driving: Social Policy for Saving Lives.* New Haven: Yale University Press; 1994 Personal Communication.

Ross, H. Laurence, R. McCleary and T. Epperlein. 1982. "Deterrence of Drinking and Driving in France: An Evaluation of the Law of July 12, 1978," *Law and Society Review.*

Russell, Francis. 1975. *A City In Terror: 1919—The Boston Police Strike.* New York: Viking.

Sampson, Robert and Jacqueline Cohen. 1988. "Deterrent Effects of Police on Crime: A Replication and Theoretical Extension," *Law and Society Review* 22: 163–189.

Schnelle, J.E, R.E. Kirchner, Jr., J.D. Casey, P.H. Uselton Jr., and M.P McNees. 1977. "Patrol Evaluation Research: A Multiple-Baseline Analysis of Saturation Police Patrolling During Day and Night Hours," *Journal of Applied Behavioral Analysis* 10: 33–40.

Schwartz, Richard and Jerome Skolnick. 1962. "Two Studies of Legal Stigma," *Social Problems* 10: 133–138.

Sellwood, A. V. 1978. *Police Strike—1919.* London: WH. Allen.

Shaw, James W. 1994. *Community Policing Against Crime: Violence and Firearms.* PhD dissertation, University of Maryland at College Park.

Sherman, Lawrence W. 1974. "Becoming Bent," in Lawrence W. Sherman, Ed., *Police Corruption: A Sociological Perspective.* NY. Anchor-Doubleday.

——. 1990. "Police Crackdowns: Initial and Residual Deterrence," in Michael Tonry and Norval Morris, Eds., *Crime and Justice: A Review of Research,* Vol 12. Chicago: University of Chicago Press.

——. 1992. *Policing Domestic Violence: Experiments and Dilemmas.* NY: Free Press.

——. 1993. "Defiance, Deterrence, and Irrelevance: A Theory of the Criminal Sanction," *Journal of Research in Crime and Delinquency* 30: 445–473.

——. 1995. "The Police," in James O. Wilson and Joan Petersilia, Eds. *Crime.* San Francisco: ICS Press.

Sherman, Lawrence W., Catherine H. Milton, and Thomas Kelly. 1973. *Team Policing. Seven Case Studies.* Washington, DC: Police Foundation.

Sherman, Lawrence W., Patrick R. Gartin, and Michael E. Buerger. 1989. "Hot Spots of Predatory Crime: Routine Activities and the Criminology of Place," *Criminology* 27: 27–55.

Sherman, Lawrence W. and Richard A. Berk. 1984. "The Specific Deterrent Effects of Arrest for Domestic Assault," *American Sociological Review* 49: 261–272.

Sherman, Lawrence W., Janell D. Schmidt, Dennis P. Rogan, Patrick R. Gartin, Ellen G. Cohn, Dean J. Collins, and Anthony R. Bacich. 1991. "From Initial Deterrence to Long-Term Escalation: Short-Custody Arrest for Poverty Ghetto Domestic Violence," *Criminology* 29: 821–50.

——. 1992. "The Variable Effects of Arrest on Criminal Careers: The Milwaukee Domestic Violence Experiment," *Journal of Criminal Law and Criminology* 83: 137–169.

Sherman, Lawrence W. and Dennis P. Rogan. 1995. "Deterrent Effects of Police Raids on Crack Houses: A Randomized, Controlled, Experiment," *Justice Quarterly* 12: 755–781.

Sherman, Lawrence W., James W. Shaw, and Dennis P. Rogan. 1995. *The Kansas City Gun Experiment: Research in Brief.* Washington, D.C.: National Institute of Justice.

Sherman, Lawrence W. and David A. Weisburd. 1995. "General Deterrent Effects of Police Patrol in Crime 'Hot Spots:' A Randomized, Controlled Trial," *Justice Quarterly* 12: 625–648.

Sherman, Lawrence W. and Heather Strang. 1996. Policing Domestic Violence: The Problem-Solving Paradigm. Paper Presented to the Conference on Problem-Oriented Policing as Crime Prevention, Stockholm, Swedish National Police College.

Skogan, Wesley. 1990. *Disorder and Decline.* New York: Free Press.

——. 1994. "The Impact of Community Policing on Neighborhood Residents: A Cross-Site Analysis," in Dennis Rosenbaum, Ed., *The Challenge of Community Policing: Testing the Promises.* Thousand Oaks, CA: Sage.

——. 1996. Paper Presented to the Conference on Problem-Oriented Policing as Crime Prevention, Stockholm, Swedish National Police College.

Skogan, Wesley and 18 others. 1995. *Community Policing In Chicago, Year Two.* Chicago: Illinois Criminal Justice Information Authority.

——. 1996. *Community Policing in Chicago, Year Three.* Chicago: Illinois Criminal Justice Information Authority.

Skolnick, Jerome and David Bayley. 1985. *The New Blue Line.* NY Free Press.

Smith, Douglas and Christy Visher. 1981. "Street-Level Justice: Situational Determinants of Police Arrest Decisions," *Social Problems* 29: 167–78.

Smith, Douglas and Patrick R. Gartin. 1989. "Specifying Specific Deterrence: The Influence of Arrest on Future Criminal Activity," *American Sociological Review* 54 (1): 94–106.

Spelman, William and Dale K. Brown. 1981. *Calling the Police: A Replication of the Citizen Reporting Component of the Kansas City Response Time Analysis.* Washington, DC: Police Executive Research Forum.

Stead, Philip John. 1977. "Patrick Colquhoun," in Philip John Stead, Ed., *Pioneers in Policing.* Montclair, NJ: Patterson-Smith.

Strang, Heather. 1996. Paper Presented to the American Society of Criminology, Chicago, November.

Sviridoff, Michelle et al. 1992. *The Neighborhood Effects of Street-Level Drug Enforcement. Tactical Narcotics Teams in New York.* NY Vera Institute of Justice.

Task Force Report. 1967. *The Police. A Report to the President's Commission on Law Enforcement and Administration of Justice.* Washington, DC: USGPO.

Tittle, Charles R. and Alan R. Rowe. 1974. "Certainty of Arrest and Crime Rates: A Further Test of the Deterrence Hypothesis," *Social Forces* 52: 455–62.

Trojanowicz, Robert. 1986. "Evaluating a Neighborhood Foot Patrol Program: The Flint, Michigan Project," in Dennis Rosenbaum, Ed., *Community Crime Prevention: Does It Work?* Beverly Hills, CA: Sage.

Tyler, Tom. 1990. *Why People Obey the Law.* New Haven: Yale University Press.

Uchida, Craig D., Brian Forst and Sampson O. Annan. 1992. *Modern Policing and the Control of Illegal Drugs: Testing New Strategies in Two American Cities. Research Report.* Washington, D.C.: National Institute of Justice.

Voas et al. 1985. From Ross 1992.

Weisburd, David and Lorraine Green. 1995. "Policing Drug Hot Spots: The Jersey City Drug Market Analysis Experiment," *Justice Quarterly* 12: 711–735.

Weiss, Alex and Edmund McGarrell. 1996. Paper Presented to the American Society of Criminology, Chicago, November.

Wilson, James Q. 1994. "Just Take Away Their Guns: Forget Gun Control," *New York Times Magazine* March 20, pp. 46–47.

Wilson, James Q. and Barbara Boland. 1978. "The Effect of the Police on Crime," *Law and Society Review* 12: 367–390.

Wilson, James Q. and George L. Kelling. 1982. "Broken Windows: The Police and Neighborhood Safety," *Atlantic Monthly* 249: 29–38.

Wilson, O. W. 1963. *Police Administration.* NY McGraw-Hill.

Wolfgang, Marvin, Robert Figlio and Thorsten Sellin. 1972. *Delinquency in a Birth Cohort.* Chicago: University of Chicago Press.

Wycoff, Mary Ann, Antony M. Pate, Wesley Skogan and Lawrence W. Sherman. 1985. *Citizen Contact Patrol in Houston: Executive Summary.* Washington, DC: Police Foundation.

Wycoff, Mary Ann and Wesley Skogan. 1986. "Storefront Police Offices: The Houston Field Test," in Dennis Rosenbaum, Ed., *Community Crime Prevention: Does It Work?* Beverly Hills, CA: Sage.

Wycoff, Mary Ann and Wesley Skogan. 1993. *Community Policing in Madison: Quality from the Inside Out. An Evaluation of Implementation and Impact.* Research Report. Washington, D.C.: National Institute of Justice.

Zimmer, Lynn. 1990. "Proactive Policing Against Street-Level Drug Trafficking," *American Journal of Police* 11: 43–74.

Lawrence W. Sherman, "Policing for Crime Prevention." Reprinted from University of Maryland, *Preventing Crime: What Works, What Doesn't, What's Promising,* Washington D.C.: Office of Justice Programs, February 1997 (NCJ 165366). ✦

Chapter 6

Crime and Disorder in Drug Hot Spots

Implications for Theory and Practice in Policing

David Weisburd
Lorraine Green Mazerolle

Weisburd and Mazerolle turn their attention to social disorder problems, particularly drug problems in some of New Jersey's most disadvantaged neighborhoods. The purpose of their study is to investigate the relationship between street-level drug hot spots, crime, and disorder problems in Jersey City, New Jersey. Broken windows theory, the guiding framework used in the research design, asserts that police should focus on minor social disorder problems as well as more serious criminal incidents. The authors argue that neighborhood "hot spots" that have more pronounced social disorder tend to be associated with drug problems and higher arrest rates.

Using a careful screening process, the authors determined that 5 percent of the streets in Jersey City showed evidence of drug activity while the vast majority of streets were drug free. They suggest that there is a need to develop new strategies to control social disorder and criminal incidents in hot spots. Though hot spots encompass a relatively small area, the population density is much higher than the rest of the city, and consequently, addressing crime and disorder hot spots could prove an effective means for greatly impacting overall city crime rates.

The policing of disorder problems has recently emerged as a central operational strategy for police departments across the country. Indeed, police departments from New York to San Francisco to Chicago are now advocating the restoration of order by targeting quality-of-life problems, aggressively dealing with disorder problems (such as panhandling, public drinking, street-level drug activity, vandalism, and public urination), and focusing on reducing fear of crime (Kelling & Coles, 1996).

Several factors have precipitated this trend in policing. First, in the 1980s local citizens began to voice their concerns about abandoned cars, graffiti, public drunkenness, street-level drug use, and other signs of social and physical incivility. Surveys of local citizens systematically revealed that residents were more concerned about quality-of-life problems than serious index crimes (such as homicide, assault, and rape), particularly when they were asked specific questions about their immediate concerns in their neighborhood (Center for Crime Prevention Studies, 1991; Kelling & Coles, 1996).

Second, community demands on the police to do something about disorder problems were given scientific support when scholars began to observe, discuss, and test the hypothesis that there was a relationship between disorder, fear, and crime (Skogan, 1990; Wilson & Kelling, 1982). Taylor and Gottfredson (1986), for example, noted that incivilities contribute to fear of crime, which in turn leads to lower levels of informal social control in a community and thus to more crime (see also Taylor, 1998; Taylor, Gottfredson, & Brower, 1984). In perhaps the most influential statement of this relationship, Wilson and Kelling (1982) argued that:

> at the community level, disorder and crime are usually inextricably linked, in a kind of developmental sequence. Social psychologists and police officers tend to agree that if a window in a building is left unrepaired, all the rest of the windows will soon be broken . . . one unrepaired broken window is a signal that no one cares; and so breaking more

> windows costs nothing. . . . We suggest that "untended" behavior also leads to a breakdown of community controls. A stable neighborhood of families who care for their homes, mind each other's children and confidently frown on unwanted intruders can change in a few years or even a few months, to an inhospitable and frightening jungle. . . . At this point it is not inevitable that serious crime will flourish or violent attacks on strangers will occur. But many residents will think that crime, especially violent crime is on the rise, and they will modify their behavior accordingly. . . . Such an area is vulnerable to criminal invasion. (p. 32)

Many criminologists and crime prevention scholars have concluded that police efforts that focus on order maintenance and disorderly behavior in high-crime communities—whether it is reflected by broken windows or graffiti, or by street-level incivilities such as prostitution or drug dealing—can result in reductions in more serious crime problems (Bayley, 1994; Kelling & Coles, 1996; Skogan, 1990).

The third factor that gave weight to the trend toward policing disorder problems was research showing the ineffectiveness of traditional policing in the form of preventive patrol (Kelling, Pate, Dieckman, & Brown, 1974), rapid response (Spelman & Brown, 1981), and investigations (Greenwood, Chaiken, & Petersilia, 1978). These research findings set the stage for widespread police adoption (at least in principle) of community policing (Greene & Mastrofski, 1988), problem-oriented policing (Goldstein,1990), zero-tolerance programs for specific crime problems (Silverman, 1999), and police priorities that sought to maintain order and respond to disorder problems (Kelling & Coles, 1996).

Finally, recent hot spots of crime research, demonstrating the spatial clustering of some crime problems (see Pierce, Spaar, & Briggs, 1988; Sherman, Gartin, & Buerger, 1989; Weisburd, Maher, & Sherman, 1993), provided a special focus for community policing and problem-oriented policing activities. Armed with knowledge that a substantial proportion of crime is found in a relatively small number of places (e.g., that 3% of all addresses accounted for 50% of all calls for service in Minneapolis; see Sherman et al., 1989), police policy makers recognized that their resources could be better utilized by focusing on hot spots of crime rather than dispersing them across beats, neighborhoods, and precincts (Sherman & Weisburd, 1995).

This article explores the relationship between street-level drug hot spots, crime, and disorder problems in Jersey City, New Jersey. Our general research question asks whether places that have a disproportionate amount of street-level drug activity also evidence disproportionate rates of other types of crime and disorder. Following the broken windows perspective, we would expect a strong spatial link between street-level drug activity, disorder, and serious crimes in places where disorder is tolerated.

Our study methodology takes a very specific spatial focus. We do not examine the spatial relationship between crime and disorder for neighborhoods, police precincts, or police beats. Rather, we examine discrete blocks or clusters of blocks within neighborhoods that we define as drug hot spots (see Sherman & Weisburd,1995; Weisburd & Green, 1995). This approach is very much consistent with recent emphasis on "place" in criminology (see Eck & Weisburd, 1995) and is particularly appropriate for examining the links between crime and disorder.

We begin the article with a description of how drug hot spots were defined in our study and provide a description of their general characteristics. We then turn to an analysis of the incidence of reported crime and disorder within such hot spots. We conclude by discussing the theoretical, policy, and practical implications of our research.

Defining the Street-Level Drug Hot Spot: A Spatial Approach

The drug hot spots used in our analysis were identified as part of an overall research effort to define and target street-level drug trafficking in Jersey City, New Jersey (Weisburd & Green, 1995). As in many other urban centers in the United States, the 1980s was a time when drug problems and community fears of drug-related crime grew dramatically in Jersey City. In 1987, when the drug hot spot project was proposed, there were a total of 3,116 drug arrests in the city, almost three times as many as were reported in 1980. To put this in perspective, in 1987 Jersey City (with a population of about 230,000) ranked higher per capita in number of drug arrests than Baltimore, San Diego, Newark, Tampa, New York City, Cincinnati, and Atlanta, all of which were among the top 10 cities for drug arrests among cities with populations of more than 250,000 (Jersey City Police Department, 1989).

In the initial phase of our study, we identified where street-level drug activity clustered in Jersey City. Our concern at this stage was not so much to define discrete drug areas as to identify potential clusters of drug activity. Because of this, we chose a unit of analysis—the intersection area—that included an intersection and all of the addresses on the blocks attached to it. We found that there were 1,553 intersection areas in Jersey City, most of which included intersections and four adjoining street segments (or blocks).

Once we had defined these intersection areas on a computer map of Jersey City, we linked them to narcotics sales arrests,[1] emergency calls for service,[2] and data from a tip line.[3] Of the total of 1,553 intersection areas in the city, 41% were linked to narcotics activity by at least one of these data sources. This, however, did not mean that such areas evidenced significant ongoing drug problems.

We understood that a lone narcotics arrest assigned to an intersection area was not a good indicator of ongoing activity. Even multiple arrests at a specific location over a week or two might be evidence of an isolated short-term problem. Similarly, one citizen tip or emergency call identifying a place as an active drug area does not provide solid evidence of drug activity. To develop a more stable measure of drug activity, we created three threshold criteria for identifying active intersection areas.[4] Intersection areas that met one of the following three criteria passed this initial screening step: at least one drug sales arrest in 2 or more of the 6 months examined, one emergency call for service for narcotics in 2 separate months during the 6 months examined and a minimum of seven or more calls, or multiple narcotics tip line responses. Ten percent of the intersection areas in Jersey City met one or more of these selection criteria.

Use of the intersection area as a preliminary unit of analysis prevented the deletion of drug locations that might have resulted from slight deviations in data-recording procedures or casual movement of offenders along street segments. However, the intersection area also meant that any event recorded on a street segment was counted in each adjoining intersection area. Thus, to define discrete drug hot spot boundaries it was necessary to return to the street block and intersection level of analysis. For the active intersection areas, 226 intersections and street segments showed some evidence of drug activity (out of a total of 4,404 street segments and intersections in Jersey City).[5] Consistent with the hot spots of crime literature (Sherman et al.,1989), just 5% of the streets in Jersey City showed evidence of drug activity, and the vast majority of the city landscape was free of ongoing drug activity as we had defined it. Even in the south district of Jersey City, which contained 42% of the segments and intersections identified as active, the majority of street segments and intersections did not meet our inclusion criteria (see Figure 6.1).

Although Figure 6.1 provides a good view of where drug activity was centered in the city, it also illustrates one of the major dilemmas confronted when trying to develop spatial analyses of crime activities as common as drug distribution. How does one treat clustering of points on the map in very large geographic areas (see also Maltz, Gordon, & Friedman, 1991)? Given the clustering of street segments and intersections in Figure 6.1, for example, we could conclude that Jersey City includes three or four very large drug areas, each covering 25 or more blocks. Alternatively, one might ask whether these large areas could be split up into distinct drug hot spots that are relatively close to each other, for example, a block or two away.

Figure 6.1
Points of Drug Sales

As an initial step in defining drug hot spot boundaries, we interviewed narcotics detectives in the Jersey City Police Department. The detectives were a natural source for information on drug hot spots because their work centers on gaining a general understanding about the way in which drug dealing in the city is organized. We also conducted observations in the drug areas, analyzed patterns of arrests for drug offenders, and examined the types of drugs found as a result of police arrests.

Detectives often disagreed on the precise boundaries of drug hot spots yet tended to have similar criteria for linking streets and intersections together to define drug market boundaries. For example, they argued that it is a mistake to view entire neighborhoods as part of large, continuous drug areas. For a number of the detectives, a series of blocks, or sometimes even a single block or intersection, may be separated from others based on the type of drug that is being sold in that place. According to the detectives, dealers tend to sell the same drug in the same area, providing a kind of specialization to market activities. These dealers do not drift considerably from one day to the next because, if they do, customers will not know where to find the drug of their choice. Although we were initially skeptical of this assumption of specialization at discrete places, our own analysis of the type of drug confiscated during arrests generally confirmed the detectives' conclusion (see Weisburd & Green, 1994).

Detectives also distinguished areas that were market centers in the same neighborhoods but were separated one from another by a small number of blocks. They argued that dealers tend to have a strong sense of territoriality that provides a degree of insulation for market boundaries. This contention was also supported in our analyses. When we examined the pattern of arrests across the active segments and intersections, we found that very few people arrested more than once for selling narcotics traversed an inactive segment or intersection to sell in an adjacent drug area (see Weisburd & Green, 1994). Indeed, people arrested in two separate areas were most likely to be arrested in different districts of the city.

Following these observations about the nature of drug distribution patterns, we used two basic criteria to construct the boundaries of street-level drug hot spots. First, taking into account the importance of type of drug in determining hot spot boundaries, we linked street segments and intersections that evidenced similar types of drug activity. Second, recognizing that sellers tended not to drift very far from their primary point of sales, we only linked active segments or intersections that were within one block and one intersection of each other. We also ensured that drug hot spots would not cut across physical barriers—such as railroad tracks or highways—that clearly divided the natural flow of drug sales activity. Overall, we identified 56 drug hot spots covering 192 segments and intersections in Jersey City (see Figure 6.2).[6]

Figure 6.2
Drug Market Boundaries

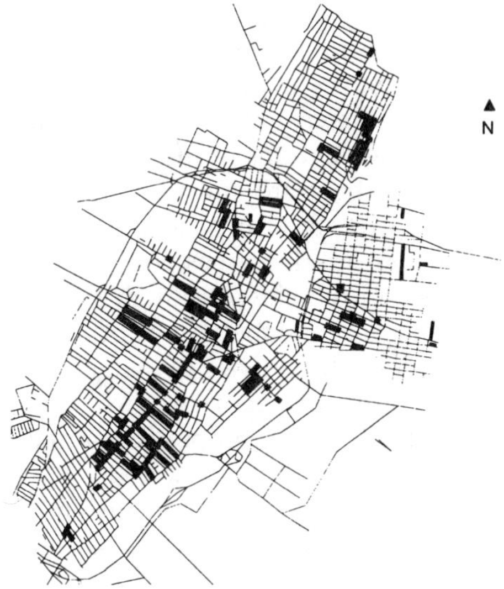

Characteristics of Identified Drug Hot Spots

The 56 drug hot spots in our study show significant variation in their physical and social characteristics. Cocaine was the prominent drug type reported for sales arrests at more than half of the hot spots. Of the drug hot spots, 6 sold primarily heroin, 3 were marijuana markets, and 10 were defined as polydrug markets. We also noted considerable diversity in the physical area covered by the drug hot spots: the majority comprised fewer than 4 segments and intersections (mean = 3.4 segments per market). Indeed, 17 markets comprised just 1 street segment or intersection. Only 2 hot spots included more than 10 segments and intersections within a single hot spot boundary.

Census data provide one way of contrasting drug hot spots with other areas in the city. We found that the average median value of the houses in our 56 markets as well as their mean rent was less than that of Jersey City houses as a whole (see Table 6.1). Examining the differences in the median value of the houses in the drug hot spots by district suggests that market characteristics reflect to some degree the neighborhoods in which they are found. Drug hot spots in the primarily middle-class north and east districts consistently showed indicators of social well-being in comparison with the less well off districts of the city. Nonetheless, in each of the districts, drug hot spot areas tended to be less well off than non-drug hot spot areas.

Overall, nearly half of Jersey City's population is defined as non-White (African American, Asian, or Hispanic). Although the propor-

Table 6.1
Selected Social Characteristics of Drug Markets (by District)

	North	South	East	West	All Drug Markets	Jersey City
Median Housing Value ($)	44,254	29,674	63,254	38,312	43,874	62,509
Mean Rent ($)	231	229	244	227	233	284
Ethnicity-race percentage						
Non-white[a]						
Residents (district)	23.0	62.5	56.5	52.0	NA	48.5
Residents (markets)	37.6	88.4	65.5	59.8	62.8	NA

a. Includes African American, Hispanic, Asian, and other race categories.

tion of non-White residents who live within the drug hot spot boundaries (62.8%) is considerably greater than that found in the city generally (48.5%), the drug hot spots again reflect to some extent the racial makeup of the communities in which they are found. In the primarily White north district, only 37.6% of residents of the drug hot spots were non-White (as contrasted with 23% of all north district residents). In the south district, where more than 60% of the residents were non-White, almost 90% of those who lived in the markets were classified as non-White. The 56 drug hot spots in our study included a slightly younger population compared with the city overall: About 29% of the drug hot spot population was under 18 years of age compared with 27% of the city residents.

Crime in Drug Hot Spots

One way to assess the spatial concentration of crime is to look at the proportion of arrests or emergency calls for service for specific offenses that fall within the drug hot spot areas.[7] The arrest category most concentrated in the drug hot spots was narcotics offenses, a fact that simply reflects the process we used to identify drug hot spots. Almost half of all arrests for narcotics (47.8 %) were found in the market areas, which made up only 4.4% of the total number of street segments and intersections in the city (see Table 6.2). Only arrests for disorderly behavior—which includes public morals offenses such as prostitution, gambling, indecency, and public drunkenness—show a similar level of concentration (41.6%). Importantly, the disorderly behavior category also includes the general category of disturbing the peace, an offense charge sometimes used against suspected drug offenders when a narcotics arrest is not supportable.

Crimes of violence such as robbery and assault, as well as possession of a weapon, were the next most common arrest categories found in the drug hot spots. For violent crimes, the drug hot spots accounted for about one-fifth of the total arrests for each crime, which is more than four times what would have been expected if arrests were evenly distributed across streets and intersections in the city. Other offenses such as burglary and theft, vandalism, and drunk driving also occurred relatively more often in market areas compared with other places in the city. Although the differences for burglary and theft were not as large in absolute terms, about twice as many burglary and theft arrests were reported as would be expected simply from the proportion of the city area covered by the drug hot spots.

One difficulty in drawing conclusions from arrest data derives from the fact that arrests for other types of crimes could have been concentrated in the drug hot spot areas simply because these were places that received a good deal of police attention. For example, the high rate of weapons charges within the drug hot spot boundaries could be explained simply by the overall quantity of police enforcement in these areas and the chance that the police could

Table 6.2
Proportion of Arrests for Selected Offenses Within the Drug Market Boundaries

Crime Type	*n* in Markets	Percentage
Narcotics (*n* = 3,252)	1,555	47.8
Robbery (*n* = 521)	105	20.2
Assaults (*n* = 1,821)	344	18.9
Weapons (*n* = 410)	82	20.0
Theft/Burglary (*n* = 2,735)	216	7.9
Vandalism (*n* = 300)	30	10.0
Drunk Driving (*n* = 273)	24	8.8
Disorderly Conduct (*n* = 772)	321	41.6

arrest a person for a narcotics offense and then, during the course of the arrest, find a weapon concealed on the suspect. Because of these concerns, we also used emergency calls for service data to compare against the crime patterns found with the arrest data.

Emergency calls to the police provide a measure of crime activity that is less affected by patterns of police enforcement (see Sherman et al., 1989; Warner & Pierce, 1993).[8] In our analysis, we included only those calls for service from citizens. Our data also identify the address of where the caller said the incident occurred, rather than the location from which the call was made. Police-initiated calls were not included in our analysis because we understood these calls to be too influenced by police perceptions of drug activity. We wanted to depict the citizen view of crime problems in this second stage of our analysis. Table 6.3 presents a summary of the proportion of emergency calls found within the drug market boundaries by crime type.

Table 6.3 shows somewhat less concentration of crime in the market areas than demonstrated with the arrest data. However, there is still a significant degree of overrepresentation for the call categories examined. About half of all narcotics calls in the city were from citizens reporting drug activity inside the drug market boundaries. Disorderly behavior (which includes public morals offenses) was the next most frequent call type recorded in the drug hot spots, followed by "nuisance" offenses (including disorderly conduct, intoxicated person, loitering, loud music, etc.). Twenty percent of all disorderly conduct calls and 16% of all nuisance calls were related to addresses within the drug market boundaries.

The proportion of violent crime calls in the drug hot spots was similar to the proportion of nuisance calls. More than 14% of all robberies and assault calls (reflected in the call category as crimes against persons) were found within the market boundaries. This is more than three times as many as the number of violent crime calls one would expect given the area of the city covered by the markets. Traffic and vehicle offenses and property crimes also show somewhat more concentration in the drug hot spots, although the concentration for these calls is only about 2% greater in absolute terms than would be expected if crime were spread evenly across the city landscape.

A second approach for examining the spatial distribution of crime is to identify the proportion of an area that evidences specific crime reports or calls. Our concern was not with the overall proportion of crime that fell within the drug hot spots but rather with the percentage of places within drug hot spot boundaries that evidenced crime activity compared with the percentage of places outside the drug markets that evidenced crime activity. Taking this approach, our findings reinforce the notion that drug hot spots are relatively crime-prone areas (see Table 6.4).

As in our earlier analyses, and again reflecting our method for identifying drug hot spot areas, narcotics arrests show the largest concentration in our 56 drug markets compared with non–drug hot spot areas. Indeed, more than 4 in 5 street segments and intersections inside the drug hot spot areas experienced at

Table 6.3

Proportion of Citizen Calls for Selected Crime Categories Within the Drug Market Boundaries

Call Category	*n* in Markets	Percentage
Narcotics (*n* = 3,019)	1,420	47.0
Crimes Against Persons (*n* = 16,621)	2,364	14.2
Property (*n* = 31,015)	2,024	6.5
Vehicle/Traffic (*n* = 26,175)	1,729	6.6
Nuisance (*n* = 22,050)	3,552	16.1
Disorderly Behavior (*n* = 2,477)	492	19.9

Table 6.4
Percentage of Segments and Intersections with Arrests and Emergency Calls for Selected Offenses Both Inside and Outside the Drug Markets

Crime Type	Market Distribution	Nonmarket Distribution
Arrests		
Narcotics	80.7	9.5
Robbery	22.3	4.7
Assaults	57.8	14.7
Weapons	23.4	4.1
Theft/Burglary	41.4	15.7
Vandalism	9.9	3.7
Drunk Driving	8.3	3.8
Disorderly Behavior	14.6	4.4
Emergency Calls		
Narcotics	85.9	14.1
Crimes Against Persons	95.8	55.0
Property	95.3	72.5
Vehicle/Traffic	91.6	68.8
Nuisance	96.8	59.9
Disorderly	61.9	17.1

least one arrest for narcotics in the 1-year period we examined. This may be contrasted with only about 1 in 10 of the street segments and intersections outside the drug hot spots. Large differences were also found for other arrest categories. Although only about 15% of the non–drug hot spot street segments or intersections revealed an arrest for assault or theft during the period we examined, almost 6 in 10 of the street segments and intersections within the drug hot spots recorded an assault arrest, and 4 in 10 streets revealed a theft or burglary arrest. Only 1 in 25 non–drug hot spot street segments or intersections included an arrest for a weapons offense, and only 1 in 20 streets included a robbery arrest. By contrast, 23% of the hot spot segments or intersections included arrests for a weapons offense, and 22% had at least one robbery arrest. Although the differences in the case of disorderly behavior, drunk driving, and vandalism are smaller in absolute terms, drug market segments and intersections are still more than twice as likely (and in the case of disorderly behavior four times as likely) to evidence an arrest for these offenses.

Emergency call data generally reinforce these basic findings. For example, although just over half of the segments and intersections outside the market boundaries had at least one call for a crime against a person during the 6-month period we examined, nearly every segment and intersection within the market boundaries experienced at least one call about a crime against a person. In the case of property, traffic, and nuisance calls, between 59% and 73% of nonmarket segments revealed calls for these offenses. However, more than 9 of 10 segments and intersections within the market areas included such calls. In the case of disorder calls, only 17% of nonmarket segments and intersections recorded a call of this type. This contrasts with 62% of the street segments and intersections within the drug markets that recorded disorderly behavior calls. Similarly, more than 80% of the places inside the market boundaries received a call about a narcotics problem. By contrast, only 14% of the street segments and intersections outside of the market boundaries recorded a call for narcotics.

Discussion and Conclusions

We sought to examine the relationship between crime and drug problems within drug market boundaries. Our research shows that drug hot spot areas include a disproportionate share of arrests and calls for police service in Jersey City. Street segments and intersections within drug hot spots were also much more likely to experience crime and disorder problems compared with non–drug hot spot areas. Overall, these findings support the idea of a spatial link between street-level drug hot spot activity, disorder, and serious crime. However, before turning to the implications of our work for policy and practice in policing we think it important to address four specific methodological and substantive concerns that might be raised regarding our analysis of crime and disorder in drug markets.

First, we recognize that the high concentration of calls and arrests within the drug hot spots does not mean that crime, drug activity, and other types of disorder are causally linked. Our data are drawn from official sources (citizen calls and arrests). As we commented earlier, the frequency of arrests for nondrug crime and disorder in drug hot spots is certainly inflated by the increased police presence in such places. In cracking down on drug crime, police are likely as well to make arrests for other types of crime and disorder. Although our findings with regard to calls for service are much less likely to be influenced by police behavior, a more definitive statement about the relationship between disorder and crime would necessitate less reactive data such as those gained through observational or self-report techniques.

Second, the uneven distribution of drug hot spots across different neighborhoods in Jersey City (see Figure 6.2) raises the question of whether the overall high rate of crime and disorder in the drug hot spots is merely a reflection of the uneven distribution of crime and disorder across different neighborhoods in the city. If this were the case, we would expect that the markets in the south district, for example, would evidence a much higher rate of arrests or calls per street segment compared with those in the lower crime areas in the north district. Review of our data does not support this position: Although the north district markets make up only 12% of the total street segments and intersections in the drug hot spots, they account for 23% of all arrests and 17% of all calls. The south district, which includes 41% of the market segments and intersections, includes only 37% of all arrests and 35% of all calls generated within the drug hot spot boundaries overall. As such, we propose that concentrations of crime and disorderly behavior in the 56 drug markets examined in this study have more to do with the drug sales activities occurring within the drug market boundaries than with the general patterns of crime and disorder problems experienced elsewhere in the city.

A third difficulty in drawing conclusions from these data derives from the fact that arrests and calls for service may have been concentrated in the drug hot spots simply because more people live in such areas. For example, there were 220,248 people in Jersey City in 1990. We estimate that at the time of our study, approximately 55,000 people lived within the 56 drug hot spots we defined.[9] Accordingly, although only 4.4% of the area of the city is covered by the drug hot spots, about 25% of the people in Jersey City live within these areas. Using population density as a means to understand the proportional distribution of crimes inside and outside the drug hot spot boundaries reveals that only disorderly behavior and nuisance problems appear overrepresented inside the drug hot spots.

Although population density provides one explanation for the overrepresentation of other crime and disorder problems in drug hot spots, the fact that drug hot spot areas have higher population density than other places in Jersey City may reflect a more general component of the broken windows hypothesis. Wilson and Kelling (1982) suggested that a broad combination of social factors contributes to neighborhood decline. Disorder is reflected not only in the physical look of a neighborhood but also in the social fabric that binds residents one to another. We find drug hot spot areas are more densely populated than non–drug hot spot areas. The drug markets have fewer single-family homes and fewer homes owned by residents. They are also places in which minorities and poor people are concentrated. Crime and disorder in such places may be more pronounced, in good part because, as sociologists have long noted, such social organization in neighborhoods is strongly related to crime in urban communities (e.g., see Reiss, 1986; Thrasher, 1927).

Fourth, our findings are limited by our examination of the concentration of crime and disorder within drug hot spots in one time period. The broken windows hypothesis suggests that there is a process of decline in urban areas that begins with minor acts of disorder and progresses to more serious crime problems. Our data suggest that street-level drug hot spot activity, disorder, and more serious crime do indeed cluster together in discrete areas. But our data do not allow us to establish the specific chain of events that led to the clustering of these crime and disorder events.

Irrespective of these methodological reservations, we believe that our findings have important policy implications for recent innovations in police crime prevention strategies. Our research suggests that street-level drug activity, disorder, and serious crime tend to cluster in specific places. The convergence of other crime and disorder within drug hot spot areas raises the promise that identifying such places can be a useful starting point for innovative policing strategies.

Our findings suggest several ways in which present police practices can be enhanced. First, the allocation of scarce police resources is an issue confronting every police agency. We suggest that careful identification of drug hot spots, using similar data (calls and arrests) and similar criteria to define the drug market locations, can assist police problem-solving efforts to tackle not only drug problems but other problems as well (notably disorder problems). Although many police agencies currently identify and strategically target generic hot spots, our research suggests that a crime-specific approach, focusing on drug problems, is a useful way for police to refine their hot spot identification processes and become more specific in the way they approach problems in these hot spots.

Second, arguably more than any other crime type, we know a considerable amount about what works and what does not in law enforcement efforts designed to tackle street-level drug market problems. For example, we know that highly organized and specified crackdown efforts can reduce drug market activity without displacement of crime (see Weisburd & Green, 1995); we know that civil remedies such as citations for building code violations, housing violations, and sewer violations work effectively to reduce drug problems (see Eck & Wartell,1998; Green, 1996; Mazerolle, Roehl, & Kadleck, 1998); and we know that working closely with place managers (Mazerolle, Kadleck, & Roehl, 1998) and landlords (Lurigio et al., 1998) shows much promise in reducing street-level drug activity. In many ways, we know more about what works to reduce street-level drug market problems than about strategies to reduce other types of crime. As such, it makes sense for the police to focus their energy on reducing drug market problems for two reasons. First, the police know what is effective in tackling street-level drug market activity. Second, knowing that other crime and disorder problems are clustered in drug market areas, the police will most likely reduce these problems in removing much of the illicit drug market traffic. We expect that a diffusion of crime control benefits will be achieved through strategic identification and enforcement inside drug market hot spots (see Weisburd & Green, 1995).

Our comments are, by necessity, speculative. More than three decades ago, Albert Reiss, Jr. (1966) suggested that sociologists must "make the scene" of deviant behavior if they are to gain real insight into its development and social organization. We believe the same approach is essential if we are to better understand why drug activity, disorder, and other crime are related at certain places. Studies will have to focus on why specific places become centers of drug activity and why specific types of crime are likely to be found in such places (e.g., see Eck, 1995).

Notes

1. Narcotics sales data include arrests made between June 1, 1991, and November 30, 1991. We examined 1,844 arrests of which 934 (51%) occurred on intersections and 910 (49%) occurred on street segments.
2. Emergency calls for service included calls made by citizens about narcotics offenses between June 1, 1991, and November 30, 1991. We did not include officer-initiated calls for service, calls that resulted from an arrest, or calls that were initiated by the police themselves. These types of calls would have significantly biased our drug hot spot identification process toward places that the police perceived were drug-dealing locations. Moreover, including the arrest data in our identification process already incorporated the police bias toward some places over others. There were 2,196 calls recorded during this time period. Of these, 1,435 (65%) identified street segments as the location of drug problems and 761 (35%) identified intersections.
3. Eighty-four narcotics tips were received by the Jersey City Police Department from June 1, 1991, to November 30, 1991. The tip line call takers received detailed descriptions from citizens about ongoing drug problems and entered details directly into the computer-aided dispatch system via a tip screen that was especially designed for the Drug Market Analysis Program.
4. Our choice of specific thresholds in each database was developed after carefully reviewing the number of intersection areas that would be included under each criterion. We also used threshold criteria that required multiple indicators either within or across the databases examined (see Weisburd & Green, 1994).
5. When we mapped the streets and intersections in the intersection areas, we noticed that 16 that were defined only by the emergency call and tip line data were adjacent to locations with narcotics sales arrest activity. We thought it unlikely that these adjacent segments or intersections were new points of drug distribution that had gone unnoticed by the police, a view that was strongly stated by Jersey City narcotics officers. Rather, we suspected that citizens identified the casual movement of offenders to or from drug areas as activity on their block. In these "close match" cases, we felt that the arrest data more accurately captured the specific location of drug sales. Accordingly, we deleted street segments and intersections that were only identified by citizen sources and were directly adjacent (within one block) to areas with sales arrest histories. We then marked these sites as subsidiary locations for later verification.
6. Beyond these criteria, we excluded locations within public housing sites and places that were defined, after further review, as unlikely to be drug distribution centers. Public housing sites were excluded because they appeared to represent a very different type of problem compared with the other markets we identified and because they were receiving special, off-duty enforcement through grants awarded to the housing authority. We also reviewed investigation and arrest report commentaries and applied a minimum threshold of three events per hot spot for inclusion in the study. Very low activity places (fewer than three events per location) generally evidenced an isolated arrest event and were often on the outskirts of larger markets. We also found that several of these hot spots were locations where the police had set up drug buys and not places with an ongoing drug problem.
7. We compared arrests made at addresses within the 56 market boundaries identified for the Drug Market Analysis Program experiment with all arrests made by the Jersey City Police Department from January 1, 1991, to December 31, and all emergency calls for service from July 1, 1991, to December 31, 1991. We included the full year of arrest information to provide as detailed a portrait of arrest activity in Jersey City as possible (N=15,381). We included only 6 months of call data (N=173,489) because the computer-aided dispatch system was not online until June 1, 1991, and thus call information prior to this date was not available. We did not use call or arrest data subsequent to this date because of possible confounding that might have developed from the

implementation of a large-scale experiment involving crackdowns on and civil remedy closedowns in drug hot spot areas shortly after this time (see Weisburd & Green, 1995).

8. Emergency call data, however, are also subject to biases, although of a different type (for discussions about the use of calls for service data, see Klinger & Bridges, 1997; Sherman et al., 1989; Warner & Pierce, 1993). For example, crimes identified by a dispatch system may represent intentional lies or a misinterpretation of events by victims or bystanders.

9. We have no direct measure of the population density inside the drug hot spot boundaries. As such, we estimate the number of people through the census data at the block level of analysis using the following procedure. A census block is a block bounded by four streets. A drug hot spot block is defined as the block face. Therefore, to extrapolate the number of people on the block face, we consistently counted the number of people on either the north census block of the block face or the east census block of the block face.

References

Bayley, D. H. (1994). *Police for the future.* New York: Oxford University Press.

Center for Crime Prevention Studies. (1991). *Drug Market Analysis Program preliminary report. The Jersey City community survey.* Newark, NJ: Rutgers University.

Eck, J. E. (1995). A general model of the geography of illicit retail market places. In J. E. Eck & D. Weisburd (Eds.), *Crime and place: Crime prevention studies* (Vol. 4, pp. 168–193). Monsey, NY: Criminal Justice Press; Washington, DC: Police Executive Research Forum.

Eck, J. E., & Wartell, J. (1998). Improving the management of rental properties with drug problems. In L. G. Mazerolle & J. Roehl (Eds.), *Civil remedies and crime prevention: Crime prevention studies* (Vol. 9, pp. 161–183). Monsey, NY: Criminal Justice Press.

Eck, J. E., & Weisburd, D. (Eds.). (1995). *Crime and place: Crime prevention studies* (Vol. 4). Monsey, NY: Criminal Justice Press; Washington, DC: Police Executive Research Forum.

Goldstein, H. (1990). *Problem-oriented policing.* New York: McGraw-Hill.

Green, L. (1996). *Policing places with drug problems.* Thousand Oaks, CA: Sage.

Greene, J. R., & Mastrofski, S. D. (Eds.). (1988). *Community policing: Rhetoric or reality.* New York: Praeger.

Greenwood, P., Chaiken, J., & Petersilia, J. (1978). *The criminal investigation process.* Lexington, MA: D. C. Heath.

Jersey City Police Department. (1989). *Identifying and controlling drug markets: The drug market analysis program.* Proposal submitted to the National Institute of Justice.

Kelling, G., & Coles, C. M. (1996). *Fixing broken windows: Restoring and reducing crime in our communities.* New York: Free Press.

Kelling, G., Pate, A., Dieckman, P., & Brown, C. F. (1974). *The Kansas City preventive patrol experiment: A summary report.* Washington, DC: Police Foundation.

Klinger, D. A., & Bridges, G. S. (1997). Measurement error in calls-for-service as an indicator of crime. *Criminology, 35,* 705–726.

Lurigio, A., Davis, R., Regulus, T., Gwiasda, V., Popkin, S., Dantzker, M., Smith, B., & Ovellet, L. (1998). More effective place management: An evaluation of Cook County's Narcotics Nuisance Abatement Unit. In L. G. Mazerolle & J. Roehl (Eds.), *Civil remedies and crime prevention: Crime prevention studies* (Vol. 9, pp. 187–218). Monsey, NY. Criminal Justice Press.

Maltz, M., Gordon, A., & Friedman, W. (1991). *Mapping crime and in its community setting: Event geography analysis.* New York: Springer-Verlag.

Mazerolle, L. G., Kadleck, C., & Roehl, J. (1998). Controlling drug and disorder problems: The role of place managers. *Criminology, 36,* 371–404.

Mazerolle, L. G., Roehl, J., & Kadleck, C. (1998). Controlling social disorder using civil remedies: Results from a randomized field experiment in Oakland, California. In L. G. Mazerolle & J. Roehl (Eds.), *Civil remedies and crime prevention: Crime prevention studies* (Vol. 9, pp. 141–160). Monsey, NY. Criminal Justice Press.

Pierce, G., Spaar, S., & Briggs, L. (1988). *The character of police work. Strategic and tactical implications.* Boston: Northeastern University Press.

Reiss, A. J. (1966). The study of deviant behavior—Where the action is. *Ohio Valley Sociologist, 32,* 1–12.

Reiss, A. J. (1986). Why are communities important in understanding crime? In A. J. Reiss & M. Tonry (Eds.), *Communities and crime* (pp. 1–34). Chicago: University of Chicago Press.

Sherman, L., Gartin, P., & Buerger, M. (1989). Hot spots of predatory crime. *Criminology, 27* (1), 27–56.

Sherman, L., & Weisburd, D. (1995). General deterrent effects of police patrol in crime "hot spots": A randomized controlled trial. *Justice Quarterly, 12,* 625–648.

Silverman, E. B. (1999). *Innovative strategies in policing.* Boston: Northeastern University Press.

Skogan, W. (1990). *Disorder and decline: Crime and the spiral of urban decay in American cities.* New York: Free Press.

Spelman, W., & Brown, D. X. (1981). *Calling the police: Citizen response of serious crime.* Washington, DC: Police Executive Research Forum.

Taylor, R. B. (1998). Crime and small-scale places: What we know, what we can prevent, and what else we need to know. In *Crime and place: Plenary papers of the 1997 Conference on Criminal Justice Research and Evaluation* (pp. 1–22). Washington, DC: U.S. Department of Justice.

Taylor, R. B., & Gottfredson, S. (1986). Environmental design, crime and prevention: An examination of community dynamics. In A. J. Reiss, Jr., & M. Tonry (Eds.), *Communities and crime* (pp. 389–416). Chicago: University of Chicago Press.

Taylor, R. B., Gottfredson, S., & Brower, S. (1984). Block crime and fear: Defensible space, local social ties, and territorial functioning. *Journal of Research in Crime and Delinquency, 21,* 303–331.

Thrasher, R. (1927). *The gang.* Chicago: University of Chicago Press.

Warner, B., & Pierce, G. (1993). Re-examining social disorganization theory using calls to the police as a measure of crime. *Criminology, 31,* 493–518.

Weisburd, D., & Green, L. (1994). Defining the street level drug market. In D. L. MacKenzie & C. Uchida (Eds.), *Drugs and crime: Evaluation public policy initiatives* (pp. 61–76). Newbury Park, CA: Sage.

Weisburd, D., & Green, L. (1995). Policing drug hot spots: The Jersey City drug market analysis experiment. *Justice Quarterly, 12,* 711–735.

Weisburd, D., Maher, L., & Sherman, L. (1993). Contrasting crime general and crime specific theory: The case of hot spot crime. *Advances in Criminology Theory, 4,* 45–70.

Wilson, J. Q., & Kelling, G. (1982). Broken windows. *The Atlantic Monthly, 249,* 29–38.

David Weisburd and Lorraine Green Mazerolle, "Crime and Disorder in Drug Hot Spots: Implications for Theory and Practice in Policing." Reprinted from *Police Quarterly,* Vol. 3 No. 3, September 2000, pp. 331–349. Copyright © 2000 by Sage Publications, Inc. Reprinted by permission of Sage Publications, Inc. ✦

Chapter 7

Focusing on Prey Rather Than Predators

A Problem-Oriented Response to Repeat Victimization

Ron W. Glensor
Ken J. Peak
Mark E. Correia

Rather than focusing on predators who commit crime, authors Glensor, Peak, and Correia approach crime according to those who are victimized most frequently. They ask, what is it about certain people that attracts criminal offenders to prey upon them?

Glensor and his colleagues note that a considerable amount of crime involves victims who suffer repeat offenses. Understanding why is an important first step in preventing future victimizations. The authors propose a problem-oriented policing approach for reducing repeat criminal victimizations using the S.A.R.A. model (scanning, analysis, response, and assessment) proposed by Herman Goldstein.

Crime is contagious.

—Louis D. Brandeis

The innocence that feels no risk is taught no caution, is more vulnerable than guilt, and oftener assaulted.

—Nathaniel P. Willis

At the zoo, there always seem to be more spectators around the lions' and tigers' cages than around those of the wildebeest and the antelope; more attention is focused on the predators than their prey. Predator behaviors are more dramatic: they stalk, pursue, attack, and devour, while prey species are comparatively dull—grazing, being constantly nervous, fleeing often, and dying (Titus, 1995).

That predators are more interesting to people than prey might explain why criminology has traditionally been more intrigued with offenders than with victims. There may also be a belief that since offenders commit the crimes, in order to control crime we must concentrate on understanding criminal motivation and behavior (Titus, 1995). These have led police to traditionally base crime control and prevention on the behavior of the offender or the locations where crimes are repeated. More recently, policing agencies in the United States have engaged in problem-solving techniques in their daily practices. The wide breadth of problem-solving policing incorporates repeat victimization as one of these essential elements (i.e., victim, offender, and location), in the analysis of crime. Yet, the police know the least about the prevalence and persistence of victimization.

Several studies (see Anderson, Chenery, and Pease, 1995; Lloyd, Farrel, and Pease, 1994; Pease, 1996; Farrel and Pease, 1993) in Great Britain have shown that encompassing repeat victimization into police practices increases our understanding of patterns of criminality and enhances prevention activities, both of which have led to great reductions in criminal behavior. In the United States, however, where problem-oriented policing has spread rapidly across the country, patterns of repeat victimization have not been as thoroughly developed nor understood and have not been assimilated into problem solving. Therefore, broadening the focus of crime prevention to include victims as well as offenders and locations would enable police officers in the United States to become more effective.

Drawing primarily upon the work and British research, this article examines the utility of repeat victimization for identifying complex crime patterns and predicting criminal activity in the United States. It begins with an overview of the research findings related to repeat victimization, followed by a discussion concerning the implementation of repeat victimization and some of the problems that might be encountered. Next, we address the issue of repeat victimization in the United States and how it may be identified, analyzed, and responded to using a problem-solving process (S.A.R.A., discussed below). Building on this information, the final section discusses the future of repeat victimization in America, and how the police can begin to incorporate this pattern of crime into their daily practices.

Repeat Victimization

Definition, Rationale, and Extent

Repeat victimization, a relatively new approach to crime analysis and prevention, occurs when the same person or place suffers from more than one incident over a specified period of time (Bridgeman and Hobbs, 1997). Just as a small percentage of offenders and locations account for a disproportionate amount of crime, so do a small percentage of victims account for a disproportionate number of victimizations. And just as repeat offenders typically commit many different types of crime, high-rate victims fall prey to a variety of victimizations (Farrell, 1995). An underlying premise of repeat victimization is that crime is not evenly distributed; that is, certain people and places are repeatedly victimized (Pease and Laycock, 1996). Consequently, repeat victimization is arguably the best single predictor routinely available to the police in the absence of specific intelligence information. In fact, Great Britain has recently adopted repeat victimization as part of the national crime prevention agenda. An awareness of its significance for the deployment of crime prevention efforts came after police examined data in the 1986 Kirkholt burglary prevention project in England (Forrester, 1988). Because too few funds were available to protect all the homes at risk, police had to identify those most at risk. The work was carried out in a public housing project north of Manchester that suffered high levels of residential burglary. What quickly became evident was that most home burglaries involved dwellings that had already been burgled at least once in the past year, and that the best predictor of a future burglary was a *past* burglary. After police took crime prevention measures, repeat burglaries were reduced to almost zero (Pease, 1996).

Looking broadly at repeat victimization, British research found that 5 percent of respondents who experienced 5 or more victimizations suffered 43 percent of all crimes reported, and that half of those victimized in 1992 were repeat victims and suffered 81 percent of reported crimes (Pease, 1996). Additional findings reported by the National Board for Crime Prevention (Anderson, Chenery, and Pease, 1994) determined the following:

- Only 10 percent of domestic violence represented an isolated event.
- Once burglarized, a residence is reburglarized at four times the rate of unburglarized homes.
- Over 39 percent of small businesses were founds to have been reburglarized at least once a year.

Though important, the above statistics do not indicate the responses taken by the police to alleviate the problem. Following is an example of how the police can take affirmative measures to address repeat victimization.

Data collected in London (Pease and Laycock, 1996) indicated that 74 of 172 (43 percent) of domestic violence incidents occurring over a 25-month period involved only about 7 percent of 1,450 households (Lloyd et al., 1994). Police took the following measures to help prevent recurrence, apprehend batterers, and enhance victims' sense of security:

- *Development and distribution of neck-pendant alarms to repeat victims.* When a person presses the button on the pendant, it dials a central station that triggers a priority response from police, opens a voice channel so the police can hear what is happening, and provide assurance that help is on the way.

- *Improvement in transfer of injunction information from courts to police.* Police knowledge of injunctions against batterers permits officers to arrive on the scene with a better understanding of their legal authority with the incident at hand.
- *Provision of support and information for victims.* Police employed a domestic violence specialist who developed safety plans for victims and helped them to improve their communication with other agencies.

These measures were warmly welcomed by police and victims alike, and several arrests were made as a result. Although the efficacy of such initiatives is difficult to demonstrate statistically, both researchers and police had no doubt about the project's worth.

Concerning offenders' rationale for choosing the persons or places, we may consider burglary as an example. Why do burglars return to burgle the same household again? One could argue that, for several reasons, they might be stupid not to return: temporary repairs to a burgled home will make a subsequent burglary easier; the burglar is familiar with the physical layout and surroundings of the property; the burglar knows what items of value were left behind at the prior burglary; and the burglar also knows that items that were taken at the subsequent burglary are likely to have been replaced through an insurance policy.

These reasons for burglaries appear to have empirical support. Anderson and his colleagues (1995) found that revictimization within 11 months for non-residential burglary was 28 percent, and for residential burglary, 16 percent. In fact, other British burglary researchers have determined that in some 80 percent of cases where more than one burglary is cleared with an arrest, the perpetrator is the same person. This is inconsistent with the long-standing, widely held view among the police that many repeat offenses are the result of criminal associates being told of residual crime opportunities.

In general, the culmination of research conducted in Great Britain on repeat victimization indicates the importance of this pattern and its utility for preventing repeat occurrences. Likewise, these findings have greatly increased our understanding of crime (see Table 7.1). Consideration needs to be given to how police utilize repeat victimization data to address recurring crime problems. That is the focus of the next section.

Table 7.1
General Findings of Research on Repeat Victimization

- An individual's past crime victimization is a good predictor of his or her subsequent victimization.
- The greater the number of prior victimizations, the higher the likelihood the victim will experience future crime (Pease and Laycock, 1996).
- Especially within crime-prone areas, a substantial percentage of victimizations consist of repeat victims (Pease and Laycock, 1996).
- The same perpetrators seem to be responsible for the bulk of repeated offenses against a victim (Pease and Laycock, 1996).
- Many factors, from police shift patterns to computer systems, conspire to mask the true contribution of repeat victimization to the general crime problem (Pease and Laycock, 1996).
- If victimization recurs, it tends to do so soon after the prior occurrence, especially for residential burglary, domestic violence, auto crimes, and retail crimes (Farrell and Pease, 1993).
- In residential burglary, 40 percent of repeat burglaries occur within one month of the previous burglary (Anderson, et al., 1995).

Application of Repeat Victimization: Methods and Problems

There are three primary sources which policing agencies employ for obtaining repeat victimization information: police records, which allow officers to use data from their crime recording system or incident logs; other agencies' records (for example to examine school crime, school records may provide a more complete picture); and interviews or surveys of crime victims providing information concerning the how (method of operation), when, and what happened (Bridgeman and Hobbs, 1997:6). This data should be collected over a 12-month period, to establish any patterns within an adequate framework of time.

After collecting the relevant data, the police can utilize several different analytical techniques to determine patterns of criminality. The first technique, location driven analysis, focuses on the geographical location of the incident or offense. The second technique, object driven analysis, is similar to location, but is used when the location is not fixed. An example is an investigation of crimes against motor vehicles which concentrates on the individual vehicle, rather than the location. Victim driven analysis concentrates on the victim since some forms of repeat victimization, such as racially motivated crimes, focus on the victim. The last technique is hot spot driven analysis. This refers to a site that accounts for a disproportionate number of crimes or incidents, and may include a single location (such as a house or a park), or a wider area, such as particular street or neighborhood. The ultimate hot spot, the "hot dot," is the individual victim who repeatedly suffers crime (Bridgeman and Hobbs, 1997:7–8).

Utilizing the above data collection methods and analytical techniques may not provide a clear picture of the extent of repeat victimization, however. Due to several reasons, the prevalence of repeat victimization may be underestimated. For example, the underreporting of crime in general is a problem that has long plagued efforts to measure its extent. People do not report all of the incidents they suffer; this exacerbates any attempt to learn the "crime picture" in general, and compounds attempts to understand repeat victimization. Secondly, many police crime recording systems do not readily identify repeat victims. Also, the police shift systems and beat areas mean that different officers are likely to deal with the same victim, thus reducing the likelihood of links being made between incidents (Bridgeman and Hobbs, 1997:2).

Repeat Victimization and Problem-Oriented Policing in the United States

As the above research findings suggest, utilizing repeat victimization to develop effective crime prevention strategies in Great Britain has shown to be quite effective. Unfortunately, police agencies in the United States have not typically focused on the victim as an important element in crime control. Although the S.A.R.A. problem-solving process can be used to identify patterns of repeat victimization within its analysis, police in the United States have primarily used offender behavior and location as the basis for crime prevention. Specifically, the problem-solving process recognizes that three elements must be present before a crime can occur: an offender (someone who is motivated to commit harmful behavior), a victim (a desirable and vulnerable target must be present), and a location (the victim and offender must both be in the same place at the same time) (see Figure 7.1). If these elements show up over and over again in patterns and recurring problems, removing one or more of these elements can stop the pattern and prevent future harms (Eck, 1992). Effective removal, however, necessitates gaining as much possible information about these three elements.

When analysis includes all three elements, a much clearer picture of crime emerges. A study on repeat victimization in 11 industrialized

Figure 7.1
The Crime Triangle

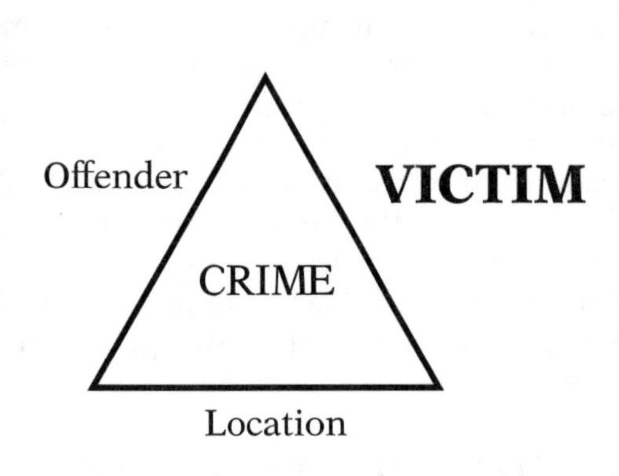

nations found that one in three residential burglaries in the United States is a repeat burglary—a proportion that surpassed all other nations in the study (Farrell and Sousa, 1997). Drawing upon the International Crime Victims Survey (Mayhew and Van Dijik,1997), this study also found that 48 percent of sexual incidents (i.e., grabbing, touching, and assault), 43 percent of assaults and threats, and 23 percent of vehicle vandalism were repeat victimizations.

Repeat victimization is not limited to the more violent crimes, however. A domestic study of white collar crime (Alexander, personal communication to Farrell and Sousa, 1997) indicated that the same people are victims of fraud and embezzlement time and time again, and that bank robberies also have high rates of repeat victimization (Pease, personal communication to Farrell and Sousa, 1997).

These studies, though somewhat limited, show the value of including repeat victimization in the problem-solving process. An important question, then, is whether problem-oriented policing can utilize patterns of repeat victimization to reduce repeat occurrences. This is the focus of the next section.

Using Problem Solving to Identify Patterns of Victimization

Problem-oriented policing was originally framed by Herman Goldstein, who argued for a radical change in policing efforts out of frustration with the dominant model for improving police operations: "More attention [was] being focused on how quickly officers responded to a call than on what they did when they got to their destination" (Goldstein, 1987:2; see also, Goldstein, 1990). Using this as a foundation, Eck (1992) and Spelman and Eck (1987) developed a problem-solving process (S.A.R.A.) to determine if problem solving could be applied to the daily practices of the police (see Figure 7.2).

Figure 7.2
Using the S.A.R.A. Problem-Solving Process to Identify Patterns of Victimization Within the Crime Triangle

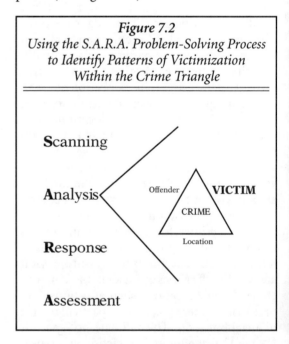

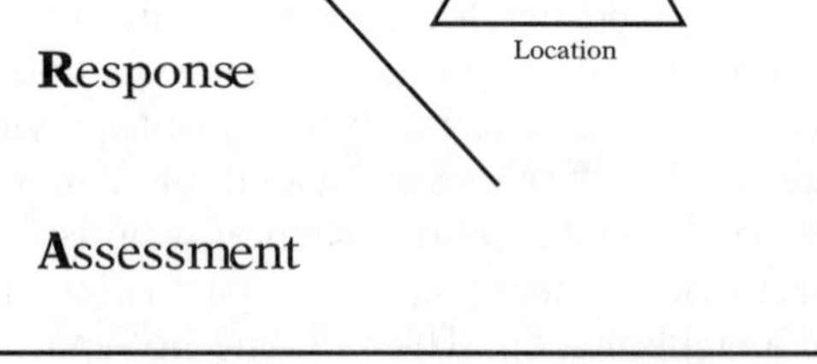

Briefly stated, this problem-solving process involves four stages: scanning, analysis, response, and assessment (Spelman and Eck, 1987:43–52). *Scanning* refers to problem identification, where officers identify recurring problems on their beats. The second stage, *analysis*, is the heart of the problem-solving process and involves the police learning as much as possible about the problem in order to identify its causes. Third is the response stage, with officers looking for long term, creative, tailor-made solutions to the problem. Finally, in the *assessment* stage, officers evaluate the effectiveness of their responses, for example, checking to see if the number of calls for service regarding the problem decreased.

The S.A.R.A. process has been used very successfully for problem-solving efforts in hundreds of communities—large, medium, and small in size—across the nation. As examples, this process was used to reduce car burglaries in Seattle, address juvenile drug trafficking in Tulsa, diminish mobile park problems in Reno, counter drugs and guns in San Diego, address crimes involving the homeless population in Savannah, and curtail mall gang problems in Lakewood, Colorado (Peak and Glensor, 1999).

The root of the problem-solving process lies in the structured analysis of problems, which leads officers to look for clusters of similar, related, or recurring incidents rather than a single incident. This type of analysis would help police identify repeat offenders, locations (hot spots), and victims. The deflection and prevention of repeat victimization lie in these responses. Spelman (1995:380) articulated the benefits of preventing repeat victimization at the patrol level:

> The primary implication of repeat offenders, vulnerable victims, and dangerous places has always been that long-term activities made sense. In the absence of special attention, these high risk people and places would remain at high risk. Thus they had a claim on a disproportionate share of police resources. Programs to target certain offenders, provide assistance to certain victims, and solve recurring problems at certain locations seem appropriate.

Discussion

Repeat victimization is not new; police officers have always been aware that the same people and places are victimized again and again. However, what *is* new are attempts abroad to incorporate repeat victimization knowledge into formal crime prevention efforts. Research has enabled the police to bring repeat victimization into clearer focus and indicated what must be done—and the kinds of information systems that are required—to identify locations and persons who need the kind of crime prevention attention that is offered through this concept.

British police forces seek to implement repeat victimization policy as daily practice. Police in the United States would also do well to recognize the value of including repeat victimization in their overall crime management policy. To do so requires several philosophical and pragmatic changes to occur (Pease, 1998). Philosophically, police departments must recognize the importance and value of repeat victimization in developing a more comprehensive picture of crime. This recognition puts crime prevention, through detection and deflection, as the sole purpose of policing (Pease, 1996). By viewing crimes as occurring in a sequence, rather than a single incident, detection will enhance future prevention efforts, and prevention will reduce the likelihood of future detection.

The identification of patterns of repeat victimization is dependent upon the available information. Pragmatically, information gathering and computer systems need to reflect repeat victimization. Therefore, greater efforts must be made to gather more information concerning the victim, including those victims who do not report their crimes to the police. This will require implementing community-based surveys to identify patterns of repeat victimization. Integrating this information with information concerning the offender and location into a single database is paramount, and will allow the police to simultaneously consider all three elements of crime offender, place and victim. This, perhaps, poses one of the greatest challenges to American police departments. Currently, very few departments have the resources and/or skills necessary to develop, implement, and maintain adequate computer databases. Those resources that do exist tend to focus on either the offender or the location.

Given that these changes will not come easily, American police departments should continue to draw upon Great Britain as a resource. Their dedication to repeat victimization can contribute greatly to American efforts. At the same time, American police departments can offer their experiences in identifying the offender and location to British police departments, who have long ignored these elements. Together, this international alliance brings all elements of the crime triangle into focus, which can greatly enhance crime prevention efforts in both countries.

References

Anderson, D., Chenery, S., and Pease, K. (1994). *Tackling repeat burglary and car crime.* Crime Detection and Prevention Papers 58. London: Home Office.

——. (1995). *Preventing repeat victimization: A report on progress in Huddersfield.* London: Home Office Police Research Group Briefing Note 4/95.

Bridgeman, C. and Hobbs, L. (1997). *Preventing repeat victimization: The police officers' guide.* London: Home Office Police Research Group.

Eck, J. (1992). A dissertation prospectus for the study of characteristics of drug dealing places. November.

Farrell, G. (1995). Preventing repeat victimization. In M. Tonry and D.P. Farrington (eds.), *Building a safer society,* (pp. 469–534). Chicago: University of Chicago Press, (1995).

Farrell, G. and Pease, K. (1993).*Once bitten, twice bitten: Repeat victimization and its implications for crime prevention.* London: Home Office, Police Research Group, 1993, p. 3.

Farrell, G. and Sousa, W. (1997). Repeat victimization in the United States and ten other industrialized countries. Paper presented at the National Conference on Preventing Crime, Washington, D.C., October 13.

Forrester, D. P. (1988).*The Kirkholt Burglary Prevention Project.* London: Home Office Police Research Group.

Goldstein, H. (1987). Problem-Oriented Policing. Paper presented at the Conference on Policing: State of the Art III, National Institute of Justice, Phoenix, Ariz., June 12.

——. (1990). Problem-Oriented Policing. New York: McGraw-Hill.

Lloyd, S., Farrell, G., and Pease, K. (1994).*Preventing repeated domestic violence: A demonstration project on Merseyside.* London: Home Office Police Research Group, Crime Prevention Unit Paper 49.

Mayhew, P. and Dijik, J.V. (1997). *Criminal Victimization in Eleven Industrialized Countries: Key Findings for the 1997 International Crime Victims Survey.* Research and Documentation Center, Dutch Ministry of Justice.

Peak, K. and Glensor, R. (1999). *Community Policing and Problem Solving: Strategies and Practices.* New York: Prentice-Hall.

Pease, K. (1996). Repeat Victimization and policing. Unpublished manuscript. University of Huddersfield, West Yorkshire, England, June 30, p. 4.

——. (1998). Repeat victimization: taking stock. Crime Detection and Prevention Series, Paper 90. London: Home Office Police Research Group.

Pease, K. and Laycock, G. (1996). *Revictimization: Reducing the heat on hot victims.* Washington, D.C.: U.S. Department of Justice, National Institute of Justice, Research Action, November.

Spelman, W. (1995). "Once bitten, then what? Cross-sectional and time course explanations for repeat victimization."*British Journal of Criminology,* 35(3):366–380.

Spelman, W. and Eck, J. E. (1987). *Problem-Oriented Policing.* Washington, D.C.: U.S. Department of Justice, National Institute of Justice.

Titus, R. M. (1995). Activity theory and the victim. Paper presented to the 4th International Seminar on Environmental Criminology and Crime Analysis, Cambridge, England, July 8, p. 1.

Ron W. Glensor, Ken J. Peak, and Mark E. Correia, "Focusing on Prey Rather Than Predators: A Problem-Oriented Response to Repeat Victimization." Reprinted from Ron W. Glensor, Mark E. Correia, and Ken J. Peak (Eds.), *Policing Communities: Understanding Crime and Solving Problems,* pp. 160–166. Copyright © 2000 by Roxbury Publishing Company. All rights reserved. ✦

Chapter 8

Screening out Criminal Offenders

An Evaluation of Crime-Free Multi-Family Housing in Tacoma

Lucy Edwards Hochstein
Quint C. Thurman

H*ochstein and Thurman evaluate the findings from an innovative approach to crime in Tacoma, Washington. This study is interesting because it concerns a crime-reduction program in a particular kind of place—multi-family housing units across the city—that limits the access of particular kinds of undesirable tenants.*

The goals of Tacoma's Crime Free Multi-Family Housing (CFMFH) project included the reduction of juvenile crime, decreases in citizen calls for police services, improvements in neighborhood perceptions of rental housing quality and safety, and increases in collaboration between local agencies, businesses, and residents. CFMFH personnel applied a multi-faceted approach to achieve project goals including Crime Prevention Through Environmental Design (CPTED) training for housing unit managers, local residents, and government agencies. Similarly, tenants were taught strategies that they might use to reduce their own personal or family vulnerability to criminal victimization. In addition, special after-school programs were established to provide youth with activities that promote increased self-esteem and social skills. The evaluation of CFMFH suggests that screening out tenant applicants with criminal histories can substantially and positively impact public safety in multi-family housing units.

Introduction

Crime and disorder problems in multi-family housing units typically pose a challenge to urban and suburban communities and their police departments. The anonymity of apartment living, compounded by lack of attachment to rented space, high resident mobility, higher than average population density, and poor applicant screening by management, seems to ensure a poor prognosis for public safety within and surrounding areas primarily composed of multi-family residences. In Tacoma, Washington an innovative response to crime and disorder in the city's most heavily populated section was to develop preventive measures for reducing criminal offender inhabitation, and thus criminal opportunities, in some of the city's most urban neighborhoods. This paper reports findings from a three-year effort to administer Tacoma's Crime-Free Multi-Family Housing (CFMFH) project.

Literature Review

Developments in public safety in the last few decades have led to a growing realization that the government, and specifically policing, cannot successfully reduce crime without assistance from citizens (Cirel et al., 1977). This view was emphasized over 30 years ago in the 1967 report from the President's Commission on Law Enforcement and Administration of Justice. Since then, advocates have persuasively argued the virtues of community crime prevention (e.g., Rosenbaum, 1986; Hope, 1995; Tonry and Farrington, 1995; Thurman et al., 2001).

One of the most influential publications in this regard dates back two decades. In Wilson and Kelling's "Broken Windows" article (1982) the authors describe efforts aimed at community-wide crime prevention as an attempt to build up areas that have fallen from previously higher levels of respectability. As noted by Rosenbaum (1988), Wilson and Kelling advocated resident mobilization, increasing interactions among residents and others, fortifying their sense of community, and increasing informal methods of policing and enforcement as key ingredients in the creation of an environment with low levels of criminal activity.

The social problem model and the opportunity reduction model proffered by Lurigio and Rosenbaum (1986:21) serve as the foundation for most contemporary community crime-prevention programs. While the former addresses the social conditions that may lead to criminal activity (Podolefsky and DuBow, 1981), such as increasing interactions, developing a sense of community (DuBow and Emmons, 1981), enforcing social norms (Greenberg et al., 1983), and identifying neighborhood boundaries (Suttles, 1972), the latter encourages activities that would reduce the potential for victimization and alters the physical environment to make it less crime-prone. In addition, the opportunity reduction model also tries to stimulate and strengthen the relationship between neighborhood residents and local police (Lurigio and Rosenbaum, 1986:22).

Community crime prevention has drawn considerable attention since the publication of Wilson and Kellings's 1982 "Broken Windows" article, which raised questions about the ability of the police to efficiently and effectively control criminal activity by the use of traditionally reactive response to crime. The authors suggested that because an environment conducive to the nurturing of criminal activity is the result of community apathy, fear, and lack of functional internal social control mechanisms, seemingly insignificant problems such as physical appearance, logistics, and community involvement should be addressed by citizens and law enforcement personnel alike, in order to maintain the integrity of a neighborhood (McGarrell et al., 1996).

Lavrakas (1985) points out that a community focus was not a major component of crime-reduction strategies until the late 1970s, when funding was provided to evaluate the their effectiveness. Accordingly, empirical research about this same period of time has been instructive. For example, the success of measures to reduce and prevent crime in poor areas suffering high crime rates tends to depend upon the involvement of those members of the community willing to make commitments to raise the standards of lifestyle and safety within their communities. Simultaneously, research foci have changed from property crimes, which require secrecy and a lack of immediate detection, to the so-called "victimless crimes" of drug activity and prostitution that often are initiated or committed in plain view. These highly visible crimes tend to be more easily detected, and hence, more frequently reported.

Despite relatively easy detection, some citizens are reluctant to enter into any kind of association with the police to reduce crime. Skogan and Annan (1993) suggest that long histories of police discrimination toward the poor and racial minorities have led many members of these groups to distrust the police. Also, police officers often are distrustful of these two groups, especially when congregated in densely populated public housing, where an officer on a service call could easily be outnumbered. This mutual attitude of distrust creates a barrier to working relationships between police and residents. Rosenbaum (1986) therefore believes that because neither the residents nor the police can effectively combat the crime situation by themselves, they must enter into a collaborative agreement involving mutual respect, problem-solving efforts, and empowerment of both citizens and officers to address problem situations in order to arrive at a positive outcome.

Applied criminological theory as exemplified by Paul and Patricia Brantingham (1981) provides an excellent vehicle for understanding and then directing community crime-prevention efforts. Their development of the theory of environmental criminology maintains that a major contributory factor in the occurrence of crime is the location where the criminal activity actually takes place. "A crime occurs when four things are in concurrence: a law, an offender, a target, and a place" (p. 7). Place is defined as ". . . a discrete location in time and space at which the other three dimensions intersect and a criminal event occurs" (p. 8). Environmental criminology involves the interaction between place and the other three dimensions that results in the production of criminal activity. It is noteworthy that Shaw and McKay (1931) also addressed the environment as a source of criminal behavior, claiming that ". . . neighborhood conditions . . . lead to individual criminal motivation" (p.18). Their approach addressed specific crime sites and focused on such aspects as building types, form, lighting, and other structural particulars.

The Brantinghams suggest that "perceived opportunity," and not motivation, results in criminal activity, and that this opportunity is made available by the mobility of the subject and his or her location at the time of the opportunity. Placement of the criminal offender, in most cases, is not by accident, and there may be a specific relationship and interaction between him and his time/place/opportunity setting that is more than mere coincidence. The examination of this relationship has the potential to provide information that could be used for determining how to manipulate or alter these variables in order to lessen criminal activity.

Interestingly, while Hope (1995:67), like the Brantinghams, agrees that "residents are frequently victimized by coresidents," he acknowledges that there has been very little research on this phenomenon. Furthermore, there has been virtually no development of policy implications that might make use of this information if proven true. Suffice it to say that when local residents know or suspect their neighbors of victimizing their neighborhood, the usual course of action is target hardening or moving to another residence (see Dugan, 1999).

The Brantinghams also discuss the negative influence of routinely visible criminal activity upon neighborhood identity. Such activity results in a multi-staged downward spiral, including: 1) perception of crime by neighborhood residents; 2) ensuing fear compounded and observed by other residents and nonresidents; and 3) undermining of neighborhood vitality due to the increase in crime, real estate values, and scarcity of investment capital due to a declining neighborhood. The Brantinghams maintain that once a neighborhood reaches this final level, the odds against its survival or successful rehabilitation are extremely high.

As the situation continues, fear of crime within a neighborhood becomes contagious, and the area declines in desirability. Accordingly, a strategy to thwart impending instability and reverse this spiral of decay is the encouragement of community participation and cooperation with law enforcement agencies to reduce crime by screening out felonious tenants and developing a plan for reducing criminal opportunities. It was in this spirit that the City of Tacoma adopted CFMFH.

Background and Program Description

Tacoma is a suburb of Seattle known regionally for its poverty and high rates of crime and disorder. Unlike most suburban communities, Tacoma is a highly urbanized city in and of itself with a substantial downtown, inner-city residential area that includes numerous apartment complexes. Many of its residents commute daily to the greater Seattle area yet spend their evenings and weekends in Tacoma where their presence results in a proportionate increase in the opportunity for criminal victimization. CFMFH seems to be one crime-reduction approach aimed at taking the battle to the inner city where the population density is greatest during the weekend and evening hours, especially in multi-family residential areas of the city that traditionally have seen only reactive styles of crime control.

In step with the idea of community crime prevention (see Tonry and Farrington, 1995), the underlying rationale for CFMFH is that if criminally active residents could be dislodged from or denied inner-city addresses in the first place then crime might be reduced or displaced (also see Hope, 1995). Accordingly, CFMFH was developed with several goals in mind. These included the reduction of juvenile crime, decreases in citizen calls for police services, improvements in neighborhood perceptions of rental housing quality and safety, and enhanced landlord/tenant relationships with the City of Tacoma.

CFMFH was initially introduced as a pilot project in 1996 through a collaborative effort with the Tacoma Police Department, the Tacoma Fire Department, Tacoma Building and Land Use Services, and the Tacoma Human Rights Department and a grant from the Washington Governor's Office of Juvenile Justice (a division of the Department of Social and Health Services). Designed to increase collaboration between local agencies, businesses, neighborhoods, and individuals to create a useful and replicable program that might be applied in any community under similar circumstances, CFMFH was developed to achieve objectives related to the education, inspection, and certification of the area's apartment communities. These included, but were not limited to: the reduction of calls for police services involving juvenile crime in particular; increases in prosocial youth activities; the provision of landlord information regarding eviction and intervention; the facilitation of voluntary certification of rental units; and the creation of city ordinances that promoted continuation of the project beyond its initial funding.

In order to achieve its objectives, CFMFH featured four main components. The landlord component required participating rental property managers and owners to attend a 16-hour training seminar on crime-prevention practices and policies for reducing the opportunity for criminal activities that typically occur on their premises. A key strategy emphasized during the training and required for certification as a CFMFH housing structure was the development of standardized procedures to screen out undesirable tenant applicants. Each apartment manager or landlord was trained to use criminal background checks paid for by a $25 application fee to regulate who was allowed to lease rental space. Only applicants without felony convictions were allowed occupancy; application fees were not returned to rejected applicants, thus creating a disincentive for felons to continue to seek residence in other CFMFH complexes once they were turned down.

Second, participants were provided a Crime Prevention Through Environmental Design (CPTED) evaluation of their property and then allowed the opportunity to apply for CPTED certification. Those sites that met the assessment criteria were expected to incur less risk for criminal activity than those that either failed to comply or did not apply for certification in the first place.

Third, the tenant education component of the program offered residents information that they might apply to reduce their own personal or familial vulnerability to criminal victimization. The fourth component was the After-School Latchkey Program. It was designed to provide youth in the targeted area with activities that promote increased self-esteem, social skills, and continuity in the rapidly changing environment of low-income housing.

Originally, CFMFH's primary focus was on neighborhoods or housing complexes that had fallen victim to urban decay. These were generally characterized by a low-income, poorly educated, elderly, single-parent, or transient population that had at one time witnessed or experienced high incidences of drug and gang activity, prostitution, and other related crime and social disorder problems. The apartment complexes in these neighborhoods were all several decades old and most were in need of extensive repair. Tenants were of all ages, ranging from children to the elderly and represented various ethnic backgrounds.

While program personnel over the years continued to focus on these first order program participants, they also expanded the scope of the program over time to include less seriously afflicted complexes. However, key program strategies continued to be education, inspection, and certification of apartment communities, with the corresponding objectives of police service call reduction, prosocial youth activities, intervention and eviction information for landlords, rental unit registration, and the creation of city ordinances in support of the program.

Research Methods

The three parts of CFMFH observed during a first-year study in 1998 remained intact in 2000. These included: 1) the comprehensive training of landlords to reduce the presence of criminal behavior and felonious individuals; 2) encouragement of CPTED practices through property evaluation; and 3) the delivery of tenant education to prevent criminal victimization. The fourth CFMFH component, implemented in the latter months of 1998 and operating in full force in 1999, was the After-School Latchkey Program that was put in place to reduce opportunities for crime among youths. Accordingly, the evaluation methodology used to conduct an assessment of the third year of Tacoma's CFMFH project was similar to that of the previous two evaluations that were undertaken in 1998 and 1999. Once again, the emphasis was upon focus group interviews, personal interviews, official report data, and direct observations to determine whether the program had any direct impact on the quality of life perceptions, police services, criminal activity, and evaluation of environmental elements directly affecting habitation.

As in previous years, the assessment conducted in 2000 followed the form of a performance audit due to a small research budget ($7,500). Aside from the issue of needed resources that were unavailable to mount a more rigorous impact assessment, we believe that the more flexible research design was justified due to the exploratory and yet compelling nature of the research topic. No published research that we know of previously existed on this topic and yet it seemed to us that determining whether or not screening out felons from apartment complexes (among the other features of CFMFH) might yield useful policy implications.

Several questions formed the basis of the performance audit. These included: 1) What are the effects of CFMFH on the perceptions of landlords, managers and tenants regarding the quality of life in their multi-family housing complexes? 2) What are the effects on crime in the neighborhood in general? 3) What effects might there be on subjective perceptions of the quality and level of police calls for service? And 4) What effects on physical and social disorder could be observed?

Of the two focus group interviews conducted in 2000, one consisted of landlords and managers, and the other of elite stakeholders (including property owners, city officials, and those involved with related programs). Judgments about the effects of CFMFH were formed during tours of apartment complexes and neighborhoods not visited in 1998 or 1999, examination of CFMFH quarterly reports, visits to After-School Latchkey Program sites, interviews with Latchkey Program personnel, an observation of a CFMFH presentation to the another municipality, and interviews of Project personnel. We also examined Tacoma Police Department calls for service data from 106 participating complexes, both before and after implementation of the project.

Findings

The data available for this assessment were collected from focus group interviews, direct observations, personal interviews, examination of calls for police service statistics data derived from those residences participating in the program, CFMFH quarterly reports, and observations of program activities, including the After-School Latchkey Program. We briefly discuss the findings from these sources in the sections that follow.

Focus Group Interviews

Although slightly different questions were asked of both the landlord and manager focus group and the elite stakeholder focus group, responses from both groups typically were optimistic and positive and conveyed support for the project and its direction. A strong concern voiced by both groups was the potential demise of the CFMFH once state funding for project personnel was withdrawn.

Landlords and managers in the first focus group included many who were interviewed in 1998 and 1999 and some new respondents. Landlords and managers indicated that they had decided to participate in CFMFH for a number of reasons, but the primary attraction was their belief that the education and contacts gained through their participation in the program would improve the appearance of their housing units, and thus increase the quality of their businesses. The focus group interview with this group revealed that these respondents were better informed about landlord/tenant laws and well-trained to recognize criminal behavior by CFMFH; it also was determined that these respondents kept informed about illicit activities in the vicinity of their buildings, especially drug-related ones. Additionally, they seemed sincerely committed to outreach beyond their own buildings to improve their neighborhoods, participate in their community, and encourage other landlords and managers to become involved in the program. They also perceived that CFMFH fostered their tenants' good citizenship and community participation.

Furthermore, respondents believed that crime rates had decreased and that this reduction was due to the fact that through CFMFH the area had assumed a more respectable identity that discouraged criminal activity. Respondents felt a closer rapport with police, and this rapport not only increased the safety of all their tenants but also helped them do a better job as managers and landlords. They admitted that law enforcement had become their ally in improving living conditions and business practices in their complexes. They also expressed concern that higher city officials, including city commissioners and the police chief, had yet to participate as actively and visibly in CFMFH as was desirable.

All of the properties of these landlord/manager focus group respondents were certified to the highest level possible in the program (Level III). No Level I or Level II certified participants were present, nor were any landlords or managers who had taken the classes and not achieved certification. The respondents reported that they found it easy to make the required improvements to their buildings and thus comply with certification criteria by making certification part of their regular maintenance program. They reported that many of their neighbors had seen the benefits and joined as well.

Each of the focus group participants was aware that the project was nearing the end of its funding period, and each was concerned that the project might be discontinued if funding for project personnel disappeared. Without the direct organization of the CFMFH personnel, they believed it would be difficult to maintain the current level of program commitment throughout the city. They feared that fewer landlords and managers would participate without direct supervision and training and that residents would no longer be educated about crime prevention. They also feared that no one specific entity would monitor certified properties to see that the standards were maintained.

Due to CFMFH, tenants in these landlords' and managers' complexes also improved. Posted program signs served to deter undesirable tenants from applying for residence, and housing appeared safer for those who were accepted as tenants. Rental contracts were modified to contain provisions for eviction for lawlessness and other situations, and evictions became far less adversarial. No longer were the majority of evictions for drugs and drunkenness, but more commonly for nonpayment and other less serious issues. Additionally, those in the rental industry felt that they had a more accurate picture of industry problems. They observed that apartment applicants had begun to select housing based upon an apartment complex's participation in CFMFH.

The landlords and managers reported that they had seen positive results from the CFMFH's After-School Latchkey Program. This program provides many after-school activities and many children attend. Besides providing a safe environment to learn and play, the Latchkey Program also was credited for diverting children from undesirable activities that result in property damage at the session sites. The after-school program also encouraged managers to involve resident children in activities.

Landlord/manager focus group responses correlated positively with tenant, landlord, and manager focus group interviews conducted in 1998 and 1999 and suggested that the high expectations and satisfaction of program participants that were noted in 2000 are consistent with data from the previous two years.

Similarly, those respondents interviewed during the elite stakeholders focus group session responded positively about the program, but understandably from a different perspective. Elite stakeholder respondents included Tacoma city officials, non-profit social service agency heads, and for-profit agency heads closely associated with rental activities in the Tacoma area. Thus, these respondents represented local government, social services, and economic interests.

While looking at CFMFH and its impact from a much broader, more encompassing perspective than the landlord-manager group, these participants nonetheless expressed positive attitudes about changes in the community and attributed them to the project. This focus group interview indicated that elite stakeholders were aware of the broader benefits of the project across the city as opposed to the landlord-manager group's more limited concern for their immediate environment and individual business interests. They viewed CFMFH as a hands-on program that existed as a unique collaboration within city government that also included non-profit and for-profit organizations, and attracted interest from outside the area. Similar to the landlords and managers, the elites also were concerned that this positive and practical program would not continue when grant funding ended.

Elite focus group respondents were encouraged by the tenant response to the program. They believed that tenants felt safer, stayed in their residences longer, and developed stronger feelings of community than they had prior to CFMFH. Many of the respondents felt that the efforts to organize and maintain the project for the past three years were enormously worthwhile, and that endeavors such as this could be a potential solution to the problems that other cities similar to Tacoma were experiencing.

Elite respondents indicated that they were reassured by the fact that overall police calls for service had decreased and noted that this trend had many positive consequences for the city: lower public safety costs to the city, a safer place to live, and consequently a more attractive venue for economic development. Although the respondents recognized that not all complexes that participated in CFMFH had experienced reduced calls for police service, they believed that calls for service at all participating complexes were more meaningful as a result and generally less serious than before training and certification were made available. In particular, they noted that police and fire calls for service related to events instigated by juveniles had been significantly reduced. They attributed this improvement to three factors: 1) the higher quality of tenants now residing in CFMFH-certified buildings; 2) the safer environment; and 3) the Latchkey activities available to younger tenants.

CFMFH's initial focus had been on multifamily housing in the highest-crime neighborhoods. However, once established in high-risk neighborhoods, the program became available to all rental properties throughout the city. City ordinances were crafted to encourage project participation. All landlords were required to register their buildings and meet minimum environmental and structural standards. In addition, a requirement was initiated for the owner or the owner's agent to live within 50 miles of Tacoma. As a result, they believed that the quality of tenants, building conditions, and respect for property had risen. Landlords appeared more responsive to tenants and city codes, and city inspectors seemed more responsive to the desire of landlords and tenants to have blight removed. Tenants also developed more positive relationships with the police and other city agencies, giving them a chance to better themselves.

The elite stakeholder respondents also voiced concerns for those who were unable to obtain housing in Tacoma due to poor credit ratings or criminal records, a predictable but unavoidable outcome of widespread CFMFH implementation. Tenants who were turned away from certified complexes were being forced to seek housing outside of the city, unless they were accepted into one of the few sheltered housing programs in the city. Fortunately, these programs not only housed tenants, but taught them how to be good renters, good neighbors, and good citizens in their community.

A final observation from both focus group interviews was that all of the participants registered requests for more education, information, and opportunities to participate in upgrading and refresher type seminars. Respondents were interested in attending refresher courses, and believed that any new knowledge would be beneficial. Additionally, many stated that refresher courses had provided them with new information they had overlooked the first time, and that each opportunity to receive new information was welcome.

Tacoma CFMFH Statistical Data

CFMFH statistical data were provided by program personnel. These data were comprised of lists of Tacoma-area properties that participated in CFMFH training, CFMFH certification, and the average monthly police calls for service for each of the certified properties. Calls for service incidents covered the spectrum from abandoned autos and noise disturbances to missing welfare checks. Time lines covered the 12 months prior to training to various numbers of months after training, some extending for more than three years.

Since 1997, 411 landlords and managers had received all three levels of CFMFH training. Of these, 118 were currently certified at Level I at the time of the performance audit, 112 were certified at Level II, and 112 were certified at Level III. Level I refers to the initial training level. In contrast, Level III represents the highest level of training offered through CFMFH.

Table 8.1
Multi-Family Housing Complexes Certified Through CFMFH

Certification Level	1997	1998	1999	Total Certified
Level I	57	86	96	118
Level II	13	20	85	112

Table 8.1 shows the number of participating multi-family housing complexes in the City of Tacoma currently certified through CFMFH and their level of certification.

Calls for police service data were available for 106 of the certified properties. As anticipated, there typically were fewer service calls at each participating area property after training and certification than before implementation of CFMFH. In 1998, 31 apartment complexes recorded an increase when compared with the 12 months before participation, while in 1997, 37 showed increases. Fifty-two showed a decrease in 1998 compared with the 12 months before training and certification, and 54 showed decreases in 1999. Twenty-four remained the same in 1998, and 15 remained the same in 1999. Both in 1998 and 1999 the number of participating properties experiencing a reduction in police calls for service was about the same as the total number of those with increased calls for service combined with those experiencing no change in the number of calls for service. That is, 49 percent in 1998 experienced decreased calls for service after program participation, 29 percent showed increases, and 22 percent remained unchanged over time. In 1999, 51 percent decreased their number of calls for service, 35 percent showed an increase

Table 8.2
Percentage of Increased Police Calls for Service at CFMFH-Certified Properties

Percentage of Increase	Number of Properties 1998	Number of Properties 1999
1–10 %	2	2
11–25 %	9	8
26–50 %	7	7
51–75 %	3	7
76–100 %	7	2
Greater than 100 %	3	11

in the number of calls for service, and 15 percent did not change over time in terms of calls for service. Tables 8.2 and 8.3 depict these results.

Table 8.2 reveals that percentages for properties with increased calls for service in 1998 and 1999 were almost evenly distributed throughout the categories and were rather small. This finding suggests that there was no single issue prompting increased calls for service, but that the increases are those that would normally be found in any relatively crime-free neighborhood. The exceptions to this are the eleven properties with over a 100 percent increase in police calls for service. It should be noted, when considering increases in calls for service, that increases may not necessarily reflect an increase in criminal activity, but instead may represent a greater awareness on the part of both managers and tenants about the infractions that justify calls to the police where no such awareness or concern had existed previously.

Table 8.3 presents the distribution of calls for police service at properties where call frequency declined over time. Table 8.3 shows that in 1999 decreased calls for police service cluster primarily in the 26–50 percent category.

Table 8.3
Percentage of Decreased Police Calls for Service at CFMFH-Certified Properties

Percentage of Decrease	Number of Properties 1998	Number of Properties 1999
1–10 %	2	4
11–25 %	17	11
26–50 %	18	23
51–75 %	9	12
76–100 %	6	4
Greater than 100 %	0	0

In 1998, they clustered between 11 and 50 percent, suggesting again that the decreases in calls for service are more significant than the increases that were observed in Table 8.2.

Key CFMFH Project Personnel Interview Data

The CFMFH grant coordinator and the Latchkey coordinator were interviewed in 2000. Interviews with these key personnel suggest that program personnel continued to work toward increasing the number of housing complexes participating in the program, while maintaining the gains made at already participating properties. Work by grant employees in this area is labor intensive. CFMFH employees regularly work more than a normal 40-hour workweek to accomplish grant goals and build on program strengths. The Latchkey Program has resolved the issues confronting it at its inception late in 1998. Since that time, the Latchkey Program increased time spent at the 1999–2000 school year sites over the previous year, and created processes for providing instruction and dealing with any participant behavior problems. For CFMFH as a whole, program personnel have been actively exploring alternative program funding options with various City of Tacoma departments. To date, the CFMFH training and certification processes have been funded through the City of Tacoma general fund, but support for participants to maintain their original high level of participation, promoting and advertising the program, and the Latchkey Program have been dependent on grant funding and in-kind donations.

Data From the After-School Latchkey Program of the CFMFH Project

Data concerning the CFMFH After-School Latchkey Program were collected through interviews with the CFMFH grant coordinator, the Latchkey Program coordinator, the Latchkey site manager, activity providers, CFMFH quarterly reports, and program observations. The Latchkey Program coordinator manages the After-School Latchkey Program, with daily activities supervised by the site manager. Program sessions were initiated after the 1998 performance audit.

Latchkey activities were directed toward nine-, ten-, and eleven-year-olds but often included the younger children being taken care of by Latchkey participants. Activities generally addressed sports and social skills, nature, and the arts, and sometimes included bicycle safety, martial arts training, conflict management and dispute resolutions skills, video-production skills, tile arts and crafts, and baby-sitter certification. There also were field trips appropriate to the time of year of each session, including a tour of Zoolights, chess tournaments, snow shoeing, and horseback riding.

During the 1999–2000 school year, Latchkey Program sessions were held at two sites—a CFMFH certified multi-family housing complex, and a community center. Sessions were held September through December at the multi-family housing site, and February through June at the community center. This brings to five the number of sites where the Latchkey Program has held sessions since its inception. According to the Latchkey coordinator, all sessions were warmly received both by participants and the organizations that provided space for the sessions. Of the five sites, one housing complex has continued to offer the Latchkey Program after the initial session provided by CFMFH. Owners of this housing complex found the Latchkey program a strong draw for new tenants, so they continued the program after Latchkey had rotated to a different site. Part of the funding for continuation was arranged by the Latchkey coordinator, who was able to link the Tacoma Health Department with the housing complex. The remaining sites wanted to continue the program, but no reliable volunteer base existed, and the sites could not acquire continuation funding.

The number of participating youths at each site varied daily and the average ranged from about 12 to 25 at multi-family housing sites to between 12 and nearly 100 at the community center. These attendance levels were the result of well-organized analysis of neighborhoods before a session site was chosen and heavy street-level marketing before the beginning of a session. The Latchkey coordinator suggested that sessions at multi-family complexes where the children lived, although they have fewer participants, were more meaningful and personalized to the needs of younger residents than those at the community center, where attendance was much higher.

As the Latchkey Program became more established and grew, its position in Tacoma gained recognition. The Latchkey Program's positive impact appears to have been integral in creating the program's partnerships with various community organizations. For example, STRIVE, a program directed toward at-risk youths, provided the program with a video-production skills instructor who lead participants in the production of a youth news program for local public access television. Tacoma Metro Parks provided instructors and materials for both 1999–2000 school year Latchkey sites. The West End Neighborhood Council provided financial backing for the tile arts and crafts. The Dispute Resolution Center instructed participants in peer mediation skills. The Tacoma Health Department contributed to the continuation of one housing complex site after Latchkey had rotated to its next site.

Discussion

Several sources of data available to assess the performance of CFMFH in 1999 were also available in 2000 with regard to CPTED training and certification, support for the maintenance of improvements, soliciting increased participation, police calls for service, and the After-School Latchkey Program. Comparison of data from all three years indicates that the project continues to yield positive results, and that ongoing efforts have enlarged the project's scope and the number of participants in CFMFH activities.

All participants in the most recent study saw the totality of program activities that make up the CFMFH Project as vital to the program's success. These respondents did not believe that those project activities funded by the city's general fund, training and certification, would be sufficient alone to maintain the high level of progress achieved by the project to date without the direction of CFMFH project personnel. In 2000, as in 1998 and 1999, CFMFH was credited by managers, landlords, and elite stakeholders alike as a force for positive physical and social change. Those persons familiar with Tacoma's multi-family housing complexes credited CFMFH with many favorable outcomes such as expanded rapport with police, a stronger sense of community, pride in apartments' premises, concern for elimination of undesirable people and activities, and increased awareness of the responsibilities involved in maintaining a positive equilibrium within the neighborhood.

Gang and drug problems in some areas of Tacoma became almost non-existent over the length of the program, and overall police calls for service continued to drop. And while calls for service have not decreased at every location, respondents were quick to attribute any increases in calls for service as an indication of a growing concern for what is going on in the neighborhood, rather than turning a blind eye to crime, or feeling helpless to act in negative situations. With managers and tenants sharing a new feeling of empowerment and of reclaiming the neighborhood came the feeling of safety and security within the home environment that respondents say did not previously exist.

Interviews and observations of participating properties suggest that improvements were not only aesthetically significant, but substantive as well. Managers, landlords, and elite stakeholders see Tacoma as both a better place for citizens of all socio-economic levels to live, and a more economically attractive place for new businesses to locate. Law abiding, low-income inhabitants now have safe places to rent in safe environments, and have been empowered to participate in maintaining the safety of their neighborhoods.

Although it still is not completely clear which determinants are most instrumental in bringing about the positive changes, it appears that project personnel and the commitment of managers and landlords appear to be key factors in the fulfillment of program goals. Their involvement and concern for the project's success serve as focal points for other participants. Managers expressed a genuine concern and personal investment in their properties, and were outspoken as to the lengths to which they would go in order to maintain the standards they have recently come to enjoy. They even encouraged others in their neighborhoods to participate and work with them to make changes that improve the environment for all their neighbors.

One secondary effect of the project is that those applicants who have been determined ineligible for CFMFH properties tenancy have been forced to move to outlying areas that have not yet adopted the program. While this may help eliminate crime problems in Tacoma apartment complexes, it may largely displace it to the fringe areas of neighboring towns.

Conclusion

Recent research by Dugan (1999) confirms that criminal victimization near a residence significantly elevates the occupants' probability of moving to a safer residential environment. Unfortunately, many law-abiding tenants who live in inner-city apartment complexes ordinarily lack the resources necessary to move or fail to have many choices from which to choose that are both safe and affordable. Furthermore, if and when they do move, there exists some risk that their vacant apartment will be re-occupied by tenants who are less law-abiding.

While admittedly the research findings that have been presented here cannot be construed as definitive, they are suggestive. Surely more rigorous evaluation methods are warranted to determine the effectiveness of CFMFH and similar community crime-prevention strategies as they might be implemented in other cities and suburban communities. However, our assessment shows the promise of the CFMFH approach to the problem of crime prevention in apartment complexes. In particular, we view the use of criminal offender background checks to screen out crime-prone tenants as a provocative policy implication worthy of additional empirical examination in the future.

References

Brantingham, P.J. and P.L. Brantingham (1981) *Environmental Criminology.* Beverly Hills, CA: Sage.

Cirel, P., P. Evans, D. McGillis, and D. Whitcomb (1977) *An Exemplary Project: Community Crime Prevention Program.* Washington, DC: Law Enforcement Assistance Administration.

DuBow, F. and D. Emmons (1981) "The Community Hypothesis," in D. Lewis (Ed.) *Reactions to Crime.* Beverly Hills, CA: Sage.

Dugan, L. (1999) "The Effect of Criminal Victimization on a Household's Moving Decision," *Criminology* 37:903–930.

Greenberg, S., W. Rohe, and J. Williams (1983) "Neighborhood Conditions and Community Crime Control," in *Community Crime Prevention.* Washington, DC: Center for Responsive Governance.

Hope, T. (1995) "Community Crime Prevention," in M. Tonry and D.P. Farrington (Eds.) *Building A Safer Community: Strategic Approaches to Crime Prevention.* Chicago: University of Chicago Press.

Lavrakas, P.J. (1985) "Citizen Self-Help and Neighborhood Crime Prevention Policy," in L.A. Curtis (Ed.) *American Violence and Public Policy.* New Haven: Yale University Press.

Lurigio, A.J. and D.P. Rosenbaum (1986) "Evaluation Research in Community Crime Prevention: A Critical Look at the Field," in D.P. Rosenbaum (Ed.) *Community Crime Prevention: Does It Work?* Beverly Hills, CA: Sage.

McGarrell, E.F., A.L. Giacomazzi, Q.C. Thurman, and R. Lincoln (1996) "Reducing Fear and Crime in Public Housing: Effects of a Drug Crime Elimination Program in Spokane, WA." Washington State University, Spokane.

Newman, O. (1972) *Defensible Space.* New York: Macmillan.

Podolefsky, A. and F. DuBow (1981) *Strategies for Community Crime Prevention.* Springfield, IL: Charles C. Thomas.

Rosenbaum, D.P. (1986) "The Problem of Crime Control," in D.P. Rosenbaum (Ed.) *Community Crime Prevention: Does it Work?* Beverly Hills, CA: Sage.

——. (1988) "Community Crime Prevention: A Review and Synthesis of the Literature," *Justice Quarterly* 5:323–395.

Shaw, C.R, and H.D. McKay (1931) *Social Factors in Juvenile Delinquency.* Washington, DC: Government Printing Offices.

Skogan, W.G. and A. Annan (1993) "Drug Enforcement in Public Housing," in R.C. Davis, A.J. Lurigio, and D.P. Rosenbaum (Eds.) *Drugs and the Community: Involving Community Residents in Combating the Sale of Illegal Drugs.* Springfield, IL: Charles C. Thomas.

Suttles, G. (1972) *The Social Construction of Communities.* Chicago: University of Chicago Press.

Thurman, Q., J. Zhao, and A. Giacomazzi (2001) *Community Policing in a Community Era.* Los Angeles: Roxbury.

Tonry, M. and D.P. Farrington (1995) "Strategic Approaches to Crime Prevention," in M. Tonry and D.P. Farrington (Eds.) *Building A Safer*

Community: Strategic Approaches to Crime Prevention. Chicago: University of Chicago Press.

Wilson, J.Q. and G. Kelling (1982) "Broken Windows," *The Atlantic Monthly* 249:29–38.

Lucy Edwards Hochstein and Quint C. Thurman, "Screening out Criminal Offenders: An Evaluation of Crime-Free Multi-Family Housing in Tacoma." Copyright © 2003 by Roxbury Publishing. All rights reserved. ✦

Part III

Challenging Issues in the Internal Police Environment

Since the inception of organizational research by management school faculty in universities across the U.S., there has been considerable discussion and debate about the "ideal type" of internal environment that might be considered optimal for organizations dedicated to achieving high employee productivity. This continues to be an important issue for a variety of bureaucratic institutions including large corporations, universities, and police departments.

Two opposing schools of management theory emerged during the previous century to guide the development of optimal organizational practices: the classical school and the behavioral school. The classical school was introduced in the first half of the twentieth century and further developed since by several theorists. By contrast, the scientific management approach proposed by Frederic Taylor focuses on the accuracy of the work process. In his field study, Taylor measured the time spent to complete routine tasks by individual workers. The purpose was simple: to find the most efficient way to complete a task. Under the scientific management approach, when efficiency improves, an organization can begin to operate more effectively, and thus become more competitive. The scientific management approach emphasized managerial efficiency and standardized workplace practices.

Proponents of the classical school emphasize the importance of bureaucracy, a concept primarily developed by German sociologist Max Weber. Weber believed that organizational rationality is an important component in the modern evolutionary process of human society. For progress to occur, government agencies must minimize the influence of human behavior (which is often unpredictable and personal) and instead embrace the values of neutrality, conformity, and impersonality. In terms of structural arrangements, bureaucracy proposes a vertical hierarchical structure with strict rules for employees and the advancement of career bureaucrats.

Luther Gulick (1937) was another key figure in the development of the classical school of thought. He outlined certain key principles concerned with organizational structure and control such as unity of command and span of control. The principles embraced by Gulick have played a prominent role in the development of the field of public administration.

American policing has been greatly influenced by the classical school of management. By the end of the 1930s, the bureaucratic (professional) model of policing had become the industry standard for organizing large police departments in the U.S., as reflected in O.W. Wilson's book, *Police Administration.* A formal organizational structure marked by hierarchical layers or ranks that operated under a highly centralized administration was well-established in police agencies across the nation. Accordingly, police officers became subject to impersonal rules designed to control their behavior.

The behavioral school of management that began in the 1930s challenged some of the classical school's key assumptions that had taken root in American policing. This group of scholars believed that humans are not only willing to work but can be motivated to complete difficult tasks. What managers need to do, therefore, is not to control their every behavior with impersonal rules and complex hierarchical structures. On the contrary, managers should empower their employees and encourage them to use personal originality, experience, and wisdom in the workplace. The behavioral school of management argues for the formation of a friendly, non-hostile environment that is healthy for those employees who are willingly to work diligently to make their individual contribution to an organization.

The emergence of Total Quality Management (TQM) is a modern example of the behavioral approach. In TQM, employees are organized into groups and empowered to tackle problems at the workplace. These employees make their own decisions on how to solve organizational problems. A basic assumption of TQM is that 80 percent of all mistakes are attributable to inadequacies in a system rather than the human operators who are employed in it.

In this section, we focus on the direction of change in the internal environment of police organizations. In essence, the following chapters discuss both when and how police organizations should make decisive changes in their internal environment to enable rank-and-file officers greater input in the jobs they do. Such input is particularly important in contemporary organizations that embrace a community policing philosophy because of the high frequency of interaction between police officers and local residents.

References

Gulick, L. 1937. "Notes on the Theory of Organization." In L. Gulick and L. Urwick (Eds.), *Papers on the Scence of Administration.* New York: Institute of Public Affairs.

Taylor, F. W. 1947. *Scientific Management.* New York: Harper and Row.

Weber, M. 1977. In H. Gerth and C. Mills (Eds.), *From Max Weber: Essays in Sociology.* Trans. and 3rd Ed. New York: Oxford University.

Wilson, O. W. 1950. *Police Administration.* New York: McGraw-Hill. ✦

Chapter 9

The Myth of the 'Military Model' of Leadership in Law Enforcement

Thomas J. Cowper

Thomas Cowper offers a new perspective for understanding the bureaucratic model of policing. Based upon fifteen years of service in the New York State Police and in the military, the author argues that the application of a military model to the field of policing has been misconceived. Historically, the military model represented the bureaucratic features of the classical school of management. In the bureaucratic mode, a hierarchical structure is the central component of organizational structure, with ranks clearly specified. According to Cowper, impersonal rules govern behavior in the military, and as a result, historically there has been little encouragement for individual originality and creativity because orders are strictly obeyed and are carried out through a rigid chain of command.

For years, students of policing have been taught that American policing is based upon a military model. Although similarities can be found in structural arrangements (e.g., the flow of information and regulatory rules), Cowper recognizes a divergence between American policing and military structures. While the military model does have rigid rules and a hierarchical structure, military leaders have long since realized the limitations of rules and the importance of unity among soldiers. Commanders of the Marine Corps, for example, strongly believe that support and input from soldiers are crucial for success on the battlefield. Consequently, military leadership has evolved while American police organizations have adhered to the more traditional military model of the past. Cowper proposes that in some respects, American policing is more military-like than the military, with decision making generally concentrated at the top of the police hierarchy.

It is a commonly accepted law enforcement notion that police agencies of the free world today are designed on the "military model" of organization and leadership. Modern analogies either lionize that model or deride it as utterly inappropriate for a civil police force. Neither view is correct: There are two military models, each based on a largely symbolic, limited, and inaccurate understanding of military doctrine and practice. One is a vicious parody, combining absurdist fiction such as Joseph Heller's *Catch-22* with a narrow view based on individual military experiences. The other is an imaginary (and inflated) heroic vision, wrapped in the flag of a different category of fiction, from the cinema accounts of Sergeant York and Audie Murphy to the *Rambo* and *Delta Force* genre. Both do a grievous disservice to both the military and the police: Each in its own way makes the military a scapegoat for the ineptitude, structural absurdities, bad management, and outright criminality in police work that are the legacies of the politicization of the American police throughout their history.

This article will not attempt to justify or defend every military practice, policy, or procedure throughout history as either good or applicable to policing. Clearly, the military has had more than its share of abusive commanders and unenlightened organizational policies. What it will attempt to do is dispel the notion of a single military leadership model that needs to be rejected—a stereotypical model based on authoritarian, centralized control of mindless subordinates conditioned to shoot first and ask questions later (Kopel & Blackman, 1997). This fallacious notion is causing many progressive police decision makers to ignore or reject a vast body of knowledge and experience—organizational structures, training and development philosophies, methods of operation, and practical leadership—that could radically improve the way law enforcement agencies conduct the business of policing. In fact, police commanders who understand strategic and tactical decision making and can incorporate effective operational planning techniques as well as organizational command and control methodologies into the conduct of police operations will increase our ability as peacekeepers to successfully resolve crisis situations without the use of military assistance, ordnance, heavy weaponry, and excessive violence.

A number of superficial similarities lend themselves to the military comparison. Police departments tend to be organized with rank structures and uniforms and incorporate many of the various accoutrements of the armed forces, designed in large measure to set cops apart from mere civilians and signal obvious membership in an organization that wields the immediate force of government. Many police executives desire for their agencies strict uniformity, respect for the chain of command, and the sharp, professional appearance of parade ground soldiers patterned after military style organization and discipline. Many individual officers themselves enjoy the apparent status and prestige afforded by a traditional association with the elite warrior class in society. Proponents of this model are quick to use symbolic "war on crime" rhetoric to justify its strict, top-down command-and-control style as essential to both the police crime suppression mandate and the requirement to control armed police officers. On the other hand, critics of the model deride it as being excessively rigid, centrally controlled by micromanaging bureaucrats, autocratic, secretive, intellectually and creatively constraining, and highly resistant to any initiative that would allow employee participation in the operational decision making process of the organization. Furthermore, many behaviorists, modern management scientists, and civil libertarians assert that the military model, this conflict-oriented, overly rigid, and centrally controlled bureaucratic organizational structure, fosters aggressive and confrontational behavior by police officers toward the public (Weber, 1999).

Time and again, the military model is held up as portraying the absolute antithesis of an enlightened, progressive, people-oriented approach to organizational management and structure. Chains of command are derided as too restrictive and rank structures as too authoritarian; uniform appearances and strict discipline are criticized for creating rigid and inflexible mindsets. Many cops themselves purge terms such as *tactics* and *operations* and *doctrine* from their vocabulary at every opportunity, lest they acquire the bankrupt trappings of militaristic brutes through mere word association. And yet, proponents of the military model continue to uphold the paramilitary tradition, imposing control and commanding authority with strict discipline and reveling in many of the customs and courtesies that have been a part of the martial lifestyle for centuries.

During the years, progressive chiefs of police have gone to great lengths to distance themselves and their agencies from the contamination of militarism. Attempts were made to substitute traditional military style uniforms with blazers and ties or non-threatening colors such as white and beige; formal titles and positions have been eliminated in some agencies, replaced with the less Spartan, more civilian appellations such as "police agent"; and the black and white full-sized patrol car has at times been traded in for less traditional, less aggressive colors and styles.[1] And yet, despite the critics, many within the policing community still desire the look and feel of strict militarism and work to maintain the appearance of policing as a sort of Spartan brotherhood of domestic warriors keeping America safe for democracy.

The community-oriented policing (COP) phenomenon has only added fuel to the fire, as many COP proponents assume that military thinking is incompatible with the philosophy of empowerment necessary for today's free-thinking and free-acting line officers. Many attempts to depart from the military model by creating new forms of organizational benevolence and workplace democracy were miserable and obvious failures. If others failed to create revolutionary new methods for running police departments, they at least succeeded in curtailing the more egregious pathologies attributed to the military model—an abusive workplace environment, top-down micromanagement, and overly aggressive, narrowly thinking, enforcement-oriented officers (Trojanowicz & Bucqueroux, 1990). And through it all, the uniforms and the mannerisms and the supposed authoritarian military style of doing business continues to be a popular organizational model for police departments.

The fundamental question that has never been asked is, Do these so called attributes, rejected out of hand by some and desperately clung to by others, truly reflect any model used or practiced by the military? Does the centralized control, micromanagement, and an authoritarian boot camp style of leadership come from actual military practice and policy? Did it ever? If so, then the efforts to distance policing from the originators and proponents of such conventions is a wise one. But if our perception of the military and its so-called model are flawed, then we are advocating a move that, at best, disregards a significantly large category of experience and learning from our collective consideration and potential benefit. At worst, it causes us to reject the very model of organization and leadership that we should be striving to emulate, because at least conceptually, organized policing and organized war fighting should be approached in very similar manners.

Both advocates and opponents of the military model base their positions on faulty assumptions and limited knowledge. The modern military is not the top-down, centrally controlled monolith that many traditional police managers cherish and forward-thinking police progressives decry. American military officers are not trained to be the arrogant martinets that generations of police supervisors have aspired to emulate, and their doctrine does not demand the blind obedience of mindless brutes commonly attributed to military culture by its many detractors. A careful and open-minded examination of current military theory and practice will reveal an approach to organization and leadership that is radically different from what both advocates of the military model and its critics within law enforcement currently believe. What is found instead is a thoroughly professional approach based on careful analysis of the arena in which they operate and a comprehensive understanding of the theories and doctrines that create success. Instead of accepting or rejecting supposed military methods and leadership models based on insufficient or inaccurate knowledge and a distorted notion of reality, we need to thoroughly examine the profession we claim to emulate.

Police organization and military organization attempt to accomplish very similar ends. Both involve the application of governmentally sanctioned force, in the ultimate sense, in the form of a combined use of men and materials organized and structured to solve a myriad of problems concerning conflicts with and resistance to that government's determined will. Both use a variety of means other than direct force to accomplish their respective missions while maintaining continuum of force options as a last resort. Both employ a wide assortment of specialists and units against multiple opponents simultaneously. Both engage in operations such as peacekeeping, humanitarian relief, and life saving, as well as the direct and forcible intervention in the affairs of others. Both must deal effectively with the civilian populations in and around their areas of operation and solve problems to succeed. And both are constrained in their efforts by externally applied Rules of Engagement that limit the amount of force they can apply at a particular time and place based on the totality of existing operational and political circumstances as perceived and determined by civilian decision makers and the law.[2]

Figure 9.1
Conceptual Similarities Between Military and Policing Professions

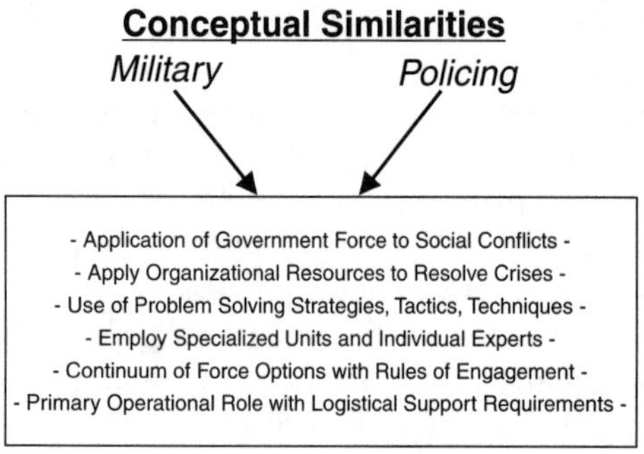

Conceptual Similarities
Military
Policing
- Application of Government Force to Social Conflicts -
- Apply Organizational Resources to Resolve Crises -
- Use of Problem Solving Strategies, Tactics, Techniques -
- Employ Specialized Units and Individual Experts -
- Continuum of Force Options with Rules of Engagement -
- Primary Operational Role with Logistical Support Requirements -

The Historical Perspective

Although it may be true that the world's military forces have produced their share of abusive autocrats and micromanaging dictators, it is equally true—but usually overlooked—that throughout history, the military has worked diligently to eliminate them from its ranks. Like businesses, the military must create atmospheres conducive to creative thinking, individual initiative, and even audacious independent action on the part of subordinates in combat, because it is essentially those human qualities that give one army the advantage over an equally formidable—sometimes a much more formidable—force. As far back as 1000 B.C., military theorists and generals wrote in great detail about what motivates men to fight and die and win in combat. No doubt that some of that writing could lend itself to the typical view of abusive and autocratic military leadership. But discounting the cultural attitudes, societal conventions, and historical realities of their day, even the early writings of ancient philosophers such as Sun Tzu indicate an understanding of leadership that goes far beyond micromanaging autocrats and sending hordes of mindless serfs in mass formations blindly to their collective deaths on the mere whim of the general.

On the contrary, many of these early military philosophers reflect a keen understanding of human nature and the elusive psychological factors within groups of human beings that compels them to endure hardship and display inordinate courage in the face of almost-certain death based solely on the inspiration of their leader and devotion to his cause or vision (Sun Tzu, trans. 1971). In 350 B.C., modern concepts such as personal and positional power, expert power, knowledge power, and information power, as opposed to reward power, coercive power, and connection power, were articulated in the writings of the Greek historian and acclaimed military commander Xenophon (as cited in Heinl, 1966), who said,

> The leader must himself believe that willing obedience always beats forced obedience, and that he can get this only by really knowing what should be done. Thus he can secure obedience from his men because he can convince them that he knows best, precisely as a good doctor makes his patients obey him.

In the declarative statement, "willing obedience always beats forced obedience," Xenophon, a military leader, identified the basic sources of power as they relate to leaders and followers in organizations. And he did so more than 2,500 years before the advent of modern research techniques and enlightened management theories.

Within military circles, this was not an isolated insight. In more modern times, the Earl of Essex wrote in a letter on September 24, 1642, "I shall desire all and every officer to endeavor by love and affable carriage to command his soldiers, since what is done for fear is done unwillingly, and what is unwillingly attempted can never prosper" (as cited in Heinl, 1966, p. 170). Clearly, then, not all of military history and culture has advocated or relied on forced and strict obedience of mindless subordinates. And in fact, the most successful military leaders and their organizations throughout history have embodied, to some extent, many of the tenets of modern democratic, participative leadership theory. General Creighton W. Abrams, aside from being a highly skilled U.S. combat officer in three wars, was most notable as a leader who encouraged his subordinates to openly question his policies and procedures and offer their own alternatives as a means to achieve employee "buy-in" and improved morale. As a tank battalion commander, he encouraged dissent among his subordinates during discussions concerning policy and procedures. Taylor and Rosenbach (1996) stated,

> Abrams made sure that his young officers were not inhibited in these discussions. In fact, stimulated by his challenges, they argued with him constantly. Usually, he would let them persuade him to do it their way. Maybe that way was not always as good as the way he would have done it, but—having argued so strongly for their own solutions—they were committed to making them work. Abrams, of course, knew this full well. (p. 122)

Perhaps, due to the life-and-death nature of the military profession, the modern armed forces of the First World nations have focused their attention heavily on leadership and its impact on structure and operations. In doing so, the modern military, particularly the American military, has radically improved the way it organizes its personnel and applies its resources to solve the various problems and accomplish the various missions necessitating its employment. Contrary to the popular notion of autocratic martinets demanding blind and unquestioning obedience from witless and uncreative followers, the modern military has continued to learn and build on the lessons learned from both historical and contemporary research regarding organization and leadership.

The Real Military Model

The modern military, far from being the creaking bastion of rigidity portrayed in the stereotype, has developed operational doctrine based on decentralization of decision making and action. The American police could be well served if they were to adopt the lessons of the real military experience, making the appropriate adaptations to reflect their different circumstances and missions. Although both institutions rely on the ability of their lower ranked personnel to make decisions autonomously, only the military instills this decision-making process within a common understanding of doctrine.

By many accounts, the Vietnam War, now more than 25 years past, was a low point in American military history, both in the strategic sense of winning wars and in the aspect of internal organizational leadership.[3] Because Vietnam was the last major long-term conflict involving the conscription of large numbers of American citizens into the armed forces during a crisis, it is only natural that the perception of many people today would be colored by that experience and by the popular depictions in the post-Vietnam media. It is the veterans of that 10-year period in our history that have shaped the popular notion of what the military is and does. Hollywood movies such as *Platoon* and *Full Metal Jacket* depict the military leadership of that specific era, perhaps correctly, as largely inept, grossly immoral, and entirely self-serving, as epitomized by Robert Duvall's character in *Apocalypse Now.* The fact that many of today's senior police leaders, line officers, and police researchers are Vietnam veterans or nonveterans who grew up during that war may do much to explain the popular notion of a single and highly undesirable military model of leadership and the mistaken belief that law enforcement should distance itself from anything even remotely associated with it.

A careful analysis of today's military reveals a radically different picture of leadership and organization. Much more than do civilian corporations and enterprises, military organizations understand the criticality of studying the field of leadership, of developing their leaders, and of understanding the complex and dynamic nature of the arena in which that leadership will be tested—conflict and crisis. Such an endeavor requires not mindless robots centrally controlled by authoritarian dictators, with no discretion to act and incapable of creative thought, but independent and audacious teams led by innovative, knowledgeable, and dynamic leaders.

The *Marine Corps' Doctrinal Publication (MCDP)-1 Warfighting* (1997),[4] written to all Marines, not simply to senior commanders and generals, states,

> An even greater part of the conduct of war falls under the realm of art, which is the employment of creative or intuitive skills. Art includes the creative, situational application of scientific knowledge through judgment and experience, and so the art of war subsumes the science of war. The art of war requires the intuitive ability to grasp the essence of a unique military situation and the creative ability to devise a practical solution.

This "employment of creative or intuitive skills" applies every bit as much to the Lance Corporal/Fire Team Leader as it does to the Captain/Company Commander or Commandant of the Marine Corps. But its value does not flow simply from the authority and willingness of subordinates to depart from established orders or procedures. The value of this ability to devise practical solutions is derived from the fundamental doctrines of the profession, a thorough understanding of unit and organizational missions, and the comprehensive knowledge base and developed experience of the practitioner on which the "art" is based. Egon Bittner's analysis of the police as "a mechanism for the distribution of non-negotiably coercive force employed in accordance with the dictates of an intuitive grasp of situational exigencies" (Kappeler, 1970/1999) attempts to grapple with the same essence. So does the problem-oriented policing movement, although we have been somewhat more successful at articulating the underlying science than in achieving its artful application on the street.

For decades, the modern military has actively and purposely worked to develop leaders who can think independently, take action without detailed supervision, and create solutions to complex and rapidly changing problems. In fact, despite the overall degradation of leadership during the Vietnam and the post-Vietnam era, even the doctrine of that day touted the knowledge and creative ability of noncommissioned officers and junior officers as our major advantage over our more centrally controlled and absolutely rigid Soviet adversaries, which we were likely to meet en masse on the plains of Europe or, in the case of the Marine Corps, on the frozen tundra and mountains of Norway or the southern flank of NATO.

Modern doctrine has evolved much further. Again, from the *MCDP-1 Warfighting* (1997),

> First and foremost, in order to generate the tempo of operations we desire and to best cope with the uncertainty, disorder, and fluidity of combat, command and control must be decentralized. That is subordinate commanders must make decisions on their own initiative, based on their understanding of their senior's intent, rather than passing information up the chain of command and waiting for the decision to be passed down.

Military commanders and leaders down to the lowest levels are mandated to take action to solve problems and accomplish any and all assigned missions without detailed orders and with little or no supervision. In addition, this mandate to take action, to take risk, is backed by a doctrinal admonition against a "zero-defects" mentality that viciously condemns and punishes even the slightest mistake, which is a common practice in most rigid and highly authoritarian organizations (*FM 100-14: Risk Management,* 1998).

But the military does not simply talk about leadership. To achieve this kind of individual skill and level of leadership development within its ranks, the military services have implemented structural and operational methods that directly encourage independent and creative action. They have proactively, rationally, and purposely developed organizational systems that foster decentralization and participative decision making. Concepts such as mission tactics (telling subordinates what needs to be done, not how to do it) and commander's intent (a device designed to help subordinates understand the larger context of their actions, allowing them to depart from the original plan in the heat of battle in a way that is consistent with the aims of the higher commander) are specific operational methodologies designed to prevent micromanagement and oversupervision of subordinates while supporting initiative at the lowest possible level.[5] *Marine Corps' Doctrinal Publication 6, Command and Control (MCDP-6,* 1997) supports the principles articulated in *Warfighting (MCDP-1,*1997), officially defining the command and control process as "a dynamic, interactive process of cooperation" that occurs vertically within and laterally outside the chain of command.

That the authoritarian, centrally controlled concept of the military still persists in the minds of both advocates and critics, in spite of concrete operational practices and detailed and comprehensive official documentation to the contrary, is puzzling. It may be indicative of widespread animosity toward and ignorance of things military resulting from the Vietnam era. Or it may be something else entirely. Whatever the cause, this misunderstanding of military organizational and leadership doctrine has significantly affected the structure and leadership of modern policing in America.

The Result of Wrong Assumptions

The primary result of this mistaken view of military leadership has been the philosophical assumptions made concerning appropriate organizational and operational methods of policing as opposed to the military. Certainly, there is the assumption of a boot camp style of leadership, as the military model has caused many police leaders and line officers alike to assume the manner or at least the outlook of a drill sergeant, the "Yes, Sir. No, Sir. Three bags full, Sir!" arrogant expectation of autocratic micro-managers. This style of leadership (not even a true representation of leadership by boot camp drill instructors) has done within policing exactly what its critics decry: created organizations that are centrally controlled and highly inflexible, characterized by top-down order transmission and bottom-up reporting; less creative and more intellectually rigid individual officers bound to tradition and regulations, unable to deal effectively with both the dynamics of modern policing theories and the communities they serve; and a more combat/enforcement-oriented force, with a resulting increase in isolation from and hostility between police and citizens. It has been justly criticized and should be replaced, as it was by the military decades ago.

The adoption of this grossly inaccurate model of leadership and organization, mistakenly attributed to the military, has obviously distorted police perceptions and leadership methodologies. Confronted with complex organizational situations and relying only on their personal experience at the lowest levels of the military hierarchy, police leaders with limited organizational training and career development use the military model as a means to obtain immediate and absolute obedience to orders without question. With limited leadership and operational training to fall back on and routinely confronted with dangerous crisis situations in their communities, many police supervisors and managers depend on an organizational structure that supports top-down decision making and total submission to ensure their authority and status within the hierarchy and retain operational control. Coupled with a faulty assumption about the military, the assertion of paramilitary status by police agencies reinforces the poor leadership practices assumed to be an essential element of that profession.

Inaccurate assumptions and mistaken beliefs about how military organizations perform have caused the police profession to ignore and neglect important organizational concepts and structures that could radically improve their ability to enhance public safety. First, the misguided rejection of the military model (or the slavish adherence to the incorrect one) has contributed to the belief that the "crime-fighter" police officer is an independent operative. Fed by media images, most spectacularly the figure of "Dirty Harry" Callahan, this is the belief that the typical street-level police officer or investigator is considered the primary crime fighter, a "lone ranger" on patrol, operating apart and in isolation from his peers and wholly removed from the ever-watchful eye of his supervisors. Working within such a model, neither the officer nor the police department benefits from the very thing that makes organizations effective—the cooperative effort of multiple agents acting in concert that produces a more effective result than the sum of the individual agents acting alone: synergy.

This model also unnaturally separates the supervisor and upper management officers from the policing mission from the moment they are promoted. Police supervisors tend to monitor (from varying distances) the activities of individually operating subordinates who are engaged in crime fighting, but they are rarely involved in the direct application of their personnel and resources to the crime-fighting effort. Instead of an organizational outlook, police officers view themselves as individual crime fighters only to the point that they become supervisors, managers, administrators, and executives within the police department. To a greater or lesser extent (depending on the agency), all those above the lowest street-level ranks merely oversee and support the individual operational functions of line-level officers. They do not contribute, in any operational sense, to the organized policing or law enforcement effort—to actual crime fighting.

Figure 9.2
Actual Contrasts Between Military and Policing Professions

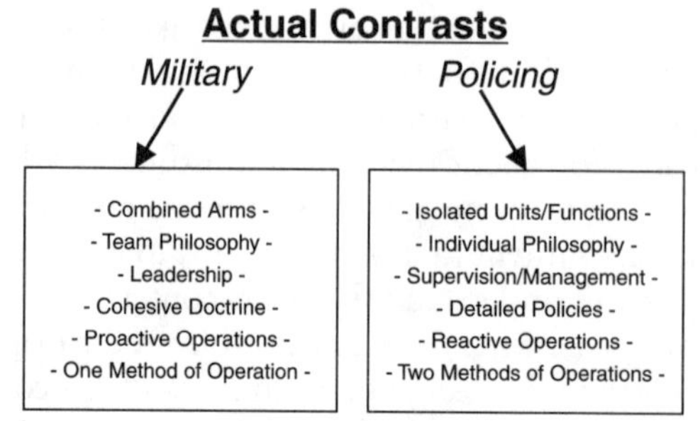

This individualized concept of organization is anathema to military professionals who view themselves as (and are by doctrine considered) "war fighters," whether they are on the front lines or on the general staff. The terms *supervisor* and *manager*, as occupational positions distinct from the war fighter, are not found in American military manuals, because supervision and management are considered merely individual components of effective leadership. All components and levels of the military hierarchy are engaged in the battle or conflict, each one planning, organizing, coordinating, and leading at his or her appropriate level or position but all working together to accomplish the operational war-fighting mission. Military personnel are either commanders or subordinates, fulfilling operational or support roles, in a line or a staff position. Not everyone is a "trigger puller," but everyone is a war fighter. And everyone up the chain of command actively participates in the war-fighting effort, not simply in supervising or managing the people involved in it.

There are numerous concepts or doctrines within the military that support and encourage this organizational war-fighting mentality that are almost completely missing in policing. The military actively employs concepts such as combined arms, which views successful war fighting as the highly coordinated employment of every organizational function or specialty in a mutually supporting manner and actively integrates all of the actions of an organization's resources and personnel to best operational advantage. Command and control, which gathers, collates, analyzes, and develops intelligence from all available information related to the warfighting effort, orchestrates operational planning and facilitates decision making based on the generated intelligence information and then coordinates and directs the timely and effective employment of those same resources toward a common goal. The concept of the commander himself, a person with extensive tactical, operational, and organizational leadership training, development, and experience in both line and staff positions, is the one person ultimately responsible for creating teamwork and the organizational and operational environment conducive to success. All of these distinctly military concepts increase the performance of organizations by improving the combined actions of the independent and creative individuals within them.[6]

Second, by automatically rejecting and/or fundamentally misunderstanding military theory and doctrine, policing has developed two completely divergent and incompatible modes of operation: the routine or daily mode of individual patrol and investigatory action, and the crisis mode of multiple unit response to serious and large-scale incidents. As previously stated, the common view of operational policing is that of the lone ranger on patrol, randomly operating in near isolation from his or her peers and largely removed from the directing/coordinating influence of his or her supervisor. This is the predominant method of operation in most departments, because crises tend to occur relatively infrequently, particularly in the smaller, suburban, and rural departments that make up the majority of American police agencies. With line-level officers operating independently and supervisors and managers doctrinally removed from the operational arena, untrained and unskilled in the art of employing personnel and resources in a combined and coordinated fashion, crisis situations have traditionally presented police departments with overwhelming challenges.

Correct use of military operational principles such as combined arms, command and control, and commandership could have significantly improved police responses during the Attica prison uprising, the MOVE confrontation in Philadelphia, the siege at the Branch Davidian compound in Waco, the Los Angeles Police Department response to the Rodney King riots, or the World Trade Organization riots in Seattle. Realizing this, the police officers themselves are beginning to learn the lessons of these and other less notable incidents by attempting to improve their own organizational response protocols. Although the police have attempted to adapt the Incident Command System (ICS) (a concept first developed by the Fire Service) to police use, it is often little more than a belated effort to organize resources during a crisis. The rudimentary police application of this process ignores the very methods of operation and leadership developed and refined over centuries by military organizations essentially for the same reasons. ICS is one method of organization that has been evolving over the past 20 years, with perhaps 10 years of significant police participation. But it suffers from structural inconsistencies and ignores fundamental organizational and operational doctrines, which tends to diminish its effectiveness and which, as already experienced by the military, could take many decades or longer to significantly improve and refine.[7]

But aside from its inherent imperfections, ICS's major flaw is that it is only used during a crisis. Because of the relative rarity of its employment, most police supervisors and managers do not generally understand how to function within it or use it properly. The traditional police dual mode methodology imposes a dangerous dichotomy between everyday operations and crisis operations. The policing solution to this dilemma (particularly in light of the police organizational methodology of removing supervisors and managers from the routine day-to-day crime fighting) has not been for sergeants and lieutenants and more senior police leaders to learn and understand ICS, the accepted system of organization and operation during larger emergencies. The predominant response has been to train one or a few specialists in the department, many times significantly junior people, to implement the ICS process at a critical incident. Senior police officials, those commanders who are ultimately responsible for the success or failure of these life-and-death situations and who receive the pay and recognition commensurate with their status, remain largely ignorant of the organizational and operational doctrine being used during a crisis. They simply and dangerously rely on operational specialists to advise them how to plan, operate, and employ their resources. The collective signal that this method of dealing with critical incidents sends throughout the profession is that if it is not important enough for our senior commanders and executives to study and understand, then it is not important.

In contrast, military organizations have one structure and one method of operation. Whether in garrison or in the field, during High Intensity Conflict or Operations Other Than War, units are organized and operations are carried out in the same manner. Commanders are always commanders; they are always involved in operations, and they always understand the operational principles governing them and their units. Individuals are intimately familiar with operational procedures because they operate, conceptually speaking, the same way day in and day out, whether it is routine training, humanitarian relief, peacekeeping, or all-out war. Police organizations could dramatically improve both their routine and crisis operations under the same type of consistent methodology.[8]

The rejection of things military by the policing profession has also drastically hindered our ability to create improvements in our current doctrine and operational methods. ICS has already been mentioned. But an even more recent "innovation" in police operations has been the concept of the COMPSTAT Process (Safir, n.d.)—the use of crime data and statistics to direct police response to crime trends and patterns and hold jurisdictional commanders responsible for efforts to reduce and eliminate them. COMPSTAT is a highly simplified form of military operational planning that uses tactical and strategic intelligence data to drive operations. It is comparatively elementary in that it fails to seek and understand the theories and concepts behind the method—the differences between tactical and strategic information/data; principles such as unity of command and combined arms operations; and the interaction and relationships between commanders, their staffs, and their operational units. It fails to address the organizational structures and operational practices (such as those mentioned above and others) that contribute to successful resolution of the identified problems. COMPSTAT is an attempt to produce genuine results by treating organizational symptoms (lack of accountability, intradepartmental coordination, bottom-up information flow) in isolation from the wider systemic factors and issues in the department that actually drive operations.

The military, philosophically accomplishing the same types of missions with the same types of resources, has developed and has been developing the theories and methods to do its job for centuries. The doctrines are sound and the methodologies are effective, albeit ever changing and improving. The philosophical concepts are directly applicable to law enforcement, with only minor and insignificant modification. Many of the operational and structural techniques are largely appropriate to our profession. Yet, it is the leadership, the kind of leadership that creates the esprit and morale and professionalism found in today's armed forces, that today's police forces should be most emulating.

Conclusion

The modern military has centuries of history, traditions, and lessons on which are based current doctrines and operational methodologies. Today's military leaders continually glean the best examples and messages from ancient historians and warfare theorists, incorporating what has been proven over the course of time to be successful into contemporary situations and practices, modifying and building on changeable ideas, and rejecting those that are or are becoming antiquated and outdated. The U.S. armed forces have an active and integrated "Lessons Learned" program that incorporates existing doctrine with detailed and open after-action critique designed to speed improvement in operational and structural methodologies. The modern military profession has solid operational and leadership doctrine on which its entire existence and methodologies are based—doctrine that is constantly being improved upon and that has directly contributed to its tactical and strategic victories over the past 20 years.

There is no doubt that the combination of the military with police in the United States would and does meet with severe opposition among the citizenry, and rightly so. This article in no way advocates the militarization of policing in America in the sense of heavy-handed storm troopers and "jack-booted thugs" usurping fundamental constitutional freedoms through combat-oriented actions. The unbridled use of total war tactics and highly destructive weaponry must be avoided within our borders, against our citizens. Military forces and police forces should always be completely separate and different organizations in a free society. In fact, the military customs, courtesies, traditions, and accoutrements, the "Yes, sir. No, sir. Three bags full, sir!" historic trappings of warrior poets that authoritative police managers treasure far more than substantive military practices, hold no relevance to policing and should be abandoned.

But there is also no doubt that conceptually, our missions and objectives are strikingly similar. Furthermore, our adversaries are becoming increasingly sophisticated and tactically adept, requiring a much more organized and capable operational response on the part of civilian police agencies if we intend to be successful without direct military support or intervention. Without dramatic improvement in the tactical and strategic organization of American law enforcement agencies, a reliance on armed military units to supplement police could be an inevitable result. As such, we should study and adopt the particular organizational and operational doctrines and methodologies that the military has developed that are applicable to our profession. A correct view of the military and the incorporation of specific military theories and practices into policing will improve the way we do business, give us a distinct strategic and tactical advantage over any criminal adversary within our borders, and make our operations safer and less prone to violent resolution. It can only benefit America's police departments, and ultimately the citizens we serve, if we look at the military model as it truly is: a highly professional and organizationally mature profession and not as the aberration that many think it is—the rigid dinosaurs of wars long lost

Notes

1. E-mail discussion with Dr. Michael Buerger, associate professor of criminal justice at Northeastern University, Boston, Massachusetts; and Alberto Melis, now chief in Waco, Texas. In referring to the "police agent" concept, Buerger referenced *The Task Force Report on the Police of the President's Commission on Law Enforcement and Administration of Justice* (1967). Departments mentioned as experimenting with various other nonmilitary modes and methods include Lauderhill, Florida; Aspen, Colorado; and San Jose, California.
2. See *FMFRP 12-41* (1989). Although not difficult to see the obvious similarities between a SWAT team conducting a hostage rescue at a failed bank robbery and the British Special Air Service conducting a hostage rescue at the Iranian Embassy in London, it is perhaps a bit more abstract to view routine police operations, particularly community policing efforts, in light of military tactics and operational leadership. But the analogy remains strikingly via-

ble. War fighting and crime fighting philosophies are not mutually exclusive.

3. See Cincinnatus (1981).
4. *Marine Corps' Doctrinal Publication (MCDP)-1 Warfighting* (1997) is the Marine Corps' foundational document concerning fundamental doctrine, that is, the philosophical framework for the way the Marine Corps conducts its business. It is required reading for all Marines and is the nexus of all other doctrinal publications. Most current Marine Corps doctrinal publications may be found on the Internet at http://www.doctrine.quantico.usmc.mil/.
5. Mission tactics is the process of assigning subordinates specific missions and leaving the manner of accomplishing those missions completely in their hands. The use of mission tactics by an organization relies on the exercise of initiative and creative thinking by subordinates and allows them the freedom to take whatever steps are necessary to solve problems and accomplish their mission based on their own available resources and the unique and rapidly changing situations that they face. To allow widely divergent subordinates this decentralized freedom of decision and action and still attain a common organizational goal in the most effective manner possible, there must be a means of focusing and coordinating the various independent subordinate efforts. Commander's intent allows subordinates to exercise their own initiative based on the immediate and uniquely changing circumstances confronting them in a way that is consistent with the higher commander's aims in accomplishing the overall mission. There are two components to any mission: the task to be accomplished and the reason behind it. Every mission has an intended purpose or the reason for accomplishing the task. With an understanding of the intent of a particular mission, responsible and free-thinking subordinates are allowed to exercise informed initiative in harmony with the commander's original desires. Situations routinely change, making accomplishment of specific tasks obsolete and perhaps even counterproductive, whereas the original intention can continue to guide actions.
6. From *MCDP-6, Command and Control* (1997): "The aim is not to increase our capacity to perform command and control. It is not more command and control that we are after. Instead, we seek to decrease the amount of command and control that we need. We do this by replacing coercive command and control methods with spontaneous, self-disciplined cooperation based on low-level initiative, a commonly understood commander's intent, mutual trust, and implicit understanding and communications."
7. The military, like policing, is organized along line and staff functions. As such, it has developed an organizational doctrine and a structure to support it that, like the Incident Command System (ICS), attempts to aid the planning and conduct of operations along with the commander's decision-making process. ICS has no fundamental organizational doctrine on which it is based and is a process and structure that does not correspond with normal police operations. Its structure tends to blur the distinctions between command and staff functions. The role and purpose of the commander, chain and unity of command, and the functional relationships between the staff, the operational units, and their mutual commander are ambiguous and confusing, particularly when implemented rarely, during crises.
8. The military views mobilized operations—for example, war, humanitarian relief, peacekeeping, nation building, and so forth—as an extended form of everyday or peacetime operations. Commanders and their units, composed of a functional staff along with the subordinate operational units that they support, are organized and operate, at least conceptually, in the same manner all the time. The tempo and urgency of operations will change with the level of crisis, but the structure and managerial/command relationships of the organization remain constant. Civilian ICS, as a separate and distinct form of organization only employed during a crisis, is inherently at odds with the basic method of daily police operations and its standard organizational structures and command relationships.

References

Cincinnatus. (1981). *Self-destruction.* New York: Norton.

FMFRP 12-41: Professional knowledge gained from operational experience in Vietnam, 1967. (1989).

Washington, DC: Department of the Navy, United States Marine Corps.

FM 100-14: Risk management. (1998). Washington, DC: Department of the Army.

Heinl, R. D., Jr. (1966). *Dictionary of military and naval quotations.* Annapolis, MD: U.S. Naval Institute.

Kappeler, V. E. (Ed.). (1999). *Police and society: Touchstone readings* (2nd ed.). Prospect Heights, IL: Waveland Press. (Reprinted from *The functions of the police in modern society,* by E. Bitmer, 1970, Chevy Chase, MD: National Institute of Mental Health.)

Kopel, D. B., & Blackman, P. M. (1997). Can soldiers be peace officers? The Waco disaster and the militarization of American law enforcement. *Akron Law Review,* 619–659. Littleton, CO: Fred B Rothman & Company.

Marine Corps' Doctrinal Publication (MCDP)-1, Warfighting (1997). Washington, DC: Department of the Navy, Headquarters United States Marine Corps.

Marine Corps' Doctrinal Publication (MCDP)-6, Command and Control (1997). Washington, DC: Department of the Navy, Headquarters United States Marine Corps.

Safir, H. (n.d.). *The COMPSTAT process.* New York: NYC Office of Management Analysis and Planning.

Sun Tzu. (1971) *The art of war* (S. B. Griffith, Trans.). London: Oxford University Press.

The task force report on the police of the president's commission on law enforcement and administration of justice. (1967). Washington, DC: U.S. Government Printing Office.

Taylor, R. L., & Rosenbach, W. E. (Eds.). (1996). *Military leadership: In pursuit of excellence* (3rd ed.). Boulder, CO: Westview.

Trojanowicz, R., & Bucqueroux, B. (1990). *Community policing.* Cincinnati, OH: Anderson.

Weber, D. C. (1999). *Warrior cops: The ominous growth of paramilitarism in American police departments* (CATO Institute Briefing Papers No. 50). Washington, DC: CATO Institute.

Thomas J. Cowper, "The Myth of the 'Military Model' of Leadership in Law Enforcement." Reprinted from *Police Quarterly,* Vol. 3 No. 3, September 2000, pp. 228–246. Copyright © 2000 by Sage Publications, Inc. Reprinted by permission of Sage Publications, Inc. ✦

Chapter 10
Reinventing Government

The Views of Police Middle Managers

Gennaro F. Vito
Julie Kunselman

The authors examine the views of police middle managers regarding the best and worst practices for reforming and maintaining operations within a public safety organization. Citing data from thirty-five middle managers attending a twelve-week course at the University of Louisville's Southern Police Institute, they report how respondents reacted to ideas from Osborne and Gaebler's 1992 book Reinventing Government.

Vito and Kunselman note that police middle managers are key figures in the organizational climate of law enforcement agencies. Accordingly, the support of middle managers in the evolution of community policing is essential. The authors assert that middle managers view partnerships with citizens, reductions in social distance between the police and local residents, and decentralization as positive developments in modern policing. However, dissimilar to other public service agencies, the police must deliver a broad range of public services and do so while balancing the public's need for social justice. The mandate of policing poses some uniquely challenging problems for the reinvention of police organizations.

Osborne and Gaebler's (1992) *Reinventing Government* is based on the premise that accountability to customers and efficient management will make government agencies more effective. The authors stressed the need to establish "entrepreneurial government" through the use of private-sector techniques such as reorganization, downsizing, privatization, and total quality management to introduce competition in the public sector. The book was a *New York Times* bestseller that influenced the National Performance Review spearheaded at the federal level by Vice President Al Gore (see Kamensky, 1996, 1998). Osborne was a major policy advisor to that effort. The challenges presented in this text have not gone unnoticed. Here, we extend the critique of the themes of *Reinventing Government* through an analysis of the views of police middle managers.

Government middle managers are singled out in *Reinventing Government* as enemies of change. They typically resist efforts to decentralize authority and establish participatory management (Osborne & Gaebler, 1992, p. 265). The assumption is that if such changes are implemented, middle managers fear the loss of their power position in the organization. Similar criticisms have been leveled against police middle managers in the implementation of community policing.

However, several authors have argued that this criticism is simplistic. It ignores the crucial role that the middle manager plays in any governmental reform effort. For example, middle managers facilitate change by performing duties that are overlooked by other functionaries, such as reconciling differences between agencies that provide related services, facilitating interorganizational service standards, and reading the community culture. These roles promote cooperation between governmental units and promote efficiency and operational change (Morgan, Bacon, Bunch, Cameron, & Deis, 1996).

The middle manager has been identified as the linchpin in police reform efforts. In their review of community policing efforts in five cities, Kelling and Bratton (1993) recommended that police middle managers be included in the planning process. Their involvement can provide instrumental leadership. If they are excluded, they can become a source of resistance. The support of police middle managers must be sought and enlisted to implement and maintain operational and organizational reform. They control the department's value system and professional environment and have the power to squash reforms such as community policing (Sparrow, Moore, & Kennedy, 1990, pp. 213–214).

Reinventing Government: A Summary

To revive the essential role that governments and public agencies play in society, *Reinventing Government* proposes 10 reforms and 36 strategies, including the following (Rainey, 1997, pp. 364–365; Russell & Waste, 1998, p. 327):

- Anticipatory government: Focus on prevention techniques for problem solving through use of strategic planning, anticipatory management, and long-range budgeting.
- Catalytic government: Government should "steer" rather than "row." Promote use of private- and nonprofit-sector resources for service delivery.
- Community-owned government: Empower communities to participate in government agencies. Ensures accountability of programs to community-based groups.
- Competitive government: Introduce competition between public and private sectors to promote efficiency of service delivery.
- Customer-driven government: Empower citizens (customers) to participate in government agencies. Ensures programs and delivery of services are tailored to customer needs.
- Decentralized government: Agency shift in hierarchical structure, that is, flattening out of hierarchical ladder to empower all agency workers to be responsible and accountable in decision-making process and program procedure.
- Enterprising government: Promotes profit-making and resource-maximizing programs as objectives of the agency.
- Market-oriented government: Promotes agency goals and services through use of economic market mechanisms.
- Mission-driven government: Guides program services and outputs using the mission of the agency rather than by following bureaucratic rules and regulations.
- Results-oriented government: Implement evaluation and performance procedures to emphasize outcomes rather than inputs.

Again, the overarching theme of these proposals is to make the government more responsive by introducing competition and a customer perspective in agency services.

Critiques of *Reinventing Government*

Critiques of the themes of *Reinventing Government* are legion in the public administration literature. Here, we focus on several elements of these critiques that are of particular relevance to policing.

One criticism of *Reinventing Government* is its use of the customer metaphor. For example, the National Performance Review stresses the need for a new customer service contract. Administrators and employees should give taxpayers the same responsiveness and consideration businesses supposedly give customers (Schacter, 1995, p. 530). Thus, government agencies should aim to satisfy their customers.

Schacter (1995) considers this a flawed analogy. She notes that many public agency clients would prefer to have no contact with the bureaucracy—for example, the "involuntary" customers of the criminal justice system. In some agencies, such as police departments, strong conflicts of interest exist that make it difficult for many departments to identify who their customers are and how they can satisfy customer needs. The customer analogy may also cause problems of equity in the provision of services. It can lead to a focus on the views of middle-class citizens who may not be concerned if agencies deliver equal services to rich and poor. In fact, equity of service has been identified as a problem in the establishment of community policing in Chicago and Houston (Skogan, 1994; Skogan & Hartnett, 1997). Community policing can be difficult in places where the community is fragmented by race, class, and lifestyle.

In place of the customer analogy, Schacter (1995) promotes the development of an "efficient citizenship" model. "Citizen-owners" must learn about the success of an entire enterprise rather than focus on how a particular agency responds to their individual demands. She calls for citizens to reinvent themselves as active citizens who take an ownership role over government and public agencies (see also Frederickson, 1996, p. 267). They must participate directly in the activities and services provided by public agencies.

Yet as Russell and Waste (1998) point out, a call for active participation is another problem surrounding the implementation of the *Reinventing Government* model. They argue that most citizens do not participate in the daily affairs of government. For example, community policing requires public participation, yet communities discovered this requirement has a significant limitation. Russell and Waste (1998, p. 335) note that even participation that follows a terrible crime quickly dissipates in most cases.

In fact, obtaining and sponsoring a high level of community involvement is a common problem in the implementation of community policing. Grinc (1994) reported on this problem in his evaluation of eight cites that were involved in innovative neighborhood-oriented policing. All program sites faced extreme difficulty in establishing a solid community infrastructure on which to build their community-oriented policing (COP) programs. The existing level of hostility between the police and the community was largely ignored or overlooked. There was a tendency to grossly underestimate the level of hostility between the police and the minority communities that have borne the brunt of past police abuses. As Buerger (1994) notes, the crucial task facing community organizations (with or without COP) is to rebuild the human capital of besieged areas.

Balancing the forces of efficiency and the desire for fairness is another challenge to reinventors. Frederickson (1996) states that reinventing government promotes "short-run increases in efficiency purchased at a likely long-range cost in administrative capacity and social equity" (p. 263). Russell and Waste (1998, p. 339) note that the criminal justice system has great difficulty squaring up such discrepancies. Efficiency typically clashes with the provision of due process of law throughout the criminal justice system. Is it desirable or wise to promote efficiency (or crime control) in a system where fairness and justice (due process of law) is a paramount value?

Finally, Rainey (1998, pp. 166–176) highlights the "blurred vision" of reinvention that fails to address the challenge of implementing the proposed changes in governmental and agency operations. Crucial issues such as empowering lower level employees, the rapid political turnover of politically elected executives and their appointees, residual skepticism about changes that have failed in the past, and the need to support and protect innovators in the system are largely ignored (see also Thompson & Sanders, 1998). Thus, the supporters of reform can be set adrift without the support they need to see it through.

This analysis extends the debate over the merits of *Reinventing Government* beyond academe to the realm of police management practitioners.

Methodology

The Administrative Officers Course at the Southern Police Institute

The data in this article reflect the views of students attending the Administrative Officers

Course (AOC) at the Southern Police Institute (SPI) at the University of Louisville. Created in 1951 under a Ford Foundation grant, the SPI is a division of the Department of Justice Administration in the College of Arts and Sciences at the University of Louisville. It is an advanced management institute whose mission is to enhance the professional development of law enforcement practitioners. It is consistently ranked among the top law enforcement educational and training schools in the world.

The AOC is a 12-week, accredited college-level educational program. Undergraduate students can receive 12 units and graduate students 9 units of credit during the 12-week course that is offered twice during the academic year. The course curriculum is designed to develop informed, effective, ethically and technically competent law enforcement managers who are capable of assuming positions of leadership in their agencies. This comprehensive managerial development program provides instruction in leadership, administrative management, personnel issues, organizational behavior, current issues in law enforcement, problem solving, and administrative law. The AOC is recognized throughout the United States as one of the four or five outstanding police management development programs in existence.

Sample

Although not a probability sample, this group of police administrators does represent 35 agencies from as far north as Alaska and as far south as Florida. Twenty-one students came from local police agencies with a mean size of 316 officers (range = 12–1,022) and serving an average population of 137,976 residents (range = 22,000–364,040). Nine students were working for county law enforcement agencies with an average size of 639 officers (range = 124–1,700), serving an average population of 561,670 citizens (range = 104,605–1 million). Five students were from state law enforcement agencies, with an average size of 1,946 officers. In terms of police organizational rank, there were 16 sergeants, 13 lieutenants, 3 captains, and 2 corporals among the respondents.

The use of this convenience sample can be questioned. These officers were volunteers—motivated administrators who were attending the SPI to further their careers in police management. Therefore, they may not be perfectly representative of the corps of police middle managers across the United States. However, it would be impossible to conduct a survey of police administrators who have read these texts in any other fashion. A sampling frame of such police administrators simply would not be available. In addition, a mailed questionnaire-type survey is unlikely to elicit the in-depth responses that were gathered for this analysis.

Method

The data for this analysis came from the answers of AOC students to take-home examination questions. These respondents were enrolled in the graduate option course JA 665: Special Topics in Policing. During the course, students were required to read *Reinventing Government.* However, neither the text nor its themes were discussed in class until the examinations were collected. The results were compiled over three semesters of classes. In the examination, students were asked to give their views of the methods and techniques presented in these texts by answering the following question:

> In *Reinventing Government,* the authors present many ideas to reform governmental operations. Select the three best and the three worst ideas that could apply to police administration. Defend your selections carefully. What is the significance of these ideas to the modern police administrator? How can police administrators use them?

Their answers were limited to 5 to 10 typewritten, double-spaced pages. They were also submitted on computer diskette. These answers were the basis of our analysis.

The responses of the participants were analyzed via content-analysis methods presented by Weber (1990). The responses were tabulated by a student in accordance with the test question. Their answers were tabulated according to whether the respondent identified an element of *Reinventing Government* as a good or bad idea for police administration. The number of responses was compiled, and a listing of categories for each idea was developed. Finally, quotations that best represented the views of the respondents were compiled for each idea.

Results

The 'Best' Ideas From *Reinventing Government*

Table 10.1 presents results of the rankings of the ideas listed in *Reinventing Government* that the police middle managers identified as "best." In accordance with the original question, we will focus on the top three ideas as ranked by the respondents. The top-ranked idea was community-owned government—to empower communities to participate in government agencies and ensure accountability of programs to community-based groups (65.7%). The reasons cited by the majority of respondents for this selection were as follows:

- It empowers the community and its citizens (15/23 = 65.2%).
- It redefines the role of the police as a community resource (15/23 = 65.2%). It grants ownership to the client (12/23 = 52.2%).

Table 10.1
Elements of Reinventing Government *Identified by Police Middle Managers as "Best"*

Type of Government	*n* (Percentage) of Respondents Selecting	
Community owned	23	(65.7)
Customer driven	19	(54.3)
Decentralized	13	(37.1)
Competitive	12	(34.3)
Anticipatory	11	(31.3)
Mission driven	9	(25.7)
Catalytic	8	(22.9)
Results oriented	8	(22.9)
Enterprising	3	(8.6)
Market oriented	2	(5.7)

Of course, the dominant police reform of the age—community policing—is an example of community-owned government in action. It may be that the popularity of this idea with the respondents is due to their familiarity and experience with community policing.

The following quotes are illustrative of the respondent's reasons for supporting the idea of community-owned government.

> The bureaucracy of the traditional style of police agency has lost sight of [empowerment]. The police created a dependency on their services to solve community issues.

> The community relied on professional police officers to solve the social crimes and the citizens in the community became dependent on this service. The idea of professionalism blinded the police and the community. The responsibility to control and take pride in a community was removed from the citizens.

Although supporting this concept, some respondents were skeptical of the ability of police departments to follow through with it.

> Although I am certain that "empowering communities" as suggested by the text is the way to go, I am not certain that [law enforcement] is organizationally prepared to accept that premise. . . . The concept is still hard for many traditionalists to accept.

Community policing also stresses the need for collaboration with citizens as coproducers and partners in public safety.

The second most popular idea (identified by 54.3% of the respondents), customer-driven government (empowering citizens as customers to participate in government agencies), is a closely aligned extension of the first. Here are the reasons listed by the majority of respondents for this selection:

- The use of customer surveys can provide valuable information to police departments (12/19 = 63.2%).

- It generates valuable feedback from customers (11/19 = 57.9%).
- It allows police to focus on citizen concerns (10/19 = 52.6%).

Once again, the aims of customer-driven government are a reflection of the norms of community policing. A significant component of community policing is the "customer satisfaction" criterion—satisfying the concerns expressed by the public (Skogan & Hartnett, 1997, p. 8).

Expressions of support for customer-driven government included the following:

> Many new and innovative ideas can be generated by feedback from citizens. For example, in our city, citizens were not satisfied with the department's response to domestic assaults. Citizens demanded more and eventually got the local city council to pass a local ordinance not only authorizing an arrest on probable cause in misdemeanor domestic assault cases but also actually mandating such an arrest. This has resulted in citizens being much more satisfied with the police response now. And none of it would have happened without the public pressure.

This quote is an example of how citizens can act as customers to get a response to a particular problem by police departments.

The third most popular idea was decentralized government, featuring a shift in agency structure to empower workers to be responsible and accountable in decision-making processes and program procedure (37.1% of the respondents). The majority of respondents fit the following categories for this ranking.

- It can increase employee job satisfaction and commitment to the job (10/13 = 76.9%).
- Here, administrators invest in employees (9/13 = 69.2%).
- It empowers workers (7/13 = 53.8%).
- It recognizes the expertise of the line worker (7/13 = 53.8%).
- It promotes police/community partnerships (7/13 = 53.8%).
- It emphasizes participatory management (7/13 = 53.8%).

These elements are yet another feature of community policing. It stresses the need for organizational decentralization to grant line officers more decision-making authority to investigate autonomously, solve neighborhood problems, and work with the public directly. In Chicago, the rank of captain was abolished under community policing. The rationale was that the departments that are committed to pushing authority and responsibility down to the neighborhood and street level often find that flattening the rank structure goes hand in hand with decentralization and increased organizational nimbleness (Skogan & Hartnett, 1997, pp. 60–62). Such implementation of community policing clearly fits the definition of decentralized government.

The following quote is representative of the support that these police middle managers expressed for decentralized government:

> Officer morale is higher in police agencies which allow the officers to make decisions about how the work is to be done (along with the community, of course). Officers appreciate the fact that their abilities are trusted, and they seem to work harder at coming up with vital solutions to important problems. Officers in these types of agencies are more flexible. Their approach to problem solving and the skills that accompany their approach are dependent upon their ability to make decisions and the recognition by management that they may sometimes fail. Police agencies that empower their officers seem to do a better job of coming up with new ideas that are more innovative and take into account the resources that are available from the public sector. They have learned teamwork as a tool for arriving at better solutions to problems.

Improving the morale of both the citizens and line staff of the police department was clearly behind the support of these police middle managers for this idea.

THE 'WORST' IDEAS FROM *REINVENTING GOVERNMENT*

Table 10.2 presents respondent rankings of the "worst" ideas in *Reinventing Government.* In accordance with the original question, we will focus on the top three ideas as ranked by the respondents. The top ranked worst idea was enterprising government (57.1%). It promotes potential profit-making and resource-maximizing programs and makes it possible for the agency to exercise initiative, especially during lean years. However, the police middle managers foresaw some problems with this approach.

- It is unethical and unfair for police departments to charge additional fees for service (12/20 = 60%).
- The police represent Public Service (9/20 = 45%).
- It raises a potential conflict. If the police focus on profit, they will lose sight of their true goals (8/20 = 40%).

These categories all reflect the idea that it is distasteful, and perhaps even dangerous, for the police to charge fees for service. It could lead to corruption and gross inequities in service delivery based on the ability to pay.

In addition, representative quotes from the respondents reveal other problems with this method.

> Traffic fines are a mainstay of government revenue, and the police are routinely accused of quota setting to generate revenues. The goals of highway safety are lost in the mix.

> Several years ago, my department started charging for several services that we had performed free for years. The department now charges $10 per person to role applicant fingerprints and $25 if we successfully unlock a car door. The total take from these two services per year is less than $3,000. This money goes into the city's general fund, and the decision to institute these charges came from city council. This money is only a drop in the bucket when compared to the department's almost $8 million budget.

Not only could the police be viewed as driven by bounties for service, but the potential gain from such enterprises could be minimal and ultimately not worth the effort. Yet, fees for service have become common in policing. For example, police departments routinely charge businesses for false burglar alarms. The false alarms become a nuisance and something of a public danger when they reach a certain point, because they can draw officers out of service. The aim of such fees is deterrence—to stop the false alarms—but they also pass on a cost to the consumer that should not be borne by the public.

Another example is the Kentucky Derby in Louisville. Churchill Downs management pays a substantial fee for increased police present during that event. However, there is a crucial difference between such fees for service on a case-by-case basis and the aggressive pursuit of revenue by a public agency. That is precisely the danger of enterprising government that these police middle managers stressed.

Table 10.2
Elements of Reinventing Government *Identified by Police Middle Managers as "Worst"*

Type of Government	*n* (Percentage) of Respondents Selecting	
Enterprising	20	(57.1)
Competitive	18	(51.4)
Results oriented	16	(45.7)
Market oriented	11	(31.4)
Mission driven	8	(22.9)
Catalytic	8	(22.9)
Community owned	2	(5.7)
Anticipatory	2	(5.7)
Decentralized	2	(5.7)
Customer driven	1	(2.9)

The second-ranked worst idea was competitive government (51.4%)—the introduction of competition between public and private sectors to promote efficiency of service delivery. The top justifications for this ranking were as follows:

- It could undermine the quality and professionalism of the police (6/18 = 33.3%).
- The police should not be focused on making money (5/18 = 27.8%).
- Personnel in competing agency may not be well trained (4/18 = 22.2%).

The following quote is an accurate illustration of the respondent's concerns about these issues:

> The goals of the criminal justice system would be better served by agencies working together and coordinating activities, rather than isolating themselves in hopes of generating more successes than an adjoining agency. By increasing emphasis on competition between departments in different jurisdictions, there may also be a tendency to push problems out of one jurisdiction into another, transplanting the problem rather than solving it.

An example of the problems associated with introducing a public-private competition in policing is Lexington, Kentucky. Under a state statute, employees of the LexCin Special Enforcement Company have become a private police force in downtown Lexington. Armed with 9 mm pistols and handcuffs, they have a "self described mission to clean up the streets outside the Triangle Center and the PNC Bank" (Associated Press, 2000, p. B4). They have arrested and taken to jail homeless persons for third-degree criminal trespass. Lexington police chief Larry Walsh argues that the LexCin employees are largely untrained and unsophisticated compared to sworn police officers: "The job of a police department and its relationship with the surrounding community is too complicated for such ambiguities" (Associated Press, 2000, p. B4). Again, the introduction of competition in the delivery of police services raises questions of equity and justice to the public at large.

Yet, competitive government was also ranked by these respondents as the fourth best idea (12 respondents, 34.3%). Some respondents had little trouble seeing the benefits of competition when public agencies other than the police were involved.

> Four years ago, our police department looked at the way it was currently purchasing, equipping, and placing into service its new patrol cars. The traditional method was to have the city shops order the cars, the equipment, and to install the equipment. The police department would be billed for the cars, the equipment, and to install the equipment. . . . The funds from the police department's budget to cover the costs would be transferred electronically. No one within the police department seemed to know what it was costing to put a police car in service, not to mention the fact that the city shops generally took several months to get the car into service. . . . Several private vendors bid along with the city shops. When the final bid was selected, the department realized a $2,700 savings per vehicle, plus the turnaround time was cut down from 3 months to 2 weeks.

Such competition for the service sought by the police department was viewed as cost-effective and beneficial.

Other respondents noted the potential of competition within the police department itself.

> Establishment of an internal grant program where Divisions compete by submitting imaginative and resourceful ideas. [This] could undoubtedly increase performance, funding projects that are useful and resourceful, rewarding innovation and increasing morale by compensating hard work.

For such reasons, the idea of competitive government was cited as both a best and worst idea.

The third worst idea listed by the police middle managers was results-oriented government—the implementation of evaluation and performance procedures to emphasize outcomes rather than inputs (45.7%). Here, measurement issues were consistently raised as a problem.

- The problem of valid, accurate measurement of police performance (11/16 = 68.8%).
- Police work is hard to define—cannot quantify service (7/16 = 43.8%).

The problems of adequately measuring effectiveness in policing are expressed in the following quotes:

> Quantity is measured but is not attached to any particular individual or group of individuals that are responsible for the results. Objectives are set on a department, division, and section level, but are not encouraged on an individual level. Quality is measured with the aid of a survey to members of the community and is used as a tool at satisfying politicians' interest in the department's performance. Cost is rarely ever measured.

> The circumstances under which police operate are constantly changing. Crime is displaced, criminals move, some programs improve the quality of life and the police then leave an area, funding is cut or changed, new leaders are installed, and the types of crimes that the public wants to give attention to change. All of these factors have direct influence on the ability of a police agency to do its job. This is why it is unfair to try and fund based on outcome.

Of course, these issues are a part of the debate surrounding the accurate evaluation of police services. Accurate criteria must be developed to assess the quality and effectiveness of current reforms such as community policing, problem-oriented policing, and COMPSTAT (see Brady, 1996; Bratton, 1998; Safir, 1997; Silverman, 1999).

Conclusion

Why are the views of police middle managers important? Reforms such as those listed in *Reinventing Government* will be implemented by these public servants. They must turn ideas into practice. Their views are based on their experience as managers who came up from the line. Although *Reinventing Government* is chock-full of examples from the field, the blanket prescriptions made must be tested by public agencies individually. Their missions and target populations are different. Methods that are appropriate for one type of agency may be disastrous for another. It is important to consider the views of managers in different agencies when such reforms are proposed.

For example, the customer analogy is particularly flawed when it is applied to police agencies. Customers demand satisfaction, and the police cannot satisfy the demands of complaining victims and/or suspects simultaneously or often individually. Complaining victims may be viewed as customers, but they may present unrealistic demands such as immediate arrest or recovery of stolen property. The police cannot always please a neighborhood that may not want certain "types of people" on their streets.

The partnership metaphor is more in order. Equity is a value that must be promoted by the police. Police officers are servants of the law, often above the wishes of a customer. Suspects may wish to avoid arrest when it is clearly called for. The suspect as client is a better analogy for the police. Clients' rights must be protected, and the use of force must be reviewed.

The only analogy worse than the customer is the ownership metaphor. Citizens who demand service because "my taxes pay your salary" are unlikely to be well received. If someone owns the police, all of society is in danger.

Overall, the views of these police middle managers reflect cautious support for the changes expressed in *Reinventing Government.* Clearly, the elements of reinvention that reflected the ideals of community policing were supported. They see great promise in the empowerment of citizens to establish a partnership with the police to improve the type and level of service delivery. A reduction in the social distance between the public and police was viewed as beneficial. The organizational structures wrought by community policing, particularly decentralization, were cited as the keys to job satisfaction and organizational efficiency. The crucial contributions of the line officer were recognized.

Respondents attacked other ideas as inequitable, unethical, or inefficient. They agreed with the critiques of reinvention that public agencies such as the police must pay strict attention to social equity in service delivery. Entrepreneurship that leads to improved efficiency, effectiveness, and customer satisfaction must be carefully balanced with justice. These issues are particularly important where police management is concerned. Their unique status as a public agency that can engage in the use of deadly force and arrest must be considered and balanced against broad, market-based reforms. The police, unlike other public agencies, do not deliver a narrowly defined good or service. As the answers of these police middle managers reflect, police reforms must be carefully considered and balanced against competing interests and the public's notion of social justice.

References

Associated Press. (2000, March 20). Private police make arrests in Lexington. *The Courier Journal*, p. B4.

Brady, T. V. (1996). Measuring what matters, part one: Measures of crime, fear, and disorder. In *National Institute of Justice: Research in action.* Washington, DC: U.S. Department of Justice.

Bratton, W. (with Knobler, P.). (1998). *Turnaround: How America's top cop reversed the crime epidemic.* New York: Random House.

Buerger, M. E. (1994). A tale of two targets: Limitations of community anticrime actions. *Crime & Delinquency, 40* (3), 411–436.

Frederickson, H. G. (1996). Comparing the reinventing government movement with the new public administration. *Public Administration Review, 56,* 263–270.

Grinc, R. M. (1994). "Angels in marble": Problems in stimulating community involvement in community policing. *Crime & Delinquency, 40* (3), 437–468.

Kamensky, J. M. (1996). Role of the "reinventing government" movement in federal management reform. *Public Administration Review, 56,* 247–256.

Kamensky, J. M. (1998). The best kept secret in government: How the NPR translated theory into practice. In P W. Ingraham, J. R. Thompson, & R. P Sanders (Eds.), *Transforming government: Lessons from the reinvention laboratories* (pp. 58–96). San Francisco: Jossey-Bass.

Kelling, G. L., & Bratton, W. J. (1993, July). Implementing community policing: The administrative problem. *Perspectives on Policing, 17.* Washington, DC: U.S. Department of Justice.

Morgan, D., Bacon, K. G., Bunch, R., Cameron, C. D., & Deis, R. (1996). What middle managers do in local government: Stewardship of the public trust and the limits of reinventing government. *Public Administration Review, 56* (4), 359–365.

Osborne, D., & Gaebler, T. (1992). *Reinventing government: How the entrepreneurial spirit is transforming the public sector from schoolhouse to state house, city hall to Pentagon.* Reading, MA: Addison-Wesley.

Rainey, H. G. (1997). *Understanding and managing public organizations.* San Francisco: Jossey-Bass.

Rainey, H. G. (1998). Ingredients for success: Five factors necessary for transforming government. In P W. Ingraham, J. R. Thompson, & R. P Sanders (Eds.), *Transforming government: Lessons from the reinvention laboratories* (pp. 147–172). San Francisco: Jossey-Bass.

Russell, G. D., & Waste, R. J. (1998). The limits of reinventing government. *American Review of Public Administration, 28,* 325–346.

Safir, H. (1997, December). Goal-oriented community policing: The NYPD approach. *The Police Chief,* pp. 31–58.

Schacter, H. S. (1995). Reinventing government or reinventing ourselves: Two models for improving government performance. *Public Administration Review, 99,* 530–537.

Silverman, E. (1999). *NYPD battles crime: Innovative strategies in policing.* Boston: Northeastern University Press.

Skogan, W. G. (1994). The impact of community policing on neighborhood residents: A cross-site analysis. In D. Rosenbaum (Ed.), *The challenge of community policing: Testing the promises* (pp. 167–181). Thousand Oaks, CA: Sage.

Skogan, W. G., & Hartnett, S. M. (1997). *Community policing in Chicago.* New York: Oxford University Press.

Sparrow, M. K., Moore, M. H., & Kennedy, D. M. (1990). *Beyond 911: A new era for policing.* New York: Basic Books.

Thompson, J. R., & Sanders, R. P. (1998). Reinventing public agencies: Bottom-up versus top-down strategies. In P W. Ingraham, J. R. Thompson, & R. P Sanders (Eds.), *Transforming government: Lessons from the reinvention laboratories* (pp. 97–121). San Francisco: Jossey-Bass.

Weber, R. P (1990). *Basic content analysis.* Newbury Park, CA: Sage.

Gennaro F. Vito and Julie Kunselman, "*Reinventing Government:* The Views of Police Middle Managers." Reprinted from *Police Quarterly,* Vol. 3 No. 3, September 2000, pp. 315–330. Copyright © 2000 by Sage Publications, Inc. Reprinted by permission of Sage Publications, Inc. ✦

Chapter 11

Sources of Job Satisfaction Among Police Officers

A Test of Demographic and Work Environment Models

Jihong Zhao
Quint C. Thurman
Ni He

The authors examine predictors of job satisfaction among police officers. Professionalized police work has often been associated with stress and burnout, largely attributable to the nature of the job itself (e.g., poor neighborhoods, disrespectful citizens, etc.). In the current study, the authors suggest job satisfaction is an important area of research in policing because satisfaction and motivation are closely related to employee productivity.

The authors suggest that identifying key sources of job satisfaction might lead to environmental improvements at the workplace and, more importantly, solutions for reducing work-related stress. Previous studies have typically treated employee job satisfaction as a unitary dimension. In the present study, the authors use three different measures of satisfaction, including satisfaction with work, supervisors, and coworkers. The findings suggest that satisfaction with work is closely related to the variety of the work itself—that is, repetitive, monotonous work may lead to job dissatisfaction. Moreover, the research indicates that autonomy and feedback are two significant predictors of satisfaction at work and with supervisors and coworkers, thus suggesting that supervisors should consider providing subordinates with sufficient independence to improve job satisfaction.

Increased interest in job satisfaction has led to a proliferation of research on this topic across various academic disciplines over the past three decades (Griffin and McMahan 1994). Jayaratne (1993), for example, reports that a key word search on "job satisfaction" from the PSYCINFO database in 1991 produced titles for more than 6,000 articles and monographs. Along this line, job satisfaction among employees of criminal justice agencies is attracting scholarly attention, as are related issues (e.g., employees' productivity, motivation, and work performance). The implementation of community policing, emphasizing participative management in which officers' problem-solving skills are applied in the community, has made research on the work environment particularly timely (Wycoff and Skogan 1993).

Several well-known theories might prove useful for explaining job satisfaction among the police (e.g., Griffin and McMahan 1994; Jayaratne 1993). Herzberg's (1968) two-factor theory of motivation, however, probably is one of the most familiar to students of American policing; it appears in almost every textbook on police administration or management currently in use (e.g., Fyfe et al. 1997; Langworthy and Travis 1994; Roberg and Kuykendall 1997; Sheehan and Cordner 1995; Swanson et al. 1993). Herzberg's theory was constructed in accordance with Abraham Maslow's well known "needs of human hierarchy," and apparently provides a useful theoretical framework for empirically assessing officers' job satisfaction (Roberg and Kuykendall 1997).

Herzberg's thesis is that an employee's job satisfaction is determined largely by his or her immediate work environment. Consequently managers should focus on that environment as a primary means of increasing employees' job satisfaction and motivation. Very little research, however, exists to verify or refute Herzberg's claims. A review of the published research on job satisfaction among police officers reveals an almost exclusive focus on officers' demographic factors such as educational level, ethnicity, gender, and rank/years of service as key independent variables associated with the employees' orientation toward police work.

Literature Review

Research on job satisfaction in policing is newer than similar research involving other professions: only about 20 published articles treating job satisfaction as a dependent variable pertain directly to policing (Buzawa, Austin, and Bannon 1994). Thus some criminal justice scholars conclude that knowledge about sources of job satisfaction among police officers lags far behind the corresponding knowledge about other occupations (Dantzker 1994; Griffin, Dunbar, and McGill 1978).

To date, much of the research on satisfaction with police work has been limited to testing the explanatory power of employees' demographic characteristics on job satisfaction and closely related dependent variables (Buckley and Petrunik 1995; Griffin et al. 1978; Jacobs and Cohen 1978; Lofkowitz 1974). Usually, four demographic variables are identified and then tested empirically.

The first demographic variable often studied is an officer's educational background. Carter and Sapp (1990) assert that the level of education among American police officers has risen substantially over the last 30 years. This rise is due, at least in part, to the assumption that an officer's ability to empathize with citizens from a variety of socioeconomic backgrounds will increase with educational attainment (Goldstein 1977). The origins of this perspective can be traced back to two presidential commissions of the late 1960s and early 1970s, which believed that education is important in doing police work in American society (National Advisory Commission 1973; President's Commission 1967).

In the past 20 years, however, scholars of policing have questioned the validity of this seemingly positive relationship between officers' education and their job performance and satisfaction. As Swanson (1977:312) observed, "The literature on police education is extensive, but it often appears bent on sustaining the notion that education for the police is good rather than on offering empirical evidence" (also see Carter, Jamieson, and Sapp 1978).

Research findings that might support this notion are mixed. Lofkowitz (1974) found that police officers' level of education was associated significantly with job satisfaction, but in an unexpected direction: Officers with master's degrees tended to demonstrate the lowest levels of positive attitudes toward their jobs. Buzawa (1984) found that the influence of education on employees' reported satisfaction was not consistent when two police departments were compared. Similar findings were reported by Griffin et al. (1978:79) in their comparison of officers with and without a college degree. In a review of research on the effects of education on police job performance, Sherman (1980) found that the relationship was weak at best. More recently, however, Dantzker (1992) found that education was associated positively with officers' job satisfaction, according to survey data from five police agencies that varied according to size and geographic region.

Ethnicity and gender are two other frequently studied variables. Historically, the organizational culture of law enforcement organizations across the United States has been indifferent to the needs of minority and female officers (Alex 1976; Haarr 1997; Martin 1994, 1995; Schulz 1995; Steel and Lovrich 1987; Sullivan 1993). Discrimination against minority and female officers persists, even though police organizations' recruitment and promotion policies have aimed at accommodation for many years (Hale and Wyland 1993; Leonard

1985; Martin 1993, 1997; Potts 1983; Steel and Lovrich 1987; Sullivan 1993). Policing, like many other professions in the United States, tends to be dominated by employees who are both white and male; thus it seems reasonable to assume that both minority and female police officers might demonstrate lower levels of job satisfaction than their white male counterparts, who set the tone for an agency's organizational culture. Research findings on these issues are inconsistent, however.

Some studies have found that minority and female police officers are among those least satisfied with their jobs (Buzawa 1984; Buzawa et al. 1994); others report mixed findings (e.g., Hunt and McCadden 1985). Belknap and Shelley (1992) concluded that a female officer's job satisfaction may be linked to the percentage of female officers employed in a given agency (also see Love and Singer 1988).

The fourth commonly identified variable in this research is years of service and/or police officer's rank. Many scholars of policing argue that alienation and cynicism are correlated positively with years of service (e.g., Gaines 1993). Similarly, almost every researcher who has studied this variable has reported that an officer's rank or length of service is associated negatively with the officer's view of the job (Burke 1989; Buzawa 1989; Buzawa et al. 1994; Dantzker 1992, 1994; Hunt and McCadden 1985; Sheley and Nock 1979). Furthermore, Dantzker (1994) observed that the negative relationship between police employees' seniority and their job satisfaction is not linear: The rate of decrease tends to level off between six and ten years of service (Allen, Hitt, and Greer 1982; Burke 1984; Neiderhoffer 1967). Langworthy (1987), however, questions the validity of research on the relationship between years of service and job alienation. He believes that the relationship between cynicism and years of service depends on the survey instrument used to collect data.

More recent attempts have been made to expand our understanding of police officers' job satisfaction by examining an officer's general attitudes about the police role, community support, and other variables as they might relate to positive attitudes toward police work (e.g., Greene 1989). Very little research, however, assesses the contribution of an officer's work environment to job satisfaction. Furthermore, when the police work environment is mentioned, it seldom is discussed as a source of job enrichment; rather, it is discussed as an obstacle. From this perspective, an officer's work environment typically is considered an important influence that shapes a police subculture negatively, impinges on discretion, and increases job stress, burnout, and alienation (see Bittner 1972; Gaines 1993; Langworthy 1987; Muir 1977; Skolnick 1966; Van Maanen 1978).

Because of the lack of research on officers' job satisfaction beyond the effects of demographic attributes, it might be fruitful to examine the work environment as an explanatory model. Such research also might prove timely, given the current enthusiasm for community policing. One premise of community policing is that it provides a supportive work environment which empowers officers to make problem-solving decisions. McGarrell and Thurman (1994), for example, assert that the relationship between officers' job satisfaction and the work environment apparently has become important because the success of community policing programs depends on participative management and the support of police officers, who must "buy into" the coproduction of order. Crank (1997a) even suggests that experienced officers who buy into community policing can do much to lead an organization to positive change (also see Crank 1997b).

In the 1990s, however, only a few studies have focused on the effectiveness of participative management and how it relates to job satisfaction. Trojanowicz and Bucqueroux (1990) found that foot patrol, as a newly reintroduced method of policing, enhances job satisfaction among the officers involved. Similarly, Wycoff and Skogan (1993) observed that officers involved with an experimental management project focusing on problem solving and a healthy workplace in the Madison (WI)

Police Department demonstrated greater overall job satisfaction and more positive attitudes toward their community. More recently, in their study of policing in Chicago, Skogan and Hartnett (1997) reported higher levels of satisfaction among officers who were engaged in community policing programs than among those who were attached to districts where community policing was not a high priority.

The Immediate Work Environment: An Important Area in Job Satisfaction Research

Almost all theories of satisfaction and motivation begin with a focus on the workplace itself. Vroom (1964) developed expectancy theory to explain the dependence on an individual's evaluation of a task assignment and level of satisfaction, based on his or her willingness to perform the expected functions of a job. Similarly, the application of assumptions about human nature in the widely cited "theory of X and Y" is correlated with the differences between two distinctive management styles in the workplace (McGregor 1960).

The two-factor theory of job satisfaction developed by Herzberg (1968) was formulated from research on 1,685 employees in 12 different investigations.[1] Findings from these investigations suggested that satisfaction in the workplace is "intrinsic" to the job with which an employee is directly involved. That is, the stimulus for employees' satisfaction is derived from job content that is found in the *work environment* (Herzberg 1968; emphasis in original).

Herzberg (1968) identified several important sources of job satisfaction in the work environment: (1) the importance of the work itself; (2) the responsibility one has while doing the work; and (3) the recognition received from doing one's work. In contrast, job dissatisfaction is a result of strict policies, overemphasis on rules, inadequate working conditions, and poor interpersonal relationships. Therefore, from a theoretical perspective, it seems reasonable to argue that a more comprehensive test of job satisfaction must include variables that measure a variety of job characteristics as well as individual employees' demographic attributes.

One of the most influential models for investigating various dimensions of the immediate job environment was developed by Hackman and Oldham (1975). One key feature of this approach is its ability to measure some of the most important dimensions that can be commonly identified in a workplace at the individual employee level. On the basis of extensive research conducted to refine their measures, Hackman and Oldham (1975) identified five "core" dimensions for evaluating the immediate work environment. They found that these core dimensions were correlated significantly with job satisfaction and employees' motivation. Key among the underlying characteristics are the *meaningfulness* of the work (to what extent the individual perceives the work as significant and important), *responsibility* for the job (how far the individual feels personally accountable for the outcomes of the work), and the extent to which the employee has *knowledge* about the results of his or her efforts.

Job meaningfulness is conceptualized as the product of three dimensions: *skill variety* (activities that challenge skills and abilities, Dimension 1); *task identity* (the extent to which the job requires completion of a "whole," identifiable piece of work, Dimension 2); and *task significance* (how substantially the job affects other people's lives, Dimension 3). Responsibility is based on the extent of the employee's *autonomy* over how he or she will perform the work (Dimension 4). Knowledge of results comes from *feedback* to the employee about the effectiveness of his or her efforts (Dimension 5) (Hackman and Oldham 1975).

Since the 1970s, the model for measuring core job dimensions and their relationship to job motivation and satisfaction has been tested extensively and applied to different work environments (Griffin and McMahan 1994; Harvey, Billings, and Nilan 1985; Idaszak and Drasgow 1987; Kulik, Oldham, and Langner 1988), including the public sector in general

(Lee and Klein 1982). Researchers have studied the relationship between job dimensions, employees' motivation, and job satisfaction in the field of corrections (Zupan and Menke 1988) and police organizations (Lurigio and Skogan 1994).

Two distinct models of job satisfaction become apparent from this discussion. The first model focuses on the relationship between an employee's demographic background and his or her level of job satisfaction. The second model originates in the school of management and emphasizes the importance of an individual's immediate work environment (Herzberg 1968). Policing research to date apparently has subscribed to the former while largely ignoring the latter. Here we apply to the policing profession Herzberg's (1968) two-factor theory that job satisfaction is a result of intrinsic work conditions, and then use multivariate analysis to examine the two models. We expect that the variation explained by all work-related variables combined will contribute more to variation in police officers' job satisfaction than will the variation in all extrinsic (demographic) variables combined. To test the models, we analyze data collected from a medium-sized northwestern police department.

Methods and Measures

The data reported here are derived from a survey of employees of the Spokane (WA) Police Department (SPD) conducted by the Division of Governmental Studies and Services at Washington State University. The study site, a regional hub for the inland portion of the northwestern United States, has a population of 188,000; 401,200 persons live within Spokane's metropolitan statistical area (MSA), according to 1995 census estimates. The median income of a Spokane resident in 1995 was approximately $33,500; the nonwhite percentage of the population is estimated at about 8 percent. The crime index for the city in 1995 was 16,484, or about 6,694 calls for service per 100,000 people living in the Spokane MSA. The SPD officer-to-citizen ratio is approximately 1.6 per 1,000 residents.

We collected data for this study from a survey instrument administered by the police department and returned directly to the university in postage-prepaid envelopes for tabulation and analysis during fall 1993. In all, 199 of 257 (77.4%) sworn employees completed and returned the instrument. Analyses comparing respondents with the actual population of SPD employees revealed that the respondents' demographic attributes matched closely those of all sworn personnel.[2]

The Dependent Variable

A review of the literature suggests that job satisfaction can be measured generically (Jayaratne 1993) or with regard to policing in particular (Dantzker 1993). Jayaratne argues that the selection of the measure should be based on the extent to which the measurement has been tested empirically. In addition, Dantzker recommends using multidimensional scales to tap job satisfaction. Given these considerations, we chose the Job Descriptive Index (JDI) on the basis of recommendations by Jayaratne (1993), Dantzker (1993), and Smith (1974). First, a measurement should be able to tap into several types of job satisfaction rather than relying on a single, unidimensional scale. Second, a measurement should be easy to comprehend and transportable across a wide variety of organizations. Finally, it is desirable to employ measures that have been widely tested and validated.

Researchers at Cornell University developed the JDI in 1959 from a large job satisfaction study (Smith 1974). It consists of a cumulative-point, adjective-checklist measure of job satisfaction that possesses adequate convergent and discriminant validity for individual analyses (Hulin 1969; Hulin and Water 1971; Quinn and Kahn 1967). This instrument can identify five types of job satisfaction: satisfaction with work, supervision, coworkers, pay, and promotion. Over the last three decades, the JDI has been used in many different settings including public organizations (i.e., Hulin 1969; Quinn and Spreitzer 1992; Smith 1974). Jayaratne (1993) reviewed 75 empirical studies randomly selected from 426 articles on job satisfaction published in 1991 and 1992; as a result, he concluded that the JDI was one of the three most frequently used survey instruments.

In the current study we used three scales of job satisfaction to measure satisfaction with an officer's work, with his or her supervisor, and with coworkers. Each scale consisted of 18 questions in which an employee was asked to rate levels of satisfaction associated with each of these three aspects. Using a direct scoring method, we weighted correct answers and then used them to compute a scale with scores ranging from 0 to 54.[3]

Independent Variables

We used two batteries of independent variables to represent the two distinct models (demographics versus work environment) concerning the primary sources of job satisfaction, as discussed earlier. Ethnicity, as one of four demographic variables, was measured by responses to an item in which respondents were asked to identify their ethnic affiliation, if any, according to the following categories: white, African American, Hispanic, or Native American. Gender was measured from the respondent's self-identification as male or female. The third demographic variable of interest, level of educational attainment, was measured on a continuum of six categories ranging from high school diploma to postgraduate college degree.

The fourth demographic variable that appears in the research literature was represented in our analysis by two separate variables: years of service and rank. We decided to use the natural log of years of service in our multivariate analysis to measure the former, and to assess rank independently.[4] A few studies that examined the relationship between rank and employees' job satisfaction show that supervisors report greater job satisfaction than do rank-and-file officers (Hunt and McCadden 1985; Sheley and Nock 1979). We coded this variable 1 for sergeants or higher, and 2 for officers.

The work environment model consisted of five dimensions: skill variety, task identity, task significance, autonomy, and feedback, as in the Job Diagnostic Survey (JDS) developed by Hackman and Oldham (1975). We measured each dimension by three variables, using a seven-point Likert scale; some variables were reverse coded.[5]

For comparison, we also examined the results of a JDS survey of two additional police departments, Departments "A" and "B." Department A is a large agency with 710 sworn officers, located in a large midwestern city. We conducted a JDS survey of all the sworn employees in Department A in fall 1996, which yielded a 53 percent response rate (370 officers). Department B is located in a city that is similar to Spokane in many respects, including geographic region and population size. We surveyed Department B in summer 1991, just before the six-month shift changes. A total of 166 questionnaires were distributed and 128 were completed, for a return rate of 77 percent.

At the agency level, the mean ratings of JDS dimensions suggest that the work environment in the Spokane Police Department closely resembled that of the other two agencies. Thus the findings reported in the next section may have implications for policing beyond Spokane itself.

Findings

In this section we provide a brief description of our data, followed by a discussion of ordinary least squares regression analysis of the effect of these two models on job satisfaction. Table 11.1 presents the frequency distributions for the explanatory and dependent variables.

In all, 199 cases were available for the analysis; minority officers accounted for about 6 percent of SPD officers. Similarly, female officers represented approximately 8 percent of all sworn officers. (The national average is 8.2 percent for cities with police forces the size of SPD; see Martin 1993.) The SPD officers' average level of educational attainment was approximately 4.0 on a seven-point scale. The logged years of service were 2.18 (natural years of service were 13.07, with a standard deviation of 8.91). Finally, 22 percent of the respondents stated their rank as sergeant or higher.

The demographic information reported for SPD matched very closely the data collected from Department B. For example, the average level of educational attainment among Department B's officers was approximately 4.18 on a seven-point scale. The natural years of service were 13.04, with a standard deviation of 8.16. Finally, 25 percent of Department B's officers reported their rank as sergeant and higher.

The five job dimensions of the JDS under the work environment model show that police officers rated higher on the dimensions related to skill variety, task significance, and autonomy than on the other two dimensions. These findings suggest that police officers do not view their work negatively. In fact, these mean ratings suggest that most officers believe they are doing a significant job with the skills necessary to accomplish the task.

A comparison of the mean ratings of the five dimensions for Spokane and for Departments A and B strongly suggests that the SPD work environment is typical for a police agency. Even the patterns of these mean ratings are very similar across the three agencies. In all three, for example, both task identity and feedback were

Table 11.1
Descriptive Statistics (N = 199)

Variables	Means	SD	*n*	%
Demographic Variables				
Ethnicity	.06	.25		
White(=0)			177	93.7
Minority(=1)			12	6.3
Gender	1.08	.28		
Male(=1)			176	92.1
Female(=2)			15	7.9
Educational attainment	4.07	1.20		
High school(=1)			8	4.0
Some college(=2)			64	32.3
Associate degree(=3)			58	29.3
B.A.(=4)			46	23.2
Some graduate(=5)			13	6.6
Graduate(=6)			9	4.5
Years of service (natural log)	2.18	1.05		
Rank	1.78	.45		
Sergeant and above(=1)			44	22.1
Officer(=2)			155	77.9
Job Dimensions	**SPD**	**Police Dept. A**		**Police Dept. B**
Skill variety	5.49 (.87)	5.35 (1.10)		5.09 (1.15)
Task identity	4.11 (1.59)	4.39 (1.35)		4.15 (1.50)
Task significance	5.73 (1.08)	5.81 (1.05)		5.77 (1.10)
Autonomy	5.59 (.96)	5.24 (1.05)		5.46 (1.14)
Feedback	4.73 (1.10)	4.26 (1.23)		4.39 (1.37)
Job Satisfaction		**Minimum**		**Maximum**
Satisfaction with work	33.20 (8.93)	8		49
Satisfaction with supervisor	41.64 (11.58)	3		54
Satisfaction with coworkers	44.19 (10.36)	3		54

Note: Alpha reliability coefficients for all eight scales—skill variety, task identity, task significance, autonomy, feedback, satisfaction with work, satisfaction with supervisor, and satisfaction with coworkers—varied from .60 to .82.

rated lower than the other three dimensions. In addition, measures of the three types of job satisfaction show that satisfaction with coworkers received the highest rating in all three agencies, and satisfaction with work, the lowest.

Table 11.2 presents the results concerning the relationship between the demographic and the work environment models on ratings of work satisfaction. For comparison, we included both unstandardized and standardized (beta) coefficients to show the contribution of each individual variable to the equation.[6]

Findings in Table 11.2 show that demographic variables by themselves explain only limited variance in job satisfaction ($R^2 = .06$). Also, ethnicity, gender, and education failed to achieve statistical significance at the .05 level of probability. Logged years of service and rank are associated negatively with officers' satisfaction with work, in agreement with findings that the literature might predict.

The addition of the five job dimension variables in the second regression equation, as represented by Model 2, substantially increased the explanatory power of the independent variables ($R^2 = .49$). With no obvious changes in either sign or size of effect of the demographic variables, the five dimensions of the work environment, when combined, accounted for over 40 percent of the variance in job satisfaction. This finding suggests that skill variety, task identity, and autonomy contribute most to the variation in officers' work satisfaction.

Table 11.3 displays the findings concerning the relationship between the two models and satisfaction with supervisors. Again, these results show that the variables constituting the demographic model explain little variance in officers' job satisfaction, with an R^2 of only .02. None of the variables representing the demographic model are statistically significant.

In contrast, the five job dimensions representing the work environment model explain a substantial amount of variance in officers' satisfaction with supervisors ($R^2 = .30$). Only two variables in this model were statistically significant, however. One variable, autonomy, explained more than one-third of the variance in satisfaction with supervisors. This suggests

Table 11.2

Regression Analysis: Satisfaction with Work as the Dependent Variable

	Model 1		Model 2	
	B	Beta	*B*	Beta
Independent Variables	Coefficients		Coefficients	
Demographic Variables				
Ethnicity	1.10	.03	2.26	.06
Gender	–.70	–.02	–2.60	–.08
Education	.39	.05	.49	.07
Years of service (log)	–1.65	–.19*	–1.57	–.18*
Rank	–3.80	–.18*	–3.12	–.15*
Job Dimensions				
Skill variety			3.35	.32*
Task identity			1.32	.23*
Task significance			1.19	.14*
Autonomy			1.78	.19*
Feedback			.24	.03
R	.24	*F* ratio = 2.15	.70	*F* ratio = 16.23
R^2	.06		.49*	

* $p \leq .05$.

Table 11.3
Regression Analysis: Satisfaction with Supervisor as the Dependent Variable

	Model 1		Model 2	
	B	Beta	*B*	Beta
Independent Variables	Coefficients		Coefficients	
Demographic Variables				
Ethnicity	−2.93	−.06	−1.96	−.04
Gender	1.79	.04	.54	.01
Education	.32	.03	.29	.03
Years of service (log)	−1.19	−.11	−.76	−.07
Rank	−.30	−.01	.61	.02
Job Dimensions				
Skill variety			1.14	.08
Task identity			−.17	−.02
Task significance			.80	.07
Autonomy			4.82	.39*
Feedback			1.60	.15*
R	.14	F ratio = .70	.55	F ratio = 7.32
R^2	.02		.30*	

* $p \leq .05$.

that a worker's perception of independence is a crucial factor in workplace satisfaction. In addition, the regression coefficient for feedback implies that satisfaction with supervisors is related closely to a worker's evaluation of the information he or she receives from supervisors.

Table 11.4 reports the findings on the influence of Models 1 and 2 on satisfaction with co-

Table 11.4
Regression Analysis: Satisfaction with Coworkers as the Dependent Variable

	Model 1		Model 2	
	B	Beta	*B*	Beta
Independent Variables	Coefficients		Coefficients	
Demographic Variables				
Ethnicity	−3.11	−.08	−2.78	−.07
Gender	−1.32	−.04	−2.61	−.07
Education	.42	.05	.47	.06
Years of service (log)	−.45	−.07	−.43	−.04
Rank	−1.54	−.06	−1.21	−.05
Job Dimensions				
Skill variety			1.01	.08
Task identity			.92	.14
Task significance			1.24	.13
Autonomy			1.71	.16*
Feedback			.48	.05
R	.12	F ratio = .53	.48	F ratio = .41
R^2	.02		.17*	

* $p \leq .05$.

workers. Here the regression coefficients suggest that the demographic variables, both collectively and individually, fail to predict variation in officers' satisfaction with coworkers. By comparison, the R^2 associated with Model 2 suggests that when the work environment model is added to the equation, it captures some variation in the dependent variable ($R^2 = .17$).

The findings from this analysis may suggest that the primary sources of satisfaction with one's coworkers cannot be explained directly by the variables representing the immediate work environment. The only variable in the equation that is significant at the .05 level is autonomy in the workplace. Autonomy was significant throughout all three regression runs despite substantial variation in explained variation, ranging from 49 to 17 percent. This finding highlights the function of autonomy in the workplace as perceived by SPD officers.

Discussion and Conclusion

The findings reported above have some important theoretical and practical implications. First, they suggest the utility of Herzberg's theory with respect to the primary sources of job satisfaction (Herzberg 1968). According to these data, job satisfaction appears to be intrinsic to an employee's work environment.

These results also indicate the relative importance of the two models. The analyses from three multiple regressions showed that Hackman and Oldham's (1975) five job dimensions explain more variation in three types of job satisfaction than do the independent variables representing police officers' demographic attributes. Furthermore, the work environment model explained more variation in job satisfaction, as measured by satisfaction with police work itself, than when satisfaction with supervisors and satisfaction with coworkers were treated as dependent variables.

Our findings strongly suggest that work environment is an essential feature of police officers' job satisfaction (Wycoff and Skogan 1993). In addition, the concept of work environment can contribute to understanding what makes working at a law enforcement agency more enjoyable. Such a perspective contrasts with previous research, which focused primarily on the negative aspects of the police work environment and on the resulting cynicism, stress, burnout, and alienation.

The current investigation also suggests that job satisfaction is multidimensional (Buzawa et al. 1994; Dantzker 1993; Huhn and Water 1971; Smith 1974). In addition, our findings suggest that different types of job satisfaction are a result of different explanatory variables. For example, police officers' satisfaction with work is associated positively with their perceptions about the importance and significance of their work, the recognition they receive, their autonomy, and the capability to do their work. By comparison, officers' satisfaction with supervisors is correlated significantly with job autonomy and with feedback from supervisors. This noteworthy finding—that feedback is significant in predicting an officer's satisfaction with his or her immediate supervisor, but not satisfaction with the job or the people at work—strongly suggests that two-way communication is necessary for improving the police work environment.

Similarly, these results highlight the importance of autonomy as a source of job satisfaction. In every regression, autonomy emerged as a significant variable related to all three types of satisfaction. In accordance with the observations of other policing scholars (e.g., Crank 1997b; Kappeler, Sluder, and Alpert 1995; Skolnick 1966), this finding suggests that police officers like to work in an environment where they enjoy considerable freedom to decide what they will do.

A traditional model of policing emphasizes control and close supervision to enhance employees' conformity and predictability (Kelling and Moore 1988; Zhao 1996). This is achieved, however, by sacrificing field officers' freedom to solve problems (Cordner 1978; Sandler and Mintz 1974). Accordingly, traditional practices may be at odds with the participative management style that is becoming more popular with the advent of community policing (Wycoff and Skogan 1993). Proponents of community policing believe that officers need more autonomy to engage in proactive, positive interactions with local residents. In addition, the importance of the work environment, particularly autonomy and feedback, is consistent with the premise of the behavioral school of management theory, concerning the importance of employees. Autonomy should become even more important as the police organization moves from a production orientation to become more employee-centered.

In general, these findings emphasize the importance of individual employees and their immediate work environment on police officers' job satisfaction. Readers, however, should be aware of a limitation of this study. As stated earlier, Spokane's police department is a medium-sized agency located in the northwestern United States. Although this department's work environment resembles closely that of two other agencies for which like data were available, our findings may have limited generalizability because of the SPD's distinctive organizational environment. For example, the SPD has been implementing community policing very aggressively since 1992 (see Oliver 1988:144–50). Therefore the work dimensions may contribute to officers' job satisfaction to a different degree than in other agencies (Swanson 1977).

We invite other scholars and practitioners of policing to join in the study of the relationship between work environment and job satisfaction in law enforcement agencies. Both longitudinal and cross-sectional studies are needed to increase the understanding of the organizational environment in police agencies and its effects on officers' job satisfaction.

Notes

1. The behavioral school of management theories represents a rich body of knowledge about the importance of individual employees in an organization. The long scholarly contribution can be traced back to the 1920s, when Mary Parker Follett (1924) wrote an article on the importance of individual employees in the workplace. The discovery of the informal work group in the Hawthorne experiment (Roethlisberger and Dickson 1939) and of the cumulative nature of authority (Barnard 1938) established the foundation for research in this school. Therefore, Maslow's theory of hierarchical needs can be viewed as the jumping-off point for later behavioral science research in job satisfaction and employees' needs. Theories have focused increasingly on individuals as a unit of analysis in organizational studies (e.g., Argyris 1973; McGregor 1960; Ouchi 1984; Vroom 1964). The primary contribution of Herzberg's two-factor theory is that it estab-

Appendix 11.1
Correlation Matrix of Dependent and Independent Variables

	1	2	3	4	5	6	7	8	9	10	11	12	13
1. Satisfaction/Work	1.000												
2. Satisfaction/Supervisor	.435*	1.000											
3. Satisfaction/Coworkers	.416*	.365*	1.000										
4. Skill Variety	.512*	.261*	.220*	1.000									
5. Task Identity	.373*	.227*	.208*	.243*	1.000								
6. Task Significance	.474*	.284*	.238*	.579*	.185*	1.000							
7. Autonomy	.430*	.451*	.266*	.333*	.397*	.293*	1.000						
8. Feedback	.365*	.296*	.158*	.349*	.487*	.370*	.274*	1.000					
9. Ethnicity	.036	–.053	–.062	–.113	.039	.010	–.031	.018	1.000				
10. Gender	.000	.054	–.023	.056	.049	.092	.019	.072	.084	1.000			
11. Education	.104	.032	.054	.006	–.027	.018	.045	–.028	.112	.194*	1.000		
12. Rank	–.146*	–.040	–.039	–.048	.000	–.040	–.040	–.006	.035	.113	–.249*	1.000	
13. Years of Service	–.130	–.084	–.038	–.102	.240	–.181*	–.005	.009	–.015	–.123	–.135	–.332*	1.000

*$p \leq .05$.

lished a direct link between an employee's immediate work environment and his or her job satisfaction. Consequently this theory has contributed substantially to research in the behavioral school of management in recent decades, including work enrichment and redesign (Hackman and Oldham 1980).

2. Data used in this analysis were collected during the second employee survey of the Spokane Police Department, which was conducted by the Division of Governmental Studies and Services (DGSS) at Washington State University. Since 1992, DGSS has systematically surveyed SPD employees to assess the work environment and employees' attitudes toward the implementation of community policing. Spokane has employed at least 257 sworn officers in the police department since December 1993. At that time, 11 officers (4.3%) were members of minorities, and 21 (8.2%) were female. Our data, collected in fall 1993, identified 12 respondents (6.0%) as members of racial minorities and 15 (7.9%) as female. We found no significant differences between our sample and the population of sworn officers in the SPD with respect to these and related background characteristics.

3. The JDI measures satisfaction with several areas of a job, including the type of work, supervisors, and coworkers. For each area a list of adjectives or short phrases is supplied; the respondent must indicate whether each word or phrase applies to the aspect of his or her job in question. If a word applies to the situation, the respondent is asked to write "yes" next to the word. If the word does not apply, the individual is asked to answer "no." If an individual cannot decide, he or she is asked to write "don't know." For a detailed discussion of the rationale, validity, and scoring method of the JDI instrument, see Smith, Kendall, and Hulin (1969, esp. pp.79–85).

4. The use of a log transformation here follows from our review of the literature, which suggested that the relationship between job satisfaction and years of service might not be linear (Allen et al. 1982; Burke 1989; Dantzker 1994). The same was true of the research on the relationship between police officers' stress and years of service (Gaines 1993; Neiderhoffer 1967). We estimated the years of service both in the original format and by log transformation. In agreement with the research literature, our results suggest that the years of service variable captured more variance in its log transformation than in its original form.

5. A JDS survey instrument appears in the appendix of Hackman and Oldham's (1980) *Work Redesign* (which also provides comparable data on the work environments of several other occupations). The authors also discuss the validity of reverse coding.

6. Multicollinearity is a potentially serious problem with ordinary least squares (OLS) regression analysis. Accordingly, the variance inflation factor (VIF) often is used to detect whether high collinearity exists between any variables. Some researchers use a VIF score of 4 or greater as an indication of severe multicollinearity (Fisher and Mason 1981; Judge et al. 1988). Our collinearity statistics showed that none of the VIF values exceeded 2; thus we concluded that multicollinearity was not a problem in our analysis (also see correlation matrix reported in Appendix 11.1).

References

Alex, N. 1976. *New York Cops Talk Back: A Study of a Beleaguered Minority.* New York: Wiley.

Allen, R., M. Hitt, and C. Greer. 1982. "Occupational Stress and Perceived Organizational Effectiveness in Formal Groups: An Examination of Stress Level and Stress Type." *Personnel Psychology* 35:359–71.

Argyris, C. 1973. "Some Limits of Rational Man Organization Theory." *Public Administration Review* 33:263–67.

Barnard, C. 1938. *The Functions of the Executive.* Cambridge, MA: Harvard University Press.

Belknap, J. and J.K. Shelley. 1992. "The New Lone Ranger: Police Women on Patrol." *American Journal of Police* 12:47–75.

Bittner, E. 1972. *The Functions of the Police in Modern Society.* 2nd ed. Washington, DC: National Institute of Mental Health.

Buckley, L.B. and M.G. Petrunik. 1995. "Socio-Demographic Factors, Reference Groups, and the Career Orientations, Career Aspirations and Career Satisfaction of Canadian Police Officers." *American Journal of Police* 14:107–48.

Burke, R. 1989. "Career Stages, Satisfaction, and Well-Being Among Police Officers." *Psychological Reports* 65:3–12.

Buzawa, E.S. 1984. "Determining Patrol Officer Job Satisfaction: The Role of Selected Demographic and Job-Specific Attitudes." *Criminology* 22:61–81.

Buzawa, E., T. Austin, and J. Bannon. 1994. "The Role of Selected Socio-Demographic and Job Specific Variables in Predicting Patrol Officer Job Satisfaction: A Reexamination Ten Years Later." *American Journal of Police* 13:51–75.

Carter, D.L., J.D. Jamieson, and A.D. Sapp. 1978. *Issues and Trends in Criminal Justice Education.* Huntsville, TX: Criminal Justice Center and Institute of Contemporary Corrections and the Behavioral Sciences.

Carter, D.L. and A.D. Sapp. 1990. "The Evolution of Higher Education in Law Enforcement: Preliminary Findings from a National Study." *Journal of Criminal Justice Education* 1:59–85.

Cordner, G. 1978. "Open and Closed Models in Police Organizations: Traditions, Dilemmas and Practical Considerations." *Journal of Police Science and Administration* 6:22–34.

Crank, J.P. 1997a. "Celebrating Agency Culture: Engaging a Traditional Cop's Heart in Organizational Change." Pp. 49–57 in *Community Policing in a Rural Setting,* edited by Q.C. Thurman and E.F. McGarrell. Cincinnati: Anderson.

——.1997b. *Understanding Police Culture.* Cincinnati: Anderson.

Dantzker, M.L. 1992. "An Issue for Policing—Educational Level and Job Satisfaction: A Research Note." *American Journal of Police* 12:101–18.

——. 1993. "Designing a Measure of Job Satisfaction for Policing—A Research Note." *American Journal of Police* 12:171–80.

——. 1994. "Measuring Job Satisfaction in Police Departments and Policy Implications: An Examination of a Mid-Size, Southern Police Department." *American Journal of Police* 13:77–101.

Fisher, J.E. and R.L. Mason. 1981. "The Analysis of Multicollinear Data in Criminology." Pp. 99–125 in *Methods in Quantitative Criminology,* edited by J.A. Fox. New York: Academic Press.

Follett, M.P. 1924. *Creative Experience.* New York: Longmans and Green.

Fyfe, J.J., J.R. Greene, W.F. Walsh, O.W. Wilson, and R.C. Mclaren. 1997. *Police Administration.* 5th ed. New York: McGraw-Hill.

Gaines, L. 1993. "Coping with the Police Job: Stress in Police Work." Pp. 338–50 in *Critical Issues in Policing: Contemporary Readings,* edited by R. Dunham and G. Alpert. Prospect Heights, IL: Waveland.

Goldstein, H. 1977. *Policing a Free Society.* Cambridge, MA: Ballinger.

Greene, J.R. 1989. "Police Officer Job Satisfaction and Community Perceptions: Implications for Community-Oriented Policing." *Journal of Research in Crime and Delinquency* 26:168–83.

Griffin, D.R., R.L. Dunbar, and M.E. McGill. 1978. "Factors Associated with Job Satisfaction among Police Personnel." *Journal of Police Science and Administration* 6:77–85.

Griffin, R.W. and G.C. McMahan. 1994. "Motivation through Job Design." Pp. 23–44 in *Organizational Behavior: The State of the Science,* edited by J. Greenberg. Hillsdale, NJ: Erlbaum.

Haarr, R.N. 1997. "Patterns of Interaction in a Police Patrol Bureau: Race and Gender Barriers to Integration." *Justice Quarterly* 14:53–85.

Hackman, J.R. and G.R. Oldham. 1975. "Development of the Job Diagnostic Survey." *Journal of Applied Psychology* 2:159–70.

——. 1980. *Work Redesign.* Reading, MA: Addison-Wesley.

Hale, D.C. and S.M. Wyland. 1993. "Dragons and Dinosaurs: The Plight of Patrol Women." *Police Forum* 3:1–8.

Harvey, R.J., R.S. Billings, and K. Nilan. 1985. "Confirmatory Factor Analysis of the Job Diagnostic Survey: Good News and Bad News." *Journal of Applied Psychology* 3:461–68.

Herzberg, F. 1968. "One More Time: How Do You Motivate Employees?" *Harvard Business Review* 46:53–62.

Hulin, C.L. 1969. "Sources of Variation in Job and Life Satisfaction: The Role of Community and Job Related Variables." *Journal of Applied Psychology* 53:279–91.

Huhn, C.L. and L.K. Water. 1971. "Regression Analysis of Three Variations of the Two-Factor Theory of Job Satisfaction." *Journal of Applied Psychology* 55:211–17.

Hunt, R.G. and K.S. McCadden. 1985. "A Survey of Work Attitudes of Police Officers: Commitment and Satisfaction." *Police Studies* 8:17–25.

Idaszak, J.R. and F. Drasgow. 1987. "A Revision of the Job Diagnostic Survey: Elimination of a Measurement Artifact." *Journal of Applied Psychology* 72:69–74.

Jacobs, J.B. and J. Cohen. 1978. "The Impact of Racial Integration on the Police." *Journal of Police Science and Administration* 6:168–83.

Jayaratne, S. 1993. "The Antecedents, Consequences, and Correlates of Job Satisfaction." Pp. 111–40 in *Handbook of Organizational Behavior,* edited by R.T. Golembiewski. New York: Dekker.

Judge, G.G., R.C. Hill, W.E. Griffiths, H. Lutkepohl, and T.C. Lee. 1998. *Introduction to the Theory and Practice of Econometrics.* 2nd ed. New York: Wiley.

Kappeler, V.E., R.D. Sluder, and G.P. Alpert. 1995. "Breeding Deviant Conformity: Police Ideology and Culture." Pp. 243–62 in *The Police and Society: Touchstone Readings,* edited by V.E. Kappeler. Prospect Heights, IL: Waveland.

Kelling, G. and M. Moore. 1988. "From Political to Reform to Community: The Evolving Strategy of Police." Pp. 1–26 in *Community Policing: Rhetoric or Reality?,* edited by J. Greene and S. Mastrofski. New York: Praeger.

Kulik, C.T., G.R. Oldham, and P.H. Langner. 1988. "Measurement of Job Characteristics: Comparison of the Original and the Revised Job Diagnostic Survey." *Journal of Applied Psychology* 73:362–66.

Langworthy, R.H. 1987. "Comment—Have We Measured the Concept(s) of Police Cynicism Using Niederhoffer's Cynicism Index?" *Justice Quarterly* 4:277–80.

Langworthy, R.H. and L.F. Travis. 1994. *Policing in America: A Balance of Forces.* New York: Macmillan.

Lee, R. and A.R. Klein. 1982. "Structure of the Job Diagnostic Survey for Public Sector Occupations." *Journal of Applied Psychology* 67:515–19.

Leonard, J. 1985. "What Promises Are Worth: The Impact of Affirmative Action Goals." *Journal of Human Resources* 20:3–20.

Lofkowitz, J. 1974. "Job Attitudes of Police: Overall Description and Demographic Correlates." *Journal of Vocational Behavior* 5:221–30.

Love, K. and M. Singer. 1988. "Self-Efficacy, Psychological Well-Being, Job Satisfaction and Job Involvement: Comparison of Male and Female Police Officers." *Police Studies* 11:98–102.

Lurigio, A.J. and W.G. Skogan. 1994. "Winning the Hearts and Minds of Police Officers: An Assessment of Staff Perceptions of Community Policing in Chicago." *Crime and Delinquency* 40:315–30.

Martin, S. 1993. "Female Officers on the Move: A Status Report on Women in Policing." Pp. 327–47 in *Critical Issues in Policing: Contemporary Readings,* 2nd ed., edited by R.G. Dunham and G.P. Alpert. Prospect Heights, IL: Waveland.

——. 1994. " 'Outsider Within' the Station House: The Impact of Race and Gender on Black Women Police." *Social Problems* 41:383–400.

——. 1995. "The Interactive Effects of Race and Sex on Women Police Officers." Pp. 388–97 in *The Criminal Justice System and Women: Offenders, Victims, and Workers,* 2nd ed., edited by B.R. Price and N.J. Sokoloff. New York: McGrawHill.

——. 1997. "Women Officers on the Move: An Update on Women in Policing." Pp. 363-84 in *Critical Issues in Policing: Contemporary Readings,* 3rd ed., edited by R.G. Dunham and G.P. Alpert. Prospect Heights, IL: Waveland.

McGarrell, E.F. and Q.C. Thurman. 1994. *Findings from the 1993 Spokane Police Department Employee Survey: Final Report.* Spokane: Washington State Institute for Community Oriented Policing.

McGregor, D. 1960. *The Human Side of Enterprise.* New York: McGraw-Hill.

Muir, W.K. 1977. *Police: Street corner Politicians.* Chicago: University of Chicago Press.

National Advisory Commission on Criminal Justice Standards and Goals. 1973. *Task Force Report: The Police.* Washington, DC: U.S. Government Printing Office.

Neiderhoffer, A 1967. *Behind the Shield: The Police in Urban Society.* New York: Doubleday.

Oliver, W.M. 1998. *Community Oriented Policing: A Systemic Approach to Policing.* Upper Saddle River, NJ: Prentice Hall.

Ouchi, W.G. 1984. *The M-Form Society: How American Teamwork Can Recapture the Competitive Edge.* Reading, MA: Addison-Wesley.

Potts, L. 1983. "Equal Employment Opportunity and Female Employment in Police Agencies." *Journal of Criminal Justice.* 11:505–23.

President's Commission on Law Enforcement and Administration of Justice. 1967. *Task Force Report: The Police.* Washington, DC: U.S. Government Printing Office.

Quinn, R.P. and P.L. Kahn. 1967. "Organizational Psychology." *Annual Review of Psychology* 18:437–66.

Quinn, R.P. and G. Spreitzer. 1992. "The Psychometrics of the Competing Values Culture Instrument and an Analysis of the Impact of Organizational Culture on Quality of Life." Pp. 115–42 in *Research in Organizational Change and Development,* edited by R.W. Woodman and W.A. Pasmore. Greenwich, CT: JAI.

Roberg, R.R. and J. Kuykendall. 1997. *Police Management.* 2nd ed. Los Angeles: Roxbury.

Roethlisberger, F.J. and W.J. Dickson. 1939. *Management and the Worker.* Cambridge, MA: Harvard University Press.

Sandler, G. and E. Mintz. 1974. "Police Organizations: Their Changing Internal and External Relationship." *Journal of Police Science and Administration* 2:458–63.

Schulz, D.M. 1995. "Invisible No More: A Social History of Women in U.S. Policing." Pp. 372–82 in *The Criminal Justice System and Women: Offenders, Victims, and Workers,* 2nd ed., edited by B.R. Price and N.J. Sokoloff. New York: McGrawHill.

Sheehan, R and G.W. Cordner. 1995. *Police Administration.* 3rd ed. Cincinnati: Anderson.

Sheley, J.F. and S.L. Nock. 1979. "Determinants of Police Job Satisfaction." *Sociological Inquiry* 49:49–55.

Sherman, L.W. 1980. "Causes of Police Behavior: The Current State of Quantitative Research." *Journal of Research in Crime and Delinquency* 17:69–100.

Skogan, W.G. and S.M. Hartnett. 1997. *Community Policing, Chicago Style.* New York: Oxford University Press.

Skolnick, J.H. 1966. *Justice Without Trial: Law Enforcement in a Democratic Society.* New York: John Wiley.

Smith, P.C. 1974. "The Development of a Method of Measuring Job Satisfaction: The Cornell Studies." In *Studies in Personnel and Industrial Psychology,* edited by E.A. Fleishman and A.R. Bass. Homewood, IL: Dorsey.

Smith, P.C., L.M. Kendall, and C.L. Hulin. 1969. *The Measurement of Satisfaction in Work and Retirement.* Chicago: Rand McNally.

Steel, B. and N.P. Lovrich. 1987. "Equality and Efficiency Tradeoffs in Affirmative Action—Real or Imagined? The Case of Women in Policing." *Social Science Journal* 24:53–70.

Sullivan, P.S. 1993. "Minority Officers: Current Issues." Pp. 331–45 in *Critical Issues in Policing: Contemporary Readings,* edited by R.G. Dunham and G.P. Alpert. Prospect Heights, IL: Waveland.

Swanson, C.R. 1977. "An Uneasy Look at College Education and the Police Organization." *Journal of Criminal Justice* 5:311–20.

Swanson, C.R., L. Territo, and R.W. Taylor. 1993. *Police Administration: Structure, Processes, and Behavior.* 3rd ed. Englewood Cliffs, NJ: Prentice Hall.

Trojanowicz, R. and B. Bucqueroux. 1990. *Community Policing: A Contemporary Perspective.* Cincinnati: Anderson.

Van Maanen, J. 1978. "The Asshole." Pp. 221–38 in *Policing: A View from the Street,* edited by P.L. Manning and J. Van Maanen. Santa Monica: Goodyear.

Vroom, V. 1964. *Work and Motivation.* New York: Wiley.

Wycof, M.A. and W.K. Skogan. 1993. *Community Policing in Madison: Quality from the Inside Out.* Washington, DC: U.S. Department of Justice.

Zhao, J. 1996. *Why Police Organizations Change: A Study of Community-Oriented Policing.* Washington, DC: Police Executive Research Forum.

Zupan, L. and B. Menke. 1988. "Implementing Organizational Change: From Traditional to New Generation Jail Operation." *Police Studies Review* 7:615–25.

Jihong Zhao, Quint C. Thurman, and Ni He, "Sources of Job Satisfaction Among Police Officers: A Test of Demographic and Work Environment Models." Reprinted from *Justice Quarterly,* Vol. 16 No. 1, pp. 153–173. Copyright © 1999 Academy of Criminal Justice Sciences. Reprinted with permission of the Academy of Criminal Justice Sciences. ✦

Chapter 12

Early Warning Systems for Police

Concept, History, and Issues

Samuel Walker
Geoffrey P. Alpert
Dennis Jay Kenney

P*olice corruption poses a tremendous cost for law enforcement agencies. The public trust of local police can be severely undermined by flagrant acts of misconduct such as those witnessed in Los Angeles in the 1990s. In addition to loss of trust, property damage due to social unrest and the civil compensation awarded through lawsuits can take their toll on police organizations and their municipalities. Here the authors discuss major findings from the implementation of a police corruption early warning system in the Miami-Dade Police Department.*

Early warning systems are defined as "data-driven programs designed to identify officers whose behavior appears to be problematic and to subject those officers to some kind of intervention" in order to reduce the likelihood of future misconduct. Several key concepts concerning early warning systems are noteworthy. First, early warning systems attempt to identify potential problem-prone officers based on their past performance in the workplace. Research consistently reveals that a small percentage of officers accounts for a large number of citizen complaints. Information on the number and characteristics of citizen complaints against officers resulting in reprimands may signal future problems of a larger scale. The authors contend that officers identified by an early warning system become candidates for interventions that may reduce the likelihood of subsequent problems.

Early warning (EW) systems have emerged as a new law enforcement administrative tool for reducing officer misconduct and enhancing accountability. EW systems are data-driven programs designed to identify officers whose behavior appears to be problematic and to subject those officers to some kind of intervention, usually in the form of counseling or training designed to correct the problematic behavior. Because of their potential for providing timely data on officer performance and giving police managers a framework for correcting unacceptable performance, EW systems are consistent with the new demands for performance evaluation raised by community policing (Alpert & Moore, 1993) and for the effective strategic management of police departments (Moore & Stephens, 1991).

The purpose of this article is to explore the concept of EW systems, the history of EW systems in American policing, and issues related to the program elements of EW systems. It reports the initial findings of a national evaluation of EW systems (Walker, Alpert, & Kenney, 1999). The evaluation involved a mail survey; municipal and county law enforcement agencies serving populations more than 50,000 people; and case studies of EW systems in three large, urban police departments.

The basic concept of EW systems is that law enforcement agencies should use data on problematic officer performance (e.g., citizen complaints, use-of-force incident reports, etc.) to identify those officers who appear to be having recurring problems or apparent problems interacting with citizens. As a retrospective, performance-based approach, an EW system is not designed to prospectively predict officer performance based on officer characteristics

(Stix, 1994). An EW system is "early" in the sense that it attempts to identify officers before their performance results in more serious problems (e.g., civil litigation, police-community relations crisis, etc.). An EW system itself does not involve formal discipline (although an officer may be disciplined for particular actions that led to identification by the system); rather, it is an attempt to warn an officer and/or correct his or her behavior. Some EW systems explicitly state that their purpose is to help officers improve their performance (New Orleans Police Department, 1998).

The intervention phase of EW systems generally consists of individual counseling by a supervisor or in a training class. It is informal in the sense that as explained above, it is not defined as a discipline within the terms of the agency's personnel procedures or collective bargaining agreement. Generally, no record of participation in an EW program per se is placed in an officer's personnel file, although the incidents that originally identified the officer (e.g., citizen complaints, use-of-force reports) do remain in the officer's file and can be considered for discipline. A separate record of participation in the EW system is generally maintained by the internal affairs or professional standards unit of the police department.

EW systems have been endorsed by the U.S. Commission on Civil Rights (1981), the International Association of Chiefs of Police (1989), private consultants on police internal investigations (Reiter, 1998), and the 1996 Justice Department Conference on Police Integrity (U.S. Department of Justice, 1997a). An EW system is incorporated in the consent decree negotiated by the Civil Rights Division of the Justice Department and the city of Pittsburgh (*United States v. City of Pittsburgh,* 1997). By 1999, an estimated 27% of all municipal and county law enforcement agencies serving populations greater than 50,000 had EW systems in place, and another 12% were planning to implement one (Walker et al., 1999).

The EW concept represents a departure from traditional police practice in which departments have been seen as punishment oriented, with innumerable rules and regulations that can be used against an officer (Westley, 1970, pp. 24–30) but with few procedures for rewarding good conduct. Alpert and Moore (1993, p. 129) argued that under community policing, police departments must develop performance measures that identify and reward "exemplary service to the community and the reduction or diffusion of violence," actions that have been essentially ignored by traditional performance evaluation systems. Apart from employee assistance programs designed to address substance abuse or family problems, police departments have done relatively little in a formal way to correct problem behavior. In the private sector, by comparison, personnel issues have become defined in terms of human resource development, with a specific emphasis on helping employees correct behavior that is not consistent with the organization's goals (Mathis & Jackson, 1999, p. 102).

The Problem Police Officer

Empirical Evidence

Interest in EW increased in response to growing evidence that in most law enforcement agencies, a small percentage of officers are responsible for a disproportionate share of citizen complaints, use-of-force incidents, or other problematic incidents. The phenomenon of the "problem officer" who receives a high rate of citizen complaints was first recognized in the 1970s. Toch, Grant, and Galvin (1975) developed a program in which Oakland, California, police officers with records of use-of-force incidents were counseled by peer officers. Goldstein (1977, p. 171) cited this program in a discussion of the need for identifying officers with a propensity for wrongdoing.

The U.S. Commission on Civil Rights (1981) published data indicating that a small group of Houston, Texas, police officers received extraordinarily high numbers of citizen complaints. In the aftermath of the 1991 Rodney King incident in Los Angeles, the Christopher Commission (1991) identified 44 problem officers in the Los Angeles Police Department (LAPD) with extremely high rates of citizen complaints. The commission commented that these officers were "readily identifiable" on the basis of existing LAPD records.

Investigative journalists have found the problem officer phenomenon in other police departments. In Kansas City, Missouri, 2% of the sworn officers were responsible for 50% of citizen complaints ("Kansas City Police," 1991). In Boston, 11% were responsible for 61.5% of complaints ("Wave of Abuse," 1992), and in Washington, D.C., a small number of officers were responsible for a large proportion of multiple discharge of firearms ("DC Police," 1998). With the exception of Kansas City, all of these reports found that police managers ignored patterns of repeated involvement in critical incidents and failed to take any kind of action against the officers with the worst records.

From Informal Knowledge to Management Tool

The concept of EW is consistent with the basic principles of personnel management and human resource development (Mathis & Jackson, 1999; Poole & Warner, 1998). Employers recruit, select, and train employees to serve effectively the goals and objectives of the organization. Effective personnel management assumes that employee performance is assessed and evaluated on a regular basis, and that the organization collects and analyzes performance data relevant for that purpose. It is also assumed that on an informal basis, each employee's immediate supervisor is familiar with the quantity and quality of the subordinate's performance (Mathis & Jackson, 1999, p. 102). Presumptively, systematic performance evaluations and supervisors' firsthand knowledge of employees is sufficient to identify those employees whose performance does not meet the organization's standards (Redeker, 1989).

Identifying problematic employees is a legitimate management goal as organizations seek to enhance the quality of the service they deliver and maintain positive relations with clients and customers. This is particularly important in human service organizations such as the police that routinely engage in a high level of interactions with citizen-clients (Bittner, 1970; Reiss, 1971). Alpert and Moore (1993, p.130) argued that the goals of community policing require police departments to develop personnel evaluation systems that reward officers who avoid using force without justification (and by implication identify and properly discipline those who use excessive force).

Police personnel evaluation systems, however, have generally failed to provide meaningful assessments of performance. As Westley (1970, pp. 24–30) noted, police departments have been punishment oriented, with few formal programs for helping individual officers improve performance and little organizational focus on officers with recurring performance problems. Standard in-service training programs are generally directed at all sworn officers and not just officers with special performance problems. Employee assistance programs (EAPs), meanwhile, are generally voluntary and directed toward officers with marital, psychological, or substance abuse problems, not officers with on-the-street performance problems (Ayers, 1990; Finn & Tomz, 1997). Thus, for example, an overly aggressive officer who receives a high rate of citizen complaints but has no off-the-job personal problems would fall outside the scope of standard EAPs.

A review of police personnel evaluation systems nearly 25 years ago found that they had serious deficiencies. In particular, the formal categories for performance assessment were vague and global (e.g., "initiative," "dependability") (Landy, 1977). A more recent report, reflecting the concerns of community policing, rendered an equally critical assessment. Oettmeier and Wycoff (1997) concluded that "most performance evaluations currently used by police agencies do not reflect the work officers do" (p. 5). In particular, they fail to address the most critical aspects of police work, notably the exercise of discretion under conditions of uncertainty and stress, with the most important decisions involving the use of deadly or physical force. The neglect of these aspects of the job is particularly important because of the unique role of the police (Bittner, 1970). And, as Alpert and Moore (1993) argued, community policing creates the need for even more comprehensive and sophisticated performance evaluation systems.

The historic failure to address problem officers is particularly notable because, as Goldstein (1977) observed, those officers "are well known to their supervisors, the top administrators, to their peers, and to the residents of the areas in which they work"; nonetheless, "little is done to alter their conduct" (p. 171). Insofar as law enforcement agencies took any kind of action, anecdotal evidence suggests that they "dumped" problem officers on racial minority neighborhoods (Reiss, 1971, pp. 167–168).

Two recent examples illustrate the extent to which some contemporary police departments have failed to collect, much less utilize, relevant data on potential officer misconduct. Prior to the 1997 consent decree with the U.S. Department of Justice (*United States v. City of Pittsburgh,* 1997), the Pittsburgh Police Bureau did not have a comprehensive department-wide database on citizen complaints, use-of-force incidents, and other problematic behavior. Similarly, prior to 1999, the LAPD did not ensure that all citizen complaints brought to the attention of the department were in fact officially recorded and eventually forwarded to a centralized office (Office of the Inspector General, 1997).

History of the EW Concept

Emergence of the Concept

The first EW programs appear to have developed independently in a number of different departments in the late 1970s. The process of development was ad hoc and experimental, without the guidance of recommended or model programs. And because these initial programs appear to have beer short lived, few records survive. Several departments began using indicators of activities to monitor officers' involvement in citizen contacts that involved use of deadly force and in response to growing public concern about that particular issue (Milton, Halleck, Lardner, & Albrecht, 1977). These initial approaches included review of arrest reports and identification of situations that involved the use of force by officers.

In Oakland, for example, records were kept on individual officers to determine whether any officers showed early signs of trouble. In addition, computers were used to determine whether any officer characteristics such as age, length of service, or education correlated with their use of force (Milton et al., 1977, p. 96). Toch et al. (1975) developed an experimental peer counseling program directed toward officers with recurring performance problems.

In New York City, information on each officer's use of force, use of firearms, complaints, discipline, sick leave, and off-duty employment was used to determine whether that officer needed further monitoring or intervention. Officers who entered the information into the files were responsible for noting trends in behavior or activities and reporting them to a supervising officer (Milton et al., 1977, p. 96).

The Kansas City Police Department, meanwhile, cross-referenced officers with their supervisors "on the theory that particular supervisory officers may be tolerating abusive behavior" (Milton et al., 1977, p. 97). The department also participated in a Police Foundation experiment in peer counseling designed to improve the performance of officers with recurring problems (Pate, McCullough, Bowers, & Ferrara, 1976).

The concept of EW systems received its first official endorsement in 1981 by the U.S. Commission on Civil Rights in its report *Who Is Guarding the Guardians.* The report was based largely on hearings with regard to police misconduct in Philadelphia, Memphis, and Houston. It included data on Houston police officers indicating that a small percentage of officers received a disproportionate share of complaints. The commission recommended that police departments create and utilize early warning systems, arguing that

> the careful maintenance of records based on written complaints is essential to indicate officers who are frequently the subject of complaints or who demonstrate identifiable patterns of inappropriate behavior. Some jurisdictions have "early warning" information systems for monitoring officers' involvement in violent confrontations. The police departments studied routinely ignore early warning signs. (U.S. Commission on Civil Rights, 1981, p. 159)

The First Permanent EW Systems

The initial experiments with EW systems appear to have been short lived, and none of those identified by Milton et al. (1977) have survived to the present. The first EW systems known to have been maintained from their inception to the present were created in the Miami Police Department and in the Miami-Dade Police Department in the late 1970s.

Miami Police Department. The Miami Police Department became concerned with its officers' behavior that generated citizen complaints in 1979, in response to a major police-community relations crisis (Porter, 1984; U.S. Commission on Civil Rights, 1984). In a May 29, 1979, memorandum to the chief, the commander of the internal security unit suggested an EW system based on the principle of organizational development. That is, the development of the organization's capacity to provide better service to the public and to reduce both citizen complaints and the perception of poor service required attention to those officers and/or department practices that created real or perceived problems with the public. This memorandum proposed a "cyclical model where the problem is diagnosed, outside professionals are consulted, strategies are developed, programs are implemented and evaluated, and results are fed back to begin the cycle again" (Ross, 1979, p. 1).

To demonstrate his idea, Commander John S. Ross had identified a list of officers, by assignment, who had two or more citizen complaints during a 2-year period (1976–1978). Ross also compiled a list of officers who had received five or more civilian complaints during that period. Armed with those data and the internal security monthly activity reports, Ross computed some interesting statistics. He found that the average number of complaints filed against a Miami police officer was .65 per year and 1.3 complaints for 2 years. He found that 5% of the officers accounted for 25% of all complaints. He noted, "If this group were suddenly removed from our department, our complaint picture could be reduced by as much as one-fourth. Obviously, this group should warrant some special attention, if we are to reduce our complaint incidence" (Ross, 1979, pp. 2–3).

At the midpoint in the study, the average Miami police officer was 32 years old with 8 years of service. The officers with five or more complaints were 27.5 years old with 4.2 years of service. The officers with the most complaints were disproportionately assigned to midnight shift. The complaint of excessive force made up 9% of complaints against all officers, but for those with two to four complaints, the complaint of excessive force made up 13% of complaints, and for those with five or more complaints, the figure increased to 16%. A similar relationship was found with complaints for harassment.

Ross (1979) suggested that commanders and supervisors should be systematically provided with information "that can be used to identify problem officers" (p. 7). He also noted that off-duty employment, including rock concerts, wrestling matches, and football games, generates a high number of citizen complaints. He reasoned that fatigue may "heighten an officer's opportunity to react in an aggressive manner" (p. 10). Ross suggested that the department should respond to these officers before they become involved in self-destructive activities or develop a trend of violating departmental orders. His proposal included more intensive supervision, counseling by outside professionals, and training in tactics and strategies. Ross (1979) concluded,

> The problem will not vanish, but it can be reduced through constant attention. The

> solutions will not be cheap, they will be time consuming, and may be difficult to implement. However, the potential is there to make a significant impact on the citizen complaint's [*sic*] against police officers. (p. 12)

The Miami EW system evolved into one of the more comprehensive approaches to monitoring police officers in the United States. Most important, it currently uses a broader range of performance indicators than other EW systems, many of which rely solely on citizen complaints as performance indicators (Walker et al., 1999). As officers are identified by the system, their supervisors are notified by official memorandum. The supervisor is then responsible for meeting with the officer and determining whether he or she needs any assistance, counseling, training, or other intervention.

The Miami EW system uses four categories of behavior as selection criteria for identifying officers (Departmental Order 2, Chap. 8). These data, which are routinely collected by the department and entered into a department-wide database, include the following:

1. Complaints—A list of all officers with five or more complaints, with a finding of sustained or inconclusive, for the previous 2 years
2. Control of persons (use of force)—A list of all officers involved as principals in five or more control-of-persons incidents for the previous 2 years
3. Reprimands—A list of all employees with five or more reprimands for the previous 2 years
4. Discharge of firearms—A list of all officers with three or more discharge of firearms within the previous five years.

An officer who is identified by the EW system is subject to a performance review by his or her supervisor. The internal affairs unit provides the supervisor with a report of each incident that caused the officer to be placed on the EW system. The supervisor evaluates these reports to determine whether the officer's behavior was consistent with professional standards (e.g., use of force justified by the circumstances, citizen complaint without merit) or whether there are behavior problems (e.g., unjustified use of force) that require attention. In this respect, the EW system is discretionary and not mandatory. Not all officers identified by the performance indicators will be referred for intervention.

In the case of officers requiring formal intervention, the supervisor then writes a memorandum recommending one of the following: reassignment, retraining, transfer, referral to an employee assistance program, fitness-for-duty evaluation, or dismissal pursuant to civil service rules and regulations. The supervisor's memorandum goes to the commander of internal affairs through the chain of command. Each reviewing supervisor must agree or disagree with the recommendation. It is important to note that, unlike some other EW systems, a number of supervisors are involved in decisions related to potential problem officers, with the result that these decisions represent a consensus of opinion.

Miami-Dade Police Department. Several events took place in the Miami area during the late 1970s that created problems for police officers in the Miami-Dade Police Department, formerly the Metro-Dade Police Department, and Dade County Sheriff's Office. The beating of an African American schoolteacher and the beating death of another African American (insurance agent Arthur McDuffie) by Miami-Dade officers aggravated existing racial tensions in the Miami area. On May 17, 1980, the four officers accused of the death of McDuffie were acquitted by an all-White jury in Tampa. Upon notification of the verdict, 3 days of riots broke out that resulted in civilian deaths and millions of dollars in property damage (Porter, 1984; U.S. Commission on Civil Rights, 1982).

As a result of the problems, the Dade County Commission enacted local legislation that made public the internal investigations conducted by the Miami-Dade Police Department. In addition, an employee profile system was adopted to track formally all complaints, use-of-force incidents, commendations, discipline, and disposition of all internal investigations. As an offshoot of the employee profile system, the Miami-Dade Police Department implemented the early identification system (EIS) under the supervision of the Internal Review Bureau. This system was created because early signs of potential problems are often not apparent to officers and may be missed by some supervisors. It is not clear what role the city of Miami's EW system had in the development of the system for the Metro-Dade Police Department.

In 1981, a system of quarterly and annual EIS reports was instituted. Quarterly reports listed officers who had received two or more complaints that had been investigated and closed, or who were involved in three or more use-of-force incidents during a 3-month reporting period. Annual reports listed employees who had been identified in two or more quarterly reports. The requirement that complaints be investigated and closed before they would qualify to be included in the quarterly report created a timing problem, because many complaints would take months before they were investigated and closed. Because of this problem, monthly reports were issued in 1992, which listed employees who had received two or more complaints during the past 60 days (regardless of disposition). It is these monthly reports that have identified officers with the most recent complaints or behavioral concerns. Major Dan Flynn (n.d., p. 2) reported that

> patterns of certain kinds of officer behavior, such as serious disputes with citizens and/or co-workers, or an above-average rate of using force, can be very predictive of more serious stress-related episodes to follow. Even though not all complaints and disputes are the fault of the involved officer, a process that enables a review of those events is invaluable. It makes it possible to reach officers who may be experiencing an escalating level of stress, before it gets out of hand and results in serious misconduct.

The monthly, quarterly, and annual reports are disseminated to the supervisors of the listed officers. The information on the list is "utilized by supervisors as a resource to determine if job stress or performance problems exist. They are designed as a resource in evaluating and guiding an employee's job performance and conduct" (Charette, n.d., p. 5). The information included in these reports is used by supervisors as one resource about an officer's performance and in conjunction with other information to provide a comprehensive picture of that officer's performance.

The immediate supervisor of any officer identified by the system receives a report on that officer. The supervisor then discusses the report with the officer and determines what further action is needed. The options include no further action or referral to departmental or outside programs, including psychological services, stress abatement programs, and specialized training programs. In 1981, 150 employees were identified in the two initial reports. In 1982, 46 employees were identified in all four quarterly reports. This decline is due to a number of factors, including the improved recruitment and selection procedures in the agency, not just the EIS. Between 1981 and 1992, departmental strength increased approximately 96%, but complaints remained at an average of approximately 300 per year. Charette (n.d.) concluded his report by noting: "A department's ability to monitor and control its employees [*sic*] conduct in a formalized tracking system, instills confidence in the employees, the organization, and the public it serves" (p.12).

Issues Related to EW Systems

The national evaluation of EW systems found that they are complex administrative tools, with a number of different goals, program elements, and potential impacts (Walker et al., 1999). There is presently no consensus of opinion among professionals with regard to any of these issues. EW systems are also high-maintenance operations requiring careful planning and a high level of ongoing administrative attention. The following section discusses the various issues related to the development and ongoing administration of EW systems.

Program Goals

EW systems are widely understood to be directed toward so-called problem officers, with the goal of reducing on-the-street police misconduct (U.S. Commission on Civil Rights, 1981). The national evaluation, however, found that the goals of EW systems must be understood in broader terms. This interpretation follows developments in private sector employment where human resource development is seen as operating at three levels: individual, group, and organization (Poole & Warner, 1998, p. 93). Consistent with that approach, law enforcement EW systems can be understood to have separate program goals related to individual officers, supervisors, and departments as a whole.

Individual Officers. EW systems are directed in part toward individual rank-and-file officers. The anticipated impact on an individual officer involves learning theory, deterrence theory, or some combination of the two.

Many EW systems are officially conceptualized as a means of helping officers. The New Orleans Professional Performance Enhancement Program (PPEP), for example, explicitly states that it is designed to help and not punish officers. The intervention phase includes a stress reduction component and a training session designed to help officers understand how to handle potentially volatile situations without incurring citizen complaints. In this respect, the anticipated impact of EW systems on officers may be characterized in terms of a learning effect.

At the same time, an implicit assumption of EW systems is that they will deter future misconduct. That is, the intervention phase will communicate to subject officers the threat of punishment in the future if their present behavior continues (Zimring & Hawkins, 1973). There is also an implicit assumption that an EW system will have some general deterrent effect on officers not subject to the system. The system theoretically communicates the threat of punishment should their performance warrant placement on the EW system.

In at least one observed police department, the EW system had a labeling effect, and officers were observed to refer to themselves as "bad boys" and to the program as "bad boys school" and "politeness school" (Walker et al., 1999). Thus, one of the dangers of EW systems is that through a labeling process (Schur, 1972), they will reinforce undesirable attitudes (and perhaps undesirable performance) among subject officers.

Deterrence theorists point out that deterrence is a communication system and that research to date has not adequately explored the extent to which a threat of punishment is perceived by its intended audience (Nagin, 1998). The same problem applies to EW systems, whether conceptualized in terms of deterrence, learning, or labeling. Thus, it is possible that some officers will be readily deterred by an EW system, some will learn from the counseling or training they receive, and some will not be affected by either process. By the same token, some officers may embrace the label of bad boy whereas others will not.

The national evaluation found that EW systems in three sites are effective in reducing citizen complaints and use-of-force reports among officers subject to intervention. The data are reported in Walker et al. (1999).

Supervisors. EW systems also have some impact on supervisors. This goal was explicitly acknowledged in two of the sites in the national evaluation (Miami-Dade and New Orleans), although in different ways, but not in the third (Minneapolis, Minnesota). The New Orleans PPEP requires the supervisor of a subject officer to monitor that individual for 6 months and to file performance evaluations every 2 weeks. Thus, the system has a formal mechanism for holding supervisors accountable for their behavior. New Orleans officials responsible for the PPEP expressed their belief that some supervisors would aggressively urge subject officers to improve their performance because further indicators of poor performance would reflect badly on them (Walker et al., 1999).

In Miami-Dade, several officials associated with the EW system explained that it "keeps things from slipping through the cracks." That is, the formal requirements of the program help ensure that a supervisor will pay closer than normal attention to an officer who is having performance problems and recognize that without such a safeguard the necessary attention may be lost in the rush of normal day-to-day work. The Minneapolis EW system paid little explicit attention to the behavior of supervisors (but see the subsequent changes in the program discussed below).

The potential impact of EW systems addresses an important issue in police management. Moore and Stephens (1991, p. 92) argued that one "particularly troubling deficiency" of traditional police management has been the lack of systems for monitoring the performance of supervisors. EW systems offer one potential remedy for that deficiency by defining specific activities related to holding officers under their command accountable. As is the case with the impact of EW systems on individual officers, however, there are a number of important but unresolved issues related to the impact of an EW system on supervisors. It is not known whether a formal monitoring process has a positive effect on supervisors or whether it is counterproductive because of the paperwork demands and a perceived intrusion into a supervisor's autonomy.

Departments. EW systems also have some impact on the organizations in which they function. Organizational development is seen as one of the key goals of human resource management (Mathis & Jackson, 1999, pp. 98–102; Poole & Warner, 1998, p. 93). The national evaluation, however, found that this was the least well-articulated aspect of EW systems. In theory, an EW system improves the overall quality of police service to the extent that it effects improvements in the behavior of individual officers. At the same time, to the extent that an EW system changes the behavior of supervisors, it has some broader impact on the department. Finally, to an unknown extent, the existence of an EW system communicates a general message about a department's values, indicating that misconduct will not be tolerated. From this perspective, an EW system can be conceptualized as one means of controlling police department use of authority in the service of a comprehensive strategic management of police departments (Moore & Stephens, 1991).

With respect to organizations, the national evaluation found that instead of affecting organizations, EW systems are more likely to be affected by the organization in which they operate. At one extreme, an EW system is not likely to be effective in a police department that has no serious commitment to accountability and integrity and where serious forms of misconduct are not punished. In this context, the EW system may well become little more than a formal bureaucratic procedure, empty of meaningful content. The potential contributions of an EW system will simply be overwhelmed by the failure of the department to investigate alleged misconduct and discipline officers appropriately. It is also possible that a poorly managed EW system will generate hostility and cynicism among officers to the extent that it harms the larger organizational environment (Omaha Police Union, 1992).

At the other end of the continuum, an EW system is most likely to be effective in a department that has high standards of accountability and, as a part of that commitment, has in place a personnel data system that captures the relevant data on police officer performance. In one of the sites in the national evaluation (Miami-Dade), the EW system was found to be simply one part of a larger personnel data system that, in turn, is part of a broader commitment to accountability. In this context, the EW system functions as a management tool that converts the data into a usable form.

The vast majority of police departments undoubtedly fall somewhere in the middle of this continuum. In many of those instances, the EW system has the potential for helping to change the organizational culture and enhancing standards of accountability. Investigating the impact of EW systems on organizations was not part of the design of the national evaluation, and no systematic data on this issue exist (Walker et al., 1999). Further research is needed on this subject.

Program Components

EW systems consist of three basic components: selection criteria, intervention, and postintervention monitoring. The national evaluation found considerable variation in each of these components. There is also at present no consensus of opinion among law enforcement specialists as to the ideal components of an EW system.

Selection Criteria. EW systems operate on the basis of a set of formal criteria for identifying problem officers and selecting them for intervention. The national evaluation found considerable variation in the selection criteria currently being used and a lack of consensus within the law enforcement community with regard to the appropriate set of criteria.

Some EW systems rely solely on citizen complaints (e.g., Minneapolis), whereas others rely on a broad range of performance indicators (e.g., Miami-Dade and New Orleans). The indicators include but are not limited to official use-of-force reports, involvement in civil litigation, and violations of administrative rules (e.g., neglect of duty).

The use of multiple indicators provides a broader base of information about an officer's performance compared with reliance on citizen complaints alone. Citizen complaints are highly underreported (Walker & Graham, 1998) and therefore are unlikely to lead to the identification of officers whose behavior legitimately requires intervention. In a number of law enforcement agencies, citizen complaints are received by an independent citizen oversight agency (Walker, 2000). In these jurisdictions, it is not necessarily the case that the law enforcement agency receives timely or complete reports on all complaints filed.

Multiple indicators are more likely to identify officers whose performance is genuinely problematic and in need of some official intervention. Departmental use-of-force reports are widely used by EW systems, but their reliability depends on the scope of a department's reporting requirements, the extent of officer compliance with those requirements, and the existence of a data system that ensures that all relevant reports are entered into the EW database.

In sum, there are a number of unresolved issues related to selection criteria, including the best set of performance indicators to be used and the management infrastructure necessary to ensure that the relevant data are entered into the EW system. The national evaluation drew no conclusions with regard to the relative effectiveness of different selection criteria.

Intervention. The intervention phase of an EW system may consist of either an informal counseling session between the officer and his or her immediate supervisor or a training class involving a group of officers (e.g., New Orleans).

With respect to individual counseling sessions, there are a number of issues related to the delivery and content of the counseling. In Minneapolis, for example, the requirement that supervisors document the counseling session was abolished after a few years. In the absence of documentation and close supervision, there is no guarantee that counseling sessions will in fact occur, that supervisors will deliver the appropriate message, or that counseling sessions will be consistent across supervisors. It is entirely possible that some supervisors simply tell their officers not to worry about it, with the result being that the goals of the EW system are undermined. Some EW systems involve higher-ranking command officers (e.g., commander of professional standards or internal affairs unit) in the counseling sessions, thereby ensuring consistency and guarding against the delivery of inappropriate messages.

Group training sessions, such as the PPEP classes in New Orleans, have the advantage of ensuring consistency of content. At the same time, however, a group approach inhibits the delivery of the appropriate message to officers who may have very different performance problems. The group approach also runs the risk of creating solidarity among officers in the class, causing them to embrace the bad boys label and reinforcing inappropriate attitudes (Schur, 1972). This effect occurred in at least one known instance (Omaha Police Union, 1992).

The national evaluation was not able to determine whether one form of intervention is more effective than other forms (Walker et al., 1999). More research on this issue is needed.

Postintervention Monitoring. Extreme variations are found among EW systems with respect to postintervention monitoring of subject officers. At one extreme are highly formal systems with considerable required documentation. At the other extreme are highly informal systems with no documentation.

The New Orleans PPEP represents a highly formal system. Subject officers are monitored for 6 months following intervention. Supervisors are required to observe subject officers on duty and to file a signed evaluation of officers' performance every 2 weeks (New Orleans Police Department, 1998). As noted above, this approach has the effect of putting supervisors on notice that their behavior is being monitored. Whether this approach has a positive effect on supervisors or is dysfunctional because of the increased paperwork requirements is not known.

Informal postintervention monitoring approaches rely on supervisors to monitor subject officers' performance and, in the event of further indicators of poor performance (e.g., citizen complaints), take whatever steps they deem necessary. In the absence of documentation or close supervision by higher-ranking officers, however, there is no guarantee that the expected informal monitoring will occur.

One of the unresolved issues related to postintervention monitoring involves striking the proper balance between a formal bureaucratic approach designed to hold supervisors accountable and an informal approach designed to enhance efficiency and flexibility.

Program Administration

The national evaluation found that EW systems are complex, high-maintenance operations, requiring a significant investment by the department in planning, personnel, data collection, and administrative oversight.

The national evaluation found that in two of the sites (Miami-Dade and New Orleans), the EW system was established with considerable initial planning and ongoing administrative attention, whereas in the third site (Minneapolis), the EW system had received little in the way of administrative attention. Yet, in that third site, developments subsequent to the evaluation period indicate that considerable new attention has been given to the EW system and that it has been substantially strengthened as a result.

The administrative demands of an EW system are illustrated by the New Orleans Police Department's PPEP, the most elaborate EW system of the three case studies in the national evaluation. The department's Public Integrity Division employs one full-time (nonsworn) data analyst and uses part of the time of two other full-time employees (one of whom is sworn) for the purpose of data entry. The Miami-Dade EW system, meanwhile, is an integral part of a sophisticated data system on police officer performance that has been developed over the course of two decades.

Conclusion

EW systems have emerged as a popular remedy for police misconduct. The national evaluation has found that EW systems exist in slightly more than one-fourth of all law enforcement agencies and are spreading rapidly.

The national evaluation also found that EW systems vary considerably in terms of their formal program content, specifically with respect to selection criteria, the nature of the intervention, and postintervention follow-up. There are many unresolved issues related to these program elements, however, and it is not possible at present to specify any one approach that is the most effective.

EW systems are a potentially important management tool for the control of police officer misconduct and for promoting standards of accountability within a law enforcement agency. The national evaluation found, however, that EW systems are expensive, complex, high-maintenance operations, requiring a significant investment of administrative resources. There is evidence that some EW systems are essentially symbolic gestures with little substantive content. There is also some preliminary evidence that well-run EW systems are effective in reducing the number of citizen complaints and problematic behavior.

An EW system is no panacea for problems of misconduct and a lack of accountability. An EW system should be seen as one part of a system of accountability. In a law enforcement agency without effective accountability measures in place, it is unlikely than an EW system will have much, if any, effect. At the same time, in an agency that has made a commitment to accountability, an EW system can serve as one of several management tools designed to curb misconduct and raise the quality of services delivered to the public.

References

Alpert, G., & Moore, M. H. (1993). Measuring police performance in the new paradigm of policing. In *Performance measures for the criminal justice system.* Washington, DC: Government Printing Office.

Ayers, R. M. (1990). *Preventing law enforcement stress: The organization's role.* Washington, DC: Government Printing Office.

Bittner, E. (1970). *The functions of the police in modern society.* Washington, DC: National Institute of Mental Health.

Charette, B. (n.d.). *Early identification of police brutality and misconduct.* Unpublished manuscript, Metro-Dade Police Department, Miami, FL.

Christopher Commission. (1991). *Report of the independent commission on the Los Angeles Police Department.* Los Angeles: City of Los Angeles.

DC police lead nation in shootings. (1998, November 15). The Washington Post, p. 1.

Finn, P., & Tomz, J. E. (1997). *Developing a law enforcement stress program for officers and their families.* Washington, DC: Government Printing Office.

Flynn, D. (n.d.). *Reducing incidents of officer misconduct: An early warning system.* Unpublished manuscript, Metro-Dade Police Department, Miami, FL.

Goldstein, H. (1977). *Policing a free society.* Cambridge, MA: Ballinger.

International Association of Chiefs of Police. (1989). *Building integrity and reducing drug corruption in police departments.* Washington, DC: Government Printing Office.

Kansas City police go after their "bad boys." (1991, September 10). *The New York Times,* p. 1.

Landy, F. (1977). *Performance appraisal in police departments.* Washington, DC: Police Foundation.

Mathis, R. L., & Jackson, J. H. (Eds.). (1999). *Human resource management: Essential perspectives.* Cincinnati, OH: Southwestern College.

Milton, C., Halleck, J., Lardner, J., & Albrecht, G. (1977). *Police use of deadly force.* Washington, DC: Police Foundation.

Moore, M. H., & Stephens, D. W. (1991). *Beyond command and control: The strategic management of police departments.* Washington, DC: Police Executive Research Forum.

Nagin, D. (1998). Criminal deterrence research at the outset of the twenty-first century. In M. Tonry (Ed.), *Crime and justice: A review of research* (Vol. 23). Chicago: University of Chicago Press.

New Orleans Police Department. (1998). *Professional Performance Enhancement Program* (PPEP). New Orleans, LA: Author.

Oettmeier, T. N., & Wycoff, M. A. (1997). *Personnel performance evaluations in the community policing context.* Washington, DC: Police Executive Research Forum.

Office of the Inspector General. (1997). *Six-month report.* Los Angeles: Los Angeles Police Commission.

Omaha Police Union. (1992, April). Bad boy/girl class notes shared. *The Shield,* p. 1.

Pate, T., McCullough, J. W., Bowers, R. A., & Ferrara, A. (1976). *Kansas City peer review panel: An evaluation.* Washington, DC: Police Foundation.

Poole, M., &Warner, M. (1998). *The IEBM handbook of human resource management.* London: International Thomson Business Press.

Porter, B. (1984). *The Miami riot of 1980.* Lexington, MA: Lexington Books.

Redeker, J. (1989). *Employee discipline: Policies and practices.* Washington, DC: Bureau of National Affairs.

Reiss, A. J. (1991). *The police and the public.* New Haven, CT. Yale University Press.

Reiter, L. (1998). *Law enforcement administrative investigations* (2nd ed.). Tallahassee, FL: Louo Reiter and Associates.

Ross, J. S. (1979, May 29). Citizen complaints against police officers (Memorandum from Commander John S. Ross to Chief Kennith I. Harms).

Schur, E. (1972). *Labeling deviant behavior.* New York: Harper & Row.

Stix, G. (1994, December). Bad apple picker: Can a neural network help find problem cops? *Scientific American,* 44–45.

Toch, H. J., Grant, D., & Galvin, R. T. (1975). *Agents of change.* New York: John Wiley.

United States v. City of Pittsburgh (W.D.P.A., 1997).

U.S. Commission on Civil Rights. (1981). *Who is guarding the guardians.* Washington, DC: Author.

U.S. Commission on Civil Rights. (1984). *Confronting racial isolation in Miami.* Washington, DC: Government Printing Office.

U.S. Department of Justice. (1997a). *Police integrity: Public service with honor.* Washington, DC: Government Printing Office.

U.S. Department of Justice. (1997b). *Police use of force: Collection of national data.* Washington, DC: Government Printing Office.

Walker, S. (2000). *Police accountability: The role of citizen oversight.* Belmont, CA: Wadsworth.

Walker, S., Alpert, G. P., & Kenney, D. (1999). *Responding to the problem police officer—A national evaluation of early warning systems.* Interim final report, National Institute of Justice.

Walker, S., & Graham, N. (1998). Citizen complaints in response to police misconduct: The results of a victimization survey. *Police Quarterly, 1,* 65–90.

Wave of abuse claims laid to a few officers. (1992, October 4). *The Boston Globe,* p. 1.

Westley, W. A. (1970). *Violence and the police.* Cambridge, MA: MIT Press.

Zimring, R. E., & Hawkins, G. J. (1973). *Deterrence: The legal threat in crime control.* Chicago: University of Chicago Press.

Samuel Walker, Geoffrey P. Alpert, and Dennis Jay Kenney, "Early Warning Systems for Police: Concept, History, and Issues." Reprinted from *Police Quarterly,* Vol. 3 No. 2, June 2000, pp. 132–152. Copyright © 2000 Sage Publications, Inc. Reprinted by permission of Sage Publications, Inc. ✦

Chapter 13

Preparing Police Officers for Success in the Twenty-First Century

Quint C. Thurman

Selecting, training, and retaining men and women to undertake the complex duties of a modern police officer comprise another set of challenges for contemporary policing. Here the author discusses these elements, their importance, and how agencies might effectively hire the best personnel to serve the public safety needs of our communities in the future.

Thurman notes that a crucial first step in the selection process is the recruitment of a diverse applicant pool that represents the social and demographic characteristics of the community in which the police agency operates. Following this, it is also important for the community to be represented in an assessment process that includes exercises aimed at determining essential cognitive and communication skills. Once applicants are selected, recruit training, field training, and advanced training are the keys to equipping personnel with the level of preparedness needed to perform well in a contemporary public safety agency that must accommodate a complex social environment.

Gerald Heuett, Jr., a Phoenix police officer and a technical advisor to the Arizona Regional Community Policing Institute, when training police about what citizens expect of them, uses an exercise that helps distinguish a professional police perspective from one that views community policing as its primary goal. He begins the exercise by asking a class of 30 or so to identify the characteristics of the ideal patrol officer. Typically they describe a person who has courage, is brave under fire, and who can be counted on to come to the aid of a fellow officer in trouble. Heuett next asks them to describe the officer they might want on the scene of a hypothetical situation involving their own son or daughter in a serious automobile crash. Here the group describes an officer in terms such as compassionate, sensitive, fair, and calm under pressure. This exercise places police officers in the same position as the citizens they serve. Heuett believes that the striking difference in the responses to the first and second questions is that in the second the participants have unknowingly answered the same way that citizens do when they are asked to describe their image of the ideal police officer. Although the police admire colleagues who exhibit bravery and know how to take charge in dangerous situations, when the people they care most about are the recipients of police services, they prefer them to be treated with compassion and fairness just the same as ordinary citizens do.

This exercise raises an interesting question. What accounts for differences in the way in which officers and the public view the role of the police in society?

Explaining the Law Enforcement Perspective Among Uniformed Personnel

Police scholars have noted differences in the orientation of the police and the public. For example, Victor Kappeler, Richard Sluder, and Geoffrey Alpert suggest that key among public-police differences is their "worldview."[1]

> The way the police view the world can be described as a "we/they" or "us/them" orientation. Police tend to see the world as being composed of insiders and outsiders—police and citizens. Persons who are not

> police officers are considered outsiders and are viewed with suspicion.[2]

People who are police officers develop their own particular *ethos,* involving three specific traits that are central to the police profession. It has been suggested that the high value placed on bravery, autonomy, and secrecy distinguish the police as an occupational group.[3]

As part of their occupation, police are expected to be brave in the face of danger, braver than any other group because they are the people who have the legitimate right to use force, and they are the ones whom the public calls when such force may be needed to maintain or restore order. Similarly, they value autonomy, that is, considerable discretion in deciding how to handle situations because no rulebook can cover every situation that an officer might encounter, nor does the administration necessarily want to control their every action. Finally, the police value secrecy in the way they obtain information and in their procedures, because they tend to view civilians as outsiders who might not understand or fully appreciate the way the police control crime.

There are at least three major explanations that might explain why police and citizens have different views about how policing should be done and what skills are needed.

One explanation for these differences might be the kind of people selected to do this job. Owing to the kinds of people drawn to careers in policing in the first place, and to the kinds of people that police departments prefer to hire, the policing profession tends to consist of people who share certain traits that make them very similar to one another and different from citizens in general.

From the author's experience, college students interested in careers in law enforcement (mostly criminal justice majors) usually choose policing for the opportunity it might present for working outdoors and because it gives them the chance to do work that helps people. Research on this topic reveals that applicants for jobs in policing come from backgrounds not all that different from the backgrounds of citizens in general. For example, scholar Lawrence Sherman writes:

> The limited evidence suggests police work attracts the sons and daughters of successful tradespeople, foremen, and civil servants—especially police. For many of them, the good salary (relative to the educational requirements), job security, and prestige of police work represent a good step up in the world, an improvement on their parents' position in life.[4]

Sherman goes on to point out that police recruits typically are drawn to policing for understandable reasons, rather than based upon personality quirks or dysfunctions:

> The motivation to become a police officer flows naturally from the social position of the people who choose policing. People do not seem to choose policing out of an irrational lust for power or because they have an "authoritarian personality." . . . Police applicants tend to see police work as an adventure, as a chance to do work out of doors without being cooped up in an office, as a chance to do work that is important for the good of society, and not as a chance to be the "toughest guy on the block."[5]

At the same time, police hiring practices in the professional style have favored applicants who appreciate rules and regulations, demonstrate a need for order, believe strongly in the legal system as a legitimate source of authority, and tend to support the idea of a chain of command as an appropriate way to manage personnel. Kappeler and his colleagues suggest that the preferences of police departments for certain traits in job applicants seem to indicate that the police favor "conformity to a middle-class life style" as one key indicator of the acceptability of prospective candidates. They even suggest that:

> Police selection practices, such as the use of physical agility tests, background investigations, polygraph examinations, psychological tests and oral interviews, are all tools to screen-out applicants who have not demonstrated their conformity to middle-

> class norms and values. Many of the selection techniques that are used to determine the "adequacy" of police applicants have little to do with their ability to perform the real duties associated with police work. . . .[6]

Furthermore, Kappeler and his colleagues conclude that, "A consequence of the traditional police personnel system is that it selects officers who are unable to identify with many of the marginal groups in society."[7]

A second explanation for differences between the worldviews of citizens and police officers is that the training received by new recruits introduces them to, and then helps them accept, a perspective that they may not have previously subscribed to as civilians. In the terminology used by sociologists, academy training serves to "resocialize" the new recruits, helping them to devalue their old way of looking at the world and replace it with a new view that fits the job and the labor force that is responsible for providing police services.

Despite the fact that official statistics refute the highly risky nature of police work, academy training tends to place a heavy emphasis on its dangerousness. This focus is accomplished primarily through the "war stories" that police trainers use to depict the dangers that lie in wait for the unsuspecting new recruit.

> Police vicariously experience, learn and relearn the potential for danger through "war stories" and field training after graduation from the police academy. In fact, an inordinate amount of attention and misinformation concerning the dangers of police work is provided to police recruits at police academies.[8]

The emphasis on the potential for danger that is supposed to alert new recruits to the need to be prepared for nearly any situation typically leads to two negative consequences. Although raising officer awareness about the unpredictability of human behavior may benefit officer safety and forewarn new recruits about the peculiarities of the career path they have chosen, the traditional academy curriculum and the war stories told by police veterans help to build a chasm between those people who are sworn to uphold the law and those other people—civilians—who are seen as potential victims, witnesses, and offenders. In so doing, the traditional curriculum reinforces and elevates the subculture of policing as the thin blue line (or as retired Minneapolis police chief Anthony Bouza calls it, the "brotherhood in blue")[9] that keeps ordered society from becoming chaotic. At the same time, the curriculum encourages police officers to be suspicious of the public as the group that will produce both unworthy victims and offensive criminals.

Traditional training practices underscore the need to maintain social distance between those in uniform ("us") versus the public ("them"), thereby justifying a gap between police officers as professionals and citizens as mere consumers of police services. Observations of academy training and data collected from academy cadets support the view that traditional training reinforces police insularity and negative stereotypes of civilians. For example, John Stratton's interviews with new police recruits colorfully illustrate the impact that training has on individual officers and their families. He quotes the wife of one police cadet undergoing training:

> Those cadets sure change a lot when they go through the academy. He's only been there six weeks and I'm trying to find a way to let him know that the kids and I are not "assholes" or "pieces of shit."[10]

A third explanation for differences in the perspectives of police and citizens is that experiences on the job ultimately shape the way police officers view their world. Bouza suggests that the nature of police work and the police subculture itself can ruin the altruism of well-intentioned new recruits. He writes:

> A wrong assumption made about the police is that they're not very adept at weeding out the palpably unfit at the entrance level. On the contrary, the thoroughness of the background investigation nearly guaran-

tees that new recruits will be qualified for the job.[11]

Speaking from his experiences, Bouza instead suggests that it is the policing experience itself that determines what kind of officer the department will produce:

> The background investigators (other cops trained for that purpose) find out an enormous amount of information about a candidate's life. Those later found to be unfit are usually exposed because of a predilection for brutality. They tend to be veterans, shaped by the agency rather than by their genes or preentrance proclivities. Most of the brutes I encountered, in three police agencies, were probably formed and subtly encouraged by the agency's culture. The background check tends to exclude the feckless, the irresponsible, and those with poor or unstable school, work, or military records.[12]

Research by James Q. Wilson is in agreement with Bouza in that it is the policing experience within an organizational setting that ultimately molds the officer and helps to shape his or her worldview.[13] What a police department expects from (and ultimately how it treats) its police officers depends to a large extent upon the perspective from which the department predicts human behavior. McGregor's Theory X and Theory Y offer a good illustration. McGregor suggests that management's beliefs about the basic orientation of workers toward their job assignments determine what managers think motivates employee performance and how best to manage them. For example, managers who subscribe to Theory X tend to believe that most employees have little enthusiasm for their assigned duties and that close supervision, combined with negative reinforcement for misbehavior, are necessary to ensure that employees do what they are told. Low expectations for employee performance based upon employees' negative attitudes toward their organization and the work in general then lead to low morale and cynicism. In contrast, proponents of Theory Y have a more optimistic image of employees. They believe that employees will perform their duties to the best of their abilities when they have input into the work they do, see great value in their work, and believe that the work they do makes a positive contribution to their organization, another group, or the greater society.[14]

Although neither perspective may fully capture all workers in a police department, researchers who write about professional-style policing tend to portray the cadre of uniformed personnel as a subculture of people who are cynical, secretive, and resistant to change. Researchers who are proponents of community policing, however, tend to be more optimistic about the capacity of the police subculture to change and adapt to community policing. Which group more accurately describes the police profession? In part, the answer probably has to do with the amount of time a department has invested in professional-style police work. For example, Theodore Ferdinand suggests that police officer "solidarity" is greatest among experienced line officers and least well-developed among academy cadets.[15] In part the answer may be that it depends on which era of policing is being discussed. Theory X seems well suited to explaining employee attitudes and behavior that result from bureaucratic styles of policing developed during the professional era, while Theory Y appears to better fit more promising expectations for police officers during the community era.

New police recruits, before they have become socialized into the subculture of policing, may approach the job with enthusiasm and energy, only to find out from more experienced employees that peer expectations for performance are less ambitious or different from what recruits anticipated. For example, John Van Maanen, a noted police scholar, writes that:

> The novice patrolman soon learns that there are few incentives to work hard. He also discovers that the most satisfactory solution to the labyrinth of hierarchy, the red tape, and unpleasantness which character-

> izes the occupation is to adopt the group standard, stressing a "lay-low-and-don't-make-waves" work ethic. And the best way in which he can stay out of trouble is to minimize the amount of work he pursues.[16]

Available research tends to support the idea of a subculture of policing that is created out of the shared experiences of the people in uniform. In fact, it is easy to imagine even the most optimistic officers being let down by constantly dealing with the kinds of circumstances that police face when doing traditional, reactive policing. Former police officer and popular novelist Joseph Wambaugh writes that the most disheartening aspect of policing has little to do with having to deal with the least desirable segment of society operating at its worst behavior, for this is to be expected, but rather, having to answer calls where the best members of society are caught at their worst moments.[17] Human behavior that falls under the category of "something-that-ought-not-to-be-happening-and-about-which-someone-had-better-do-something-now," as Egon Bittner has referred to it, taxes the police officer's ability to view the general public in a positive light.[18]

In addition to the kinds of situations that new patrol officers encounter in the field with civilians, the negative attitudes of their colleagues also fuel their cynicism toward the public and the department they work for. Van Maanen's interview with one veteran patrol officer illustrates how the traditional police subculture views itself with respect to the administration and the people they are sworn to protect:

> . . . You gotta learn to take it easy. The department don't care about you and the public sure as hell ain't gonna cry over the fact that the patrolman always gets the shit end of the stick. The only people who do care are your brother officers. So just lay back and take it easy out here. Makes things a lot smoother for us as well as yourself.[19]

Similarly, police cynicism can be fueled by poor management, as Bittner has noted:

> Because police superiors do not direct the activity of officers in any important sense they are perceived as mere disciplinarians. Not only are they not actually available to give help, advice, and direction in the handling of difficult problems, but such a role cannot even be projected for them. Contrary to the army officer who is expected to lead his men into battle—even though he may never have a chance to do it—the analogously ranked police official is someone who can only do a great deal to his subordinates and very little for them. For this reason supervisory personnel are often viewed by the line personnel with distrust and even contempt.[20]

Nevertheless, with all the negatives that have been written about the policing subculture, it is not necessarily true that the subculture as a whole is uniformly bad in itself or bad for policing. For example, John Crank argues that seasoned police officers have a great deal to offer in the implementation of community policing if only the administration will trust them to use their street skills and experience for the sake of organizational change.

Crank eloquently describes the positive features of the police subculture:

> Seasoned officers are culture carriers, the department's living traditions acted out daily. They have acquired a practical understanding about people on their beat. They know how to deal with them. They have "toolkits" of solutions to the everyday, garden-variety problems to which they are long accustomed. They have a sense of when to speak softly, when to use command voice, when to ignore, or when to look closer. They know the saturnine alleys, the quiet roads where lovers sneak away, the fields where teenagers go to drink on Saturday night, the safe havens, and the areas that need pressure. They chafe at the limits of their ability to respond to problems—to arrest bad guys, to provide activities for young people.[21]

For Crank, and for community policing, the police subculture holds a great deal of promise for policing reform:

> The key to successful community policing lies in the way that administrators engage a street cop's heart. The rank and file need to be involved in some capacity in all planning sessions, in the development of training programs, and in he ongoing evaluation of their work. They must be given self-accountability.[22]

In addition to making full use of an officer's innate abilities and skill, policing in a community era attempts to expose police personnel to a wider assortment of people and positive experiences than was customary in the professional era. Rather than meeting only victims, witnesses, and offenders, in community policing officers are broadly exposed to contacts with citizens interested in and supportive of public safety. Community policing encourages favorable interactions with the public that tend to reaffirm the high value of the police to the community. In short, community policing invites the police to initiate contact with business people, local residents, civic group leaders, and religious leaders, among others, rather than simply reacting to calls from dispatch or patrolling the streets solely to deter and detect lawbreakers. That is, community policing means the police are coactive, as well as reactive and proactive.

Hiring Practices

Policing in any era requires officers who are fully functional and well-trained to deliver the appropriate services at the right time. In a nutshell, it requires good training, knowledge of the law, an awareness of departmental policies and procedures, and most important, discretion. As Keith Haley has noted, however, there is much more to good policing than training by itself. An important first step is selection. "Communities must select recruits who have both the potential for learning the requisites of police work and the motivation to serve citizens and visitors in their localities."[23] After all, he adds, "Police officers are community leaders with broad discretion."[24]

In order to appreciate good policing, it is useful to understand how police departments choose the people whom they entrust to do such an important job. Indeed, if community policing represents a new and different way to deliver police services, it might be asked whether we need to hire different people from those hired in the past to do this different job.

In the professional era, police officers were selected on the basis of objective measures of their ability to do the job. Applicants were screened for acceptability based upon their clean criminal record, a background check, a favorable psychological profile, high scores on a standardized test, physical qualifications, and a personal interview. Such a process was far better than the procedure during the political era when selection often was based on who was voted into a local political office or depended on an influential person whom an applicant or a family member might know. The professional era's more objective measures allowed for a fairer appraisal of an applicant's abilities and helped to ensure that the people who were hired were adequately qualified for the job.

The selection process used in most departments today continues the practices of the professional era. Although the current practices are noticeably more equitable, additional improvement is needed to make them better suited to choosing personnel during the community era.

Recruitment

Recruitment and assessment are two preliminary steps in the hiring process in any era. It is at these stages that a pool of applicants from which people will eventually be hired and trained is formed.

Recruitment today involves the posting, advertising, and promoting of available positions to the public. Job announcements are placed in accordance with a city or county's policies for posting such notices. They give information about deadlines, how to apply, and the job description itself.

In order to ensure an optimum pool of candidates, job openings may also be advertised in local newspapers and trade journals. Recruiting officers may visit local or regional colleges and universities in order to seek qualified applicants. As Chris Eskridge has noted, the selection of college-educated applicants in particular offers many advantages to police departments. College-educated recruits tend to have a greater awareness of social and ethnic problems, draw fewer citizen complaints, receive higher satisfaction ratings from the public, and tend to be "less authoritarian" in their approach to others. Furthermore, Eskridge notes that college-educated police officers seem to make better workers overall, demonstrating "higher levels of morale and better work attitudes," which probably accounts for the fact that they are more likely to be promoted than those without college experience.[25]

Advertising and promotion are especially crucial in the community era in order to encourage a wide diversity of applicants. Not only should the police adequately represent their communities in terms of racial and ethnic diversity, they should also have a knowledge of community values and needs and show tolerance for the wide variety of people who live there.

Potential applicants from the community who may not have been attracted to the idea of working in a professionally oriented department might be drawn to the prospect of serving their community in a department that is committed to the broader and more comprehensive role of community policing. It is up to the department for the most part to define for the community what it is looking for in a successful applicant and to encourage a broad cross-section of eligible citizens to apply.

Assessment

Once the job applicant pool has been established, the selection process moves to the assessment or "screening-in" stage.

> Screening-in applicants denotes a process through which only the best of the qualified applicants are considered for employment. Screening-out applicants, by contrast, involves removing all unqualified applicants from the applicant pool and then considering for employment anyone who is at least minimally qualified—those who are not screened out.[26]

Larry Gaines and Victor Kappeler note that job applicants can be assessed according to minimum standards and testing procedures that help to determine which qualified candidates are more highly desirable than others as job prospects:

> Police employment standards vary from department to department, but may include requirements relating to vision, hearing, age, height, weight, biographical characteristics, educational levels, residency, and the absence of a history of drug use.[27]

In comparison to preemployment minimum standards, testing creates a situation in which candidates compete against each other rather than against some preestablished standard. The two most commonly used tests in police selection are the written test and the oral interview.[28]

After reviewing much of the literature on selection and testing, Gaines and Kappeler conclude that the hiring process for police officers poses a difficult challenge for departments: "Selection should be considered a balancing act in which numerous problems and forces are constantly weighed and considered."[29] Although this statement holds true for police departments during the professional era, it is particularly appropriate for those agencies trying to hire well-rounded and qualified applicants during the community era.

Three key improvements are needed at the screening-in, or assessment, stage to make the hiring process more compatible with the need to find personnel well-suited to the challenge of policing in a community era. First, police departments must encourage innovation in order to promote change. Departments moving away from a military-style bureaucracy will have to reevaluate their testing procedures. For example, they may want to consider ways to ensure that candidates who display creativity and risk-taking abilities will not necessarily be scored below those who value structure and certainty over all else. Similarly, they may want to examine how well the standardized forms they use test for problem-solving ability.[30]

A second improvement that is needed involves bringing the community into the assessment process itself. Citizen representatives can help with the screening to identify those candidates who might work well with diverse groups and who display strong attachments to the community that will help the police develop strong partnerships with community groups. Citizen advisory boards can be helpful in selecting new employees. Lacking such boards, representatives from civic groups can be recruited to participate in oral board interviews of job applicants or even to spend a few days at a time to help conduct mini-assessment centers, similar to how many police chiefs are selected around the country.[31]

Although involving the community in the assessment process is more difficult and time consuming than not doing so, weighing the long-term benefit of hiring the right person for the job against the cost of putting the wrong person in the field makes the additional time spent well worth it. After all, having community input at this stage helps to bond the community to the new recruit immediately when he or she becomes a uniformed officer.

A third improvement that is needed during assessment is to test applicants for important communication skills. Professional-style police work has demanded contact with citizens under adverse conditions that require the use of voice to control situations, console victims, interview witnesses, and interrogate suspects. Verbal skills become even more important in today's police forces. Officers will meet citizens from a wider variety of economic and social backgrounds, since much of the time the officers will be making contacts on their own rather than simply answering calls. Also, they will be expected to speak at public functions and make public addresses, something earlier patrol officers rarely ever did.

Training for Success

After the right people to do the right job have been hired, they must be trained. According to 1993 data collected by the Bureau of Justice Statistics (BJS) through the Law Enforcement Management and Administrative Statistics (LEMAS) program, formal police training was a requirement for newly hired police recruits in nine out of 10 police departments. Furthermore, since the departments that did not require training tended to be small, the 90 per cent of the departments that required training accounted for 99 percent of all sworn police personnel in the United States.[32]

Although smaller police departments tend to require less training, the typical new recruit is exposed to a minimum of 457 training hours and up to a maximum of 1,176. According to the LEMAS data, an average recruit will undergo 425 hours in an academy setting and another 215 hours in the field, for a combined average of 640 training hours. Furthermore, the numbers are higher for new sheriffs' deputies. BJS estimates that on average, new deputies received approximately 750 total training hours in 1993.[33]

Requiring a substantial number of hours of training is not to say that all training is uniformly effective. For example, Vance McLaughlin and Robert Bing write that:

> Strangely enough, police training continues to vary throughout the United States. There is considerable disagreement with regard to the rigor of these programs and time allocation for them. The state of Missouri, for example, requires 150 hours of training in smaller departments, while Hawaii requires 790 hours (plus four months of field training). Moreover, the focus on mandatory training has regrettably been on the number of hours at the expense of quality and skill retention. As a result, many P.O.S.T. Councils have less than rigorous standards. In many programs, for ex-

> ample, the curriculum for recruits is written at the sixth-grade level.[34]

The goal of academy training is to introduce newly hired applicants to a wide range of subjects over the span of a few short weeks. They are expected to learn about criminal statutes, proper arrest procedures, officer safety, personal defense, firearms, and pursuit driving, among other technical skills. Although much of their training is considered crucial in preparing new recruits for life on the streets as a uniformed officer, the reliance on such skills for officer survival leaves little room for newer subjects that may prove equally, if not more, useful to officers expected to succeed at community policing. After all, research has documented that police officers spend disproportionately little of their time doing "real police work," that is, detecting and apprehending criminals and investigating crimes. For example, Priss Dufford notes that most of a patrol officer's daily activities (75 percent to 90 percent) are spent on noncriminal activities.[35]

Subjects directly related to community policing and other useful topics are not usually taught in police academies or are given only scant attention. One reason for this lack stems from a crowded curriculum that has little room for newer subjects unrelated to officer safety or nonlegal matters. The reliance on a traditional curriculum and the reluctance to incorporate new training subjects, however valuable they might be, is due primarily to the idea that policing is a particularly dangerous occupation. On the one hand, there is the potential for danger in the form of personal injury or even death to the officer or someone being protected. Understandably, then, training devoted to officer safety under adverse conditions commands one of the highest priorities of time and attention at the academy. On the other hand, the potential for danger of a different type also demands training time and attention. That danger is the threat of lawsuits against an individual officer or the department. Accordingly, knowledge of the law is another major area of emphasis in the academy.

Another reason for the lack of new subjects is that police trainers are unfamiliar with them because they themselves were schooled in a more traditional approach.

Also, community-policing related topics are given little attention in academy classrooms because of the challenging nature of the subject matter itself. In contrast to fairly concrete, easily demonstrable technical skills that can be learned through rote exercises (such as pursuit driving, firearms training, CPR, and a host of other, similar activities) and legal procedures that are covered in lectures based on law books, the central themes of community policing are difficult to teach. Information about how best to know your community and how to engage in problem solving involves concepts and principles that are fairly abstract. Because the subject matter of community policing generally requires more listening than hearing and more thinking than memorizing, it poses a considerable challenge to both teachers and recruits.

Other forms of training that might help officers work successfully with their colleagues and the public pose similar kinds of challenges. Consequently, for example, training in public speaking and facilitating small and large meetings are not routinely offered to new recruits. Former police chief Anthony Bouza echoes the need for police to acquire good communication skills and stresses their importance over the course of an officer's career:

> The ability to get up and speak effectively in front of a group; skill in dealing with the press; a grasp of the issues needed to cope with unions, prosecutors, the various publics, and others—all should be provided through arduous preparation and training. Yet, there is little evidence that American policing is even aware of this challenge, much less rising to meet it.[36]

Not only must the curriculum be expanded if community policing is to succeed, there also may be a need to train new recruits to accept a certain amount of risk. Risk-taking in the face of professional-style practices that have the endorsement of a strong police subculture will challenge new recruits to be morally courageous. Bouza suggests that:

> Training recruits in the importance of moral courage, such as is so piously and consistently included in the widely ignored code of ethics that every police agency adopts as its credo, is as important as teaching the recruit to cope with street dangers, yet police training usually neglects this critical aspect. In fact, it might be held that the opposite message is being transmitted, that the thing to be is a "stand-up guy."[37]

Furthermore, Bouza writes that:

> If cops are to develop the moral courage it takes to cleanse their agencies of corruption and brutality, they are going to have to learn that courage takes many forms, and that the type needed for such reforms is different from the street heroism they value so dearly.[38]

Field Training

Field-training officers (FTOs) are responsible for supervising freshly trained recruits (often referred to as rookies) during the initial stages of their probationary period of employment. It is at this point that new recruits actually are exposed to patrol duties and situations on the street that training can not fully prepare them for. It is at this point that they begin to develop a sense of discretion and autonomy that undergirds the patrol experience. It is here that they also are most directly exposed to the subculture of policing. As Van Maanen writes:

> During a newcomer's first few months on the street he is self-conscious and truly in need of guidelines as to his actions. A whole folklore of tales, myths, and legends surrounding the department is communicated to the novice by his fellow-officers, conspicuously by his FTO. Through these anecdotes—dealing largely with "mistakes" or "flubs" made by policemen—the recruit begins to adopt the perspectives of his more experienced colleagues.[39]

One particular challenge for departments committed to community policing is the traditional practice of assigning less experienced officers to the most undesirable work schedules. In most departments, rookie officers are first assigned to patrol during third, or graveyard shift (11 p.m. to 7 a.m.). As day shift (7 a.m. to 3 p.m.) and swing shift (3 p.m. to 11 p.m.) slots become available, more senior personnel assigned to third shift bid for them, leaving graveyard slots to those with less seniority, including rookies.

Rookie officers trained in community policing are in great need of practicing what they have learned with the community groups that may have had a hand in selecting them. Unfortunately, assigning them directly to the third shift means that most officers will have greatly reduced chances of interacting with civic and volunteer groups, who normally do not have meeting times that fit the 11 p.m. to 7 a.m. work schedule. Even if there are few such opportunities during the graveyard shift, officers assigned that time need even greater innovation and dedication in order to do community policing with much success.

In-Service Training

Once new recruits have settled into their roles and advanced beyond the probationary period of employment, the amount of supervision given to their work in the field drops off dramatically, as Van Maanen's research in one department shows:

> In Union City, as in all large city departments, the work of patrolmen is difficult, if not impossible, to evaluate. There are the required annual patrolman performance ratings submitted by the sergeants, but these are essentially hollow paper exercises in which few men receive low marks.[40]

Officers who seem to keep as busy as others doing similar work are mostly left alone to work through their shifts. Although daily reports that officers prepare for sergeants are routinely monitored, most departments fail to scrutinize individual officers closely except under unusual circumstances (e.g., cases involving deadly force or a citizen complaint) or during regularly scheduled evaluations (usually annual) of officer performance that typically are not all that telling, as Van Maanen's words suggest.

With very little personalized assessment of officer performance by the department, officers must look to other sources for feedback about how well they are doing their jobs. The usual sources include their colleagues and the wide assortment of citizens with whom they might come in contact on any given day. However, in-service training sessions sometimes provide officers with opportunities to examine specific police practices and assess how well they may be performing certain duties.

In-service training is meant to help officers achieve one or more of four goals. First, it may help them maintain seldom used skills such as pursuit driving, self-defense tactics, or firearms training. Second, it may help them sharpen skills that are used more frequently but may have fallen off, such as those having to do with proper arrest procedures, investigating traffic accidents, and preserving evidence. Third, in-service training may provide officers with information about changes in procedures and practices that result from new legal statutes or changes in previous laws. Finally, it may introduce them to advancements in the field or innovative ways to think about criminal detection, crime prevention, problem solving, and community mobilization.

Most departments require sworn personnel to acquire 40 or so hours of in-service training annually. Although such training could be used to teach community policing, few departments have required such training or even made it available to those who might wish it.

Officers working in many departments are guaranteed access to the amount of training that will meet their annual in-service training requirement, usually at little, if any, cost to them. The academies that train new recruits often supply in-service training as well, using many of the same instructors teaching many of the same subjects. Although there may be a need in the field for different kinds of training, many officers prefer to select courses on subjects with which they are familiar; similarly, many trainers seem to prefer teaching popular topics that they are experienced in teaching.

Such popular in-service courses typically revolve around officer safety. Another popular subject involves criminal investigation because many officers are interested in promotion to the rank of detective. Furthermore, changes in legal statutes and procedures occasionally necessitate in-service training that all officers must acquire.

Training that meets annual in-service requirements that is not offered free of charge or required by the department or that is too conceptual, not seemingly applicable, or difficult to teach is difficult to sell to the rank and file. To the extent that community policing training to date remains undeveloped or is largely unavailable, many of the nation's police have had only limited exposure to it through in-service training. In addition, few academies offer advanced community policing or devote much time to related topics such as strategic planning, organizational change, and community mobilization. A challenge for academies in the future is to make such topics more accessible to active and veteran patrol officers.

Unfortunately, the limitations noted above do not pertain only to the men and women who patrol our streets and highways, but also seem to apply to the personnel who supervise or command them. Bouza writes that:

> The education and training of police managers, nationally, has been not only appallingly deficient, but wrongheaded. In common with most American education, the system, such as it is, is vocationally centered, with lots of courses on what can only be called the oxymoron of "police science." Law, procedures, regulations, and technical requirements are heavily weighed. The emphasis, a not-altogether-mistaken one, is on developing an effective technician. These skills are essential, but they must be accompanied by an understanding of the

broader context within which events take place.[41]

Conclusion

Similar to the question that Heuett asks in his training exercise, we might ask police officers how they might describe the difference between someone who is rewarded for being a "good" police officer and someone whom they might recognize as a "great" police officer. The replies typically identify a good patrol officer as someone who writes a lot of tickets, gets good "numbers" (meaning numbers of arrests, citations, or whatever else their supervisor is looking for), or maybe has made a big bust. In contrast, the great ones are always the ones everybody looks up to or the ones everyone wanted to be like when they first started out as a rookie. The great ones seem to know how to handle every situation. They are viewed as problem solvers and respected as leaders. Where the good numbers cop might be viewed as efficient, it is the truly great cop who goes beyond efficiency and is seen as effective.

The author has occasionally followed with a second question about which kind of officer might be ideally suited to community policing. The answers from uniformed officers are not all that surprising. They still admire the qualities that made great cops two dozen years ago. Those same qualities are still needed for patrolling the streets in a community era. We still need people in uniform who can do a comprehensive job as a police officer under the variety of circumstances they encounter today.

It is to be expected that the people who have always done well as police officers will naturally excel at policing in a community era. But modern police departments have to be more deliberate in attracting, selecting, and training applicants to do well at community policing. These applicants will not only have to excel in the demands of professional-style policing, but also be able to show their peers, supervisors, and the public that they are up to new challenges.

Notes

1. Victor E. Kappeler, Richard D. Sluder, and Geoffrey P. Alpert, "Breeding Deviant Conformity: Police Ideology and Culture," in *The Police and Society: Touchstone Readings*, ed. Victor E. Kappeler (Prospect Heights, IL: Waveland Press, 1995), pp. 243–262 [p. 243].
2. *Ibid.*, pp. 243–244.
3. *Ibid.*
4. Lawrence Sherman, "Learning Police Ethics," in *Policing Perspectives: An Anthology*, eds. Larry K. Gaines and Gary P. Cordner (Los Angeles: Roxbury, 1999), pp. 301–310.
5. *Ibid.* p. 304.
6. Kappeler, Sluder, and Alpert, "Breeding Deviant Conformity."
7. *Ibid.* p. 246.
8. *Ibid.*
9. Anthony V. Bouza, *The Police Mystique: An Insider's Look at Cops, Crime, and the Criminal Justice System* (New York: Plenum Press, 1990).
10. John G. Stratton, *Police Passages* (Manhattan Beach, CA: Glennon, 1984).
11. Bouza, *The Police Mystique*, p. 69.
12. *Ibid.* p. 69.
13. James Q. Wilson, *Varieties of Police Behavior* (Cambridge, MA: Harvard University Press, 1968).
14. Douglas McGregor, "The Human Side of Enterprise," in *Classics of Organizational Behavior*, ed. W. E. Natemeyer (Oak Park, IL: Moore, 1978), pp. 12–18.
15. Theodore H. Ferdinand, "Police Attitudes and Police Organization: Some Interdepartmental and Cross-Cultural Comparisons," *Police Studies*, 3 (1980):46–60.
16. John Van Maanen, "Kinsmen in Repose: Occupational Perspectives of Patrolmen," in *The Police and Society: Touchstone Readings*, ed. Victor E. Kappeler (Prospect Heights, IL: Waveland Press, 1995), pp. 225–242 [p. 235].
17. Joseph Wambaugh, *Floaters* (New York: Bantam Books, 1996).
18. Egon Bittner, "Florence Nightingale in Pursuit of Willie Sutton," in *The Potential for Reform in the Criminal Justice System* (Beverly Hills: Sage, 1974), pp. 17–44 [p. 30].
19. Van Maanen, "Kinsmen in Repose," p. 238.

20. Egon Bittner, "The Quasi-Military Organization of the Police," in *The Police and Society: Touchstone Readings,* ed. Victor E. Kappeler (Prospect Heights, IL: Waveland Press, 1995), pp. 173–183 [p. 179].
21. John P. Crank, "Celebrating Agency Culture: Engaging a Traditional Cop's Heart in Organizational Change," in *Community Policing in a Rural Setting,* eds. Quint C. Thurman and Edmund F. McGarrell (Cincinnati: Anderson, 1997) pp. 49–57 [p. 50].
22. *lbid.*p. 57.
23. Keith N. Haley, "Training," in *What Works in Policing: Operations and Administration Examined,* eds. Gary W. Cordner and Donna C. Hale (Cincinnati: Anderson, 1992), pp. 143–155 [p. 143].
24. *Ibid.* p. 143
25. Chris Eskridge, "College and the Police: A Review of the Issues," in *Police and Policing: Contemporary Issues,* ed. Dennis J. Kenney (New York: Praeger, 1989), pp. 17–25 [p. 20].
26. Larry K. Gaines and Victor E. Kappeler, "Selection and Testing," in *What Works in Policing: Operations and Administration Examined,* eds. Gary W. Cordner and Donna C. Hale (Cincinnati: Anderson, 1992), pp. 107–123 [p. 109].
27. *Ibid.* p. 112.
28. *Ibid.* p. 118.
29. *Ibid.* p. 121.
30. Ricky S. Gutierrez and Quint C. Thurman, "Selecting, Training, and Retaining Officers to Do Community Policing," in *Community Policing in a Rural Setting,* eds. Quint C. Thurman and Edmund F. McGarrell (Cincinnati: Anderson, 1998), pp. 75–83.
31. *Ibid.*
32. Bureau of Justice Statistics, *Law Enforcement Management and Administrative Statistics, 1993: Data for Individual State and Local Agencies with 100 or More Officers* (Washington, DC: U.S. Department of Justice).
33. *Ibid.*
34. Vance McLaughlin and Robert Bing, "Selection, Training, and Discipline of Police Officers," in *Police and Policing: Contemporary Issues,* ed. Dennis Jay Kenney (New York: Praeger, 1989) pp. 26–33 [p. 29].
35. Priss Dufford, *Police Personal Behavior and Human Relations: For Police, Deputy, Jail, Corrections, and Security Personnel* (Springfield, IL: Charles C. Thomas, 1973).
36. Anthony V. Bouza, *The Police Mystique,* p. 129.
37. *Ibid.* p. 72.
38. *Ibid.,* p. 72.
39. John Van Maanen, "Kinsmen in Repose," p. 236.
40. *Ibid.,* p. 233.
41. Anthony V. Bouza, *The Police Mystique,* p. 128.

Quint C. Thurman, "Preparing Police Officers for Success in the Twenty-First Century." Adapted from Quint C. Thurman, Jihong Zhao, and Andrew Giacomazzi, *Community Policing in a Community Era: An Introduction and Exploration,* pp. 168–190. Copyright © 2001 by Roxbury Publishing Company. All rights reserved. ✦

Part IV

Challenging Issues in the External Police Environment

An essential feature of police work, especially in the current community policing movement, is building close relationships with local communities and neighborhoods. Communities and neighborhoods comprise the external environment in which a local police agency operates. In turn, when studying the interaction between local police organizations and the external environmental, there are three primary components that shape the police-community relationship.

The first component of the police-community relationship involves the interdependence of the two entities. Police departments must adapt to their external environment. Unlike private companies that can choose their individual environment (e.g., by relocating to a different city if a company is unhappy with the current community), public agencies like the police have no choice but to accept the environment as a whole and respond to the demands of their constituents. How well they do so has serious consequences for resource allocation, longevity of personnel, and ultimately, public safety.

The second component concerns the reciprocity between police and the external environment. Police departments typically lack the clout to dominate an external environment. Community influence, on the other hand, exerts significance influence on police organizational behavior. For example, it is generally accepted that the root causes of crime are structural conditions such as poverty, unemployment, and so forth. This means that the ability of police to control crime is constrained. Though citizens often view the police as a panacea for local crime problems, the reality is that policing's contribution to crime reduction tends to be marginal at best under ordinary circumstances.

The final component relates to demands from the external environment for change over time. Social change is normative and evolutionary, and drives police work in many ways, such as prioritizing policing practices. In the 1980s, for example, domestic violence became a primary focus of local communities nationally. Politicians and legislatures passed a number of laws regarding domestic violence. Accordingly, local police agencies made domestic violence one of their top priorities. We have been witness to a similar pattern concerning sex offenders in the 1990s, and more recently racial profiling has captured center stage.

The shift in importance of certain social issues exerts significant impact on local police agencies that cause police organizations to respond in kind. Failure to adapt may impair the legitimacy afforded police departments and make police agencies look bad in the eyes of their constituents. However, change is not easy. Under normal conditions, few individuals volunteer to change their behavior unless absolutely necessary. Similarly, change brings unforeseeable risk as well. In this section, five articles are presented that focus on the challenging issues that have forced police organizations to transform themselves by adopting new procedures or operational standards. These issues are challenging because major changes are required for local law enforcement agencies to adapt to the intense demands of their external environments. ✦

Chapter 14
Crime Fighting as Myth

Anthony V. Bouza

Anthony Bouza, a former Minneapolis police chief, provides his personal views on police work, the public, and the role of law. Essentially, he argues that the external environment exerts significant influence on police operations. This is particularly true in police search and seizure law. Bouza asserts that when Supreme Court cases set legal boundaries for police activities, the procedural guidelines are not always clear.

The police response to crime when procedural elements are imprecise and operational standards indistinct contributes to the difficulty of law enforcement. A further source of trouble stems from the nature of policing against the backdrop of a crime-control mandate. Bouza asserts that "Cops rarely do well when their authority is questioned." This challenge mainly originates from the external environment, particularly from the residents of poor neighborhoods where law enforcement is often the primary means of keeping peace and order. However, it is in just such an environment that police authority is likely to be questioned. Bouza's own personal experiences and perspectives on police work, public expectations, and the law make for a unique and provocative analysis of the state of American policing in a complex society.

No sane person would say it, but, the reality of urban policing in the last third of the twentieth century—and very likely for some years ahead—has been trying to control the urban underclass, which is mainly black. Riots and street crime—at appalling and ever-increasing levels through the seventies, eighties, and half of the nineties—terrified the overclass and left it shaken. The booming economy probably eased some of the pressures by reducing the number of homeless and employing many of the formerly excluded, but the maldistribution of prosperity's bounty has kept a significant portion of the population at poverty levels.

Is it a surprise that the overclass knows how to get what it wants? It hires and fires, pays and withholds, rewards and punishes. And America, as the centuries segue, is still run by white men. How else to explain their absence from the ramparts of mass protest movements anywhere? With rare exceptions (as when they were to be shipped out to fight an unpopular war in Vietnam) white American males have seen little need to storm the barricades.

In this environment the overclass, nervous about disorders and personal attacks, pressured the police to act. The cops, under a rapidly unfolding series of Supreme Court restrictions, often inspired by justice William O. Douglas (if, rightly in a way, credited to the redoubtable Chief Justice Earl Warren), had to adjust—and they did.

Constitutional Issues[1]

The police can't just crash in and take the evidence, secure in the knowledge that, as before *Mapp v. Ohio* in 1961, the terms of its recovery would not be questioned in state courts (and, when it was questioned in federal court for the previous forty years, the evidence was blithely shifted into a state prosecution, under something hallowed as the "Silver Platter Doctrine"). It is a remarkable testament to the unblinking hypocrisy and moral corruption of the pre-Warren court years that tainted evidence, which federal judges threw out as inadmissible, could be handed over by the Feds to local police agencies for use in state courts, where the illegally obtained evidence was not only accepted, but even welcomed.

The reason wags hold that bad cases make bad law is that the issues that wind their way up to the Supreme Court often involve society's less savory elements. It is the Larry Flynts who define free speech issues at the Supreme Court level, not the local bishops.

A case that illustrated a number of key principles involved a sex shop operator who sought my legal services in the late nineties. His place featured nude dancers and booths where guys could feed coin machines to keep a sexy video going while they masturbated. The dancing and videos were legal and it was impossible, given the privacy of the booths, to catch the patrons in the act. The odors, in these confined spaces, were putrid.

Cops would inspect the place and, being libidinous in the extreme, very likely experienced secret titillation in the process. I base this view on the fact that whenever we confiscated pornographic videos, I'd have to limit their viewing to evidentiary purposes or the cops would get goggle-eyed as they became riveted to the images on the screen. I became an early believer in the addictive properties of porn.

The owner took to filming the inspecting crews of cops as they made their rounds in his premises, a legal but dangerous practice. Cops rarely do well when their authority is questioned.

Mostly these encounters proceeded without incident, but the owner inevitably came across a thumper who roughed him up, pushed him out and brought him, face first, down onto the sidewalk, hard, as he twisted his arms to handcuff him. He was charged with interfering with officers, assault (the cop claimed to have been grazed by the owner's video camera as they maneuvered in the tight quarters), and resisting arrest. The real charge should have been failing the attitude test, but this hasn't been included in the codes yet.

The charges in this blatantly false arrest were immediately thrown out by the first judge reviewing the incident. So the owner sued.

I saw it as a classic First Amendment free speech issue and took the case. I had, by then, become inured to giving expert testimony in such issues on behalf of other than prime clients.

After reviewing all of the material I did something I'd never done before, and haven't since—I asked his lawyer if I could meet with the man to discuss settling. The lawyer was happy to agree.

The city had offered about a quarter million dollars and we all thought they could be jacked a bit higher. I told the guy I thought the case was winnable and that he had right on his side. But I warned him that the cops' versions would be very different from his, that his robust appearance belied the injuries he was claiming, and that white juries loved cops, especially in uniform and testifying as to the risks they ran, every day, on behalf of folks just like the jurors. The jury might very easily accept their version of events, notwithstanding the fact that all the charges had been summarily dismissed. Given his employment, the cops' likely testimony, the city's offer, and his appearance, I urged him to settle.

He surprised me with his vehemence. He said he only came to listen because he respected me so much, but he wouldn't settle at that level, or near it, if they put a machine gun to his head.

We went to trial.

I was very tough on the stand but, as I addressed the jury and sought eye contact, their averted bodies conveyed a troubling message of rejection. We lost.

I was bitterly disappointed because I felt the cops had been testilying, the jury had been taken in, and, most importantly, a great chance to underline the First Amendment right of free speech had been lost.

The sex operator suffered the additional indignity of his lawyer's, and my, fees.

Public Morals

Many in the police would believe that enforcing moral values is a key element of fighting crime. The most slippery slope in law enforcement is what is delicately referred to as vice. Laws are generally pretty malleable: Think of the Supreme Court's tortured locutions over the meaning of this or that section in our codes. But it gets positively labyrinthine when sex enters the picture. Wisely, the Supreme Court has mostly avoided the question, being content to set such guidelines as defining pornography (tricky question) in such phrases as "lacking any artistic merit," "appealing exclusively to prurient interests," "lacking any social value," and being beneath "community standards."

What this approach has accomplished is to lend enormous flexibility to our sex laws, enabling enforcement to shift with prevailing social winds. It has also had the effect of encouraging questionable enforcement actions that injure segments of our population in their rights.

Citizens tend to think of the law as rigid and immutable, but in reality it is not only plastic but amenable to priority scaling that enables the enforcers to pretty much pick and choose in accord with personal philosophy. This is why the police chief's outlook is so critical.

In secretly favoring the existence of gay bathhouses in Minneapolis, I was at 180 degrees from the agency and my predecessors, who had waged merciless warfare against these enclaves. My experience had taught me that, were it possible to eliminate these dens, the activities that took place in them would pop up in men's rooms all over the city. Uninterested citizens and their children would be forced to witness sex acts or be otherwise disturbed. Sequestration and privacy removed the activities from public view or access.

And therein lay the key—protecting the larger public from offensive behavior. No one wants to be subjected to intrusions into their privacy. I frequently received complaints from neighbors that cruising motorists were propositioning them. Tied to this was my sense that prostitutes bore the brunt of punishments in a system sustained and driven by johns. If women were importuned by passing motorists trolling for fellatio, I'd act and send undercover female officers to dress and saunter the streets saucily and arrest the johns for "soliciting for prostitution." These johns often turned out to be respectable blue-collar types—even civil servants—and, in one notable case, a police sergeant. When I was awakened with the news, there was an expectant silence. Would I extend professional courtesies? was the unstated question.

"Well, what would you do if he was a civilian?" I asked.

"Book him."

"You have your answer."

He was, of course, acquitted by a gullible jury of sympathetic whites. The public morals/vice/sex/pornography questions centered, for me, on the first word of the equation—public. I'd strike at street conditions involving the importuning of women, but tolerate off-street behaviors in bathhouses.

I wouldn't allow a billboard showing coitus, defining that as "lewdness" despite the amorphous nature of the term. I was seeing scenes of pretty explicit sex on the screen, but Hollywood had adopted an admission code that protected the public from innocent exposures to something not so innocent. And, besides, the sex occurred in the artistic context of a story that could easily be described as socially or artistically meaningful. If something wasn't egregiously offensive and public I was always inclined to tolerate it. I believed flag burners were exercising a constitutional right, even as I found the practice very distasteful. It wasn't my tastes that were at stake. I thought the Brooklyn Museum "Sensation" exhibit in 1999 depicting the Virgin Mary defiled by elephant dung a legitimate expression of artistic freedom, as was a photograph of the immersion of a crucifix in urine.

America wisely allows traffic in Nazi artifacts and explicitly describes the socially harmful and dangerous incitement of hate messages it forbids. I would have prosecuted—and did—the presentation and sale of clearly pornographic matter whose only object was an appeal to sexual urges, and which was, after all, against the law. I could see the point of setting limits but felt we ought to allow whatever wasn't clearly and generally accepted as dangerously wrong.

Would I have allowed a museum to display a male figure with an erection? A painting of a couple in an explicit sex act? Where does censorship begin and end? No right is without limits. We limit freedoms for the sake of order and civilization. Freedom of religion cannot encompass human sacrifice.

A Supreme Court justice once said he couldn't define pornography but he knew it when he saw it, and a writer once allowed she wouldn't object to any sex act unless "it frightened the horses."

If artistic meaning can be found, if the exhibit is sequestered such that an innocent wouldn't stumble onto it, and if the surrounding society seems generally accepting, I'd conclude yes, allow it and defend the rights of all by protecting the rights of the artist.

It isn't always understood that such freedoms, in every case, have limits. Incitement to riot, threats, noisy disturbances, and the hoary shouting of "fire" in a crowded theater are all forbidden by law—as is pornography. The meanings shift—James Joyce's great work *Ulysses* was once banned as pornography—but the constant is that there are limits. The protection of children is widely accepted as legitimate grounds for legislatively limiting adult behavior toward them.

In the NYPD, we even convicted a black militant of anarchy in the sixties, for advocating the killing of judges in a speech we tape recorded. He might have found more mercy if his advocacy had focused on another profession, such as bankers.

Still, the activism of the Warren Supreme Court in the sixties created slow changes in police actions and in defining rights and limits that had been mostly honored in their breaches rather than in their observances.

After *Miranda v. Arizona*[2] in 1966, the police were compelled to demonstrate the voluntariness of confessions and admissions (acknowledgments of guilt without rising to the level of a full-blown and detailed mea culpa). Grillings and third degrees were out. Deception and manipulation were not.

Other decisions circumscribed police powers, but they had (we can see this in retrospect, decades after their issuance) the surprising effect of making cops more skilled, more professional, and more effective. Evidence now had to be meticulously gathered. Suspects were more skillfully, professionally questioned. Search warrants had to be secured. Lawyers had to be brought into the process. All of these requirements obliged the police to refine their responses and train their members, or suffer humiliating defeats in court.

Training and innovative techniques were adopted and a tremendous national competitiveness arose as to who could develop the most cunning—and legally permissible—crime countermeasures. The courts became the filters through which police actions had to pass.

The decisions also coincided with President Lyndon Johnson's appointment of a President's Commission on Crime that, with its 1967 report, changed policing's national landscape while introducing such startling innovations as 911. It was the last such national undertaking and there haven't been any similar presidential initiatives since.

Innovations abounded.

In 1973, Detroit cops analyzed stick-ups to the point where they could predict, with almost the regularity of a monthly mortgage payment, the appearance of usually two "worthies" at the liquor store or chocolate shop, with guns, threats, and worse. These robbers would not only terrorize the hapless workers, but sometimes pistol-whip or shoot them.

Could the human imagination conceive of a worthier target for police aggressiveness? In the ironies of history, it came to pass that the answer, surprisingly, was yes.

The Detroit Police Department inaugurated a program with a catchy acronym—STRESS.[3] The use of sexy titles became one of the more baleful features of police ingenuity in combating street crime. The phrase stood for "Stop the Robberies, Enjoy Safe Streets." And it worked—but, alas, too well.

This stakeout unit, staffed with sharpshooters, would simply post several of these cops in the back room of the soon-to-be-robbed location.

With a dependability they might profitably have brought to more quotidian enterprises, the pistoleros would arrive and announce a holdup. The victim would transmit the signal and fall to the floor as the cops emerged with shotguns, shouting "Freeze—Police!" The stunning surprise often paralyzed or galvanized the criminals into flight, noncompliance, or shooting at the armor-protected cops, resulting in a very unequal gun battle the criminals invariably lost.

The body count soared. The black community charged the cops with being judge, jury, and executioner. Controversy flared as a mayoral campaign loomed.

A black candidate—in this now mostly black city that whites had fled in unprecedented numbers—ran on the promise of eliminating STRESS, narrowly won over a white former police commissioner, and kept his pledge. He was reelected repeatedly.

In other cities black mayors and black police chiefs were under similar but less direct pressures, and whites frequently had more behind-the-scenes influence. The innovations being adopted—like the aforementioned stakeouts—impinged disproportionately on black male suspects. People were getting mugged, so the cops decided to replicate the experience and disguised themselves in the fashion of likely victims. They profiled the victimization patterns and sent out cops dressed as little old ladies, drunken white businessmen, and other likely targets—and they were regularly mugged. The muggers were arrested and a disproportionate number were black males. In Minneapolis, a city with a population of less than 5 percent adult black males in the eighties, produced arrest rates of 85 percent black males. The operations leading to mugging arrests were called *decoy units.*

All of this was going on simultaneously with the relative impunity of white-collar criminals, feeding into the black community's resentment over becoming the cynosure of police operations.

Decoys and Strangers

Two incidents illustrate the fears inspired by stranger to stranger crimes of violence as well as the challenges—sometimes met and sometimes avoided—that they represent for the police.

In the first, a young woman is walking from church to the subway on a Sunday morning in July 2000, when a stranger carrying a three- or four-pound concrete block comes up behind her, smashes her on the head—cracking her skull—and flees. She survives the attack and the police, quite properly, go with a full-court press.

The second case is a slasher who emerges from the bushes in a secluded area of Prospect Park in Brooklyn, after midnight, and attacks four males, individually, over the course of four months in early 2000. The victims suffer nonfatal but serious wounds inflicted with clubs and knives. In an area known to attract gays, the assailant may have been a "gay basher"—a familiar criminal type most likely driven by homophobia to attack homosexuals.

These cases . . . cry out for decoy operations that replicate the victimization patterns—setting out police undercover [officers], with back-up team and protection, to deflect the attack from helpless civilians to armed-and-ready cops. The cases involve repeated acts of violence by recidivists on strangers, the ideal setting for decoys.

There was no talk of decoys in the latter case as everyone lapsed into the convenient bromides of more police coverage.

In avoiding the risks and complexities of decoy tactics, police executives throw blue at the problem and hope it'll go away. And what are the risks of using such aggressive tactics as sending cops out dressed as victims, to get mugged, anyway? I found out as I implemented the practice in Minneapolis in the eighties.

Every six months or so a group of black ministers, civil rights leaders, politicos, and other activists would ask to meet with the mayor and me. They complained bitterly that 85 percent of the muggers we arrested in decoy operations were black males, in a city where they constituted about 5 percent of the population. They demanded the operation be closed down.

The mayor looked to me to respond and I said they were mugging us, we weren't mugging them, and I wouldn't stop.

The mayor added, "I let the chief run the department and I'll look into any specific complaint of abuse if you have one." They didn't.

That would conclude the matter for another six months or so.

These were good, decent, caring people who, in my view, exerted unwise influence to eliminate a sound program. They succeeded with my successors.

In urban America, homes were burglarized and televisions and such cleaned out. The cops hit upon the notion of opening stores and get[ting] the word out that they'd buy stolen goods. A steady parade of burglars would tender their pelf, be secretly photographed and identified, and weeks later—after a large enough haul of suspects had been identified—rounded up. These were called *sting operations.*[4]

And, of course, undercover cops posing as addicts infiltrated drug operations and made large seizures and lots of arrests. This became—and is mainly alone in continuing to be—a genuine war on drugs.

The elimination of stakeouts, decoys, and stings across the police landscape has been accomplished in stealth and silence; it is one of the gritty little pills chiefs have had to swallow, and silently. One invariable response, when the question arises, is, "Oh, yes, we certainly are still doing those," and they may even be able to produce front organizations that appear to fit the bill. The reality is that no one in American policing is pursuing really aggressive anti-street-crime tactics as the new century begins.

In trying to fight crime, police chiefs have always had to contend with the resistance of police unions and the rigidities of civil service. To these, in recent years, has been added the resistance of black leaders who resent the disproportionate appearance of black males among those swept up by decoy, sting, and stakeout units.

Of tangential interest, yet critical in establishing the importance of politics in policing, is the fact that this period, mainly the sixties and seventies, was also the high-water mark of police and federal infiltration of subversive—and sometimes only activist or unpopular—groups. The decline of aggressive anticrime operations was mirrored in the abandonment of what were called intelligence-gathering missions.

Notes

1. James A. Inciardi, *Criminal Justice* (New York: Harcourt Brace Jovanovich, 1987).
2. Linda Greenhouse, "Miranda Decision Has Its Day in Court," *New York Times,* April 20, 2000; "Saving the Miranda Rule," *New York Times,* April 19, 2000.
3. "STRESS," *New York Times,* March 10, 1972.
4. Geane Rosenberg, "F.B.I. Casts a Wide Net with Plenty of Tangles," *New York Times,* February 9, 2000.

Anthony V. Bouza, "Crime Fighting as Myth." Reprinted from Anthony V. Bouza, *Police Unbound: Corruption, Abuse, and Heroism by the Boys in Blue,* pp. 73–82 (Amherst, NY: Prometheus Books). Copyright © 2001 Anthony V. Bouza. Reprinted by permission of the publisher. ✦

Chapter 15

What We Know About Police Use of Force

Kenneth Adams

K*enneth Adams' review of the issues surrounding police use of force touches on an important and timely policing topic. Nothing angers community members more than abuse of authority by police officers, especially when it involves abusive force. This is particularly true for neighborhoods with high minority concentrations. American citizens cling to their civil liberties and are highly critical of a government that is too powerful or intrusive. Consequently, and unlike most countries in the world, there is no centralized police force in the U.S. Nevertheless, the more than 17,000 different police organizations operating in the U.S. are alike in that they have the legal authority to use force in order to compel compliance of ordinary citizens within their jurisdictional boundaries.*

Police departments, large or small, must pay close attention to the use-of-force issue. In his review, Adams examines the research on the topic. His first discovery is that the police use of force is relatively infrequent. Second, police use of force often takes place in poor neighborhoods where the relationship between police and local residents is strained. Third, his review of the literature suggests that overall, officers' personal characteristics, such as ethnicity, age, and gender, have little effect on the decision to use force. Finally, the available evidence indicates that a small proportion of officers account for a large percentage of use-of-force complaints.

Ambrose Bierce, a social critic known for his sarcasm and wit, once described the police as "an armed force for protection and participation."[1] In this pithy statement, Bierce identifies three critical elements of the police role. First, by describing the police as "armed," their ability to coerce recalcitrant persons to comply with the law is emphasized. Because police carry weapons, it follows that the force they use may have lethal consequences. The capacity to use coercive, deadly force is so central to understanding police functions, one could say that it characterizes a key element of the police role.

Second, the primary purpose of police is protection, and so force can be used only to promote the safety of the community. Police have a responsibility for safeguarding the domestic well-being of the public, and this obligation even extends in qualified ways to protecting those who violate the law, who are antagonistic or violent toward the police, or who are intent on hurting themselves. In dealing with such individuals, police may use force in reasonable and prudent ways to protect themselves and others. However, the amount of force used should be proportional to the threat and limited to the least amount required to accomplish legitimate police action.

Third, the concept of participation emphasizes that police and community are closely interrelated. Police are drawn from the community, and as police they continue to operate as members of the community they serve. The community, in turn, enters into a solemn and consequential relationship with the police, ceding to them the power to deprive persons of "life, liberty, and the pursuit of happiness" at a moment's notice and depending on them for public safety. Without police, the safety of the community is jeopardized. Without community support, police are dispossessed of their legitimacy and robbed of their effectiveness.

This three-element definition of police makes it easy to understand why abuse of force by police is of such great concern. First, there is the humanitarian concern that police are capable of inflicting serious, even lethal, harm on the public. Second, there is the philosophical dilemma that in "protecting" the whole of society, some of its constituent parts, meaning its citizens, may be injured. Third, there is the political irony that police, who stand apart from society in terms of authority, law, and responsibility, also are part of society and act on its behalf. Thus, rogue actions by a few police, if condoned by the public, may become perceived as actions of the citizenry.

Recent developments in policing have elevated concerns about police use of force beyond ordinarily high levels. In particular, community policing, which is becoming widespread as a result of financial incentives by the federal government, and "aggressive" policing, which is becoming widely adopted as a solution to serious crime problems, have come to the fore as perspectives of choice by policing experts. Community policing emphasizes the role of the community as "coproducers" of law and order in conjunction with the police. Communities naturally vary in attributes, and they vary in how they are defined for the purposes of community policing. Consequently, some communities look to add restrictions on police use of force, while others are satisfied with the status quo, and still others seek to ease current restrictions. Regardless of the community's orientation on this issue, community policing means increased levels of accountability and responsiveness in key areas, such as use of force. Increased accountability hinges on new information, and new information stimulates debate.

The other emerging perspective is "aggressive" policing, which often falls under the rubric of broken windows theory, and, as a strategic matter, is concerned with intensifying enforcement against quality-of-life and order maintenance offenses. The influence of aggressive policing can be seen in the proliferation of "zero tolerance" enforcement strategies across the nation. The concern is that the threat posed by petty offenders may be exaggerated to the point that use of force becomes more commonplace and abuses of force more frequent.

The Violent Crime Control and Law Enforcement Act of 1994 mirrored congressional concern about excessive force by authorizing the Civil Rights Division of the U.S. Department of Justice (DOJ) to initiate civil actions against police agencies when, among other conduct, their use of force reaches a level constituting a pattern or practice depriving individuals of their rights. DOJ exercised that authority when, for example, it determined that an urban police department engaged in such conduct and negotiated a consent decree that put in place a broad set of reforms, including an agreement by the department to document its use of force and to implement an early warning system to detect possible abuses.[2]

Use-of-force concerns also are reflected in the attention the media give to possible instances of police abuse. An accumulation of alleged abuse-of-force incidents, widely reported in the media, encourages overgeneralization by giving the impression that police brutality is rampant and that police departments across the nation are out of control. For example, Human Rights Watch states, "Allegations of police abuse are rife in cities throughout the country and take many forms."[3]

Before considering the details of recent research efforts on police use of force, it is useful to summarize the state of our knowledge.[4] We know some details about police use of force with a high degree of certainty. These items represent "facts" that should frame our understanding of the issues. Other details about police use of force we know in sketchy ways, or the research is contradictory. These items should be subject to additional research using more refined methods of inquiry. Finally, there are some aspects of police use of force about which we know very little or next to nothing. These items represent critical directions for new inquiry.

As is often the case with important policy questions, the information that we are most confident of is of limited value. In many cases, it does not tell us what we really need to know, because it does not focus squarely on the important issues or is subject to competing interpretations. Conversely, the information that is most critical for policy decisions often is not available or is very difficult to obtain. Such is the case with police use of force. The issues that most concern the public and policymakers lack the kinds of reliable and solid information that advance debate from the realm of ideological posturing to objective analysis. Nonetheless, it is important to take stock of our knowledge so that it is clear which issues can be set aside and which should be the target of efforts at obtaining new knowledge.

What, then, is the state of knowledge regarding police use of force? We begin with issues about which we have considerable information and a high degree of confidence in our knowledge. Discussed next are issues where knowledge is modest and considerably more research is merited. Finally, we conclude with issues that are critical to debates over police use of force and about which little knowledge exists.

What We Know with Substantial Confidence About Police Use of Force

Police Use Force Infrequently

Whether measured by use-of-force reports, citizen complaints, victim surveys, or observational methods, the data consistently indicate that only a small percentage of police-public interactions involve the use of force. As Bayley and Garofalo observed, police-citizen encounters that involve use of force and injury are "quite rare."[5]

Because there is no standard methodology for measuring use of force, estimates can vary considerably on strictly computational grounds. Different definitions of force and dif-

Working Definitions

Police use of force is characterized in a variety of ways. Sometimes, these characterizations are functionally interchangeable so that one can be substituted for another without doing injustice to the factual interpretation of a statement. At other times, however, differences in terminology can very consequential to a statement's meaning. For example, "deadly force" refers to situations in which force is likely to have lethal consequences for the victim. This type of force is clearly defined and should not be confused with other types of force that police use.

In contrast, "police brutality" is a phrase used to describe instances of serious physical or psychological harm to civilians with an emphasis on cruelty or savageness. The term does not have a standardized meaning; some commentators prefer to use a less emotionally charged term.

In this report, the term "excessive force" is used to describe situations in which more force is used than is allowed when judged in terms of administrative or professional guidelines or legal standards. Criteria for judging excessive force are fairly well established. The term may also include within its meaning the concept of illegal force.

Reference also is made to "excessive use of force," a similar, but distinctly different, term. Excessive use of force refers to high rates of force, which suggest that police are using force too freely when viewed in the aggregate. The term deals with relative comparisons among police agencies, and there are no established criteria for judgment.

"Illegal" use of force refers to situations in which use of force by police violated a law or statute, generally as determined by a judge or magistrate. The criteria for judging illegal use of force are fairly well established.

"Improper," "abusive," "illegitimate," and "unnecessary" use of force are terms that describe situations in which an officer's authority to use force has been mishandled in some general way, the suggestion being that administrative procedure, societal expectations, ordinary concepts of lawfulness, and the principle of last resort have been violated, respectively. Criteria for judging these violations are not well established.

To varying degrees, all of the above terms can be described as transgressions of police authority to use force.

ferent definitions of police-public interactions will yield different rates[6] (see "Working Definitions" box). In particular, broad definitions of use of force, such as those that include grabbing or handcuffing a suspect, will produce higher rates than more conservative definitions. The Bureau of Justice Statistics' (BJS) 1996 pretest of its Police-Public Contact Survey resulted in preliminary estimates that nearly 45 million people had face-to-face contact with police over a 12-month period and that approximately 1 percent, or about 500,000 of these persons, were subjected to use of force or threat of force.[7] When handcuffing is included in the BJS definition of force, the number of persons increases to 1.2 million.

Expanding and contracting definitions of "police-public" interactions also work to affect use-of-force rates but in an opposite way from definitions of force. Broad definitions of police-public "interactions," such as calls for service, which capture variegated requests for assistance, lead to low rates of use of force. Conversely, narrow definitions of police-public interactions, such as arrests, which concentrate squarely on suspects, lead to higher rates of use of force.

The International Association of Chiefs of Police (IACP) is in the process of compiling statistics on use-of-force data being submitted by cooperating agencies. These data indicate that force is used in less than one-half of 1 percent of dispatched calls for service. From this point of view, one might well consider police use of force a rare event. This figure is roughly consistent with the preliminary estimate reported by BJS, although the IACP figure is subject to the reporting biases that may exist in police agency data. Furthermore, IACP data are not yet representative of the national picture because of selection bias; the estimate is based on a small percentage of police departments that voluntarily report information on use of force.

Garner and Maxwell found that physical force (excluding handcuffing) is used in fewer than one of five adult custody arrests. While this figure hardly qualifies as a rare event, it can be considered low, especially in light of the broad definition of force that was used.

In characterizing police use of force as infrequent or rare, the intention is neither to minimize the problem nor to suggest that the issue can be dismissed as unworthy of serious attention. Society's ends are best achieved peaceably, and we should strive to minimize the use of force by police as much as possible. However, it is important to put police use of force in context in order to understand the potential magnitude of use-of-force problems. Although estimates may not completely reassure everyone that police are doing everything they can to minimize the use of force, the data do not support the notion that we have a national epidemic of police violence.

Another purpose for emphasizing the infrequent nature of police use of force is to highlight the methodological challenges of trying to count or study infrequent events. In this regard, methodological approaches can vary considerably in terms of cost efficiency, reliability, and precision of information obtained. In BJS's 1996 pilot household survey of 6,421 persons, 14 respondents, or roughly 1 in 450, said that they were subjected to use of force or threat of force by police over a year's time. The household survey approach has the benefit of providing national-level estimates based on data that are free of police agency reporting biases. However, as noted by BJS, the preliminary estimates derived from such a small number of respondents are subject to a wide margin of error. This issue is particularly important if one is interested in tracking changes over time, because a very small change in reporting can have a very large impact on estimates. In the survey's continuing development, the next pilot test will use a sample about 10 times the size of the 1996 pilot test as well as involve a redesigned questionnaire.

Police Use of Force Typically Occurs at the Lower End of the Force Spectrum, Involving Grabbing, Pushing, or Shoving

Relatively minor types of force dominate statistics on police use of force. Garner and

Maxwell observed that police use weaponless tactics in roughly 80 percent of use-of-force incidents and that half the time the tactic involved grabbing the suspect. Alpert and Dunham found that in Miami 64 percent of use-of-force incidents involved grabbing or holding the suspect. In the BJS pilot national survey, it was estimated, preliminarily, that about 500,000 people were "hit, held, pushed, choked, threatened with a flashlight, restrained by a police dog, threatened with or actually sprayed with chemical or pepper spray, threatened with a gun, or experienced some other form of force."[8] Three-fifths of these situations, however, involved only holding. Finally, Pate and Fridell's survey of law enforcement agencies regarding use of force and civilian complaints also confirms that minor types of force occur more frequently than serious types.[9]

As a corollary finding, when injuries occur as a result of use of force, they are likely to be relatively minor. Alpert and Dunham observed that the most common injury to a suspect was a bruise or abrasion (48 percent), followed by laceration (24 percent). The kinds of police actions that most captivate the public's concerns, such as fatal shootings, severe beatings with fists or batons that lead to hospitalization, and choke holds that cause unconsciousness or even death, are not typical of situations in which police use force. These findings reassure us that most police exercise restraint in the use of force, even if one has concerns over the number of times that police resort to serious violence. From a police administrator's point of view, these findings are predictable. Officers are trained to use force progressively along a continuum, and policy requires that officers use the least amount of force necessary to accomplish their goals.

Another affiliated finding is that police rarely use weapons. According to Garner and Maxwell, 2.1 percent of adult custody arrests involved use of weapons by police. Chemical agents were the weapons most frequently used (1.2 percent of arrests), while firearms were the weapons least often used (0.2 percent of arrests). Most police departments collect statistics on all firearm discharges by officers. These data consistently show that the majority of discharges are accidental or are directed at animals. Only on infrequent occasions do police use their firearms against the public. One implication of these findings is that increased training in how to use standard police weapons will be of little value in dealing with day-to-day situations that involve use of force. Training, if it is to be effective in reducing the use of force, needs to focus on how to gain compliance without resorting to physical coercion.

Use of Force Typically Occurs When Police Are Trying to Make an Arrest and the Suspect Is Resisting

Research indicates that police are most likely to use force when pursuing a suspect and attempting to exercise their arrest powers. Furthermore, resistance by the public increases the likelihood that police will use force. These findings appear intuitively sound given the mandate that police have regarding use of force. Police may use force when it is necessary to enforce the law or to protect themselves or others from harm. The findings also seem logical in view of police training curriculums and departmental regulations. Alpert and Dunham find that police almost always follow the prescribed sequence of control procedures they are taught, except when suspect resistance is high, in which case they tend to skip the intermediate procedure.

The conclusion that police are most likely to use force when dealing with criminal suspects, especially those who are resisting arrest, is based on four types of data: arrest statistics, surveys of police officers, observations of police behavior, and reports by the public about their encounters with police.

Arrest statistics show that resisting-arrest charges often are involved in situations in which officers use force. The interpretation of this finding is ambiguous, however, because officers may bring such charges in an attempt to justify their actions against a suspect. Some commentators would even argue that resisting-arrest charges are a good indication that police officers acted inappropriately or illegally. Because we are relying on official reports by officers who are involved in use-of-force incidents, and because they have self-interest in presenting the situation in the most favorable light possible, we cannot rely on arrest records alone in determining what happened.

Fortunately, other research is available to help clarify the situation. The pilot national household survey by BJS included a series of questions about the respondent's behavior during contact with police.[10] The preliminary analysis revealed that of the 14 respondents in the sample who reported that police used or threatened force against them, 10 suggested that they might have provoked the officer to use force. The provocative behaviors reported by suspects include threatening the officer, assaulting the officer, arguing with the officer, interfering with the arrest of someone else, blocking or interfering with an officer's movement, trying to escape, resisting being handcuffed, and resisting being placed in a police vehicle.

Research by Alpert and Dunham confirms that criminal suspects are not always cooperative when it comes to arrest. In almost all (97 percent) cases in which police officers used force in a Florida jurisdiction, the suspect offered some degree of resistance. In 36 percent of use-of-force incidents, the suspect actively resisted arrest, and in one-quarter of the incidents the suspect assaulted the officer. The researchers observed that the most common type of suspect force was hitting or striking a police officer (44 percent).

Garner and colleagues, after using statistical controls for more than 50 characteristics of the arrest situation, the suspect, and the police officer, found that forceful action by suspects was the strongest and most consistent predictor of use of force by police.[11] Furthermore, they found that while 22 percent of arrests involved use of force by police, 14 percent of arrests involved use of force by suspects. Police officers in Phoenix completed a use-of-force survey after each arrest to generate these data.

Finally, Bayley and Garofalo tallied 36 instances of force used by police or suspects out of 467 police-public encounters observed firsthand by researchers.[12] They found that in 31 incidents police used force against suspects and in 11 incidents suspects used force against police.

One implication of the research is that the decision to use some level of force probably has legal justification in most cases. Force is likely to be used when suspects resist arrest and attempt to flee. Also, in a significant number of instances, suspects use force against the police. These findings leave open the issue of excessive force, since issues of proportionality are not clearly addressed. However, the findings do suggest that many debates over excessive force will fall into gray areas where it is difficult to decide whether an officer acted properly, because there is credible evidence that the use of force was necessary.

What We Know with Modest Confidence About Police Use of Force

Use of Force Appears to Be Unrelated to an Officer's Personal Characteristics, Such as Age, Gender, and Ethnicity

A small number of studies suggest that use of force by police is not associated with personal characteristics, such as age, gender, and ethnicity. Bayley and Garofalo concluded that use of force is not related to age, although it may be related to experience.[13] Worden, in an analysis of observational data on 24 police departments in 3 metropolitan areas, concluded that the personal characteristics of police officers do not have a substantively significant effect on use of force.[14]

Likewise, Garner and colleagues reported that the race of suspect and officer is not predictive of use of force.[15] However, they found that incidents involving male police officers and male suspects are more likely to involve force. Alpert and Dunham found that officer characteristics are of little utility in distinguishing between force and nonforce incidents. Hence, gender and ethnicity appear unrelated to use of force. Given the limited research in this area, these conclusions should be accepted with caution and additional verification of these findings is needed.

It is widely accepted in criminology that violence, along with a wide variety of other risk-taking and norm-violating behaviors, is a young man's game. Thus, we should expect that young, male police officers should use force more than their female colleagues or older officers. The fact that this is not clearly the case seems surprising.

A lack of relationship between age and gender, on the one hand, and use of force, on the other, may be a function of police hiring and deployment practices. Retirement plans keep the age of police officers lower than that of most other occupations, and seniority, which is derivative of work experience, often brings more choice in work assignments, including duties that limit one's contact with criminal suspects on the street. Both these tendencies serve to constrain variation in the age of police officers who are exposed to potentially violent situations. This may attenuate the relationship between age and use of force. However, it is equally plausible that young male officers are assigned to high-crime areas where frequent use of force is necessary to gain compliance. Finally, it is possible that exposure to the police culture works to encourage the use of force, thus counterbalancing the decline in aggressivity that comes with age as demonstrated in criminological studies. More research is needed to disentangle these relationships.

The finding that an officer's race is unrelated to the propensity to use force runs counter to the argument that racial animosity lies at the heart of police abuse. Indeed, Alpert and Dunham's research indicates that officers are more likely to use force against suspects of their own race. The lack of relationship between race and use of force, as well as between gender and use of force, is probably disheartening to those who argue that integration of police agencies along racial and gender lines will do much to reduce the incidence of police violence. Again, more research is needed to understand the situation of minority and female police officers with regard to their use of force.

Use of Force Is More Likely to Occur When Police Are Dealing with Persons Under the Influence of Alcohol or Drugs or with Mentally Ill Individuals. More Research Is Needed

Police come across a wide variety of situations in their work. They encounter problems that range from relatively minor to serious to potentially deadly. They also interact with people exhibiting various mental states, including persons who are hysterical, highly agitated, angry, disoriented, upset, worried, irritated, or calm.

Two situations that often give police officers cause for concern are when suspects appear to be under the influence of alcohol or drugs and when civilians appear to suffer from serious mental or emotional impairments. The concern stems from the fact that in such situations a person's rational faculties appear impaired. In dealing with problem situations, officers most often talk their way, rather than force their way, into solutions. For this reason, when a civilian is in a highly irrational state of mind, the chances of the police officer having to use force presumably increase and the possibility of injury to both officer and civilian increases as well.

Research carried out for the President's Commission on Law Enforcement and Administration of Justice observed that alcohol use by either a suspect or an officer increased the chances that force will be used.[16] Garner and colleagues found that alcohol impairment by suspects was a consistent predictor of police use of force, while drug impairment predicted increased use of force for some but not all measures of use of force.[17] In contrast, Alpert and Dunham observed that alcohol or drug impairment of suspects was unrelated to police use of force or subsequent injury. That finding is interesting because, although impaired civilians did not demonstrate an increased propensity to resist an officer's actions, when they did resist they were more inclined to do so by actively resisting or assaulting the officer.

Part of the disparity in findings between the President's Commission's research and more recent studies may be attributed to the fact that police officers today are better trained in how to deal with impaired civilians. Most police officers now receive training in a variety of violence reduction techniques, and this development is partly attributable to concerns over the President's Commission's findings and over the frequency with which police now are called to respond to large-scale violence, such as riots.

Questions about how police deal with civilians who appear to have impaired mental states are important from administrative and practical points of view. Police officers are expected to exercise restraint in dealing with impaired civilians, while at the same time they need to be cautious about protecting their safety as well as the safety of other civilians. This puts them in a precarious situation, one in which mistakes of judgment or tactics can have grave consequences.

From a practical standpoint, police regularly encounter civilians with impaired mental states, which makes the problem more than academic. Alpert and Dunham found that in 42 percent of use-of-force situations, suspects appeared to be under the influence of alcohol or drugs. Overall, the research on whether police use force more frequently in relation to civilians with impaired mental states is inconsistent. Further investigation, with an emphasis on implications for training, could reduce the risk of force and injury for both police officers and civilians.

A Small Proportion of Officers Are Disproportionately Involved in Use-of-Force Incidents. More Research Is Needed

We often are told that a small number of people are responsible for most of the productive or counterproductive work in an organization. For example, we hear about the 80/20 rule in organizational management. That is, 20 percent of the workers account for 80 percent of the work. Policing has its counterpart explanation for deviant or illegal behavior. It is called the rotten apple or rogue officer theory, and it is often used to explain police corruption. Recently, a variation of this theory has become the principal explanation for use-of-force problems in police departments. In this context, we speak of "violence-prone" police officers and we point to these individuals as the reason why a department has problems with the use of force.[18]

People with extraordinary work performance, either good or bad, are noticeable when compared with their colleagues, and their salience leads us to think that their work is highly consequential to the good fortunes or misfortunes of an organization. The utility of this perspective for police managers attempting to deal with illegitimate use of force lies in the presumed concentration of problem behaviors in the work force. If only a handful of police officers accounts for most of the abuses, then effective solutions targeted at those individuals should deal with the problem. The nature of the solution, be it employee selection, training, oversight, or discipline, is less important than its degree of effectiveness and its ability to be directed at the problem group of employees.

The Christopher Commission, which investigated the Los Angeles Police Department subsequent to the Rodney King incident, highlighted the "violence-prone" officer theory.[19] The Commission, using the department's database, identified 44 officers with 6 or more civilian allegations of excessive force or improper tactics in the period 1986 through 1990. For the 44, the per-officer average for force-related complaints was 7.6, compared with 0.6 for all officers identified as having been involved in a use-of-force incident for the period January 1987 through March 1991. The 44 officers were involved in an average of 13 use-of-force incidents compared with 4.2 for all officers reported to be using force.

Put another way, less than one-half of 1 percent of the department's sworn officers accounted for more than 15 percent of allegations of excessive force or improper tactics. The degree of disproportion (30:1) is striking and suggests that focusing efforts on a handful of officers can eliminate roughly 1 out of 7 excessive force incidents. This finding has led many police departments to implement early warning systems designed to identify high-risk officers before they become major problems. Most of these systems use administrative records, such as disciplinary records and citizen complaints, to monitor officer performance for possible problems.

The concept of an early warning system for risk management of problem police officers is not new. In the early 1980s, a report on police practices by the United States Commission on Civil Rights found that "[e]arly warning information systems may assist the department in identifying violence-prone officers."[20] Consequently, it was recommended that "[a] system should be devised in each department to assist officials in early identification of violence-prone officers."[21]

Until recently, these systems received limited acceptance, owing in part to concerns over possible abuses. The abuses include use of inaccurate information, improper labeling of officers, misuse of confidential records regarding discipline and other personnel matters, and social ostracism by peers and community for officers identified as problematic. There also were concerns about limited resources and about increased legal liability for the organization and individual officers.

As Toch observes, the violence-prone officer paradigm often is based on a variety of loosely articulated theories of violent behavior.[22] The theories include concepts such as racial prejudice, poor self-control, and ego involvement. Furthermore, these theories often overlook the possibility that greater-than-average use of force may be a product of situational or organizational characteristics.

For example, an officer's work assignment may involve a high-crime area that contains a high proportion of rebellious offenders. Also, divisive, dehumanizing views of the world, such as "us-them" and "good guy–bad guy," that facilitate violent behavior may be supported by the organizational culture. Further, administrative views of work roles and products, communicated formally or informally, that emphasize crime control through aggressive police behavior may encourage confrontational tactics that increase the chances of violent behavior by either civilian or police officer. Unless the reasons for violence propensity are accurately identified, the effectiveness of interventions targeted at violent police officers is a hit-or-miss proposition.

Of the 44 officers identified by the Christopher Commission in 1991, 14 subsequently left the department as of October 1997. Of the 30 remaining officers, two had a use-of-force complaint that was sustained after review between 1991 and 1997.[23] This low number may be due to a variety of reasons, such as difficulties in sustaining citizen complaints, reassignment of work duties, negative publicity leading to a change in behavior, or greater circumspection when engaging in misconduct. However, the finding also may reflect regression to the mean. This is a statistical phenomenon postulating that extreme scores gravitate toward the mean or average score, thereby becoming less extreme over time.

For example, groups of police officers who receive many citizen complaints, or who are disproportionately involved in the use of force, or who frequently are given poor performance ratings, will tend to become "better" over time, in the sense of statistically looking more like the "average" officers, even if nothing is done about these problems. Statistical regression represents a serious threat to the validity of early warning systems based on the assumption that extreme patterns of behavior persist over extended periods of time.

What We Do Not Know About Police Use of Force

The Incidence of Wrongful Use of Force by Police Is Unknown. Research Is Critically Needed to Determine Reliably, Validly, and Precisely How Often Transgressions of Use-of-Force Powers Occur

We do not know how often police use force in ways that can be adjudged as wrongful. For example, we do not know the incidence of excessive force, even though this is a very serious violation of public trust. We could pull together data on excessive force using police disciplinary records and court documents, for example, but the picture would be sketchy, piecemeal, and potentially deceiving. When it comes to less grave or less precise transgressions, such as "improper," "abusive," "illegitimate," and "unnecessary" use of force, the state of knowledge is even more precarious.

In discussing this issue, we will concentrate on excessive force, because these transgressions are of utmost concern to the public and because well-established professional and legal criteria are available to help us evaluate police behavior. Notwithstanding a generally agreed-upon terminology, we should recognize that developing a count of excessive force that is beyond all dispute is an unworkable task. This is so because difficult judgments are involved in deciding whether use of force fits the criteria for these categories in a given situation, and reasonable people will disagree in such judgments. We clearly need more accurate, reliable, and valid measures of excessive force if we are to advance our understanding of these problems.

Academics and practitioners both tend to presuppose that the incidence of excessive force by police is very low. They argue that, despite their shortcomings, agency statistics provide a useful picture of the use-of-force problem. These statistics show that most officers do not engage in force on a regular basis, that few people are injured by police use of force, that only a small number of people complain about police misconduct involving use of force, and that only a handful of these complaints are sustained.

The argument has appeal. We believe that the vast majority of police officers are professionals who respect the law and the public. If use of force is uncommon, civilian complaints are infrequent, and civilian injuries are few, then excessive force by police must be rare. That conclusion may indeed be correct, but to the extent that it hinges on official police statistics, it is open to serious challenge.

Current indicators of excessive force are all critically flawed. The most widely available indicators are civilian complaints of excessive force and civil lawsuits alleging illegal use of force. Civilian complaints of excessive force are infrequent, and the number of substantiated complaints is very low. These figures are consistent with the argument that excessive force is sporadic. However, complaint mechanisms are subject to selection and reporting biases, and the operation of complaint systems, which typically is managed by police, wields considerable influence on whether people will come forward to complain.

Civil lawsuits against police are exceedingly rare relative to the number of times that police use force. Because the legal process is highly selective in terms of which claims get litigated, lawsuits are a very unreliable measure of illegal use of force. With both civilian complaints and lawsuits, small changes in administrative practices can have a large impact on the magnitude of the problem measured in these ways.

The difficulties in measuring excessive and illegal force with complaint and lawsuit records have led academics and practitioners to redirect their attention to all use-of-force incidents. The focus then becomes one of minimizing all instances of police use of force, without undue concern as to whether force was excessive. From this perspective, other records, such as use-of-force reports, arrest records, injury reports, and medical records, become relevant to measuring the incidence of the problem.

From a theoretical perspective, understanding all use-of-force incidents helps us to put wrongful use of force in perspective. However, because political, legal, and ethical issues are very serious when we are dealing with excessive force, pressures to know the incidence and prevalence of these events with precision will always be present.

As a corollary of our current inability to measure excessive force, we cannot discern with precision changes in the incidence of these events over time and across places. This means that we can neither determine whether excessive force problems are getting better or worse nor determine the circumstances under which those problems are more or less severe.

The Impact of Differences in Police Organizations, Including Administrative Policies, Hiring, Training, Discipline, and Use of Technology, on Excessive and Illegal Force Is Unknown. Research Is Critically Needed in This Area

A major gap in our knowledge about excessive force by police concerns characteristics of police agencies that facilitate or impede this conduct. Although many of the conditions that arguably lead to excessive or illegal force by police seem obvious, or appear to be a matter of common sense, we still greatly need systematic research in this area. We need to know, for example, which organizational characteristics are most consequential, which characteristics take on added significance in various environments, and which characteristics are redundant or derivative of other characteristics.

Many formal aspects of the organization—such as hiring criteria, recruit training, in service programs, supervision of field officers, disciplinary mechanisms, operations of internal affairs, specialized units dealing with ethics and integrity, labor unions, and civilian oversight mechanisms—plausibly are related to levels of officer misconduct. It makes sense that poorly educated, badly trained, loosely supervised, and inadequately disciplined officers are likely to be problematic, and that when such officers are in the majority, the organization is on the road toward disaster. Yet, we lack research that systematically addresses these questions.

Less formal aspects of police organizations—officer morale, administrative leadership, peer culture and influence, police-community relations, relations with other government agencies, and neighborhood environments—also plausibly have a part in levels of officer misconduct. Alienated officers who do not have a clear vision of their role and responsibilities and who are working in disorganized agencies and interacting with the public under stressful circumstances probably are more likely to abuse their authority, including their authority to use force. Research that systematically addresses these questions is lacking.

Methodological investigation of relations between organizational elements and use-of-force transgressions will help explain police misconduct at a theoretical level. More importantly, research on these questions will allow us to deal effectively with police misbehavior. Faced with serious misconduct problems in a police agency, we need to focus scarce resources on those aspects of police organizations that are most clearly related to ensuring proper conduct of officers with regard to use of force. Generalized efforts to reform police organizations that are expected to reduce misconduct problems tend to be inefficiently focused and thus appear clumsy, inadequate, and misinformed.

Research must focus on establishing the relative cost-effectiveness of various strategies to reduce or eliminate police misconduct. Furthermore, only strategies that are solidly grounded in theory, practice, and empirical research will provide reliable solutions with predictable costs and benefits.

Influences of Situational Characteristics on Police Use of Force and the Transactional Nature of These Events Are Largely Unknown. More Research Is Necessary

Research on police-citizen encounters reveals that use of force by police is situational and transactional. That is, police respond to circumstances as they first encounter them and as they unfold over time. For example, Bayley and Garofalo observed that the situations most likely to involve police use of force are interpersonal disturbance and violent personal crime.[24] Beyond this, however, we do not know much about the types of events that enhance the likelihood that police will use force.

Similarly, we have noted that when suspects attempt to flee or physically resist arrest police are more likely to use of force. We also noted that in many cases both police and suspects use force against each other. However, these findings do not address the transactional nature of police-public encounters in that they do not describe the step-by-step unfolding of events and interactions. Knowing that police use force if suspects physically resist arrest, it matters if police use force without provocation and the suspect responds by resisting or vice versa.

A variety of situational elements plausibly are related to police use of force. If police are called to a scene where there is fighting, they may have to or believe they have to use force to subdue the suspects. If they are called to a domestic dispute where emotions are running high, they may have to or believe they have to use force to gain control of the situation. If they are called to intercede with a civilian who is recklessly brandishing a weapon, they may have to or believe they have to use force to protect themselves and others. Use of force in such circumstances may be justifiable, but to the extent that it is predictable, we can prepare officers for these encounters and devise alternative strategies that minimize or eliminate the use of force.

Some situational factors may increase the chances that force of questionable legitimacy will be used. For example, officers sometimes use force on the slightest provocation following a high-speed car chase, when adrenaline levels are high. They may use force more frequently when they are alone, because they feel more vulnerable or believe that they can get away with it. They may use force more frequently as a way of emphasizing their authority when suspects are disrespectful or when there is a hostile audience to the encounter. At this point, however, knowledge about the types of police-citizen encounters in which police are likely to use force is rudimentary.

Police-public encounters are transactional in the sense that all the actors in a situation contribute in some way to its development and outcome. Understanding the transactional nature of police use of force is important because it emphasizes the role of police actions in increasing the chances that force will be used.

From this perspective, it is possible to minimize the use of force by modifying the behavior and tactics of police officers. By understanding the sequences of events that lead police to use force, we can gain a greater degree of control over those situations and possibly redirect the outcome. But we have only a basic understanding of the transactional nature of use-of-force situations, despite the fact that sequences of actions and interactions are highly germane to determining whether use of force was excessive or illegal. . . .

References

Geoffrey P. Alpert and Roger G. Dunham, "The Force Factor." In *Use of Force by Police, National Institute of Justice—Research Report.* (Washington DC: U.S. Department of Justice) October 1999 pp. 45–60.

Joel H. Garner and Christopher D. Maxwell, "Measuring the amount of force used by and against its police in six jurisdictions." In *Use of Force by Police, National Institute of Justice—Research Report* (Washington DC: US. Department of Justice) October 1999 pp. 25–44.

Notes

1. Bierce, Ambrose, *The Devil's Dictionary,* New York: Dover, 1958: 101.
2. "Justice Department Consent Decree Pushes Police to Overhaul Operations," *Pittsburgh Post-Gazette,* March 1, 1998, C-1.
3. Based on an investigation in 14 cities, Human Rights Watch described the brutality situation as follows: "[p]olice officers engage in unjustified shootings, severe beatings, fatal chokings, and unnecessarily rough physical treatment in cities throughout the United States, while their police superiors, city officials and the Justice Department fail to act decisively to restrain or penalize such acts or even to record the full magnitude of the problem." Human Rights Watch, *Shielded from Justice: Police Brutality and Accountability in the United States,* New York: Human Rights Watch, 1998: 1, 27.

4. A previous summary of research on police use of force can be found in McEwen, Tom, *National Data Collection on Police Use of Force,* Washington, DC: U.S. Department of Justice, Bureau of Justice Statistics and National Institute of Justice, April 1996, NCJ 160113.
5. Bayley, David H., and James Garofalo, "The Management of Violence by Police Patrol Officers," *Criminology,* 27(1) (February 1989): 1–27; and Bayley, David H., and James Garofalo, "Patrol Officer Effectiveness in Managing Conflict During Police-Citizen Encounters," in *Report to the Governor,* Vol. III, Albany: New York State Commission on Criminal Justice and the Use of Force, 1987: B 1–88.
6. Adams, Kenneth, "Measuring the Prevalence of Police Abuse of Force," in *And Justice For All: A National Agenda for Understanding and Controlling Police Abuse of Force,* ed. William A. Geller and Hans Toch, Washington, DC: Police Executive Research Forum, 1995: 61–97.
7. Greenfeld, Lawrence A., Patrick A. Langan, and Steven K. Smith, *Police Use of Force: Collection of National Data,* Washington, DC: U.S. Department of Justice, Bureau of Justice Statistics and National Institute of Justice, November 1997, NCJ 165040.
8. Ibid.
9. Pate, Anthony M., and Lorie A. Fridell, with Edwin E. Hamilton, *Police Use of Force: Official Reports, Citizen Complaints, and Legal Consequences,* Vols. I and II, Washington, DC: The Police Foundation, 1993.
10. Greenfeld, Lawrence A., Patrick A. Langan, and Steven K. Smith, *Police Use of Force: Collection of National Data.*
11. Garner, Joel, John Buchanan, Tom Schade, and John Hepburn, *Understanding Use of Force by and Against the Police,* Research in Brief, Washington, DC: U.S. Department of Justice, National Institute of Justice, November 1996, NCJ 158614.
12. Bayley, David H., and James Garofalo, "The Management of Violence by Police Patrol Officers"; and Bayley, David H., and James Garofalo, "Patrol Officer Effectiveness in Managing Conflict During Police-Citizen Encounters."
13. Ibid.
14. Worden, Robert, "The 'Causes' of Police Brutality," in *And Justice For All: A National Agenda for Understanding and Controlling Police Abuse of Force,* 31–60.
15. Garner, Joel, John Buchanan, Tom Schade, and John Hepburn, *Understanding Use of Force by and Against the Police.*
16. Reiss, Jr., Albert J., *Studies on Crime and Law Enforcement in a Major Metropolitan Area,* President's Commission on Law Enforcement and Administration of Justice, Field Survey No. 3, Washington, DC: U.S. Government Printing Office, 1967.
17. Garner, Joel, John Buchanan, Tom Schade, and John Hepburn, *Understanding Use of Force by and Against the Police.*
18. Toch, Hans, "The 'Violence-Prone' Police Officer," in *And Justice For All: A National Agenda for Understanding and Controlling Police Abuse of Force,* 99–112.
19. Independent Commission on the Los Angeles Police Department, *Report of the Independent Commission on the Los Angeles Police Department,* Los Angeles, CA: Independent Commission on the Los Angeles Police Department, 1991.
20. United States Commission on Civil Rights, *Who's Guarding the Guardians? A Report on Police Practices,* Washington, DC: United States Commission on Civil Rights, 1981: 159.
21. Ibid.
22. Toch, Hans, "The 'Violence-Prone' Police Officer," 112.
23. Office of the Inspector General, Los Angeles Police Commission, "Status Update: Management of LAPD High-Risk Officers," Los Angeles: Los Angeles Police Commission, 1997.
24. Bayley, David, H., and James Garofalo, "Patrol Officer Effectiveness in Managing Conflict During Police-Citizen Encounters."

Kenneth Adams, "What We Know About Police Use of Force." Reprinted from Kenneth Adams, "Use of Force by Police: Overview of National and Local Data," *National Institute of Justice Research Report,* October 1999. ✦

Chapter 16

A National Survey of Pursuits and the Use of Police Force

Data from Law-Enforcement Agencies

Dennis Jay Kenney
Geoffrey P. Alpert

P*olice pursuits attract considerable public attention, as evidenced by Hollywood's depictions of heroic police officers diligently pursuing "bad guys," narrowly missing pedestrians, and leaving behind a wide swath of mayhem and destruction. In reality, police hot pursuits are usually the last resort for capturing a fleeing suspect.*

In their study, Kenney and Alpert summarize data from a national survey on pursuits and the police use of force. Their findings suggest that while most police departments across the nation have a departmental policy on pursuit, most agencies do not require officers to file reports on police use of hot pursuits. Second, there remains no consensus among departments over whether hot-pursuit engagement should be restricted or permitted for any offense. In addition, the authors report exceptionally high rates of officer and citizen injury as a result of hot pursuits.

Nationally, very little is known about police pursuit driving. The National Highway Traffic Safety Administration (NHTSA) maintains some statistics, but they are limited to pursuit-related deaths as captured by the Fatal Accident Reporting System (FARS). Prior to 1994, this system received information from local agencies only when a pursued vehicle or its driver was involved in a fatal crash. There were 347 pursuit-related deaths reported in 1993. In 1994, the reporting system was modified to include a driver-level factor, "in pursuit." While this modification will increase the number of fatal accidents that qualify for the "pursuit-related" category, other reporting problems remain. In fact, the *FARS Newsletter* reported that "These changes will maximize our ability to recognize fatalities on the file related to police pursuit; still, we won't be able to record all pursuits resulting in fatalities. Again, some do not qualify as 'accidents'; others may not be reported on the FAR as involving any pursuit" (FARS 1993, 2). In other words, some incidents do not fit into the FARS definition and the investigating agency may not report others properly. A possible consequence of the improved system was the increase to 388 pursuit-related deaths reported in 1994. Though the NHTSA is working diligently to improve data collection and retrieval, the number of pursuit-related deaths in the United States remains unknown. Certainly, the number of pursuits with outcomes other than a death is unclear and insufficient information exists to even estimate their totals. Likewise, nothing is known about other aspects of pursuits on a national basis.

Equally limiting as our lack of knowledge about pursuits is the absence of information about other areas of police force. For example, in discussing the use of firearms, Geller and Scott (1992) have described the current research:

> More is known now about the nature and frequency of shootings in which police are involved, although we have nothing resembling a comprehensive, continuous na-

tional picture of these violent police-citizen encounters. Even police insight into the nature, extent, causes and prevention of police shootings tends to draw on anecdotal rather than systematic information, and insight is highly localized. . . . This state of affairs poses a dilemma for public policy makers, who do not have the luxury of waiting for systematic data or tactical advances before making concrete decisions about how the police are supposed to conduct themselves. The atmosphere surrounding the "deadly force debate" is charged with emotion, fear entrenched assumptions, class- and race-based suspicions and virtually intractable value conflicts. (p. 1)

Beyond anecdotal impressions, the most comprehensive national look at use-of-force issues can be found in a recent survey conducted by Pate and Fridell (1993). From their research, they report that "despite the importance of these issues, relatively little is known about the extent to which police use force, the types of force used, the extent to which force results in citizen complaints . . . and the extent to which those complaints are determined by the departments to be justified" (p. 31).

Their survey, the authors contend, "provide[s] the first national data on these topics." Still, limited, however, they report that many agencies do not require reports for most types of force. They also show that training, number of incidents, rates of force, complaints about force, and the justification of those complaints vary significantly among agencies (Pate and Fridell 1993, 153). Since the survey reported here focused on many of these same questions, reference to responses concerning the use of force will be offered for comparison to pursuit.

Though what we know about police use of firearms and use of less-than-lethal force is limited, the quantity and quality of information concerning pursuits are at least a decade or so behind (Alpert and Fridell 1992). It is the purpose of this chapter to begin addressing these voids by describing the results from the first national survey on police pursuits and the use of police force.

What We Know Beyond Fatalities

In 1992, the Bureau of Justice Statistics published its Law Enforcement Management and Administrative Statistics for 1990. In its section for large agencies (more than 100 officers), each agency was asked if it maintained a pursuit policy. Ninety-nine percent of the agencies reported having one. Unfortunately, there was no indication of the nature or quality of the policy or when it was implemented. With one important exception, no other national-level data were found.

In an effort to address similar issues nearly twenty-five years ago, Fennessy and Joscelyn (1970) attempted a national survey of both state police and municipal departments serving cities with populations over 100 thousand. Unfortunately, after receiving only limited responses (40%) with information that was "inadequate, inconsistent, and sometimes suspicious," they concluded their effort to define "the national implications of hot pursuit with an historical data collection approach" to be unworkable. Specifically, the issues they encountered were summarized as follows:

- an absence of a consistent definition of "hot pursuit."
- a lack of a consistent standard for charging violators apprehended after a pursuit.
- police records systems that are not designed for such analysis.
- inconsistent reporting by officers of unsuccessful pursuits.
- records-keeping procedures intended primarily for officer and agency defense.

To replace their survey, the authors turned instead to a four-site field study using research staff to systematically collect data during a one-month time frame at each site. From that, they extrapolated to the nation as a whole. While more recent studies have provided other important perspectives on police pursuits (Nugent et al. 1989; Shuman and Kennedy 1989; Alpert and Fridell 1992; Kennedy,

Homant, and Kennedy 1992; Homant and Kennedy 1994a; Falcone 1994; Payne and Corley 1994), none, so far, have overcome the obstacles found by Fennessy and Joscelyn (1970) to offer a national picture. We believe that the present work fills that gap by reporting information from a national sample of law-enforcement agencies.

Methods

The national survey on pursuits and use of police force was conducted between October 1994 and May 1995. The purpose of the survey was to collect pursuit and use-of-force information from police agencies throughout the country. For consistency, we requested that each agency apply the standard definition adopted by the International Association of Chiefs of Police (1990) in its *Model Policy* for vehicular pursuits: "An active attempt by an officer in an authorized emergency vehicle to apprehend fleeing suspects who are attempting to avoid apprehension through evasive tactics." Specifically, the instrument asked about the following:

1. mandated vehicle pursuit policies, both local and statewide.
2. pursuit data collection and incident analysis.
3. incidents resulting in accidents, injuries, assaults on officers, or reports of officer misconduct.
4. policies governing pursuit actions, options, alternatives, and terminations.
5. training provided to pursuing officers.
6. procedures, if any, for pursuit reviews and/or investigations.
7. discipline and litigation resulting from pursuits.

Similar information on police uses of other forms of force was requested as well. In all, this eight-page instrument contained fifty items, though many included multiple parts and/or requested open-ended answers.

A sampling frame of 800 municipal and county police agencies was selected. Using a national mailing list compiled by the International City Managers Association, a randomly selected group consisting of 40 percent large agencies (N = 320) and 60 percent smaller jurisdictions (N = 480) was selected for an initial mailing. For our purposes, the point of division between large and small jurisdictions was placed at 100 thousand population.

Once selected, our survey group was examined for obvious duplications and inaccuracies before the initial mailing. From this review, twenty-six agencies were removed from the sampling frame. Included were agencies that no longer existed or had been merged or consolidated into larger jurisdictions or departments. Our remaining sample now consisted of 774 agencies. With our first wave of mailings, another thirty-six surveys were returned by the post office as undeliverable, although accurate addresses for eight of these were identified. Though many of the missing jurisdictions were unknown to project staff, our estimate is that all were from sparsely populated communities. In all, our first-wave survey sample consisted of 746 law-enforcement agencies.

Each survey in the initial wave was addressed to the responding agency's chief executive and included a requested return by the second week of November 1994. Our survey instructions requested that the chief executive designate the persons appropriate for the instrument's completion. With our instructions we acknowledged that the information requested was quite detailed and might require a longer time for some agencies to complete.

While a one-month completion date was requested, responses were returned regularly throughout the month of November. As such, project staff decided to postpone a second mailing for approximately one week until the returns from the first wave were exhausted. In fact, by the last week of November, 322 responses (43%) had been received. Following several days with no additional returns, a second wave mailing to the 424 nonresponding agencies was completed with additional instructions stressing the importance of the project. For this wave, a completion date of 20 December 1994 was requested to encourage departments to complete the instrument before the Christmas holidays. By the end of the year, an additional sixty-eight responses were received, bringing the response rate to more than 52 percent. During January 1995, PERF staff contacted the remaining 356 agencies by telephone.

From the telephone contacts, project staff located another nine agencies that no longer existed independently. This further reduced the sample total to 737. Many others reported a change in their chief executive and explained that they had not received the survey request since personalized mail was forwarded to the addressee. In those cases, the request for participation was repeated and a copy of the survey instrument was sent to the new executive by fax. Other agencies reported that they had simply failed to complete their questionnaires. Where it was still available, staff requested that they do so; where it was not, a third copy was faxed to them as well. From these requests, another forty-six instruments were received, raising the overall response rate to more than 59 percent. Of the remaining 301 nonresponding agencies, only seventeen (2%) reported a desire not to participate. The other 284 (38%) informed us that they could not supply the requested information because their agencies did not collect it. As such, we are reluctant to label this group nonrespondents.

In sum, contact was made with 737 agencies, of which 436 completed useable data, 284 reported they did not collect or maintain the information, and 17 refused to participate. It is important to recognize that 38 percent of the agencies reported that they could not provide the necessary information because it was not collected. This is a discouraging figure that reflects the generally poor state of record keeping as it relates to pursuit-driving information. It is encouraging that only seventeen agencies (2%) that may have had the requested information available refused to provide it.

In all, our respondent sample included 149 agencies (34%) employing 1 to 25 sworn officers, 97 agencies (22%) with 26 to 150 sworn officers, 100 agencies (23%) with 151 to 500 sworn officers, 49 agencies (11%) with more than 500 sworn officers, and 41 agencies (10%) that did not report their size.

The National Survey of Pursuit

Nearly all the agencies (91%) reported having written policies governing pursuit situations, though the dates that their current policies were implemented varied considerably from as early as 1970 to as recently as 1995. Most, however, had implemented their current pursuit policy since 1990 (57%) while a sizable group (42%) had done so since 1992. Further, nearly half (48%) reported having modified their pursuit policy within the past two years. Most of those (87%) noted that the modification had made the policy more restrictive than the earlier version. Similarly, most of the responding agencies (72%) had their pursuit policies reviewed by a legal authority prior to its adoption. Table 16.1 compares the availability of pursuit policies, policy modifications during the previous two years, and policies on the use of force by police by the type and size of agency responding.

Similarly, the data in Table 16.2 compare the availability of statistics and other data on pursuits and use-of-force incidents. From these data, municipal agencies and larger agencies are more likely to routinely collect such information, a difference that may be related to the frequency of occurrence for these events. In addition, those agencies that collect such data apparently do so voluntarily, since only 11 percent of our respondents reported that their data-collection programs for pursuits are state mandated. Interestingly, while respondents from ten states advised that they operated under a state requirement, in only two of those states (California and New Jersey) were the responding agencies in agreement. For example,

Table 16.1
Pursuit and Use-of-Force Policies by Agency Type

	Pursuit Policy		Policy Modified in Past Two Years		Use of Force Policy	
	Yes	No	Yes	No	Yes	No
Agency Type						
City	271 (95%)	14 (5%)	143 (51%)	138 (49%)	267 (93%)	19 (7%)
County	103 (87%)	15 (13%)	54 (46%)	63 (54%)	110 (92%)	9 (8%)
Unknown	21 (81%)	5 (19%)	12 (52%)	11 (48%)	20 (77%)	6 (23%)
Agency Size						
Below 100 Officers	203 (89%)	24 (11%)	95 (43%)	128 (57%)	208 91%)	20 (9%)
101–500 Officers	114 (100%)	—	72 (63%)	42 (37%)	113 (99%)	1 (1%)
501–2,500 Officers	44 (98%)	1 (2%)	25 (56%)	20 (44%)	44 (96%)	2 (4%)
Over 2,501 Officers	3 (100%)	—	1 (33%)	2 (67%)	3 (100%)	—

in Minnesota, while eight departments reported a state-mandated pursuit data-collection program, three others apparently were not aware of such a requirement. In six other states, only one responding agency believed data collection was required. From this, it would appear that the value of pursuit and use-of-force data, and the issues and requirements of collection, have not yet been clearly defined at local departmental levels.

Table 16.2
Availability of Pursuit and Use-of-Force Statistics

	Pursuit Data		Use-of-Force Data	
	Yes	No	Yes	No
Agency Type				
City	105 (37%)	180 (63%)	121 (44%)	152 (56%)
County	26 (22%)	91 (78%)	43 (38%)	71 (62%)
Unknown	4 (15%)	22 (85%)	11 (42%)	15 (58%)
Agency Size				
Below 100 Officers	46 (20%)	181 (80%)	69 (32%)	148 (68%)
101–500 Officers	58 (50%)	57 (50%)	62 (56%)	49 (44%)
501–2,500 Officers	25 (56%)	20 (44%)	28 (65%)	15 (35%)
Over 2,500 Officers	3 (100%)	—	3 (100%)	—

Analyzing Pursuit-Policy Elements

Recall that nearly one-half of the responding agencies reported modifying their pursuit policies within the past two years and that in nearly each instance the result was a more restrictive policy than the one in place before the modification. Even so, when the individual elements of each agency's policy are examined, interesting differences emerge. For example, while departments were evenly split over permitting pursuits for any offense (48%), some restricted officer chases to incidents involving violent felonies (16%). Most permitted only marked vehicles to conduct a pursuit (58%), and a few restricted pursuing speeds to a specific maximum over the speed limit (11%). Overwhelmingly, supervisors were assigned the responsibility of terminating a pursuit (79%), while most agencies also placed responsibility on the officers involved (69%). Many (40%) required that pursuits be terminated once a suspect's identity becomes known.

Beyond these cumulative results, however, some agencies clearly had differing expectations. Municipal agencies, for example, were significantly more likely to restrict pursuits to felony incidents (19%) than were their county counterparts (11%). Similarly, municipal agencies restricted pursuits to marked vehicles (64% versus 53%) and imposed supervisory responsibility (85% versus 77%) far more often than did county departments.

Among those who had modified their policies within the past two years, the differences were even more remarkable. For example, 68 percent restricted pursuits to marked vehicles. Of those with unchanged policies, however, only 54 percent imposed a similar limit. At least 89 percent of those with revised policies gave the supervisor responsibility for deciding whether to terminate a chase, though fewer than 77 percent of those agencies whose policies that had not changed had a similar requirement. While significant for all types of responding agencies, the patterns of policy change were most pronounced between county and sheriff's departments. As such, among those who had recently modified their policies few significant differences between city and county policy were found. From those where recent modifications had not occurred, however, county officers were consistently less restricted on either their pursuit actions or supervision. Table 16.3 demonstrates these differences.

In addition to when they can pursue, recent policy modifications appear to have imposed changes on how officers pursue as well. When asked about alternatives allowed, nearly one-half (42%) reported that roadblocks were permitted, though more (47%) advised that pursuits should be terminated once the offender's license plate number was determined. Far fewer permitted vehicle immobilization techniques (5%), channelization efforts (20%), ramming (12%), or had portable barrier strips

Table 16.3
Policy Differences by Agency Type

Agency Type	Restrictive	Discretionary	Discouragement
City	43%	52%	5%
County	39%	59%	1%

	Policy Modified			*No Policy Change*		
Agency Type	Marked Veh. Only	Supv. Resp.	End if Susp. Id.	Marked Veh. Only	Resp. Supv.	End if Susp. Id.
City	70%	91%	44%	57%	80%	42%
County	64%	89%	49%	44%	79%	36%

available (15%). While few differences based on agency size or type could be found, county officers were significantly more likely to be permitted to employ roadblocks (55% versus 43%), spinouts (10% versus 3%), or barrier strips (30% versus 10%) than officers from municipal departments. Similarly, mid-sized departments (501 to 2,500 officers) were significantly more likely to employ road blocks (67%), but less likely to have barrier strips available than were agencies of any other size.

A Review of the Incidents

Though only 135 (31%) of the agencies systematically maintain police pursuit statistics or data, 308 (71%) could provide estimates of the numbers of pursuits their officers had engaged in during 1993, the last full year prior to the survey. The figures ranged from zero (N = 34) to 870 pursuits, with large agencies obviously experiencing greater numbers of incidents than smaller ones. When pursuit incidents per officer were examined, however, it was the smaller and municipal agencies that experienced the highest rates of pursuing. Despite this, the rate of pursuit-related accidents increased substantially with agency size. Table 16.4 presents pursuits and related accidents by agency type and size.

Pursuit Training and Accountability

Despite an awareness that pursuits do occur and the understanding that they can result in accidents or injuries, many departments acknowledged taking only limited steps to prepare their officers for pursuits. Similarly, there was a conspicuous lack of institutional review of pursuit incidents. As a result, a general absence of corrective measures should not be surprising. For example, although 60 percent of the agencies responding provide entry-level pursuit-driving training at the academy, the average time devoted to these skills was estimated at less than fourteen hours. The remaining 40 percent of the agencies reported no preservice pursuit training. Once in service, the agencies with training averaged just over three hours per year of additional training. In contrast, nearly 83 percent of these agencies required in-service training in the use of force which averaged more than eight hours per year. These differences exist despite the fact that 12 percent reported five or more incidents each during the previous year where vehicle pursuits ended with one or more suspects fleeing from officers on foot, nearly 16 percent had one or more pursuits result in assaults on officers, and almost 13 percent had at least one pursuit result in an intentional ramming of a police vehicle. Interestingly, the county agencies provided an average of nearly two additional hours of academy-based pursuit-driving training to entry-level officers although they have a pursuit-related accident rate nearly 40 percent below the municipal departments.

Table 16.4
Pursuits and Pursuit-Related Accidents by Agency Type and Size

		Per 1,000 Pursuits				
	Pursuits per 1,000 Officers	Accidents	Ofc. Injuries	Susp. Injuries	Other Injuries	Deaths
Agency Type						
City	112	324	25	70	19	2.4
County	105	198	27	82	24	8.6
Agency Size						
Below 100	181	164	22	72	20	4.1
101–500	109	297	26	71	18	5.7
501–2,500	124	394	46	129	30	3.2
Over 2,501	99	577	24	61	26	2.0

The mid-sized departments (501 to 2,500 officers), on the other hand, have a pursuit-related accident rate more than twice that of the small departments (less than 100 officers), yet on average offer less than half the in-service training in pursuit driving. The agencies that have modified their pursuit policies within the past two years required from their officers both more hours of training in pursuit decision making (both entry and in-service) and practical exercises at a driving track or similar setting than agencies not having modified their policies recently.

Beyond training for such situations, our responding agencies reported important differences in their follow-up evaluations once an actual pursuit incident had occurred. While most (89%) routinely conducted some follow-up, for many that amounted to nothing more than an informal supervisory review (33%) or a report addressing the incident by the pursuing officer (47%). Others, however, require a formal supervisory review (46%), while a few (8%) initiate an internal investigation into all incidents. Internal investigations were more commonly used in response to pursuits resulting from inappropriate actions or that ended in an accident or injuries.

Disciplining Officers

Given their regularity, it is probably inevitable that officer error and misconduct will sometimes result from vehicle pursuits. In fact, slightly more than 12 percent of the agencies reported having to discipline officers at least once during 1993 for pursuit-related actions. The actual discipline offered ranged from simple counseling with an oral reprimand to the termination of two officers.

Beyond internal actions, nearly 16 percent of our sample of police agencies advised that during 1993 they had been involved in litigation resulting from pursuits (Table 16.5). Eighteen (2.5% of the sample; 26% of those involved in litigation) of those agencies either lost or settled the actions against them. Munic-

Table 16.5
Involvement in Pursuit-Related Litigation During 1993

	Involved		Lost or Settled	
	Yes	*No*	*Yes*	*No*
Agency Type				
City	53 (20%)	216 (80%)	13 (5%)	247 (95%)
County	11 (9%)	106 (91%)	3 (3%)	109 (97%)
Agency Size				
Below 100 Officers	10 (4%)	217 (96%)	2 (1%)	223 (99%)
101–500 Officers	31 (30%)	73 (70%)	6 (6%)	91 (94%)
501–2,500 Officers	20 (49%)	21 (51%)	5 (14%)	31 (86%)
Over 2,501 Officers	1 (100%)	—	1 (100%)	—
Policy Status				
Modified in Past Two Years	44 (22%)	154 (78%)	12 (6%)	180 (94%)
No Recent Modifications	25 (12%)	177 (88%)	6 (3%)	187 (97%)

ipal agencies, agencies that had modified their pursuit policies within the past two years, and larger agencies were more likely to be involved in such actions, though only agency size was associated with significant differences in the legal outcomes. Unfortunately, we were unable to determine whether the previously reported pursuit-policy modifications were a result of the litigation during 1993.

Earlier we noted that training requirements and intensity were generally greater for use-of-force issues than for pursuits. While the risks to others posed by police chases may be greater, our results suggest that the responses (both internal and external) to force incidents are more serious. For example, while 12 percent of our respondent agencies administered discipline for pursuit-related actions, more than 18 percent employed discipline in response to a police use of force. Further, nearly 5 percent of our agencies reported disciplining officers five or more times during 1993, whereas fewer than 2 percent did so with such frequency in response to pursuit violations. In addition, the range of disciplinary action was more limited for pursuits than uses of force. Where disciplinary actions for pursuit-driving violations normally involved some form of a reprimand (82% of all actions taken), the actions taken for use-of-force violations included reprimands alone (7% of actions taken), reprimands with suspensions, demotions, or terminations (44%), suspensions alone (25%), additional training (10%), and termination or retirement (7%).

Finally, when combined, pursuits and the uses of force that result can be especially problematic. During 1993, 25 percent (109) of our sample departments experienced police pursuits that resulted in officers using force, in addition to the pursuit itself, to apprehend a suspect. In only a few of those incidents (24), however, were allegations filed that the force used was excessive or unreasonable. In twelve of those cases, those allegations were sustained. Fortunately, the trends for the future appear positive, as most (68%) of the participating agencies see either no change or a decrease in complaints of excessive pursuit related force over the past two years.

Conclusion

The responses to our national survey revealed or reinforced several important trends. First, it is critical for law-enforcement agencies to create and maintain systems to collect information on pursuit driving. The inability of many to respond to our questions was discouraging. Second, the fact that most agencies had policies was favorable; however, the overall quality and direction of those policies was questionable, since some departments had instituted theirs as many as twenty years ago. More favorably, we note that many agencies have updated their policies and most who have made them more restrictive than those previously in effect. Third, the necessary training for pursuits needs rethinking. It is obviously unwise for our law-enforcement agencies to expect officers to make proper and appropriate decisions with minimal or no training. Similarly, the supervisory aspect of each agency's policies should be reviewed and enforced. Finally, the requirements that officers justify their actions or have a supervisor evaluate their pursuit (after-action reports) needs more attention. When actions are found to be inappropriate, officers often do not receive meaningful discipline for problem pursuits. Perhaps as a result, litigation in pursuit is a real and serious concern.

References

Alpert, G., and L. Fridell. (1992). *Police Vehicles and Firearms.* Prospect Heights, Ill.: Waveland.

Bureau of Justice Statistics. (1992). *State and Local Police Departments—1990.* Washington, D.C.: Author.

Falcone, D. (1994). Police Pursuits and Officer Attitudes: Myths and Realities. *American Journal of Police* 13 (1): 143–155.

Fatal Accident Reporting System (FARS). (1993). Coding Focus. *FARS Newsletter,* September, 2.

Fennessy, E., Jr., and K. Joscelyn. (1970). A National Study of Hot Pursuit. *Denver Law Journal* 48: 389–403.

Geller, W., and M. Scott. (1992). *Deadly Force: What We Know.* Washington, D.C.: Police Executive Research Forum.

Geller, W., and H. Toch, eds. (1995). *And Justice for All.* Washington, D.C.: Police Executive Research Forum.

Homant, R., and D. Kennedy. (1994a). Citizen Preferences Concerning Police Pursuit Policies. *Journal of Criminal Justice* 22: 415–458.

Homant, R., and D. Kennedy. (1994b). The Effect of High-Speed Pursuit Policies on Officers' Tendencies to Pursue. *American Journal of Police* 13: 91–111.

International Association of Chiefs of Police. (1990). *Model Policy: Vehicular Pursuit.* Washington, D.C.: Author.

Kennedy, D., R. Homant, and J. Kennedy. (1992). A Comparative Analysis of Police Vehicle Pursuit Policies. *Justice Quarterly* 9: 227–246.

Nugent, H., E. Connors, J. T. McEwen, and L. Mayo. (1989). *Restrictive Policies for High Speed Pursuit Pursuits.* Washington, D.C.: U.S. Government Printing Office.

Pate, A., and L. Fridell. (1993). *Police Use of Force: Official Reports, Citizen Complaints and Legal Consequences.* Washington, D.C.: Police Foundation.

Payne, D., and C. Corley. (1994). Police Pursuits: Correlates of the Failure to Report. *American Journal of Police* 13: 47–71.

Shuman, I. G., and T. Kennedy. (1989). Police Pursuit Policies: What Is Missing? *American Journal of Police* 10: 21–30.

Wells, L. E., and D. Falcone. (1992). Organizational Variations in Vehicle Pursuits by Police: The Impact of Policy on Practice. *Journal of Criminal Justice Policy Review* 6: 311–333.

Dennis Jay Kenney and Geoffrey P. Alpert, "A National Survey of Pursuits and the Use of Police Force: Data from Law-Enforcement Agencies." Reprinted from Dennis Jay Kenney and Robert P. McNamara (Eds.), *Police and Policing: Contemporary Issues,* 2nd ed., pp. 156–169. Copyright © 1999 by Dennis Jay Kenney and Robert P. McNamara. Reproduced with permission of Greenwood Publishing, Inc., Westport, CT. ✦

Chapter 17
The Establishment of a Police Gang Unit

An Examination of Organizational and Environmental Factors

Charles M. Katz

Charles Katz's study on the establishment of a gang unit in a large metropolitan area makes a unique contribution to the study of gangs and police behavior. Katz applies an institutional theory of management to explain the relationship between one municipal police organization and its response to the demands from its external environment.

Briefly summarized, institutional theory focuses on organizational response to demands from the external environment (e.g., citizens, organizations, news media, etc.). In a simple environment, an organization such as a police agency knows how to react to ordinary demands from the public. However, in more complex situations, organizational leadership becomes less certain about the best adaptation to "fit" an environment that has shifted or changed.

Based on data collected from a variety of sources, Katz found that the formation of a specialized unit to deal with a growing gang problem was only marginally successful. He argues that the gang unit was created primarily for the purpose of gaining public support from constituents outside the organization rather than as an effective means to resolve the city's gang problem. Simply put, the creation of a gang unit was a demonstration to local residents that the police department was taking their concerns seriously, although there was little expectation that the unit could solve this significant social problem.

In response to the rising concern about gang problems, many law enforcement agencies have established special gang units to apprehend gang members and deter gang-related activity. In 1999, the Law Enforcement and Management Administrative Statistics (LEMAS) survey reported that among large agencies with 100 or more sworn officers, special gang units existed in 56% of all municipal police departments, 50% of all sheriff's departments, 43% of all county police agencies, and 20% of all state law enforcement agencies (Bureau of Justice Statistics, 1999: Table C).[1] These findings lead to an estimate of approximately 360 police gang units in the country.[2] The recency of this phenomenon can be further seen by the fact that over 85% of specialized gang units have been established in the past 10 years (Katz et al., 1998).

Although specialized police gang units represent a new feature in American policing, it is part of an overall trend among many police departments to create specialized units to address unique law enforcement problems, such as repeat offenders, domestic violence, and hate crimes (e.g., Boyd et al., 1996; Bureau of Justice Statistics, 1999; Martin, 1986). Such specialized units are said to be created to focus departmental resources, energy, and skill on a particular community problem. Additionally, such an approach is intended to be a symbolic act to the community, potential offenders, and police officers that the police department is taking a specific problem seriously (Meyer, 1979; Scott, 1995).

It appears that for similar reasons, many police officials and gang scholars have called for the consolidation of gang control functions within police departments (e.g., Burns and

Deakin, 1989; Huff and McBride, 1993; Jackson and McBride, 1985; Rush, 1996). They have argued that assigning the primary responsibilities of the gang problem to a police gang unit will increase the technical efficiency and effectiveness of a police department's response toward its community's gang problem. They point out that consolidation of gang control functions will permit officers, through training and experience, to develop highly technical skills that would not otherwise be possible. They also claim that consolidation of gang control functions allows police organizations to distribute gang-related work orderly and rationally, which better enables police departments to develop and coordinate their response to community gang problems.

Despite the justifications for this organizational approach, little consensus exists as to why police gang units are created and why they have responded to local gang problems in the way that they have over the past 10 years. Many police officials and scholars have argued that specialized gang units have been created for rational reasons, attributing the rise of gang units to the growing number of gangs, gang members, and gang-related problems in communities across the country (Burns and Deakin, 1989; Huff and McBride, 1993; Jackson and McBride, 1985; Weisel and Painter, 1997). Others, however, have argued that the gang problem in many communities is relatively minor, and that the police response to gangs has been fueled by police departments in their quest for federal funding, or as the result of racial stereotyping (McCorkle and Miethe, 1998; Zatz, 1987).

The present study seeks to advance our understanding of some of the issues, problems, and events that shape and define a police department's response to its community's gang problem. Although police officials, researchers, and citizens frequently express their beliefs as to how and why police agencies have responded the way they have toward community gang problems, little systematic research has been done that has investigated these beliefs. This paper uses a multimethodological approach to examine the factors that shaped a Midwestern police department's response to its community's gang problem. This study seeks to extend previous research by examining both organizational and environmental factors associated with the establishment of a specialized police gang unit. The theoretical issue explored in this study is the utility of the institutional perspective for understanding police organizational behavior.

The remainder of the literature review is divided into two sections. The first section outlines the concept of institutional theory and its contribution to understanding change in organizations. The second section discusses prior research as it relates to the establishment of police gang units.

Theoretical Background

Institutional Theory

Institutional theory (Aldrich, 1999; Crank and Langworthy, 1992; Tolbert and Zucker, 1996) holds promise for understanding the police organizational response to the gang problem. Within the institutional perspective, which has been most thoroughly explicated in the general organizational behavior literature, it is argued that the structure and activities of an organization do not necessarily reflect rational adaptations to environmental contingencies. That is, organizations do not create structures or engage in operational activities simply because they are more efficient or more effective. Instead, institutional theorists argue that organizational structures and operational strategies reflect the values and beliefs that are shared by powerful actors, called sovereigns, who have the capacity to influence the policies, decisions, and financial resources of the organization (Abell, 1995; Christensen and Molin, 1995; DiMaggio and Powell, 1991; Scott, 1995). Sovereigns for police agencies include such actors as the mayor, city council members, police unions, special interest groups, citizens, and other criminal justice agencies.

Meyer and Rowan (1977) refer to the ideas and beliefs that are shared by an organization's institutional environment as myths. Myths, in this context, are ideas and beliefs that have not been objectively tested, but are considered to be truths or social facts because they are known and accepted by all within the institutional environment. In this context, myths are rational in that they identify problems and express solutions to those problems (Scott, 1992). Scott (1977: 14) further explains, however, that "these beliefs are myths in the sense that they depend for their efficacy, for their reality, on the fact that they are widely shared, or are promulgated by individuals or groups that have been granted the right to determine such matters."

Accordingly, institutionalists argue that for organizations to establish legitimacy, organizational structures and operational activities must be performed in accordance with the myths that are held by sovereigns in their institutional environment (Christensen and Molin, 1995; Crank, 1994; Friedland and Alford, 1991). Those organizations that conform to the ideas and beliefs that are prescribed to them by their environment are more likely to obtain "cultural support" and, henceforth, to improve their chances for organizational resources and survival (Meyer and Rowan, 1977; Ogle, 1998). Conversely, those organizations that do not conform to the ideas and beliefs that are held by their institutional environment are at risk of being perceived as useless or unimportant, and they may lose any legitimacy that was previously granted by their institutional environment (Crank and Langworthy, 1992).

Crank and Langworthy (1992), who were some of the earliest researchers to argue for the importance of examining policing from an institutional perspective, suggested that much of the structure and activities that are seen in police organizations are influenced by, or may be the result of, institutional considerations. They go on to argue that effectiveness and efficiency are issues of limited importance in a noncompetitive environment. Instead, Crank and Langworthy maintain that for a police organization to achieve and maintain legitimacy, it must engage in those activities that are widely thought to be right, good, and effective. For example, the authors point out that the police continue to use random preventative patrol despite a relatively well-known body of research that suggests this operational activity is not technically efficient or effective in reducing crime. They argue, instead, that preventative patrol has continued to be used because it illustrates to the police department's institutional environment that the police are, in fact, acting like the police and that they are doing what is right and what is expected to be done. Accordingly, Crank and Langworthy claim that to understand police organizational structures and operational strategies, we must focus on how the police acquire and manage legitimacy.

Acquiring and Managing Legitimacy

In a recent review of institutional theory, Suchman (1995) suggests that there are three primary ways that organizations acquire and manage legitimacy—namely, conform to environments, select among environments, and manipulate environments. With respect to conforming to environments, Suchman argues that officials that seek legitimacy for their organization oftentimes find it easiest to alter their structure so that the organization appears as if it is conforming to the beliefs and values of its environment. He explains that organizations can conform to environments, for the purpose of obtaining legitimacy, in a number of ways. One strategy might be to alter the structure of the organization in an effort to "signal" to their institutional environment. A number of organizational theorists have argued that as environments become more complex, organizations are more likely to use structure to communicate, both internally and externally, that they are responding to market changes and sovereign tastes (Greenwood and Hinings, 1996; Meyer, 1979; Scott and Christensen, 1995). In the case of specialized police units, for example, Crank and Langworthy (1992) hypothesized that specialized units are often created for ceremonial purposes rather than to increase the effectiveness or the efficiency of the department. In particular, they argued that specialized units are created in an effort to communicate to the public, potential criminals, and officers that a particular problem is being taken seriously.

Another strategy might be for the organization to make use of previously established networks that are already viewed as legitimate. Suchman (1995) maintains that by an organization closely aligning itself with personnel or other entities that have already achieved a high level of legitimacy, they can achieve legitimacy. Applying this principal to police organizations, Crank and Langworthy (1992) hypothesized that this might be the reason police organizations (as well as special units) become highly involved in relational networks. They argue that these relationships not only provide a means of establishing connectedness among organizational units, but also result in a ceremonial reaffirmation of organizational legitimacy.

Still another strategy that an organization might use to conform to its environment, for the purpose of obtaining legitimacy, is engaging in a process known as mimetic isomorphism (see also DiMaggio and Powell, 1991). Mimetic isomorphism occurs when an organization models itself after other organizations that are perceived as legitimate for the purpose of enhancing its legitimacy (DiMaggio and Powell, 1991; Donaldson, 1995; Suchman and Eyre, 1992). Mastrofski and Uchida (1993), for example, argued that recent innovations in policing, such as the creation of special units and the adoption of community policing strategies, have done little to increase technical outputs. Instead, they argue that many police organizations are adopting these new reforms for the purpose of enhancing their legitimacy so that they may ensure the flow of organizational resources. The authors explain that by adopting new organizational structures or strategies that have been institutionally accepted by similar organizations, even if they are only symbolic or ceremonial in nature, it conveys an image of operational effectiveness.

Although passively conforming to an organization's institutional environment is a means of gaining legitimacy, Suchman (1995) points out that organizations often use more active strategies to gain legitimacy. He argues that one of the simplest ways for an organization to obtain legitimacy is for it to select the environment that will accept it without having to make any significant or meaningful changes. In other words, instead of the organization conforming to its institutional environment, it simply selects a different environment that will value the outputs that it provides. However, Suchman argues that many organizations are not permitted to select their environment in which to operate. In these cases, he argues that organizations often choose to buffer themselves from their institutional environment by decoupling activities.

Traditionally, organizational theories have emphasized that structural arrangements and technical activities are tightly coupled (Donaldson, 1995; Zhao and Maguire, 1999)—that is, that the technical activities carried out by the organization conform to a consistent and clear set of expectations. However, the institutional perspective holds that variation, or conflicting values, can occur within the institutional environment (Greenwood and Hinings, 1996). As a consequence, institutionalists argue that organizations like the police are better served if they decouple their structures from their activities (Crank and Langworthy, 1992). This approach allows the organization to continue to engage in its core activities while engaging in activities that have little association with the routine activities that take place in the organization (Christensen and Molin, 1995; Garud and Kumaraswamy, 1995; Orton and Weick, 1990).

This might explain why some police departments establish specialized units when the magnitude of a problem may not justify a greater level of law enforcement. Some researchers have suggested that sovereigns closely associate specialized units with the "war on crime" (Sparrow et al., 1990). By creating a specialized unit, administrators are able to respond publicly and decisively to an emerging problem as identified by their social and political environments. Such a strategy allows the police to selectively respond to environments that will garnish them legitimacy while allowing them to attend to core technologies.

Lastly, Suchman (1995) argues that organizations may respond to external demands by manipulating their environment. In this case, the values and beliefs of sovereigns in the organization's institutional environment are not necessarily incorporated into an organizational response. Instead, the organization seeks to promote or create new myths for the purpose of obtaining resources and support. Oliver (1991) further explains that manipulation is opportunistically and intentionally used by organizations to co-opt or control sovereigns in their institutional environment for the purpose of shaping the expectations of their social reality.

Organizations that engage in this type of organizational behavior are said to operate in an enacting mode (Weick,1995). Daft and Weick (1984) explain that "the enacting mode reflects both an active, intrusive strategy and the assumption that the environment is unanalyzable" (p. 288). As such, they argue that because the institutional environment is unanalyzable, organizations must socially construct their environment. Weick (1979, 1995) and his colleagues (Daft and Weick, 1984; Orton and Weick, 1990; Weick and Roberts, 1993) maintain that organizations that operate in an enacting mode aggressively develop programs that they believe are marketable. As a consequence, these organizations do not necessarily alter their organizational structure or operational activities because of environmental contingencies, but they construct an environment that will highlight the importance and value of their organization.

These principals, as applied to police organizations, are highlighted by Crank (1994) in his essay on institutionalization in policing. He hypothesized that the rapid adoption of community policing by police departments across the nation was largely driven by their need to regain legitimacy that had been lost during the professional era. In particular, he argued that police organizations have acted as entrepreneurs, influencing their institutional environment by constructing and guiding "nostalgic" myths of the police and how they should operate while making only a few organizational and operational changes. Likewise, some preliminary research suggests that police organizations may also establish special units for the purpose of manipulating their environment. This will be further discussed in the next section.

Prior Studies of the Police Response to Gangs

Although a relatively large amount of research has examined gangs, gang members, and gang-related activity, little research has examined the nature of the organized response to the gang problem. Most of what we know about the police response to the gang problem has come from the media and police officials. Interestingly, even academic pieces have almost exclusively relied on newspaper accounts and professional trade magazines as their primary sources of information (e.g., Klein et al., 1995; Spergel, 1995).

The few studies that have examined the factors that influence the creation of police gang units have typically been focused at the macrolevel. This research has primarily been limited to mail surveys of police leaders. These studies asked police officials if their community has a gang problem and, if they do, to identify their department's particular strategy for dealing with gangs. Such studies have reported that departments that claim to have a gang problem are significantly more likely to have established a specialized gang unit (Curry et al., 1992; Needle and Stapleton, 1983). Nonetheless, a number of academics have questioned the veracity of such data, arguing that police agencies have a vested interest in claiming a worsening gang problem (Bursik and Grasmick, 1995; Hagedorn, 1990).

At least two gang researchers, who both used a moral panic perspective to understand the police response to gangs, have found evidence that the police have become actively involved in the social construction of gang problems at the local level. Zatz (1987) examined the police response to gangs in Phoenix, Arizona, using data obtained from social workers, media reports, and court records. She claimed that the Phoenix community was not faced with a serious gang problem at the time that the gang unit was created, but that police officials established the gang unit and constructed the gang problem in an effort to campaign for federal dollars. She argued that the police department, through the media, successfully constructed a social image of gang members as dangerous, crime-prone Chicano youths that threatened the safety of the Anglo community. She further asserted that the police department also released information warning the public that the gang problem would escalate in the future if the police did not respond. Data obtained from court records and social service agents, however, indicated that gang members did not pose a significant threat to the community at the time, and that police departmental claims of a serious gang problem were grossly exaggerated for the purpose of obtaining organizational resources.

McCorkle and Miethe (1998) reported similar findings in their examination of legislative records, media accounts, and official crime data in Las Vegas, Nevada. The authors argued that the gang problem in Las Vegas was grossly overexaggerated by the police department in an effort to acquire resources and repair their poor image. In particular, they reported that at the time police officials made claims of a growing gang problem, the police department was under considerable financial pressure because of a growing community and was concurrently undergoing serious scrutiny by political officials and community members as the result of a number of police misconduct charges. Accordingly, the authors argued that police officials linked national reports of a growing gang problem to concerns of increasing crime rates in Las Vegas in an effort to divert attention away from the problems of the police department and justify the need for additional police resources.

Although the conclusions of the above two studies are consistent with the moral panic perspective, the findings are also supportive of the institutional perspective—in that the authors found that the police sought to manipulate their environment for the purpose of ensuring organizational resources and survival. However, unfortunately, because the authors did not use the institutional perspective as a framework for analysis, the research failed to take into consideration many of the organizational and environmental factors that may have contributed to the creation of the police gang units. For example, the researchers primarily relied on data obtained from newspaper articles to determine the organizational motivation of police officials and data from court records to determine the extent of the objective threat posed by gang members.

Although the above research provides some insight into the factors that might have influenced the police departments to create specialized gang units, the researchers failed to include data from two central sources: the police organization (or police officials) and sovereigns. As such, there has been a lack of research that has systematically examined the creation process from the perspective of the police organization. It would seem imperative that when attempting to understand how and why a police organization responds to a gang problem that it would be necessary to take into consideration how the organization, and those in the organization, made sense of their reality at the time that the gang unit was created, and how this reality shaped the gang unit's response to the gang problem. Similarly, it would also seem important to take into consideration how sovereigns might impact the police response to gangs. As noted in the above section, research that does not take into consideration the institutional environment in which an organization operates fails to fully capture how the organization conceptualizes, comprehends, and makes sense of the social system in which it operates (Weick, 1995; Weick and Roberts, 1993).

The Present Study

The present study uses a conceptual framework grounded in institutional theory to add to the limited research that has focused on the police response to gangs. Several of the propositions and principals noted earlier in the literature review serve to inform research aimed at identifying and examining the factors that lead to the establishment of a specialized police gang unit. The principal goal of the present study is to describe how one police agency's gang unit was created and to examine the forces that drove the agency to establish the gang unit while ascertaining the utility of the institutional theory framework for this purpose. The second purpose is to examine how these forces influenced the gang unit's response to the community's gang problem. The goal here is to illustrate how the gang unit's response to the gang problem was affected by the factors that led to the unit's creation.

Setting and Methods[3]

Setting

The present study takes place in a large Midwestern community, hereafter called Junction City (a pseudonym). The economic base of Junction City consists of a combination of light manufacturing, service industries, and agricultural-related business. Although Junction City is a fairly prosperous community with a low unemployment rate and a relatively high median household income, a relatively large number of its residents still live below the poverty line (Slater and Hall, 1996). In terms of ethnic composition, the community is diverse, but very similar to national patterns. Caucasians make up approximately 80% of the community (compared with 80.3% for the nation), African Americans make up about 15% (compared with 12.1%), Asians make up 1% (compared with 2.9%), and Hispanics make up about 3% (compared with 9%) (Slater and Hall, 1996). The city's crime rate is somewhat below other major Midwestern cities (e.g., Chicago, Kansas City, and St. Louis) and has remained fairly stable over the past 10 years (Crime in the United States, 1996).

The Junction City Police Department has about 800 full-time employees, more than 600 of whom are sworn officers. The police department's gang unit currently operates within the Special Investigations Bureau. The unit comprises 13 individuals, 10 sworn and 3 nonsworn, and is divided into two shifts.[4] Almost all of the officers and civilian personnel (10) work "B" shift from 8:00 a.m. to 4:00 p.m. Only three officers work "C" shift from 2:00 p.m. to 10:00 p.m. The Junction City Police Department's gang unit is not physically located at Central Headquarters. Instead, it is housed in the northeastern section of the city, a geographic location that is predominantly African-American and is believed to be the center of much of the community's gang activity.

A Multimethodological Research Design

The research design in this project was purposefully constructed to gain a comprehensive view of how and why the police responded to the gang problem in Junction City. In particular, the present study brings together multiple sources of data (e.g., field observations, in-depth interviews, and documents) to focus on a single point and to help explain, clarify, and corroborate issues of question (Lincoln and Guba, 1985; Merriam, 1988).

Field Observations. Approximately 300 hours were spent in the field accompanying gang unit officers from the Junction City Police Department between October 1996 and June 1997 (See Table 17.1). Most of the fieldwork in the present study was with the gang unit officers. After an initial meeting with all of the gang unit personnel, it was agreed that the project would be most benefited by accompanying gang unit officers, and not the supervisors, on their normal shifts. As a result, approximately 253 hours were spent with seven gang unit officers, 20 hours with two gang unit supervisors,

Table 17.1
Data Collection

Type of Data	Number	Date Collected
Interviews with Police Administrators		
Past Chief of Police (1982–1989)	1	June 1997
Lieutenant in Charge of the Gang Unit	1	April 1997
Gang Unit Data		
Field Observation	289 Hours	October 1996–June 1997
Interviews with Gang Unit Officers and Sergeants	9	January–May 1997
Review of Documents		
Official Documents	62	October 1996–June 1997
Newspaper Articles	162	January 1987–July 1997
Interviews with Nongang Unit Personnel		
Internal Personnel	8	March–June 1997
Network Tracking Personnel	16	March–June 1997
School Administrators	14	March–June 1997
Special Interest Group Administrators	7	March–June 1997

and 16 hours with two civilians in the gang unit.

Using an ethnographic research method, officers were accompanied during their regular shift, which averaged 8 hours. A notebook and pencil were used to record field notes that consisted of both descriptive and reflective data. The descriptive data recorded in the field notes included observations and discussions that took place on the job. The notes included areas covered by the interview instrument (as discussed below) as well as other areas, such as how the officers spent their time, the role of the gang unit officer, any contacts gang unit officers made during their shift, informal relationships that developed between gang unit officers and those in their internal and external environment, as well as decisions that were made by gang unit officers.[5]

Throughout the ride-along, reflective data were also recorded. These notes included the "personal thoughts, speculation, feelings, problems, ideas, hunches, impressions, and prejudices" (Bogdan and Biklen, 1992: 121) of the researcher. In a sense, these notes were used as potential hypotheses to be tested. In particular, the reflective (as well as descriptive) data were continually analyzed as the study progressed. This constant comparative method allowed for the adjustment and modification of observational focus over the course of the study for the purpose of checking and testing emerging ideas (Lofland and Lofland, 1995).

Interviews with Gang Unit Officers. In-depth interviews were used to supplement the observations of the gang unit officers. The interview schedule did not emerge from the fieldwork portion of the study. Instead, the main purpose of the interview schedule was to add insight into the daily lives of the gang unit officers and to further aid in understanding the gang problem from the perspective of the gang unit officer. In particular, the interviews were designed to extract subjective reactions from the officers regarding what they consider to be the realities of their work situation, what they feel they must do to effectively perform their job, and what they perceive they actually do on the job.

Because officers tend to be guarded against outsiders, I accompanied the officers for three months before supplementing the ethnographic observations with the interviews. This approach was intended to familiarize and create a comfort level between myself and the officers before the interviews. It appears that this approach was successful in that during many of the interviews officers commented on subjects that I believe they would not have if I had not been familiar to them. It was not unusual for an officer to preface a comment by saying "between you me and the flag pole" or "don't put this in your book, but the reality is that. . . ."

Interviews were conducted with all 10 of the gang unit officers during their normal working hours. The interviews with the seven investigators and the two sergeants comprised 120 questions and focused on seven major areas: officer characteristics and background, why the officer chose the gang unit, their perceptions of the gang unit, the history of the gang unit, the organizational structure of the gang unit, program activities performed by the gang unit, and the goals, objectives, and policies of the gang unit. The interview with the lieutenant in charge of the gang unit focused on the organizational constructs of the gang unit. These questions were directed toward the background of the gang unit, personnel selection, measures of success, and budgetary issues.

Interview data were collected systematically, but in a way that allowed flexibility for discovery. Efforts were made to encourage the officers to bring in outside information not called for from the interview schedule. The interviews lasted approximately six hours and usually took two working days to complete. Once again, paper and pencil were used to record the interviews.

The Review of Documents.

Official Documents. Sixty-two official documents produced by the gang unit and the police department were used for the present study. These included such documents as the gang unit's standard operating procedures (SOP), annual reports, interoffice communications, intelligence and training bulletins, sign-in sheets, grants obtained by the gang unit, booklets produced by the gang unit, and statistics kept by the gang unit. Because no central depository exists for these documents in either the gang unit or the police department, the documents were collected as they presented themselves. Most of the documents were collected as a result of "putting the word out" that I was looking for anything that was related to the history and development of the gang unit. Several documents were also obtained through questioning officers about a particular area of interest. Occasionally, when a question was asked that an officer was unable to answer, we would both attempt to find a document that may aid in the requested information.

These documents are intended to serve as both primary and secondary research materials. They serve as primary research materials in that they are used to document how the officers in the gang unit have been directed to conduct themselves. In other words, the official documents produced by the gang unit or the police department are expressive of the organizational arrangements and may also place the organization in a historical context. For example, the gang unit's SOPs from 1988 to 1996 serve as sources of data communicating the organization's official mandate and how their mandate may have changed over time.

Official documents such as sign-in sheets and bulletins distributed by the gang unit and police department serve as secondary research materials. Documents such as sign-in sheets help define not only the gang unit's community, but also those with which it has frequent contact and possible influence. These documents shed additional light on the common practices and beliefs of the gang unit and illustrate how the gang unit has changed over time. Furthermore, statistics kept by the gang unit are illustrative of the scope of the local gang problem and assist in constructing the realities of the community's gang problem, or at least the realities as documented by the police department. Accordingly, the official documents provide a rich source of support for the findings derived from the observations and interviews (Jorgensen, 1989; Marshall and Rossman, 1995).

At the completion of the project, participants made assurances that all available documents were presented to the researcher. However, because the police department and gang unit [do] not have a central depository or a method of cataloguing documents, it is not possible to assess the representativeness of the sample of documents collected because of the hard-to-define population. An examination of the data indicates that some types of documents may be more representative of their population than are others. For example, although many types of documents (e.g., sign in sheets, statistical reports) were produced at regular intervals and appeared to be representative, other types of documents (e.g., interoffice memoranda) were produced at irregular intervals, and because of the time that has passed between the creation of the gang unit and the collection of the data, it is not possible to assess their representativeness.

Newspaper Articles. The present study also made use of 162 articles obtained from local newspapers between January 1987 and July 1997. The newspaper articles were not only intended to provide a historical record of the development of the gang unit in terms of its organizational mandate and role, but also to provide additional insight into the various external forces that may have affected the gang unit's response to the city's gang problem. Because the newspaper serves as a forum for the community to speak about its concerns, newspaper articles may also provide a rich source of data on how those in the community feel about the gang unit. Accordingly, the newspaper articles offer a different view of the city's gang problem and may offer different opinions as to how the gang problem should be approached and how the gang unit should respond to the city's gang problem.

Several methods were used to locate articles related to the gang unit. The first was a computer search using the Lexus newspaper indexing system with the key terms "gang," "unit," and "police." Although these search terms brought up several hundred articles, which oftentimes only provided vague references to the gang unit, only articles that provided insight to the police response to gangs were extracted. The second method of obtaining newspaper articles on the gang unit was sifting through old newspaper articles that the gang unit had collected from 1989 through 1991. The newspaper articles collected by the gang unit, however, were mostly articles discussing the success of a particular gang unit investigation or a headline story of a documented gang member who either had been killed or apprehended by the police. The last method of collecting newspaper articles related to the gang unit was simply reading the local newspaper during my time in the field and clipping those articles that offered some insight into the police response to gangs in Junction City.

Interviews with Non-Gang Unit Personnel. Forty-six non-gang unit personnel, representing the internal (e.g., fellow police officers/insiders) and external environments (e.g., nonpolice officers/outsiders) of the gang unit were also interviewed. The main purpose of the interviews with non-gang unit personnel was to add further insight into the gang unit's response to the community's gang problem. The interview schedule comprised 17 questions and focused on five major issues: (1) perceptions of the gang problem in the respondent's community; (2) the nature of the relationship between the respondent's unit/ agency and the gang unit; (3) influences the gang unit had had on the respondent's unit/agency; (4) advantages to the unit's/agency's relationship with the gang unit; and (5) problems that the unit/agency had had with the gang unit. Accordingly, interviews were designed to obtain subjective reactions, both positive and negative, from those who had had contact with the gang unit.

Two methods were used to decide who should be interviewed. The first was that during the observational portion of the study, an ongoing log was kept of those persons with whom the gang unit had contact with or who were heard as having an influence on the gang unit. The second method of determining who should be interviewed was accomplished by asking the gang unit officers whom they felt should be contacted to gain further insight into the gang unit. As a consequence of these observations and suggestions, 8 officers representing seven units within the police department, 16 members of the Law Enforcement Network/Tracking System (a.k.a. Gang Task Force), 14 school administrators, and 7 individuals representing eight special interest groups were interviewed. Interestingly, the officers' suggestions of who should be contacted were almost identical to the list that had previously been compiled from observations in the field.

Analysis

Using the qualitative analytic strategies outlined by Schatzman and Strauss (1973), data analysis began early in the research process. From the inception of the study, data were continually reviewed, coded, and organized both chronologically and categorically. This "analytic cycle" allowed us to continually test emerging ideas as well as to identify patterns, relationships, and processes. Additionally, the "constant comparative method" was used to analyze the data after the completion of the project. This process involves "unitizing" and "categorizing" information units (Glaser and Strauss, 1967). These categories and units of meaning were identified and coded after carefully reading the field notes, interviews, and documents collected during the study. To assist in this process, all of the data, with the exception of the documents obtained from the police department, were entered into a computer using the NUD*IST (non-numerical unstructured data indexing searching and theory-building) program. The NUD*IST software program allowed for the coding of data so that "chunks of data" could be pulled out and formed into meaningful categories and patterns.

Several strategies were employed to ensure that the interpretation of the findings were accurate. First, the present study triangulated multiple sources of data. In other words, data from different sources were used to corroborate and clarify the research in question (Lincoln and Guba, 1985; Marshall and Rossman, 1995; Merriam, 1988). Second, the present study used a participatory mode of research. Gang unit officers and police officials were included in all phases of the research project—from the qualitative nature of the research design to the interpretation of the data—in an effort to ensure that the data were accurately collected and interpreted and to ensure that important issues were not missed. Third, several experienced researchers were used as peer examiners. These individuals periodically reviewed data collected from the field to provide a check on researcher bias.

The Creation of the Gang Unit

It appears that social and political factors were largely responsible for the creation of the police gang unit in Junction City. The gang unit was established in 1988, a time when public policy discussion surrounding gangs was common. This can be seen by the number of national and local news reports on gangs. Nationally, before 1985, fewer than 50 newspaper articles a year were published about gangs. By 1988, the number of newspaper articles on gangs increased to more than 900 a year (Palumbo et al., 1992: 3). Similarly, in Junction City, the local newspaper only published one article on gangs in 1986 and 1987; however, in 1988, more than 55 articles on gangs appeared in the local newspaper.

A number of key community stakeholders argued that as a result of the national exposure on gangs, many people in Junction City had begun to see a local gang problem. For example, the Chief of Police stated, "Everything people looked at appeared to be gang-related, whether it was a crime or anything else." As a result, he claimed that he had begun to feel pressure from community and political leaders, as well as police officers, to do something about the gang problem. Some, he stated, had even suggested that he was "just like the rest of the chiefs around the nation who were in denial about the gang problem." The Chief of Police, however, argued adamantly that he was not in denial, but he simply did not believe that there was a significant gang threat to the community at the time.

At the same time, some community leaders began to believe that the police department was not taking an aggressive enough stance against a potential gang problem. In particular, because of political instability among key municipal leaders, the Chamber of Commerce decided to take a leadership role in addressing the gang issue. The Chamber of Commerce feared that if gangs were not prevented, they could take a foothold and hinder the attraction of business to the community. With this in mind, the Chamber of Commerce put together a task force in April 1988 that comprised representatives from many of the city's largest corporations, as well as community leaders from the local school system, police department, and public housing.

Shortly after the community task force on gangs was established, the Guardians, an African-American police officers association, publicly proposed an all African-American gang squad to deal with the gang problem in the African-American section of the city. Their proposal was publicly endorsed by a local African-American state senator, an African-American city council member, and a group of African-American business and community leaders. The Guardians argued that the police department was not being responsive to the needs of the African-American community in Junction City with regard to the gang problem. For example, the President of the Guardians was quoted as saying

> What the police department has done so far hasn't impacted the African-American community. We're talking about a serious problem of gang activity and youth violence in the African-American community. We're not fabricating this. We are not trying to slander the police department in any way. We're just saying that we can do a better job in this particular area. (Local Paper, May 25, 1988: 17)

As a result, the Guardians proposed that an 8- to 10-person unit, staffed entirely with African Americans, would better address the city's gang problem.[6] They claimed that "we have a vested interest [in the African-American] community. Most of us live here. We have doors open to us that won't be opened to them (white officers)" (Local Paper, May 25, 1988: 17). Proponents of this position also maintained that African-American officers would be better able to gather intelligence on gang-related activities because of their close connections to community members (Local Paper, June 5, 1988). The Chief, however, rejected this proposal, because he felt that an all African-American gang squad would be a step in the wrong direction, and that he should not succumb to such public pressure (Local Paper, June 5, 1988).

Press releases and interviews with police officials suggested that the organization of the community task force and the public proposal by the Guardians to establish a gang squad was the major turning point in the police response to gangs. Because community leaders, as well as certain segments of the police department, began to recognize publicly that the city had a gang problem, it became difficult for the Chief of Police not to develop an organizational response. In an interview, the Chief of Police agreed, stating that although he still did not believe that the city faced a serious gang problem, "various public elements had an impact on my decision to establish a gang unit." Accordingly, approximately 45 days after the community Task Force was put together and two weeks after the Guardians publicly proposed an all African-American gang unit, the Chief of Police announced the creation of the gang unit.

Assessing the Gang Problem

To assess the magnitude of the gang problem in Junction City at the time that the gang unit was created, as well as to examine the changes in gang-related behavior over time, gang-related intelligence and official records collected by the police department were analyzed. Although it would be preferable to have gang-related crime data for the period before the creation of the gang unit through the present time, the systematic documentation of gang members, gangs, and gang-related incidents was not collected by the police department until 1990. Accordingly, departmental intelligence reports and interviews with police officers are used to examine the nature of the gang problem in Junction City before 1990.

Intelligence records suggest that the gang problem in Junction City was minimal in 1988, the year the gang unit was created. In January 1988, the Chief of Police ordered an assessment of the gang problem in Junction City. The final report indicated that a gang problem in Junction City existed that deserved monitoring and direct intervention; however, little evidence was found in the report that suggested that gangs posed a significant threat to the community. In fact, the most serious example used to illustrate the seriousness of the gang problem was that an officer was knocked over in an attempt to prevent a fistfight between two gang members (Interoffice communication, January 25, 1988). The passage reads as follows:

> I have noticed that some or all of the [gang] members have exhibited signs of deviant anti-social behavior. This deviant anti-social behavior has manifested itself in terms of assault, destruction of property—motor vehicle, disorderly conduct, and burglary. A good example of this behavior was demonstrated to one of our most experienced and articulate officers, John Timmes. On 28 December, 1986, Officer Timmes was knocked to the ground by a 17 year-old member of the Lords of Violence when Officer Timmes attempted to break up a fight at 17th and State Street. (Interoffice communication, January 25, 1988: 2)

Shortly after the assessment, the Chief of Police established a temporary, four-officer Youth Coordination Committee under the direction of the Narcotics Unit.[7] The creation of this unit was not made public, and it was originally constructed to operate for a 30-day period for the purpose of evaluating the nature of the gang problem in Junction City. Intelligence records compiled by the unit indicated that gang membership in Junction City was restricted to 16 to 30 hard-core gang members from the Los Angeles area, as well as 150 youths who "associated" with the gang members (Interoffice communication, March 18, 1988). Additionally, intelligence records at this time indicated that "gang activity carried out by gang members in Junction City [was] limited to the wearing of gang colors and to the writing of gang-related graffiti" (Interoffice communication, 1988: 1).[8]

To further examine the operational context of the gang unit, the gang unit's statistics were used to assess the magnitude of the gang problem from 1990 to 1996. As seen in Table 17.2, 12% to 42% of the city's homicides were gang motivated. Gang statistics for crimes other than homicide illustrate that gang members were involved in a relatively small proportion of the total incidents in the city. In particular, gang members account for only about 5% of narcotics-related arrests (i.e., possession, sales). Similarly, over the past six years, gang members had generally been involved in less than 5% of total reported incidents for the crimes of robbery, misdemeanor assault, and felony assault. The only crime for which gang participation appeared to be increasing is misdemeanor assault. In 1990, gang members were involved in less than 1% of all misdemeanor assaults, whereas in 1996 gang members were involved in more than 6% of all misdemeanor assaults reported in Junction City.

On the basis of the data provided here, it appears that the magnitude of the gang problem was minimal at the time that the gang unit was created and that gang-related crimes, while having increased slightly since the establishment of the gang unit, still represent a relatively small proportion of total crimes. The only exception appears to be for gang-motivated homicides, which have not steadily increased or decreased, but appear to be cyclical in nature—with periods of higher rates of gang-motivated homicides followed by periods of relatively few gang-motivated homicides. However, caution should be used when interpreting these data. Data obtained from gang units have been found to be unreliable in the past and may inflate the prevalence of gang-related crime (Katz, 1997; Maxson and Klein, 1990). For example, the Junction City gang unit records all incidents, with the exception of homicide, as gang-related if a gang member is involved in the incident. Maxson and Klein (1990) have found that such member-based definitions

Table 17.2
Gang-Related Activity as Reported by the Junction City Police Department's Gang Unit, 1990–1996

Activity		1990	1991	1992[b]	1993	1994	1995	1996
Homicide	Number of Gang-Related Incidents	—[a]	12	3	5	14	13	6
	Number of Total Incidents	11	35	35	32	33	39	27
	% Gang-Related	—	34.2	12	15.6	42.4	33.3	22.2
Sexual Assault	Number of Gang-Related Incidents	6	12	5	6	16	5	12
	Number of Total Incidents	217	204	213	209	217	80	114
	% Gang-Related	.02	.4	2.3	2.8	7.3	6.2	10.5
Felony Assault	Number of Gang-Related Incidents	2	98	52	140	161	95	62
	Number of Total Incidents	2,307	2,366	2,601	2,906	2,762	2,670	3,801
	% Gang-Related	.00	4.1	1.9	4.8	5.8	3.5	1.6
Misdemeanor Assault	Number of Gang-Related Incidents	11	111	68	117	192	193	265
	Number of Total Incidents	3,565	3,321	3,646	4,155	4,604	4,890	4,051
	% Gang-Related	.00	3.3	1.8	2.8	4.1	3.9	6.5
Robbery	Number of Gang-Related Incidents	11	22	13	19	43	31	20
	Number of Total Incidents	604	634	678	752	918	808	822
	% Gang-Related	1.8	3.4	1.9	2.5	4.6	3.8	2.4
Narcotics	Number of Gang-Related Incidents	14	95	85	95	125	53	163
	Number of Total Incidents	1,818	1,865	1,886	1,683	2,249	2,889	3,361
	% Gang-Related	.00	5.1	4.5	5.6	5.5	1.8	4.8
Documented Gang Members		—	886	1,228	1,313	1,423	1,690	1,920
	% Increase			38.6	6.9	8.3	18.7	13.6

a. Information not available.

b. NIVERS reporting system was implemented September 6, 1992. As a result, all statistical data for the department were not collected from September 6, 1992 through December 31, 1992, and therefore were not available for this analysis.

may inflate the prevalence of gang-recorded crime by a factor of two. With this in mind, it seems reasonable to suggest that these findings illustrate that even if gang crime has increased in Junction City, the overall proportion of gang crime is small and has not changed substantially over time.

The Achievement of Legitimacy

Although the above section described how the police department's institutional environment affected the establishment of the gang unit, this section describes the early history of the gang unit and the strategy that was implemented by the unit to respond to the community's gang problem. As will be argued below, it appears that because the gang unit was created as a result of pressure placed on the police department by various sovereigns in its institutional environment, instead of for reasons of technical rationality, the newly established gang unit was faced with a number of competing ideas and beliefs that significantly affected its organizational structure and operational strategies.

When the gang unit was initially created, it was staffed with one sergeant [and] four plain-clothed investigators, and organizationally placed in the community relations unit. Officers, in and out of the gang unit, indicated that this was to "Get out there and let the community know that we were out there, and doing something." As a result, gang unit officers, at the time, spent most of their time informing the community about the city's gang problem in an effort to prevent gangs from developing. One administrator summed up the police response to the gang problem by stating that

> If a problem came up they [gang unit officers] would go to the meeting and talk about the problem and tell the crowd what the department was trying to do about it. They also educated the public about gangs. While they did not have the manpower to educate it was their mandate.

In an interview with the Chief of Police, he stated that he chose this strategy because he did not want to give the perception to the public that he was ignoring the problem; yet, at the same time, he did not want to overreact. Therefore, he responded in this manner to "show that he was concerned, but not too concerned."[9]

In response to the African-American community's concerns, minority officers were purposefully selected for the gang unit. At the time the gang unit was created, the unit comprised three African-American officers, one Hispanic officer, and one white officer. It was believed that the minority officers would have greater rapport with the minority community—the community believed to be hit hardest by the gang problem—and that they would be more sensitive to issues facing the minority community. In addition, the gang unit was physically placed in a substation in the northeastern section of the city to provide greater access to the minority community. The substation was also intended to increase the informal contact between the officers and the community. It was hoped that the informal contact would lead to better communication between the police and the public, and send a message that the police department was being responsive to the African-American community's needs and demands.

Legitimacy Challenged

Within the first two years, the gang unit's legitimacy was continuously challenged. The data suggest that it was not individuals or organizations outside of the police department that challenged the necessity of the gang unit, as has been suggested by some police officials and researchers (see Spergel, 1995), but that the gang unit lacked support from the administrators and police officers in the Junction City Police Department. Interviews with past and present gang unit officers suggested that until recently, the gang unit was extremely unpopular among many administrators and officers in the police department. It was not uncommon for officers to state that "we were treated like a red-haired stepchild" or "we were the bastard child of the police department." It appears that the lack of support experienced by the gang unit was largely a result of the initial strategy chosen by the Chief of Police and Gang Unit Commander, which conflicted with the expectations of police administrators and police officers of what the gang unit should do and what those in the gang unit should look like.

First, a number of the officers attributed the gang unit's lack of support to the gang unit's organizational mandate of community relations. Many of the officers explained that this "soft-touch" approach was resented by many of the police officers who thought that the gang unit was not taking a strong enough stance against the gang problem. For example, one officer explained, "We were never taken seriously back then because all we did is talk about the problem, but we never actually did anything." Another officer similarly stated, "Back then they [other officers] did not like us because we did not do anything. Before we were thought of as a joke because of the lack of enforcement, all we did was prevention stuff. We were never a threat to the kids on the street."

Second, many of the gang unit officers attributed the unit's lack of support to the disproportionate number of minority officers that were placed in the gang unit. Officers believed that by selecting a disproportionate number of minority officers, the unit was viewed as a "showpiece" that was designed for public image instead of to respond to the city's gang problem. As a result, many of the officers felt that the minority officers selected for the unit were unqualified and were only selected to accommodate the minority community, which, at the time, was publicly calling for an all African-American gang unit that would be sympathetic to the African-American community's needs.

Based on these perceptions, the officers in the gang unit were viewed as unreliable and unprofessional. One officer commented that

> When I was in the narcotics unit, the gang unit officers would not record or share any of their information. It was ridiculous. That's what their job was all about. Also, whenever I called them for help on a search warrant, they would not even show up to lend me a hand. They just left me out there hanging.

Another officer stated, "They were just jack-offs. When they went on trips, they would get into a lot of trouble. They also had a bad reputation on the street. I guess what I am saying is that they were just bad officers all around."

Some officers, both in and out of the gang unit, also openly stated that because the unit was predominantly African-American, the officers were thought to be corrupt. Specifically, it was rumored that these officers were giving away classified information on the local gang problem. It was believed that because officers in the gang unit were predominantly African-American, they were more likely to associate with gang members, and, therefore, would be more likely to share confidential information with gang members. One former African-American gang unit officer explained:

> There was not a lot of trust because of the number of minority officers that were in the gang unit. For example, I was kicked out of the gang unit twice.[10] One commander kept writing up reports to internal affairs saying that I was leaking information. He also said that I was not recording all the information that I knew about gang members. I even think that my phone was tapped. He [the commander] thought that because all of the search warrants that we were doing were coming up empty that I was leaking it [classified information] to them [the gang members]. But the reason that the searches weren't coming up with any drugs was because gang members simply were not selling drugs in Junction City.

Another Hispanic officer in the unit stated that

> Back then everyone thought that we were corrupt because we were a minority unit. They thought that because we were black and Hispanic that somehow we were more likely to give gang members information. That's why we had no support. We had a crappy office. We did not even have phones or enough cars. All four of us would drive around in one car. INTERVIEWER: What do you mean no phones? RESPONDENT: Ya, we had to use a pay phone forever. It was not until the mayor visited us and wanted to make a call and couldn't that we got some phones.

Although these rumors of corruption were never substantiated, the officers, particularly the minority officers, argued that they illustrated the serious problems that the gang unit faced in its formative years.

Legitimacy Regained

In the summer of 1990, the Chief of Police appointed a new African-American commander to the gang unit. Upon arrival, the commander recognized that the gang unit was faced with serious opposition within the police department. He explained that

> When I came to the unit the perception was that we [the gang unit] were the battered child of the Junction City Police Department. This was largely because we did not do anything. We were a support unit, like we are now, but nobody wanted our help then because they did not know what we did.

Accordingly, the lieutenant instituted a number of organizational changes and operational strategies that remain in effect today in an effort to receive support from administrators and police officers in the Junction City Police Department, as well as sovereigns outside of the police department, such as local school officials, key community groups, and other criminal justice agencies.

Changes in Personnel. In an effort to gain legitimacy among those in the police department, the lieutenant first made significant personnel changes. He "strongly encouraged" all but one of the officers to leave the unit, and brought in new officers whom he believed would add credibility to the unit's image. The lieutenant argued that the only way he could change the status of the gang unit within the police department was to diversify the unit racially. He explained that "units are evaluated and judged by the friends that they keep in the police department. And, because we were a minority unit, we did not have many friends, and, therefore, we did not receive a great deal of support. So, to get support, we diversified." The lieutenant further explained that as a result, he purposefully selected a number of Caucasian officers who were highly respected throughout the police department in an effort to gain credibility among the officers and administrators within the Junction City Police Department. This strategy led to the recruitment and assignment of eight officers to the gang unit.[11] Of the eight officers, five were Caucasians who had previously worked in the most prestigious units in the police department. Specifically, two of the Caucasian officers transferred into the gang unit from the homicide unit, two from the narcotics unit, and one from the organized crime unit. It was argued that if the unit was to be a "real gang unit," it had to have officers with occupational specialties that were more applicable to dealing with gang-related problems and not just public relations.

However, the lieutenant also selected three minority officers who had a significant amount of experience in community relations. The supervisors in the unit all explained that although it was important to have Caucasians in the unit for organizational support, minority representation was still important so that the unit "would be representative of the community they serve." The officers in the gang unit agreed, arguing that both African-American and Hispanic citizens are more likely to trust officers of their ethnic background. One Hispanic officer explained that "when you talk to Hispanics, you have to know and be familiar with their culture. For example, when you are dealing with a Hispanic family, you always talk to the man of the house, never presenting your position to the kid or to the mother." Others stated that some African-American youths will not even talk to Caucasian officers and that it was necessary to have African-American officers in the unit to deal with such issues.

Changes in Operational Strategy. In an effort to gain legitimacy among those in the police department, the gang unit also made significant changes in its operational strategy. This included the gang unit being organizationally moved from the Community Relations Bureau to the Special Investigations Bureau. This placed the gang unit organizationally parallel to other enforcement-related units, such as the Criminal Investigations Unit, Organized Crime Unit, and Vice and Narcotics Unit. This gave the gang unit, organizationally speaking, an image that its primary emphasis was crime control instead of community relations. Administrators in the department commented that such a move gave additional confidence to those inside and outside of the police department that the primary role of the gang unit was law enforcement.

As a consequence, the gang unit's original community relations mandate was replaced with one that was more oriented toward a crime-fighting image. In particular, gang unit officers were instructed to allocate approximately 50% of their time toward intelligence activities, 25% toward enforcement activities, and 25% toward educational activities (Gang Unit Standard Operating Procedures, no date). The gang unit was also reconfigured as a support unit, and it was mandated to assist other units and organizations with gang-related problems and issues (e.g., gang investigations, patrolling known gang areas). The gang unit's standard operating procedures manual outlines its mission as follows:

> The gang unit has the mission of assisting other Junction City Police Department Investigative Units, the Uniform Patrol Bureau and other [criminal justice] agencies in resolving gang related crimes and diminishing gang related violence. The gang unit stresses emphasis in three specific areas to accomplish this mission. They are Intelligence, Education, and Enforcement. (Gang Unit Standard Operating Procedures, no date: 2)

Accordingly, although the gang unit redefined its mandate to include more law enforcement–oriented activities in an effort to conform to the expectations of officers and administrators in the police department, it also changed its operational strategy to one that placed a premium on building partnerships with individuals and organizations both inside and outside of the police department.

This operational strategy of building partnerships by the gang unit appears to have been taken for two reasons. The first is that it promoted an image of operational effectiveness. By establishing and maintaining partnerships with organizations that have already acquired a high degree of legitimacy, the gang unit gained and maintained legitimacy through association with these organizations. For example, the gang unit's enforcement-related activities were found to be primarily conducted in conjunction with units such as homicide and weed and seed—both of which were well supported by sovereigns both inside and outside of the police department. Similarly, the education and intelligence-related activities performed by the gang unit were largely observed to be conducted in coordination and cooperation with such established institutions as local schools, community groups, and criminal justice agencies that lent organizational support to the gang unit. Therefore, by closely aligning itself with organizations that had already achieved a high level of legitimacy, and by giving the appearance of usefulness to these organizations, the gang unit gained and maintained legitimacy.

The lieutenant in charge of the gang unit confirmed this observation. He continually mentioned that by associating with organizations that had already acquired a high degree of legitimacy, the gang unit would receive organizational support itself. For example, in one conversation he stated that

> I may look stupid but I'm a smart guy. To get this unit out from the garbage heap I started to build relationships. . . . For example, I teamed up with Tom Barkue for more clout.[12] Barkue has more influence than most people in this town. He was the one who got me the space in this building. Because the community liked Barkue and knew that he was on the right track, when I moved over to this building the community thought highly of me.

The second purpose of developing partnerships with sovereigns in their institutional environment was that the gang unit acquired the ability to recruit clients (i.e., gang members) through its organizational partners. In the 289 hours (equivalent to 36.1 working days) that were spent with the officers in the gang unit, only 14 contacts were observed between gang unit officers and gang members. Furthermore, nine of these contacts occurred on one day in which the gang unit cooperated with the weed-and-seed unit in a hot-spot operation. Therefore, if one excludes the nine contacts made during the hot-spot operation, an operation that was conceived and organized by the weed-and-seed unit, only five contacts were observed between gang unit officers and gang members. Accordingly, it appears that this lack of contact with gang members made it difficult for gang unit officers to gather information on gang members—which was their primary organizational mandate. As a consequence, it appears that gang unit officers developed partnerships with other agencies in an effort to recruit clients.

This was observed in a number of strategies used by officers in the gang unit. One strategy was their efforts to have patrol officers refer gang members to the gang unit for documentation. Another strategy was presentations to community groups, school officials, and law enforcement personnel in which gang unit officers educated their audience on how to identify gang members and the importance of contacting the gang unit in the event of such an identification. Still another was the Network Tracking Program (a.k.a. Gang Task Force) established by the gang unit, in which participating criminal justice agencies were encouraged to refer individuals' names for documentation or risk being excluded from the program.

This strategy lent legitimacy to the gang unit in that it enabled the gang unit to collect and document gang-related information that illustrated the increasing severity of the gang problem. By forming relationships with organizations that had the ability to identify and refer potential clients (i.e., gang members), the gang unit was able to come into contact with clients that it otherwise would have not been able to contact. Such an organizational strategy gained legitimacy for the gang unit by categorizing more individuals within the purview of the gang unit, and thereby demonstrating the need of the gang unit to their institutional environment.[13]

Conclusions and Implications

Using data obtained from a multimethodological research design, the police response to gangs in Junction City was examined. The purpose of the study was to examine the factors that led to the creation of a specialized police gang unit, and how these factors influenced the gang unit's response to the community's gang problem. The results from the present study lend support for the institutional perspective. In particular, the data suggest that the gang unit was created as a consequence of pressures placed on the police department from various powerful elements within the community, and that once created, the gang unit's response to the community's gang problem was largely driven by its need to achieve and maintain legitimacy among various sovereigns in their environment. Three general points may be made concerning the findings from this study.

First, although the results of the present study are consistent with the institutional perspective, the findings are at odds with others that have also found that institutional considerations have had an impact on the creation of police gang units. Zatz (1987) and others suggest that the creation of specialized police gang units has largely been a consequence of the police manufacturing myths about the gang problem for the purpose of obtaining financial resources. They further argued that these myths are perpetuated and maintained through the processing of racial stereotypes. However, data from the present study suggest that the Junction City Police Department did not actively participate in the social construction of the local gang problem (i.e., manipulating their institutional environment). Instead, the police department acted in a responsive manner incorporating the beliefs and ideas of those in their institutional environment. The data illustrated that the police department created the gang unit under pressure from key community stakeholders. As such, it appears that the police department attempted to manage its legitimacy by conforming to its environment and establishing a gang unit (i.e., decoupling structure and activities), which was organizationally structured and operationally oriented to communicate to their institutional environment that the police department was responding to the community's gang problem.

Interestingly, the results of the present study suggest that the African-American community played a major role in shaping the police response to gangs in Junction City. In particular, the data revealed that the African-American community was one of the foremost advocates of establishing the gang unit and wanted the gang unit to focus its efforts on the African-American community. Although such a finding is counterintuitive, it may reflect dual concerns within the African-American community: first, that African-American community members might feel more vulnerable and fearful of gang-related problems, and second, the perception by African Americans that African-American neighborhoods receive too little police protection. Although data were not available to examine these issues as part of the present study, past research has found that those in African-American communities are significantly more fearful of being victimized and are significantly more likely to be victimized than are those living in Caucasian communities (Skogan and Hartnett, 1997; Skogan and Maxfield, 1981; Walker et al., 1996). Accordingly, it might be that members of the African-American community in Junction City viewed crime as a major issue facing their community and that gangs contributed to much of their community's crime problem. Although the factors that might contribute to this perception are many (see Klinger, 1997), the data revealed that the African-American police officers association and African-American political leaders supported the belief that gangs were responsible for a disproportionate amount of the crime in the African-American community. Such a position by these individuals may have reinforced or lent legitimacy to the fears of African-American community members.

Second, with respect to the factors that influenced the gang unit's response, it appears that the common theme that unites these findings is that the gang unit's response was extremely susceptible to coercive pressures placed on it by its institutional environment. In particular, the findings of the present study suggest that because the gang unit was created as a result of institutional considerations, instead of as a result of rational considerations, its organizational structure and operational activities were largely a function of ceremony more so than a reflection of the organization's need to act in a rational or effective manner. This was particularly evident by the unit's emphasis on creating and maintaining relational networks with officials/organizations that had already achieved a high level of legitimacy, as well as the structural and strategic changes that the unit made in an attempt to conform to sovereigns' beliefs as to what the gang unit should look like and how it should behave. Indeed, as argued by organizational theorists in the past (Crank and Langworthy, 1992: 360; Meyer and Scott, 1992; Orton and Weick, 1990; Scott and Christensen, 1995; Weick, 1995), through ceremonial displays of legitimacy, and by oftentimes incorporating competing ideas and beliefs into its organizational structure and operational activities, the gang unit was able to convey an image of operational effectiveness when it was otherwise unable to demonstrate success in a normative fashion.

The findings suggest that the officers within the Junction City Police Department may have had the most significant impact on the gang unit's organizational structure and operational activities. Although organizational theorists in the field of policing have typically discussed sovereigns in terms of those operating outside of the police department (e.g., mayors, city council members, special interest groups) (for exception, see Crank and Rehm, 1994), the results of the present study indicate that the gang unit was influenced and shaped by the interorganizational system in which it is located. Namely, the data illustrated that for the gang unit to achieve and maintain legitimacy, it had to adhere to and demonstrate a commitment to the professional, political, and social beliefs of the officers in the police department. Such a finding suggests that the police response to gangs must not only be understood in terms of the broader social system in which the police are located, but also must be understood in the context of police culture.

Finally, the findings from the present study call into question the state of specialized police units. First, the findings challenge the perspective that specialized police units are necessarily created as the result of organizations seeking to improve their technical efficiency and effectiveness. In particular, many have suggested specialized police units are the natural consequence of police departments responding to a unique and increased workload, and they are a result of police organizations seeking to devise the most efficient and effective organizational structure. However, the findings from the present study suggest that some specialized police units may be created as a consequence of pressures that are placed on the police department, instead of the police organization actively seeking to improve its technical efficiency and effectiveness.

Second, the findings from the present study challenge the notion that specialized police units necessarily increase technical efficiency and effectiveness. In particular, researchers in the past have argued that the formation of special police units can result in a more successful police response by focusing departmental resources, energy, and skill on a unique law enforcement problem. However, the findings from this study, as well as others (Walker and Katz, 1995), have demonstrated that many of these units might receive minimal support from police departments in terms of administrative support. This in part may be because these special police units are created as a result of external pressures placed on the police department, instead of for reasons of technical efficiency or effectiveness. Accordingly, some special police units may receive only a "bare minimum" of support from police administrators and officers because of the lack of technical effectiveness and efficiency that they are believed to bring to the department. Therefore, future research should not only examine the factors that lead to the creation of special police units, but also the internal support that these units receive when they are created.

Two potential limitations should be noted before the interpretation of the findings is complete. First, the findings of the present study should not necessarily be generalized to other communities. A number of studies have demonstrated that a community's gang problem is unique and may not be similar to another community's. Accordingly, a police department's response to a gang problem may be highly reflective of the nature of the local gang problem, or it may be the result of a unique sociopolitical climate that exists within a given community or police department. Second, although the findings presented here appear to reflect an accurate account of the police response to gangs in Junction City, it is possible that the data were contaminated by the presence of the investigator. Specifically, officers in the gang unit may have altered their behavior, or they may not have provided truthful responses during conversations, interviews, and debriefings, which in turn may have had an impact on the information presented in this study. However, it should be noted that the validity of the present study was increased through repeated observations of gang unit personnel over an extended period of time and by bringing together multiple sources of data.

Future research should continue to examine the impact that key community stakeholders and organizations have on the creation of specialized police units and how they continue to affect the unit once created. Furthermore, future research on the police response to gangs should focus on racial considerations, both inside and outside of the police department, which may influence the police response to gangs. Although researchers have spent much time focusing on ethnicity and its relationship with the gang problem, little research has focused on how the role of ethnicity has affected the police response to gangs.

In conclusion, although these findings lend considerable support for the institutional perspective, they nevertheless should caution researchers in generalizing about the factors that might influence a police department's response toward a community's gang problem. The findings of this study, coupled with those of others (Curry et al., 1992; McCorkle and Miethe, 1998; Weisel and Painter, 1997; Zatz, 1987), suggest that considerable variation might exist with respect to the factors associated with the creation of gang units, and how these factors might influence a police department's response to gangs. Future research should examine the impact that internal and external forces have on the police response to gangs and how these forces may be geographically and temporally contingent.

Notes

1. For a discussion of validity problems relevant to specialized units and the LEMAS data, see Walker and Katz (1995).
2. The estimate of 360 gang units was determined as follows: 56% of the 454 police departments (254), 50% of the 167 sheriffs' offices (83), 43% of the 30 county police departments (13), and 20% of the 49 state law enforcement agencies (10). A specialized unit was defined in the survey as an organizational unit that has at least one person assigned on a full-time basis.
3. For a fuller discussion of the setting and methods used in the present study, see Katz (1997).
4. Accordingly, the number of personnel in Junction City's gang unit is very similar to other gang units across the country. Curry et al. (1992) reported that the median size gang unit in the United States is 10 personnel. They further reported that only approximately 20% of the established police gang units have 20 or more personnel.
5. It should be noted that as rapport developed between the officers and myself the officers became active participants in the research process. They often stated, "Here is something you should know about," or "Come with us, we're doing something you may not have seen yet." Additionally, the longer I spent with the officers, the more I participated in what was viewed as gang unit work. Over the course of my time with the gang unit, I participated in searching vehicles and houses, helped with presentations to local schools, and assisted in documenting gang members in the gang information system.
6. One reviewer questioned whether the gang problem in Junction City was played down because it was perceived to be a minority problem. The data, however, did not indicate that a racial disparity existed in the perception of the seriousness of the gang problem or that the police department denied the existence of the gang problem because it was believed to be an African-American problem. Instead, the data supported the contention that the gang problem was consistently downplayed by the department because of the Chief's beliefs that the magnitude of the gang problem in Junction City was not large enough to justify the establishment of a gang unit or to even consider it a "moderate" problem.
7. Data suggest that the Youth Coordination Committee was initially placed in the Narcotics Unit because of the perception by many officers that the gang problem was primarily being fueled by gang members from outside of the community that came to Junction City for the purpose of selling drugs. Accordingly, the department initially viewed the role of drugs as central to understanding the community's gang problem and therefore attempted to evaluate the seriousness of gang problem under the auspices of the Narcotics Unit. Decker and Kempf-Leonard (1991) have reported similar findings in their examination of the St. Louis Police Department.
8. The Youth Coordination Committee's findings were confirmed through data obtained from media reports, interviews with key police officials, and official records, which all suggested that gang-related assaults and homicides were minimal, if not nonexistent in Junction City at this time.
9. Although space does not permit a lengthy discussion of the gang unit's mission at this time, gang unit officers also engaged in intelligence and enforcement activities. In particular, gang unit officers documented gang members and were responsible for some enforcement-related activities, such as patrolling known gang areas and collaborating with other units within the department on gang-related problems (e.g., serving search warrants, criminal investigations). However, these activities were subordinate to its community relations mandate.
10. The officer was reinstated both times because the allegations were found to be unsubstantiated by the internal affairs unit.
11. Six months before the new commander was appointed to the gang unit, the gang unit was allocated five additional officers. Although it is unclear why, the lieutenant suggested that it was because the gang unit was shifting to more of a law enforcement mandate that required more officers. However, the lieutenant was unsure of the reasons, and no other data were available to verify the lieutenant's belief.
12. Tom Barkue, an African American, was the head administrator for the Department of Public Housing in Junction City. His position

in Junction City was thought of as somewhat unique because of his popularity among both the African-American and the Caucasian communities.

13. As discussed earlier, many researchers and police officials have claimed that such partnerships are created for rational purposes. They argue that these partnerships allow for improved communication, which can assist in the arrest, prosecution, and conviction of gang members. They also claim that the communication that results from these partnerships can lead to the prevention of gang-related activity through awareness and education (Brantley and DiRosa, 1994; Burns and Deakin, 1989; Huff and McBride, 1993; Jackson and McBride, 1985; Rush, 1996). However, interviews with Junction City Police officers, school administrators, and officials from other criminal justice agencies indicated that these formalized partnerships served few rational purposes. For example, of the 16 gang task force members, 12 stated that gangs were either no problem or a minor problem for their agency. Similarly, observations revealed that with the exception of the homicide unit, only two intelligence-related contacts were observed between gang unit officers and other officers in the Junction City Police Department. School administrators also indicated that there was little need for communication with the gang unit because of the lack of gang activity that took place in their schools.

References

Abell, Peter. 1995. The new institutionalism and rational choice theory. In W. Richard Scott and Soren Christensen (eds.), *The Institutional Construction of Organizations.* London: Sage.

Aldrich, Howard. 1999. *Organizations Evolving.* London: Sage.

Bogdan, Robert C. and Sari K. Biklen. 1992. *Qualitative Research for Education: An Introduction to Theory and Methods.* Boston, Mass.: Allen and Bacon.

Boyd, Elizabeth, Richard Berk, and Karl Hamner. 1996. Motivated by hatred or prejudice: Categorization of hate-motivated crimes in two police divisions. *Law and Society Review* 30:819–850.

Brantley, Alan and Andrew DiRosa. 1994. Gangs: A national perspective. *FBI Law Enforcement Bulletin* May:1–17.

Bureau of Justice Statistics. 1999. *Law Enforcement Management and Administrative Statistics, 1997: Data for Individual State and Local Agencies with 100 or More Officers.* Washington, D.C.: U.S. Government Printing Office.

Burns, Edward and Thomas J. Deakin. 1989. A new investigative approach to youth gangs. *FBI Law Enforcement Bulletin* October:20–24.

Bursik, Robert J. and Harold G. Grasmick. 1995. Defining gangs and gang behavior. In Malcolm W. Klein, Cheryl L. Maxson, and Jody Miller (eds.), *The Modern Gang Reader.* Los Angeles, Calif.: Roxbury.

Christensen, Soren and Jan Molin. 1995. Origin and transformation of organizations: Institutional analysis of the Danish Red Cross. In W. Richard Scott and Soren Christensen (eds.), *The Institutional Construction of Organizations.* London: Sage.

Crank, John. 1994. Watchman and community: Myth and institutionalization in policing. *Law and Society Review* 28:135–351.

Crank, John and Robert Langworthy. 1992. An institutional perspective of policing. *The Journal of Criminal Law and Criminology* 83:338–363.

Crank, John and Lee Rehm. 1994. Reciprocity between organizations and institutional environments: A study of Operation Valkyrie. *Journal of Criminal Justice* 22:393–406.

Crime in the United States: 1995. 1996. Washington, D.C.: U.S. Government Printing Office.

Curry, G. David, Richard A. Ball, and Robert J. Fox. 1994. *Gang Crime and Law Enforcement Recordkeeping.* Washington, D.C.: U.S. National Institute of Justice.

Curry, G. David, Richard A. Ball, Robert J. Fox, and Darryl Stone. 1992. *National Assessment of Law Enforcement Anti-Gang Information Resources. Final Report.* Washington, D.C.: U.S. National Institute of Justice.

Daft, Richard and Karl Weick. 1984. Toward a model of organizations as interpretive systems. *Academy of Management Review* 9:284–295.

Decker, Scott and Kimberly Kempf-Leonard. 1991. Constructing gangs: The social definition of youth activities. *Criminal Justice Policy Review* 5:271–291.

DiMaggio, Paul and Walter Powell. 1991. The iron cage revisited: Institutional isomorphism and collective rationality in organizational fields. In Walter Powell and Paul DiMaggio (eds.), *The New Institutionalism in Organizational Analysis.* Chicago, Ill.: University of Chicago Press.

Donaldson, Lex. 1995. *American Anti-Management Theories of Organization.* Cambridge, U.K.: Cambridge University Press.

Friedland, Roger and Robert Alford. 1991. Bringing society back in: Symbols, practices, and institutional contradictions. In Walter Powell and Paul DiMaggio (eds.), *The New Institutionalism in Organizational Analysis.* Chicago, Ill.: University of Chicago Press.

Garud, Ragud and Arun Kumaraswamy. 1995. Coupling the technical and institutional faces of Janus in network industries. In W. Richard Scott and Soren Christensen (eds.), *The Institutional Construction of Organizations.* London: Sage.

Glaser, B. and A. Strauss. 1967. *The Discovery of Grounded Theory.* Chicago, Ill.: Aldine.

Greenwood, Royston and C.R. Hinings. 1996. Understanding radical organizational change: Bringing together the old and the new institutionalism. *Academy of Management Review* 21:1022–1054.

Hagedorn, John H. 1990. Back in the field again: Gang research in the nineties. In C. Ronald Huff (ed.), *Gangs in America.* Newbury Park, Calif.: Sage.

Huff, C. Ronald and Wesley D. McBride. 1990. Gangs and the police. In C. Ronald Huff (ed.), *Gangs in America.* Newbury Park, Calif.: Sage.

Jackson, Robert K. and Wesley D. McBride. 1985. *Understanding Street Gangs.* Costa Mesa, Calif.: Custom.

Jorgensen, Danny. 1989. *Participant Observation: A Methodology for Human Studies.* Newbury Park, Calif.: Sage.

Katz, Charles M. 1997. *Police and Gangs: A Study of a Police Gang Unit.* Ph.D. Dissertation. University of Nebraska at Omaha.

Katz, Charles M., Edward R. Maguire, and Joseph B. Kuhns. 1998. A macro-level analysis of the creation of specialized police gang units: An examination of rational, social threat, and resource dependency perspectives. Presented at the annual meeting of the American Society of Criminology, Washington, D.C.

Klein, Malcolm W., Cheryl Maxson, and Jody Miller (eds.). 1995. *The Modern Gang Reader.* Los Angeles, Calif.: Roxbury.

Klinger, David. 1997. Negotiating order in patrol work: An ecological theory of police response to deviance. *Criminology* 35:277–306.

Lincoln, Yvonna S. and Egon G. Guba. 1985. *Naturalistic Inquiry.* Beverly Hills, Calif.: Sage.

Lofland, John and Lynn Lofland. 1995. *Analyzing Social Settings: A Guide to Qualitative Observation and Analysis.* Belmont: Wadsworth.

Marshall, Catherine and Gretchen Rossman. 1995. *Designing Qualitative Research.* Newbury Park, Calif.: Sage.

Martin, Susan. 1986. Policing career criminals: An examination of an innovative crime control program. *The Journal of Criminal Law and Criminology* 77:1159–1182.

Mastrofski, Stephen D. 1994. Community policing and police organizational structure. Paper presented at the Workshop on Evaluation Police Services Delivery, Centre for Comparative Criminology, University of Montreal, November 2–4.

Mastrofski, Stephen D. and Craig D. Uchida. 1993 Transforming the police. *Journal of Research in Crime and Delinquency* 30:330–358.

Maxson, Cheryl and Malcolm Klein. 1990. Defining and measuring gang violence. In C. Ronald Huff (ed.), *Gangs in America.* Newbury Park, Calif.: Sage.

McCorkle, Richard and Terrance Miethe. 1998. The political and organizational response to gangs: An examination of a "Moral Panic" in Nevada. *Justice Quarterly* 15:41–64.

Merriam, Sharan. 1988. *Case Study Research in Education: A Qualitative Approach.* San Francisco, Calif.: Jossey-Bass.

Meyer, John and Brian Rowan. 1977. Institutionalized organizations: Formal structure as myth and ceremony. *American Journal of Sociology* 83:340–348.

Meyer, John and W. Richard Scott. 1992. Centralization and the legitimacy problems of local government. In John W. Meyer and W. Richard Scott (eds.), *Organizational Environments.* London: Sage.

Meyer, Marshall. 1979. Organizational structure as signaling. *Pacific Sociological Review* 22:481–500.

Needle, Jerome and William Stapleton. 1983. *Police Handling of Youth Gangs: Reports of the National Juvenile Justice Assessment Centers.* Washington, D.C.: U.S. Government Printing Office.

Ogle, Robin. 1998. Theoretical perspectives on correctional structure, evaluation, and change. *Criminal Justice Policy Review* 9:43–51.

Oliver, Christine. 1991. Strategic responses to institutional processes. *Academy of Management Review* 16:145–179.

Orton, J. Douglas and Karl E. Weick. 1990. Loosely coupled systems: A reconceptualization. *Academy of Management Review* 15:203–223.

Palumbo, D. J., R. Eskay, and M. Hallet. 1992. Do gang prevention strategies actually reduce crime? *The Gang Journal* 1:1–10.

Rush, Jeffery P. 1996. The police role in dealing with gangs. In J. Mitchell Miller and Jeffery P. Rush (eds.), *Gangs: A Criminal Justice Approach.* Cincinnati: Anderson.

Schatzman, Leonard and Anselm Strauss. 1973. *Field Research: Strategies for a Natural Sociology.* Englewood Cliffs, N.J.: Prentice-Hall.

Scott, W. Richard. 1977. Effectiveness of organizational effectiveness studies. In Paul S. Goodman and Johannes M. Pennings (eds.), *New Perspectives on Organizational Effectiveness.* San Francisco, Calif.: Jossey-Bass.

——. 1992. Organization of environments: Network, culture, and historical elements. In John W. Meyer and W. Richard Scott (eds.), *Organizational Environments.* London: Sage.

——. 1995. Introduction: Institutional theory and organizations. In W. Richard Scott and Soren Christensen (eds.), *The Institutional Construction of Organizations.* London: Sage.

Scott, W. Richard and Soren Christensen (eds.). 1995. *The Institutional Construction of Organizations.* London: Sage.

Skogan, Wesley and Susan Hartnett. 1997. *Community Policing Chicago Style.* New York: Oxford University Press.

Skogan, Wesley and Michael Maxfield. 1981. *Coping with Crime.* Beverly Hills, Calif.: Sage.

Slater, Courtney M. and George E. Hall (eds.). 1996. *County and City Extra Annual Metro, City, and County Data Book.* Lanham, Md.: Bernan Press.

Sparrow, Malcolm, Mark Moore, and David Kennedy. 1990. *Beyond 911: The New Era for Policing.* New York: Basic Books.

Spergel, Irving A. 1995. *Youth Gang Problem: A Community Approach.* New York: Oxford University Press.

Suchman, Mark C. 1995. Managing legitimacy: Strategic and institutional approaches. *Academy of Management Review* 20:571–610.

Suchman, Mark C. and D. Eyre. 1992. Military procurement as rational myth: Notes on the social construction of weapons proliferation. *Sociological Forum* 7:137–161.

Tolbert, Pamela and Lynne Zucker. 1996. The institutionalization of institutional theory. In Stewart Clegg, Cynthia Hardy, and Walter Nord (eds.), *Handbook of Organizational Studies.* London: Sage.

Walker, Samuel and Charles M. Katz. 1995. Less than meets the eye: Police department bias crime units. *American Journal of Police* 14:29–48.

Walker, Samuel, Cassia Spohn, and Miriam DeLone. 1996. *The Color of Justice.* Belmont: Wadsworth.

Weick, Karl E. 1979. *The Social Psychology of Organizing.* Reading, Mass.: Addison-Wesley.

——. 1995. *Sensemaking in Organizations.* Thousand Oaks, Calif.: Sage.

Weick, Karl E. and Karlene H. Roberts. 1993. Collective mind in organizations: Heedful interrelating on flight decks. *Administrative Science Quarterly* 38:357–381.

Weisel, Deborah and Ellen Painter. 1997. *The Police Response to Gangs: Case Studies of Five Cities.* Washington, D.C.: Police Executive Research Forum.

Zatz, Marjorie S. 1987. Chicano youth gangs and crime: The creation of a moral panic. *Contemporary Crises* 11:129–158.

Zhao, Solomon and Edward Maguire. 1999. *Chapter Two.* Unpublished manuscript.

Charles M. Katz, "The Establishment of a Police Gang Unit: An Examination of Organizational and Environmental Factors." Reprinted from *Criminology,* Vol. 39 No. 1, 2001, pp. 37–73. Copyright © 2001 American Society of Criminology. Reprinted by permission. ✦

Chapter 18
Racial Profiling

Issues and Implications for Police Policy

David L. Carter
Andra J. Katz-Bannister

Racial profiling continues to be a controversial issue in American policing. Here the authors provide a comprehensive overview of existing knowledge about this important topic with implications for the development of meaningful policies in the future.

Carter and Katz-Bannister first address a definitional dilemma that surrounds the issue of racial profiling. What do we really mean by the term? They next trace the historical development of the concept and then highlight the need for a formal response from police organizations regarding the utility of criminal profiling. In particular, they argue that more training is needed to accommodate changes in operational procedures and an evolving organizational culture.

Driving While Black has become an all too common euphemism for the allegation that police officers stop and detain citizens of color solely on the basis of race or ethnicity. At one extreme of the continuum, minority group members portray most police behavior as being motivated by racial prejudice. At the other end, police officers typically argue that their behavior is not influenced by race at all; that they make investigative stops solely on the reasonable belief that the person is involved in some kind of criminality. Minority group members assert that police officers stereotype all people of color as being involved in crime. Police officers respond that there is more criminality in poor communities and that a disproportionate number of minorities live in poor neighborhoods, thus the probability of a minority group member being stopped will increase. The points and counterpoints continue; however, in disputes, absolute points rarely exist. Rather, the truth lies somewhere in the middle of the continuum[1] (see Figure 18.1).

Evidence from the authors' experience and research suggests that the notable majority of police officers do not consciously make decisions to conduct traffic or investigatory stops of people based exclusively on race or ethnicity. However, demography is too frequently one of

Figure 18.1
Continuum of Racial Profiling

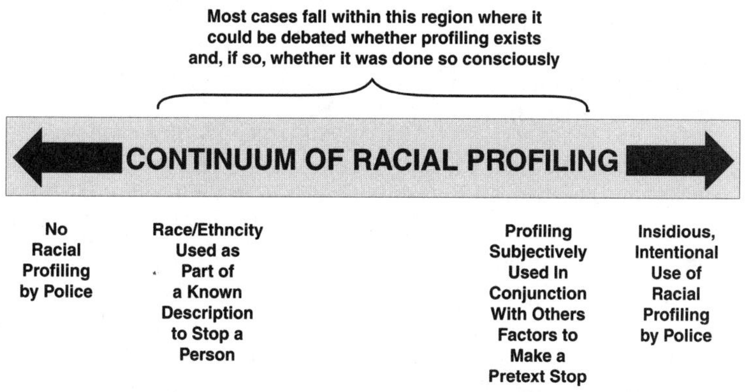

the factors considered by officers when assessing whether a person is "suspicious." Consequently, it is probable that race or ethnicity is an unconscious decision blended with other facts which is the basis for police action rather than being overt or insidious discriminatory behavior. Nonetheless, such stops are improper behavior, albeit a product of factors other than "institutionalized racism" or conscious targeting of minorities.

Without question, racial profiling is an important social topic which has emerged in many venues. On June 9, 1999 President Clinton stated:

> Today, I am directing my Cabinet agencies to begin gathering detailed information on their law enforcement activities. The Justice Department will then analyze this data to assess whether and where law enforcement engage in racial profiling and what concrete steps we need to take at the national level to eliminate it anywhere it exists.[2]

The issue was also one of the central discussions at both the 1999 and 2000 semi-annual meetings of the Police Executive Research Forum (PERF). Furthermore, it received an important national forum when discussed in the second presidential debate.[3] Consistent with this trend, the American Civil Liberties Union stated:

> One of the ACLU's highest priority issues this year [2000] is the fight against the outrageous practice of racial profiling. Our recently released report, *Driving While Black: Racial Profiling On Our Nation's Highways,* documents this practice of substituting skin color for evidence as a grounds for suspicion by law enforcement officials.[4]

The debate is more complex than simply arguing whether the police are discriminatory or not. Factors related to social psychology, occupational socialization, and law are integral to understanding and remedying the problem. The intent of this chapter is to provide an objective, policy-oriented view of racial profiling based on an empirical assessment of issues which can serve as the basis for a police department's implementation of an anti–racial profiling policy.

What is Racial Profiling?

Simply stated, the concept argues that the police target minorities—mostly Blacks[5] and Hispanics—for exploratory stops to determine if they are involved in criminality. It is generally asserted that police officers use a "pretext stop"—typically a minor traffic or vehicle equipment infraction—as the "legal reason" to stop a person of color for what is really an exploratory investigation. Thus, racial profiling may be defined as: "any police-initiated action that relies upon the race, ethnicity, or national origin of an individual rather than the behavior of that individual or information that leads the police to a particular individual who has been identified as being engaged in or having been engaged in criminal activity."[6]

The Idea of Profiling

In law enforcement, a profile refers to a combination of unique demographic and behavioral patterns which are based on an analysis of objective information that suggests a probability beyond randomness that a person who manifests these characteristics, attributes, and behaviors is likely to be involved in a specific type of criminal offense.

Perhaps the earliest widespread familiarity with law enforcement profiling emerged from the research of the FBI's Behavioral Sciences Services Unit (BSSU) examining serial murderers and serial rapists. Based on research conducted by the BSSU Team, investigators learned how to interpret an array of crime scene clues and evidence to develop a list of traits and behaviors that would uniquely describe the offender. These traits—collectively known as the profile—would be used as a tool to guide the investigation. Thus, specific identifying offender information was not known, yet the profile was used to focus the investigation toward people who matched these collective attributes even though there may not be specific evidence linking the individual to a particular crime. The profile was expressly developed as an investigatory tool.

Profiles have also been used by the U.S. Customs Service to identify potential offenders at U.S. Ports of Entry.[7] Based on an analysis of data from a history of arrests and seizures, customs officials have developed profiles that define characteristics and behaviors for different types of offenders. The profiles differ based on offenses—drug smugglers versus antiquities smugglers versus those trying to avoid customs tariffs are examples.

When used by law enforcement, offender profiles are typically explicit and based on an analysis of known offenders. The weakness, however, is in the application of the profile's protocol by an officer. This has important implications for officer training, supervision, and performance evaluation.

As an illustration, the idea of racial profiling has a portion of its roots in a tactical intelligence protocol called "Operation Pipeline." This lengthy protocol, developed jointly by the Drug Enforcement Administration (DEA) and Arizona Highway Patrol, gave officers a wide range of variables which, in combination, suggested that the person possessing those variables was a probable drug trafficker. When employed correctly, the protocol identified drug traffickers with a reasonable degree of consistency. However, the process was time consuming and awkward to employ, particularly if an officer was following a target and attempting to assess variables in the protocol while traveling down the road.

While Operation Pipeline has not been scientifically evaluated, anecdotal evidence suggests that in application officers truncated the protocol, isolating selected variables rather than using the total protocol. As an example, in the allegations of profiling by the New Jersey Highway Patrol (NJHP), it was alleged that NJHP officers would select variables such as a young black male driving a rental car. Even though the protocol may include these variables, the protocol would include additional variables such as location, time, furtive conduct, position of the car (suggesting weight), and other factors; these were essentially ignored. Had the NJHP officers received comprehensive training on application of the protocol, the importance and need for using all protocol variables and had on-going, proactive supervision monitoring their behavior, then the allegations of racial profiling would likely have carried less weight by evidence of a high proportion of arrests for offenses for which the profile was designed to target.

The important point to note is that offender profiling, per se, is not improper. Indeed, it can serve the best interests of a community and be an efficacious tool for law enforcement if it is based on objective information and applied properly by law enforcement officers.

Legitimate Policies of 'Targeting' Different Areas of the Community

A significant law enforcement trend is the use of crime analysis and crime mapping to aid police in the reduction of crime. Perhaps the best known initiative is the New York City CompStat (*Comp*uterized *Stat*istics) program where timely, on-going analysis of reported crime is used by precinct commanders to employ targeted enforcement tactics to stop specifically identified crime trends. While there are a number of elements in the CompStat process, the concept's premise is to increase police accountability for crime reduction by *offender targeting* and *targeting geographic areas of a community* where problems are identified through crime analysis.

A "target" is essentially a profile. However, it is a specifically defined profile based on expressly known characteristics associated with crime trends. Officers are instructed to use those profiles in a specific manner in the belief that it will suppress—or at least displace—criminality and capture offenders.

CompStat is the *strategy* that is used to develop profiles based on known data. Police officers "on the street" use *tactics*—such as directed patrol or problem solving—as the methods to operationalize the strategy. For example, research on directed patrol dates back thirty years. It has been found that when officers concentrate their efforts on specifically defined behaviors and offenders (i.e., profiles), then the targeted crime trend will either be displaced or suppressed. Perhaps the best-known example of this practice is the Selective Traffic Enforcement Program (STEP) where an analysis is done of traffic accidents. At locations where there are multiple accidents on a consistent basis, the data are assessed to document the location, time of day, day of week, and the most common type(s) of traffic violations contributing to the accidents. Officers are given this information and told to observe the locations during peak accident times and write citations for the types of violations found in the accident analysis. The point to note is that locations and driver behaviors are targeted—or profiled—based on objective data analysis for an explicit reason. The result is fewer traffic accidents at the targeted locations.

Similar types of targeting/profiling are done for criminal offenses and nuisance calls. For example, if there is a series of burglaries, crime analysis will identify consistent trends which link the different burglaries together. Most burglars are repeat offenders, so it is likely that a large number of burglaries will be cleared with one arrest (just as future burglaries can be prevented by incapacitating the offender). In many such cases, forensic evidence and investigative leads may suggest a profile of the offender. This may include gender, race/ethnicity, age, vehicle type, and collateral information (e.g., if the burglar uses a large hammer to break in doors, officers would look for such a hammer when investigating suspects). Thus, if the analytic information indicates that the burglar was a black male, 17–23 years of age and driving a light-colored, mid-sized, four-door car, in a general area where the burglaries are occurring (including a "trend line" of likely future burglaries), then this would be a profile that has a legitimate basis for officers to use to conduct an investigative stop.

The important points to note are:

1. Profiles can serve a legitimate purpose for law enforcement and crime prevention.

2. The profiles must be based on objective data analysis that includes multiple descriptive variables which can isolate a narrow range of possible offenders thereby providing a legitimate investigatory stop.

3. The profile must be of sufficient detail to make a reasonable person believe there is reason warranting further investigation for the crime(s) associated with the profile.

4. Officers using this profile will likely conduct legitimate investigatory stops of people who match the profile characteristics but who are not involved in the crime(s).

5. It is proper for officers to stop, detain, conduct a frisk for weapons, and conduct an investigatory questioning of people matching the profile to determine if an individual is a true suspect in the crimes.

6. Officer behavior may include safety procedures (e.g., getting occupants out of a car; having multiple back-up officers; placing one's hand on the weapon) that may be deemed offensive to the person stopped but are necessary and reasonable safety precautions—depending on the crimes involved—until the person stopped is in a safe position and/or until the officer is satisfied that the person stopped is not the criminal suspect or a safety risk.

7. Officers have the obligation to fully inform the person stopped of the reasons for the stop; to take actions which are reasonable for investigation and safety, but are not overly intrusive; to apologize to persons stopped who, based on the officer's investigation, are not involved in the crime(s) being investigated; and to provide the person stopped with the officer's name and badge number, if requested.

Thus, the integration of objective data-based profiling provides the police with legal and managerially sound strategies and tactics which can be used to reduce crime and apprehend offenders. The obligation of the police is to ensure all appropriate safeguards are in place to ensure the propriety and effectiveness of these tactics. The obligation of the public is to recognize that such strategies are legitimate and are in the community's best interest even though there are instances wherein such tactics will be offensive to the individual.

Problems with Data Collection That Must Be Considered

Because of problems associated with improper police use of profiles in traffic stops, the national movement—including explicit state laws—is to collect circumstantial and demographic information about drivers whom police stop. Legislation from Missouri is often cited as the model statute for police data collection. The statute states, in part, "Each time a peace officer stops a driver of a motor vehicle for a violation of any motor vehicle statute or ordinance, the police officer shall report [demographic, arrest and search] information to the law enforcement agency that employs the officer."[8] The intent is for police agencies to analyze these data to determine if there are anomalies suggesting that traffic stops are based on race/ethnicity or other discriminatory variables. In addition, the *Traffic Stops Study Act* was introduced in the U.S. Congress in 1999[9] and reintroduced in 2000 to document driver demographics and police activity (e.g., enforcement action, searches) in traffic stops. Similarly, the *Law Enforcement Trust and Integrity Act of 2000*[10] addresses issues associated with police-minority relations, including racial profiling. Clearly, the trend is to collect data on police traffic stops in order for some assessment to be made about police stops of minority group members.

Police officers tend to oppose the idea of data gathering as part of a racial profiling monitoring policy for two primary reasons.[11] First, such a policy infers that all officers profile minorities—as expressed in community meetings the authors facilitated, many people of color are convinced this is true. One community member commented, "We don't need a study to find out if racial profiling exists. We *know* it exists" (emphasis in original statement).

The presumption of guilt about officer behavior is not only offensive to officers, it undermines the sense of fundamental fairness stressed in the justice system. Those who call for and support data collection argue that officers themselves are undermining this same sense of fairness by stopping people simply based on race or ethnicity. These views represent dichotomous positions that are difficult to reconcile to both groups' satisfaction. A policy goal should be to fully educate officers that data collection is intended to be a check on officer behavior which can as easily exonerate the police as it can convict them.

It is naive to say that if officers are doing their job properly, they have no need to worry about the collective demographic results of their traffic stops. Just as some officers will profile racial and ethnic minorities, there are also minority group members who will "profile" all officers as being brutal or attempt to use the racial profiling controversy in the hope of being released from a citation. The knife cuts both ways and all parties must recognize this.

Police leaders, elected officials, and citizens must recognize there will likely be a chilling effect on officer-initiated activity when a police department begins collecting demographic data during traffic stops. Officers have repeatedly expressed concern that they will be labeled as racists if "their numbers don't look right." The safest way to prevent this, in many officers' minds, is to significantly decrease proactive work and only respond to calls. While this decreases service to the community, officers state, "that must be what the community wants."

The second reason officers are concerned about data collection lies in the well-known axiom of statisticians: Statistics can lie. The critical element of data collection in traffic stops is not the data, per se, but the *interpretation* of the data. As an example, let us say that a white male police officer's traffic stop data show that 85% of all persons he stopped for traffic violations were black. What this means depends on the interpretation. Several interpretations can arise as examples:

1. The officer is generally stopping blacks for equipment violations and whites for moving violations, thus he is using the traffic violations as a pretext stop, therefore he is profiling.

2. The officer is generally stopping blacks for equipment violations and whites for moving violations, however, the area is poor and residents are predominantly black. Because of poverty, there is a greater likelihood that vehicles remain in disrepair, thus more equipment violations among the residents and less likelihood the officer is profiling.

3. The officer is assigned to an area where 95% of the residents are black. Because only 85% of the traffic stops were black, the officer was either not profiling or perhaps the officer was intentionally stopping more white drivers to make his statistics "look better."

4. The area where the traffic stops are made is 65% black; however, there is a large commuting workforce of blacks and most stops are for moving violations during rush hour, thus the likelihood the officer is not profiling.

5. An analysis of traffic accidents shows that most accidents occur between 4:00 p.m. and 6:00 p.m. on weekdays at a given intersection as a result of drivers making illegal left turns. Analysis of the officer's traffic citations shows that the citations issued are for left turn violations during the peak traffic problem hours, and therefore are not based on profiling.

On the theme of interpretation, a common concern of officers was expressed by the question, "What percentage of people from different races will be acceptable for my traffic stops?" Herein lies the difficulty of interpreting the data. There is no standard that can be used to definitively conclude that racial profiling is occurring. As will be discussed later, any comparative standard for data is inherently dynamic, varying by time, geography, transience, reported crime, and calls for service. Despite this analytic complexity, data collection of traffic stops is an important empirical tool for monitoring officer behavior. However, the interpretative standard will be variable and viewed in aggregate form.

As noted previously, some members of the minority community state that there is no need to collect data because they know from their personal experience that officers use profiling. There is no doubt that this is a sincere belief; however, policy and personnel actions cannot be taken without some form of objective evidence. Thus, both collection and interpretation of the data are critical ventures with long-ranging implications for the community, officers, and the department as a whole.

The issue of interpreting statistics from demographic data collection is therefore critical. While the data should be public record, it must be recognized that this leaves open opportunities for all people—e.g., police supporters, police critics, and the media—to draw their own conclusions. Even if the intent is to interpret the data accurately, it must be recognized that such interpretations are complex and cannot simply be a matter of comparing officer stops to general demographic characteristics of an area. Interpretation must consider such factors as:

1. Actual population demographics

2. Accuracy of Census data

3. Transient population in area (e.g., major streets)

4. Demographic changes in the area based on time (e.g., employers and businesses)

5. Calls for service received by the police from the community (e.g., suspicious persons, prowlers, etc.)
6. Community complaints received by the police (e.g., speeding traffic, open air drug markets, prostitution, noise, etc.)
7. Reported crime in the area (including types of crime, when crimes are occurring, known suspects' characteristics, etc.)
8. Accuracy of information reported by officers

If officers are improperly stopping drivers by considering race or ethnicity as a criteria to stop, then police officials clearly want the practice to end. If an officer's behavior is the product of insidious discriminatory practices, then the officer should be disciplined. If the officer's behavior is a product of unconscious consideration of race/ethnicity as one factor in an equation to stop motorists, then closer supervision and training may be the best remedies. One must be careful, however, to avoid generalization of all police practices based on spurious incidents.

Beyond the philosophical issues addressed above, there is a pragmatic issue that must be addressed: the cost of the data collection process. Citizens and city officials alike must recognize that there are expenses associated with data monitoring. While each traffic stop form may only take about thirty seconds to complete, when multiplied by the number of officers, by the number of forms completed in a year's time, it can become a surprisingly high time commitment. Add to this the time involved in processing the forms, the printing costs, and analysis time, which is very labor intensive, and one can see that the costs rise quickly.

Discussing issues of race is always a sensitive process—it makes people uncomfortable and there is always a fear of offending someone or being given an unfair label. Despite this sensitivity, if the issues are not openly discussed, then progress cannot be made. On this theme, one may find that statistically racial and ethnic minorities may indeed be stopped more frequently, but not necessarily due to police profiling. Police departments deploy officers proportional to demand. There is typically a disproportionate amount of reported crime and calls for services in impoverished areas of all American cities. Unfortunately, minorities—notably blacks and Hispanics—live disproportionately in lower income neighborhoods. As a consequence, there are higher levels of contact between the police and minority communities. Factors such as these must be part of any data interpretation.

Issues and Concerns of Perceptions

Advertising works because all human beings "judge books by their covers." That is, people make quick judgments about others based on a wide range of factors: age, gender, race/ethnicity, clothing, car, manner of speaking, behavior, the attitude one displays, background of the person making the judgment, and any number of other subtle variables. Moreover, humans tend to generalize their judgment—stereotyping—to a wide range of people: the police are all brutal; young black males wearing Fubu clothing are involved in drugs; or blondes are slow-witted.

In focus groups of officers and comments from citizens in the community—both of which the authors facilitated—both displayed stereotyped perceptions, which are the essence of the conflict associated with racial profiling. Police and citizens alike must understand the premises of this process. First, perceptions are based upon the *limited information that a person receives.* Second, that information is *interpreted* using *one's own experiences, which are inherently limited.* Third, a *judgment is made* about the incident and *applied to all persons of the same group.*

For example, police training has traditionally taught officers that effective tactical patrolling includes being aware of people "who do not fit the area." The assumption has been that such a person has a likelihood of being involved in a crime, and so warrants a stop and investigation by the officer. The conclusion that a person "does not fit an area"[12] is a perception based on a stereotype, whether it is a teenaged black male driving an old car in a predominantly white, middle-class neighborhood (the assumption being that the youth may be casing homes for burglaries or looking for a car to steal) or a white person driving an upscale car in a predominantly black, low-income neighborhood (the assumption being that the person is looking for an open-air drug market). The important point to note is that in both cases officers are frequently acting on perceptions and stereotypes rather than fact-based observations that suggest a person is involved in criminality. The Fourth Amendment has the provision of "particularity"—in these cases, the officers must be able to articulate particular facts and behaviors that make the officer believe the person has committed, is committing, or is about to commit a crime. Without such reasons, and relying simply on a perception, the stop of a person is improper.

Conversely, citizens also have inaccurate perceptions of officers and stereotype those perceptions to all police. A belief expressed multiple times in community meetings was that there was "institutionalized racism in the police department." There is no doubt that those expressing that perception sincerely believe it. However, the basis for that perception typically comes from several sources—including unsubstantiated word of mouth or "urban legends"—and is stereotyped. For example, a common complaint is that when officers stop a black male, one or two back-up police cars appear and that the officer may approach the car with his or her "hand on their gun." A common citizen perception is that the officer's behavior is predicated on the fact that the driver was black. On the issue of a back-up officer, the citizen must realize that this is common procedure used for most car stops, particularly at night—officers, by practice, will provide back-up regardless of the demographic characteristics of the driver. While the citizen knows he or she did not commit a crime, the officer does not know this until the investigatory stop is completed. Typically, the officer will not place his or her hand on a weapon without some reason—for example, the car that is stopped may match the description of one wanted in a crime. The two diverse perceptions collide, creating conflict. Communication becomes an important key to resolving this conflict, as does the recognition of perceptions.

Both the community and police must recognize that their beliefs are based on stereotyped perceptions. Both must develop empathy for the views of the other and both must recognize the limitations of their perceptions. The burden on the public is that if a citizen believes that an officer's behavior is improper, the citizen must file a complaint with the police department. If there is a problem officer, little action can be taken without a formal record, including complaints. The burden on officers is to ensure that official actions are based on legitimate reasons which can be clearly articulated as being crime-related, not just perceptions, including traditional police practices that have since become antiquated. Investigations based simply on "suspicion" (i.e., perceptions) are improper relics of past police procedures that must cease.

While there is debate about the existence of racial profiling[13] and the exact character of the problem, there are clearly significant beliefs that must be addressed. For example, in December 1999, the Gallup Organization released a Social Audit Poll on Black/White Relations in the U.S. Among the findings were:

> The majority of white, as well as black, Americans say that racial profiling is widespread in the United States today. Fifty-nine percent of a sample of national adults aged 18 and older say that racial profiling is widespread. Eighty-one percent of the American public say they disapprove of the practice. Americans were asked if they had ever been stopped just because of their race or ethnic background. More than four out of ten blacks responded "yes." For blacks, such incidents are not isolated events.

> About six out of ten of those who say they have been stopped because of their race say it has occurred three or more times, including 15% who say it has happened eleven or more times. For whites, the numbers who have been treated unfairly by any of these three entities is very small: 7% for local police. For blacks, the numbers are larger. Almost three out of ten blacks—27%—say they have been treated unfairly by their local police. The differences by age and gender on this message of perceived treatment by police are profound: Again, the largest perceptions of unfair treatment come with young black men, particularly in relationship to their local police. More than half—53%—of black men 18–34 say that they are treated unfairly by the local police in their area.[14]

These data show the American public believes there is a problem and that problem must be addressed.

Objective and Empirical Documentation

As noted previously, citizens concerned about racial profiling repeatedly stated in community meetings that "a study is not needed" because they "know racial profiling occurs." These conclusions are based on anecdotal experiences that have been generalized (i.e., stereotyped) to the entire police population. While this belief may be unshakable among those who hold it, the fact remains it is a perception.

Policy and personnel actions must be based on empirical evidence that is objectively documented. If unconscious racial profiling is occurring because of residual effects of antiquated police practice or the misapplication of law, then the department must have empirical evidence that documents the character and extent of the problem. Without this information, effective remedies cannot be implemented. Similarly, if a police officer is involved in improper behavior, both standards of law and collective bargaining agreement provisions assure the officer of explicit rights, including objective, documented evidence supporting the specific allegations of misconduct. The burden of proof is on the department to show misconduct has occurred, which requires more than allegations or generalized beliefs.

The important point to note is that in both the cases of departmental policy change and allegations of officer misconduct, the police department can rely on neither stereotyped perceptions nor emotional exhortations. There is no alternative except to collect, analyze, and document evidence to fully and objectively understand the true nature of the problem before remedies can be imposed.

Management Responsibilities and Remedies

Police departments have the responsibility to respond to concerns of the community as well as to proactively monitor officer behavior. A clear trend is that communities are asking police agencies to ensure accountability of officers to contemporary standards of law and procedural behavior in the course of conducting traffic stops. As a result, several management responsibilities focus on these issues.

It must be recognized that regardless of the actions and remedies that are taken to eliminate racial profiling, the chance that it will reoccur nonetheless remains. An analogy of a common issue illustrates this point. There are explicit guidelines about when an officer can pursue a fleeing car. The officer must make a quick judgment—if the officer decides to pursue, and a subsequent investigation finds that the pursuit was not justified under policy, any discipline must be weighed in relation to the facts known to the officer at the time, the type of judgment the officer used, and any collateral injury or damage resulting from the pursuit. That is, the departmental response is balanced with the facts. A similar balance must occur in allegations of racial profiling. To be sure, the department will respond to founded allegations, but the remedy must be weighed in consideration of all the facts. Because of this, and the complexity of issues associated with this problem, the police departments should employ multiple approaches to ensure accountability and respond to improprieties.

Leadership

A police organization needs to have leadership at all levels of the organization for new initiatives to be successfully implemented. The chief of police must provide the stimulus for change and set the tone for the department. In Lansing, Michigan, this is being accomplished through definitive statements and actions by the chief clearly demonstrating that:

1. there will be no tolerance for racial profiling in Lansing;
2. there will be a traffic stop data collection initiative to monitor officer behavior;
3. if anomalies appear to exist with respect to the demography of those stopped for traffic violations, appropriate corrective action will be taken on a continuum ranging from supervisory action to discipline;
4. input from officers will be gathered prior to the implementation of policy to determine the issues, concerns, and observations police officers have with respect to issues of racial profiling;
5. input from the community will be gathered prior to the implementation of policy to determine the issues, concerns, and observations citizens have with respect to racial profiling.

Once the chief sets the tone and values for the department, leadership continues throughout the organization. Every person in managerial and supervisory positions has the responsibility to reinforce the chief's tone and carry these leadership values throughout their responsibilities. Informal leaders in the department must similarly reinforce these values in order to ensure that the department's culture is consistent with the chief's vision. Thus, leadership is the first key step in assuring accountability on racial profiling issues.

Data Collection

It was noted previously that there is a clear national trend to collect demographic data of drivers stopped for traffic offenses. There are both philosophical and practical reasons for a police department to implement a traffic stop data collection system. Practically, given that several states already have legislation requiring such data collection by police departments, it appears that such a mandate nationwide is inevitable. As such, a planned, measured initiative designed and implemented by the police department will be easier to integrate and more fully address the particular needs of Lansing.

Philosophically, data collection will provide information that permits the monitoring of police practices to empirically measure what, if any, types of problems exist; the nature of those problems; trends associated with identified problems; unique characteristics associated with profiling problems; and documentation of any particular individual showing a pattern of improper behavior in order for the department to resolve problems.

Training/Resocialization of Officers

To change operational procedures and the organizational culture, a key mechanism is training. The training foundation begins with inculcating the issues, values, and tone reflecting the chief's vision. Building on this is a foundation of substantive information which is used to address issues and procedures that will be changed.

To begin, contemporary issues and arguments associated with racial profiling are gleaned from research on a national scale. Using this framework, the police officer focus groups and community meetings provide specific insight on the issues directly in the city while identifying unique local concerns. These materials are collectively integrated into a training program that permits explanation, discussion, and understanding of racial profiling in the community. This is followed by training on the specific police department policies and procedures as well as the practical process of completing and submitting the traffic stop data collection report.

Training is only the first step in resocialization—that is, changing the organizational culture. Desired changes in attitudes and processes must be continually reinforced and policy standards must be adhered to. All parties must recognize, however, that the change process for all institutions is slow. While procedural changes can be implemented immediately, attitudinal change is significantly more complex and can take a great deal of time. As long as progress is being made, all parties must be patient.

Training the Community

It was suggested in community meetings that training sessions also be held for community members. The intent of these sessions would be to explain police policies and practices in order to provide more insight on police behavior and practice. Such training merits consideration as not only public education but also as a mechanism to open dialogue.

Supervision

The resocialization discussed previously unquestionably requires effective supervision. This includes observing officer behavior, discussing issues and problems, and providing direction when subordinates are not following either the letter or spirit of policies and values of the department. Personnel in supervisory positions have the responsibility to reinforce the chief's vision and to enforce departmental directives. Supervision is a critical ingredient for successful organizational change.

Evaluation

There are four forms of evaluation that need to be considered in this initiative. *Process evaluation* assesses whether a new policy, procedure, or practice is operating the way it was intended. For example, are the traffic stop data forms being completed, collected, and processed in an efficient and effective manner? Frequently such processes need fine-tuning once in the implementation phase. Process evaluation identifies problems which need to be corrected.

Outcome evaluation measures the aggregate effect of the policy, procedure, or practice. Thus, as previously discussed, assessments will be made of the traffic stop data to identify any anomalies in traffic stop processes and impose remedies for those anomalies.

Performance evaluation refers to specific assessment of individual officers by supervisors to determine the quality of their work as stipulated by policy, procedures, and organizational values. If problems exist, supervisors have the responsibility to provide a remedy to ensure that the officer's on-duty performance and behavior meet the standards and expectations of the department.

Complaint monitoring exists at two levels. The first is the investigatory follow-up allegations of officer misconduct made by a citizen. Departmental internal affairs directives provide guidance on these processes. The second type of monitoring is to look at aggregate complaint data to determine if any trends exist. For example, if there is a disproportionately high number of complaints against a specific officer, even if the officer is exonerated, there may be factors that need to be addressed in the officer's behavior, such as his or her communication style with the public. As another example, if there is a disproportionate number of complaints against officers who work for a specific sergeant, closer examination may find that the sergeant is an ineffective supervisor. Whenever any discernible trends exist in complaints, the trends warrant closer analysis to learn if there are subtle problems that need to be addressed.

Technology

While different forms of technology can be used to record and analyze traffic stops, perhaps the most important technology for ensuring accountability is a front window–mounted video camera with a videotaping system. Widely available for years, these systems provide important independent evidence that can be used to document racial profiling incidents as well as to exonerate officers who may be accused of the practice. In addition, the cameras have a preventive component in that officers may be more cognizant to evaluate criteria used to stop drivers to ensure they are not profiling. In this regard, President Clinton's 2000 Crime Bill included the provision of "$10 million to help police departments purchase more video cameras to protect both the safety of officers and the rights of the individuals they stop."[15]

For in-car cameras to accomplish their goals, policies and procedures must be in place to control the cameras' use. For example, explicit policy must stipulate that cameras are turned on for all traffic stops and remain on until the driver leaves the scene. There must also be policy on videotape retention and storage. Finally, supervisors must ensure that officers are adhering to this policy on all traffic stops and take corrective action should a subordinate not use the cameras as directed.

Certainly other technologies should be explored as a means to support anti–racial profiling policies: a database to monitor complaints and serve as an "early warning system"; the ability for citizens to submit complaints via police department web pages; and on-line education programs for the police and community alike are all examples of technological applications.

Conclusion

Racial profiling is not just a police issue—it is a social issue that has persistently existed in many forms: loan applications, service in restaurants, access to educational opportunities, and access to housing are examples. As a microcosm of society, it is not surprising that conflicts in police-minority relations have continued. Importantly, the greater concern for racial discrimination related to law enforcement stems from the authority vested in the police to use force against citizens and deprive people of their liberty: this is anathema to our free society and as such must be monitored carefully. This initiative seeks to accomplish this end in Lansing.

Footnotes

1. For a balanced view of issues see: *Policy.com: The Policy News and Information Service* [online]. Available from World Wide Web: (http://www.policy.com/news/dbrief/dbriefarc253.asD).
2. See: (http//www.whitehouse.gov/WH/Work/060999.html).
3. Wednesday, October 11, 2000, Wake Forest University, Winston-Salem, North Carolina.
4. See: (http://www.aclu.org/profiling/).
5. Throughout this paper the authors use the descriptor "black" rather than African-American because "black" is a more accurate descriptor. For example, blacks from Canada, the United Kingdom, and the Caribbean would not be accurately described as "African-American."
6. Ramirez, D.A., J. McDevitt, and A. Farrell. (2000). *A Resource Guide on Racial Profiling Data Collection Systems.* Unpublished report. Washington: U.S. Department of Justice.
7. Customs and Immigration services of most developed countries use some form of profile to identify potential offenders. The effectiveness of these profiles has been the subject of debate with Customs officials noting their substantially different authority and responsibility compared to local law enforcement.
8. Revised Statues of Missouri, Section A, Chapter 560, Section 650.
9. House Resolution 1443, Rep. Conyers (D-MI) and Senate Bill 821, Sen. Lautenberg (D-NJ).
10. Introduced in the House in March 2000 by Rep. Conyers (D-MI).
11. Concepts in the following discussion are based on the article: Hoover, Larry. (2000). "Why Police Resist Collecting Race Data on Traffic Stops." *Police Labor Monthly,* (July) Vol.19, No. 2, Justex Systems, Huntsville, TX.
12. Harris refers to this as "Rational Discrimination." See: Harris, D. (1999). "The Stories, the Statistics, and the Law: Why 'Driving While Black' Matters." *Minnesota Law Review.* Vol. 84, No. 2:265–326; refer to p. 294.
13. Dichotomous views can be found in: Strossen, N., I. Glasser, and K. Clark. (2000). *Driving While Black: Racial Profiling on Our Nation's Highways.* New York: American Civil Liberties Union. McQuiggan, F. (2000). *Racial Profiling: Who Is Stereotyping Whom?* [online]. Available from World Wide Web: (http://www.domelights.com/racprof1.htm).

14. See: (http://www.gallup.com/poll/releases/ar991209.asp).
15. See: (http://www.whitehouse.gov/WH/Work/060999.html).

David L. Carter and Andra J. Katz-Bannister, "Racial Profiling: Issues and Implications for Police Policy." Copyright © 2003 by Roxbury Publishing Company. All rights reserved. ✦

Part V

Innovations, Boundary Spanning, and Capacity Building

Organizational innovation involves any alteration of individual behavior, operational activity, or management style. In a loose sense, innovation, also referred to as organizational change, seeks to improve police operations.

There are two key types of organizational innovation or change. The first involves adaptation to a change in an organization's external environment. Innovations of this type are directed toward finding a "fit" between an organization and its environment for the purpose of growth or survival. Factors that influence this type of organizational innovation include technological change, environmental variation, or change in the political landscape. In a certain sense, this kind of innovation implies that an organization is primarily forced to respond to the demands of its environment.

The second type of innovation is a result of planned change. This usually begins with a careful evaluation of the organizational environment. External experts are often hired as consultants to conduct the evaluation. If a police department decides to implement a fear-reduction program in a high-crime neighborhood, for example, researchers first conduct surveys and interviews of local residents to identify the neighborhood's top problems. Similarly, surveys and/or interviews with police officers may offer additional information on how to create specific programs to solve identified problems. Researchers then propose a process for program implementation. This type of innovative program requires serious planning and substantial resources (personnel and equipment) in order to complete the process. Commitment from top administrators, therefore, is an essential component to ensure success.

In terms of initial response to demands from external environment, James Thompson (1967) developed a conceptual framework that is briefly explained in the chapter by Jihong Zhao and Quint Thurman that appears in this section. Thompson argued that every organization has core operations that are stable over time. Police executives tend to fiercely protect core operations because changes at the core may lead to significant and sometimes unanticipated changes throughout the organization.

Because few organizations truly want to undergo dramatic changes even when the external environment may demand it, they will tend to create a few innovative programs that attempt to respond to the environment's demands, but simultaneously protect their core operations from being forced to change. If time proves these "boundary-spanning units" useful, the innovations may become part of core operations. If not, they will be dropped. Thus, the unwanted, unforeseeable consequences of change can be avoided to the extent possible.

Applying Thompson's theory to American policing, innovative programs (such as storefront stations, victim contact programs, and problem-solving units) are largely independent of the core operations of police work, which already include randomized patrol and detective work. If an innovative program is successful, Zhao and Thurman's study suggests that it will be incorporated into the police agency's core operations.

Reference

Thompson, J. 1967. *Organizations in Action.* New York: McGraw-Hill. ✦

Chapter 19
The Nature of Community Policing Innovations

Do the Ends Justify the Means?

Jihong Zhao
Quint C. Thurman

Here the authors examine modern policing from the perspective of James Thompson's theory of organizational change and ask, is the core mission of policing changing? If so, how might we be able to tell?

For several decades the core mission of professional policing has been crime control. Analyzing data from a national survey of police chiefs collected in three-year intervals over a period of several years, Zhao and Thurman asked respondents to rank their agencies' priorities in terms of crime control, order maintenance, and public service. Their findings suggest that while police organizations are seeking to be innovative in the external police environment, public safety agencies largely continue to embrace crime control as a primary organizational priority.

Introduction: Ends and Means of Police Innovations

Scholars and practitioners alike have contributed much in the last two decades to the debate concerning the need for organizational change and innovations in American policing, particularly in terms of movement away from a professional model to one that is more "community-oriented" (Kelling and Moore 1988). As a result, many contemporary police agencies now aspire to community-oriented policing (COP) as an ideal organizational form that noticeably differs from a traditional or bureaucratic approach. It is widely believed that this reconceptualization of the relationship between the police and citizens is crucial for redefining the police's proper role as public service providers in a modern democratic society (Angell 1971).

Central to the COP philosophy is the reprioritization of the core mission or "ends" of American policing in terms of public safety functions, and correspondingly, the creation of new means to achieve such ends. Thus, the sequence of the three primary functions of American policing—crime control, order maintenance and nonemergency services (Wilson 1968; Walker 1983)—should be rearranged to better meet the needs of American citizens. Some scholars have called change in the priorities of police functions a paradigm shift (e.g., Sykes 1986; Kelling 1988; Weisburd et al. 1988). Several reasons that justify such a reprioritization of organizational ends have been identified. These include (1) the recognition that order maintenance is the essential function of police in a free society (Goldstein 1977, 1987); (2) the understanding that the coproduction of order between police and citizens is instrumental in controlling crimes (Kelling and Stewart 1989; Moore 1992; President's Commission on Law Enforcement and Administration of Justice 1967); and (3) the acknowledgment that the police cannot control crime using the traditional approach (Kelling et al. 1974; Greenwood et al. 1977).

Reprioritizing police functions is further supported by research findings that police officers spend little time on crime control (Wilson 1968; Walker 1983; see Sherman 1993 for a critical review). Consequently, Eck and Rosenbaum (1994: 7–8) observe:

> These functions—crime control, emergency aid, nonemergency services, and jus-

> tice—have not been discarded by community policing advocates. Instead, community policing rearranges priorities among functions and adds new ones. Nonemergency services take on greater importance. Crime control, emergency aid and justice become less prominent relative to nonemergency services for four reasons.

As they argue, these reasons are as follows: (1) a small proportion of police work is devoted to the crime control function; (2) the police have limited capacity to control crime; (3) the public shows more concern about nonemergency and quality-of-life problems than about crime control activities, per se; and (4) the causes of crime are disorder and decline (cf. Skogan 1990).

In terms of corresponding means, Lurigio and Skogan (1994: 315) point out that COP reprioritization of police functions "translates into a variety of specific operations and practices." More specifically, Weisel and Eck (1994) (also see Bayley 1994) suggest that "almost all of the agencies had previous experience with concepts related in form to community policing: citizen liaison groups; park, walk, talk activities; Neighborhood Watch meetings; foot patrol; storefronts; bike patrol units; and other activities" (p. 56).

Even so, this notable shift in police priorities to COP has not remained immune from criticism. For example, Riechers and Roberg (1990: 108) argue that "the assumptions and goals of community policing are not always compatible." In a similar vein, Klockars (1988: 214) states that COP is "best understood as the latest in a fairly long tradition of circumlocutions whose purpose is to conceal, mystify and legitimate police distribution of nonnegotiable coercive force." In response to Bittner's (1970) typology of American police functions, Klockars concludes that the very nature of American police makes it impossible for them to change (cf. Price 1977). Similar criticism concerning police control and co-production of order may be found in the works of Manning (1988) and Mastrofski (1988). The central argument is that the police's core mission never changes—crime control remains the top priority.

Since the 1990s, however, many criticisms of COP have disappeared from prominent discussion within both academic and professional circles. Rosenbaum et al. (1994: 331) observe that "today, one would need to search high and low to find a critic of community policing." Similarly, Sadd and Grinc (1994: 42) notice that police departments across the nation "are jumping on the community policing bandwagon without having a clear conception of what community policing is all about."

Unfortunately, if scholars and practitioners do not investigate critical concerns about COP, such as the prioritization of police functions and the relationship between the means and the ends of the police role, then COP may look like a "done deal" before consensus exists on what is to be done (Roberg 1994: 254). This paper raises the concern that scholars and practitioners of American policing may be unable to constructively investigate the COP movement because very little knowledge exists about the process of such change in general and about its nature in particular (Reiss 1992).

In this paper, the authors use James Thompson's theory of organizational change as a theoretical framework to investigate the core mission of American policing. The authors first examine prioritization of police functions and then address the relationship between these priorities (ends) and the means used to try to achieve them. A primary aim of this analysis is to assess the utility of Thompson's theory of organizational change as applied to the COP movement that currently is sweeping American society.

Thompson's Theory of Organizational Change

Four Major Organizational Components

In his classic book, *Organizations in Action,* Thompson (1967) provides a theoretical framework for understanding why organizations behave in predictable ways. Thompson maintains that under the norm of rationality, organizations will tend to exhibit similar, predictable behavior under certain shared preconditions. The starting point for theorizing about organizational action is to understand an organization's four major components and the interrelationships that exist among them.

The first and most important component is an organizational domain that may be conceptualized as the core mission or principal values that an organization seeks to achieve (also see Meyer 1975). Accordingly, the domain justifies the organization's existence and explains why organizations differ from one another.[1]

> Domain consensus defines a set of expectations both for members of an organization and for others with whom they interact, about what the organization will and will not do. It provides, although imperfectly, an image of the organization's role in a larger system, which in turn serves as a guide for the ordering of action in certain directions and not in others. (Thompson 1967: 29)

Consequently, the "domain consensus" (or sense of purpose) to a considerable extent determines an organization's course of action in a society. For example, public agencies differ from private concerns in good part because their core missions are very different. Within the realm of public agencies, moreover, law enforcement organizations share a similar organizational domain that differs from those of other public agencies (e.g., schools, hospitals, sanitation departments, etc.) with respect to their primary social service functions.

A second key organizational component that Thompson identified is the use of technology. Generally speaking, this organizational dimension is defined in terms of the availability of technology to provide an essential means for an organization to achieve its core mission. For example, substantial technological improvement in telecommunications companies has made long distance and international calls possible for customers. This, in turn, opens new frontiers in the telecommunications industry. Given their own particular domain as a focus of attention, organizations are constantly searching for ways to improve the technology used to achieve their core mission.

A third major organizational component concerns the task environment. The task environment is conceptualized as that part of the external environment that an organization targets for operations. Organizations vary in their task environments because their domains and/or technological assets are different. For example, primary schools' task environment involves the education of children from six to 12 years old; this is part of the global external environment that defines the schools' task environment. In essence, the task environment limits the operational space that an organization tries to control in its external environment.

A final key organizational component involves the organization's technical core. According to Thompson, the technical core may be thought of as a coordinating plan that provides the link between the organizational domain, the technology and the task environment. The purpose of the technical core is to organize and coordinate an organization's diverse units to achieve the organization's mission (i.e., the successful coordination and processing of raw materials from the input to the output stage in a predictable fashion). For example, in a primary school, the core mission defines a task environment and directs attention to the available classroom of technology; the raw materials here are children in a certain age group. The technical core's function is to successfully process these raw materials from the input stage (e.g., when students enter the school system) to the output stage (namely, when they graduate). The technical core provides the grounds for the rational determination of roles, expectations and processes in the organization, and it enables the organization to standardize its operations and achieve its mission in a predictable way.

Technical Rationality Vs. Organizational Rationality

Thompson points out that it is improper to characterize organizations as operating solely in either a closed system or an open system. Actually, both types of systems may be found in an organization. Organizations continually try to locate their technical core within a closed system to achieve technical rationality by reducing uncertainty:

> Perfection in technical rationality requires complete knowledge of cause/effect reactions plus control over all of the relevant variables, or closure. Therefore, under norms of rationality (Prop. 2.1), organizations seek to seal off their core technologies from environment influences. (Thompson 1967: 24)

Technical rationality is a preferred means for an organization to evaluate its performance. However, most organizations cannot completely seal the technical core off from external influences. Under normal conditions, an organization cannot evaluate its performance based solely on technical rationality (e.g., cost/benefit analysis), and as a result, concerns about technical rationality are supplemented by the need to consider organizational rationality:

> With clearly imperfect technologies, technical rationality cannot be assessed with confidence, and the organization must fall back to a less precise but fundamental question: does the unit contribute to the organization's needs? . . . Evaluations of this sort are typically made of maintenance or troubleshooting crews, nursing services, instructional teams in schools and universities. . . . (Thompson 1967: 95)

The more complex the external environment confronting an organization, the more likely the organization is to use organizational rationality (which is based on estimated needs or processing necessities rather than cost/benefit or technical rationality) to guide its activities.

The Nature of Organizational Change: A Response to Uncertainty

After outlining the major components of Thompson's theory and identifying two levels of rationality, the next matter of concern is to explain the nature of organizational change set forth by Thompson. Organizational change is defined here as an organization's alteration of operations to continue to achieve its core mission. Thompson (1967) suggests that among the primary causes of organizational change are uncertainties or constraints stemming from the organization's technical and task environment components. These uncertainties constitute a threat to the rationality on which an organization must depend. For example, an organization's task environment boundaries are defined by the domain in which a certain part of the external environment exists. Uncertainties or constraints tend to obscure task environment boundaries, and as a result, confusion may arise regarding fundamental questions.

Thompson (1967: 68) points out that "generally, we may say that organizations find their environmental constraints located in *geographic space* or in the *social composition* of their task environments" (italics in original). Thus, the more complex the social composition an organization faces in the external environment, the more restraints or uncertainties it will have in its task environment. Furthermore, Thompson suggests that, compared with other types of organizations, government agencies face more uncertainties or constraints. Public agencies are "captive" organizations by their nature. Unlike private organizations, which can move or redefine their core mission to change or update their task environment, public agencies are not free to make similar changes:

> The most dramatic example of constraints, perhaps, arises in the case of governmental organizations [that] are captives of a particular population. The public school system treated badly by its mandatory population may lose all of its members, but the organization as such cannot move to another community; it must stay home and fight the "in-law battle." (Thompson 1967: 30)

Thompson correctly notes that captive organizations have no choice but to respond to constraints, even though there is no hope that they will ever escape the unpredictability of the external environment. Police organizations are a typical example of such a captive organization, as described by Thompson.

Initial Response to Uncertainties: Boundary-Spanning Units and Programs

Confronted with uncertainties from the external environment and operating under the ubiquitous norms of rationality, an organization will seek to make changes to stabilize the external environment. Generally speaking, an organization uses one or two approaches (or a combination) in times of uncertainties: organizations seek to either improve technology or move to expand their task environment. Thompson notes the following in this respect:

> The more an organization is constrained in some sectors of its task environment (Prop. 3.4), the more power it will seek over remaining elements of its task environment. When the organization is unable to achieve such a balance (Prop. 3.5), it will seek to enlarge its task environment. (Thompson 1967: 38)

An organization's primary purpose in seeking to enlarge its task environment is to protect its technical core by buffering itself against the uncertainties of its external environment. Commonly used strategies to enlarge its task environment induce the creation of new units and programs that expand the previous operational space to include new frontiers. This is particularly true in captive or public organizations. For example, Thompson notes that "community hospitals, prisons, city governments, and public schools all exhibit this device of creating new elements in the task environment to offset other constraints within it" (Thompson 1967: 37).

Under the norm of rationality, the primary function of these new units or programs is to serve as "surveillance" agents or "sensors." They help an organization to estimate the impact of uncertainties and formulate strategies for dealing with them. The efficiency and effectiveness of "boundary-spanning" units are not judged by clear cost/benefit rationality criteria, but rather by the much vaguer standard of organizational rationality (e.g., outside recognition, appearance of influence). Thompson (1967) suggests that those surveillance units act with relative independence and autonomy: "Here, we would expect boundary-spanning units to be differentiated functionally to correspond to segments of the task environment, and each to operate on a decentralized basis to monitor and plan responses to fluctuations in its sector of the task environment" (p. 73). (Interestingly, there is relatively little cooperation among and between these units and those responsible for core mission duties because of highly differentiated monitoring and sensor functions.)

In addition, given the fact that enlarging the task environment by those boundary-spanning units serves to protect an organization's technical core, any substantial change caused by absorbing these units into routine operation will take place only when an organization is certain that it can sufficiently control that enlarged portion of the task environment. Thompson (1967) observes that if these various assumptions about rationality and boundary-spanning are true, then similar behavior or patterns of activities will appear among organizations that are confronted with similar technological and environmental problems.

Thompson's theoretical framework provides a set of propositions that may be applied to an analysis of the nature of organizational change in contemporary American policing. First, police organizations are indeed mission-driven. Police agencies' *domain* relatively defines their societal role. Second, police agencies' *technical core* operations are important for accomplishing their core mission. Third, under the threat of uncertainties and constraints from the external environment, police organizations will try to *improve technology* and *expand their task environments* to protect the technical core. Fourth, given police agencies' captive status, the more turbulent the external environment confronting them, the more enlarged the task environment they must seek to stabilize the external environment. Fifth, the lower the level of cooperation and association of boundary-spanning units within police organizations, the less likely that these units will become routinized inside the technical core. In other words, the change that boundary-spanning units accomplish is mainly symbolic, rather than fundamental to the organization's core mission. Finally, similar patterns of boundary-spanning will occur among those police departments that face a similar external environment.

Method and Measures

The data used in this paper were derived from a national survey of police chiefs conducted by the Division of Governmental Studies and Services (DGSS) at Washington State University. DGSS has conducted surveys at three-year intervals since 1978. The cities in the sample were selected from those initially included in a representative national survey of police chiefs in cities with over 25,000 residents, conducted by the International City Management Association in 1969. The sample included 281 municipal police departments in 47 states. The representativeness of regions and the sizes of cities were considered in selecting the sample. Included in the database for this study was the sixth survey of municipal police departments, conducted in 1993.

After three waves of mailings, 228 (81 %) of 281 police departments completed and returned the survey. Either a police chief or an appointed representative was asked to rate 16 police activities, including crime control, order maintenance and service functions. The 16 activities were mainly derived from the index Wilson developed in his study, *Varieties of Police Behavior* (1968). Each item was rated on a four-point scale, ranging from "very low priority" to "high priority."

Similarly, respondents were asked to identify from a list the presence or absence of 12 COP programs compiled from a review of the relevant literature (e.g., Skolnick and Bayley 1986; Goldstein 1990; Brown and Wycoff 1987; Moore 1992). These 12 COP programs represent the extent of police organizational change in terms of *externally focused* innovation. Externally focused innovation includes the reorientation of police operations and crime prevention activities to adjust the organization's influence and improve its relationship with the external environment (Huber et al. 1993).

The Nature of Contemporary Organizational Change in American Policing

The following discussion applies Thompson's theoretical framework to the analysis of contemporary American policing. Previous findings suggest that the primary causes of changes taking place in police organizations stem from the external environment, particularly the extent of social disorganization present in a community—in Thompson's terms, the *social composition* of the organizational environment (Zhao et al. 1994; Sadd and Grinc 1994; Kelling and Wilson 1982; Skogan 1990).

Research findings consistently suggest that uncertainties emanating from the external environment influence police organizations to initiate and then implement *externally focused* COP innovations. To understand and explain such change, it is important to analyze the domain or core mission of American policing, which provides the justification for what police should and should not do.

The Domain of American Policing

Kelling and Moore (1988) suggest that the history of American policing may be categorized according to three distinctive phases—namely, the political, the bureaucratic and the community-oriented eras. Furthermore, they argue that a set of new core missions or domains may be identified in each phase, which provides an explanation for why American police organizations have evolved as they have over time.

A review of the literature suggests that consensus exists among scholars of American policing concerning police agencies' core missions during the first two phases of police history. Walker (1977, 1980) states that the core mission of American policing in the political era was order maintenance (cf. Wilson 1968; Monkkonen 1992), as exemplified in Lane's (1992: 8) vivid description of policing in that phase:

> But in most cases the new police did serve the purpose intended, generally proving their ability to obey orders and deal effectively with hostile crowds of pro- or anti-slavery men and women, Irishmen and natives, whatever their own political views or ethnic affiliations.

Furthermore, Lane suggests that during the political era, police organizations nationwide were not mandated to be professional and independent forces exclusively focusing on crime control functions. He notes that "no political faction wanted independent or impartial law enforcement; the real issue was simply which faction, and which level, would direct the force" (1992: 12).

Common agreement among scholars also may be found with respect to the core mission of American policing during the bureaucratic era. The law enforcement function, particularly crime control, served as police organizations' primary core mission in this phase (cf. Kelling and Moore 1988; Walker 1977; Reiss 1992).

Disagreement concerning the core mission of American policing is evident when attention shifts to the current community-oriented phase. The review of literature at the beginning of this paper identified two distinctive perspectives concerning the core mission of American policing in contemporary society. Scholars of COP forcefully argue that the core mission or priorities have fundamentally changed since the 1970s (Goldstein 1987; Trojanowicz and Bucqueroux 1990; Kelling 1988; Moore 1992).

The reprioritization in the core mission that these scholars see reflects a departure from crime control and a movement toward service and community order maintenance. Evidence that supports this argument, mainly derived from some rather impressive research, includes (1) the extensive implementation of COP innovations across the nation (Trojanowicz and Bucqueroux 1990); (2) the link between COP innovations and the core mission in many agencies (Wasserman and Moore 1988); and (3) the broadly recognized failure of crime control strategies (Skolnick and Bayley 1986).

However, other scholars persuasively argue that the basic nature of American policing has not changed in any fundamental way during the past two decades (e.g., Klockars 1988; Riechers and Roberg 1990). Manning (1988) points out that COP innovations represent "the drama of control," while Mastrofski (1988) highlights the potential danger of COP innovations aimed at expanding police control in a free society, particularly in disadvantaged communities.

However, despite the exchange of rhetoric among scholars of these two perspectives with respect to the core mission of contemporary American policing, "a lot of heat but little light" has been produced on this important issue—namely, what is currently the core mission of American policing?

In their recent study of the core mission of American policing in 50 states, Burton et al. (1994: 690) found that the law enforcement function remains the primary mandate of state legal codes. They observed that "22 states (44%) mandate only the role of law enforcement for their police. This is the most common police role as defined in state legal codes." Twenty-four states mandate their police forces to perform both law enforcement and order maintenance functions, while only three states require police to exclusively perform an order maintenance function. Finally, only one state, New York, requires the police to perform the service function—that is, assisting citizens in a broad sense. From Burton et al.'s findings, it could be argued that the police's core mission remains predominantly one of law enforcement, a mission that a state's legal code mandates.

In this study, 16 survey items were mainly derived from a similar study of police organizations that James Q. Wilson conducted in 1968. Police departments were asked to prioritize local problems ranging from violent crimes to the provision of services to citizens. A principal-component-analysis statistical technique was used to analyze the underlying factors associated with the various police functions identified in the 1993 survey (that is, the retention of factors with eigen values greater than one). Furthermore, the commonly used approach of varimax orthogonal rotation was adopted for presentation of these data because this approach is more appropriate than other techniques for undertaking exploratory analysis (Kim and Mueller 1978: 48–50). Five distinctive factors were found and are reported in Table 19.1.

The findings reported in Table 19.1 indicate the presence of five clear factors or empirically clustered aspects of mission. These factors correspond very closely to the aspects of police mission over which the debate has been waged. Table 19.2 shows the priority ranking afforded these factors in the 1993 survey.

Findings from Table 19.2 reveal that the top priority police organizations identified is law enforcement, with particular attention to violent or street crimes. The service function is given the lowest priority of the five factors. This suggests that police organizations clearly know their core mission in American society (which their legal codes also mandate). Furthermore, these findings support the claim of some scholars that the core mission of American policing has remained largely unchanged during the past 50 years or more. Accordingly, the findings appear to suggest that COP advocates may be victims of wishful thinking concerning the broad movement toward the values implicit in the COP model.

Table 19.1
Factor Analysis: Police Priorities in Operation

Factor	Loading	Percentage of Variance	Eigen Value
1. Services			
a. Fire, power out, tree down	.76		
b. Accident, illnesses, ambulance calls	.74		
c. Lost and found	.66		
d. Stray animals	.57		
e. Drunkenness	.47	28.2%	4.52
2. Order Maintenance			
Neighborhood trouble	.83		
Family trouble	.66		
Vagrancy	.43	8.1%	1.84
3. Property Crime			
a. Burglary	.80		
b. Property damage	.69		
c. Vandalism	.60	11.4%	1.26
4. Gang			
a. Drugs	.78		
b. Street crimes	.63	6.3%	1.07
5. Violent Crime			
a. Robbery	.82		
b. Rape	.75		
c. Stranger assault	.68	6.9%	1.02

Total Variance Explained = 60.9%

Table 19.2
Mean Ratings of Priorities in Police Operations

Factors	Mean (Standard Deviation)
Violent Crime	3.77 (.35)
Gang	3.53 (.54)
Property Crime	2.82 (.53)
Order Maintenance	2.76 (.52)
Service	2.36 (.60)
N = 215	

1 = very low priority, 2 = low priority, 3 = moderate priority, 4 = high priority

Technology, Task Environment and Technical Core: A Case Study of American Policing

After defining the core mission of American policing as mainly law enforcement, the next step is to conceptualize COP innovations based on Thompson's theoretical framework. If the domain is clear to American police chiefs, how are they coping with their captive status in a period of broad social change?

In the bureaucratic era, the technological improvements available to police organizations were extensive. Reiss (1992) suggested that innovations in technology were closely linked to the fulfillment of the core mission, law enforcement:

> Each technological change—from the telephone, patrol car and two-way radio transmission to the computer—has had significant impact on internal organization and operation of police departments. . . . Adaptations to social technologies, such as those of organizational behavior and risk analysis, while less pervasive, are becoming characteristic modes of rational technocratic administration in police departments. (p. 83)

Furthermore, Reiss (1992: 84) suggests that "much of the technocratic emphasis in policing derives from a model of proactive and reactive crime control" (for a review, see Manning 1992). The proponents of the bureaucratic model of policing strongly believed that the increased use of technical inventions could create professional police organizations that were highly effective at law enforcement (e.g., Vollmer 1936; Wilson 1950). The adoption of technological innovations reflects the application of technical rationality in police operation. For example, the effectiveness of handling calls that officers field may be measured by length of response time, and productivity may be evaluated by the number of arrests per shift. These typical measures provide the standard criteria for success among police organizations nationwide.

Consistent with improvements in technology, the bureaucratic model's task environment changed from an order maintenance function to a law enforcement function. During the early phase of the bureaucratic model, many boundary-spanning units were established in accordance with the core mission, including motorized patrol, crime investigation, vice, crime lab, and traffic divisions. Because these units could presumably provide effectiveness in the law enforcement function, and because their activities could be measured by technical rationality criteria, in time they were institutionalized as permanent operating units in the police agency task environment. In sum, the bureaucratic model's task environment had relatively clear boundaries that limited the scope of police work to law enforcement.

Manning (1992: 358) points out the following: "The core technology of police, their decision making, is fundamental, not easily altered, and multiply determined, and it is the mode of decision making that determines what information is available to other officers." Similarly, by applying Thompson's theoretical framework, he suggests that police organizations' technical core involves the process of moving information from the input stage to the output stage (cf. Reiss 1992). In this research, the technical core is defined beyond that limited scope. Police departments' technical core should include the essential features of a bureaucracy, such as a paramilitary organizational structure, a span of control, a division of labor, and a process of evaluating employees. The key point here is that these features provide essential technical rationality in police organizations. Furthermore, the technical core definition of task makes the adoption of technical innovations possible in the task environment and constitutes a central control mechanism in a closed system (Reiss 1992). For example, standardized operational procedures enable police administrators to evaluate officers' performance based on technical rationality. The essential element of technical rationality is uniformity as opposed to diversity, and centralization as opposed to decentralization.

Uncertainties and Expansion of Task Environment: Change Since the 1970s

Many scholars suggest that the core mission of American policing has been under criticism since the late 1960s and early 1970s, when urban disturbances forced the police into a conflict they had tried to avoid for a long time (Moore 1992). At the same time, escalating crime rates cast doubt on the police's effectiveness in controlling crime. Furthermore, Goldstein (1977) went so far as to argue that the current mission of American policing represents an anomaly in a free society.

All these uncertainties from the external environment threatened police organizations' technical core and domain, particularly in large cities where uncertainties from the external environment were most salient (e.g., most disturbances in the late 1960s took place in large, racially diversified cities). To reduce these uncertainties to a minimum, police agencies had two primary choices based on Thompson's theoretical framework. First, they could use more technological innovations, thereby achieving technological rationality. Alternatively, they could enlarge their task environment. In doing the latter, they hoped to stabilize the external environment.

Unfortunately, technical innovations, combined with traditional crime-fighting strategies, seemed to be relatively ineffective in the 1970s and 1980s. Several significant studies of wide distribution suggested that the improvement of technologies and crime-fighting strategies might have little or no association with the effectiveness of the law enforcement function—the core mission of police. The direct consequence of these research findings is that police organizations quite likely cannot continue to use technical rationality to evaluate their performance within a closed system of organizational logic. Manning (1992) observes that the trend to use technological innovations is ongoing. However, police administrators nationwide are much less confident than their predecessors in the 1950s concerning the effectiveness and efficiency of such innovations.

Similarly, the bureaucratic model's task environment is under great pressure as crime rates increase, particularly for violent street crimes. Wilson and Kelling's "Broken Windows" theory forcefully asserts that disorder is an important factor that leads to crime (cf. Skogan 1990). Furthermore, Goldstein (1987) highlighted the weakness of police operations that focus on incidents rather than the problems underlying the incidents. One obvious consequence is that task environment boundaries have become less clearly defined over time.

The problems found in both the technical and the task environments directly threaten the technical core of police organizations in many cities, particularly in socially disorganized communities. To protect the technical core and ensure the integrity of the core mission, police departments must expand their task environment. The purpose of such expansion is to stabilize the external environment by covering more variables that were not part of the police responsibility previously. As Thompson suggested, the more turbulent the external environment confronting a police department, the greater the expansion in task environment the police organization must seek. This expansion is symbolized in the creation of boundary-spanning units. These units' primary purpose is to buffer the uncertainties from the external environment that threaten the technical core, so that police organizations' core mission may remain more or less untouched. Thus, boundary-spanning units become useful tools for achieving organizational rationality because the task environment's imperfect technologies and unclear boundaries remain unresolvable obstacles.

Thompson's observations are fully consistent with the empirical findings discussed earlier. COP externally focused innovations are more likely to occur in socially disorganized communities because the turbulent environment of these communities poses more uncertainties, which, in turn, threaten the technical core. It is noteworthy that there is no comparable set of explanatory variables that predicts the occurrence of COP internally focused change.

The findings reported earlier suggest that the core mission of American policing has changed very little since the early days of this century. The next step in the analysis is to investigate the association among COP innovations. Thompson's framework (1967) would suggest that there will be limited interconnections among these innovations because their major function is to monitor and buffer against the external environment, as opposed to changing police agencies' technical core. If COP externally focused innovations represent a well-planned change, then moderate or high correlations will be observed among a set of programs or strategies that constitute the definitive elements of COP innovations. Table 19.3 reports findings concerning the intercorrelations among COP innovations (for a complete list and frequency distribution of COP programs see Appendix 19.1).

Findings from Table 19.3 highlight two important points. The first concerns the lack of association among elements of reorientation of police operations and programs. Many police departments reported using various innovations to reorient their operations. However, either weak or no correlations exist among these COP innovations. For example, foot patrol is often considered one of the most celebrated programs in the COP model. Despite the fact that most police organizations (88.4%) reported using this program, it has no correlation with other COP innovations other than being a special task unit. This finding suggests that the effectiveness of foot patrol programs is judged more on organizational rationality grounds—social recognition—than on whether such programs support the use of other strategies that might help make COP an organizational core mission. Furthermore, no clear pattern has been identified that might

Table19.3
Correlation Matrix of COP Innovations: Externally Focused Change

	Newsletter	Foot Patrol	Storefront	Boundary-Spanning Unit	Victim Programs	Education	Fixed	Survey	Block	Business	Meeting	Volunteer
Newsletter	—	.07	.03	.03	.11*	.13*	.02	.12*	.03	.08	.06	.16***
Foot Patrol	—	—	.10	.20***	−.04	.06	.12*	.11	−.06	.01	.11*	.06
Storefront	—	—	—	.02	.00	−.09	.12*	.21***	.06	.20**	.22***	.06
Boundary-Spanning Unit	—	—	—	—	.18**	.33***	.28***	.07	.17**	.13**	.22***	.01
Victim Programs	—	—	—	—	—	.03	.13*	.12*	−.05	.28***	.12*	.24***
Education	—	—	—	—	—	—	.15**	.17**	.21***	.11*	.25***	.13*
Fixed	—	—	—	—	—	—	—	.15**	.22***	.21***	.37***	.18**
Survey	—	—	—	—	—	—	—	—	−.01	.17**	.26***	.21***
Block	—	—	—	—	—	—	—	—	—	.21***	.30***	−.04
Business	—	—	—	—	—	—	—	—	—	—	.31***	.24***
Meeting	—	—	—	—	—	—	—	—	—	—	—	.29***
Volunteer	—	—	—	—	—	—	—	—	—	—	—	—

* p<.05 ** p<.01 *** p<.001

constitute a set of core operational and/or program reorientations. This is consistent with Weisel and Eck's (1994: 54) finding: "It should be emphasized here that there is no single model of community policing being identified, advocated or studied."

A second observation involves crime prevention programs. Moderate correlations exist among crime prevention programs compared with the reorientation of police operations programs. This finding may suggest that, to a certain extent, crime prevention programs are implemented in accord with a somewhat planned approach in police organizations nationwide.

The findings reported in Table 19.3 suggest that police organizations are trying to enlarge their task environment by implementing new programs that were not previously included in their scope of activity. They are more likely using these innovations in a trial-and-error strategy to stabilize the external environment, rather than as part of a well-planned effort to control the enlarged task environment. In other words, police organizations seem to be uncertain about the effectiveness and consequences of new programs, but willing to give them a try. However, the effectiveness of innovations is judged more by outside recognition of their value than by technical rationality rooted in the cost/benefit analysis of technical core activities.

Conclusion

This paper has focused on the proper conceptualization of the nature of the COP movement in contemporary American policing. James Thompson's theoretical framework was applied in identifying the core mission of American policing. The survey results concerning the priorities of police functions suggest rather strongly that American police agencies' core mission has remained relatively unchanged over the past 50 years.

The theoretical analysis focused on the key components of police organizations as they arise under the ubiquitous norms of technical and organizational rationality. A key issue is how to best understand police organizational response to the myriad uncertainties arising from the contemporary external environment, particularly those with their roots in social disorganization. It appears from the findings that COP innovations are a direct result of police organizations' responsiveness to their external environment. Given the fact that uncertainties constitute a threat to police agencies' technical core and domain, these agencies try to protect their technical core by reducing uncertainties from the external environment as much as possible. In this regard, they are trying to enlarge the task environment to erect buffers between the technical core and environmental uncertainties. Generally speaking, police organizations have been successful at protecting their technical core, or at least part of it, throughout the history of professional law enforcement:

> As we approach the [21st] century and ponder changes of the century almost past, it would be easy to conclude that the basic structural organization of policing today resembles rather closely that in place at the beginning of this century. (Reiss 1992: 55)

Organizational change is a "traumatic and unsettling" process (Pfeffer 1982: 229). Under the norm of rationality, few organizations choose to undergo substantial changes if there are no life-threatening uncertainties from the external environment. Furthermore, most organizations prefer to implement change on a marginal, incremental basis (see Zhao et al. 1994). Moreover, under the norm of rationality, most organizations would prefer to pursue technical rationality rather than attempt the more difficult challenge of effecting organizational rationality (Thompson 1967). Police organizations apparently are no exception in this regard.

One may argue that contemporary police organizational change stems primarily from boundary-spanning innovations. The process of such change is based on a trial-and-error approach rather than on a self-imposed, intentional redefining of the core mission of policing. However, should these boundary-spanning units prove able to stabilize uncertainties from the external environment, it is predicted that substantial organizational change in American policing will occur as the boundaries of the task environment are redefined. Modification of the technical core and the domain should then follow (see Moore 1992).

This paper does not suggest that implementation of the COP model is always superficial; rather, it is likely that the COP model is evolving slowly where COP innovations have produced positive results. Even so, the development of this philosophical shift is far from what scholars of the change perspective have claimed.

The conclusions to be drawn from this study highlight the complexity inherent in the slow process of organizational change currently under way in American policing. It took approximately 50 years of change before the bureaucratic model crystallized in the 1950s. During this transition, a considerable number of boundary-spanning units appeared and were later institutionalized into American law enforcement practices and police agency structure. The same phenomenon may be occurring again as police organizations try to be more responsive to their external environments. It may take another 30 years for the COP model to be finalized with respect to organizational domain, technical core and task environment. Reiss (1992: 94) observes:

> Yet the rhetoric of contemporary policing characterizes the dilemma of police organizations and administrators at the close of the [20th] century. The dilemma of modern policing seems to lie in determining whether to continue opting for rational bureaucratic administration centering on crime events and their control or, rather, to transform policing in a community and social problem-centered bureaucracy that is accountable to local groups.

More precisely, the findings suggest that little substantial organizational structural change has taken place in American policing in recent years, despite all of the discussion of COP. This means that American policing is likely engaged in a long process of evolution rather than a fast-moving revolution. Although many scholars of policing might say that the direction of change is favorable, it appears to be more creeping incrementalism than decisive advancement.

Note

1. In his book, Thompson uses the term *domain* in a more restrictive sense. In this research, *organizational domain* means an organization's guiding principle and core missions. Furthermore, similar types of organizations may be identified based on their core missions.

Appendix 19.1
Frequency Distribution of Externally Focused Change: COP Programs

	Yes	No
1. Community Newsletter	49.8%	50.2%
2. Foot, horse patrol	88.4%	11.6%
3. Storefront station	41.4%	58.6%
4. Special task unit	91.6%	8.4%
5. Victim contact program	62.8%	37.2%
6. Education of public	98.1%	1.9%
7. Fixed assignment	87.0%	13.0%
8. Citizen survey	62.3%	37.7%
9. Block watch	97.7%	2.3%
10. Business watch	65.1%	34.9%
11. Block meeting	86.5%	13.5%
12. Volunteer program	68.4%	31.6%

N = 215

References

Angell, J. 1971. "Toward an Alternative to the Classic Police Organizational Arrangement: A Democratic Model." *Criminology* 8:185–206.

Bittner, E. 1970. *The Functions of Police in Modern Society.* Washington, D.C.: National Institute of Mental Health.

Brown, L., and M. Wycoff. 1987. "Policing Houston: Reducing Fear and Improving Service." *Crime and Delinquency* 33:71–89.

Burton, V., J. Frank, R. Langworthy, and T. Barker. 1994. "The Prescribed Roles of Police in a Free Society: Analyzing State and Legal Codes." *Justice Quarterly* 10:683–695.

Eck, J., and D. Rosenbaum. 1994. "The New Police Order: Effectiveness, Equity and Efficiency in Community Policing." In D. Rosenbaum (ed.), *The Challenge of Community Policing: Testing the Promises.* Thousand Oaks, Calif.: Sage Publications. Pp. 3–23.

Goldstein, H. 1977. *Policing a Free Society.* Cambridge, Mass.: Ballinger Publishing Co.

——.1987. "Toward Community-Oriented Policing: Potential, Basic Requirements and Threshold Questions." *Crime and Delinquency* 33:6–30.

——. 1990. *Problem-Oriented Policing.* New York: McGraw-Hill.

Greenwood, P., J. Chaiken, and J. Petersilia. 1977. *The Criminal Investigation Process.* Lexington, Mass.: D.C. Heath.

Huber, G., K. Sutcliffe, C. Miller, and W. Glick. 1993. "Understanding and Predicting Organizational Change." In G. Huber and W. Glick (eds.), *Organizational Change and Redesign: Ideas and Insights for Improving Performance.* New York: Oxford University Press.

Kelling, G. 1988. "Police and Community: The Quiet Revolution." *Perspectives on Policing.* No. 1. Washington, D.C.: National Institute of Justice and Harvard University.

Kelling, G., and M. Moore. 1988. "From Political to Reform to Community: The Evolving Strategy of Police." In J. Greene and S. Mastrofski (eds.), *Community Policing: Rhetoric or Reality?* New York: Praeger. Pp. 1–26.

Kelling, G., A. Pate, D. Dieckman, and C. Brown. 1974. *The Kansas City Preventive Patrol Experiment. A Summary Report.* Washington, D.C.: Police Foundation.

Kelling, G., and J. Stewart. 1989. "Neighborhoods and Police: The Maintenance of Civil Authority." *Perspectives on Policing.* No. 1. Washington, D.C.: National Institute of Justice and Harvard University.

Kim, J., and C. Mueller. 1978. *Introduction to Factor Analysis: What It Is and How to Do It.* Beverly Hills, Calif.: Sage Publications.

Klockars, C. 1988. "The Rhetoric of Community Policing." In J. Greene and S. Mastrofski (eds.), *Community Policing: Rhetoric or Reality?* New York: Praeger. Pp. 239–258.

Lane, R. 1992. "Urban Police and Crime in Nineteenth-Century America." In M. Tonry and N. Morris (eds.), *Criminal Justice: A Review of Research.* Vol 15. Chicago: University of Chicago Press. Pp. 1–50.

Lurigio, A., and W. Skogan. 1994. "Winning the Hearts and Minds of Police Officers: An Assessment of Staff Perceptions of Community Policing in Chicago." *Crime and Delinquency* 40:315–330.

Manning, P. 1988. "Community Policing as a Drama of Control." In J. Greene and S. Mastrofski (eds.), *Community Policing: Rhetoric or Reality?* New York: Praeger. Pp. 27–45.

——. 1992. "Information Technologies and the Police." In M. Tonry and N. Morris (eds.), *Criminal Justice: A Review of Research.* Vol. 15. Chicago: University of Chicago Press. Pp. 349–398.

Mastrofski, S. 1988. "Community Policing as Reform: A Cautionary Tale." In J. Greene and S. Mastrofski (eds.), *Community Policing: Rhetoric or Reality?* New York: Praeger. Pp. 47–68.

Meyer, M. 1975. "Organizational Domains." *American Sociological Review* 40:599–615.

Monkkonen, E. 1992. "History of Urban Police." In M. Tonry and N. Morris (eds.), *Criminal Justice: A Review of Research.* Vol. 15. Chicago: University of Chicago Press. Pp. 547–580.

Moore, M. 1992. "Problem Solving and Community Policing." In M. Tonry and N. Morris (eds.), *Criminal Justice: A Review of Research.* Vol. 15. Chicago: University of Chicago Press. Pp. 99–157.

Pfeffer, J. 1982. *Organizations and Organization Theory.* Boston: Pitman.

Reiss, A. 1992. "Police Organization in the Twentieth Century." In M. Tonry and N. Morris (eds.), *Criminal Justice: A Review of Research.* Vol. 15.

Chicago: University of Chicago Press. Pp. 51–97.

Riechers, L., and R. Roberg. 1990. "Community Policing: A Critical Review of Underlying Assumptions." *Journal of Police Science and Administration* 17:105–114.

Roberg, R. 1994. "Can Today's Police Organizations Effectively Implement Community Policing?" In D. Rosenbaum (ed.), *The Challenge of Community Policing: Testing the Promises.* Thousand Oaks, Calif.: Sage Publications. Pp. 249–257.

Rosenbaum, D., S. Yeh, and D. Wilkinson. 1994. "Impact of Community Policing on Police Personnel: A Quasi-Experimental Test." *Crime and Delinquency* 40:331–353.

Sadd, S., and R. Grinc. 1994. "Innovative Neighborhood-Oriented Policing: An Evaluation of Community Policing Programs in Eight Cities." In D. Rosenbaum (ed.), *The Challenge of Community Policing: Testing the Promises.* Thousand Oaks, Calif.: Sage Publications. Pp. 27–52.

Sherman, L. 1993. "Why Crime Control Is Not Reactionary." In D. Weisburd and C. Uchida (eds.), *Police Innovation and Control of the Police: Problems of Law, Order and Community.* New York: Springer-Verlag. Pp. 171–189.

Skogan, W. 1990. *Disorder and Decline: Crime and the Spiral of Decay in American Neighborhoods.* Berkeley, Calif.: University of California Press.

Skolnick, J., and D. Bayley. 1986. *The New Blue Line: Police Innovations in Six American Cities.* New York: The Free Press.

Sykes, G. 1986. "Street Justice: A Moral Defense of Order Maintenance Policing." *Justice Quarterly* 3:497–516.

Thompson, J. 1967. *Organizations in Action.* New York: McGraw-Hill.

Trojanowicz, R., and B. Bucqueroux. 1990. *Community Policing: A Contemporary Perspective.* Cincinnati: Anderson Publishing Co.

United States. 1967. *President's Commission on Law Enforcement and Administration of Justice: The Challenge of Crime in a Free Society.* Washington, D.C.: U.S. Government Printing Office.

Vollmer, A. 1936. *The Police and Modern Society.* Berkeley, Calif.: University of California Press.

Walker, S. 1977. *A Critical History of Police Reform.* Lexington, Mass.: D.C. Heath.

——. 1980. *Popular Justice: A History of American Criminal Justice.* New York: Oxford University Press.

——. 1983. *The Police in America: An Introduction.* New York: McGraw-Hill.

Wasserman, R., and M. Moore. 1988. "Values in Policing." *Perspectives on Policing.* No. 8. Washington, D.C.: National Institute of Justice and Harvard University.

Weisburd, D., J. McElroy, and P. Hardyman. 1988. "Challenges to Supervision in Community Policing: Observations on a Pilot Project." *American Journal of Police* 7:29–50.

Weisel, D., and J. Eck. 1994. "Toward a Practical Approach to Organizational Change: Community Policing Initiatives in Six Cities." In D. Rosenbaum (ed.), *The Challenge of Community Policing: Testing the Promises.* Thousand Oaks, Calif.: Sage Publications. Pp. 53–72.

Wilson, J. 1968. *Varieties of Police Behavior. The Management of Law and Order in Eight Communities.* Cambridge, Mass.: Harvard University Press.

Wilson, J., and G. Kelling. 1982. "The Police and Neighborhood Safety: Broken Windows." *Atlantic Monthly* 249:29–38.

Wilson, O.W. 1950. *Police Administration.* New York: McGraw-Hill.

Zhao, J., C. Simon, and Q. Thurman. 1994. "The Impact of Internal Organizational Factors on Contemporary Organizational Change in American Policing." Paper presented at the 1994 annual meeting of the Academy of Criminal Justice Sciences, Chicago.

Jihong Zhao and Quint C. Thurman, "The Nature of Community Policing Innovations: Do the Ends Justify the Means?" Copyright © 1996 Police Executive Research Forum. Reproduced with permission. ✦

Chapter 20
Problem-Oriented Criminal Investigation

Brian Forst[1]

B*rian Forst argues for the inclusion of problem-solving approaches in criminal investigations. The reader might recall from a previous chapter that problem-oriented policing (POP) is widely regarded as one of the most significant recent contributions to contemporary policing. Proponents of POP assert that crime incidents are actually symptoms of greater problems, such as underlying social disorder. In contrast, traditional policing focuses on the surface of problems (e.g., crime incident), while ignoring the root causes of crime.*

Forst argues that police detectives should also use problem-solving techniques to help them identify and then solve patterns of problems. By tradition, detective work is reactive in nature. That is, a police investigator is assigned to a particular case and then goes about its resolution until it can be solved or until he or she must abandon it. While each criminal case has its own unique elements, Forst argues that a problem-solving approach can be useful in criminal investigations to help understand patterns of criminal activity so that future patterns may be identified proactively.

> Fortunately, it is not necessary to surround creativity with mystery and obfuscation. No sparks of genius need be postulated to account for human invention, discovery, creation. These acts are acts of the human brain, the same brain that helps us dress in the morning, arrive at our office, and go through our daily chores, however uncreative most of these chores may be. Today we have a substantial body of empirical evidence about the processes that people use to think and to solve problems, and evidence, as well, that these same processes can account for the thinking and problem solving that is adjudged creative.
>
> —Herbert A. Simon (1985: 4)

Introduction

Although the central role of criminal investigators is to solve crimes that have already occurred, many of the day-to-day problems confronting criminal investigators can be alleviated through more conscious investments in identifying and solving *patterns* of problems. Problem-oriented policing has changed much about how police think about and do their work toward this end, but it has been applied primarily as a strategy for patrol operations. Some criminal investigation problems that lend themselves to this strategy are unique to particular settings, and some are common to criminal investigation generally. Specific areas of opportunity for substantial improvement in problem-oriented investigation include collaboration with patrol officers, shift of focus from offenses to offenders and locations, and a more coherent use of modus operandi files and related data sources. This chapter explores the application of problem identification and problem solving tools to these and other issues in criminal investigation.

The problem-oriented approach is one of the most significant strategies in contemporary policing. Defined in 1979 by Herman Goldstein,[2] problem-oriented policing aims to shift from a predominantly reactive mode of policing to a more preventive mode that identifies problems that often lead to crime, fear of crime and dissatisfaction with police, and nips them in the bud before they blossom into criminal episodes to which police must later react.[3] Crime hot spots and neighborhoods experiencing disorder and decline are examples of environments that lend themselves to problem-oriented policing strategies.

Such a focus on crime prevention is neither new nor revolutionary. Municipal police departments in the United States routinely handled problems of public health and disorder in the 19th century. The Reform Era of the early 20th century and the Professional Era of the mid-20th century effectively put an end to such preventive activity, focusing instead on random patrols designed to respond rapidly to calls for service and catch crimes in progress. Following the crime explosion of the 1960s and research that revealed that random patrols were not as effective in preventing crime as had been widely assumed throughout most of the 20th century, police departments in Madison, Wis., Newport News, Va., Baltimore County, Md., and elsewhere began experimenting successfully in the 1980s and 1990s with programs designed to take a more proactive position to identify and solve problems in high-crime areas.[4]

While each "problem" has its unique elements, calling for any of several solutions drawn from a wide variety of options, the problem-oriented approach has identifiable stages that characterize virtually every application. Each stage is conducted with a distinct purpose:[5]

1. *Define problems* specifically, so that they can be clearly understood and communicated to others.
2. *Collect information* both from within and outside the usual department sources.
3. Engage in a broad *search for solutions.*

Relevance to Criminal Investigation

The application of preventive, problem-oriented approaches to criminal investigation is inherently limited. Criminal investigation is, after all, primarily about solving crimes that have already occurred. The investigator gets involved typically after preventive policing strategies have already failed. Moreover, the investigator responds to a single incident, while "problems" in problem-oriented policing are clusters of related incidents, not single incidents (Goldstein 1990: 66).

Nonetheless, the stages noted above—problem identification, data collection and problem solving—apply to most investigations as well. An unsolved crime is a problem, one that prior research has found depends for a solution more on whether the victims and witnesses identify the offenders, than on keen powers of detective reasoning and intuition, or cutting-edge forensic analysis (Greenwood et al. 1975). By investing generally in the building of closer ties with the community, the police can encourage critical sources of information to come forth when they are needed to help in solving particular crimes. Problem-solving processes are called for, moreover, to reveal *patterns* of crime, so that future crimes that follow such patterns can be prevented.

In the natural course of conducting a long series of investigations, detectives become aware of patterns that may provide opportunities for crime prevention. Such patterns can often be more quickly and sharply identified through crime analysis, the process of identifying and describing trends and patterns in the commission of crimes based on analysis of data (Reuland 1997; Reinier et al. 1977). Of particular interest in crime analysis are the following questions: *Where* have particular kinds of crimes been occurring? *When* have they been occurring—at particular times of day, day of week or month, season of the year, or under particular sets of circumstances? What specific *similarities* and *dissimilarities* exist among crimes that have been occurring at crime "hot spots"? Which of the similarities suggest a particular offender or group of offenders? What do similarities among or patterns about the victims suggest? For example, is the same type of vehicle being broken into? Are elderly people being targeted? Who might have additional information regarding these patterns—information that could solve the crime or lead to a solution? While the patterns unearthed by addressing such questions may occasionally be distinct enough to permit predictions of specific crime occurrences, they are more likely only to suggest areas that should be closely monitored at certain times.

John Eck has described instances of detectives taking such a larger view of investigative work. One example is that of a detective in Newport News, Va., who speculated that half of the homicides in that city (those following domestic disputes) may be preventable through more effective early intervention strategies. By bringing together local experts in the field of domestic violence to review current procedures and explore opportunities for more effective intervention, the detective helped to develop a new program that forced targeted couples into mandatory counseling (Eck 1996).

Specific data sources can be especially useful in crime analysis. Crime reports give basic information about the category of crime, time and place of occurrence, and the victim. Dispatch records provide basic data about the response to each reported incident to which a unit or units were sent. Activity summaries supply information about what was observed at the scene, names of witnesses and suspicious persons, and dispositions of each matter. Modus operandi files, used to help solve new crimes, furnish information about commonalities among crimes, both those committed by specific offenders known to the department and those committed by unidentified offenders. These various data sources typically vary in degrees of computer readability and reliability, depending on the department.

Some jurisdictions have developed their own unique data systems useful for supporting crime analysis. The state of Washington created a system in 1990 to assist in solving homicides: the Homicide Investigation and Tracking System (HITS). Allowing for as many as 250 data elements in a single record, the system documents information about victims, crime scene details and persons arrested for the crime (Keppel and Weis 1993).

Because a problem-oriented approach is more generalized than the by-the-book approach common in policing, it has implications for a different set of management conventions. It calls, first, for a more decentralized decision-making authority. Investigators and patrol officers cannot be expected to find creative solutions to problems when they must obtain approval from a supervisor at each and every decision point. For major decisions, approval will be needed, which suggests a second requirement: a problem-oriented strategy requires training and policy guidance of mid-managers so that they can respond effectively to questions from less senior personnel.

Perhaps most important, a problem-oriented approach entails risks. It requires that management be willing to experience occasional failures—especially personnel time spent on activities that yield no apparent results—to prevent future crimes. When an officer's, detective's, or unit's occasional failures outweigh the value associated with problems identified and solved over a period of months, it becomes appropriate to review the specific problem-solving objectives and procedures employed by the individual or unit. Such a review may turn up any of several possible flaws: inadequate training in problem solving, objectives that do not contribute significantly to the larger goals of the unit, insufficient use of available information sources, or simply lack of commitment to the approach, sometimes to an extent that "problem solving" is used as a ruse for malingering.

When problem solving or crime analysis unearths problems or patterns that may be endemic to the larger community, it is important that the insights be disseminated (by way of internal memoranda, bulletins, and "hot sheets," with maps) to other individuals and units who may be able to use the information. Resources may be reallocated, decoys and stings may be established, targets may be hardened, and decisions and policies may be reconsidered in the light of such information.

Specific areas of opportunity for substantial improvement in problem-oriented investigation include collaboration with patrol officers and others, shifts of focus from offenses to offenders and locations, and a more coherent usage of modus operandi files and related data sources. Each of these areas is addressed in turn below.

Improved Coordination

Detectives almost never solve crimes without help from others. They typically receive a case from the patrol officer who conducted a preliminary investigation at the crime scene. They often work with officers from other jurisdictions to exchange information about suspects in a case or series of cases. They work closely with patrol officers assigned to the beats in which the crime occurred to obtain information from other informed sources in the area—information that often turns out to be the difference between a solved and an unsolved crime.

Coordination has become critically important in most contemporary settings. Communities have turned increasingly to private solutions to crime prevention, and for serious commercial and residential crimes, police investigators must work effectively with private security agents for information leading to solved crimes, and to the prevention of future crimes. Community policing strategies also call for increased coordination with public and private institutions (social service agencies, churches, public utilities, and so on) to solve crimes, aid victims and prevent future crimes. Patrol officers often perform many of these coordinating activities, but investigators cannot always leave these matters for patrol officers to do alone.

Coordination begins with effective communication. Communication is sometimes formal and sometimes informal. Formal communication is preferable in a variety of circumstances: when important information needs to be given precisely and systematically, when the information needs to be preserved, or when sensitive information cannot be effectively presented in person, for example, because it may be easily distorted or misunderstood. Informal communication is more in order when flexibility is needed, when real meanings must be conveyed that are not clear in formal modes, when formal modes are too costly, or when a personal touch is needed to stimulate unity.

Effective communication serves a multitude of purposes. It informs and educates, providing essential information clearly. It serves to unite, often by resolving controversy and facilitating the redress of grievances. It motivates by showing respect and assurance, avoiding threats, soliciting ideas, giving reasons behind directives and basic information, and by listening as well as transmitting information. It can improve operations by stimulating useful feedback information and cooperation.

Detectives can, in short, more accurately identify problems, obtain better information about them, and develop more effective solution strategies by improving their coordination with others who have information and insights about the problems.

Shift in Focus from Offenses to Offenders and Locations

Case-oriented investigation is the traditional reactive method of handling an unsolved crime. Usually the result of a patrol officer's response to a call for service, the investigation's magnitude is determined primarily by the gravity of the offense rather than the dangerousness of the suspect or the relationship between the current crime and other matters of concern in the area. Serious crimes generally lend themselves to case-oriented investigation.

Case-oriented investigations do not ignore offender information or information about problems in the area that may be related. Information about offenders and related problems can help lead to the crime's solution and the offender's arrest Those matters, however, are not the primary information goals of case-oriented investigation. They are subordinated to the primary goal of case-oriented investigation: obtain information to solve a single crime. Thus, the focus of case-oriented investigation is on the physical evidence, information provided by victims and witnesses about suspects, information about a suspect's vehicle, the recovery of stolen property, and modus operandi information that can lead to a solution of the crime.

Case-oriented investigations are often required even in environments that make full use of preventive strategies. Such investigations can, in any case, employ modern methods of crime solving, including the use of *solvability factors* to focus resources on the most effective aspects of the case (Greenwood et al. 1975).

Offender-oriented investigations focus on people who are known to have committed specific crimes and may be suspected of having committed several others in the area. This tactic is more proactive than the case-oriented strategy, it anticipates and heads off new crimes by targeting resources on people who have already established themselves as offenders. The basic concept of an offender-oriented approach derives from a widely observed finding that a few offenders are responsible for a disproportionate number of crimes, and that investigative resources can be more productively applied to cases involving those offenders than to cases involving the less frequent and less dangerous offender.[6]

Investigators have long appreciated the value of offender-oriented investigation. The Federal Bureau of Investigation, following Henry Fielding's published descriptions of wanted persons in *The Covent Garden Journal* and Allan Pinkerton's publication of a "rogues' gallery" of offenders, created its list of "Ten Most Wanted" in the United States in the 1930s. Several local police departments followed suit.[7] Even prosecutors set up programs focusing on repeat offenders and major violators in the 1970s.[8] While some of those lists and programs targeted offenders who had been put there primarily because of the nature of a single crime rather than a series of crimes, the strategies were nonetheless offender-based rather than offense-based.

National data bases such as that maintained by the National Criminal Information Center (NCIC) can be especially helpful in supporting offender-based investigation strategies. The Violent Criminal Apprehension Program (VICAP) is a national program run by the FBI to link homicide cases committed by the same offender (Green and Whitmore 1993). Systems such as California's CAL-ID and the Automated Wants and Warrants System (AWWS), and Michigan's Law Enforcement Information Network (LEIN) provide somewhat comparable offender-based information at the state level. Effective offender-based systems are typically automated, with fingerprint data, criminal history records, and information about crime locations, stolen property, license registration, and DNA patterns of convicted sex offenders (Reaves 1995).

More Coherent Use of Modus Operandi Files and Related Data Sources

Well-designed and carefully maintained modus operandi (MO) files often prove useful as well. Modus operandi files provide information about the method of operation of suspects associated with particular cases: method of entry, tools and weapons used, victim characteristics and behaviors, crime scene condition and so on.

Although the use of MO files appears to vary substantially from department to department, they can be used to identify offenders in new cases, sometimes by linking characteristics of the new cases to patterns that show up in prior solved cases. The files can be used also to link new cases to patterns that show up in prior unsolved cases, providing opportunities to combine information from different crimes to build a stronger basis for solving a series of crimes committed by a single offender. Such linkages can be used to set up surveillance and undercover operations to catch the offender in a subsequent crime, or to prevent further crimes by increasing security for victims or targets that fit the prior patterns.

Conclusion: Taking Greater Advantage of Problem-Oriented Investigation Opportunities

Problem-oriented strategies can be used to improve contemporary criminal investigation in several ways. One is to expand effective collaborations both within police departments, by investigators working more effectively with patrol officers, and also with investigators and officers in other law enforcement agencies. This involves not only more effective personal outreach to break down artificial territorial boundaries within and between departments, but improvements in data-sharing technologies and activities as well. Offenders who commit crimes in several different jurisdictions pose substantial problems across the map. They often evade capture due to failures of different jurisdictions to coordinate with one another and share data. Problems confronted by investigators in several places can be solved simultaneously by improving the flow of information from department to department.

Another way to expand problem-oriented investigation opportunities is to improve the quality of information contained in existing data systems, including MO files. Modus operandi files could be improved through standardized data and organization of information, and systematic procedures for correcting and updating the data. Recent estimates suggest that the likelihood that an offender in a new case had been arrested previously (hence should be in the MO file) is considerably higher than is widely understood, and it rises substantially with increases in the probability of arrest and the average number of offenses in a criminal career.[9] Improving MO files could have a multiplier effect: better MO files could induce increases in solution rates, increasing the probability of arrest, which could turn induce victims to report crimes at a higher rate, thus providing still greater increases in the likelihood that the offender in a new case will be apprehended.

Criminal investigators are generally less visible to the public than are patrol officers. Their lower profile status may allow them to focus more on solving crimes, but it may also tend to produce insularity, reducing incentives to build closer relationships with the community, as has become more common in patrol operations employing community- and problem-oriented policing strategies. Aspects of crime solving may be inherently more reactive than preventive, but problem-oriented policing is only superficially more relevant to patrol operations than to detective work. Investigators and patrol officers alike are bound to improve their performance by combining a focus on offenses with one on offenders and locations.

By combining traditional crime-solving methods with conscious investments in the identification and solution of *patterns* of problems that lie beneath the surface of one apparently unrelated case-oriented investigation after another, the thoughtful investigator and effective investigative unit can improve their ability to not only solve crimes, but to prevent them as well.

Notes

1. The author wishes to thank John Eck, Michael Planty and Ross Swope for their helpful comments on an earlier draft.
2. Goldstein's 1979 article in *Crime and Delinquency* was substantially expanded and updated in a 1990 book.
3. Goldstein (1990) defines a problem in policing as a cluster of similar, related or recurring incidents, a substantive community concern, or a unit of police work.
4. George L. Kelling et al. (1974) document the failure of a random patrol strategy in Kansas City in the 1970s. Eck and Spelman (1987) document successes with problem-oriented policing strategies in Newport News and Baltimore in the 1980s. The 1987 Baltimore County experiment is described by Taft (1986).
5. Eck and Spelman (1987) have identified four steps to the problem-solving process: 1) *scan-*

ning, to identify the problem; 2) *analysis,* to learn about the causes, scope and effects of the problem; 3) *response,* to act toward a solution to the problem; and 4) *assessment,* to establish whether the response was effective.

6. In 1972, researchers at the University of Pennsylvania reported that 18 percent of all boys born in Philadelphia in 1945 accounted for 52 percent of all the offenses known to have been committed by the group (Wolfgang et al. 1972). Similar results were found by the University of Pennsylvania team in a replication of the earlier research using the 1958 cohort of all children born in Philadelphia (Wolfgang 1980). Comparable findings of disproportionality were obtained in a longitudinal study of offenders in London (Farrington 1983), and in a study of offenders arrested in the District of Columbia during the period 1971–75 (Williams 1979).
7. A noteworthy example is the Washington, D.C., Repeat Offender Program (ROP), created in the 1980s. Police Foundation researchers found that the number of offenders sentenced to prison increased substantially when targeted by ROP (Martin and Sherman 1986).
8. The federal government created a program in 1975 that provided financial support to local-level "career criminal" prosecution programs. (Forst 1995, pp. 372–3)
9. Using current population, arrest rate and offending estimates from the Uniform Crime Reports, National Crime Victimization Survey and offender self-report data, the likelihood is about 55 percent that the offender in a new stranger rape case was previously arrested for the same offense (Forst and Planty 1997).

References

Eck, J. 1996. Rethinking Detective Management. In *Quantifying Quality in Policing,* edited by L. T. Hoover. Washington, D.C.: Police Executive Research Forum.

Eck, J., and W. Spelman. 1987. Who Ya Gonna Call? The Police as Problem-Busters. *Crime and Delinquency* 25:31–52.

Farrington, D.P. 1983. *Further Analyses of A Longitudinal Survey of Crime and Delinquency.* Washington, D.C.: National Institute of Justice.

Forst, B.1995. Prosecution and Sentencing. In *Crime,* edited by J.Q. Wilson and J. Petersilia. San Francisco: Institute for Contemporary Studies.

Forst, B., and M. Planty. 1997. *Investigating Crime: The Utility and Coverage of Modus Operandi Files.* Paper delivered at the 49th annual meeting of the American Society of Criminology, San Diego, November 1997.

Goldstein, H. 1979. Improving Policing: A Problem-Oriented Approach. Crime and *Delinquency* 25:236–58.

Goldstein, H. 1990. *Problem-Oriented Policing.* New York: McGraw-Hill.

Green, T. J., and J. E. Whitmore. 1993. VICAP's Role in Multiagency Serial Murder Investigations. *The Police Chief* 60 (June):38–45.

Greenwood, P., J. M. Chaiken, J. Petersilia, and L. Prusoff. 1975. *The Criminal Investigation Process.* Santa Monica: Rand Corporation.

Kelling G. L., A. Pate, D. Dieckman, and C. E. Brown. 1974. *The Kansas City Preventive Patrol Experiment: A Summary Report.* Washington, D.C.: Police Foundation.

Keppel, R. D., and J.G. Weis. 1993. *Improving the Investigation of Violent Crime: The Homicide Investigation and Tracking System.* National Institute of Justice Research in Brief. Washington, D.C.: U.S. Department of Justice.

Martin, S. E., and L. W. Sherman. 1986. Selective Apprehension: A Police Strategy for Repeat Offenders. *Criminology* 25:155–73.

Reaves B. A.,1995. *Law Enforcement Management and Administrative Statistics.* Washington, D.C.: U.S. Department of justice, Bureau of Justice Statistics. Pp. 169–80.

Reinier, G. H., T. J. Sweeney, R. V. Waymire, R. A. Newton III, R. G. Grassie, S. M. White, and W.D. Wallace 1977. *Integrated Criminal Apprehension Program: Crime Analysis Operations Manual.* Washington, D.C.: Law Enforcement Assistance Administration.

Reuland, M. M. (ed.). 1997. *Information Management and Crime Analysis.* Washington, D.C.: Police Executive Research Forum.

Simon, H. A. 1985. What We Know About the Creative Process. In *Frontiers in Creative and Innovative Management,* edited by R.L. Kuhn. Cambridge, Mass.: Ballinger.

Taft, P. B., Jr. 1986. *Fighting Fear: The Baltimore County COPE Project.* Washington, D.C.: Police Executive Research Forum.

Williams, K. 1979. *The Scope and Prediction of Recidivism.* Washington, D.C.: Institute for Law and Social Research.

Wolfgang, M. E. 1980. Some New Findings from the Longitudinal Study of Crime. *Australian Journal of Forensic Science* 13:12–29.

Wolfgang, M. E., R. M. Figlio, and T. Sellin. 1972. *Delinquency in a Birth Cohort.* Chicago: University of Chicago Press.

Brian Forst, "Problem-Oriented Criminal Investigation." Reprinted from T. Shelley and A. Grant (Eds.), *Problem-Oriented Policing*, pp. 399–412. Copyright © 1998 Police Executive Research Forum. Reproduced with permission. ✦

Chapter 21
Geographic Profiling

D. Kim Rossmo

Since the early 1990s, large police agencies have tried to incorporate promising modern technologies that have policing applications. The well-known stories of applying modern technology to police work include computerized crime mapping techniques that rely on sophisticated computer software and data mining procedures to describe and analyze crime incidents in specific geographic locations. Computerized crime mapping is capable of helping police organizations examine seemingly unrelated relationships among crime incidents in order to identify patterns.

Rossmo introduces the reader to a particularly innovative approach to managing crucial information that will help criminal investigators successfully solve serial violent crimes. Geographic profiling is a relatively new innovation that melds environmental criminological theory with a practical application to help investigators determine a geographically based pattern of criminal victimization. Once established, this pattern can then be used along with other information to develop probability models for determining the location of a serial offender's base of operations.

Introduction

When the throat of Victorian prostitute Polly Nichols was slashed in Buck's Row on August Bank Holiday, 1888, horrified London newspapers warned of a 'reign of terror' (Rumbelow, 1988). Jack the Ripper was certainly not the first or last of his type, but the unsolved mystery of the Whitechapel murders still symbolizes our lack of understanding of such dangerous predators. Equally important, the very nature of their crimes makes these criminals difficult and challenging to apprehend.

One of the most problematic aspects of predatory violent crime is the volume of tips and suspects generated through their investigation. Traditional police methods are not always sufficient and detectives need alternative tactics to assist them in these types of cases. Geographic profiling, a strategic information management system designed to support investigative efforts in cases of serial murder, rape and arson, is one such approach.

Investigative Difficulties

> For heaven's sake catch me before I kill more. I cannot control myself. (Message written in lipstick on the living room wall of Frances Brown, victim of serial murderer William Heirens; Kennedy, 1991)

The investigation of serial violent and sexual crime is complex and difficult. Most murders are solved because they involve intimates and the search for the offender begins with the victim's family, friends and acquaintances. There is no such victim-offender relationship, however, in stranger sexual crime.

The police must therefore delineate likely groups of potential suspects, a process referred to as 'framing' (Kind, 1987) or establishing the circle of investigation (Skogan & Antunes, 1979). Such an effort typically involves the inspection of those parties with relevant criminal or psychiatric records, the accumulation of intelligence and the collection of suspect tips from members of the public. Because these investigative efforts can produce large numbers of potential suspects, often totaling into the hundreds and even thousands, problems with information overload usually develop.

> Although a modern police force can fill rooms with details of possible suspects, they still have the enormous problem of finding the vicious needle in their haystack of paper. (Canter, 1994)

The still unsolved Green River Killer case in Seattle, Washington, involved the murder of 49 prostitutes. To date the police have only had the resources to investigate two-thirds of the 18,000 names in their suspect files (Montgomery, 1993). Detectives have gathered 8,000 tangible items of evidence from the crime scenes and a single television special on the case generated 3,500 tips. In Britain, the nationwide search for the Staffordshire serial murderer amassed details on 185,000 people over the course of 11 years before the child-killer was finally caught (Canter, 1994).

The Narborough Murder Enquiry, a massive four-year manhunt, obtained close to 4,000 blood samples for DNA testing prior to eventually charging Colin Pitchfork with the deaths of two teenage girls (Canter, 1994; Wambaugh, 1989). The Yorkshire Ripper inquiry accumulated 268,000 names, visited 27,000 houses, and recorded 5,400,000 vehicle registration numbers (Doney, 1990; Nicholson, 1979).

A corollary to the problem of information overload is the high cost associated with any extensive, long-term investigation. The final tally for the Atlanta Child Murders case was more than $9 million (Dettlinger & Prugh, 1983), while the Yorkshire Ripper inquiry cost an estimated £4 million (Doney, 1990). The Green River Task Force has so far accumulated expenses of approximately $20 million (Montgomery, 1993).

It is important for police detectives to know which crimes are connected so that information between related cases can be collated and compared. An inability to recognize connections and confusion over which crimes should form part of a series has occurred in several investigations. This problem has been termed 'linkage blindness' (Egger, 1984).

Several other investigative difficulties exist that complicate efforts to connect linked crimes and to identify and apprehend serial killers, rapists and arsonists (Egger, 1990; Holmes & De Burger, 1988; James, 1991; O'Reilly-Fleming, 1992). Such problems include: (a) the learning process inherent in serial offending; (b) false confessions; (c) copycat crimes; (d) public fear, media interest and political pressure; (e) personnel logistics; (f) multiple agency coordination; and (g) resource and cost issues.

Geographic Profiling

Several investigative approaches to these problems have been developed by police agencies, including psychological profiling and computerized crime linkage analysis systems (Copson, 1995; Johnson, 1994). Geographic profiling is an information management strategy designed to support serial violent crime investigation (Rossmo, 1995a). This service is provided by the Vancouver Police Department's Geographic Profiling Section to police forces and prosecuting offices (MacKay, 1994; Thompson, 1996). The first such profile was prepared in 1990 and to date, requests have come from a variety of federal, provincial, state and local law enforcement agencies across North America and Europe, including the Royal Canadian Mounted Police (RCMP), the Federal Bureau of Investigation (FBI), and New Scotland Yard. The cases have involved crimes of serial murder, serial rape and sexual assault, serial arson, bombings, bank robbery, sexual homicide and kidnapping.

The location of a crime site can be seen as an important clue, one that can provide valuable information to police investigators. Geographic profiling focuses on the probable spatial behavior of the offender within the context of the locations of, and the spatial relationships between, the various crime sites. A psychological profile provides insight into an offender's likely motivation, behavior and lifestyle, and is therefore directly connected to his/her spatial activity. Psychological and geographic profiles thus act in tandem to help investigators develop a *picture* of the person responsible for the crimes in question. It should be noted that not all types of offenders or categories of crime can be geographically profiled. In appropriate cases, however, such a spatial analysis can produce practical results.

A psychological profile is not a necessary precursor for a geographic profile, although the insights it may provide can be quite useful, particularly in cases involving a small number of offences. Geographic profiling has both quantitative (objective) and qualitative (subjective) components. The objective component uses a series of scientific geographic techniques and quantitative measures to analyze and interpret the point pattern created from the locations of the target sites. The subjective component of geographic profiling is based primarily on a reconstruction and interpretation of the offender's mental map.

The main quantitative technique used in geographic profiling is a computerized process termed criminal geographic targeting (CGT) (Rossmo, 1993, 1995b). By examining the spatial information associated with a series of crime sites, the CGT model produces a three-dimensional probability distribution termed a 'jeopardy surface,' the 'height' of which at any point represents the likelihood of offender residence or workplace.... The jeopardy surface is then superimposed on a street map of the areas of the crimes . . . ; such maps are termed 'geoprofiles' and use a range of colors to represent varying probabilities. A geoprofile can be thought of as a fingerprint of the offender's cognitive map.

The system's underlying algorithm was developed from research conducted at Simon Fraser University in the area of environmental criminology (Rossmo, 1995e). The process relies on the model of crime site selection proposed by Brantingham and Brantingham (1981), and is also informed by Cohen & Felson's (1979) routine activities approach. The CGT algorithm employs a distance-decay function $f(d)$ that simulates journey to crime behavior. Each point (x,y) located at distance d from crime site i, is assigned a probability value $f(di)$. A final value for point (x,y), representing the likelihood of offender residence, is determined by summing the N values for the point produced from the N different crime sites—the more locations, the better the performance.

By establishing the probability of the offender residing in various areas and displaying those results on a map, police efforts to apprehend criminals can be assisted. This information allows police departments to focus their investigative activities, geographically prioritize suspects, and concentrate patrol efforts in those zones where the criminal predator is most likely to be active.

The Profiling Process

A geographic profile fits into a typical criminal investigation in the following sequence.

1. Occurrence of a crime series.
2. Employment of traditional investigative techniques.
3. Linkage analysis determining which crimes connected.
4. Preparation of a psychological profile.
5. Construction of a geographic profile.
6. Development of new investigative strategies.

The preparation of a geographic profile involves the following operational procedure: (a) examination of the case file, including investigation reports, witness statements, autopsy reports and, if available, the psychological profile; (b) inspection of crime scene and area photographs; (c) discussions with investigators and crime analysts; (d) visits to the crime sites when possible; (e) analysis of neighborhood crime statistics and demographic data; (f) study of street, zoning and rapid transit maps; (g) analysis; and (h) report writing (Holmes & Rossmo, 1996).

In addition to the offence locations and times involved in a crime series, some of the other elements that need to be considered in the construction of a geographic profile include crime location type, target backcloth, and offender hunting style. These three considerations are the most important and are discussed in detail below. Other factors include location of arterial roads and highways, presence of bus stops and rapid transit stations, physical and psychological boundaries, zoning and land use, neighborhood demographics, routine activities of victims, and displacement.

Crime Locations

Most of the geography of crime literature treats the concept of crime site as a single location. Depending upon the type of crime, however, there may be various locations connected to a single offence. Each of these has a potentially different meaning to the offender and, consequently, distinctive choice properties (Newton & Swoope, 1987; Ressler & Shachtman, 1992). In homicide, for example, such location types include (a) victim encounter, (b) attack, (c) murder, and (d) body dump sites. While these particular actions could all occur at one place, in many cases they are divided up between two or more different locations.

Eight possible crime location sets can result from combinations of these four different crime site types. For example, Canadian sex killer Paul Bernardo encountered and attacked his victims on the street, strangled them in his home, and then dumped their bodies at remote sites (Burnside & Cairns, 1995; Pron, 1996). The specific location set for a given crime is a function of victim selection and encounter site characteristics, but it also implies something about the offender, how he/she searches for victims, and the associated level of organization and mobility. Generally, the greater the organization and mobility of the offender, the greater the potential complexity (i.e. the more separate locations) of the crime location set. Research has also shown a high level of consistency in the geographic modus operandi of serial offenders, as most repeatedly employ the same crime location set (Rossmo, 1995a). This implies that the concept of crime location set could be used as an assessment characteristic for the linking of serial offences.[1]

While all crime scene types are important in the construction of a geographic profile, every site type may not possess an equal degree of relevance in all cases. Some locations, particularly in homicides, are not known to investigating police officers. Prior to the apprehension of the offender, these places can only be determined through evidence recovery or witness statements. In a typical unsolved homicide the police know the body dump site (which may or may not be the murder scene) and the place where the victim was last seen. In some circumstances, they may only know one of these locations.

Target Backcloth

Brantingham & Brantingham (1991) suggest that the structure of the target or victim backcloth is important for an understanding of the geometric arrangement of crime sites. The target backcloth is equivalent to the spatial opportunity structure. It is configured by both geographic and temporal distributions of *suitable*—as seen from the offender's perspective—crime targets or victims across the physical landscape. The availability of such targets might vary significantly according to neighborhood, area or even city, and can also be influenced by time, day of week and season (Brantingham & Brantingham, 1984).

Because victim location and availability play key roles in the determination of where offences occur, non-uniform or 'patchy' target distributions can distort the spatial pattern of crime sites. Victim selections that are non-random, or based on specific and rare traits, will require more searching on the part of the offender than those that are random, non-specific and common (Canter, 1994; Davies & Dale, 1996; Holmes & De Burger, 1988). For example, if an arsonist prefers to select warehouses as targets, their availability and distribution, geographically determined by city zoning bylaws, will have a strong influence on where the crimes occur. If the arsonist has no preferences, then the target backcloth will probably be more uniform as houses and buildings abound, at least in urban areas. The target sites of a predator who seeks out prostitutes will be determined primarily by the locations of *hooker strolls,* while the attack sites of an offender who is less specific could well be found anywhere.

A uniform victim spatial distribution means that the locations of the crimes will be primarily influenced by the offender's activity space; otherwise, crime geography is more closely related to the target backcloth. In the extreme cases of an arsonist for hire or a contract killer, victim location totally determines crime site. The consideration of victim characteristics thus plays an important role in the development of an accurate geographic profile.

The target backcloth is influenced by both the natural and built physical environments as these affect where people live. Housing development is determined by such factors as physical topography, highway networks, national boundaries, city limits, land use and zoning regulations. The Werewolf Rapist, Jose Rodrigues, lived in Bexhill on the south coast of England during his series of 16 sexual assaults. With no potential victims situated in the English Channel to the south, he was forced to confine his attacks to locations north of his residence, resulting in a distorted target pattern. Such problems could be compensated for through the appropriate topological transformation of the physical space within and surrounding the offender's hunting area.

Hunting Typology

> Throughout accounts of serial murders run themes of adventurous risk in the stalking of human prey by stealth or deception, the excitement of the kill. . . . The egoism of the hunter permits the degradation of potential victims to the level of wild game. The planning, excitement, and thrill of the hunt overrides all other considerations except eluding capture. (Green, 1993)

Predatory criminals employ various hunting styles in their efforts to seek out and attack victims. These, in turn, affect the spatial distribution of the offender's crime sites, suggesting that any effort to predict offender residence from crime locations must consider hunting style. It was therefore important to ascertain those methods of hunting that produce target patterns inappropriate for this type of spatial analysis. Previous classifications of serial crime geography have only been descriptive of the final spatial pattern and not of the processes that produced those outcomes. It was therefore necessary to develop a hunting typology relevant to serial offenders. While this scheme was constructed from an exploratory data analysis of serial murderers, it is informed by the geography of crime theory and is applicable, for the purposes of geographic profiling, to certain other types of predatory crime.

While a murder can potentially involve several different types of crime locations, experience has shown that victim encounter and body dump sites are most important in terms of an investigation-oriented geographic analysis. These are the location types most likely to be discovered by the police; attack and murder scenes, if different from encounter and dump sites, are usually known only to the murderer. The hunting typology is therefore concerned with offender behavior *vis-à-vis* these particular crime locations

Search and Attack Methods. The serial killer hunting process can be broken down into two components, (a) the search for a suitable victim, and (b) the method of attack. The former influences selection of victim encounter sites, and the latter, body dump sites. The proposed hunting typology results from the categories produced by the combination of these elements.

The following four victim search methods were isolated:

1. *Hunter*—defined as an offender who sets out specifically to search for a victim, basing the search from his/her residence.
2. *Poacher*—defined as an offender who sets out specifically to search for a victim, basing the search from an activity site other than his/her residence, or who commutes

or travels to another city during the victim search process.

3. *Troller*—defined as an offender who, while involved in other, nonpredatory, activities, opportunistically encounters a victim.

4. *Trapper*—defined as an offender who assumes a position or occupation, or creates a situation that allows him/her to encounter victims within a location under their control.

The following three victim attack methods were isolated:

1. *Raptor*—defined as an offender who attacks a victim upon encounter.

2. *Stalker*—defined as an offender who first follows a victim upon encounter, and then attacks.

3. *Ambusher*—defined as an offender who attacks a victim once he or she has been enticed to a location, such as a residence or workplace, controlled by the offender.[2]

Hunters are those criminals who specifically set out from their residence to look for victims, searching through the areas in their awareness space that they believe contain suitable targets.[3] The crimes of a hunter are generally confined to the offender's city of residence. Conversely, *poachers* travel outside of their home city, or operate from an activity site other than their residence, in the search for targets. The differentiation between a hunter and a poacher, however, is often a difficult and subjective task.

The terms 'hunter' and 'poacher' are similar to the 'marauder' and 'commuter' designations used by Canter & Larkin (1993) in their study of serial rape in England. *Marauders* are individuals whose residences act as the focus of their crimes. *Commuters*, on the other hand, travel from home into another area to commit their offences. It was hypothesized that marauders would have homes situated within their offence circle, while commuters would have homes located outside. Only 13% of the 45 British serial rapists were found to have their home base situated outside of the offence circle.

The FBI, however, observed that 51% of 76 US serial rapists lived outside of the offence circle (Reboussin, Warren & Hazelwood, 1993; Warren, Reboussin & Hazelwood, 1995). Alston (1994) had similar findings in a study of 30 British Columbia stranger sexual assault series; in 43% of the cases the offence circle did not contain an offender activity node. The inconsistency in these findings may be attributable to differences between European and North American urban structure, neighborhood density and travel behavior (Warren, Reboussin & Hazlewood, 1995).

One of the problems with the circle hypothesis is its determination of hunting behavior solely from crime site point pattern (see Alston, 1994, for a discussion of other associated problems). In cases involving large numbers of offences, the rapist may have commuted to several different areas in various directions, creating an offence circle that contains their residence, and in cases involving small numbers of crimes, a marauder may have found all of his/her victims through traveling by chance in the same direction, resulting in an offence circle that excludes their home base. Offence circles could therefore lead to both commuter and marauder designations, depending upon what point in a serial rapist's career they were generated.[4]

This happened in both the Yorkshire Ripper and the Boston Strangler cases (Burn, 1984; Davies & Dale, 1996; Frank, 1966). In other instances, a non-uniform target backcloth may force a commuter pattern regardless of the offender's hunting style. Davies & Dale (1995) warn 'that the commuter and marauder models may just be extremes of a continuum of patterns determined by topography and target availability'. Because of these problems, a more subjective interpretation of offender hunting style is used here to classify serial criminals as either hunters or poachers.

Trollers are those offenders who do not specifically look for victims, but, rather encounter them during the course of other, usually routine, activities. Their crimes are often spontaneous, but many serial sex offenders have fantasized and planned their crimes in advance so that they are ready and prepared when an opportunity presents itself ('premeditated opportunism').

Trappers either assume positions or occupations where potential victims come to them, or entice them by means of subterfuge into their homes or other locations under their control. This may be done through entertaining suitors, placing want-ads, or taking in boarders. Black widows, 'angels of death' and custodial killers are all forms of trappers, and most female serial murderers fall into this category (Hickey, 1986; Pearson, 1994; Scott, 1992; Segrave, 1992).

Raptors, upon encountering a victim, attack almost immediately. *Stalkers* follow and watch their targets, moving into the victim's activity space, waiting for an opportune moment to strike. The attack, murder, and body dump sites of stalkers are thus strongly influenced by their victims' activity spaces. *Ambushers* attack those they have brought or drawn into their 'web'—some place where the offender has a great deal of control, most often his/her home or workplace. The victims' bodies are usually hidden somewhere on the offender's property. While victim encounter sites in such cases may provide sufficient spatial information for analysis, many ambushers select marginalized victims whose disappearances are rarely linked, even when missing person reports are made to the police.

Hunting Style. Target patterns are determined by offender activity space, hunting method, and victim backcloth. One of the main purposes of the hunting style typology was the identification of those situations where an analysis of the relationship between offender activity space and crime location geography is appropriate. This allows for the elimination of those cases where such an analysis is impossible or redundant. Poachers, for example, who live in one city and commit their crimes in another, may not reside within their hunting area. Stalkers, whose crime locations are driven more by the activity spaces of their victims than by their own, will not usually produce target patterns amenable to this type of spatial investigation.

Table 21.1 shows the matrix produced by a cross-tabulation of the search and attack methods, and the suitability of the resultant cells for a geographic analysis based on encounter and body dump sites. The matrix uses a sliding scale of designations (yes, possible, doubtful, and no) to refer to suitability likelihood. A designation of redundant refers to a situation where such an analysis is possible, but trivial. For example, the offender's address could be accurately determined from an analysis of the body dumpsite locations of a trapper serial killer (e.g. one who entices victims into his/her home, murders them, and then buries

Table 21.1
Serial Offender Hunting Typology and Geographic Analysis Feasibility

	Search Method			
Attack Method	**Hunter**	**Poacher**	**Troller**	**Trapper**
Encounter sites				
Raptor	Yes	Doubtful	Yes	Redundant
Stalker	Yes (if known)	Doubtful	Yes (if known)	Redundant
Ambusher	Yes	Doubtful	Yes	Redundant
Body dump sites				
Raptor	Yes	Doubtful	Yes	Redundant
Stalker	Possibly	No	Possibly	No

their bodies in the backyard or basement), but such a circumstance negates any need for a spatial analysis. The cases of Belle Gunness, who poisoned her suitors, and Dorothea Puente, who murdered her elderly tenants, are examples of this type of situation.

As there appears to be a correlation between search and attack methods, actual serial criminals tend to fit into some cells more often than others. For example, hunter/raptors and trapper/ambushers are much more common than hunter/stalkers or trapper/raptors. Also, the suitability ratings in Table 21.1 are only suggestive, as individual cases may vary significantly from one another in terms of their spatial details.

Investigative Strategies

Various investigative strategies can be employed in a more effective and efficient manner through a geographic profile, and some examples are discussed below (Rossino, 1995c, 1996). The choice of a given tactic is dependent upon the specific circumstances in a particular case. As most of our public and private record systems contain address data, it is probable that additional investigative techniques will be developed over time. Indeed, several of the approaches presented below were proposed by police detectives themselves.

Suspect Prioritization. Geographic and psychological profiles can help determine which suspects, leads and tips should be prioritized during a major crime investigation. This is particularly important in cases suffering from information overload. More than one murder inquiry identified the correct suspect but failed to realize it at the time.

Patrol Saturation and Static Stakeouts. Areas in the geoprofile most probably associated with the offender can be used as the basis for establishing directed or saturation patrolling efforts and static police stakeouts. This tactic is most viable in those cases where the crimes are occurring during specific time periods. Barrett (1990) describes how Kentucky police, correctly anticipating the movement of a serial killer through the pattern of his crimes, set up roadblocks in a park to question late night motorists. This tactic gathered over 2000 names for the purpose of cross-comparison with other investigative information.

Through a geographic analysis of the crime sites in the Atlanta Child Murders, Dettlinger came to the conclusion that the killer was commuting along certain city routes (Dettlinger & Prugh, 1983). But his suggestion that stakeouts be established at the crucial points in this spatial pattern went unheeded by police, and five more bodies would be dumped near these locations before Task Force officers staking out a Chattahoochee River bridge pulled over Wayne Williams.

Neighborhood Canvasses. A geoprofile can be used for optimizing door-to-floor canvasses in urban areas and grid searches in rural areas. Similarly, information requests have been mailed out to target areas established through the prioritization of postal carrier walks. For example, LeBeau (1992) notes the case of a serial rapist in San Diego, who was arrested through canvassing efforts in an area targeted by analysis of the crime locations. The Vampire Killer, serial murderer Richard Trenton Chase, was caught in the same manner after a psychological profile predicted that he would be living near a recovered vehicle stolen from one of his victims (Biondi & Hecox, 1992; Ressler & Shachtman, 1992).

Police Information Systems. Police computerized dispatch and record systems often contain information of potential importance to an investigation. Offender databases, records management systems (RMS), parolee lists, computer aided dispatch (CAD) systems and the like can be strategically searched by address or location with a geoprofile (Bralian, Valcour & Shevel, 1994; Fowler, 1990; Pilant, 1994; Rebscher & Rohrer, 1991; Skogan & Antunes, 1979).

Outside Agency Databases. Parole and probation offices, mental health outpatient clinics, social services offices, and certain commercial establishments are often useful sources of information. Determining which of these are located in the area where the offender most likely lives can assist police investigations.

Postal Code Prioritization. Postal or zip codes can be prioritized with a geoprofile and then used to conduct searches and rankings of address databases. The following case illustrates one example of how this tactic has been used. During the investigation of a sexual murder police learned of a suspicious vehicle seen prowling the area of the attack on the evening of the crime. The only information witnesses could provide concerned the make and color of the automobile. A geographic profile was prepared, postal codes ranked, and this information then used to optimally search Department of Motor Vehicles computer records.

Even with just a three parameter search—(a) vehicle make, (b) vehicle color, and (c) registered owner address postal code—this procedure still served as an efficient discriminating method, resulting in only a few dozen records from hundreds of thousands of vehicles. Offender description, and zoning and socio-economic data, further refined the suspect search.

Task Force Computer Systems. A major crime inquiry may lead to the creation of a task force involving dozens of police officers investigating tips and following up leads. The resulting information is often entered and collated on some form of computerized database such as the Home Office Large Major Enquiry System (HOLMES), used by British police forces for managing large volumes of investigative case data (Doney, 1990; US Department of Justice, 1991).

These operations usually suffer from information overload and require some form of data prioritization (Keppel & Birnes, 1995). A geoprofile can determine the street addresses, postal codes and telephone numbers from those areas where the offender most likely resides. This process can also be linked to information available in CD-ROM telephone directory databases listing residential and business names, telephone numbers, addresses, postal/zip codes, business headings and standard industrial classification codes.

Sex Offender Registries. Sex offender registries, such as exist in Washington State (Popkin, 1994; Scheingold, Olson & Pershing, 1992), are a useful information source for geographic profiling in cases of serial sex crimes. By providing a list of addresses of known violent sex criminals, such registries can be used with a geographic profile to help prioritize suspects. The US Violent Crime Control and Law Enforcement Act of 1994:

> . . . requires states to enact statutes or regulations which require those determined to be sexually violent predators or who are convicted of sexually violent offenses to register with appropriate state law enforcement agencies for ten years after release from prison, or risk the reduction of Federal grant money. (US Department of Justice, 1994)

Peak-of-Tension Polygraphy. In suspicious missing persons cases presumed to be homicides, with known suspects, polygraphists have had success using peak-of-tension tests in narrowing the search area for the victim's remains (Cunliffe & Piazza, 1980; Hagmaier, 1990; Lyman, 1993; Raskin, 1989). By exposing the suspect to questions concerning the type of location where the victim's body might have been hidden (e.g. cave, lake, marsh, field, forest, etc.), a deceptive response can help focus the search. The process often involves the use of maps or pictures. The utility of peak-of-tension polygraphy is enhanced when the procedure is directed by a geographic profile.

Bloodings. During certain sexual murder investigations the British police have conducted large-scale DNA testing of all men from the area of the crime (DNA Database, 1995). The first such case was the Narborough Murder Enquiry, when 'all unalibied male residents in the villages between the ages of 17 and 34 years would be asked to submit blood and saliva samples voluntarily in order to "eliminate them" as suspects in the footpath murders' (Wambaugh, 1989).

Close to 4,000 men from the villages of Narborough, Littlethorpe and Enderby were tested during the investigation. Considerable police resources and laboratory costs can therefore be involved in such 'bloodings'. A geographic profile could efficiently direct the testing process through the targeting and prioritization of residents by address or postal code. The use of such a systematic strategy would result in a more effective and less expensive DNA mass screening sampling procedure.

Trial Court Expert Evidence. In addition to analyzing the geographic patterns of unsolved crimes for investigative insights, the spatial relationship between the locations of a crime series and a suspect's or accused offender's activity sites can be assessed in terms of the probability of their congruence (Rossmo, 1994). When combined with other forensic identification findings (e.g. a DNA profile), such information can increase evidential strength and therefore the probability of guilt. Geographic profiling thus has application in both the investigative and criminal trial stages.

Conclusion

> We were just hunting humans. I guess because we thought they were the hardest things to hunt, but humans are the easiest things to hunt. Sad to say, but it's true. (Convicted Canadian murderer; Boyd, 1988)

The ease with which such offenders hunt humans has its roots in the basic nature of our society. We simply do not expect to encounter seemingly random violence during the course of our daily lives. Even the offenders themselves may not understand why they do what they do. Albert DeSalvo, the Boston Strangler, could not explain his hunting processes to interviewers.

> I was just driving—anywhere—not knowing where I was going. I was coming through back ways, in and out and around. *That's the idea of the whole thing. I just go here and there. I don't know why.* (Frank, 1966)

But while we may not understand them, it is still imperative that we know how to catch them.

Geographic profiling is a strategic information management system used in the investigation of serial violent crime. This methodology was designed to help alleviate the problem of information overload that usually accompanies such cases. By knowing the most probable area of offender residence, police agencies can more effectively utilize their limited resources, and a variety of investigative strategies have now been developed to maximize the utility of this process for unsolved cases.

> Some of our [offender profiling] hypotheses . . . seem now to have passed into the general realm of established detective knowledge. . . . It is this gradual building of elements of certainty by scientific rigor that is the object of the researchers. (Copson, 1993)

But it is also the interaction between academic research and the police field that allows an investigative methodology to grow and develop. The importance of geography for criminal investigation and offender profiling strikes a chord within practitioners, a resonance best explained by an old police truism: 'When all else fails, return to the scene' (Barrett, 1990).

Notes

1. ViCLAS, the RCMP computerized linkage analysis system, was designed with certain geographic profiling requirements in mind. It is possible to conduct queries, amongst other search criteria, based on crime location set similarities.
2. This typology is remarkably similar to Schaller's (1972) description of certain hunting methods used by lions in the Serengeti, where he observed ambushing, stalking, driving (direct attack) and unexpected (opportunistic) kills.
3. Wesly Allan Dodd, a serial killer executed for the murder of three children in the state of Washington, wrote in his diary, 'Now ready for my second day of the hunt. Will start at about 10 a.m. and take a lunch so I don't have to return home'. He was worried, however, that if he murdered a child in the park through which he was searching, he'd lose his hunting ground for up to two to three months (Westfall, 1992).

4. The probability that the N crimes of a marauder will appear to be those of a commuter is approximately: $(2^n - 1)/(2^{2n} - 2)$. The odds that such a pattern could happen by chance is not insignificant for low values of n. For example, in a series of 4 crimes the probability is equal to 23%.

D. Kim Rossmo, "Geographic Profiling." Reprinted from Janet L. Jackson and Debra A. Bekerian (Eds.), *Offender Profiling: Theory, Research and Practice*, pp. 159–175. Copyright © 1997 by John Wiley & Sons Limited. Reproduced by permission of John Wiley & Sons Limited. ✦

Chapter 22
Veering Toward Digital Disorder

Computer-Related Crime and Law Enforcement Preparedness

Mark E. Correia
Craig Bowling

On a local or city level, most police detectives don't even know where to begin when investigating computer-related crimes. In many instances, the cases are shuffled off to the computer guy, namely the officer or officers who have let it be known that they are not intimidated by a personal computer, and whose experience with them usually doesn't go much further than Microsoft Excel or, for the more advanced, the ability to navigate Compuserve.

—Chris Goggans, aka computer underground member "Eric Bloodaxe" (quoted in Icove, Segeer, & Vonstorch, 1995)

The primary function of police in society is to maintain peace and order. When social change takes place, police must respond accordingly. The authors highlight the necessity of innovation in police work as technological changes impact modern society. For example, they note that just as home computer use has increased since the early 1990s, so has the incidence of computer-related crime (e.g., hacking, Internet child pornography, and software piracy). The authors assert that American society has entered the age of "digital disorder."

Correia and Bowling investigate the preparedness of law enforcement agencies in the information age. Data collected from a survey of 278 police agencies in 47 states are presented to examine in particular how well law enforcement agencies are prepared to investigate cyber crimes. Their findings suggest that law enforcement agencies are not adequately prepared for computer-related crime investigations, even though the incidence of cyber crime is expected to rise. They conclude with a discussion of the implications of their study and highlight the need for policing agencies to rethink the prioritization of computer-related crime in the twenty-first century.

A recent episode of the popular television series "Law and Order" depicted NYPD detectives attempting to examine a computer at a crime scene. Upon initial analysis, the detectives discovered the system to be password protected and thus inoperable. Consequently, the detectives were left somewhat confounded.[1] Although fictional, this scenario appears to mirror reality as today's law enforcement officers increasingly find themselves involved in investigations wherein computers are both tools and targets of criminal activity. Examples of this new trend in criminality include the following:

- "computer-related attacks" increased by 22% between 1996 and 1997 (Zuckerman, 1998);
- 62% of survey respondents reported security breaches in their computer systems during the previous 12 months (Computer Security Institute/ Federal Bureau of Investigation, 1999);
- worldwide losses due to software piracy in 1998 are estimated at nearly $11 billion (Business Software Alliance, 1999);

- Dutch hackers penetrated Defense Department computers during the Gulf War, obtaining information on U.S. troop movement which they later tried, unsuccessfully, to sell to Iraqi intelligence (Christensen, 1999); and
- investigators were often forced to examine subject Internet usage and computer hardware during the rash of deadly domestic school shootings in 1998 and 1999.

The perpetrator of such cyber crime varies from the domestic teen hacker to the international organized crime actor. For example, in Edmonds, Washington, local police and secret service agents seized a computer from a teenager who, while online, obtained more than 300 credit card numbers that were used to make numerous purchases. During Operation Cheshire Cat, an investigation that involved law enforcement agencies in 11 other countries, special agents with the U.S. Customs Service simultaneously raided sites in 22 states after uncovering an extensive and sophisticated international Internet-based child pornography ring known as Wonderland (Fields, 1998). Russian mobster Vladimir Levin, with the aid of an insider, transferred millions of dollars from Citibank accounts in New York to foreign destinations from St. Petersburg, Russia.

Federal government systems have increasingly come under attack with the proliferation of computers. The Defense Information Systems Agency (DISA) reported that Defense Department computers were attacked more than 250,000 times in a 1-year period and that attacks on non-classified Department of Defense systems, by both domestic and foreign suspects, have escalated. On a similar front, Operation Eligible Receiver illustrated the vulnerability of both government and private sector computers.[2]

In May and June of 1999, *.gov* Web sites came under attack from self proclaimed hacker groups in retaliation for recent enforcement activity by the Federal Bureau of Investigation (FBI). The U.S. Senate and the Department of Interior Web sites were defaced and numerous domain name service (DNS) attacks were launched against the FBI site. The attackers, some of whom were located abroad, vowed to continue attacks against any and all federal computer networks. Similarly, White House computer systems came under attack shortly after the inadvertent bombing of the Chinese embassy in Belgrade during the Kosovo-Serbia conflict in May of 1999. Some of the cyber attacks launched against the White House are believed to have originated from China.

These cases provide just a sampling of the scenarios facing law enforcement. Unfortunately, the dynamic nature of high technology places law enforcement at a grave disadvantage. Due to the rigid organizational structure of police agencies, administrative issues such as equipment procurement, training, and funding tend to handicap the law enforcement officers (Bowling, 1997a,1997b). Criminals, often free of the ruinous limitations of close-ended and mechanistic systems, regularly use the latest versions of operating systems, software, and hardware, whereas their antithetic counterparts in law enforcement are forced to make due with antiquated technology. Policing under such conditions only exacerbates the ever-widening technology gap between the good guys and the bad guys.

In an effort to provide further insight into policing during the information age, this analysis draws on theoretical concepts and empirical data and applies these to pragmatic issues surrounding law enforcement's exposure to computer-related crime. Although it has been suggested that law enforcement is not prepared for computer-related crime, empirical data scarcely exists to verify or nullify such a claim.[3] In a shift away from qualitative and anecdotal evidence, we draw on a nationwide baseline exploratory study of municipal police departments.

Setting the Stage

As previously discussed, the permeation of computers throughout society has made technology, once a tool available only to researchers and scientists, accessible to millions. As of 1998, an estimated 45% of American households now have computers (Web Trend Watch, 1999). An annual study conducted by Nielson Media Research and CommerceNet found that as of June 1999, 92 million Americans and Canadians (16 years and older) have Internet access, up from 79 million the year prior ("Change is Good," 1998). Internet-related e-commerce is also rapidly increasing, as spending levels in 1999 were at approximately $33.1 billion and projected to reach $61 billion annually by 2002 (Gregory, 1997; "Online retailing in North America," 2000). These increases, coupled with current evidence, suggest that the success of businesses and governmental agencies may be contingent on the viability and security of their telecommunication and computer networks. The increased reliance on computer technology amplifies the vulnerability of the modern infrastructure to cyber crime.

This vulnerability has provided a new arena for criminal activity. Just as the criminal element did not hesitate to take advantage of previous technologies (e.g., the automobile and the telephone), so too has the computer become a tool for the propagation of nefarious activity. Unlike inventions during the industrial age, which would take years to achieve mass implementation (Toffler, 1980), inventions during the information age can take a mere 3 to 6 months before becoming fully available to the public (Button, 1993). When this dynamic technology collides with the rigidity of police agencies, law enforcement agents often find it difficult to keep pace with the rapid technological advances (Bowling, 1997a).

This also highlights current and future problems facing law enforcement, that is, a mechanistic organization operating in a hyper-dynamic environment (Bowling, 1997b).[4] If this situation continues, as is expected because computing power doubles every 18 months, and police agencies are unable to secure adequate resources, the next century will prove to be the most difficult era yet for law enforcement.

Digital Disorder: Broken Windows in Cyberspace

Attempted break-ins, trespassing, sex-related commerce, harassment, stalking, vandalism, money laundering, theft, and child pornography—surely one would agree that if these crimes were occurring in any given neighborhood, a police presence would be necessary, and without police, escalation of criminal activity would most likely continue. Yet in the neighborhood known as cyberspace, these "broken windows" abound and the police are seldom to be found (Sussman,1995). Furthermore, prosecutors at the local and federal level have been unwilling, in most cases, to prosecute computer-related crime cases (see McEwen, 1989).

With the proliferation of computers and large networks such as the Internet, practitioners and academics are forced to reconceptualize the notion of disorder (Bowling, 1997a, 1997b). Graffiti, abandoned cars, dilapidated buildings, public drunks, litter, and sex trade business are joined by new forms of disorder specific to the information age. Spam e-mail, pornographic Web sites, #hackphreak and #kidpics on Internet relay chat (IRC), alt.pictures.erotica.animals, online stalking, and DNS attacks all constitute examples of a new form of disorder—*digital disorder* (Bowling, 1997a). Composed of data, digital disorder poses a difficult challenge to law enforcement's quest to maintain order and has led Kevin Manson (1997) of the Financial Fraud Institute at the Federal Law Enforcement Training Center (FLETC) to remark that law enforcement has now become the "thin digital blue line."

The concept of digital disorder has its roots in the real world hypothesis of disorder put forth by Wilson and Kelling (1982) and expanded on by Skogan (1990). Just as disorder in the physical world entices criminals, the digital variant is interpreted by the more serious cyber criminal that "no one cares." Similar to the pimp or drug pusher who views the first unfixed broken window as a signal to move in and peddle his trade, unreported malicious computer trespass and the like are perceived by computer criminals as an opportunity to move toward more serious computer-related crimes.

The growing presence of sex sites on the Internet is an example of a digital broken window. Just as the sex industry has embraced past technological revolutions (e.g., telephones and VCRs), it has now begun to construct a formidable presence in cyberspace. In 1998, online sex sites generated approximately $970 million and forecasts suggest the medium will reach $3.12 billion by 2003 ("Sex-on-the-Web Industry," 1999). It might be argued that the proliferation of sex trade sites on the Internet is a form of digital disorder. For example, what many perceived as simply an overabundance of "nudie" pictures on the Internet, in actuality may have served as a social cue (e.g., broken window) to others that no one cares. Such a cue may have facilitated the presence of child pornography to its current standing on the Internet and promoted the accelerated pace of organized crime participation in sex-related Internet commerce (see Carter & Katz, 1997).

Hence, it appears that Skogan's (1990) discussion of the impact of red light districts and sex trade businesses on neighborhoods and their role in citizen perceptions of increased disorder can now be applied to cyberspace. Consequently, one may argue that a decline in cyber-spatial neighborhoods may have been and continues to be expedited by the expansion of pornographic sites (both legal and illegal) on the Internet.

The information age brings a new dimension to policing, a dimension wherein law enforcement lags years behind the technology. With criminals not hesitating to procure new technologies, it is safe to suggest that the onset of the next millennium will bring increased incidents of digital disorder.

Law Enforcement: Prepared?

> Expense of training, equipment, and software continue to cause law enforcement to lag years behind.
>
> —Survey respondent

Local law enforcement officers are usually the first responders to crimes; hence, their ability to effectively examine and secure computers at crime scenes is of paramount importance. As previously noted, the dynamic nature of high technology makes it difficult for law enforcement officers to keep pace with current and developing technologies. Organizational obstacles faced by policing agencies in dealing with computer-related crime are difficult to identify, though numerous suggestions have been forwarded. Lack of understanding, foresight, and scarce funding have been recognized as primary reasons why law enforcement's position is tenuous at best (Button, 1993; Fitzpatrick, 1995; Tafoya, 1997b). A secondary problem is that because technology is entering law enforcement from the bottom up, administrators are often unaware of the technological issues facing those in the field (Clark & Dilberto, 1996).

Change within law enforcement organizations has been characterized as arduous, often occurring only when they are faced with the propinquity of outside pressure or when their domain consensus is threatened (Guyot, 1979; Thompson, 1967; Zhao, 1996). Given this historical trend, changing organizational dynamics to focus on computer crime is going to be a daunting task in an era where street crimes produce the highest levels of fear among citizens and capture the lens of the media and the focus of policy makers (Kappeler, Blumberg, & Potter, 1996).

Externally, another challenge is that victims of computer-related crime often do not contact the police because they perceive such agencies as technologically inept and thus incapable of such investigations (Carter & Katz, 1996; Quade & McEwen, 1996). Just as effective policing of traditional crime is highly dependent on citizen trust and cooperation, so too is the effective policing of computer-related crime. It has been argued that law enforcement "is combating 21st century technology with 19th century laws," further inhibiting their effectiveness (McKenna, 1996). Taken together, these obstacles and the escalation of computer-related crimes has led Carter and Katz (1996) to state that if "the trend of computer crime over the last five years provides any indication of the future, law enforcement's problems have just begun" (p. 1; see also Button, 1993; Tafoya, 1986).

Although such qualitative evidence suggests that law enforcement is not prepared to effectively manage computer-related crime, quantitative research has been lacking to either substantiate or displace this belief. Thus, we have attempted to fill this void with a baseline-exploratory study examining the state of preparedness of municipal police departments in dealing with computer-related crime and to uncover the underlying issues: Below, the findings and analysis of this survey are presented, as well as suggestions that may better prepare law enforcement agencies to more effectively police that which may prove to be the most formidable challenge in modern society—computer-related crime.

Method

The results of a nationwide sample of 278 municipal police departments in 47 states are reported here. The sample includes municipal police departments (populations over 25,000) that were originally included in a 1969 survey of police chiefs administered by the International City Managers Association. The surveys were addressed to the chiefs of the departments, but many names were filled out by individuals responsible for research in the agency. A modified Dillman (1978) Total Design Method was employed for the self-administered mail surveys. This process entails a pretesting of the survey instrument, use of appropriate graphics, and repeated mailings to nonrespondents. The agencies were surveyed in two mailing waves over a 6-month period during the spring and summer of 1997, resulting in a response rate of 83%.

In terms of analysis, contingency tables and correlations were employed to assess the associations between the dependent and independent variables. Lastly, OLS regression was used to assess the causal relationships between departmental characteristics and their level of preparedness.

Variable Coding

Dependent Variables

Three dependent variables were incorporated to measure the priority that police agencies place on computer-related crime. The first measure asked about the current priority and the second addressed the anticipated priority 2 years from now. Originally, these measures included a 4-point Likert-type scale ranging from *very low* to *high* priority (see Table 22.1). For analytical purposes, each variable was recoded, with *very low* and *low* in one category and *moderate* and *high* another category.

Organizational change within an agency is indicative of a commitment to pursue certain goals (e.g., community policing; Zhao, 1996). Hence, it was necessary to assess whether agencies had undergone organizational restructuring to address computer-related crime. The majority of questions in this section were categorical ("yes" or "no") and asked whether the department had changed their standard operating procedures (SOPS), training, or recruitment due to computer-related crime; if they had developed a specialized unit (existing on the department's organizational chart) for this type of crime; and if not, were there plans for the development of such a unit. The creation of an overall measure to assess organizational adjustment in regard to computer-related crime proved to be highly reliable ($\alpha = .72$).[5]

Independent Variables

In terms of the independent variables, three general classifications were incorporated into the analysis. The first addressed issues regarding investigations of computer-related crime. The three questions in this area were categorical ("yes" or "no") and inquired as to whether the department had been involved with such investigations over the past year, whether these investigations entailed contacting agencies from other states, and if the investigations included contacting agencies from other coun-

Table 22.1
Variable Coding and Descriptive Statistics (N = 222)

Variable	Category	Value	*n*	%
Dependent priority	Low	1	153	68.9
	High	2	69	31.1
Anticipated priority	Low	1	84	38.2
	High	2	136	61.8
Organizational adjustment	Low	1	190	85.6
	High	2	32	14.4
Independent priority	Very low	1	47	21.2
	Low	2	106	47.7
	Moderate	3	64	28.8
	High	4	5	2.3
Anticipated priority	Very low	1	15	6.8
	Low	2	69	31.4
	Moderate	3	112	50.9
	High	4	24	10.9
Investigative activity	Low	3	78	35.1
		4	66	29.7
		5	62	28.0
	High	6	16	7.2
Expected increase	Yes	1	168	78.5
	No	0	46	21.5
Population	< 50,000	1	48	22.5
	50,000 to 100,000	2	57	26.8
	100,001 to 250,000	3	63	29.6
	250,001 to 500,000	4	29	13.6
	> 500,000	5	16	7.5

Note: Missing data are excluded from these analyses.

tries. For analytical purposes, these indicators were scaled to create an overall measure of investigative activity ranging from low to high.[6]

If a unit existed, agencies were prompted to respond to questions regarding the training of members, membership in the High Technology Crime Investigations Association (HTCIA), and the number of staff dedicated to the unit (a continuous variable).

Lastly, departments were asked if the agency expected an increase in computer-related crime. All of these questions were categorical with possible responses of "yes" or "no."

In addition to these general categories, the scaled versions of priority, anticipated priority, and organizational adjustment were also used as independent variables.

Data Analysis

Findings from this baseline study appear to provide support for the commonly held belief that law enforcement agencies are not adequately prepared for computer-related crime investigations and order maintenance in the information age. For example, Table 22.1 reveals that only 31% of all responding agencies ranked this type of crime as either a moderate or high priority. More agencies, however, indicated that they expected the level of departmental priority to increase (61.8%) within 2 years.

Somewhat to our surprise, the data indicate that a significant proportion of respondents have been involved in some type of computer

Table 22.2
Relationship Between Levels of Investigation and Specialized Units (N = 222)

		Involved in Computer-Related Investigation			
		Yes	**%**	**No**	**%**
Plans for unit	Yes	14	82.4	3	17.6
	No	105	58.7	74	41.3
Specialized unit***	Yes	26	100		
	No	118	60.8	76	39.2

Note: χ^2 = 15.366. Missing data are excluded from these analyses.
*** $p < .001$

crime investigation (65.2%), of which 44.6% entailed contacting agencies in other states and 11.2% involved contacting law enforcement agencies in other countries.[7] This appears to illustrate the ageographical (Christy, 1997) and ajurisdictional (Post, 1995) nature of computer-related crime, which contributes to the blurring of agency jurisdiction and responsibility.

Crosstabs were used to assess the relationships between the nominal level variables and the chi-square statistical test was employed to assess significance. In general, the findings suggest that familiarity with or exposure to computer-related crime is indicative of increasing organizational preparedness. For example, of those agencies that reported having a specialized unit, all have been involved in computer-related crime investigations, and those agencies that have not been involved in such an investigation reported not having any specialized units (see Table 22.2).

Although the vast majority of agencies reported not having a specialized unit (found on the organizational chart), higher proportions of agencies reported an expected increase in computer-related crime, regardless of unit development. Not surprisingly, Table 22.3 indicates that nearly 96% of those agencies with a specialized unit expect this type of criminal activity to increase in the future. This same table also reveals that 76% of those agencies without a specialized unit expect an increase in this type of crime; yet analysis shows that these same agencies do not plan on developing a specialized unit. One might conclude that regardless of future expectations, citizens, public officials, and some law enforcement agencies may not be willing to devote the time and/or resources necessary to investigate and prepare for computer-related criminal activity.

Nearly 64% of the agencies that rank this crime category as having higher priority also expect an increase in such crime (see Table

Table 22.3
Relationship Between Development of a Specialized Unit and an Increase in Computer-Related Crime (N = 213)

		Expected Increase			
		Yes	**%**	**No**	**%**
Specialized unit*	Yes	25	96	1	4
	No	142	76	45	24

Note: χ^2 = 5.511. Missing data are excluded from these analyses.
* $p < .05$

Table 22.4
Relationship Between an Expected Increase in Computer-Related Crime and Level of Current Priority (N = 214)

		Current Priority			
		Higher	%	Lower	%
Expected increase*	Yes	107	63.7	61	36.3
	No	46	85.2	8	14.8

Note: χ^2 = 10.957. Missing data are excluded from these analyses.
* $p < .05$

22.4).[8] This is significantly different than those agencies reporting low priority and expecting an increase (36%, $p < .05$). Similar findings are reported in Table 22.5, which shows that there is a significant difference between agencies that expect a higher priority ranking of these crimes and also expect an increase (72%), compared with those agencies that expect a low priority ranking and also expect an increase (15%, $p < .001$).

In terms of correlations, the data indicate that higher levels of investigation are significantly related to higher levels of organizational adjustment ($p < .05$), higher levels of current priority and anticipated priority ($p < .01$), and cities with larger populations ($p < .05$; see Table 22.6).

The finding that higher levels of organizational adjustment are significantly related to higher levels of priority and anticipated priority ($p < .01$) was anticipated. Due to the cross-sectional design of the study, it is unknown whether organizational adjustment preceded the higher levels of priority or visa versa. The data indicate significant associations between increases in city populations and organizational adjustment ($p < .01$) and anticipated priority ($p < .05$). This was expected given that larger police departments tend to have access to more resources and newer technology.

Two models were constructed to assess the effects of the independent variables on departmental levels of priority and anticipated priority. Results reported in Table 22.7 suggest that many of the independent variables are significant indicators. In terms of the first model, current priority, policing agencies that had experienced more investigations ($p < .001$) and expected an increase in computer-related crime ($p < .01$) were significantly more likely to increase the level of organizational priority in regard to computer-related crime.

A similar pattern is found in the second model predicting levels of anticipated priority.

Table 22.5
Relationship Between an Expected Increase in Computer-Related Crime and Anticipated Priority of Computer-Related Crime (N = 212)

		Anticipated Priority			
		Lower	%	Higher	%
Expected increase***	Yes	46	27.7	120	72.3
	No	38	70.4	16	29.6

Note: χ^2 = 32.724. Missing data are excluded from these analyses.
*** $p < .001$

Table 22.6
Relationship Between the Dependent and Independent Variables (N = 222)

	1	2	3	4
Investigation scale (1)				
Organizational scale (2)	.340**			
Priority (3)	.443**	.318**		
Anticipated priority (4)	.382**	.300**	.668**	
City population (5)	.142*	.168*	.090	.119*

Note: Missing data are excluded from these analyses.
* $p < .05$. ** $p < .01$.

Table 22.7
OLS Regression Results for Police Preparedness (N = 222)

Model	**Priority**	**Anticipated Priority**
Investigative activity	.381 (.053)***	.270 (.054)***
Expected increase	.275 (.111)*	.245 (.506)***
Population category	.042 (.040)	.015 (.041)
df	212	210
R^2	.283	.268

Note: Missing data are excuded from these analyses.
* $p < .05$. *** $p < .001$.

Again, those agencies that have participated in investigations (p < .001) and expected increases in computer-related crime (p < .001) were significantly more likely to hold higher levels of anticipated priority for computer-related crime.

Overall, the analysis indicates that American municipal law enforcement agencies are not adequately prepared for computer-related crime. More disturbing is that many agencies, despite expecting an increase in this type of criminal behavior, do not plan on developing any specialized units to address this steadily increasing problem plaguing America. Nor does the level of current or anticipated priority effect organizational changes that may enhance the ability to counter computer-related crimes.

Policy Implications: What Might Be Done?

> Law enforcement can only rise above reacting to change by resolutely adopting a long-range perspective.
>
> —William Sessions (1990)

Due to the exploratory nature of this research, this study has neither answered all questions nor addressed all issues facing law enforcement in the information age, specifically in regard to computer-related crime. Rather, our aim is to provide greater insight and understanding into some of the issues currently facing law enforcement and to aid municipal police departments in taking the neces-

Table 22.8
OLS Regression Results for Organizational Change (N = 222)

Model	Organizational Adjustment I	Organizational Adjustment II
Investigative activity	.159	.188
	(.036)*	(.034)*
Expected increase	–.116	–.108
	(.073)	(.076)
Priority	.139	
	(.046)	
Population category	–.009	–.016
	(.026)	(.026)
Anticipated priority		.107
		(.044)
df	186	184
R^2	.097	.079

Note: Missing data are excuded from these analyses.
* $p < .05$.

sary steps toward becoming more effective in dealing with computer-related crime.

This endeavor is not meant to suggest that police agencies are mere technophobes incapable of effectively investigating high-tech crime. On the contrary, we believe that just as law enforcement has adapted to the automobile, radio, and telephone, so too can they become a formidable foe of the cybercriminal. Numerous changes, however, will have to occur to overcome the numerous challenges. First, unlike earlier technologies, computer technology advances and changes at a far greater rate, brings the conception of boundaries crashing down, and is currently accessible by millions of people worldwide. These unique characteristics are problematic for agencies that are traditionally mechanistic in both structure and operation. As previously discussed, police organizations will continue to fall behind the technology curve if closed-ended approaches to the likes of training and technology refresh remain as "unofficial" standard operating procedures. The importance for implementing an open-ended and organic approach to computer-related crime is highlighted when one realizes that law enforcement will soon be forced to deal with the first generation of computer-literate criminals.[9]

In terms of policy, the question arises as to how law enforcement can conduct computer-related crime investigations in an era of devolution and resource-deprived public organizations, leaving them without necessary equipment and training.[10] Furthermore, it is not solely computer-related crimes that will be hampered if this situation does not change, but many other forms of traditional criminal investigations that also require the use and knowledge of computers (e.g., murder suspect who keeps a journal on his computer, money laundering records, drug dealers who use e-mail and computer databases). Hence, the lack of necessary equipment and training in this area will have serious consequences on the investigative effectiveness of police agencies.

Not addressing the current and forthcoming issues will prove to be incredibly problematic for law enforcement and hamper the reduction of the ever-widening technology gap between the good guys and the bad guys. As Coutorie (1995) noted, "If nothing is done until it becomes politically important enough to target, law enforcement will be hopelessly behind the learning and technology curves to address the problem" (p. 27).

Although by no means a panacea, adopting the tenets of TOPSS is an integral approach to effectively manage with computer-related crime: *t*ask forces (interagency), *o*rganic systems (promotes adaptability in a dynamic arena), *p*rivate-public sector cooperation (Federal Computer Investigative Committee, High Technology Investigative Association, The Agora, and Computer Technology Investigators Northwest), *s*pecialized units (U.S. Secret Service Electronic Crimes Branch, U.S. Customs Cybersmuggling-C3, and the National Infrastructure Protection Center), and *s*trategic and long-range planning (Button, 1993; Tafoya, 1986, 1990, 1997a, 1997–1998; Toffler, 1980).[11] Implementing TOPSS will better enable agencies to know what to expect from the technology and provide the tools necessary to commit to the future (Fitzpatrick, 1995, p. 18).

In addition to TOPSS, law enforcement management must acknowledge that computer-related crime is indeed an important issue that demands immediate attention (e.g., funding, training, etc.). Although those at the lower levels of the organization appear to be more familiar with the impact of the technological advances (Clark & Dilberto, 1996), administrators must get up to speed on information age variables that are currently affecting law enforcement on a broader scale. This requires law enforcement to embrace a more open-ended and organic system model with respect to agency organization and domain consensus to adjust to this hyperdynamic environment (Bowling, 1997a, 1997b), despite law enforcement's previous failures to embrace this type of change (Thompson, 1967; Zhao, 1996). Remaining rigid in a rapidly revolving environment will prove disastrous.

The often-held belief that law enforcement is inadequately prepared to handle computer crime had until now been primarily qualitative and anecdotal. Utilizing quantitative data, this baseline study provides somewhat of a clearer picture as to where municipal police departments find themselves in a time when computer-related crime is taking society by storm. Currently, the data suggest law enforcement, specifically on the municipal level, is not prepared to effectively handle computer-related crime, nor, for the most part, is it preparing for such crime.

Future research must continue in areas where we have an incomplete understanding. For example, a more comprehensive and universal definition of computer crime (consider adding to the UCR), the ability to identify forthcoming technologies, and the examination of county prosecutors' preparedness for computer crime are all needed (as Frank Clark has noted, local law enforcement must have the blessing of the district attorney's office to pursue such investigations). Meanwhile, exploration of funding issues and the possibilities of online community policing (e.g., virtual cop shops) should be explored.

At the dawn of the third millennium, the Net-gen will be the first generation of computer literate criminals, providing a daunting challenge for law enforcement. However, we are of the belief that law enforcement is up to the challenge in that if the likes of TOPSS is examined, developed, and adhered to, we will witness the accession of the first generation of computer-savvy crime fighters—the cybercops of the 21st century.

Notes

1. The authors note that generally, only specialists in a controlled setting should conduct forensic analysis of computers. To prevent tainting or losing evidence, the fictional detectives at the scene should not have tampered with the computer.
2. National Security Agency (NSA) red teams posing as North Korean operatives were able to penetrate Department of Defense (DOD) and public sector systems (e.g., power grid computers).
3. For the purposes of this study, computer-related crime has been defined as "any violation of criminal law that involves knowledge of computer technology for perpetration, investigation, and prosecution" (Parker, Smith, Turner, & Sherizan, 1989). However, it should be noted that a universally accepted definition does not exist—thus often hampering discussion and research of this topic.

4. See Burns and Stalker (1961) and Katz and Kahn (1966) for discussions on mechanistic-organic systems and open-ended and closed-ended organizations. These works are relevant in understanding the current dilemma law enforcement faces.
5. The scaled measure consists of four indicators: specialized training, High Technology Crime Investigations Association (HTCIA) membership, specialized unit, and a change in standard operating procedures. The measure ranges from 4 (*low levels of change*) to 8 (*high levels of change*). These were then collapsed into two categories, with 4 through 5 representing 1 and 6 through 8 representing 2.
6. Reliability analysis showed this measure to be moderately reliable with an alpha of.63.
7. Such a high percentage might be attributed to the lack of understanding and yet to be agreed on universal definition of what constitutes a computer-related crime. We used the definition found in the Department of Justice–National Institute of Justice Computer Crime Resource Manual, which was reprinted on the front page of the survey instrument. This table has been excluded but can be obtained from the authors.
8. Two variables were recoded for this analysis. The question regarding current priority and expected priority were collapsed into two categories. The first category, *low priority,* included the responses to *very low priority* and *low priority,* whereas the second category, *higher priority,* included the responses to *moderate priority* and *high priority.* This recoding was necessary to statistically analyze the relationships between these two variables and the other categorical variables in the analyses.
9. In a recent poll, 71% of children opted to retain their computer when asked whether they would rather keep their TV or their PC ("Change is Good," 1998).
10. See the Steve Jackson Games case (Manson, 1995; Sterling, 1992) for an example of might happen if investigators are not adequately trained.
11. A central component of TOPSS is the ability of agencies to create interagency task forces and dedicated units with the department (Conly,1989; McEwen,1989). Such endeavors, however, pose numerous challenges. For example, it requires different levels of government to cooperate and work with one another and also poses funding and jurisdictional problems. Though difficult, such developments are necessary to effectively combat computer-related crime.

References

Bowling, C. (1997a). *Digital disorder and policing in the next millennium: Examining issues of concern for law enforcement in the information age and beyond.* Submitted in partial fulfillment for the degree of Master of Arts in Criminal Justice, Washington State University.

Bowling, C. (1997b). *The Internet, digital disorder, and police agencies: A survey of theoretical and pragmatic issues in the cyber-age.* Paper presented at the Annual Meeting of the Academy of Criminal Justice Sciences, Louisville, KY.

Burns, T., & Stalker, G. (1961). *The management of innovation.* London: Tavistock Institute.

Business Software Alliance. (1999, May 25). *1998 Global Software Piracy Report* [Online]. Available: http://www.bsa.org

Button, L. (1993, June). The future of computer crime and law enforcement. *NIJ/NCJRS—Command College Class XVI.* Sacramento, CA.

Carter, D., & Katz, A. (1996, December). Computer crime: An emerging challenge for law enforcement. *FBI Law Enforcement Bulletin* [Online]. Available: http://www.fbi.gov

Carter, D., & Katz, A. (1997). *Computers as a tool of international organized crime.* Paper presented at the Annual Meeting of the Academy of Criminal Justice Sciences, Louisville, KY.

Change is good. (1999, January). *Wired,* p. 163.

Christensen, J. (1999, April 6). *Bracing for guerrilla warfare in cyberspace* [Online]. Available: www.cnn.com

Christy, J. (1997, August 6–8). *The escalation of the terrorist threat.* Paper presented at the XII Annual Symposium on Criminal Justice Issues, Chicago, IL.

Clark, F, & Dilberto, K. (1996). *Investigating computer crime.* Boca Raton, FL: CRC Press.

Computer Security Institute/Federal Bureau of Investigation. (1999, March 5). *Issues and trends: 1999 Computer Security Institute/Federal Bureau of Investigation computer crime and security survey* [Online]. Available: http://www.gocsi.com

Conly, C. (1989). *Organizing for computer crime investigation and prosecution.* (National Institute of Justice). Washington, DC: U.S. Department of Justice.

Coutorie, L. (1995). The future of high-technology crime: A parallel Delphi study. *Journal of Criminal Justice, 23,* 13–27.

Dillman, D. (1978). *Mail and telephone surveys: The total design method.* New York: Wiley-Interscience.

Fields, G. (1998, September 3). 12 country raid busts child porn ring. *USA Today,* p. 4A.

Fitzpatrick, C. (1995, October). Managing computer resources. *Police Chief, 62,* 18–20.

Gaines, L., Kappeler, V., & Vaughn, J. (1997). *Policing in America.* Cincinnati, OH: Anderson. (Reprinted from *A Delphi forecast of the future of law enforcement,* by W. Tafoya, 1986.)

Gregory, S. (1997). *1998 tech guide* (pp. 66–80).

Guyot, D. (1979). Bending granite: Attempts to change the rank structure of American police departments. *Journal of Police Administration, 7* (3), 253–284.

Icove, D., Segeer, K., & Vonstorch, W. (1995). *Computer crime.* Sebastopol, CA: O'Reilly and Associates.

Kappeler, V., Blumberg, M., & Potter, G. (1996). *The mythology of crime and criminal justice.* Prospect Heights, IL: Waveland.

Katz, D., & Kahn, R. (1966). *The social psychology of organizations.* New York: Wiley.

Manson, K. (1995). Steve Jackson games: The privacy protection act in cyberspace. FLETC *Legal Bulletin* [Online]. Available: http://www.well.com.user.kfarrand.lud.htm

Manson, K. (1997). *Robots, wanders, spiders, and avatars: The virtual investigator and community policing behind the thin digital blue line.* Paper presented at the Annual Meeting of the Academy of Criminal Justice Sciences, Louisville, KY

McEwen, T. (1989). *Dedicated computer units.* (National Institute of Justice). Washington, DC: U.S. Department of Justice.

McKenna, P. (1996). Hacker crackers. *The Airman.*

Net populated swells to 92 million. (1999, June 18). [Online]. Available: http://www.wired.com

Online retailing in North America reached 33.1 billion in 1999 and is projected to top 61 billion in 2000. [Online]. (2000). *Shop.org.* Available: http://www.shop.org

Parker, D., Smith, D., Turner, G., & Sherizan, S. (1989). *Computer crime: Justice resource manual* (National Institute of Justice). Washington, DC: U.S. Department of Justice.

Post, D. (1995). Anarchy, state, and the Internet: An essay on law-making in cyberspace. *Journal of Online Law* [Online]. Available: http://www.jol.org

Quade, S., & McEwen, J. (1996). *Research needs for computer crime (draft).* Alexandria, VA: Institute for Law and Justice.

Sessions, W. (1990, January). Commentary. *FBI Law Enforcement Bulletin,* 59, 1.

Sex-on-the-Web industry set to multiply. (1999, May 24). *Foxnews.com* [Online]. Available: http://www.foxnews.com

Skogan, W. (1990). *Disorder and decline: Crime and the spiral of decay in American neighborhoods.* Berkeley: University of California Press.

Sterling, B. (1992). *The hacker crackdown: Law and disorder on the electronic frontier.* New York: Bantam.

Sussman, V. (1995, January 23). Policing cyberspace. *U.S. News & World Report,* 118, 54–61.

Tafoya, B. (1986). *A Delphi forecast of the future of law enforcement* (Doctoral dissertation, University of Maryland, 1986). College Park, MD: University of Maryland.

Tafoya, W. (1990, January). The future of policing. *FBI Law Enforcement Bulletin, 59,* 13–17.

Tafoya, W. (1997a, August 6–8). *The escalation of the terrorist threat.* Paper presented at the XII Annual Symposium on Criminal Justice Issues, Chicago, IL.

Tafoya, W. (1997b, October). Policing high-tech crime. *Crime and Justice International, 13,* 6.

Thompson, J. (1967). *Organizations in action.* New York: McGraw-Hill.

Toffler, A. (1980). *The third wave.* New York: William Morrow.

Web Trend Watch. (1999). *More families buying PCs: Computer sales surge again.* Available: http://www.mediainfo.com

Wilson, J., & Kelling, G. (1982, March). Broken windows: The police and neighborhood safety. *Atlantic Monthly, 249,* 29–38.

Zhao, J. (1996). *Why police organizations change.* Police Executive Research Forum.

Zimbardo, P (1969). The human choice: Individuation, reason, and order versus deindividuation, impulse, and chaos. In W. Arnold & D. Levine (Eds.), *Nebraska symposium on motivation* (pp. 237–307). Lincoln: University of Nebraska Press.

Zuckerman, M. (1998, March 4). Computer attacks up 22% since 1996. *USA Today*, p.1A.

Mark E. Correia and Craig Bowling, "Veering Toward Digital Disorder: Computer-Related Crime and Law Enforcement Preparedness." Reprinted from *Police Quarterly*, Vol. 2 No. 2, June 1999, pp. 225–244. Copyright © 1999 Sage Publications, Inc. Reprinted by permission of Sage Publications, Inc. ✦

Chapter 23

Technological Challenges and Innovations in Police Patrolling

Delores E. Craig-Moreland

D*elores Craig-Moreland takes a closer look at how technological innovations might be incorporated into modern patrol work. She asserts that inputting, storing, and retrieving pertinent information will have a significant impact on management and planning among rank-and-file officers in the field in the near future.*

Craig-Moreland examines several modern technological innovations that seem to have great utility in police operations. For example, Enhanced 911 and computer-assisted dispatch enable officers to pinpoint the location of callers and respond quickly. Similarly, mobile personal computers show great promise for opening new communication channels among patrol officers. Mobile personal computers also give officers access to a variety of forms of information such as driver's license checks, database inquiries, and the retrieval of suspect photo images.

The invention of digital cameras has favorably impacted police work. Photos of crime scenes can now be stored electronically and conveniently retrieved when needed. In addition, car-mounted digital cameras or camcorders enable officers to document key aspects of arrests and traffic stops. Having this capacity may help to verify an officer's version of a controversial event or even deter problematic behavior in the first place, as officers and citizens who know they are being recorded may think twice before acting unlawfully.

The use of computers and other technology to support police patrol functions has been a work in progress since the Law Enforcement Assistance Administration (LEAA) days of the 1970s. While LEAA was disbanded in the 1980s, evidence of its impact can be seen to varying degrees in the myriad of federal, state, and local law enforcement agencies. Research such as URBIS, a multi-year study of government use of computers, showed a large expansion in use of computers in the 1970s and the 1980s. A 1997 survey by the Department of Justice reported that the period from 1993 to 1997 saw the percentage of local police departments using in-field computers increase from 13 to 29 percent. Departments reporting use of in-field computers employed 73 percent of all U.S. officers in 1997.

In reviewing the history of technology and law enforcement, Samuel Walker (1997) noted some of the earliest technology to impact law enforcement included Automated Fingerprint Identification System (AFIS) and Automated Video Identification System (AVIS), both of which increased ease of information storage and exchange between officers and departments. Since then, the availability of terminals in patrol cars has rapidly accelerated the infiltration of technology in patrol work. The purpose of this paper is to describe some of the current applications of technology in patrol, and some of the key issues associated with technological advances in policing.

Records

Ken Peak and Ron Glensor (1999) have pointed out that the ability of police patrol units to resolve an incident to which they respond is driven by information, frequently of a very limited nature. Access to records has always been a vital part of police patrol work because it allowed the patrol officer to discover information that was crucial to proper exercise of discretion in dealing with citizens. These contacts between patrol officers and the general public all represented general order maintenance and presented officers with opportunities to apprehend persons wanted as suspects or by the courts.

One of the earliest uses of computers in law enforcement was records storage and retrieval. Records that have been stored on computers include arrests and incident reports, driving citations, warrants, and convictions. Storing such information on computers made it readily available, as long as the user knew how files were organized and accessed. However, most records are organized by case, and accessed by the name of the person for whom the record was created. This hierarchical structure limits access to those who know that key piece of information, making it difficult for officers to search for records by the date or type of an event.

Access to such records usually required a call into some central records office that did checks of vehicles by license tag, warrants by the name of a driver or licensed person, etc. If the number of clerks available to answer such queries was limited, backlogs were possible. Some departments found lengthy periods of waiting for a vehicle check led to long vehicle stops. Each such event reduced the number of available officers on patrol. Current software is structured in a more relational manner, allowing for flexible inquiry.

With personal computers mounted in patrol vehicles, software now allows direct query by the officer. This can be achieved by direct submission of the vehicle tag, the driver's name, etc. Time delay in receiving a response is usually in seconds, and information is typically very up to date. According to research reported by Northrop, Kraemer, and King (1995), patrol officers reported that the search for and retrieval of records from computer files is their most frequent use of computers.

Patrol officers spend a significant amount of time completing incident reports. Software such as Automated Law Enforcement Incident Report (ALEIR) combines word processing and data processing. It facilitates the creation of an incident report, and it allows management personnel to sort and review activity by type of crime, or any other pertinent crime statistic.

Patrol Vehicle Location and Dispatch of Assistance

The system of dispatch of assistance has remained fairly constant since the advent of 911 systems. A call is received, the dispatcher gathers critical information, identifies the location and nearest vital service, and transmits a call for service. In the case of police calls, departments have differed in methods of dispatch, ranging from "any available unit" dispatch to assignment of specific units to respond. The ongoing challenge has always been to know who is available to handle a particular call. Large departments have relied on beats and sectors to cover large populations and geographic areas. Of course, the problem is that occasionally there will be multiple calls for service in one area. In the past, this led to lengthy response times.

Enhanced 911 (E911) and computer-assisted dispatch (CAD) make it possible to display all police calls for assistance. With mobile personal computers and monitors in patrol cars, officers can select and tag a call to take, according to other activity. This CAD system allows experienced officers to select calls with consideration given to other calls being worked. The officer can make a decision to stay available because it is possible to anticipate a need for backup at another call. The officers can also see how long a call has been waiting for service.

Departments that use this method have discovered that CAD has an added advantage in that the transmission of the call information cannot be monitored on a police scanner. If a high priority call, such as a robbery in progress, comes in it can be serviced by dispatching officers via scrambled voice transmission. Under these conditions, any voice dispatch is an automatic signal for a high priority call.

Crime Solving Through Technology

Some of the more advanced uses of technology are available to assist patrol officers in dealing with street crime. ShotSpotter is a new monitoring system of acoustic sensors that can detect and pinpoint gunfire (ShotSpotter, 2003). It can cover several square miles with one system, is weatherproof, and serves as a deterrent in high-crime neighborhoods. It can locate the point at which gunshots were fired by means of triangulation; the location is displayed on a computerized map of the community. Dispatchers can listen to a brief audio clip to verify that the event was in fact gunfire. Officers then can be directed to the precise location of the gunfire source.

Newspaper reports in the Portage, Wisconsin area have detailed another high-tech police tool. When two teenage boys tried to break into a government building, a cleaning lady witnessed the crime suspects. Rather than taking her to the police department to look at the photos of known suspects and previous felons, a patrol officer with no prior experience used "FACES" software for suspect sketching. The sketch then was made available to patrol officers via mobile computer and both juveniles were apprehended before the evening was over (WISCTV, 1999).

Theft of automobiles continues to be a high-volume crime. Electronic tracer devices such as LoJack or CarTracker are built around a small transmitter randomly located on the automobile. Once the motor vehicle is reported stolen, the transmitter is activated via remote, thus providing police with its exact location.

Technology also can be used to build a "fingerprint" system for weapons, storing the exact markings produced by a specific gun on a shell casing. With the advances in this technology, information could be stored on manufactured firearms to create their unique impact on shell casings. This same technology would provide the basis for comparing and making "hits" to identify the specific firearm used in a crime. Thus, if the only thing at a crime scene is a shell casing, as is often the case, this still would provide a rapid link to the firearm used in the crime.

Digital cameras have made dramatic changes in the field of photography. Much of the work of preserving information at a crime scene involves photo images. Continuously operating digital cameras mounted in patrol cars can sometimes record a critical piece of information before the event in question. Retrieval after the fact can be vital in reconstructing some activities. These digital images can improve officer safety and serve as material for training, assist in accident reconstruction, and can corroborate officer statements about potential liability situations. Digital cameras also can be fixed at intersections to perform similar functions, to allow for the reconstruction of accidents, and to verify frequency of violations, etc. An example of another application of the digital cameras is the Falls Church, Virginia program named CrossingGuard. This program uses video cameras to detect cars crossing through interesections at red lights, and records a brief video sequence of violations, including close-up color images of license plates. The system transmits the images digitally via regular phone lines to the central processing facility. An interesting safety feature of CrossingGuard is that it can extend the red light in the other direction to allow the violator to safely proceed through the intersection. The instant replay of the violation is clear-cut evidence of the violation, and completely objective.

Computer Voice Stress Analyzer or CVSA is another example of technology in law enforcement. This functions in a manner similar to the lie detector of old. It confirms patterns of voice stress consistent with truthfulness or dishonesty. A Palm Beach (FL) detective reported using high voice stress levels as a support to get an admission of guilt from a suspect in an arson case. It also supported the innocence of another suspect. While it is not generally available for use by patrol, its availability to sort out the truth may help to "encourage" a higher level of honesty from the beginning of an investigation.

Crime Analysis and Patrol Planning

A number of police departments such as those in Long Beach, California (Binkley, 1991) and Tacoma, Washington (Parrott & Stutz, 1991) have installed geographic information systems (GIS) to support routine functions such as producing beat maps, planning patrol strategies, and maximizing efficiency in the service of warrants.

By coupling GIS with E911 and CAD, law enforcement officials can gain a much better understanding of the nature and magnitude of their crime problems. For instance, a GIS system can answer questions about the size and scope of burglary problems, according to each beat or precinct. Geographic information systems have thus been used to analyze high-volume crimes which are associated with career criminals (Binkley, 1991). This information can be used for planning special patrols likely to encounter these career criminals (for further discussion of GIS mechanics see Rogers and Craig,1994). In its most sophisticated form, police departments can make use of geographic profiling (Rossmo, 2000). GIS information can be merged with crime analysis to identify specific offenders who commit crimes serially.

Challenges

Developments in technology related to computers advance so rapidly that it is a serious challenge to avoid being swept away by a tide of new products. Every day there are new software packages being offered to law enforcement. Applications are almost endless, ranging from report generating to browsing everything from the penal code to police sketches. The most effective way to handle these opportunities appears to be the path taken by the Los Angeles County Sheriff's Department (Pilant, 2000). The organization has formed a technology committee, which constantly searches for technology solutions to current problems. They seldom consider some new form of technology just because it is new. By reviewing department problems and weighing the ability of a new application to deal with such problems, the field of products to consider remains manageable. At the same time, a constant state of openness allows the department to be open to things they have not thought of, with a view to relevance.

The rapid development of computers and other forms of technology for law enforcement leads to the question of law enforcement readiness to use such technology. Computer literacy is improving among those recruited for law enforcement because it is improving in society as a whole. But computer literacy among officers cannot be assumed. A random sample of some police department web sites indicated that computer literacy has not become a necessary skill among recruits. Specific job-related training is probably sufficient for use of mobile personal computers, but may not lead to innovative use of computers by law enforcement. With increases in cybercrime, patrol officers can be expected to need specific knowledge of computers that will allow for the securing of computers at crime scenes (Correia & Bowling, 2000).

Ironically, the computer may be the answer to the training needs of patrol officers. Web-based education programs are being offered specifically for law enforcement officers, bringing the top law enforcement instructors in the country and their classes to life on the computer. Dynamic computer-based training for this specialized application is now a reality.

Another challenge in using technology is the rather hostile environment presented by patrol. Consideration is mainly focused to the rather delicate nature of most electronic devices and the sometimes rough conditions experienced in patrol vehicles. Patrol vehicles experience vibrations, extreme changes in temperature, and lots of bouncing and bumping along. Mobile docking stations can be customized to include whatever technology is available and to facilitate rapid installation and removal of equipment. Such stations include ports to connect personal computers, some form of power adapter/source, and some form of mounting plate. The military defense industry and aerospace have dealt with these challenges in the past and may be a source of innovation related to durability, which may benefit law enforcement.

Patrol use of technology results in a challenge to the courts to deal with technology. In the case of digital cameras, not every jurisdiction allows digital photography as a means of representing a crime scene or critical evidence. CVSA is at the moment a tool for the use of crime investigators and its standing in court proceedings has not yet been decided. The future of technology as a tool of patrol will rest to some extent on the relevant standards of evidence set by the courts.

Summary

The information age has subsumed law enforcement. It is no longer possible to function in the world of law enforcement without computers. Computer literacy may not be a requirement of recruits, but it is a virtual (no pun intended) certainty that every patrol officer will experience on-the-job training to use in-field computers. They will be making use of computers to reconstruct accidents, locate gunfire, collect and preserve evidence, etc. The applications are more or less limitless. The answer to this opportunity is very similar to the answer to law enforcement in general: get organized. A team of knowledgeable individuals who are familiar with the work of patrol and crime investigation teams are in a position to review new technology for its relevance to ongoing operations. They are also in a position to understand the potential of new offerings.

References

Binkley, L. L. (1991) Futuristic System Helps Long Beach Corner Career Criminals. *Police Chief 58* (4), 2–5.

Correia, Mark E., and Bowling, Craig. (2000) Veering Toward Digital Disorder: Computer-Related Crime and Law Enforcement Preparedness. *Police Quarterly 2* (2), 225–244.

Northrop, Alana, Kraemer, Kenneth L., and King, John L. (1995) Police Use of Computers. *Journal of Criminal Justice 23* (3) 259–275.

Parrott, R., and Stutz, F. P. (1991) Urban GIS Applications. In D. J. Maguire, M. F. Goodchild, and D. W. Rhind (Eds.), *Geographic Information Systems: Principles and Applications.* New York: John Wiley and Sons, Inc. (2): 247–260.

Peak, Kenneth J., and Glensor, Ronald W. (1999) *Community Policing & Problem Solving: Strategies & Practices.* Upper Saddle River, New Jersey: Prentice Hall.

Pilant, Lois (2000) Spotlight On . . . Evaluating and Purchasing New Technologies. *Police Chief LXVII* 4 , 46–54.

Rogers, Robert and Craig, Delores. (1994) Geographic Information Systems in Policing, *Police Studies 17* (2), 67–78.

Rossmo, D. K. (2000) *Geographic Profiling.* Boca Raton, FL: CRC Press Inc.

ShotSpotter. 2003. *Technology Overview: Detecting Gunshots Acoustically* [online]. Avaliable from Word Wide Web: (http://www.shotspotter.com/technologyoverview.htm).

Walker, Jeffery T. (1997) Re-Blueing the Police: Technological Changes and Law Enforcement Practices. In M. L. Dantzker (Ed.) *Contemporary Policing: Personnel, Issues, and Trends.* Boston: Butterworth-Heinemann. 257–276.

WISCTV. 1999. *Computer Sketches Aid Portage Police* [online]. Cited September 13, 1999. Available from World Wide Web: (http://www.wisctv.com).

Delores E. Craig-Moreland, "Technological Challenges and Innovations in Police Patrolling." Copyright © 2003 by Roxbury Publishing Company. All rights reserved. ✦

Part VI

Police Deviance and Ethical Issues

Underlying the issue of police misconduct is the question: Who polices the police? The founding fathers of our nation shared a fear of strong, centralized government power that resonates in the American polity to this day. Accordingly, a decentralized government with considerable local authority and control are the hallmarks of American society.

Unlike its European counterparts, the U.S. lacks a centralized police force. Few other local government agencies are empowered to carry firearms and have the authority to use force, even lethal force, to compel the legal compliance of citizens. Even with local control and decentralization of police forces in America, the public is still wary of a police force that might exceed its legal authority. And such concern is warranted. After all, those entrusted with police powers, no matter how well they are trained, are mere human beings vulnerable to the vagaries and temptations associated with the human condition.

Police deviance varies from minor violations of department policies to an intentional breaking of the law for personal gain or satisfaction. Opportunities for deviance can arise whenever officers are engaged in interactions in the field out of the watchful eye of a supervisor, and even more frequently when officers are exposed to the dark side of society in undercover cases involving vice and drugs.

Ethical issues deal with what a police officer should or should not do, but do not necessarily involve a breach of the law. Historically, police administrators have attempted to use professionalism to educate and train police officers. For example, in his field study of a medium-sized police department, Muir (1977) interviewed officers with a variety of questions in an attempt to understand the nature of police work. He concluded that a good police officer with high moral character is an individual who performs his or her work with passion and professionalism. Further, the most important characteristic of an exemplary police officer is the willingness to serve with compassion. The following four selections help the reader understand many of the issues surrounding ethical police behavior and police officer deviance.

Reference

Muir, W. 1977. *Police: Streetcorner Politicians.* Chicago: University of Chicago Press. ✦

Chapter 24
When Badges Get Too Big

Identifying and Misidentifying Police Misconduct from Citizen Complaints

Kim Lersch

This study of citizen complaints about police misconduct is both informative and timely. First, the author points out that stories covered by the news media are seldom accurate, typically failing to reflect the true nature of an incident. Second, she notes that an area of citizen complaints which has attracted very little empirical scrutiny concerns non-lethal police-citizen encounters. What little is known is that race/ethnicity, age, and sex are all significantly related to citizen reporting of police misconduct. For example, African-American citizens tend to be more likely to complain about police misconduct than other racial or ethnic groups.

Lersch also finds that young male officers receive a disproportionate number of complaints for excessive force compared to female officers. It is also noteworthy that there is a positive correlation between an officer's productivity (number of arrests) and the number of citizens' complaints—the more tickets an officer writes, the more likely he or she is to draw citizen complaints. In a similar vein, patrol officers who work closely with citizens on a daily basis are more likely to receive complaints than their counterparts who work as criminal investigators.

Introduction

In the Fall of 1991, I started my graduate education in sociology. Discussions of the Rodney King incident, which had occurred only a few months earlier, became the center focus of a number of my courses. While obviously violent police misconduct was nothing new, this was one of the first times that such an incident had been captured on film and broadcast to living rooms across the world. Not since the urban unrest of the 1960s had the American public focused so much attention on police misconduct, especially involving minority citizens. And, like many other young impressionable students of police behavior, I became hooked on police misconduct issues.

As luck would have it, I enrolled in several courses with a professor by the name of Joe Feagin, a radical sociologist who specializes in race/ethnic relations. Dr. Feagin encouraged my interest in police misconduct and offered to work with me on a thesis in the area. One of the more interesting facts that quickly surfaced when I started my research was that there was (and still really is) no reliable data source that provides information on the national level of incidents of police misconduct. Think about this for a moment. A police administrator reviews his use of force reports and excessive force complaints, concerned that the level of force his agency employs may be higher than other agencies'. There is no government agency or centralized clearinghouse that compiles such information; there are no comparison rates or mean figures that can be used to judge whether or not an agency is higher or lower than average. Given the importance of the phenomenon of police misconduct, this is a very interesting fact.

Recognizing a void in our knowledge of police misconduct, Dr. Feagin suggested that I try to compile a data source that provided nationwide information on violent police/citizen encounters. It was decided that I use an on-line database called Lexis/Nexis and review major newspaper accounts of police brutality, noting such variables as officer race, citizen race, circumstances surrounding the encounter, and other pertinent information. While this was an interesting undertaking, I quickly found that media accounts of police misconduct are not viewed as a reliable source of data. We were finally able to get an article published based on this data (see Lersch and Feagin, 1996), but not until the manuscript (and especially the data source) had been thoroughly raked over the coals by reviewers from other journals.

While I was still interested in police misconduct, I realized that I needed a more defensible source of data for my dissertation. It was then that I began my research on citizen complaints against the police. Citizen complaints are viewed as an official source of information concerning the police and, as a data source, are viewed more favorably than media accounts. However, the use of citizen complaints as a valid and reliable indicator of acts of police misconduct is not beyond critique. As will be discussed later in this chapter, there are some very real problems with equating a citizen complaint with an act of misconduct. However, this practice occurs all the time. Whenever a police shooting occurs, more often than not a television reporter will say something like, "In his fifteen years of service, Officer Jones has had eight citizen complaints filed against him, none of them sustained." What does this mean? Is that a lot? Does the lack of substantiated complaints imply a police cover-up, lack of evidence, or what?

It is the purpose of this chapter to provide an overview of what we know about citizen complaints. General information concerning the types of complaints filed, who files them, as well as typical characteristics of the accused officers will be presented. Additionally, a critique of the validity of citizen complaints will be provided. Hopefully, the next time you hear a statement made by a reporter regarding the eight prior complaints that an officer has on his permanent record, you will have a much better understanding of what those eight complaints may (or may not) mean concerning the actual behavior of the officer.

Police Misconduct and Citizen Complaints: The Basics

To better understand misconduct of police officers, researchers have turned to a number of methods such as the use of observational studies, analyses of surveys of citizens and/or police officers, studies of official police records, and examinations of citizen complaints. Each data source has its own unique problems related to whether or not the data provides an accurate picture of what actually happened in a particular police-citizen encounter.

While this chapter will describe some of the various issues related to the validity of citizen complaints, one of the positive aspects of this particular data source is that it provides data on non-lethal encounters with the police. A great deal of research exists that examines the use of deadly force by police officers. We know quite a bit about officers who are involved in deadly force incidents, citizens who have been targeted for deadly force, situational aspects of the encounter, and the effects of written policies on an officer's decision to use deadly force.

One of the reasons why we know more about the use of deadly force is the availability of data. Contemporary law enforcement agencies maintain records on the use of deadly force, and these records are readily available to the public. We do not know as much about non-lethal incidents involving officers. Violent police-citizen incidents are a relatively rare occurrence and, when they do occur, the encounters often take place out of the public eye (Bayley and Garofalo, 1989; Fyfe, 1989; McLaughlin, 1992). Additionally, many violent incidents go unreported by both the officer and the citizen involved.

Analyses of citizen complaints of misconduct allow the researcher to examine a variety of allegations. While complaints may allege the improper or excessive use of force, others may accuse officers of illegal searches, unlawful arrest, threatening or intimidating demeanor, rudeness, theft of property from a crime scene, or even throwing ice down the blouse of a waitress. Because of the wide variety of allegations that can occur, in order to statistically analyze the data researchers often collapse or combine categories of allegations. This introduces a problem when one tries to compare results of studies based on data collected from different agencies and the researchers have used different categories for complaints.

Recognizing the lack of consistency in classifications of complaint types across studies, it is still helpful to look at the types of complaints filed by citizens. Pate and Fridell (1993), in a review of the relevant literature on police use of force, reported rates of violent misconduct allegations as low as 17.5 percent in Washington State Departments (Dugan and Breda, 1991) to a high of 66.4 percent in "Metro City" (Wagner, 1980). With respect to complaints of a nonviolent nature, Dugan and Breda (1991) reported that 41.8 percent of the complaints filed against Washington State Agencies were for alleged "verbal misconduct." Littlejohn (1981) in a review of the city of Detroit Police Department, reported a rate of 24 percent for demeanor related complaints. Griswold (1994) found that only 13.9 percent of the complaints filed against a police agency in Florida involved allegations of discourtesy or harassment, but this percentage included both internal police complaints as well as citizen allegations.

Citizen Characteristics

Beyond the types of complaints, researchers have also examined the characteristics of citizens who have filed the complaint of misconduct. When citizen characteristics have been discussed in previous studies, many researchers have focused on the race of the citizen filing the complaint. While the results of these studies have not achieved full consensus, many reports have found that minority citizens, especially African Americans, are more likely to file complaints against police officers. This trend is not all that surprising, given the level of tension and conflict that exists between the police and minority citizens.

Racial disparity in the evaluations of police performance is nothing new. In one of the early studies of citizen ratings of the police, Bayley and Mendelsohn (1969) reported that minority citizens rated the performance of the police at a lower level than did whites, even when controlling for age, gender, and other background influences. Since the advent of public opinion polls in the 1960s, minorities have consistently rated police performance lower than white Americans (Cox, 1996; Flanagan and Vaughn, 1995; Smith, Graham, and Adams, 1991; Walker and Katz, 2002). According to a 1970 Harris poll, only one-fifth of the African American respondents felt that local police officers applied the law equally; 62 percent felt the police were against African Americans; 73 percent felt their local law enforcement officers were dishonest; and 67 percent felt police officers were more concerned with injuring African Americans than with preventing criminal acts (Feagin and Hahn, 1973). Other more recent polls suggest that African Americans are more likely than whites to report harassment and to know someone who is a victim of police misconduct (Bessent and Taylor, 1991; Kappeler, Sluder, and Alpert, 1994). Further, blacks are more likely than whites to report suspicion and lack of confidence in the practices of the police (Johnson, 1997).

Given the lower evaluations that have been provided by minority citizens in public opinion polls, it is not surprising that in many studies minority citizens were overrepresented among complainants of misconduct. Between 1987 and 1990, a total of 4,400 complaints of misconduct were filed against the Los Angeles Police Department. While black citizens in the city of Los Angeles comprise only 13 percent of the city population, 41 percent of the complaints against officers were filed by blacks (Rohrlich and Merina, 1991). In my dissertation data that was collected from a large police agency in the southeastern United States, while minority citizens accounted for 22.2 percent of the city population, 50.5 percent of the complaints against the agency were filed by minorities (Lersch, 1998a). Other researchers (Kerstetter et al., 1996; Wagner, 1980; Walker and Graham, 1998) have found similar overrepresentation of minority citizens among complainants. Pate and Fridell (1993) found that blacks were overrepresented among complainants of excessive force when the officer involved was employed with a municipal or county agency. With respect to state agencies, whites were found to be slightly overrepresented among complainants.

So, given the fact that minorities tend to file more complaints against the police, does this mean that minorities experience higher levels of police misconduct than whites? The answer to this question is really beyond the scope of this chapter. However, one of the problems that exist when examining complaints of misconduct based on citizen race is that there may be racial differences in the definition of what sort of behaviors constitute "police misconduct," especially with respect to the use of force. In a poll conducted by *Time* magazine in the wake of the Rodney king incident, while 92 percent of the African Americans surveyed felt that excessive force had been used against King, only 72 percent of Caucasians voiced a similar belief (Lacayo, 1992).

The use of racial slurs, profane or abusive language and other forms of verbal abuse have been defined as "police brutality" by many citizens, especially among minority citizens (Adams, 1995; Locke, 1995; President's Commission on Law Enforcement and Administration of Justice, 1967; Worden, 1995). Locke (1995: 134) notes that "in some quarters, any unwarranted or unwelcome police conduct may constitute brutality." Broad definitions concerning what sorts of behaviors constitute a charge of "police brutality" may artificially inflate allegations of excessive force.

Officer Characteristics

The characteristics of officers have been analyzed. Previous studies have examined for relationships between the gender, race, age, tenure, and education of officers and the occurrence of citizen complaints. The findings are summarized in the next section.

Gender. With the passage of the Equal Employment Opportunity Act of 1972, women began to enter the male-dominated field of policing in significant numbers. While women continue to be a minority in law enforcement agencies, since 1972 their numbers have increased from 4.2 percent of the sworn personnel to just below 9 percent (Lanier, 1996).

Coinciding with the arrival of more women police officers was a host of studies that compared the attitudes, performance, and evaluations of male and female officers. Possible behavioral differences between the male and female officers were explored from every angle, including the initiation of citizen encounters, number of arrests, commitment to public service, and ability to diffuse potentially violent situations. These investigations did not produce consistent results. While some studies found differences between male and female officers, others did not.

However, there appears to be one area in which a fair amount of consistency has been reported with respect to differences between male and female officers: citizen complaints, especially in allegations involving the improper use of force. Steffensmeier (1979) found that the presence of female officers on patrol resulted in a decreased number of citizen complaints and an overall reduction in police violence. Van Wormer (1981) stated that male officers were more likely to generate citizen complaints, provoke incidents of violence, and be involved in brutality cases. Conversely, female officers did not present a violent, threatening image to the general public, were found to avoid assaults, and seemed to produce an overall calming effect. Similarly Grennan (1987) found that female officers in male-female patrol teams were more effective in calming a potentially violent situation. It has also been demonstrated that female officers are less likely to be involved in deadly force incidents (Horvath, 1987).

In its review of the practices of the Los Angeles Police Department, the Christopher Commission detected a number of officers whose names appeared repeatedly in personnel complaints, reports of officer-involved shootings, and in use of force reports. Of the 120 officers with the most citizen complaints of excessive force, all of the officers were male (Independent Commission on the Los Angeles Police Department, 1991). Similarly, in the research that I conducted based on the citizen complaints filed against a large police agency, male officers were the more likely targets of citizen complaints (Lersch, 1998b). When a colleague and I looked at only the problem-prone officers who had received a high number of citizen complaints, all of the officers were male (Lersch and Mieczkowski, 1996). Hickman, Piquero and Green (2000) found that the strongest predictors of citizen complaints were gender (male), marital status (single) and whether or not the officer had repeatedly failed polygraph tests.

Race. The literature concerning the race of the officer and the incidents of complaints has not demonstrated a clear pattern (Riksheim and Chermak, 1993). While some studies have reported that black officers are more likely to use unjustified force and are more likely to be involved in on-duty shootings, these occurrences may be due to the overrepresentation of black officers in high crime areas (Sherman, 1980; Fyfe, 1981). Friedrich (1980) reported that while black officers were more likely to use reasonable force against citizens, they were less likely to use excessive force than their white peers. Similarly, Worden (1992) found that black officers were more likely to use force but less likely to use improper force in dealings with citizens.

Pate and Fridell (1993), in an extensive study of complaints of excessive force, found no definite pattern with regard to the race of the officer named in the complaint.

The responding sheriff's agencies reported that the officers who had been accused of violent misconduct were reflective of the agency in terms of race. However, the county, city, and state agencies reported that minority officers were more likely to be accused of excessive force than the white officers.

Things get even more complicated when one wishes to look at the relationship between the race of the officer and the race of the citizen. Some researchers have found that complaints against the police tend to be intraracial in nature: that is, white citizens complaining against white officers or black citizens complaining against black officers. In his classic study, Reiss (1968) found that violent altercations between offenders and officers tended to be intraracial in nature. Carter (1986) found that Hispanic officers were more likely to discriminate against Hispanic citizens than white citizens.

In one study that was based on my dissertation data, minority citizens were more likely to file complaints against a minority officer (Lersch and Mieczkowski, 1996). For me, this intraracial tendency was fairly surprising. I really expected that I would find a large number of complaints filed by minority citizens against white officers. However, this is one of the problems when trying to use citizen complaints as an accurate reflection of what is actually happening on the streets. Not every incident of police misconduct is reported. If an individual does choose to file a complaint, he or she assumes that an agent of the department will not retaliate against them and, ultimately, something will be done in response to their complaint.

The fear that some people have of the police is very real. This may be a difficult fact for many white, middle-class folks who have been brought up with visions of Officer Friendly to understand and accept. A Latino man who works at the University approached me recently to share a very negative experience that he had had with one of our local police officers. Based on "Juan's" account, it was clear that the officer had acted inappropriately. I encouraged him to contact Internal Affairs and file a complaint. Juan's eyes opened wide, and asked me if I was nuts. "The officer will come after me," he said. "The cop will find out where I live, what kind of car I drive, where I work." Juan was clearly afraid of retaliation. The end result was that no complaint was filed, although Juan had clearly experienced an act of inappropriate conduct.

So, to return to the intraracial nature of the complaints: Perhaps the reason that minority citizens are more likely to file complaints against minority officers is because a minority citizen may feel more confident that the complaint will be addressed, whereas a complaint filed by a minority citizen against white officers would more likely be ignored. Given the lengthy history of mistrust and animosity between minority citizens and the police, this could be a feasible interpretation. However, because citizen complaints only reflect the "misconduct known to the police" and not the true level of misconduct, we really have no idea what the real explanation for the intraracial tendency is.

Age, Tenure, and Education. The age of the officer may have an effect on his or her manner in dealing with citizens, although research has not provided consistent results. Cohen and Chaiken (1972) found that officers in a single birth cohort who were oldest at the time of their appointment were less likely to have complaints filed against them for discourtesy, racial slurs, or excessive force. Conversely, Alpert (1989) found that age had no influence on the decision to use force in the arrest of a citizen or in the use of deadly force.

Tenure has been associated with the manner in which officers react to citizens. It has been reported that older, more experienced officers present a calmer demeanor when dealing with the public, while officers with fewer years of experience initiate more contacts with citizens, are more likely to make arrests, and tend to patrol more aggressively (Forst, Lucianovic, and Cox, 1977; Friedrich, 1980). Smith, Graham, and Adams (1991) found that while older officers perceived heightened levels of citizen respect, if an officer worked in a specific area for an extended period of time, he or she was more likely to feel at risk of citizen abuse.

No matter what one's chosen profession, it is generally assumed that inexperienced employees will make rookie mistakes. Policing is no different. While working with a local supervisory level police officer on a research project in which she wished to examine the relationship between misconduct and education, the supervisor was adamant about only looking at officers who had at least five years of experience with this particular agency. The supervisor's rationalization was that after a few years, the officer's "true" behavior would surface. Any citizen complaints received prior to that were just "rookie" mistakes and were not reflective of the officer's working personality. However, the relationship between age and tenure is more complex.

Age and tenure can be closely tied together. The general trend is for older officers to also have more years of experience. This is not always the case. Let's say there are two officers, both with six years of experience. Officer Smith, a high-school drop out, grew tired of working as an assistant manager at the local burger joint, earned his GED and joined the police department on his 19th birthday (some agencies still will hire officers at the ripe old age of 19). Officer Jones joined the department after a four-year stint in the military, where he spent a great deal of time overseas. With the assistance of the G.I. Bill, he then went to college and earned a 4-year degree. At the age of 26, Jones became a police officer. Would you expect these two officers who have the same length of service to have similar problems arise when dealing citizens? Probably not.

Previous studies have found that officers with advanced degrees were less authoritarian, received fewer citizen complaints, and were less likely to be accused of unnecessary physical force (Bowker, 1980; Carter and Sapp, 1990; Dalley, 1975). Some of thc arguments supporting an increased educational requirement in the hiring of officers include the development of greater understanding and tolerance for minorities as well as allowing for additional experiences for maturity (Mahan, 1991). When studies only look at tenure and/or age and do not control for educational attainment or military experience, the direct causal effects of these variables are difficult to trace.

So, What's the Problem with Citizen Complaints?

I began to analyze citizen complaints because I wanted a more "official," reliable, valid source of data on police misconduct. I contacted a large police agency and, for several months, camped out in the Internal Affairs office where I combed through three years of citizen complaints. Unfortunately, when I started digging into the complaints, I quickly realized that there are some very real problems with equating a citizen complaint with an act of misconduct.

There was the complaint from the women who accused the detective sent to her home of incompetence. Apparently, this woman regularly summoned the police to her home for a variety of unfounded criminal complaints. On this particular occasion, a window that was found cracked open was, in her mind, a clear indication that someone had tried to break into her house. The detective that was sent to her home found no fingerprints and nothing missing, and determined that no crime had been committed. When the Internal Affairs detective investigated her complaint, the woman told the IA investigator that on television, at least two detectives are always sent to investigate complaints. She had only been sent one detective, and this one was clearly not qualified.

Then there was the complaint of rudeness, incompetence, and dereliction of duty filed against an officer. The complainant, a white male who resided in a rather affluent area of this particular city, was clearly disturbed by the behavior of the officer who had been dispatched to his home. When the IA detective (who happened to be white) looked into this allegation, the complainant shared with the detective that the real problem was that the officer was African American, and that he did not want an African American officer sent to his home. The citizen wanted to be assured that the next time he called the agency, only white officers would be dispatched. The IA detective suggested that the citizen either move or handle criminal matters on his own, because the agency would dispatch the next available officer to his home, no matter what the race, ethnicity or gender of that officer (good for the agency!).

Unfortunately, I could go on and on with these sorts of citizen complaints. "The officer was rude to me when he gave me my ticket. And, by the way, don't these officers have better things to do than give law-abiding citizens like me traffic violations? So what if I was doing 30 over in a school zone." "The officer was lazy—she refused to arrest the punk next door. I know that kid stole some things from my garage. What do you mean, you need more evidence than my gut feeling to make an arrest?" "I want to file a complaint of excessive force—when the officers arrested my mentally unstable and intoxicated daughter, they hog-tied her and put her in the back of the cruiser. I realize that she was biting, kicking, and punching, but did they have to tie her up like that?" "The officer refused to help me. I wanted to evict my tenants and she refused to arrest them"—a civil matter beyond the powers of an officer.

The problem with these types of complaints is that while the allegations were not sustained, the complaints still become a permanent part of an officer's record. The morning that I was writing this section, a local police officer was arrested at his estranged wife's home for domestic violence. The local news broadcaster reported that the officer had been named in two complaints of excessive force, which sounds bad to the average Joe Public. Do these complaints reflect "real" uses of excessive force, or did someone complain that their handcuffs were too tight?

The Issue of Overreporting

Overreporting of acts of misconduct is a concern. Arguably, it may be just as important to examine the motivations of the citizen filing a complaint as it is to look at the allegation against the officer. Why is this citizen filing a complaint against the officer? Citizens file complaints for any number of reasons. They are angry because they feel singled out for a ticket or arrest. They may not have a clear understanding of the legal constraints on an officer's behavior. Or, as discussed by Adams (1995), a citizen may file a complaint with the hope of securing an upper hand in the plea bargaining process. And, as stated previously, there may be definitional differences based on race and social class as to what sort of behavior constitutes an act of misconduct.

As evidence of overreporting, some critics point to the low substantiation rate of citizen complaints (Adams, 1995). After an allegation is investigated, it is usually given one of four possible findings: exonerated; not sustained; sustained; or unfounded. These rulings are defined as follows:

- **Exonerated:** The acts that provided the basis for the complaint or allegation occurred; however, investigation revealed that they were justified, lawful, and proper.
- **Not sustained:** The investigation failed to disclose sufficient evidence to prove the allegations made in the complaint.
- **Sustained:** The investigation disclosed sufficient evidence to prove clearly the allegations made in the complaint.
- **Unfounded:** The investigation conclusively proved that the act or acts complained of did not occur.

When researchers have examined complaints of misconduct, the substantiation rates typically fall between 0 and 25 percent, with a reported norm of 10 percent or less (Pate and Fridell, 1993). This means that, on average, 90 percent of the allegations of misconduct are either not supported by the available evidence or are not determined to be acts of misconduct at all.

Complaints as Productivity Measures

As an interesting twist to the overreporting issue, some agencies view citizen complaints as a productivity measure. On several occasions when I've done presentations on citizen complaints, I have been stopped by high-ranking law enforcement officials. Their initial comment was that the officers with greater numbers of complaints were just young, more aggressive officers performing their duties to the best of their abilities. Far from being problem officers, these individuals were the only officers who were performing their duties and earning their paychecks. Not only does this explanation absolve the individual officer receiving the complaint from any wrongdoing, but it also relieves the department of any blame for condoning the misconduct of its officers.

There is a kernel of truth to this view. Given the nature of the function of the police, it has been argued that citizen complaints are inevitable (Wagner and Decker, 1997). Police officers, in their role as the social control agents of the state, are often put into situations that place them in direct conflict with citizens. By definition, police officers must enforce the law and arrest those who violate the law. These sorts of adversarial encounters can lead to unpleasant situations, and, when the mechanisms are in place for a citizen to file a complaint against a police officer, it is not unreasonable to assume that some citizens will take advantage of the opportunity to voice their displeasure.

There is also some data to support this evaluation of citizen complaints as a measure of aggressive policing. In the first wave of data collection that I did for my dissertation, I found that a small group of officers accounted for a disproportionate number of citizen complaints. When a colleague and I examined this group of officers further, we found that officers with a high number of complaints were significantly younger and had fewer years of experience when compared to officers with fewer complaints (Lersch and Mieczkowski, 1996). Further, these problem-prone officers were more likely to have complaints filed against them as a result of a proactive encounter with a citizen. That is, the complaints resulted after the officer initiated the encounter on his own accord—traffic stops, investigations of suspicious persons, etc.

To explore this relationship further, I went back to the agency and collected additional data not only on citizen complaints, but on standard measures of officer productivity such as number of arrests, number of traffic citations, and number of field interrogation reports. A number of very interesting findings emerged from this data. First, whether or not an officer received a complaint seemed to be strongly related to assignment: While the agency employed over 500 sworn law enforcement personnel, only 117 officers had received a citizen complaint in the 12-month period of analysis. The vast majority of these 117 officers (85 percent) were assigned to the patrol division. Of the 18 officers that were not, several were assigned to the traffic unit and others were in the canine unit. The accused officers, as a function of their assignments, were therefore in positions to regularly find themselves in potentially negative confrontations with citizens, which would put them at greater risk for receiving citizen complaints. This would support the contention that citizen complaints are inevitable given the function of the police.

Second, there did seem to be a relationship between the productivity of the officers and the number of complaints they received. One of the officers with the highest number of complaints for the year was a traffic officer who was regularly featured in the local press for his innovative and highly successful ways to catch speeders. Armed with his trusty radar gun, he would hide in trees, disguise himself as a construction worker, or sit at the bus stop dressed as a tourist. In fact, significant positive correlations were found between the total number of citizen complaints and all of the traditional productivity measures. The number of felony arrests, misdemeanor arrests, traffic citations, juvenile status offense arrests, and the number of field interrogation reports were related to the number of citizen complaints. More active and aggressive officers had higher number of citizen complaints (Lersch, 2002).

The findings of this particular study should not be used to support the flat dismissal of citizen complaints as frivolous and vindictive. One serious issue remains concerning this data source: There is no means by which to accurately assess the behavior of the officer. Just because an officer is highly productive and has received a higher number of citizen complaints, this does not automatically imply that the citizens are just reacting to their negative experience of receiving a ticket, being arrested, or being stopped and interrogated on the street. The citizen may be filing the complaint with greater motivation than just to get even with the officers or to deflect attention from the citizen's own behavior. In addition to writing the citation or making the arrest, the officer may have acted poorly.

Few Citizen Complaints Mean No Problems, Right?

If an agency receives a high number of citizen complaints, what does this mean? As a further challenge to the validity of citizen complaints as a measure of actual police behavior, the better the police/community relationship, the more complaints the agency will receive. Citizen complaints reflect not only an evaluation of the behavior of the individual officer, but the confidence that the citizen has with the police agency to monitor the behavior of their own (Pate and Fridell, 1993). As an example of how complicated these issues can become, I was asked once to evaluate a community policing effort that was to be based in a minority community. As one of the evaluative measures, I wanted to examine the number of citizen complaints that was filed by residents in the target area. I had hoped that the number of complaints would go up, not down. As odd as it might sound, an increase in the number of citizen complaints may reflect a highly successful community policing effort.

Areas with poor community relations often proudly point to their relatively low number of citizen complaints as evidence that they are doing nothing wrong. This may not be the case at all. The reason we've all seen the Rodney King videotape was because George Holliday, the man who had taped the incident, was treated with indifference when he contacted the Foothill Station of the Los Angeles Police Department. Holliday informed the officer who answered his call that he had witnessed the beating. The officer asked no questions about the incident, nor did he offer to take down a formal complaint. Paul King, brother of Rodney, also tried to file a complaint in person at the Foothill station. He too was met with uncooperative officers, this time at the supervisory level, who made no record of the complaint (Skolnick and Fyfe, 1993).

When I started working at my first "real" job as an assistant professor, the chair of my department invited me to have lunch with her and the chief of the largest local police agency, a department with about 100 sworn officers. During lunch, my chair explained to the chief that I studied citizen complaints against the police. The chief then proudly invited me to come down and examine the eight complaints that had been filed against his agency in the past year. My immediate gut reaction was that something was wrong—where were the rest of the complaints? About a year later, I got my answer.

The headlines of the local papers were filled with the story of an African-American male homeowner who had tried to file a complaint of misconduct against several patrol officers. It seems that the officers were responding to a call in which an intoxicated black male was disturbing the peace. Unfortunately for the officers, they went to the wrong address. According to the papers, the officers were very rude and threatening in their interaction with "Mr. Adams," who was innocently unloading groceries from his car. The incident began to escalate until Mr. Adams finally retreated into his home, where he promptly called the police to file a complaint. At police headquarters, the complaint call was transferred to "Lieutenant Jones," who was very concerned about the complaint and patiently promised Mr. Adams that his complaint would be taken seriously and the officers would be disciplined. When Mr. Adams called the agency several weeks later to follow up with Lieutenant Jones, he was informed that Jones had retired about six months ago. No official complaint had ever been recorded.

An agency can do a great deal to discourage a citizen from filing a complaint of misconduct (Walker, 2001). Complaint procedures that are complicated, intimidating, or otherwise difficult to use will have an impact on the reporting rate (for a discussion of various complaint systems, see Perez and Muir 1995). It is not unheard of for citizens to be told when they are filing a complaint that if the internal investigation rules the complaint to be unfounded, the citizen may be charged with filing a false police report. In communities where English is not the primary language, agencies may not have informational posters and pamphlets on how to file a complaint in the residents' native tongue.

Just as overreporting is a problem, underreporting of acts of police misconduct is clearly a concern. Walker and Bumphus (1992) reported that only one-third of the people who believe that they have been mistreated by police officers pursue the matter by filing an official complaint, which would imply that we are missing the majority of misconduct incidents. Critiques of this nature are roughly comparable to the validity concerns when using the Federal Bureau of Investigation's Uniform Crime Reports as a measure of criminal activity in the U.S.; one is only able to evaluate and analyze the crimes known to the police.

It is very difficult to know how many citizens experience acts of police misconduct and choose not to report it. Evidence is hard to come by. In one of the few studies that report actual figures, Walker and Graham (1998), in an analysis of data collected as part of the 1977 Police Services Study, noted that only 36 percent of the respondents who had experienced or witnessed an act of police misconduct chose to take any kind of formal action. More recently, in the research that I did that examined the relationship between the number of complaints an officer received and the officer's productivity, I may have inadvertently found some evidence to support the underreporting criticism (Lersch, 2002). One of the productivity measures concerned the number of field interrogation reports, which would seem to be a potentially very negative encounter. A field interrogation is conducted when an individual is acting in a suspicious manner, but there is not enough evidence to make an arrest. Prostitutes, suspected drug dealers, and loiterers are common targets for a field interrogation. Some officers had a comparatively high number of FIRs, while many others had posted none at all. When the distribution of total field interview reports was presented to several experienced officers with this particular agency, the common response was that the officers with high numbers of FIRs were simply harassing people.

Interestingly, when I looked to see whether or not there was a relationship between the number of demeanor-related complaints an officer received (which included allegations of non-violent harassment) and the number of FIRs issued, there was no significant relationship. If the patrol officers define this activity as a potential tool of harassment, why is this not reflected in the complaints? It may very well be that citizens who find themselves targets of FIRs choose not to file complaints. This finding may reflect a tendency for citizens to underreport allegations of misconduct. Given the nature of this particular activity, a citizen who has just been identified by the police as a potential criminal may not wish to draw additional attention to him- or herself, and may ultimately choose not to file a complaint of misconduct.

Should We Throw the Baby out with the Bath Water?

Given all of the problems with citizen complaints as a reflection of actual police behavior, why should researchers examine them at all? The purpose of this chapter is not to encourage agency administrators to dismiss citizen complaints as a reflection of officer productivity, citizen retaliation, or a positive community policing effort—anything other than the possible inappropriate behavior of the officer. The examination of citizen allegations of misconduct is an important tool in the overall evaluation of officer performance. However, it is clear that citizen complaints are but one measure of police behavior (Alpert and Walker, 2000). While some officers may accumulate a higher number of citizen complaints due to their high level of activity and aggressive style of policing, other officers may receive complaints because they have crossed the line of proactive policing and engaged in harassment. While agencies should not ignore citizen complaints, it is important that citizen complaints be used in conjunction with other indicators, such as internally initiated allegations of misconduct, peer evaluations, and overall performance measures.

References

Adams, K. (1995). Measuring the prevalence of police abuse of force. In W.A. Geller, and H. Toch, (Eds.), *And Justice for All: Understanding and Controlling Police Abuse of Force,* Police Executive Research Forum, Washington, DC, 61–98.

Alpert, G. (1989). Police use of deadly force: The Miami experience. In R. Dunham and G. Alpert (Eds.), *Critical Issues in Policing,* Waveland, Prospect Heights, IL, 480–495.

Alpert, G. and Walker, S. (2000). Police accountability and early warning systems: Developing policies and programs. *Justice Research and Police, 2,* 59–72.

Bayley, D. and Garofalo, J. (1989). The management of violence by police patrol officers. *Criminology, 27,* 1–23.

Bayley, D. and Mendelsohn, H. (1969). *Minorities and the Police: Confrontation in America.* New York: Free Press.

Bessent, A.E. and Tayler, L. (1991, June 2). Police brutality—Is it no problem? *Newsday,* p. 5.

Bowker, L. (1980). A theory of the education needs of law enforcement officers. *Journal of Contemporary Criminal Justice, 1,* 17–24.

Carter, D. (1985). Hispanic perception of police performance: An empirical assessment. *Journal of Criminal Justice, 13,* 487–500.

Carter, D. and Sapp, A. (1990). The evolution of higher education in law enforcement: Preliminary findings from a national study. *Journal of Criminal Justice Education, 1,* 59–85.

Cohen, B. and Chaiken, J. (1972). *Police Background Characteristics and Performance: Summary.* Rand Institute, New York.

Cox, S.M. (1996). *Police: Practices, Perspectives, Problems.* Boston: Allyn and Bacon.

Dally, A. (1975). University vs. non-university graduated policemen: A study of police attitudes. *Journal of Police Science and Administration, 3,* 458–468.

Dugan, J.R. and Breda, D.R. (1991). Complaints about Police Officers: A Comparison among Types and Agencies, *Journal of Criminal Justice, 19:* 165–171.

Feagin, J.R. and Hahn, H. (1973). *Ghetto Revolts: The Politics of Violence in American Cities.* New York: The MacMillan Company.

Flanagan, T.J. and Vaughn, M.S. (1995). Public opinion about police abuse of force. In W.A. Geller and H. Toch (Eds.) *And Justice for All: Understanding and Controlling Police Abuse of Force.* (pp. 113–132). Washington, D.C.: Police Executive Research Forum.

Forst, B., Lucianovic, J. and Cox, S. (1977). *What Happens After Arrest? A Court Perspective of Police Operations in the District of Columbia.* Institute for Law and Social Research, Washigton D.C.

Friedrich, R.J. (1980). Police use of force: Individuals, situations and organizations. *The Annals of the American Academy of Political and Social Science, 452,* 82–97.

Fyfe, J. (1989). Police/citizen violence reduction project. *FBI Law Enforcement Bulletin* (May 18–23): 23–29.

——. (1981). Race and extreme police-citizen violence. In J. Fyfe (ed.) *Readings on Police Use of Deadly Force,* Police Foundation, Washington, D.C.

Grennan, S.A. (1987). Findings on the role of officer gender in violent encounters with citizens. *Journal of Police Science and Administration, 15,* 78–85.

Griswold, D.B. (1994). Complaints against the police: Predicting dispositions. *Journal of Criminal Justice, 22,* 215–221.

Hickman, M., Piquero, A. and Greene, J. (2000). Does community policing generate greater numbers and different types of citizen complaints than traditional policing? *Police Quarterly, 3,* 70–84.

Horvath, F. (1987). The police use of deadly force: A description of selected characteristics of intrastate incidents. *Journal of Police Science and Administration, 15,* 226–238.

Independent Commission on the Los Angeles Police Department. 1991. *Report of the Independent Commission on the Los Angeles Police Department.* Los Angeles: Independent Commission on the Los Angeles Police Department.

Johnson, J. (1997, September). Americans' views on crime and law enforcement: Survey findings. *National Institute of Justice Journal, 223,* 9–14.

Kappeler, V.A., Sluder, R.D., and Alpert, G.P. (1994). *Forces of Deviance: Understanding the Dark Side of Policing.* Prospect Heights, IL: Waveland Press.

Kerstetter, W.A., Rasinski, K.A., and Heiert, C.L. (1996). The impact of race on the investigation of excessive force allegations against police. *Journal of Criminal Justice, 24,* 1–15.

Lacayo, R. (1992, May). Anatomy of an acquittal. *Time,* 30–32.

Lanier, M. (1996). An evolutionary typology of women police officers. *Women & Criminal Justice, 8,* 35–57.

Lersch, K.M. and Feagin, J.R. (1996). Violent police-citizen encounters: An analysis of major newspaper accounts. *Critical Sociology, 22,* 29–51.

Lersch, K.M. and Mieczkowski, T.M. (1996). Who are the problem prone officers? An analysis of citizen complaints. *American Journal of Police, 15,* 23–44.

Lersch, K.M. (1998a). Predicting citizen race in allegations of misconduct against the police. *Journal of Criminal Justice, 25,* 1–11.

——. (1998b). Exploring gender differences in citizen allegations of misconduct: An analysis of a municipal police department. *Women & Criminal Justice, 9,* 69–79.

——. (2002). Are citizen complaints just another measure of officer productivity? An analysis of citizen complaints and officer activity measures. *Police Practice & Research: An International Journal, 3,* 135–144.

Littlejohn, E.J. (1981). The civilian police commission: A deterrent of police misconduct. *Journal of Urban Law, 59,* 5–62.

Locke, H.G. (1995). The color of law and the issue of color: Race and the abuse of police power. In W.A. Geller and H. Toch, (Eds.) *And Justice for All: Understanding and Controlling Police Abuse of Force* (pp. 133–150). Washington, D.C.: Police Executive Research Forum.

Mahan, R. (1991). Personnel selection in police agencies: Educational requirements for entry level. *Law and Order,* 282–286.

McLaughlin, V. (1992). *Police and the Use of Force: The Savannah Study.* Westport: Praeger.

Pate, A.M. and Fridell, L.A. 1993. *Police Use of Force: Official Reports, Citizen Complaints and*

Legal Consequences, Police Foundation, Washington, DC.

Perez, D.W. and Muir, W.K. 1995. Administrative review of alleged police brutality. In W.A. Geller and H. Toch, (Eds.), *And Justice for All: Understanding and Controlling Police Abuse of Force,* Police Executive Research Forum, Washington, DC, 205–222.

President's Commission on Law Enforcement and Administration of Justice (1967). *A National Survey of Police-Community Relations: Field Surveys V.* Washington, D.C.: U.S. Government Printing Office.

Reiss, A.J. Jr. (1968). Police brutality—Answers to key questions. *Trans-Action,* July–August, 10–19.

Riksheim, E.C. and Chermak, S.M. (1993). Causes of police behavior revisited. *Journal of Criminal Justice, 21,* 353–382.

Rohrlich, T. and Merina, V. (1991, May 19). Racial disparities seen in complaints to LAPD. *Los Angeles Times,* p. 1.

Sherman, L. (1980). Causes of police behavior: The current state of quantitative research. *Journal of Criminology and Delinquency, 17,* 69–100.

Skolnick, J.H. and Fyfe, J.J. (1993). *Above the Law: Police and the Excessive Use of Force.* New York: Free Press.

Smith, D.A., Graham, N., and Adams, B. (1991). Minorities and the police: Attitudinal and behavioral questions. In M.J. Lynch and E.B. Patterson (Eds.) *Race and Criminal Justice* (pp. 22–35). New York, NY: Harrow and Heston.

Steffensmeier, D.J. (1979). Sex role orientation and attitudes toward female police. *Police Studies, 2,* 39–42.

Van Wormer, K. (1981). Are males suited to police patrol work? *Police Studies, 3,* 41–44.

Wagner, A.E. (1980). Citizen complaints against the police: The complainant. *Journal of Police Science and Administration, 8,* 247–252.

Wagner, A.E. and Decker, S.H. (1997). Evaluating citizen complaints against the police. In R. Dunham and G. Alpert (eds.), *Critical Issues in Policing: Contemporary Readings* (3rd edition). Prospect Heights: Waveland Press, Inc.

Walker, S. (2001). *Police Accountability: The Role of Citizen Oversight.* Stamford: Wadsworth.

Walker, S. and Bumphus, V. (1992) The effectiveness of civilian review: Observations on recent trends and new issues regarding the civilian review of the police. *American Journal of Police, 11,* 1–26.

Walker, S. and Graham, N. (1998). Citizen complaints in response to police misconduct: The results of a victimization survey. *Police Quarterly, 1,* 65–89.

Walker, S. and Katz, C. (2002). *The Police in America: An Introduction* (4th ed.). New York, NY: McGraw Hill.

Worden, R.E. (1995). The "causes" of police brutality: Theory and evidence on police use of force. In W.A. Geller and H. Toch (Eds.) *And Justice for All: Understanding and Controlling Police Abuse of Force* (pp. 31–60). Washington, D.C.: Police Executive Research Forum.

Kim Lersch, "When Badges Get Too Big: Identifying and Misidentifying Police Misconduct from Citizen Complaints." Copyright © 2003 by Roxbury Publishing Company. All rights reserved. ✦

Chapter 25
When Strings Are Attached

Understanding the Role of Gratuities in Police Corruptibility

Brian L. Withrow
Jeffrey D. Dailey

Introduction

Withrow and Dailey examine police ethics from a theoretical perspective by exploring the etiology of police corruption. Though corruption stories often make headline news, corruption tends to be a broadly defined concept that raises the question, what do we mean when we use the term police corruption? *For example, Delattre (1996) has argued that police officers should never, under any circumstances, receive any gratuity, tip, or extra recognition for doing the job they are paid to do. And yet, nearly all of the stories that appear on the front page of the newspaper involve very serious breaches of public trust in the police.*

The authors point out that a major dilemma for contemporary police administrators concerns the recent philosophical shift to community policing, which encourages police officers to initiate close relationships with local residents. These collaborative relationships with citizens and citizen groups may increase the likelihood that officers will be offered extra compensation for the work they do in a variety of forms. Withrow and Dailey examine the "slippery slope" thesis that corruption begins with minor gratuities and eventually leads to larger, big-ticket items given in appreciation for work well done—or, far worse, for intentionally overlooking violations of the law.

Believing the "slippery slope" argument too limited to fully explain police deviance, the authors offer a new theoretical model to conceptualize police corruption, utilizing a three-layer system to define the relationship between all parties to police misconduct.

One of the most important aspects of modern policing is the necessity of forging strong interpersonal alliances between police officers and the public. Indeed, many departments report considerable success in reducing crime and the fear of crime through community- or problem-oriented approaches that are in a large part dependent upon strong external relationships. The support for forging community alliances is so strong that one would be hard pressed to find a contemporary police administrator that cautions officers against "getting close to the public." However, during the earlier part of the twentieth century, many "progressive" police administrators advocated that the police should distance themselves from the community. In the latter part of the nineteenth century political leaders highly and inappropriately influenced police organizations. In effect, many municipal police agencies were little more than private security forces for political bosses. The abusiveness of this situation led many police administrators (August Vollmer and later O.W. Wilson) to advocate a strong separation between police officers and the public. It was believed that when police officers got too close to the public, the potential for corruption through the transference of minor gratuities and eventual cooptation rendered the individual police officer ineffective. Administratively, these concerns were manifested in a reduction of foot patrol (also influenced by the advent of the motor vehicle), beat and shift rotation and absolute departmental prohibitions against the acceptance of gratuities. Delattre (1996) summarizes this perspective by arguing exhaustively that the police should never, under any circumstances, receive any gratuity, tip or extra recognition for doing their job.

This presents a potential problem for contemporary police administrators. For example, how can an administrator encourage officers to develop interpersonal relationships with local merchants (e.g., convenience store operators) while prohibiting officers from accepting free cups of coffee when visiting these businesses to identify solutions to community problems? Doesn't it seem *normal* for a business owner to offer a visitor a cup of coffee while discussing problems of mutual concern? If so, could this potentially corrupt the officer? How would an officer tactfully decline an offer of genuine kindness? In response to this, Kania (1988) argues that police officers should be *encouraged* to accept gratuities to the extent that their acceptance forges community relations.

The purpose of this article is to offer a model that provides guidance to police administrators in finding a balance between these two diametrically opposite positions. The model more comprehensively explains the essential nature of this limited yet common form of police corruption. Specifically, this article argues that previous explanations of police corruption are incomplete because they 1) fail to consider the critical role played by the giver of gratuities, and 2) erroneously determine the level of corruption by the value of the gift exchanged.

Overview of the Literature

There is considerable agreement among scholars on the meaning of the term *corruption* (see McMullen 1961; Souryal 1979; Goldstein 1977; Feldberg 1985; Kleinig 1996;). In effect, they argue that corrupt actions include three features. First, corrupt acts are forbidden by law, departmental policy or an ethical standard. Second, corrupt acts involve the misuse of a police officer's legitimate authority. Third, corrupt acts include some actual or anticipated reward or gain (Barker and Carter 1994).

There is considerable debate among scholars and practitioners on why police officers engage in corrupt acts. Most research on the cause of police corruption can be categorized into one of three explanations. First, there are those that consider the nature of police work as the primary causal factor of corruption. The stress, psychological trauma and physiological demands of police work can and do have an affect on even the most resilient individual. The manifestation of these factors can result in behavior that would normally be considered corrupt (see Kleinig 1996; Souryal 1979). Second, some researchers consider weaknesses in the moral character or integrity of the individual officer as the primary cause of corruption. This argument is based in part on the reality that even though all police officers are subjected to essentially the same occupational stress, not all officers become corrupt (see Delattre 1996; Souryal 1979). Third, and most predominant, is the perspective proposing that organizational stress and structural variables are the primary causes of corruption. Specifically, proponents of this explanation argue that the inherent pervasiveness of the police subculture encourages and sustains its members participation in corruption (see Gentile 1998; Kleinig 1996; Delattre 1996).

Overwhelmingly, the research attempting to explain the process of corruption focuses on the structure of the police organization or the dynamics of the police subculture. Kappler, Sluder and Alpert (1994) in an argument similar to Sykes and Matza's (1957) Techniques of Neutralization, propose that the police subculture instructs officers on the use of several neutralization techniques to justify illicit activities. Delattre (1996) explains police corruption in terms of its structural motivations.

1. A young person of high ideas, but little exposure to realities that challenge naive expectations of human decency,
2. enters a world that exposes the worst in people, and
3. is trained and influenced by senior colleagues who have lost faith in police work, and

4. if the young person must establish some mutual trust and reliance with colleagues that are corrupt, and
5. their supervisors are unlikely to support efforts to behave honorably, and
6. the likelihood of sanction is negligible, then
7. the young officer will accept the status quo and become corrupt.

By far the most interesting explanation of the process of corruption is the *slippery slope* perspective. This perspective proposes that the acceptance of minor gratuities begins a process wherein the recipient's integrity is gradually subverted and eventually leads to more serious unethical conduct. Sherman (1985) observes that novice police officers quickly recognize the importance of the social bonds between members of the department. Some young officers may initially rationalize that the acceptance of minor gratuities (e.g., free coffee or half-priced meals) is necessary for acceptance into the police subculture. Once the officer has survived this moral dilemma, it becomes easier to engage in more serious forms of deviance (e.g., free drinks from bartenders). Thus begins a slippery slope whereupon the officer is faced with increasingly greater moral dilemmas.

Critical Analysis of the Literature

Most research on police corruption reaches at least one of the following conclusions:

1. The value of the item or service exchanged between the giver and receiver appears to define the relative seriousness of the corruption. For example, more expensive gifts are either the result or cause of more severe levels of corruption.
2. With some notable exceptions, the role of the giver is largely ignored. Culpability for corruption is primarily focused on the police officer, the police subculture and/or the department.

These conclusions are somewhat useful in describing how corruption typically starts and grows within a police organization. They offer plausible explanations of the process by which a police officer might initially engage in petty bribery and eventually progress into extreme forms of criminal behavior. However, for several reasons these findings neither fully explain the nature of corruption, specifically the acceptance of gratuities, nor provide adequate insight in to the function of corruptibility.

First, throughout the literature on police corruption the focus of discussion (and blame) is almost exclusively on the public official (i.e., the police officer). Admittedly, the integrity of police officers should be of great concern to citizens in a free society. The police routinely exercise wide-ranging authority with limited supervision. Furthermore, the potential social and personal harm that can result from unregulated police authority is considerable. However, the authors take issue with the fact that the participation of the giver is noticeably absent in almost all discussions of police corruption and argue that the giver is an essential participant in police corruption.

Second, individuals in all human organizations are susceptible to peer pressure. Police officers are not essentially more or less susceptible to peer pressure than any other professionals. To blame peer pressure for the onset and continuation of corruption requires that we also accept the notion of corruption as a norm within the police organization. Although there are several celebrated cases of systemic corruption in some of the nation's largest police organizations, there is no evidence suggesting corruption is pervasive in *all* police organizations. Peer pressure may be an important variable but it is not a *necessary* factor leading to corruption.

Third, the slippery slope perspective somewhat limits our understanding of the dynamics of corruption. This perspective does not consider the possibility that an officer, predisposed to do so, could *begin* with higher levels of corruption. But more importantly, the slippery slope argument does not consider the role of the giver in the process leading to higher forms of corruption. This explanation focuses entirely on the police officer's role. The model outlined below substantially improves the slippery slope explanation of the dynamics of corruption.

Fourth, in most discussions on police corruption, the value of the material object exchanged between an officer and an individual in some way defines the relative level of corruption. The model presented below is not dependent upon the value of the item exchanged. In fact, the model proposes that the value of the material object exchanged is for the most part irrelevant to the level of social harm. In this regard the model is consistent with Cohen (1986:25) who writes,

> If the value alone determined the seriousness of taking gratuities, we might end up with an equation of four hundred cups of coffee to the television set.... This suggests that it is not primarily the value of what is taken that will differentiate these cases as exploitive or not.

A Model of Circumstantial Corruptibility

The research outlined in the previous section is useful for explaining the process of corruption. However, the common conclusions of this research substantially limit our ability to understand the essential nature of corruption and the function of corruptibility. The model outlined herein responds to these criticisms. This model, called a Model of Circumstantial Corruptibility, expands our understanding of corruption by answering the following questions.

1. At what point does the exchange of a gift or service between a giver and a receiver constitute corruption?
2. What factors determine the relative harmfulness of corruption?

The following definitions are presented to assist the reader with our intended meanings of the terms and concepts essential to the model.

Exchange—the transfer of something of value from one person to another.

Corruptible exchange—the transfer of something of value from one person to another wherein the giver expects something in return for the item or service and the receiver, in violation of prior responsibilities, accepts the item or service as well as the terms of the exchange. The terms of the exchange may either be implicit or explicit.

Corruption—the merger of a giver offering a gift or service with the expectation of a return from the receiver and a receiver, in violation of prior responsibilities, willing to accept the gift of service as well as the terms of the exchange.

Corruptibility—the capacity for both the giver and receiver to achieve a particular level of corruption as defined by its potential harm to society.

The Essential Elements of the Model of Circumstantial Corruptibility

The Model of Circumstantial Corruptibility proposes that the level of corruption (as defined by its relative harmfulness to society) attained by the participants of a corruptible exchange is influenced by two, and only two, elements—the role of the giver and the role of the receiver. In this section the essential elements of the model are defined. In addition, the functionality of the model is discussed in detail.

The Role of the Giver

The role of the giver is one of two essential elements or circumstances that determines the level of corruptibility. In every exchange, the giver assumes one of the following roles.

Presenter—offers a gift voluntarily without any expectation of a return from the receiver.

Contributor—furnishes something toward a result. In this role the giver expects something in return for his contribution. However, in this role there is some level of voluntariness present in the exchange.

Capitulator—involuntarily responds to the demands of the receiver.

The level of voluntariness the giver assumes during the exchange primarily determines the giver's role. When in the *presenter* role, the giver has the highest level of voluntariness. Conversely, while in the *capitulator* role, the giver responds involuntarily to the receiver.

The Role of the Receiver

The role of the receiver is the other of the two essential elements or circumstances that determines the level of corruptibility. In every exchange, the receiver assumes one of the following roles.

Acceptor—receives a gift humbly and without any residual feelings of reciprocity.

Expector—looks forward to the gift and regards it as likely to happen. Will be annoyed by the absence of the gift.

Conqueror—assumes total control over the exchange and influence over the giver.

The receiver's role is primarily determined by the level of influence he or she exerts onto the giver during the exchange. While in the *acceptor* role, the receiver exerts no control over the exchange or the giver. Conversely, while in the *conqueror* role, the receiver exerts total control over the exchange as well as the giver.

The Function of the Model

The function of the model is centered on the intersection of the giver and receiver, each assuming his own role, around an exchange. For example, when the giver assumes the role of the *presenter* and the receiver assumes the role of the *acceptor,* the result is a *giving* exchange. At this level, the giver voluntarily offers a gift without any expectation of a return from the receiver. The receiver, exerting no influence on the giver, accepts the gift. As long as the giver and receiver continue to assume these roles, corruption cannot and does not occur. However, if the giver and receiver assume other roles, corruptibility progresses to higher levels of social harm along a *hierarchy of wickedness.* The levels on the hierarchy of wickedness are defined as follows.

Bribery—the act or practice of giving or taking something of value wherein the giver expects something in return for his gift and the receiver, in violation of prior responsibilities, agrees to conform his behavior to the desires of the giver.

Exploitation—the act or practice of unjustly or improperly using another person for one's own profit or advantage.

Each level in this hierarchy is associated with the intersection of certain roles assumed by the giver and receiver. The following figure illustrates the relationships between the roles of the giver and receiver and the levels on the hierarchy of wickedness.

Figure 25.1
A Model of Circumstantial Corruptibility

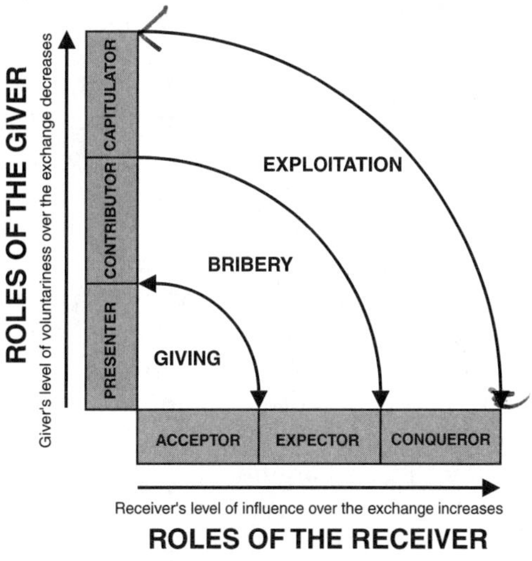

The confusion of roles between givers and receivers is inevitable. For example, a merchant may genuinely offer a free cup of coffee to a police officer simply in appreciation of the officer's contribution to the overall safety of the community. The officer may incorrectly perceive that the gift "has strings attached" and refuse the gift. Role confusion, although possible, will be mitigated by several factors. First, police officers are particularly keen at recognizing behavioral clues that offer insight into an individual's motivation. In fact, an officer's survival depends on identifying and proactively responding to potentially threatening patterns of behavior. Second, behavior (and our perception of its motivation) occurs in a context. If the officer has visited the establishment frequently and never received any consideration, then a single cup of coffee would not likely be considered a potential bribe. Conversely, if the establishment has a special cup reserved only for police officers then it is reasonable to assume that the establishment is actively *recruiting* the presence of police officers within its property. Third, role renegotiation is a common occurrence in human interaction. Often roles are renegotiated informally and nonverbally. This process is largely dependent upon who is in charge of the exchange. The directional arrows located along the curved lines in Figure 25.1 indicate who controls each level of an exchange.

Professionals familiar with the literature on gratuities should note the similarities of our model to Kania's (1988) typology. Like Kania, we argue that the intentions of givers in connection with the intentions of receivers should define the nature of an exchange. In addition, our "roles" of givers and receivers are heavily influenced by Kania's "perceptions" of givers and the police. However, the Model of Circumstantial Corruptibility is distinguishable from Kania's typology in several ways. First, a major theme of Kania's argument is that the police should be *encouraged* to accept *minor* gratuities to the extent necessary to foster good public relations. We make no such argument. Instead we would encourage the police to consider the role of the giver as well as their own intentions when deciding whether or not to accept a gratuity. In certain circumstances, our model would consider the exchange of *any* gratuity as ethical, regardless of its value. Second, our model is more parsimonious and communicable than Kania's. It collapses Kania's ten relationships into three yet retains the same level of instructive detail. Importantly, one of the relationships that Kania defines as ethical we define as unethical. Third, our model heightens the influence of the giver by explaining more comprehensively how givers affect the nature of an exchange and at what point givers themselves engage in corrupt acts. Kania's typology never defines a giver's participation as unethical unless the police improperly accept a gratuity. Fourth, we prefer to use the term *roles* rather than *perceptions* because in the final analysis we believe how individuals actually behave is more important for defining the nature of an exchange, especially in retrospect. In addition, the term *roles* is intended to communicate more of an active participation than does the term *perceptions.* Fifth, our model more fully explains the power dynamic between givers and receivers and how this dynamic defines the level of corruption. At the lowest level of corruption, the giver maintains control over the behavior of the receiver. The giver offers a gratuity or bribe and the receiver performs in a way consistent with the wishes of the giver, yet inconsistent with his or her prior responsibilities. This is the onset of the lowest (albeit offensive) level of corruption. At some point it is possible for a receiver to establish control over the giver and demand payment for current and/or future services. These exploitive acts are the most extreme forms of corruption.

Application of the Model

The traditional academy approach for preparing officers to confront potential gratuity and corruption problems tends to focus on developing individual resistance skills. While at the academy, recruits are typically instructed how to "just say no" and politely refuse all gratuities or considerations offered to them. However, it is difficult for an individual to refuse a bona fide gift. We are taught in our culture to be gracious and to "never look gift horses in the mouth." This often results in confusion on the part of new officers on what is acceptable behavior. On one hand, officers are taught never to accept a gratuity and, on the other, they are taught the value of maintaining close ties to the community. What better way to get to know a local merchant than to accept a gratis cup of coffee while discussing the merchant's safety and security needs? There is a very real possibility than an officer's refusal, no matter how polite, may alienate an officer with a merchant (Kania 1988).

The application of our model at the street level relies primarily on awareness training. Police officers should be aware of the dynamics of corruption and the potential compromise of gratuity acceptance. But more importantly, these officers should understand how givers, typically merchants, can and do attempt to misappropriate the services of the police department through the manipulative and seemingly generous offering of relatively minor gratuities. Police officers are well trained for and capable of judging the intentions and motivations of other persons. In a very real sense an officer's survival is dependent upon this skill. Indeed many police officers have developed informal strategies for refusing gifts. Some officers insist on paying full price. Others will leave the difference between the amounts charged (i.e., half price) and the actual amount owed in the tip to the waitperson. In extreme cases some officers simply avoid patronizing certain businesses that insist on offering gratuities.

At the administrative level the issue of gratuities becomes more acute. Many departments attempt to regulate thc acceptance of gratuities through a strict prohibition policy. Promulgation of such a strict policy is relatively easy. However, in most situations compliance is next to impossible. Police officers typically work at considerable distance from routine supervision. Merchants that offer gratuities are not usually willing to report officers for violating strict prohibition policies. Why should they? More often than not, strict prohibition policies are only useful *after* an officer has been compromised and there is a need, pursuant to an official sanction, to tie the behavior to a violation of policy.

A few departments attempt to control corruption by imposing a dollar limit on gratuities. This policy is based on the notion that the value of the gratuity is directly proportional to its power to corrupt. Instead, the change of behavior or role assumed by the receiver, e.g., the relative level of influence exerted by the receiver to insure the delivery of the gratuity, is a more important indicator of the seriousness of corruption than the value of the item or service exchanged. For this reason, the policy focus should be on an officer's or merchant's actual behavior. For example, frequent, or even chronic, patronage of one particular restaurant, especially by officers from faraway beats, may indicate that the establishment is offering something more than good food and courteous service. It is wholly within the rights of management to question the motivations of overly generous merchants.

Recognizing givers as a potential threat to the equity and fair accessibility of policing services provides administrators with another line of defense against possible corruption—the givers themselves. Limiting the number of on-duty police officers that may frequent a place of business at any one time is an important first step in responding to merchants that attempt to *commandeer* policing services through the offering of gratuities. Police leaders should not be discouraged from proactively contacting merchants that flagrantly offer gratuities in order to encourage officers to frequent their places of business. Ultimately, it is conceivable that a department may designate some places of business off limits to any officer not on official business (i.e., responding to a call for service).

One of the considerable accomplishments of the community era of policing has been the enlistment of private citizens, neighborhood groups and business associations into the fight against crime. Many communities report substantial reductions in the fear of crime and even in the rate of crime due to creative police and community partnerships. Often community groups and business associations are more than willing to support proven crime control or fear-reduction strategies, but not necessarily for altruistic reasons. For example, recognizing the value of bicycle patrol, a group of merchants representing the restaurant/entertainment district may offer new bicycles to the police department. Of course these bicycles are to be used exclusively within the local entertainment district, especially on weekend nights. One national fast food chain even sets aside a booth in the dining area for local police officers. Some restaurants even reserve these booths with engraved signs including the officers' names and equip them with telephones, facsimile machines and laptop hookups. These public gestures of support are potentially thinly veiled attempts to misallocate public policing services.

The administrative response to such gestures is relatively simple. If it is a gift then there can be no expectation on the part of the giver as to how the gift is to be used by the receiver. If the merchants or neighborhood associations wish to donate bicycles to the police department then they must be told that this equipment may be used in other areas of the city considered more in need of this type of enforcement strategy.

Final Thoughts

The purpose of this article is to present a model that more comprehensively explains the essential nature of a limited but common form of police corruption, specifically the acceptance of gratuities. Previous explanations of police corruption are incomplete because they fail to consider the important role of the giver and overemphasize the value of the gift. In addition to more completely explaining the process of this limited form of corruption, we believe this model provides more insight for police practitioners. This is particularly important for administrators who are interested in developing strategies that are dependent upon positive relationships between the police department and the community.

Finally, this article is not an attempt to replace the work of previous researchers. Instead, the model presented is intended to expand upon previous models, specifically by including the role of the giver, limiting the importance of the value of the gift, and substantially improving our understanding of corruption and the function of corruptibility. In doing so, the model is intended to offer subsequent researchers an additional method of inquiry and administrators with another option for controlling the pervasive nature of corruption.

References

Barker, T. and Carter, D.L. 1994. *Police Deviance, Third Edition.* Cincinnati, OH: Anderson Publishing Company.

Cohen, H. 1986. "Exploiting Police Authority." *Criminal Justice Ethics* 5(2): 23–30.

Delattre, E. J. 1996. *Character and Cops: Ethics in Policing, Third Edition.* Washington, D.C.: The AEI Press.

Feldberg, M. 1985. "Gratuities, Corruption, and the Democratic Ethos of Policing: The Case of the Free Cup of Coffee." Pp. 267–276 in *Moral Issues in Police Work,* edited by F. A. Elliston and M. Feldberg. Totowa, NJ: Rowan and Allanheld.

Goldstein, H. 1977. *Policing in a Free Society.* Cambridge, MA: Ballinger.

Kania, R. R. E. 1988. "Should We Tell the Police to Say 'Yes' to Gratuities?" *Criminal Justice Ethics.* Summer/Fall: 38–48.

Kappler, V. E., Sluder, R.D. and Alpert, G.P. 1994. *Forces of Deviance: Understanding the Dark Side of Policing.* Prospect Heights, IL: Waveland Press.

Kleinig, J. 1996. *The Ethics of Policing.* Cambridge, MA: Cambridge University Press.

McMullan, M. 1961. "A Theory of Corruption." *Sociological Review* 9: 181–201.

Sherman, L. W. 1985. "Becoming Bent: Moral Careers of Corrupt Policemen." Pp. 253–265 in *Moral Issues in Police Work,* edited by F. A. Elliston and M. Feldberg. Totowa, NJ: Rowan and Allanheld.

Souryal, S. S. 1979. "Etiology of Police Corruption." *Police Chief* December: 77–79.

Sykes, G. and Matza, D. 1957. "Techniques of Neutralization: A Theory of Delinquency." *American Journal of Sociology* 22: 664–670.

Brian L. Withrow and Jeffrey D. Dailey, "When Strings Are Attached: Understanding the Role of Gratuities in Police Corruptibility." Copyright © 2003 by Roxbury Publishing Company. All rights reserved. ✦

Chapter 26
Police Sexual Misconduct

Tim Maher

In this chapter the author examines the issue of on-duty sexual misconduct perpetrated by police officers. Police sexual misconduct (PSM) is a form of police deviance that to date has not been widely studied. Here Maher shares research findings from a recent study of sworn personnel from law enforcement agencies in the St. Louis metropolitan area.

Using a snowball technique to develop his sample, Maher personally interviewed forty police officers about their knowledge of PSM incidents concerning eight categories of PSM behaviors. His research lends insight into the occurrence of sexually motivated nonsexual contacts, voyeurism, sexual contacts with crime victims, sexual contacts with criminal offenders, sexual shakedowns, citizen-initiated sexual contacts, and officer-initiated consensual sexual contacts. Maher concludes that PSM is widespread, but that steps can be taken and policies adopted that might help to reduce this form of police deviance in the future.

Introduction

Police deviance refers to a wide variety of police activities inconsistent with an officer's authority that violate the standards of ethical conduct the public expects from members of the criminal justice system. It encompasses a number of behaviors for which an officer can be disciplined, terminated, sued, or criminally prosecuted. Many forms of police deviance (e.g. brutality, discrimination, and drug corruption) have received substantial public and scholarly attention. This is not the case for police sexual misconduct. Only recently have academics become aware that some police officers abuse their position in pursuit of personal sexual interests.

Police sexual misconduct compromises the integrity of the law enforcement community and interferes with police officers' ability to effectively perform their duties. The combination of police authority, an unsupervised atmosphere, and the frequent isolated contact with the public helps create situations whereby police officers have ample opportunity to participate in various forms of sexual misconduct. In addition, some scholars argue that because policing is dominated by a masculine culture, and police have a monopoly on state-sanctioned violence, a basis for sexual victimization is created.[1]

This chapter examines on-duty police sexual misconduct (PSM). It begins by providing an operational definition of "police sexual misconduct." Previous studies of PSM are then reviewed, and the extent and nature of PSM is examined, with a specific focus on a study of the perceptions of St. Louis metropolitan area police officers about levels of PSM and factors that contribute to this behavior. Finally, implications of this study and other research are discussed, including recommendations for creating a future agenda to help criminal justice officials and researchers develop a more comprehensive and universal conceptualization of PSM, better methods of measurement, and more effective approaches for controlling this behavior.

Defining Police Sexual Misconduct

A lack of uniformity exists in descriptions of deviance and police deviance, which has created a problem in precisely defining these terms and makes it equally difficult to define PSM. General definitions of deviance referring to violations of society's norms create a problem because not all people agree on what is deviant and what is not. This probably applies to PSM as well, because rules and standards governing this behavior are not clear, and not all "on-duty sexual behavior" is necessarily viewed as deviant by individual officers, police social groups or police administrators.

Generally, police behavior is guided by two sets of standards. The first, "external rules or standards" includes constitutional, criminal, common, and civil laws, as well as public opinion. The second, "internal rules or standards," includes departmental policies, procedures, practices, and regulations.[2] Although these standards guide police behavior, the police culture plays an important role and greatly influences the extent to which these standards are followed and enforced.

No single existing definition of PSM is comprehensive enough to address all forms of this behavior. In addition, none of the definitions used in the past is narrow enough to address only those incidents of PSM that occur while officers are on duty. Therefore, the following definition was developed by gathering and elaborating on information provided in police deviance literature and by incorporating general principles of acceptable police behavior:

> Any behavior by a police officer, whereby an officer takes advantage of his or her unique position in law enforcement to initiate or respond to some sexually motivated stimuli. This behavior must include physical contact, verbal communication, or a sexually implicit or explicit gesture directed toward another person. The behavior must have occurred while on-duty in relation to an officer's official or unofficial duties.

Some acts of PSM occur while an officer is off duty, but result from contact initiated while the officer was on duty. In addition, several courts hold that some police officers can be held civilly liable for acting under the "color of law" while off duty, especially if a department requires that officers are "always on duty."[3] Although it is recognized that off-duty PSM may be no less deviant than the on-duty variety, this chapter focuses exclusively on PSM that occurs while the officer is on duty acting in an official capacity.

Police Sexual Misconduct Literature

While not extensive, some research has focused on PSM, primarily police sexual violence. Barker (1978) examined several forms of police deviance, including sexual misconduct.[4] He found that fifty officers and civilian employees from a small southern city police department believed that 31.84% of the city's officers had sex while on duty. Kraska and Kappeler (1995) examined on-duty police sexual violence.[5] They established a continuum for police sexual violence based on the "obtrusiveness of the police behavior." They examined 124 cases of sexual violence, of which thirty-seven cases involved rape and sexual assault, taken primarily from federal litigation cases and a national news media source. They also examined the institutional and cultural support for these behaviors and concluded that the dual elements of police secrecy and reporting obstacles for victims make it difficult to gather data on this topic. They stress that sociocultural links exist between police sexual violence and the structural position of police in society, and that we must avoid viewing police crime as simply an aberration committed by just a few bad officers.

Kappeler and Vaughn (1997) assessed police sexual violence as it relates to municipal liability.[6] They contend that along with the possibility of criminal consequences, there is a high likelihood of municipal liability for police sexual violence. They indicate that civil liability is currently more common than criminal litigation for police sexual violence. They contend that police executives have a duty to prevent, recognize, and act on incidents of sexual violence in their agencies, and that police supervisors should be proactive and investigate any sign of sexual violence even when a pattern of abuse has not yet been established.

Vaughn (1999) also explored civil liability under state tort laws against police officers engaged in sexual violence.[7] He maintains that governmental agencies must take police officers' deviant acts more seriously and that the need exists for systematic data collection so that police sexual violence can be routinely monitored.

McGurrin and Kappeler (2002) argue that state officials do not respond adequately to police sexual violence.[8] They suggest a link exists between police sexual violence and state structural support. They propose that the state's failure to intervene and limit harms by police officers directed at women constitutes a political form of sanctioned violence.

These studies represent important steps in advancing our understanding of PSM. However, because they rely on data from cases in which the victims made public their victimization, through the criminal justice process, the courts, or the media, they exclude much PSM that has not been exposed through these institutional mechanisms. Cases involving police officers participating in sexual misconduct are similar to other hidden populations, such as drug users whose activities are clandestine and concealed from mainstream society. Much PSM is known only to those who participate in the behavior and to police officers with access to these hidden populations. In addition, much of the research has focused on police behavior involving *sexual violence,* thereby excluding less intrusive but still ethically questionable behavior, such as pulling over a driver to get a closer look at the occupants, running a computer check on a vehicle license plate to determine where the attractive driver lives, or having sex in a patrol car.

The Extent of PSM

The full extent of this behavior is unknown. Many victims choose not to report incidents of PSM, fearing retaliation by the police or not being believed. Still others fear being blamed for the incident. Some victims also fear the depersonalization and humiliation of "secondary victimization," by which victims of some crimes, especially sexual violence, are subjected to negative and embarrassing experiences in the criminal justice system.[9] Other victims do not report PSM because they are unaware they have been victimized or they do not think the behavior is serious enough to report.

Some PSM is not reported because it involves consensual behavior, and the willing participation of "the victim." Although these incidents usually do not involve serious criminal behavior, they do generally violate principles of acceptable behavior common to law enforcement. In addition, many of these incidents violate minor laws, and in some cases police department rules, regulations, or policies.

Police officers and police organizations also hamper efforts to learn more about the extent of PSM. The "police culture" shapes and drives police behavior and opinions. Manning (1989:360) defined police culture as the "accepted rules, and principles of conduct that are situationally applied, and generalized rationales and beliefs."[10] Although all subgroups teach group members norms and values of their group, the isolation and separation of police officers from the public caused by their unusual work schedules and the continued formal socialization process of police work creates a subculture that is especially powerful. It sets them apart from general society and greatly influences their lives and careers. The police code of secrecy, or the "blue wall of silence," is a product of the police subculture and prevents outsiders from learning about police business. Generally, the code of secrecy refers to the practice of police officers not discussing police business with others, especially the behavior of officers on their same shift.[11] Some analysts contend that police departments and officers allegedly cover-up, remain silent, or ignore incriminating matters associated with police behavior.[12]

Although the "blue wall of silence" creates an obstacle for anyone attempting to learn about secret information from police officers, Sapp (1994) successfully interviewed police officers in several states about PSM.[13] He reported that most officers do not take advantage of the opportunity to engage in PSM, although a sufficient number do participate to create a problem worthy of study. He argues that the secrecy surrounding PSM must be removed, and that the problem will not be eliminated until the "boys will be boys" attitude among police administrators and supervisors is abandoned. His work demonstrates important steps in identifying PSM as a problem, and suggests that some police officers may be willing to discuss this topic with people outside the law enforcement community. However, Sapp and other researchers have not specifically explored actual levels of PSM, leaving the public and criminal justice officials to wonder about the extent of this problem.

Noting this omission, I concluded an urgent need existed to conduct a study to measure levels of PSM and identify those factors that contribute to officers' decisions to engage in or refrain from such behavior. Because much PSM remains secret, it became necessary to breach the "blue wall of silence." Interviewing active police officers is perhaps the best method to determine the extent of this problem; however, accomplishing this is no simple task and requires gaining access to the police subculture.

Making the initial contact may be the most difficult aspect to gaining access to hidden populations. Therefore, I took advantage of my status as a former police officer and used a methodological approach commonly referred to as a "chain-referral" or "snowball sample."[14] I began by contacting police officers I knew and then asked them to refer other officers I did not know to participate in my research. Limitations do exist when using a chain-referral method of data collection, but given the potential difficulties in accessing hidden populations, certain limitations must be accepted.

The St. Louis Metropolitan Area PSM Study

A total of forty officers from fourteen police agencies in the St. Louis metropolitan area participated in the study. I was personally acquainted with sixteen of the officers. Nineteen of the officers were assigned to the patrol division, thirteen officers were assigned to detective units, four officers held the rank of sergeant, and two officers held the rank of lieutenant. Thirty-five of the study participants were male and five were female. Although not random, the sample does reflect differences in agency size, officer rank, and experience roughly typical of officers employed with police departments in the St. Louis metropolitan area.[15]

All officers in the study completed a survey questionnaire and participated in a personal interview. The surveys were designed to obtain information about officers' knowledge of PSM, including their perceptions of the extent of this behavior, as well as their opinions about factors that may influence officers' decisions to engage in or refrain from PSM. During the interviews officers were asked to elaborate on their survey responses. Interviews were not tape recorded, and therefore officers' responses were reconstructed as accurately as possible from handwritten notes.

Study participants were asked to provide information about their first-hand and second-hand knowledge of PSM in St. Louis metropolitan area police departments. First-hand knowledge is defined as having personally participated in PSM, personally witnessed PSM, or having another officer relate an incident of PSM in which they themselves participated. Second-hand knowledge is defined as being told about an incident of PSM by a third party. Officers were asked to report the number of incidents for eight categories of PSM. Those categories are:

1. *Nonsexual contacts that are sexually motivated.* Behaviors that are sexually motivated without direct sexual actions or inferences. These behaviors may or may not be recognized as sexually motivated by the citizen. An example of this type of behavior may include making a sexually motivated traffic stop, whether it is valid

or invalid, for the purpose of getting a closer look at or information from an occupant of a vehicle.

2. *Voyeuristic contacts.* Behavior involving an officer seeking out opportunities to view unsuspecting citizens partially clad or nude. Examples of this behavior include looking in windows of houses or buildings, and seeking out parked cars in hopes of observing sexual activities of the occupants.

3. *Contacts with crime victims.* Behaviors that involve an officer who takes advantage of the opportunity to contact a crime victim in part for the purpose of initiating sexual contact with that victim. Examples of this behavior include unnecessary callbacks or visits to a crime victim, and taking advantage of the susceptible emotional state of a sex crime victim.

4. *Contacts with offenders.* Behaviors that involve using police authority to take advantage of suspected offenders including any sexually motivated harassment by an officer. Examples include unnecessary searches, frisks, and pat-downs, or rubbing against a suspect in an arrest situation for the purpose of sexual gratification.

5. *Contacts with juveniles.* Behavior that involves an officer accepting or initiating sexual contact with any juvenile. This also includes any sexually motivated harassment by an officer.

6. *Sexual shakedowns.* Behavior that involves the demand for sexual service from an unwilling citizen involved in some illegal activity. The citizen yields to the demands solely on the basis of police authority to arrest. An example of this misconduct is demanding sexual service from a suspect in exchange for the officer not arresting the suspect.

7. *Citizen-initiated sexual contacts.* This behavior involves an officer accepting any sexual contact initiated by a citizen.

These seven categories served as the basis of my research and were first used by Sapp (1994) in his study of police sexual misconduct.[16] An additional category was included.

8. *Officer-initiated consensual sexual contacts.* Any behavior that involves sexual contact between an officer and citizen where the officer initiated the contact and the citizen willingly participates.

Officers reported a total of 8,306 first-hand incidents and a total of 12,456 second- hand incidents, for a combined total of 20,762 incidents reported by forty officers in the study, or an average of 519 reported incidents per officer. The combined years of service for all forty officers was 532, so they reported an average of thirty-nine incidents per officer per year.

The frequency of incidents of PSM ranged considerably among responding officers. Two officers in particular reported exceptionally high numbers of incidents. Officer #17 reported having knowledge of 3,470 first-hand and second-hand incidents over a four-year career, averaging 868 incidents per year. Officer #19 reported a total of 1,446 incidents over a two-year career, averaging 723 incidents per year. Although I have no reason to doubt the truthfulness of any study participant, due to the exceptionally high number of incidents reported, these two cases were treated as outliers. When removed from the data, the average number of incidents reported per officer per year dropped from thirty-nine to thirty. Some officers reported very low numbers of incidents, averaging only three incidents per year. However, these cases did not fall far enough away from the mean to be treated as outliers. The total number of police sexual misconduct incidents reported by officers in the St. Louis metropolitan area study appear in Table 26.1.

Several factors might account for the large discrepancy in reported incidents between officers, including the possibility that some po-

Table 26.1
Knowledge of PSM Reported by Forty Police Officers

	First-Hand Knowledge			Second-Hand Knowledge		
Service Misconduct Category	*Last Year*	*Ever*	*Per Year Service*	*Last Year*	*Ever*	*Per Year Service*
Nonsexual Contacts	213	3481	6.54	374	3901	7.33
Voyeuristic	122	1426	2.68	259	3032	5.69
Contacts with Juveniles	2	66	.12	2	47	.08
Contacts with Crime Victims	35	242	.45	74	202	.37
Sexual Shakedowns	1	11	.02	4	40	.07
Contacts with Offenders	27	168	.31	9	314	.59
Citizen-Initiated Contacts	110	1150	2.16	246	1899	3.56
Officer-Initiated Contacts	161	1762	3.31	436	2841	5.34
Total	**671**	**8306**		**1709**	**12456**	
Mean Total Per Year	16.77	15.59		42.72	23.03	

lice departments simply experience higher levels of PSM. Although there is little doubt that this is true to some extent, this study did not discover a large discrepancy in average frequency of reported incidents among the 14 agencies represented in the data.

It is more likely that all police departments experience some PSM, but there are large differences between officers' knowledge of PSM within the same agency. Survey participants were asked whether they believed officers in their respective departments were likely to report a similar number of incidents. Many officers suggested that there would be differences and that an officer's knowledge of PSM is likely to be influenced by shift and assignment. Eighty-eight percent of respondents reported that more PSM is likely to occur among officers assigned to the patrol unit and more likely to occur on the night shift (11pm–7am).

Some survey participants suggested that certain officers might have less knowledge of PSM because they are less sociable. In addition, some officers are recognized as having high ethical standards, and are frequently shielded from such behavior by other officers because they do not want them to know about the behavior. One survey participant had this to say:

> Everybody on the department knows I don't approve of that behavior. They also know if I observe them involved in sexual misconduct, I will report it. Therefore, I don't have a lot to report to you in this survey. However, I do think there is more sexual misconduct occurring at my department than I know about.

The majority of PSM incidents do not involve serious criminal conduct. Incidents involving juveniles, sexual shakedowns, and contacts with offenders account for only 3% of the total incidents reported. Noncriminal, consensual contacts initiated by either the officer or citizen account for 33% of the sexual misconduct. Incidents involving nonsexual contacts, voyeuristic behavior, and contacts with crime victims, all of which could in some cases be classified as minor criminal conduct, account for the majority, or 63.8% of all incidents reported.

The lack of reported serious criminal conduct could be interpreted in two ways. First, officers may not be willing to report serious criminal conduct involving police officers for fear of incriminating themselves or fellow officers. Second, there may be relatively few serious criminal incidents actually occurring. Although a large percentage of the PSM reported in this study is not of a serious criminal nature, the less serious incidents are no less wrong, deserve attention, and should not be tolerated.

It is important to mention that in some cases it was necessary for officers in the St. Louis study to provide approximations for numbers of incidents they reported. This is especially true for the more experienced officers who were required to recall numbers of PSM incidents from careers that span many years. It is also likely that some of the reported incidents were not mutually exclusive and some of the same incidents were probably reported by more than one officer. Exactly how much duplication in reported incidents occurred is unknown. However, duplication is more likely to be the case among officers who are employed at the same agency as opposed to officers who work at different police departments.

How officers define PSM determines levels of reported incidents. Only one officer in the survey reported having seen a definition for PSM, but could not recall the source. No officer from any of the 14 departments represented in this sample reported having knowledge of a specific written departmental policy on PSM. These findings are contrary to the work of Barker and Wells (1982), who found that of 307 police agencies in a southern state, only 35% of the chiefs reported that their department had no written rules regulating "sex on duty."[17] Consequently, participants in this study received virtually no official guidance or information to construct a definition of PSM. Even without specific policies, however, the definitions provided were generally similar. Common to many of the definitions was the distinction between consensual and nonconsensual behavior. When interviewed about their definitions, there was a general consensus that any on-duty sexual behavior was wrong. There was, however, little agreement on exactly what behaviors constitute on-duty sexual behavior. Officer #14 provided this comment:

> It's difficult to define police sexual misconduct. I have been a cop for over fifteen years, and I have never given it much thought. I believe it is similar to pornography, I know it when I see it.

Officers in the St. Louis study were not specifically asked the number or percentage of officers whom they believed had sex on duty, but were asked to estimate the level of participation for each of the eight categories of PSM addressed in the study. On average, they reported that 36.5% of all officers with whom they were associated participated in at least one of the eight forms of misconduct, a figure very close to the prevalence measure reported in prior research.[18]

Study participants were also asked to rate a set of nine factors to assess what factors influence officers' decisions to participate in or refrain from PSM. The rating scale ranged from 1 to 4, with 1 being not important and 4 being very important. The mean scores for these nine factors are listed in order of significance from most influential to least.

1. Personal morals and values (mean score = 3.8)
2. Self-control (mean score = 3.7)
3. Concern over reaction of spouse or significant other (mean score = 3.2)
4. Availability of misconduct opportunity (mean score = 2.9)
5. Disciplinary measures taken by department (mean score = 2.8)
6. Climate of department and or squad assignment (mean score = 2.8)
7. Lack of adequate supervision (mean score = 2.7)
8. Officer peer pressure (mean score = 2.5)
9. Normal written policy of department on sexual misconduct (mean score = 2.4)

None of the factors received an average rating of 1, which suggests that all nine factors play at least some role for some officers' decisions to engage in or refrain from PSM. However, some factors appear to play a more significant role in this decision-making process. Overall, officers believe that factors related to one's personal morals and values, and self-control are most influential in their decisions to engage in PSM. This implies that officers choose to engage in sexual misconduct based primarily on a personal decision and discounts the influence and support of the police organization and culture. This lends support to the police myth of the "rotten apple."[19] This myth suggests that police deviance is isolated, a single rotten apple in a barrel of good apples, and that police deviance and misconduct are viewed as singular aberrations and not as being widespread or in any way supported by the state, police organization, or a deviant subculture. The "rotten apple" myth has been and continues to be promoted by police administrators and management; therefore, officers in this survey may simply be reflecting a widely held view that they have been socialized to accept.

The availability of misconduct opportunities provided by police work also ranked high on this list. Much PSM occurs at night, under the cover of darkness, when few people are around to interrupt or discourage such behavior. In addition, prior research suggests that the opportunity for PSM is enhanced by the existence of lonely suitors seeking attention, or other willing participants such as young groupies who initiate sexual contacts because they are attracted to the uniform, weapon, or the power of police officers.[20]

Those factors related to the organizational and social structure of policing received mixed ratings. Peer pressure from fellow officers to participate in PSM received the second lowest rating. While peer pressure to engage in PSM may be considered low by officers, the police culture may create an atmosphere in which officers are encouraged to be tolerant of or indifferent to PSM, even if they themselves do not participate. This atmosphere may be similar to other institutions where people in authority take advantage of their positions and engage in sexual misconduct. Inappropriate sexual behavior involving authority figures like scout leaders, athletic coaches, therapists and religious leaders is well documented.[21]

The recent priest scandal confronting the Catholic Church provides a good example. Although the Catholic Church condemns such behavior, church officials may have also condoned it by covering up, failing to report, or otherwise failing to deal with abusive priests. The failure of the Catholic Church to root out and punish abusive priests may have created an atmosphere that drew some men to the priesthood because of the misconduct opportunities and the belief that their behavior would not be treated criminally. Similar dynamics may operate in policing. Although pressure to engage in PSM may not be significant, there may be pressure not to report such conduct due to the police culture "code of secrecy." One officer in the study had this to say:

> Most police departments definitely operate in a "macho man" atmosphere. Lots of cops openly talk about their sex lives and sexual conquests, including those while on duty. If you don't like what you are hearing, then you better learn to ignore it or get up and walk away. You should not go to a supervisor to complain, and you definitely better not go outside the department to complain. I am not talking about molesting a child or something serious, but if you hear about something minor, like having sex on duty, then you should just keep it to yourself.

A police department's formal written policy on PSM ranked as the factor least likely to influence an officer's on-duty sexual behavior. None of the departments in this study had a formal written policy on PSM. When interviewed, survey participants generally concluded that most officers know that PSM is wrong, and if this behavior is detected, it may result in some form of discipline. However, PSM is rarely officially detected, and most officers said they did not believe discipline would be severe for most forms of PSM. This supports the findings of McGurrin and Kappeler (2002), who suggest that there is a relative lack of response by state officials to police sexual violence.[22] Klockars, Ivkovich, Harver, and Haberfeld (2000) did not specifically address PSM in their study of police integrity, but did report that police officers regard nonserious rule violations as warranting little or no discipline.[23]

Finally, officers were asked whether they would report a fellow officer for PSM. All but one respondent stated that it would depend on the severity of the violation. They stated that if the incident involved a serious violation of the law, for example rape, sexual assault, or sex with a juvenile, they would most likely report the incident. Conversely, if the incident involved something less serious, it was unlikely they would report it, even if the incident involved a minor violation of the law or a police department rule or regulation. This included supervisors who stated it was unlikely they would formally handle a minor violation of PSM and that they would probably handle the situation informally.

This willingness among police officers to report some violations of PSM and not others provides an example of ethical relativism, which suggests that people in different circumstances have different expectations of one another based on what they learn as a result of cultural traditions and socialization.[24] Police officers face many ethical dilemmas during their careers and must learn, primarily from other officers, how to react to situations and individuals, while keeping in mind potential gains and losses. Officers frequently confront situations in which there is no clear course of action. They may be torn between doing what is legally correct and what they feel is a more sympathetic course of action. Examples include whether to arrest a minor in possession of alcohol, or whether to arrest a homeless person for trespassing when the person is attempting to stay warm in cold weather. Many officers also report that they are confronted by dilemmas regarding fellow officers, their families, or friends. Many report differences in how they handle situations involving other officers and indicate they are more reluctant to report some incidents because they do not want to get fellow officers in trouble.[25] While the use of discretion in policing is common, some observers contend that increased scrutiny for the more serious ethical dilemmas facing police officers is warranted.[26]

Summary and Implications

The available research suggests that many police officers engage in on-duty police sexual misconduct. Although most of the misconduct may not involve serious criminal behavior, much of the behavior does qualify as minor crime and violates widely accepted ethical standards commonly associated with law enforcement.

Having established that PSM is relatively common, what should be done to address this matter? To begin, all police personnel should be educated about sexual misconduct and its effects on policing. The research suggests that only the most severe forms of PSM are considered problematic by police officers and their supervisors. Not until the secrecy surrounding PSM is removed and police administrators, supervisors, and officers confront this problem and take it more seriously, will the true extent of PSM be discovered and legitimate efforts made to control it.

Second, law enforcement should adopt clear policies and procedures that address and regulate PSM and all unethical behavior. Walker (1999) reports that formal written policies are currently the dominant approach to controlling police behavior and police officers are more likely to respect and follow the rules if formally adopted.[27] Other researchers suggest that policies help establish uniformity in policing and create a formal framework for controlling police behavior.[28] Many police agencies do not have a formal written policy on PSM. Two nationally recognized leaders on police policy, the International Association of Chiefs of Police (IACP), and the Commission on Accreditation for Law Enforcement (CALEA) also report that they have no specific model policy recommendations for PSM.

This formal lack of acknowledgement of PSM may be telling. First, it may indicate that police officials do not believe PSM is a significant problem, and therefore is not worthy of a formal policy. Second, the police culture may indirectly encourage PSM, or at the very least create an environment in which officers are reluctant to report fellow officers for sexual misconduct because they do not want to get their fellow officers in trouble or they believe the administration is not really concerned about PSM. Finally, formal policies addressing PSM likely will be developed and become standard in policing only when law enforcement is significantly pressured by the public, media, and the courts. Recent attention drawn to other problem areas of policing, such as racial profiling and police pursuits, demonstrate the powerful role outside interest groups can play in affecting police policy.[29]

A broader, more systematic approach must be adopted by law enforcement to help define, measure, and control PSM, especially in its more common manifestations. This will require a concerted effort by both local and national law enforcement agencies, as well as input from police personnel, unions, and associations. National organizations like the IACP and CALEA could play an important role in this effort and lead the way by adopting a model policy for PSM. These policies would help to create a better understanding of the issue and would assist all people, but especially police administrators and personnel in the process of constructing a more universal conceptualization of PSM, thereby allowing for better management and control of sexual misconduct.

Third, the apparent availability of misconduct opportunities provided by police work suggests that police administrators must urge supervisors to take a more proactive role in controlling PSM. In addition, better screening of police applicants could help to identify and weed out those individuals who may have a propensity towards this type of behavior.

Finally, more attention by researchers is needed to address a problem that has long been neglected. Police sexual misconduct must be more clearly defined, so it can be more accurately measured and better controlled.

Notes

1. McGurrin and Kappeler, 2002.
2. Kappeler, Sludder and Alpert, 1998.
3. Vaughn and Coomes, 1995.
4. Barker, 1982.
5. Kraska and Kappeler, 1995.
6. Kappeler and Vaughn, 1997.
7. Vaughn, 1999.
8. McGurrin and Kappeler, 2002.
9. Murram, Hellman and Cassinello, 1994.
10. Manning, 1998.
11. Reuss-Ianni, 1982.
12. Goldstein, 1975; National Bulletin on Police Misconduct, 1992.
13. Sapp, 1994.
14. Erickson, 197; Heckathorn, 2002; Sudman, 1976.
15. St. Louis County Police Department, 2000.
16. Sapp, 1994.
17. Barker and Wells, 1982.
18. Barker, 1978.
19. Sherman, 1980.
20. Sapp, 1997.
21. Flowers, 1994; Goldstein, 1987; Grenz and Bell, 1995.
22. McGurrin and Kappeler, 2002.
23. Klockars, Ivkovich, Harver and Haberfeld, 2000.
24. Kleinig, 1996.
25. Pollock, 1996.
26. Pollock and Becker, 1996.
27. Walker, 1996.
28. Kappeler, Sludder and Alpert, 1998.
29. Frick, 1997; Homant and Kennedy, 1994.

References

Barker, T. and Wells, R. O. (1982). Police Administrators' Attitudes Toward the Definition and Control of Police Deviance. *FBI Law Enforcement Bulletin,* March, 102–111.

Barker, T. (1978). An Empirical Study of Police Deviance Other than Corruption. *Journal of Police Science and Administration*, 6, 264–272.

Erickson, B. H. (1979). Some problems of inference from chain data. *Sociological Methodology*, 10, 276–302.

Flowers, R. B. (1994). *The Victimization and Exploitation of Women and Children: A Study of Physical, Mental, and Sexual Maltreatment in the United States*. Jefferson, N.C: McFarland & Company, Inc.

Frick, R. (1997). Callifornia's Police Pursuit Immunity Statute: Does It Work? *Police Chief*, 64, 36–43.

Goldstein, H. (1975). *Police Corruption: A Perspective on Its Nature and Control*. Washington DC: Police Foundation.

Goldstein, S. L. (1987). *The Sexual Exploitation of Children: A Practical Guide to Assessment, Investigation, and Intervention*. New York: Elsevier.

Grenz, S. J. and Bell, R. D. (1995). *Betrayal of Trust: Sexual Misconduct in the Pastorate*. Downers Grove, IL: InterVarsity Press.

Heckathorn, D. D. (2002). Respondent-Driven Sampling II: Deriving Valid Population Estimates From Chain-Referral Samples of Hidden Populations. *Social Problems*, 49, 11–34.

Homant, R. J. and Kennedy, D. B. (1994). Citizen Preferences and Perceptions Concerning Police Pursuits. *Journal of Criminal Justice*, 22, 425–435.

Kappeler, V. E., Sludder, R. D. and Alpert, G. P. (1998). *Forces of Deviance: Understanding the Dark Side of Policing*. Prospect Heights, IL: Waveland Press.

Kappler, V. E. and Vaughn, M. S. (1997). Law Enforcement: When the Pursuit Becomes Criminal—Municipal Liability for Police Sexual Violence. *Criminal Law Bulletin*, 33, 352–376.

Kleinig, J. (1996). *The Ethics of Policing*. Cambridge: Cambridge University Press.

Klockars, C. B., Ivkovich, S. K., Harver, W.E. and Haberfeld, M. R. (2000). *The Measurement of Police Integrity*. Washington DC: National Institute of Justice.

Kraska, P. B. and Kappeler, V. E. (1995). To Serve and Pursue: Police Sexual Violence Against Women. *Justice Quarterly*, 12, 85–111.

Manning, P. K. (1998). The Police Occupational Culture in Anglo-American Societies. In L. Hoover and J. Dowling (Eds.), *Encyclopedia of Police Science*. New York, NY: Garland.

McGurrin, D. and Kappeler V. E. (2002). Media Accounts of Police Sexual Violence: Rotten Apples or State-Supported Violence? In K. M. Lersch (Eds.), *Policing and Misconduct*. Upper Saddle River, NJ: Pearson Education.

Murram, D., Hellman, R. and Cassinello, B. (1994). Prevalence of negative attitudes among police officer's toward rape victims. *Adolescent and Pediatric Gynecology*, 8, 89–91.

National Bulletin on Police Misconduct (1992). Sexual Misconduct by Officer—Department's Policy of Silence. December.

Pollock, J. M. (1996). Ethics and Law Enforcement. In Dunham, R. D. and Alpert, G. P. (Eds.), *Critical Issues In Policing*. Prospect Heights IL: Waveland Press.

Pollock, J. M. and Becker, R. (1996). Ethical Dilemmas in Police Work. In Braswell, M., McCarthy, B. and McCarty, B. (Eds.), *Justice, Crime and Ethics*. Cincinnati, OH: Anderson Publishing.

Reuss-Ianni, E.(1982). *Two Cultures of Policing*. New Brunswick, NJ: Transaction Books.

Rubington, E. and. Weinberg, M. S. (1995). *Deviance: The Interactionist Perspective*. Needham Heights, MA: Allyn & Bacon.

Sapp, A. D. (1997). The Seductions of Sex. In Crank, J. P. (Eds.), *Understanding Police Culture*. Cincinnati, OH: Anderson Publishing Co.

——. (1994). Sexual Misconduct By Police Officers. In Barker, T and Carter, D. L. (Eds.), *Police Deviance*. Cincinnati OH: Anderson Publishing Co.

Sherman, L.W. (1980). Causes of Police Behavior: The Current State of Qualitative Research. *Journal of Research in Crime and Delinquency*, January, 69–96.

St. Louis County Police Department (2000). *Facts on St. Louis County Police Services*. St. Louis County Police.

Sudman, S. (1976). *Applied Sampling*. New York: Academic Press.

Sykes, G.M., and Matza, D. (1957). Techniques of Neutralization. *American Sociological Review*, 22, 664–670.

Taylor, L. (1985). *In the Underworld*. London: Unwin.

Vaughn, M. S. (1999). Police Sexual Violence: Civil Liability Under State Tort Law. *Crime and Delinquency*, 45, 334–357.

Vaughn, M. S. and Coomes, L. (1995). Police Civil Liability Under Section 1983: When Do Police

Officers Act Under Color of Law? *Journal of Criminal Justice*, 23, 395–415.

Walker, S. (1996). *The Police in America.* Boston: McGraw-Hill College.

Tim Maher, "Police Sexual Misconduct." Copyright © 2003 by Roxbury Publishing Company. All rights reserved. ✦

Chapter 27

Drug Use and Drug-Related Corruption of Police Officers

David L. Carter

Carter reviews the literature on drug-related corruption among police officers, highlighting the extent of drug-related corruption, its possible causes, and policies that might be effective in reducing the problem.

The author distinguishes two distinct groups involved in drug-related police corruption. The first operates within a "user-driven cycle," and includes officers whose drug use begins recreationally. Recreational drug use, according to Carter, prompts confiscation of drugs from drug dealers for an officer's personal use. The second category of officers operates within a "profit-driven cycle," and includes both users and non-users. These officers rely on drug raids to secure drugs primarily for resale.

Carter asserts that drug-related police corruption has become a much larger problem in the past ten years, because police officers have more exposure to drug money and illegal drug markets today than ever before. Carter suggests that police administrators need to be attentive to drug-related corruption and attack the problem by implementing new policies and more adequate training.

The corruption ofpolice officers is a problem which spans cultures, countries, and generations in that it is based in human weaknesses and motivations. Because even the lowest ranking police officer can exercise wide power and because there are people who want to take advantage of that power, the threat of corruption is inevitable. Administrators must recognize that no matter how aggressively the problem is controlled, investigated and penalized, there will always be someone in the organization who will become susceptible to corruptive influences.

This is not meant to be a cynical view of the problem, but a practical one. It is the practical administrator who will be the most successful in combating corruption and keeping its influence at a minimum. Denying that the problem exists or failing to investigate it aggressively will result in a more devastating impact. As one police manager told the author,

> We probably could have stopped this problem sooner if we'd been able to accept the fact that we had some [corrupt] officers. As it stands now, the corruption has spread like a bad infection.

While many elements of corruption can be examined, this chapter focuses only on one aspect: that related to drugs.

The Pathology of Corruption

Police corruption includes a wide variety of prohibited behaviors—either crimes or departmental rule violations—committed under the auspices of a police officer's position. Goldstein defined corruption as

> . . . acts involving misuse of authority by a police officer in a manner designed to produce personal gain for himself or others. [It] is not limited to monetary gain, because gain may be in the form of services rendered, status, influence, prestige, or future support for the officer or someone else. (1975:3–5)

Important elements of this definition are "police authority" and "personal gain." Thus, corruption involves some type of transaction between the officer and another person. The nature of that transaction can be complex and circumstances will vary significantly. Particularly problematic in some cases of drug-related corruption is determining when both of these elements exist together.

The cause of corruption is not a simple issue. There is always the proverbial "bad apple" who somehow slipped through the department's selection process. However, more disturbing are the cases of officers who have good work records and appear dedicated yet they slip into a mode of corrupt behavior. Administrators are frequently at a loss to explain how this occurred to a "good officer." Many factors could contribute to this, including:

- Greed
- Personal motivators such as ego, sex, or the exercise of power
- Tolerance of the behavior by the community
- Socialization from peers and/or the organization
- Inadequate supervision and monitoring of behavior
- Lack of clear accountability of employees' behavior
- No real threat of discipline or sanctions

No single factor is likely to "cause" corrupt behavior. Instead, the behavior appears to evolve from the interactive effects of several of these variables.

A Typology of Drug-Related Corruption

Drug-related corruption of police officers is particularly problematic. While overall incidents of corruption appear to have declined, the cases of drug-related corruption have notably increased. The reasons are complex and offer challenges for the police and community together in order to minimize their impact. To better understand the breadth of the problem, the author has developed the following typology.

Type 1 Drug Corruption: In Search of Illegitimate Goals

The Type 1 goals are defined as "illegitimate" in that an officer is seeking to use his/her position as a police officer simply for personal gain. Examples of this type of corruption would include:

- Giving information to drug dealers about investigations, undercover officers, names of informants, planned raids and so forth in exchange for a monetary payment.
- Accepting bribes from drug dealers in exchange for actions such as non-arrest, evidence tampering, perjury, or contamination of evidence.
- Theft of drugs by an officer from the police property room or laboratory for personal consumption or sale of the drug.
- The "seizure" of drugs without arresting the person possessing the drugs with the officer's intent of converting the drugs to personal use.
- Taking the profits of drug dealers' sales and/or their drugs for resale.
- Extorting drug traffickers for money or property in exchange for non-arrest or non-seizure of drugs.

Research by the author indicates that there are two distinct behavioral cycles—not necessarily mutually exclusive—motivating Type 1 corrupt acts. These motivations are classified as "cycles" because of a distinct recurring and reinforcing process. For example, after an officer's initial corrupt act he/she would fear being detected. After the fear decreased and another opportunity occurred, the officer would perform another improper act. Again, a period of fear of apprehension—albeit a shorter one—followed by another incident. The failure to be detected apparently reinforces the officer's feeling of invulnerability from detection. As time increases, the frequency of misconduct would cyclically increase until an undefined saturation point is reached and the officer feels that no further risks could be taken.

User-Driven Cycle. In these cases an officer starts as a "recreational" user of drugs, typically buying the substances for personal consumption from a dealer. The officer's behavior evolves to a point when he/she decides that instead of buying the drugs they can be "confiscated" from users/dealers or taken from the police property room. This decision appears to be the product of several factors which interact. One is the increasing cost of drug use. A second factor is opportunity: the officer concludes that it is cheaper to convert seized drugs for personal use rather than to buy them. Finally, officers begin to worry that their occupational identity may be discovered by drug dealers (if not already known) leading to blackmail.

Profit-Driven Cycle. Officers involved in this form of corruption include both users and non-users of drugs. The intent in this form of corruption is purely monetary. The primary motivation for becoming corrupt is the vast amount of unaccountable and untraceable money involved in the illicit drug trade coupled with the opportunity, by virtue of police authority, to seize these monies. This is further compounded by the fact that the source of the money is illegal activity. During the course of research on the topic, officers involved in corruption tended to make comments along the line that "it's not fair" or "it's not right" that drug traffickers had far more money than the officers who were "working for a living" or who were "risking their lives."

To give perspective on the amounts of money involved, one former undercover narcotics investigator now assigned to a task force to investigate drug corruption stated, "When you're looking at on-going [drug] deals of even medium to small size quantities, $100,000 is a small score for a bribe in drug trafficking today." In another case, ten officers from one police department made two robberies of cocaine from drug traffickers. In just these two robberies, the officers made over $16 million among them. The amounts of money are staggering—and tempting.

Type 2 Drug Corruption: In Search of Legitimate Goals

Strikingly different is the second form of corruption—in search of legitimate goals. Since corruption is the abuse of one's position for personal gain, it may be argued that, in the case of drug corruption, "gain" is not only money, tangible goods, and services but may also be an organizational benefit—perhaps a form of "winning" or "revenge." Examples of Type 2 corrupt behavior include:

- False statements to obtain arrest or search warrants against "known" drug dealers/traffickers
- Perjury during hearings and trials of drug dealers
- "Planting" or creating evidence against "known" drug dealers
- Overt and intentional entrapment
- Falsely spreading rumors that a dealer is a police informant, thus placing that person's safety in jeopardy

The characterization of "legitimate goals" is from the perspective of the officer. There are persons whom officers "know" are involved in drug trafficking, however, the police are consistently unable to obtain sufficient evidence for arrest. Similarly, there are "known" criminals who have been found not guilty in court because the government has not been able to prove its case—frequently because evidence has been excluded on "technicalities." The officers see these recurring circumstances and become frustrated because the trafficker is "beating the system." This is compounded by the tendency to perceive legal strategies during hearings and trials as "unfair manipulation of the law" by attorneys.

The Type 2 corrupt officer's self-determined goal is to prosecute and incarcerate the drug traffickers. However, Type 2 corruption occurs when the attempt to accomplish this *legitimate goal* is through *illegitimate means.* When the goal (conviction) is achieved the officer receives the satisfaction that he/she "won." This form of revenge is psychologically rewarding and, obviously, improper.

It is argued that in the case of Type 2 corruption, the acts are not only for the personal psychological gain of the officer but also in support of organizational goals through which the officer may be rewarded by commendations, promotions, and/or recognition. It may also be argued that this form of corruption is for organizational gain via the arrest and prosecution of known serious, often dangerous, drug traffickers.

Type 2 corruption is further compounded because this behavior is not traditionally perceived as being corrupt. There is a degree of informal organizational tolerance for behavior which gets "known" traffickers off the street or seizes the traffickers' cache of drugs. This tolerance complicates the determination of wrongdoing and undermines the commitment toward integrity which was discussed in the previous section.

An officer's exposure to drug-related situations as well as the opportunity for either type of corruption will be largely dependent on the officer's assignment. While the opportunity for corruption may be found in many assignments, clearly patrol officers and drug investigators have the greatest exposure to corruption-related situations.

Illicit Drug Use by Police Officers

Just as drug-related corruption has surfaced, the problem of employee drug use has emerged in law enforcement (just as it has in virtually every other occupation.) While instances of alcohol abuse have been well documented as they relate to police officers, scrutiny of drug effects, other than alcohol, have been less prevalent. The obvious distinction between alcohol and illicit substances is the unlawful nature of the latter. Not only must concern be directed toward the behavioral effects associated with drug use, but also the abrogation of duty and trust by the officer who has violated the law through drug possession. Furthermore, concern must be given to the threat posed by the association with drug dealers-this alone can place an officer in a compromising position.

Recreational Drug Use

The most frequent issue related to officer drug abuse is "recreational" use. Recreational use of drugs is a somewhat broad characterization. Admittedly, it is a term which may not be completely inclusive of all drug use, particularly in cases of addiction. For the present discussion, recreational use is defined as drug use that does not involve corruption and where use was initially a product of the desire to experience the expected exhilaration, psychoactive effects, physiological effects and/or mood changes associated with drug consumption. Under this definition, drug use may include both on-duty and off-duty use of illicit narcotic and non-narcotic controlled substances as long as corruption is not involved.

On-Duty Drug Use

The extent of on-duty drug use by officers is simply not known. An intuitive assumption is that some on-duty use occurs; however, it appears to be relatively rare. When it does occur, the potential ramifications are widespread. The most serious implication is that an officer may use deadly force or be involved in a traffic accident while under the influence. Other effects of on-duty use include poor judgment in the performance of the officer's duties, an increase in behavior related to liability risks, participation in other forms of misconduct, and having a negative influence on co-workers and the community with whom the officer has contact. In one case the author discovered during the course of research on the topic, a patrol officer in a major Midwestern city was found using cocaine while on duty. During the internal affairs investigation the officer admitted he had regularly used cocaine on-duty for over one year. The officer said he felt co-workers would be able to tell from his behavior when he was "high," so each time after he "snorted" cocaine he would "chase it" with whiskey. He knew fellow officers would "cover for him" if they thought he was an alcoholic, therefore, he masked the cocaine's behavioral influences with the odor of alcohol. This experience, which provides insight into the occupational culture of policing, serves as an extreme example of how on-duty substance abuse can occur without being discovered.

On-duty drug use can also occur if the problem becomes systemic within the work group. In one moderate-sized Midwestern city, about thirty officers were identified as being involved in a "user's ring" (most of whom did not use drugs on duty.) Drug use became so pervasive that there was tolerance for its use, even on duty. While some officers in the group did not like the on-duty use, they would not inform on those using drugs during working hours because of the strong implication they would be discovered as drug users, albeit during off-duty hours. The implication from this experience is that in light of the police subculture, if off-duty use becomes pervasive, there is an increased likelihood of on-duty use among the officers involved.

In perhaps the only empirical study of the subject, Peter Kraska and Victor Kappeler discovered on-duty drug use during the course of working with a southwestern police department on another project. Through the use of unstructured self-report interviews, departmental records, and personal observations they found that 20 percent of the officers in the department used marijuana while on duty twice a month or more. Another 4 percent had used marijuana at least once while on duty. Moreover, 10 percent of the officers reported they had used non-prescribed controlled substances (including hallucinogenic drugs, stimulants, or barbiturates) while on duty. (This may not be an additional 10 percent of the officers; it may include some of the marijuana users.) Most of the officers involved in this behavior were between the ages of 21 and 38 and had been police officers for 3 to 10 years.

One may hope that the high incidence of on-duty drug use found in this study was an exceptional occurrence. If not, the problem may be greater than we believe. Certainly, the findings dispel the myth that drug use is a problem found only in the police departments of the nation's largest cities. Based on this, and other research, it is also reasonable to assume that those agencies which have had more serious drug-related problems—notably corruption—have also experienced on-duty drug use.

Drugs of Choice

In cases where police drug use has been documented, marijuana appears to be the most common drug used. The preference for marijuana is most likely because of its comparatively minor addictive nature, its limited long-term effects, the ease of obtaining it, its comparatively low cost, and, importantly, the lesser social stigma associated with the use of marijuana when compared with other drugs. Cocaine is clearly the second most frequently used drug and appears to be fairly prevalent. The best explanation for this seems to be its availability, its prevalent use in many social situations, and the generally greater sense of exhilaration provided by cocaine compared to marijuana.

There is also some evidence of abuse of non-prescribed or falsely prescribed pharmaceutical subsustances. Amphetamines and barbiturates fall into this category, typically where officers have used the drugs as a way of coping with various personal problems. In some cases, stimulants have been used to help keep officers "alert" (or awake) when they have been working excessive hours in a second job or going to school. This form of substance abuse appears to have different dynamics than marijuana or cocaine use. Interestingly, officers showed greater tolerance for protecting officers who used amphetamines and barbiturates as opposed to other controlled substances, despite the fact the use of those substances is illegal. There were no indications of a significant problem with synthetic hallucinogenic drugs or heroin.

As a final note, some police administrators have expressed concern that an increasing number of officers may be using illicit anabolic steroids. Their concern, while somewhat focused on the illegal use, is primarily directed toward the reported behavioral effects of steroids. Specifically, some research has indicated that regular steroid users become violent and aggressive. The implications of these effects in law enforcement are obvious. Interestingly, new police programming may indirectly contribute to this problem. With more departments participating in competitive physical competitions, such as the Police Olympics, which include weight lifting, martial arts, running, and similar activity, in addition to rewarding physical fitness, the appeal of the conditioning effects of steroids is powerful. This is an important area for police executives to carefully explore.

Substance Abuse as a Job-Related Condition

Questions have arisen of whether officer drug use could be a job-related condition. There have been two primary arguments on which this assertion is based: police stress and the officer's job assignment.

The rationale the stress argument posits is that as a result of the high levels of stress in policing, some officers have resorted to drug use as a coping mechanism. Despite the wide array of research on police stress there is no scientific evidence to support this claim. In fact, the author would argue that drug abusing officers would experience greater stress since there is always the fear that an officer's drug abuse may be discovered. This, of course, would likely end in discipline or termination. If stress was, in fact, a major cause of police drug use, then it is likely that higher levels of drug use would have been discovered over the past two decades. Furthermore, evidence from police disciplinary actions and labor arbitrations where officer drug use is at issue does not suggest that stress was a cause.

The second issue of job-relatedness is more problematic. This argument states that officers who are working undercover drug investigations with frequent and on-going exposure to drugs may become socialized in the "drug culture." That is, constant interaction in the environment of drug use and transactions reduces the adverse socio-moral implications of drug consumption while at the same time reinforcing the permissibility of its use.

It is clear that undercover officers do, in fact, become socialized into the drug culture based on language, dress, and other behaviors which carry over to the officer's off-duty time. Officers who work undercover in prostitution, gambling, and bootlegging tend to diminish the social impact and "wrongfulness" of these behaviors. Given these factors and our knowledge about the socialization process in general, it is reasonable to assume that officers could be similarly assimilated into the drug culture. This is reinforced by the knowledge that if an officer is going to be accepted into a social group, he/she must appear to ascribe to that group's norms. While the process may begin as a masquerade for the officer, constant exposure to the culture combined with the stress of the environment may reasonably lead to acceptance of drug use (and other improper behaviors) at the social level even though the officer recognizes that they should not be accepted at the legal level. Generally, the longer an officer is in such an environment the more acceptable that group's values and norms become. While empirical research is virtually non-existent on this issue, anecdotal evidence from research conducted by the author gives credence to this process occurring.

The Corruption-Culture Milieu of Police

Despite the significant differences in the motivations and behaviors involved in the different forms of corruption and drug use, the author has observed eight operational constructs which permeate each type of corruption. These factors appear to have cumulative interactive influences which continually reinforce each type of behavior. That is, left uncontrolled, these factors can contribute to an environment wherein corruption will flourish.

Opportunity Structure

In situations that confront police officers in their positions of authority, there are opportunities for them to "profit" from the exercise of their authority. Barker (1994) observed that the opportunity structure provides the police officer with many situations to observe and/or participate in a wide range of illicit activities. In addition, the police come into contact with many people who are criminal (or on the periphery of criminality) during the officers' normal work routine under conditions of little or no supervision. Kraska and Kappeler observed that three variables related to the opportunity structure of policing add to the police officers' vulnerability. First is the duration and intensity of exposure to the criminal element of a society. Second is the police officer's relative freedom from supervision. Third is the uncontrolled availability of contraband and opportunities to convert situations (such as the investigation of a burglary at a business) to personal gain with minimal risks. The corrupt officer is one who exploits these opportunities.

Abrogation of Trust

Based on the literature of police ethics, organizational values, labor arbitrations, and case law, it is clear that there is a higher standard of integrity required of police officers than of the "average citizen" (Carter, 1988). The essence of that standard is reflected in the officer's oath of office and the concomitant trust citizens place in police officers as result of their unique authority. On the matter of corruption Klockars has emphasized that, "What is corrupted in police corruption is the special trust police enjoy by virtue of their occupation" (1983:334). Officers' violations of law or their failure to afford due process and equal protection to citizens is a fundamental abrogation of lawful duties which erodes public trust. Because of the critical public safety role the police hold in our global societies, the trust given to a police officer's position is one which should be carefully upheld.

Rationalization

A telling remark by a police officer interviewed by the author sheds light on how corrupt behavior is rationalized. The officer, who had taken money from a drug dealer, simply observed that "it was just drug money," implying that there was a different standard for the taking of illegally earned money compared to lawfully obtained wealth. Another common rationalization is that corruption "was not hurting anyone," again with the implication that there is a different standard of equity or justification when money is taken from a "known criminal" than other persons. Perhaps because in the back of their minds officers recall their oath of office, they tend to rationalize their corrupt acts.

Invulnerability Factor

Essentially, this is the perception that because of an officer's position and authority, he/she will not be implicated in the misconduct. The officer's easy access to information, camaraderie, and the power to influence others contribute to this perception. Perhaps the epitome of this factor can be illustrated in one officer's statement: "Who's going to take the word of a [criminal] over a cop?" The officer felt he was "safe"—invulnerable from allegations by criminals—and would not be caught.

'The Code of Secrecy'

The literature on policing has thoroughly examined the "code of secrecy" within the police culture (see Barker and Carter, 1994; Blumberg and Niederhoffer, 1985; Kennedy, 1977). The "code," although it has variations, is generally described as a cultural norm that prohibits the discussion of "secrets" and behaviors with those outside of the defined social group (which may vary, depending on the social group). The group's parameters may be defined by shift, assignment, rank, or simply employment by a police organization. The parameters may also be defined on the basis of participation in the occupational group activities. That is, an officer who does not subscribe to the "code" or adhere to its rules may be ostracized from the social group. The influence of peer pressure to "belong" and the social sanctions associated with ostracism make the "code" a powerful cultural dynamic.

Despite the seriousness of police corruption, there still appears to be some reluctance to inform on such officers. When corruption was mentioned by officers who were interviewed in the author's research, the honest officers simply tended to disassociate themselves but not report the corrupt officer to the department. Interestingly, an officer who informs on a fellow officer may be labeled a "rat" who cannot be trusted. The "rat" may even experience more ostracism than the officers involved in the corrupt behavior (see McAlary, 1987; Knapp Commission, 1973). In one city, an officer who was not involved in any form of misconduct observed another officer taking a bribe. The "straight" officer did not report the corrupt officer nor did he say anything about the bribe until he was interviewed by Internal Affairs during an investigation of the corrupt officer. When asked why the officer had not come forward, the Internal Affairs investigator stated,

> . . . he didn't fear getting shot, he didn't fear getting hurt [on the job]; he *did* fear the repercussions of turning in a fellow officer even under these circumstances.

Market Forces

Just as market forces can drive an economy, they can also influence corrupt behavior. Police officers control the commodity of "police authority." Whether the officer independently decides to exercise authority unlawfully (such as taking money from a drug dealer) or whether the officer is induced to a corrupt act by another person, depends to some extent on the risk-benefit ratio. Even the most honest officers have been tempted on occasion to commit a corrupt act. If an officer has the opportunity to "earn" two or three times his annual salary through one corrupt act, temptation becomes stronger. The officer will weigh the risks and benefits of the situation—sometimes even momentarily—to decide his course of action. Included in this "weighing" process are social responsibility, ethical standards, peer influences, and different potential ramifications of the act. Hopefully, the proper factors will weight the scale in that direction. In too many cases, however, officers have succumbed to the temptation, deciding the benefits outweigh the risks.

Inadequate Organizational Controls

Many police organizations simply have not provided sufficiently rigorous supervision and training on matters related to the dynamics of corruption. Similarly, insufficient investigative audit controls are used to monitor case development and officer behavior. Following the review of an extensive drug corruption problem in one city, the police department implemented a new anti-corruption program. The Deputy Chief, in commenting on the program, said,

> We found we had to go back to the basics. We simply did not have enough accountability nor enough training. We were lax, putting these things on the back burner so we could concentrate on crime and handling calls. It's apparent we paid dearly for that misjudgment.

Persistence of the Corruptive Patterns

Even with the threat of investigation and the self-awareness of one's misconduct, it appears extraordinarily difficult for an officer to stop his/her corrupt behavior once it is started. Following this line of thought, Goldstein noted what he called the "addictive element" of corruption: "Once an officer has agreed to accept the [personal gain] of corruption, he usually becomes addicted to the system" (1975:27). Stated differently, corruption becomes habitual. This author argues that this "corruptive habit" has a reinforcing effect in that the officer must further rationalize his/her behavior when the opportunity arises for a corrupt act. Similarly, because of the difficulty of breaking out of the patterns, the feeling of invulnerability must be heightened.

Policy Implications

Police managers need to be certain that there is effective supervision of officers. This includes frequent interaction between the supervisor and subordinate and stringent requirements of accountability on behalf of the officer. In police organizations where corruption is known to be a chronic problem, special supervisory vigilance should be in place. Supervisors should be trained in the "behavioral signs" of corrupt behavior and be required to monitor behavior in circumstances or at crime scenes where opportunities for corruption are highest. Aggressive supervision can be both a preventive policy and a tool to detect corruption.

Training and reinforcement of ethics and professional responsibilities should be provided in periodic training sessions to officers of all ranks. The police organization should articulate organizational values and ensure those values permeate all policies, procedures, and supervisory actions. Training and supervision should also reinforce the officers' role and responsibility to equitably enforce the law, emphasizing that all people are treated the same regardless of whether they are law-abiding citizens or "known criminals." Policies and procedures should clearly reflect this position.

A timely and aggressive internal investigations process and discipline system can reduce impressions of "invulnerability" by officers as well as increase the perception of risk associated with corrupt behavior. If an employee understands the department will not tolerate corruption and this is reinforced by a reputation of aggressive internal controls, then the invulnerability factor will be significantly reduced.

The department needs to have an open environment where communications between personnel at all ranks is open and invited. Having an open organization minimizes the need for "secrets." Similarly, supervisors who engender open communications and trust will minimize the effects of the "code of secrecy" as manifest through peer pressure. In addition, having a mechanism for "rumor control" can minimize gossip and misperceptions which, in turn, reduces the environment of secrecy. Finally, through effective leadership and expectations of responsible, ethical behavior, an environment of professional accountability will emerge which reduces reliance on the "code of secrecy."

The department must be particularly sensitive to areas of police behavior which are uniquely vulnerable to corrupt behavior. Constant scanning of the environment to identify corruptive risks should be done in order to counteract those factors. Increasing risk of detection and certainty of punishment should be a paramount factor. The inculcation of values and reinforcement of social responsibility should be done on an on-going basis. Finally, all policies related to the identification, investigation, and adjudication of police misconduct should be periodically reviewed to ensure they are being followed and are consistent with contemporary issues, practices, problems and law.

A Further Perspective on Policy

Understanding factors that motivate officers to become involved in corrupt acts can aid the implementation of both preventive and detection programs. Similarly, understanding factors which contribute, even indirectly, to the potential for corruption can facilitate organizational responses to counteract negative trends.

A consistent finding of the author's research was that organizations—when initially confronted with evidence of corruption—tended to *deny* the problem, creating an obstacle to effective policy development. Another consistent issue was the effect of the police working environment on officer misconduct. The concern was that if an officer's misbehavior was significantly influenced by the occupational environment, policy responses would have to deal with this. Both of these issues warrant greater attention.

Organizational Denial

As noted above, when confronted with indications that police officers are involved in corruption, there is a tendency of administrators to deny the problem. Typically, the denial is not to avoid negative publicity nor is it to "cover up" the problem. Rather, the denial occurs because administrators have difficulty believing that officers are involved in corrupt behavior (Carter and Stephens, 1988).

When asked about drug corruption, comments from police administrators were "I can't believe it," "I can't understand it," and "The allegations can't be true." One administrator stated,

> The last problem I ever thought I'd face is my officers robbing drug dealers *for drugs.* I mean, the reports are here—it's in black and white—but my mind just can't accept it. I don't know if I let [the officers] down or they let me down. Something definitely went wrong in the system somewhere.

This reaction reflects two important things. First, it clearly illustrates the denial, which is a manifestation of the organizational trauma associated with officer corruption. On this subject a captain, who was a 24-year municipal police veteran, stated "I guess I'm just from another generation—I just don't understand [it.]"

A second reaction is what might be categorized as organizational confusion and the lack of preparation to manage corruption problems. Many police departments have generic disciplinary procedures and codes of conduct, but tend to have inadequate policies, procedures, training, supervision, support resources, and administrative control to detect and respond to officer corruption. The lack of planning for potential corruption tends to contribute to programming that is reactive, based on intuitive and emotional reasoning rather than a fully outlined strategy to deal with the problem. As a result, the problem lingers and conflicts occur regarding what the department should do to resolve the situation.

While departments were not eager to publicize their corruption problems, they typically did not mislead the media. In some circumstances, conflicting reports were given from the police department. However, this appeared to occur because the department did not have a complete grasp of the problem and organizational denial tended to cloud its objectivity.

Environmental Factors

Early theories of corruption viewed it "as a result of interaction between the police organization and its environment [with] the causal emphasis placed on the environment" (Sherman, 1983:369). The environment encompasses the organizational and social dynamics of the police officer's work life. It is a variable that includes the community political organization, the structure of local government, norm conflicts, and the values of the local culture. Similarly, Goldstein's observation on the police officer's working environment was that,

> [the] average police officer . . . sees the worst side of humanity. He is exposed to a steady diet of wrongdoing. He becomes intimately familiar with the ways people prey on one another. In the course of this intensive exposure he discovers that dishonesty and corruption are not restricted to those the community sees as criminal. He sees many individuals of good reputation engaging in practices equally dishonest and corrupt. (1975:25)

In light of the literature on environmental causes of misbehavior and inferences from the impact of occupational socialization on an individual's behavior, a critical question could reasonably be asked: If the officer is policing an environment where crime is prevalent and the people with whom the officer has the most frequent contact are criminal or social problems, might this be an influence on the officer's behavior? The answer is not definitive, however, such a circumstance is an important variable which appears to have a contributing influence.

As one illustration, the greatest potential for drug-related police corruption exists for narcotics and vice officers. They receive even less supervision than patrol officers and are not only constantly exposed to the "drug culture" but are also expected to participate in that culture as a charade. In the gamesmanship of undercover work, some officers tend to confuse their own cultural norms with the norms of the criminal culture they have penetrated. The buying and selling of drugs become second nature, as do the language and social perspective (i.e., values and norms) of that culture.

In one case, the author spoke with an undercover narcotics officer about the practice of "simulation," that is, pretending to smoke marijuana during the course of an undercover assignment as a means to help legitimize the officer's role. The officer reported that

> Simulation is crap—any user knows if you're smoking or faking, and you can bet they're watching the new guys to see if you're taking a real hit. If I'm at a [drug] deal and I try to simulate, I might as well be wearing a sign that says COP. . . . So you've got to take a real hit to sell yourself. Anyway, it's just a hit of marijuana—it's got less bite than tequila.

The officer went on to report that he, along with another undercover narcotics officer, had smoked marijuana—which they had seized during their undercover work—while off-duty. Perhaps what was most striking about the officer' statements was that he did not appear to recognize the serious impropriety of his acts. In fact, he implied that his department should permit undercover drug officers to smoke marijuana in the course of investigations to help maintain their credibility. In the author's opinion, this officer's occupational environment contributed to his misconduct; however, it is impossible to assign a causal weight to such environmental factors.

When this officer's statement was told to a police supervisor from another agency (who formerly worked undercover narcotics), the supervisor stated: "That guy's got a problem. He's been in too long without anybody keeping an eye on him." It is not argued here that the environment has a wholesale influence on undercover officers. Rather, the environment must be viewed in light of individual socialization and organizational factors which influence behavior.

How can the environmental variable be dealt with in dealing with a corrupt officer? Should the police department share some of the responsibility for the officer's wrongdoing? Do these environmental factors mitigate the officer's liability for corrupt acts? These are difficult questions which require closer direct examination of social, legal, moral, and administrative issues. With respect to the control of these factors, Manning observed,

> it is very simple at one level: control the targets, the money, the evidence, the informants and train and supervise the officers. At another level [this] is very difficult to carry off because the individual officer-based model predominates. (1983)

According to Stoddard, the inference to be drawn from these environmental factors is that we should ". . . see police corruption as something that is not an individual problem but a problem of the occupation and its organization; something in the nature of police work itself" (1983:334).

Control of Corruption

Based on a wide array of literature and the causes enumerated above, there are a number of factors which can be introduced to minimize and control corruption.

Leadership by the Chief of Police

The police chief must establish a clear standard for the department that corruption will not be tolerated in any form. Corruption must be defined for the officers so there is no question about those acts which are prohibited. It must also be clear that officers are expected to act in a lawful and ethical manner which includes reporting officers involved in corrupt behavior (i.e., breaking the "code of secrecy"). Furthermore, the chief must be firm in the commitment that disciplinary action and criminal prosecution will be swiftly and surely taken against offending officers.

Management and Supervision

Managers and supervisors have the responsibility to reinforce the chief's tone of integrity, commend officers for ethical behavior, and lead by example. Supervisors and managers must also monitor officers, particularly those in assignments which are of a higher risk for corruption, to ensure their behavior is lawful. When any suspicion arises about a subordinate's behavior, the manager or supervisor must take immediate action to solve the questions.

Supervisory Training

Supervisors need to receive training on such areas as recognizing the signs of corruption, employee assessment, and inculcating values in subordinates. Too often supervisors are given these responsibilities, but are not told how to fulfill them. In-service training must also include "updates" on police policy, liability law, and related factors which change in the policing environment.

Organizational Control and Information Management

The department should establish a system which monitors officer behavior to ensure all police personnel are following procedures related to stops, detention, arrests, storing evidence and recovered property, conducting computer checks, and any other aspect of police procedure which is subject to abuse. Irregularities should be more closely examined, particularly where patterns of irregularities exist. All suspicious activities should be documented and investigated according to established internal investigations policy.

Internal Auditing and Informants

Two corruption-related problems arise with informants: The improper use of departmental money to pay informants and the use of informants to perform improper acts on behalf of the officer. To avoid these problems, careful controls must be in place to audit both money and interaction between officers and informants. Any "secret" or "confidential" funds for informants and undercover operations must have rigid controls for accountability.

Internal Affairs

The police Internal Affairs function is designed to investigate allegations of wrongdoing by police officers. Internal Affairs investigators must be familiar with the different types of corruption which occur, know how to investigate corruption cases, and be vigilant in their investigations. Too frequently, these cases are difficult to investigate because of the unwillingness of people to testify.

Drug Enforcement Units

As noted previously, because of the vast amounts of money involved in unlawful drug transactions, officers working in Drug Enforcement Units are particularly susceptible to corruption. Supervision, audit controls, and a policy of regular personnel turnover in these units will help reduce the potential for corruption.

Evidence Handling and Storage

While most police departments have procedures for marking and storing evidence to maintain the chain of custody for evidence in court, these procedures typically do not provide a comprehensive control of evidence. Procedures must be established to comprehensively control property beginning with the time it is seized, not when it arrives at the police station. Supervisors should also monitor officer conduct when property is seized. Care should also be taken to periodically monitor property in storage to ensure it has not been tampered with.

An Early Warning System

Based on the research related to officer corruption, certain behaviors have emerged which are indicative of misconduct. Purchases which appear to be beyond the officer's financial means, changes in the officer's social behavior, and allegations from informants that an officer might be "on the take" are illustrations of these indicators. Utilizing these types of information, the department may develop an "Early Warning System" which monitors the indicators—particularly for officers in highly susceptible assignments. In this way, corruption can be dealt with before it becomes extensive. Moreover, such a system may serve a preventive role as well.

Training

Officer training on matters related to corruption, integrity, ethics, and social responsibilities should be provided on a periodic basis to keep awareness of the problem omnipresent. For officers working in undercover assignments, training should be provided which explicitly addresses the threats of corruption in the assignment, how to avoid corruption, and actions to take when corruptive advances are made toward the officer.

Discipline

When officers are found to have been involved in corruption, discipline should be swift, sure, and substantial. This reinforces the chief's commitment to having a "clean" department and shows that there will be no toleration for corrupt behavior.

Corruption, perhaps more than any form of misconduct, undermines the public confidence in the police. It represents a complete violation of the public trust and an absolute abuse of the authority the public has vested in officers. When corruption flourishes in a department, the integrity of the entire police department is drawn into question. As a result, stringent controls play an important role in maintaining public confidence and effectiveness of the policing function.

References

Alpert, Geoffrey P. and Roger C. Dunham. 1992. *Policing Urban America.* 2nd. ed. Prospect Heights, IL: Waveland Press.

Barker, Thomas. 1994. "Peer Group Support for Occupational Deviance." In Thomas Barker and David L. Carter, *Police Deviance.* 3rd ed. Cincinnati, OH: Anderson Publishing Company.

Blumberg, Abraham and Elaine Niederhoffer (eds.) 1985. *The Ambivalent Force.* 3rd ed. New York: Holt, Rinehart and Winston.

Carter, David L. 1990. "An Overview of Drug-Related Misconduct of Police Officers: Drug Abuse and Narcotic Corruption." In Ralph Weisheit, *Drugs and the Criminal Justice System.* Cincinnati, OH: Anderson Publishing Company.

——. 1990. "Drug-Related Corruption of Police Officers: A Contemporary Typology." *Journal of Criminal Justice.* 18:85–98.

——. 1988. *Controlling Off-Duty Behavior. Higher Standards of Integrity for the Police.* Paper presented at the annual meeting of the Academy of Criminal Justice Sciences. San Francisco, California.

Carter, David L. and Darnel Stephens. 1988. *Drug Abuse by Police Officers: An Analysis of Critical Policy Issues.* Springfield, IL: Charles C. Thomas, Publisher.

Commission to Investigate Allegations of Police Corruption and the City's Anti-Corruption Procedures. (Knapp Commission.) 1973. *Report of the Commission.* New York: George Braziller.

Dombrink, John. 1994. "The Touchables: Vice and Police Corruption in the 1980s." In Thomas Barker and David L. Carter, *Police Deviance.* 3rd ed. Cincinnati, OH: Anderson Publishing Company.

Goldstein, Herman. 1975. *Police Corruption: A Perspective on its Nature and Control.* Washington, DC: Police Foundation.

Klockars, Carl (ed.) 1983. *Thinking About Police: Contemporary Readings.* New York: McGrawHill.

Kenney, Dennis J. and James O. Finckenauer. 1995. *Organized Crime in America.* New York: Wadsworth Publishing Company.

Kraska, Peter and Victor Kappeler. 1988. "A Theoretical and Descriptive Examination of Police On-Duty Drug Use." *American Journal of Police.* 7:60.

Sherman, Lawrence. 1983. "Scandal and Reform." In Carl Klockars, *Thinking About Police: Contemporary Readings.* New York: McGraw-Hill.

Stoddard, E.R. 1983. "Blue Coat Crime." In Carl Klockars, *Thinking About Police: Contemporary Readings.* New York: McGraw-Hill.

David L. Carter, "Drug Use and Drug-Related Corruption of Police Officers." Reprinted from Larry K. Gaines and Gary W. Cordner (Eds.), *Policing Perspectives: An Anthology*, pp. 311–323. Copyright © 1999 by Roxbury Publishing Company. All rights reserved. ✦

Part VII

The Challenges Ahead

This section focuses on the future challenges facing American policing. Predicting future trends in police organizations is especially difficult given the complex structural variation in law enforcement agencies, the strong influence of a demanding external environment, and the uncertain nature and scope of local politics. For example, at the turn of the previous century, few anticipated the coming of a professional model of policing that would dominate police services for the next fifty years.

Over the past two decades, changes in public safety have been significant. In the late 1970s, most police administrators and scholars agreed that American policing needed to adapt to a dynamic external environment. Two of the main pillars of the professional model—preventive patrol and detective work—were proven to be ineffective in controlling local crime or reducing social disorder. New operational activities had to be developed in response.

The role of the federal government in the reformation of public safety has proven significant as well. The passage of the 1994 Violent Crime Control Act and the endorsement of community policing by the Clinton Administration made the transition to community policing attractive and feasible to many agencies across the nation. Grant funding totaling $9 billion was used to assist local law enforcement agencies in their implementation of community policing initiatives, the largest sum of monetary support bestowed upon policing by the federal government in American history. More than 75,000 community-oriented policing officers were hired with these funds; in addition, numerous technological innovations were deployed in over 12,000 law enforcement agencies, all funded by the Office of Community Policing Services since its creation in 1994.

Despite funding for these "boundary-spanning units," as Thompson would call them, there has been very limited change in the organizational structure of law enforcement agencies. Few police agencies have seriously attempted to make significant changes in their rank system, their span of control, or the nature of the primary form of communication (e.g., chain of command) in their organizations. Not a single police agency claims to have totally restructured its organization in order to implement community policing. And while some departments have attempted to geographically reassign their detectives or revise personnel evaluation methods by paying attention to problem solving and innovation, no systematic pattern of reform in police organizational structure is currently in evidence.

We believe that the greatest changes that lay ahead for police organizations will be in the area of technological adaptation. Today's law enforcement agencies have improved in their ability to use technology. Traditionally, research and planning units were mainly created to compile departmental data or reports for top administrators. Now, many of these units also devote their energies to crime mapping, web maintenance, and even program evaluations. Laptop computers have been installed in patrol cars to improve communication among officers and to allow quicker information access. We also believe that the police will continue to implement innovative programs to combat local disorder problems. While we cannot predict the exact impact of these programs on crime reduction in the future, we anticipate that there will be considerable public acceptance of new and innovative strategies as long as the innovations that are developed do not infringe upon dearly held civil liberties.

Reference

Thompson, J. 1967. *Organization in Action.* New York: McGraw-Hill Book Company. ✦

Chapter 28
The Future of Policing

David H. Bayley
Clifford D. Shearing

Here the authors note a divergence between "police" and "policing," and argue that the former should be defined as any public law enforcement agency that is authorized by state law to carry out legal police functions. "Policing," in contrast, refers to a method of keeping peace and order. The authors argue, therefore, that private police, a rapidly growing resource, also perform policing work.

Much discussion in the article centers on the erosion of social control by public police forces. They note that over the past thirty years, "The police and policing have become increasingly distinct. . . . In the United States, for example, there are three times more private security agents than public police officers." Anticipated changes include an increase in civilian employees who do policing work in the years ahead, as police agencies hire more civilians to perform crime prevention and technical support functions.

Bayley and Shearing also observe that community policing, with its openness to the external environment, represents another major reform in American policing. Accordingly, they assert that more police administrators seem to realize the value of participative management and empowerment of police officers in the workplace. This development marks a significant change from a traditional professional model of policing in which chain of command and span of control are highly valued.

Finally, the authors believe that how public police perform their duty is related to three important social issues. Public safety is the primary issue, because the effectiveness of current change is closely associated with controlling crime. The other two issues are equity and human rights. Can the police in the U.S. control crime and simultaneously promote social equity? What about their sensitivity to human rights? Because there is a close association between social disorganization and crime in a community, law enforcement activities are apt to be concentrated in economically disadvantaged neighborhoods where residents are most vulnerable to abuse of authority and criminal victimization. These issues are crucial for determining citizen trust in the police and support for effective public safety measures.

Modern democratic countries like the United States, Britain, and Canada have reached a watershed in the evolution of their systems of crime control and law enforcement. Future generations will look back on our era as a time when one system of policing ended and another took its place. Two developments define the change—the pluralizing of policing and the search by the public police for an appropriate role.

First, policing is no longer monopolized by the public police, that is, the police created by government. Policing is now being widely offered by institutions other than the state, most importantly by private companies on a commercial basis and by communities on a volunteer basis. Second, the public police are going through an intense period of self-questioning, indeed, a true identity crisis. No longer confident that they are either effective or efficient in controlling crime, they are anxiously examining every aspect of their performance—objectives, strategies, organization, management, discipline, and accountability. These movements, one inside and the other outside the police, amount to the restructuring of policing in contemporary democratic societies.

The restructuring of policing, which is already well advanced, has profound implications for public life, especially on the level and distribution of public safety, the vitality of civil rights, and the character of democratic government. Yet, despite the fatefulness of these changes, there has been hardly any public debate on the future of policing. If Thomas Jefferson was right that the price of liberty is eternal vigilance, then the current silence about these issues is a source of great risk for democratic societies.

In order to begin a debate that is long overdue, we first describe in greater detail the pluralizing of policing and the changing character of public policing. Second, we examine the impact of these developments on society and government. Third, we predict the likely future of policing by pinpointing the factors shaping each movement. Finally, we specify the policies that are needed ensure that the current restructuring of policing serves the broad interests of a developed democratic society.

It is very important to be clear about what we mean when we talk about policing. We are not concerned exclusively with "the police," that is, with people in uniforms who are hired, paid, and directed by government. We are interested in all explicit efforts to create visible agents of crime control, whether by government or by nongovernmental institutions. So we are dealing with polic-*ing,* not just *police.* At the same time, we say *explicit* attempts to create policing institutions so as not to extend our discussion to all the informal agencies that societies rely on to maintain order, such as parents, churches, employers, spouses, peers, neighbors, professional associations, and so forth. The activities of such people and institutions are undoubtedly critically important in crime control, but they have not been explicitly designed for this purpose. They are rarely objects of explicit crime policy. So the scope of our discussion is bigger than the breadbox of the police but smaller than the elephant of social control. Our focus is on the self-conscious process whereby societies designate and authorize people to create public safety.

The End of a Monopoly

In the past 30 years the state's monopoly on policing has been broken by the creation of a host of private and community-based agencies that prevent crime, deter criminality, catch lawbreakers, investigate offenses, and stop conflict. The police and policing have become increasingly distinct. While the customary police are paid, the new policing agents come in both paid and unpaid forms. The former are referred to as private security; the latter as community crime prevention.

To complicate matters further, private security—the paid part of private policing—comes in two forms: people employed by commercial companies who are hired on contract by others and persons employed directly by companies to work as security specialists. Private police now outnumber the public police in most developed countries. In the United States, for example, there are three times more private security agents than public police officers (Bayley 1994).[1] There are twice as many private police as public police in Canada and in Britain (Johnston 1992). In all countries for which there is information, the private security sector is growing faster than the public. This has been true since the early 1960s, when the contemporary rebirth of private security began. Businesses and commercial firms, by the way, are not the only customers for private security. Private guards are now often used to guard many government buildings, including police stations.

The increase in the numbers of private police reflects a remarkable change in their status (Shearing 1992). Through World War II, private security was looked on as a somewhat unsavory occupation. It had the image of ill-trained bands of thugs hired by private businesses to break strikes, suppress labor, and spy on one another. The police, as well as the public, viewed private security companies as a dangerous and unauthorized intrusion by private interests into a government preserve. Since World War II, however, a more tolerant attitude has developed, with private security seen as a necessary supplement to the overburdened public police. In the past few years especially, governments have gone beyond passive acceptance to active encouragement of commercial private security. There now seems to be a general recognition that crime is too extensive and complex to be dealt with solely by the police and that the profit motive is not to be feared in policing.

In recent years private policing has also expanded under noncommercial auspices as communities have undertaken to provide security using volunteered resources and people. A generation ago community crime prevention was virtually nonexistent. Today it is everywhere—citizen automobile and foot patrols, neighborhood watches, crime-prevention associations and advisory councils, community newsletters, crime-prevention publications and presentations, protective escort services for at-risk populations, and monitors around schools, malls, and public parks. Like commercial private security, the acceptability of volunteer policing has been transformed in less than a generation. While once it was thought of as vigilantism, it is now popular with the public and actively encouraged by the police. Because these activities are uncoordinated, and sometimes ephemeral, it is hard to say how extensive they are. Impressionistically, they seem to be as common as McDonald's golden arches, especially in urban areas.

Policing has become a responsibility explicitly shared between government and its citizens, sometimes mediated through commercial markets, sometimes arising spontaneously. Policing has become pluralized. Police are no longer the primary crime deterrent presence in society; they have been supplanted by more numerous private providers of security.

Searching for Identity

During the past decade, police throughout the developed democratic world have increasingly questioned their role, operating strategies, organization, and management. This is attributable to growing doubts about the effectiveness of their traditional strategies in safeguarding the public from crime.

The visible presence of the police seems to be stretched so thin that it fails to deter. Police devote about 60% of their resources to patrolling but complain about running from one emergency call to another, often involving noncriminal matters. The scarecrow has grown tattered in relation to the prevalence of crime. At the same time, regrettably few villains are caught in relation to crimes committed: 21% in the United States, 26% in Britain, and 16% in Canada (1992 statistics).[2] Even fewer receive any sort of punishment through the criminal justice system. Crime pays, as scarcely more than 5% of crimes committed in the United States result in the imprisonment of the criminals involved. Because the police know all this, they are desperately searching for new approaches, responding in part to the competition they face from private security whose strategies overwhelmingly favor prevention over detection and punishment. The central question underlying police soul-searching is whether they can become more effective in truly preventing crime.

One answer to this has been community policing. Its philosophy is straightforward: the police cannot successfully prevent or investigate crime without the willing participation of the public, therefore police should transform communities from being passive consumers of police protection to active co-producers of public safety. Community policing changes the orientation of the police and represents a sharp break with the past. Community policing transforms police from being an emergency squad in the fight against crime to becoming primary diagnosticians and treatment coordinators.

Although community policing has gotten most of the publicity in recent years, many police believe that law enforcement, their traditional tool in crime fighting, can be made more efficient. This approach might be called crime-oriented policing. It involves developing smarter enforcement tactics so that crime will not pay. Some examples include the setting up of fencing operations to catch habitual thieves and burglars; harassing drug markets so as to raise the cost of doing business; monitoring the activities of career criminals and arresting them for minor infractions of the law; cracking down unpredictably on criminal activity in particular locations; installing video cameras on public streets; and analyzing financial transactions by computer to spot cheating and fraud.

Police are also discussing, and sometimes implementing, a strategy that is a hybrid of community-oriented and crime-oriented policing. It is referred to as order-maintenance policing and involves stopping the disorderly, unruly, and disturbing behavior of people in public places, whether lawful or not. This suppressive activity not only reassures the public, demonstrating the limits for unacceptable behavior, but reduces the incidence of more serious crime (Wilson & Kelling 1982; Skogan 1990). The New York City Police Department employed this strategy against the "squeegy men" who extorted money from motorists by washing the windshields of cars stopped at traffic lights and asking for donations. The New York City Transit Police reduced the incidence of robbery on the subways by undertaking an energetic campaign against fare-beaters who vaulted over turnstiles. In both cases, the police reduced menacing activity that frightened law-abiding citizens and warned off criminals who would take advantage of what seemed to be unguarded territory (Kelling & Coles 1994). Like community policing, order-maintenance policing requires diagnosis and problem solving, but like traditional policing, it emphasizes law enforcement. It might be called community policing with a hard edge.

In addition to rethinking their standard strategies, the police are themselves helping to blur the line between government and nongovernment policing. For example, some police departments now sell the protective services they used to give away. Rather than considering police protection as a public good, free to all citizens, police are increasingly taking the view that people who derive a commercial benefit from police efforts should pay for it. Accordingly, ordinances have been enacted requiring private burglar-alarm companies to be fined or charged a fee if their electronic systems summon police to false alarms more than a specified number of times. Police are also beginning to charge fees for covering rock concerts, professional sporting events, and ethnic festivals. In some cities, businesses have banded together to pay for additional police patrols in order to get the protection they think they need.

In a development that is found across northern America, police not only sell their protective services but allow their own officers to be hired as private security guards—a practice known as "moonlighting." Many American police regularly work two jobs, one public, the other private. Indeed, moonlighting is considered a valuable perquisite of police employment. What this means is that the pluralizing of policing is being directly subsidized in the United States by public funds. Private policing uses police that have been recruited, trained, and supported by government. When acting as agents of private entities, police retain their legal authority and powers.

Not only do public police work as private police but civilians—nonpolice people—increasingly share responsibilities within public policing. Special Constables in Great Britain and Cadets, Police Auxiliaries, and Reserves in the United States often work on the street alongside regular police personnel. Though they serve without pay, and often without weapons, they are virtually indistinguishable in appearance from police. Some communities in Britain have hired able-bodied unemployed persons to patrol the streets, and others have deployed partially trained police officers as community liaison officers (Johnston 1994).

Furthermore, work traditionally performed by uniformed officers has increasingly been given to civilian employees. Usually these are jobs that don't require law enforcement, such as repairing motor vehicles, programming computers, analyzing forensic evidence, and operating radio-dispatch systems. Of all police employees, 27% in the United States are now civilians; 35% in Great Britain; 20% in Canada and Australia; and 12% in Japan (Bayley 1994). A variation on this is to contract out—privatize—support functions altogether, such as publishing, maintaining criminal records, forensic analysis, auditing and disbursement, and the guarding of police premises. Police departments are also beginning to use senior citizen volunteers to provide specialized expertise as pilots, auditors, chemists, or computer programmers.

Some communities employ special support personnel, often dressed in uniforms similar to those of the police, in frontline functions as well. The most common of these are the now ubiquitous parking-meter patrols. But uniformed civilians also conduct crime-prevention classes, make security inspections of premises, provide follow-up counseling to crime victims, resolve neighborhood disputes, and advise about pending criminal matters (Skolnick & Bayley 1986).

The innovations that are being made in operational strategies as well as the increasing use of civilians in police work have important implications for the management and organization of the police. For example, police increasingly resent being used by government as an omnibus regulatory agency. So, in an effort to save money and focus on crime prevention, many departments are considering reducing the scope of regulatory activity, such as licensing bars and nightclubs, enforcing parking regulations, maintaining lost and founds, organizing neighborhood watches, conducting crime-prevention seminars, and advising property owners about protective hardware (Johnston 1994; Bayley 1985).

Police are also beginning to recognize that the traditional quasi-military management model, based on ranks and a hierarchical chain of command, may not accommodate the requirements of modern policing. Several forces have recently eliminated redundant supervisory ranks, and almost all are talking about the value of participative, collegial management. This involves decentralizing command and allowing subordinate commanders to determine the character of police operations in their areas. There is also a great deal of talk about treating the public as customers and about measuring performance by surveys of public satisfaction rather than exclusively by the number of crimes and arrests.

Finally, police are being subjected to more intense and rigorous supervision by both government and nongovernment agencies than has ever been true in the past. In Britain, Canada, and Australia civilian review boards have recently been created that can independently investigate instances of police misbehavior, especially those involving allegations of brutality. In the United States, too, 66 major police departments had civilian review by late 1994 and the number was steadily increasing (Walker & Wright 1994). From the police point of view, the unthinkable is happening: the behavior of individual officers is now subject to civilian oversight, including, in some jurisdictions, determining blame and the severity of punishment.

Moreover, great attention is now being given to developing mechanisms for the systematic evaluation of the quality of police service. Checklists of performance indicators have being developed and national databases assembled to assist the evaluation exercise. Private management consultant firms are now regularly hired to assist local governments in evaluating police. Accrediting organizations have been set up nationally as well as in several American states and Canadian provinces to develop standards of police performance and organization.

Taken together, the pluralizing of policing and the search by the public police for a new role and methodology mean that not only has government's monopoly on policing been broken in the late 20th century, but the police monopoly on expertise within its own sphere of activity has ended. Policing now belongs to everybody—in activity, in responsibility, and in oversight.

What's at Stake

Does it matter that policing is being reconstructed? Should we care that policing is pluralizing and that the public police are having an identity crisis? Yes, we should. These developments have fateful consequences for the level of public safety, for access to public security, for human rights, and for accountability. Let us examine restructuring's implications for each of these.

Safety

Expanding the auspices under which policing is provided increases the number of security agents. If visible policing deters, then communities should be safer if there are private uniformed security guards and designated civilian patrols and watchers to supplement the public police. If the expansion of private policing was occurring at the expense of public police, of course, then safety would not be enhanced. But that does not appear to be happening. Relative to population, there are more police in developed democracies in 1995 than in 1970 despite the growth in private security. It seems reasonable to conclude, therefore, that pluralizing has made communities safer.

Pluralizing the sources of policing affects not only the quantity of policing but its quality as well. Although both public and private police rely on visibility to deter criminality, private police emphasize the logic of security, while public police emphasize the logic of justice. The major purpose of private security is to reduce the risk of crime by taking preventive actions; the major purpose of the public police is to deter crime by catching and punishing criminals.

Arrest is the special competence and preferred tool of the public police. By using it quickly and accurately, they hope to deter criminality. Private police, on the other hand, both commercial and community based, have no greater enforcement powers than property owners and ordinary citizens. Thus, their special competence and preferred tool is anticipatory regulation and amelioration. By analyzing the circumstances that give rise to victimization and financial loss, they recommend courses of action that will reduce the opportunity for crime to occur. These recommendations are followed because they become conditions for employment or participation. For a secretary in an office, locking doors and keeping a purse in a desk drawer is a condition of employment; for a teenager in a shopping mall, wearing shoes and not playing loud music are conditions of access; for a retailer, not selling goods on the sidewalk in front of his store is a condition for acceptance by the local business community; and for airline passengers, passing through a metal detector is a condition of travel. Because such regulations are legitimized by the fiction of being self-imposed, as opposed to being mandated by government, they avoid most constitutional challenge.

There is a closer connection between the end—safety—and the means—policing—with private police, both commercial and volunteer, than with public police. Governments protect communities by providing police and then limiting their authority; private institutions and informal communities protect themselves by determining what circumstances produce crime and then finding people who know how to change them (Shearing 1996). Private police are more responsive than public police to the "bottom line" of safety. If safety is not increased, private police can be fired. For public police the bottom line is not safety but clearance rates. But even here failure has few negative consequences. Police are not fired for not achieving this objective.

The public police are beginning to recognize the inherent limitations of their justice-based approach. Through community policing and order-maintenance policing, the public police are developing strategies for reducing disorder and the opportunities for crime that are similar to the practices readily accepted by commercial and informal communities from private police.

Both quantitatively and qualitatively, then, the pluralizing of policing should increase public safety.

The gains in public safety from the soul-searching currently unsettling public policing are less predictable. It depends on which way they go: more of the same, crime-oriented law enforcement, order maintenance, or community policing. Improvements in crime prevention will require commitment to experiment with new approaches and a willingness to subject them to rigorous evaluation. What is required is a shift in the logic of policing from one that conceives of it as remedying past wrongs to one that seeks to promote security.

Equity

The pluralizing of policing promises to increase public safety and has already done so in some places. The problem is that pluralizing under market auspices at present does not improve security equally across society. It favors institutions and individuals that are well-to-do. Commercial policing not balanced either by voluntary neighborhood crime prevention or by public policing following a preventive, presumptive logic leads to the inequitable distribution of security along class lines. If public safety is considered a general responsibility of government, perhaps even a human right, then increased reliance on commercial private policing represents a growing injustice.

The effects of pluralization under commercial auspices would be even more harmful if the prosperous sectors of the community who pay most of the taxes were to withdraw resources from the public sector, objecting that they were paying twice for security—once to the government and once again to hired private security. If this were to occur, the government's ability to develop qualitatively improved policing for the poor would be undermined. It might even be difficult to maintain existing levels of police service. Sam Walker (1976) has argued that this has already occurred and explains the chronic underpolicing of lower- and middle-income neighborhoods throughout American history. It may also be happening today in the form of tax revolts, such as Proposition 13 in California. Undoubtedly the people who are most interested in reducing taxes are those who feel relatively secure and spend most of their time in privately protected places.

That people are calculating the cumulative costs of policing would be unambiguously indicated if communities began to ask for vouchers from the government to spend on policing, public or private, as has happened in public education. In such a system, communities could opt out of the public sector, or substitute an alternative public supplier of police services. The contract system of policing in Canada is like this, although communities must choose exclusively among government suppliers. Despite the popularity of the idea of privatization in the public sector, no government we know of has allowed communities to use public money to substitute private for public police. As we will argue shortly this provides one element in a response to the injustice of the growing inequality of access to security.

Some of the efforts the public police are making to restructure themselves may help to solve the equity issue, others will not. If police concentrate on law enforcement, the dualism between rich and poor will be exacerbated. The rich will be increasingly policed preventively by commercial security while the poor will be policed reactively by enforcement-oriented public police. Moreover, since there seems to be a qualitative difference in the efficacy of these approaches—deterrence versus prevention—the poor will also be relatively less secure. There are three ways theoretically to prevent this inequitable dualism from arising, given the unavailability of market mechanisms for poor people.

First, the numbers of traditional police could be increased in poor high-crime areas. Unfortunately, this might be as unpleasant for the poor as the dualism itself, because it would lead to an intensification of traditional law enforcement.

Second, the public police could adopt the community policing model for economically poor high-crime areas. Community and order-maintenance policing incorporates many of the adaptive, consensual, ends-oriented practices of private security. Unfortunately, despite pronouncements to the contrary, police are often reluctant to adopt such policies in high-crime areas where they are already feeling hard pressed and where the efficacy of new approaches is unproven. Although community policing in theory is a powerful way to provide preventive policing for the poor, it may be distributed across cities in such a way that it reinforces rather than offsets the growing inequity in public security along class and racial lines.

Third, communities themselves might spontaneously develop their crime-preventing capacities. The chances of community-based pluralizing offsetting the defects of public policing are difficult to predict. Mobilization takes place more easily where people trust one another, possess leadership skills, have a stake in their communities, and are organized politically to achieve it. Although such efforts are growing by leaps and bounds, their efficacy, especially in high-crime areas, is unproven (Rosenbaum & Heath 1990; Skogan 1990).

The mobilizing activities of the public police through community policing are probably necessary, therefore, to offset the emerging dualism. This alone is likely to be of limited value, however, because experience so far suggests that community policing is harder to introduce in poor than in affluent neighborhoods. The irony may be that community policing compensates for the emerging dualism best where it is least needed and worst where it is most needed.

Human Rights

Because government is deeply distrusted in Anglo-American tradition, the powers of the police are circumscribed; their activities closely monitored. Private commercial policing and community-based private security, on the other hand, are apt to be more intrusive, premonitory, and presumptive than public policing. They impose the more onerous and extensive obligations of custom and public opinion. The pluralizing of policing, therefore, increases the informal regulatory control of crime. This, indeed, is the strength of policing under nonstate auspices: social pressure rather than law ensures discipline.

Seen in these terms, community policing, which is community-based crime prevention under governmental auspices, is a contradiction in terms. It requires the police, who are bound by law, to lead communities in informal surveillance, analysis, and treatment. Community policing is a license for police to intervene in the private life of individuals. It harnesses the coercive power of the state to social amelioration. This represents an expansion of police power, and is much more in keeping with the continental European than with the Anglo-American traditions of policing. Community policing may be an answer to the dualism brought by pluralizing but at the risk of encouraging the "vigilantism of the majority" (Johnston 1994).

Community policing, and its cousin community-based crime prevention, are attractive solutions to the problem of security inequity in a society where policing is being pluralized. But both impose costs. Community-based crime prevention, like commercial private policing, imposes social rather than governmental constraints. Community policing, on the other hand, couples social pressure with government direction. The mitigating factor is that community policing, as we note below, can provide for some measure of "bottom-up" accountability if it is developed in ways that encourage and permit genuine citizen participation.

Democracy

Democratic principle requires that police be accountable so that they serve the interests of the people. This is surely no less true for policing generically, which, as we have just seen, determines in a practical way the balance between freedom and order that people experience. At first glance, pluralization would not seem to pose a problem for accountability. Commercial private security is accountable to the market. If customers don't like what their security experts do, they can fire them. This alternative is not available for public police, who can only be fired by revolution. The problem with this view is that the accountability provided by markets accrues to buyers of private security and not to all the people who might be affected by it. Private security inevitably serves employers better than workers, owners better than patrons, and institutions better than individuals. The great advantage of public policing in democratic countries is that it is accountable to every citizen through the mechanisms of representative government.

Furthermore, the pluralizing of security under commercial auspices changes the social basis on which policing is organized. In democratic countries, police have been created to serve the interests of people territorially defined. Public policing is based on geographical communities. Private police, by contrast, serves primarily interest communities, that is, communities united by function rather than geography. It follows that the decentralization of policing that occurs through pluralizing is very different from the decentralization that occurs when government does it. The former is more selective in social terms; the latter includes everyone.

Voluntary community crime prevention, the other way in which pluralizing is occurring, does not suffer from the defect of social selectivity. The social basis for it is the same as under government, namely, people territorially defined. The problem with volunteer private policing, however, is its organizational informality. It may fail to represent the interests of people who are inarticulate, unorganized, and marginalized. The volunteers in private policing are likely to have interests that may differ from those of people who decline to participate. Community crime prevention is policing by the self-appointed, which is what people usually think of as vigilantism.

In sum, commercial private policing provides accountability through the formal mechanism of contracts but on the basis of social interests that may exclude many citizens. Volunteer private security provides accountability through informal mechanisms organized on the basis of citizenship that may or may not include everybody. Public policing provides accountability through formal mechanisms organized on the basis of citizenship that, in principle, cover everyone. Unless new alternatives are developed, it follows that accountability is best achieved through public policing operating according to principles of community policing. Community policing supplements the customary accountability of representative political institutions with grassroots consultation, evaluation, and feedback.

Trade-Offs

What trade-offs among these qualitatively different features—safety, equity, human rights, and accountability—does the current restructuring of policing present?

Broadening the auspices under which policing is organized, especially substituting private for governmental ones, probably raises the level of public safety because it increases the number of security agents and also substitutes a preventive security paradigm for a deterrent one. However, pluralizing increases safety at the cost of equity. This can be offset if community policing is strongly implemented in disorganized poor communities afflicted by crime.

Pluralized policing, however, is less constrained by formal rules and, therefore, puts the rights of the people it polices at risk. Pluralized policing is more security conscious than rights conscious.

Pluralized policing, under both commercial and community auspices, is only fictively consensual and democratic. Although it represents and empowers new groups, it does so on the basis of social interest rather than citizenship, and it provides haphazardly for the representation of all who might be affected by it. Pluralized policing inevitably shifts power away from government, but it does not necessarily distribute it to more people. Community policing, on the other hand, combines the traditional accountability of representative government with the informal accountability of volunteer crime prevention.

The point to underscore is that the changes occurring in policing are more than technical adjustments in the way policing is delivered. They represent the restructuring of government itself and the redistribution of power over one of government's core functions. By shifting policing to new auspices through markets, community action, and police reform, the nature of governance is changing.

The Likely Future

Recognizing that fundamental changes are being made in policing that have profound consequences for the quality of civic life, is it possible to predict what the future holds? What balance among the overlapping and competing movements of pluralization and reformation will emerge? Will a new and stable equilibrium be found between state and nonstate policing? Might the state reassert itself, once again dominating policing? Could the public police become increasingly marginalized, confined to the policing of poor inner cities? And what will the character of public policing become—enforcement oriented, community based, or some new combination?

The current restructuring is driven by the public's concern about security. It is hardly an accident that the expansion of private security as well as the development of community policing coincided with rising crime rates throughout the developed world. If the threat to security were to decline significantly, the impetus to restructuring would be largely removed. This is unlikely to happen. Crime, notwithstanding the recent decline in overall rates in some countries, will continue to rise and even perhaps get worse for two reasons. First, crime is disproportionately committed by young males between the ages of 15 and 25. Twenty-nine percent of serious crime in the United States is committed by people under 19.[3] This group will rise by over 20% in the next decade. In Canada 14% of crime of violence and 25% of crimes against property are committed by people 12 to 17 years old (Statistics Canada 1993). Second, the violence of crime has been increasing. During the past 10 years the rate at which American teens are murdered has doubled (Blumstein 1994). The homicide arrest rate for white youths rose by 80% during the past decade, for black youths 125%. This rising lethality can be traced to the increased availability of sophisticated firearms that in turn is related to the penetration of drug markets into poor urban neighborhoods (Butterfield 1995). Unless circumstances change fundamentally, the violence of crime will continue to be perceived as a serious threat.

Furthermore, whatever happens to crime objectively, the public's fear of crime will certainly not decline. Because crime is fascinating, the media can be counted on to continue to exploit and exaggerate it. Only criminologists and police seem to know that crime is not randomly distributed in society; that it is not a national problem affecting everyone to the same extent. Crime is concentrated in particular localities characterized by unemployment, poverty, poor education, and single-parent homes. Crime has indeed risen and become more deadly during the last generation, but it has only marginally worsened for most of us. Unfortunately, because there seems to be no economic incentive, or political one either, for pointing this out, the public will continue to be terrorized by the exploitation of crime news (Chermak 1995).

Assuming that crime and the fear of crime are unlikely to decline, can we expect governments to adopt policies that would rectify the underlying conditions, the so-called root causes, that breed crime? If this happened, then the restructuring of policing would be less imperative. This, too, is unlikely for several reasons. The political mood . . . is certainly against large-scale social intervention by government. Rising crime rates are often considered to be evidence that Great Society programs have failed. Ironically, then, the very rise in crime that impels the restructuring of policing may have helped convince people that social programs undertaken by government are a waste of money. Conservative social theorists also argue that government doesn't know how to remedy criminogenic conditions. Social programs are as likely to be counterproductive as they are wasteful (Murray 1988; Wilson 1983). The political hostility to amelioration is also fueled by a general perception that taxes are too high. Tax revolt has become a permanent condition, and placating it an enduring political necessity. All governments seem resigned to doing less with less for the foreseeable future.

For demographic, social, and political reasons, then, the threat of crime will intensify. The search for security will not diminish but may grow in desperation. How, then, will government and the larger community provide for its intense desire for security?

First, government is unlikely to be able to respond effectively through traditional law enforcement programs. It will certainly not be able to do so through simply increasing the number of public police. Most research over the past 30 years has failed to show a connection between variations in the numbers of police and the incidence of crime.[4]

At the same time, the cost of increasing the "visible presence" of the police, that is, police on the streets, remains dauntingly high. Because of staffing and deployment rules, 10 additional officers must be hired in order to get one extra uniformed police officer on the streets around the clock throughout the year (Bayley 1985). The incremental cost of a unit of "visible presence" on American streets is, therefore, about $500,000—10 times a patrol officer's average annual salary plus benefits. Few governments are going to be willing to make such investments.

Moreover, the distributional requirements of democratic politics ensure that additional police officers will not be concentrated in high-crime neighborhoods where their marginal utility would be highest, but will parcel them out in dribs and drabs so that every politician can claim to have gotten some police for his or her constituency. The allocations made under the 1994 Crime Control Act in the United States show this clearly. Distributional politics reduces the effectiveness of public expenditures on policing in any democratic society.

Democratic governments are also limited in their ability to respond to crime by political values. In the Anglo-American tradition, government is distrusted. As a result, public pressure to "get tough" on crime invariably encounters stiff resistance from people concerned about civil liberties. Governments may sometimes enact Draconian policies, but in the long run they swing back and forth between punishment and due process. Deterrence, which will continue to dominate the efforts of modern democratic governments to control crime, clashes with the very precepts on which government has been established. Democratic societies may fear crime, but they fear authoritarianism more.

We believe, therefore, that democratic governments are unlikely to be able to allay the public's desperate need for safety through the criminal justice system. The demand for security is unlikely to be met by governmental action, whether through amelioration or deterrence.

Second, we are unsure but skeptical of the ability of Western societies to respond to the demand for order by spontaneous crime-preventive activities undertaken by communities. Our skepticism arises out of the value Western societies place on individualism. Westerners want to be free not only from government constraint but from social constraint as well. Because people in Western countries, unlike the Japanese, Chinese, and Koreans, place great importance on individual development and freedom, they do not readily submit to the informal discipline of groups (Bayley 1985, 1991). If they do so, it is for short-term instrumental ends, such as winning a game, obtaining emotional support for a particular problem, making useful contacts, or obtaining particular advantages. The capacity of families, neighborhoods, schools, churches, and employers to discipline their members and to organize against crime and disorder is weak in individualistic societies. Although the vitality of community crime prevention in Western democratic countries currently is impressive and heartening, its staying power and its effectiveness are doubtful. Experience so far indicates that efforts at community organization are difficult to sustain after initial enthusiasm wears off. Moreover, the rigorous research so far done on community crime prevention has failed to show substantial benefits.

Individualistic democratic societies are caught between a rock and a hard place with respect to crime control. On the one hand, they are limited by their political values from authoritarian controls and, on the other, they are limited by their cultural values from the discipline of informal social control.

Third, caught in this bind, it is inevitable that Western democratic societies will continue to resort to the marketplace for security solutions. Free enterprise capitalism is the mechanism the West must rely on to compensate for the deficiencies of governmental control and social cohesion in controlling crime. Market-mediated private security is the natural response of societies like ours, just as privatization generally has been to problems of health, education, research, information dissemination, and income support. Security can hardly not become "commodified" in individualistic democratic societies. There is no other place to turn.

Commodification of security has been encouraged by the rise of "mass private property" in the latter half of the 20th century—meaning facilities that are owned privately but to which the public has right of access and use (Shearing & Stenning 1983). These include shopping malls, educational campuses, residential communities, high-rise condominiums and apartments, banks, commercial facilities, and recreation complexes. The world is no longer divided simply between privately owned space used by its owners and the numerous public streets used by the public. By blurring the distinction between the public and the private, mass private property attenuates and marginalizes government's responsibility for security. It constricts government efforts at preventive policing to clearly public venues. Preventive policing in mass private property has become the responsibility of security specialists bought privately through the market.

If we are right that governments cannot provide satisfactory public safety, that neighborhoods will have only haphazard success in doing so, and that mass private property will continue to dominate urban space, then market-based private security will inevitably increase relative to public policing. It may even begin to cannibalize public policing if affluent people become more reluctant to pay twice for safety. It follows, therefore, that there will be no avoiding the emergence of dualistic policing stratified by race and class. The affluent will be protected by private security agents organized by interest groups and operating according to preventive principles backed up by the requirements of specialized membership or participation; the poor will be protected by a weakened public police operating according to principles of deterrence based on procedurally limited law enforcement. Western democratic societies are moving inexorably, we fear, into a Clockwork Orange world where both the market and the government protect the affluent from the poor—the one by barricading and excluding, the other by repressing and imprisoning—and where civil society for the poor disappears in the face of criminal victimization and governmental repression.

Fourth, there is one more factor that may powerfully influence the security trends outlined here, namely, outbreaks of collective violence, especially in large cities. The United States has already experienced serious but isolated instances of this—the "Rodney King" riots in Los Angeles, the Thompkins Park and Crown Heights riots in New York City, and the Liberty City riots in Miami. But collective violence is happening in quieter, more pervasive ways that is not so easily recognized. Gang violence in some inner-city neighborhoods has attained the dimensions of an ongoing riot. The former Mayor of Washington, DC, formally requested the deployment of the National Guard in August 1994. And Americans asked why the Army and Marines were sent to Somalia when the United States had its own gang warlords terrorizing inner-city neighborhoods. England now has "slow riots" in the summer in which unemployed youths from public housing estates regularly burn tires, cars, and sometimes buses "for fun."

Collective violence, whether in the form of short, intense riots or persistent, endemic criminality, powerfully reinforces the dualistic tendencies in the current restructuring of policing. Portrayed as unpredictable and random, such violence scares the well-to-do and demonstrates the impotence of the police. This encourages further privatization along class lines. At the same time, collective violence weakens community crime prevention impulses among the disadvantaged by polarizing communities and weakening trust among neighbors and even family members. Furthermore, in the face of collective violence, governments become less willing to allow poor communities to develop self-defense capabilities (Bayley 1975, 1985). Collective violence is inevitably perceived in political terms. The standard response of governments is, therefore, to centralize policing power rather than allow it to be decentralized among what appear to be unpredictable and politically untrustworthy communities.

Collective violence not only drives a wedge deeper between the rich and the poor; it undercuts the ability of the state to more equitably distribute security among the rich and the poor by undermining the capacity and enthusiasm among the public police for community policing. Persistent collective violence causes the police to centralize decisionmaking, adopt a military style of command, emphasize law enforcement, deploy heavier weaponry, patrol in groups rather than as individuals, take preemptive action, and distrust the public. Collective violence also makes commanders cautious about tying down officers in community development work. They want to save resources for "the big event," which weakens their capacity for flexible adaptation and problem solving, both of which are essential elements of community policing.

Collective violence is like a bus waiting to broadside the evolution of policing in the late 20th century. If it hits, there may be nothing anyone can do to prevent the emergence of a dualistic system of policing.

Fateful Choices

The fear of crime, the absence of ameliorative social policies, the ineffectiveness of deterrence, the rise of mass private property, and the commodification of security are powerful forces shaping the future of policing. The dualistic tendencies in policing are almost certain to be strengthened, with consequent distortions of equity, human rights, and accountability. In the face of these developments, can modern democratic, individualistic societies provide humane policing equitably for all their members? We believe they can, but only if two policies are adopted.

First, it is necessary to enable poor people to participate in markets for security. For this to happen it will be necessary to develop mechanisms to provide for the reallocation of public funding for security. The objective should be to provide poorer communities with the ability to sustain self-governing initiatives.

One way of achieving this would be through block grants to poor communities so that they can participate in the commercial market for security. Not only does this level up access to security, it vests directive authority in the people most affected. If appropriate mechanisms for community self-government are created, block grants raise the likelihood that policing will be responsive to the wishes of the community. Block grants would encourage poor communities to develop security regimes that fit their problems and mores in the same way that private security adapts to the goals of businesses. In effect, communities would be given security budgets that they could spend on various mixtures of public and private policing. Distributional problems between rich and poor might still arise, of course, particularly if the rich refused to pay. All policies that have any prospect of mitigating the growing class differences in public safety depend on the affluent segments of our societies recognizing that security is indivisible. The well-to-do are paying for crime now; but they have not learned that they will save more by leveling up security than by ghettoizing it.

Second, community policing must become the organizing paradigm of public policing. Through community policing governments can develop the self-disciplining and crime-preventive capacity of poor, high-crime neighborhoods. Community policing incorporates the logic of security by forging partnership between police and public. Since safety is fundamental to the quality of life, co-production between police and public legitimates government, lessening the corrosive alienation that disorganizes communities and triggers collective violence. Community policing is the only way to achieve discriminating law enforcement supported by community consensus in high-crime neighborhoods.

Community policing faces substantial obstacles and will not be easy to achieve. Most police are still not convinced it is needed, and research so far is equivocal about its success. The latter may be attributable more to failures in implementation than defects in the program. Community policing requires substantial revision of organizational priorities within the police and is managerially demanding. It requires new styles of supervision and new methods of evaluating performance. Although community policing sounds appealing, few politicians have the nerve to force community policing on reluctant police departments. They would rather give unrestricted grants to police agencies, thereby earning credit for being tough on crime while not challenging standard operating procedures. Finally, as we have noted, community policing is hardest to achieve in the places that need it most. In terms of resources, it requires government to take the security problems of the poor as seriously as it does the security problems of the rich.

Both of these policies—community block grants and community policing—highlight a fundamental question: does government have the wisdom, even if it has the will, to guide the course of security's restructuring without making it worse? Vouchers and community policing will work to offset the socially divisive effects of restructuring only to the extent that they empower communities to take responsibility for themselves and, in some cases, to heal themselves. This requires government not only to reform the police but to redistribute political power with respect to one of the core functions of government. This is a lot to ask, because faced with shortcomings in public safety, governments will be tempted to enhance directiveness rather than encourage devolution. To avoid this, a radical rethinking of the role of government is required.

Fortunately, while the inclination of government to stipulate rather than facilitate remains strong, there is a widespread and growing movement to challenge this. Just as the past is prologue to the continued restructuring of policing, so, too, there seems to be a growing realization in democratic, individualistic societies that in order to create a more humane, safe, and civil society, government must be reinvented, specifically, that grassroots communities must be made responsible for central aspects of governance. The rethinking of security that our proposals require is consistent with this rethinking of governance. Restructuring is a problem that may contain the seeds of its own solution.

Notes

1. In the United States there are about 2 million private security people as opposed to about 650,000 sworn police.

2. These calculations based on clearances for U.S. Index crimes or their near equivalents in Britain and Canada—homicide, rape, aggravated assault, robbery, burglary, larceny, and auto theft. U.S. Bureau of Justice Statistics 1993; United Kingdom Home Office 1992; and Statistics Canada 1993.

3. "After the Respite, Crime Rises," *Albany Times Union*, 14 Dec. 1994, p. 1.

4. This conclusion has recently been challenged by Stephen Levitt who has demonstrated for the first time that hiring additional police may be cost effective (Levitt 1994a, 1994b). Levitt's analysis shows that in large American cities each additional officer prevents between 7 and 10 crimes per year, at an annual saving that is

$150,000 more than the cost of the officer's hire.

References

Bayley, David H. (1975) "The Police and Political Development in Europe," in Charles Tilly, ed., *The Formation of National States in Western Europe.* Princeton, NJ: Princeton Univ. Press.

——. (1985) *Patterns of Policing. A Comparative International Policing.* New Brunswick, NJ: Rutgers Univ. Press.

——. (1991) *Forces of Order: Policing Modern Japan.* Berkeley: Univ. of California Press.

——. (1994) *Police for the Future.* New York: Oxford Univ. Press.

Blumstein, Alfred (1994) "Youth Violence, Gangs, and the Illicit-Drug Industry." Unpub., Carnegie-Mellon Univ., Pittsburgh (July 26).

Brogden, Michael, & Clifford Shearing (1993) *Policing for a New South Africa.* London: Routledge.

Butterfield, Fox (1995) "Grim Forecast on Rising Crime," *New York Times,* p. A24 (19 Feb.).

Chermak, Steven M. (1995) *Victims in the News.* Boulder, CO: Westview Press.

Johnston, Les. (1992) *The Rebirth of Private Policing.* London: Routledge.

——. (1994) "Policing in Late Modern Societies." Paper for the Workshop on Evaluating Police Service Delivery, Montreal (Nov.).

Kelling, George L., & Catherine M. Coles (1994) "Disorder and the Court," *Public Interest,* p. 57 (Summer).

Levitt, Steven D. (1994a) "Reporting Behavior of Crime Victims and the Size of the Police Force: Implications for Studies of Police Effectiveness Using Reported Crime Data." Unpub., Harvard Univ. (Aug.).

——. (1994b) "Using Electoral Cycles of Police Hiring to Estimate the Effect of Police on Crime." Unpub., Harvard Univ. (Nov.).

Murray, Charles (1988) *In Pursuit of Happiness and Good Government.* New York: Simon & Schuster.

Rosenbaum, Dennis P., & Linda Heath (1990) "The 'Psycho-Logic' of Fear-Reduction and Crime-Prevention Programs," in John Edwards et al., eds., *Social Influence Processes and Prevention.* New York: Plenum Press.

Shearing, Clifford (1992) "The Relation between Public and Private Policing," in M. Tonry & N. Morris, eds., *Modern Policing.* Chicago: Univ. of Chicago Press.

——. (1996) "Reinventing Policing: Policing as Governance," in O. Marenin, ed., *Policing Change: Changing Police.* New York: Garland Press.

Shearing, C. D., & Philip Stenning (1983) "Private Security: Implications for Social Control," 30 *Social Problems* 493.

Skogan, Wesley G. (1990) *Disorder and Decline.* New York: Free Press.

Skolnick, Jerome H., & David H. Bayley (1986) *The New Blue Line.* New York: Free Press.

Statistics Canada (1993) *Canadian Crime Statistics, 1993.* Ottawa: Statistics Canada.

United Kingdom Home Office (1992) *Criminal Statistics: England and Wales, 1992.* London: HMSO.

U.S. Bureau of Justice Statistics (1993) *Sourcebook of Criminal Justice Statistics, 1993.* Washington: Bureau of Justice Statistics.

Walker, Samuel (1976) "The Urban Police in American History. A Review of the Literature," *J. of Police Science & Administration,* pp. 252–60 (Sept.).

Walker, Samuel, & Betsey Wright (1994) "Civilian Review of the Police: A National Survey." Washington: Police Executive Research Forum.

Wilson, James Q. (1983) *Crime and Public Policy.* San Francisco: ICS Press.

Wilson, James Q., & George L. Kelling (1982) "Broken Windows: The Police and Neighborhood Safety," *Atlantic Monthly,* pp. 29–38 (March).

David H. Bayley and Clifford D. Shearing, "The Future of Policing." Reprinted from *Law and Society Review,* Vol. 30, Number 3 (1996). Copyright © 1996 by The Law and Society Association. Reprinted by permission of The Law and Society Association. ✦

Chapter 29
The Future of Policing in a Community Era

Jihong Zhao

> Twenty years from now you will be more disappointed by the things that you didn't do than the ones you did do. So throw off the bowlines. Sail away from the safe harbor. Catch the trade winds in your sails. Explore dreams. Discover.
>
> —Mark Twain

Jihong Zhao speculates about the future direction of community policing in American policing agencies. The large-scale implementation of hundreds of community policing programs over the past few years can be viewed as a favorable sign of progress. In the late 1990s, these programs often captured media attention locally and even nationally. The exposure of police officers to successful community policing programs is significant in that the implementation of community policing can cultivate a new generation of police officers and police leaders who are accepting of the community policing philosophy.

At the same time, there are other developments that make the future of community policing uncertain. The first concerns an increase in paramilitary policing units in police agencies across the nation. While police agencies across the U.S. have attempted to improve relations between police and the public, they have also moved quickly to establish paramilitary units, particularly in medium-sized departments where violent crime is infrequent. Such a development seems to be at odds with a community policing model of citizen engagement. In addition, the role of police unions in promoting community policing is unclear. Traditionally, unions have resisted change and innovation in organizational settings. It remains to be seen where police unions will weigh in on the issue of community policing.

What is the direction of community policing in the twenty-first century? A similar question was asked at the start of the twentieth century when modern policing was in its infancy. Predicting the future of any occupation or organization is a formidable task that is fraught with difficulty. For example, many innovations in the criminal justice system that once were predicted to have far-reaching effects have failed to do so. In his book, *Sense and Nonsense About Crime,* noted scholar Samuel Walker studied the impact of 20 such innovations proposed by either liberals or conservatives and found that very few of them met with expectations.[1]

In that light, it might be wiser not to speculate about the future of American policing. However, aside from the fact that the author finds the challenge irresistible, two other reasons for doing so are compelling. First, I believe that a fairly accurate forecast of police departments over the next five years is possible because community policing is well underway as a new style of policing. The concept of community policing and its implementation has a history that spans two decades if the pilot studies on foot patrol in Flint, Michigan, and Newark, New Jersey, are considered.[2]

A second reason that I believe that prediction is warranted is that the implementation of community policing has been accompanied by a strong emphasis on research evaluation, especially over the past five years. As discussed in previous chapters, we can draw on the results from several studies to inform our predictions based upon information that is both theoretical and practical.

Where Community Policing Is Now and Where It Is Going

Before any prediction can be made, it is important to know what is the pattern of change in community policing. In chapter 4, three stages of organizational change proposed by Robert Yin were introduced.[3] The first stage involves initiation, that is, the implementation of innovative activities. In this stage an organization tries a variety of innovations and then assesses their respective utility. Effective innovations are retained, while ineffective ones are discontinued.

James Thompson noted that during the initiation stage, these innovative programs are isolated from the core of an operation.[4] This means that innovations are not deliberately integrated into the formal organizational structure. In addition, they are evaluated by organizational rationality based upon social recognition rather than by technical rationality based on a cost-and-benefit analysis, even though the latter is more certain.

The pattern of change in community policing is similar to what Thompson predicted about the initiation stage of organizational change. As discussed in the previous chapters, the change process always starts with the adoption of innovative programs. The number of programs will differ depending on the size and location of the police department. The New York Police Department, for example, may implement more programs than a medium-sized police department because it is much larger and is located in a very dynamic environment.

Innovative programs such as foot patrols and storefront police substations are generally set up by a designated unit, which, to a large extent, is isolated from core police operations such as patrol and criminal investigations. This isolation allows police administrators to have better control of new programs before they can decide to expand the scope, change the focus, or even terminate the programs without disturbing the normal operations of the department.

A review of the literature on community policing suggests that a majority of innovative programs are rarely implemented more widely than by a special unit.[5] The primary means of evaluating innovative programs is customer satisfaction. This evaluation is usually done by conducting a variety of citizen surveys and interviews about their contacts with beat police officers. The effectiveness of these programs is then determined according to organizational rationality. Does this program generate social recognition? Do residents like the program?

After 20 years of community policing, there has been no irrefutable evidence that it significantly reduces crime in a community. This means that technical rationality based upon a cost and benefits analysis cannot be applied to community policing innovations. The bottom line is this—despite some 20 years of efforts, community policing as a form of organizational change still remains largely at the initiation stage.

Most of the research in policing suggests that community policing is the future model for American policing in the twenty-first century. Consequently, community policing should progress naturally toward the second stage identified by Yin, the institutionalization of change.

Institutionalization has several important aspects. The first concerns organizational structure. To institutionalize community policing, the structure of police departments needs to be modified so that innovations may be integrated. Innovative units must become a formal part of patrol operations or criminal investigations rather than remain as isolated units. The second is that evaluation of community policing should move beyond simply measuring citizen satisfaction. Although it is extremely valuable to learn what local communities think of a police program, technical rationality must be achieved, and clearly defined measures to facilitate institutionalization should be developed. The third aspect, as discussed in earlier chapters, concerns the culture of police departments, which must be altered in a direction consistent with community policing.

The next sections present the positive, negative, and uncertain forces that affect the institutionalization of community policing. The purpose is to examine the feasibility of community policing in the near future.

Positive Forces

In order to predict whether or not the institutionalization of community policing will be the future of American policing, it is necessary to examine the competing forces of change and evaluate the possible outcomes. Four specific forces seem to favor the change to community policing.

More Community Policing Programs

First, community policing programs are very popular with police executives, other community leaders, and the public as evidenced by the considerable increase in these programs over the past five years. Recent studies show that community policing is widespread, having been adopted not only in a few large police departments but also in medium and small departments that traditionally have followed the winds of change.[6] In addition to the expansion of community policing, there also is a wider variety of community policing programs in place compared to the previous five years.

In the 1980s, the primary focus of community policing programs was to reduce citizen fear of crime and social disorder. For example, an important factor behind the implementation of the foot-patrol program in the Houston Police Department was to reduce the fear of crime; an evaluation of the program found that it was effective in reducing public fear of crime.[7] At that time, only a handful of community policing programs were identified as such, including foot patrol, special units, and neighborhood watch.[8] Recent developments have substantially expanded the variety of programs available.[9] The Resolving Conflict Creatively Program (RCCP) implemented in the New York City and Boston Police Youth Corps are examples.[10]

The expansion of community policing programs makes organizational change in policing more visible to the public and the news media. It seems fair to say that the longer police departments can keep up the momentum of innovation, the more likely it is that innovations will be institutionalized.

Strong Support From the Federal Government Since 1994

The second positive force behind institutionalization of community policing has been the very strong endorsement of the federal government since the passage of the Violent Crime Control and Law Enforcement Act in 1994. This statute represents "an investment of more than $30 billion over six years. . . . [It] is the largest Federal anti-crime legislation in the Nation's history."[11] As a direct result of this legislation the federal government is actively involved in the national implementation of community policing. In addition, this act subsidized the hiring of an additional 100,000 officers who must promote community policing goals in their departments. A key example of this effort includes the establishment of the Office of Community Oriented Policing Services (OCOPS or COPS). A primary goal of COPS is to ensure the institutionalization of community policing innovations in police departments across the country. COPS coordinates and supervises federally subsidized community policing programs and oversees evaluations. The creation of 35 community policing regional training institutes across the nation is another important step taken to expand the scope of implementation.[12]

Similarly, as a direct result of the 1994 Crime Act there has been more money available for research and evaluation than at any other time in the history of American policing. Many of COPS' grants to local departments, for example, include provisions for research and evaluation. There has been a substantial increase in research activities to document the progress of community policing. In sum, the direct involvement of the federal government, particularly the Clinton administration, provided much-needed funding and technical support for the implementation of community policing.

The Use of Technology

A third positive force for change is the increase in the use of advanced technology in community policing. Since the early 1990s, community policing innovations have extended to the use of hi-tech tools for combating urban crimes and reducing social disorder. Computerized statistics (CompStat) is a good example of this development. Police departments in several large cities such as Boston, Indianapolis, and Chicago have used CompStat and computer-mapping technology to disseminate information to all ranks of officers to make them all accountable for fighting crime. The best-known use of CompStat was in New York in 1993 under the leadership of then police commissioner William Bratton. During his brief tenure, Bratton chided his sworn personnel: "No one ever lost his job over not having the right answers. No one gets into trouble for crime being up in their precinct. People got in trouble if they didn't know what the crime was and had no strategy to deal with it."[13]

As the first step in CompStat, personnel from each of the 76 New York City precincts, nine police service areas, and 12 transit districts compiled a statistical summary of the week's crime incidents. Next, the information on arrests, summons activity, use of firearms, and victims was forwarded to central headquarters. These data included the specific times and locations of the crimes, and police activities. The CompStat unit in the department loaded the information into a citywide database for an analysis of crime patterns. A weekly CompStat report was then generated to present a concise summary of crime incidents and other important performance indicators.

The next step in CompStat involved crime strategy meetings attended by senior administrators, all the precinct commanders, and supervisors of specialized investigative units. These meetings were usually convened every two weeks from 7 A.M. to 10 A.M. in the command and control center. Every commander was expected to be called on at random to make his or her presentation approximately once a month. During the presentation, the commander had to analyze the pattern of crime incidents in the area, potential problems, and the strategies adopted or planned to deal with them. The presentation was aided with a computerized "pin mapping" technology that displayed crimes, arrests, and quality-of-life data in a series of visual formats including charts, graphs, and tables. During the presentation, the senior administrators frequently asked commanders questions and looked for solutions.[14]

The significance of using CompStat is that the precinct commanders and supervisors were held accountable for an increase or decrease in local crimes and social disorder. Therefore, they were forced to develop new strategies to reduce neighborhood crimes. At the same time, the lower level of management also was held responsible for their respective areas because the "pin mapping" was able to display crime patterns at the street level. CompStat became the crucial link that demanded accountability at every level of the department.

New York City mayor Rudolph Giuliani observed that

> CompStat transformed the Department from an organization that reacted to crime to a Department that actively works to deter offenses. Before CompStat, the Department's 76 precinct commanders were isolated from the Department's top executives. Under the CompStat system, precinct commanders meet with the Police Commissioner and other high-ranking members of the Department at semiweekly meetings to identify local crime patterns, select tactics, and allocate resources. Arrests are no longer the measure of effective policing—commanders are now responsible for deterring crime.[15]

Similarly, the Chicago Police Department adopted the Information Collection for Automated Mapping (ICAM) computer program. This program has two primary features. First, it can produce a map of reported offenses of a particular type in an area, or it can generate a list of the 10 most frequently reported offenses in a patrol beat. Second, it can generate a map and conduct a search of a particular type of offense. The unique part of the ICAM program is that the computer terminals can be installed at the district level, and supervisors and patrol officers can have access to ICAM. In essence, the availability of this high-tech program facilitates the problem-solving efforts of the department. The ICAM program has been well received in Chicago. It is estimated that 20 percent of all officers use ICAM regularly, and 60 percent use it occasionally. From June 26 to July 25, 1995, a total of 6,689 queries were requested in the department, or 223 queries per day.[16]

The Crime Rate Is Down

The fourth positive force for change is that crime rates are down. No matter what happens, police departments are essentially evaluated by the local crime rate because the public believes that crime is the most important component of their job description. It is one thing for a police department to establish a few outreach programs and improve the quality of life in a community, but it is another if the crime rate remains the same or rises; then pressure falls on the police to respond appropriately.

A primary reason for the police to move toward community policing is that, for most of the 1960s and 1970s, the rates for both violent and property crimes were up significantly. Since the early 1990s, however, the crime rate has been declining. According to the *Uniform Crime Report,* for example, the crime index rate fell for the sixth straight year in 1997 and was down almost 17 percent from 1991. In addition, the violent crime rate declined 7 percent, continuing the downward trend since 1994.[17] In nearly all major cities, including New York, Los Angeles, and Chicago, the number of murders has dropped significantly. In turn, the continuing decline of crime rates has captured the attention of almost all major news networks and received extensive coverage. American cities are becoming safer.

Who should be given the credit for this declining crime rate? Unquestionably, the implementation of community policing has received much of the praise. In a recent public address, President Clinton stated, "In 1997, crime decreased for the sixth straight year thanks in part to community policing. Our commitment to American's law enforcement officers is working to keep our streets and communities safe."[18] To date, law enforcement agencies have added more than 88,000 community policing officers to patrol the streets, and the public seems to have responded favorably to this trend. Although other factors, such as the aging of the baby boomer generation, might also account for declining crime rates, community policing is widely perceived to be at least partially responsible.[19]

Even at the local level, the reduction of crime has been attributed to community policing innovations. Since 1993, overall crime was down more than 43 percent in New York City. The city's murder rate at the time was at its lowest level since the late 1960s, and Mayor Giuliani gave much of the credit to the NYPD and its new methods for dealing with crime and incivilities: "A very critical component of the success of the New York City Police Department has been an innovative style of police management called CompStat."[20] Although some might debate whether or not CompStat and community policing are synonymous, this New York style of meeting the public-safety needs of its citizens has been credited with achieving miraculous results.

Similarly, in Boston, the police and juvenile probation officers joined hands and created an innovative program, Operation Night Light, to prevent juvenile probationers from getting into trouble again and again. At night, police and juvenile probation officers visited each probationer's residence to make sure the person stayed at home. Since the inception of the program, the number of juveniles killed by gunfire has greatly diminished. In fact, from July 1995 to December 1997, not a single boy or girl in the city was murdered. Much of this success has been attributed to Operation Night Light.

In sum, the decline of crime has provided the police with a favorable external environment. They can show the nation that community policing is working and that people are benefiting from these innovative programs. All four of these positive forces keep the momentum of community policing moving forward toward institutionalization.

Negative Forces

Ambiguity About COP

The first negative force that impedes change concerns the ambiguity surrounding the definition of community policing. What is community policing anyway? Questions remain. Police administrators and quite a few scholars have a hard time defining the term despite the popularity of community policing across the nation. John Eck and Dennis Rosenbaum argue that, "One reason for its popularity is that community policing is a plastic concept, meaning different things to different people."[21] Furthermore, Mark Moore has suggested that, "It is important that the concept mean something, but not something too specific . . . the ambiguity is a virtue."[22] However, it is exactly the virtue of looseness as a concept that may act as an impediment to its institutionalization.[23]

Today, it is difficult to reject community policing as a welcome reform because every program implemented in a police department can be labeled a community policing innovation of one type or another. At the same time, it is difficult to accept it as a legitimate reform movement as long as its definition remains largely elusive. For example, after almost two full decades of implementation, there is not a single department that can claim to have implemented community policing completely, to have institutionalized its principles throughout the department. Community policing remains a loosely defined concept, with definitions that vary from broad abstraction to narrow specificity.

As discussed in an earlier chapter, three distinctive theories might explain the institutionalization of the police during the professional era. They are: (1) scientific management articulated by Taylor, focusing on one best way and technical rationality;[24] (2) the "ideal-type" of bureaucracy suggested by Weber, emphasizing the structural rationality of management;[25] and (3) Gulick's organizational-supervision approach that proposes a chain of command and span of control.[26] As previously suggested, the institutionalization of the bureaucratic style of policing was guided by a clearly developed theoretical framework for a specific structural arrangement.

Community policing, however, lacks this theoretical refinement. The theoretical framework continues to remain relatively undefined or "plastic," as more new programs labeled community policing are added nearly every day. The authors believe that this confusion at the theoretical level threatens to impede the institutionalization of community policing.

The Largely Unchanged Organizational Structure

The second negative force that impedes the institutionalization of community policing concerns structural change in police departments. In general, organizational structure can be defined as "the enduring characteristics of an organization reflected by the distribution of units and positions within the organization and their systematic relationships with each other."[27] This definition suggests that an organizational structure is relatively permanent. Unlike innovative programs that can easily be modified or dropped, the structure of an organization, especially the core structure, is not very easy to change over a short period of time.

Peter Blau identified two dimensions of organizational structure based on a study of 53 public employment security agencies.[28] As discussed in an earlier chapter, the horizontal dimension has two components: spatial differentiation and occupational differentiation.

Spatial differentiation is the extent to which an organization's tasks are divided among subordinate units, for example, the number of different units in a police department. Occupational differentiation is the number of different specialties available in an organization, that is, the extent of the division of labor. The number of specialists (e.g., crime lab specialists and computer analysts) is greater in the New York Police Department, for example, than in the Omaha Police Department.

The vertical dimension, or hierarchy, concerns the distribution of authority, reflecting the degree of managerial control. In a police department, organizational hierarchy can be assessed by the number of ranks from police officer at the bottom to the chief at the top. It is assumed that the more levels in the hierarchy, the more formalized the organizational structure. The more formal the structure, the less likely it is to institutionalize innovations.

As previously mentioned, three anthologies published since 1994 focus on community policing.[29] They contain many influential research studies but only a few of them refer to the relationship between structural change and the institutionalization of community policing. Among these few, there is a consensus that organizational hierarchy impedes innovations.[30] Little research is available on the relationship between reducing organizational hierarchy and community policing innovations. Research is very limited on how to incorporate community policing programs into the formal structure of a police department. Very little has been written on the need to increase the horizontal structure of a police department and flatten the vertical structure if community policing is to be institutionalized. Studies on this topic tend to focus on evaluation of community policing programs.

Uncertain Forces

The Increase in Paramilitary Policing Units

About three decades ago, Egon Bittner argued that the use of force is the defining feature of American police.[31] Therefore, he argued, crime control will always be the core function of police work. This view of American policing seems to rule out any substantial deviation from the bureaucratic or professional model because community policing promotes the idea of police/community partnerships to produce order. In addition, community policing recommends a reprioritization of police functions to make controlling social disorder and provision of services more important.

The purpose of a paramilitary policing unit (PPU) or Special Weapons and Tactics (SWAT) unit in a police department is straightforward. These highly trained law enforcement bodies can be swiftly deployed with an impressive use of force. During the last 10 years when students of American policing were focusing mostly on an expansion of community policing, there also has been a less noticeable trend toward the militarization of some components of the American police. Peter Kraska and Louis Cubellis conducted a survey of police departments serving small jurisdictions of 25,000 to 50,000 citizens.[32] The 40 items of the survey were designed to collect data on the formation, prevalence, and activities of PPUs in small cities that had not previously had a paramilitary emphasis. More than half of the departments completed and returned the survey. Kraska and Cubellis noted three important findings. First, they found a rapid expansion of PPUs in these departments between 1985 and 1995 (an increase of 157 percent). More and more departments have established PPUs to call on for hostage situations, acts of terrorism, civil disturbances, and high-risk search and arrests—infrequent activities in small cities. Second, the establishment of a PPU was not linked to worsening conditions because there was no increase in crime rates, drug use, fear of crime or the economic problems in these small cities. Third, in Kraska and Cubellis' opinion, the emergence of the PPU represents a pent-up desire to return to an earlier era that was characterized by the wars on drugs and crime. In the light of these findings, one might conclude that rather than becoming more open and progressive, the police culture may be returning to a more paramilitaristic orientation and one that proved largely ineffective in dealing with the conditions and causes of crime in the 1970s.

The author believes that the growth of PPUs constitutes an uncertain force affecting the institutionalization of community policing, because any incident involving the police use of force can lead to conflict between police and residents in a community, particularly minority residents. The history of police-community relations in this country is replete with examples of peaceful demonstrations turning violent because of an inappropriate police action or because a controversial court decision appeared to exonerate police misconduct. The fact that PPUs are being established in small cities not as a result of an increase in crimes or social disorder but as an appeasement to a paramilitary culture suggests a grave error may be in the making. It could force a showdown between factions who embrace a community problem solving approach and factions who wish to return to the narrower mission of law enforcement and reactive policing.

The Role of the Police Unions

Research in community policing is almost completely silent on the relationship between police unions and organizational change. Police unions have played an important role in the history of American policing. In general, unions are not advocates for change. Unions tend more toward fighting for the benefits of ordinary employees and for power sharing with management.[33]

Unions operating in the public sector have similar interests to those in the private sector. Labor relations often take on the character of intense and tough "battles" with management to settle a host of issues connected primarily to the economic interests of employees.[34] In the recent history of police unions in America, there has been a tough "war" between management and unions concerning economic benefits and management discretion.[35] Recent research confirms that the collective bargaining by police unions does produce economic benefits for police officers.

In police departments that use collective bargaining, a number of management issues such as the allocation of manpower and structural change need the approval of police unions. In addition, any new department policies concerning disciplinary actions and employee benefits usually involve the participation of police unions. If unions are to play an important role in such managerial issues, then they might be expected to be heavily involved in the process of structural and operational changes brought about by community policing. For example, community policing encourages police officers to know their beats and interact with local residents, which could mean a longer shift assignment for individual officers. At this point, however, there is little information about the role of police unions in the implementation of community policing. The role of PPUs and police unions in the institutionalization of community policing will be determined over time.

The Future Direction of Community Policing

If organizational change is represented as a continuum between the bureaucratic style of policing during the professional era at one end and the community policing style of the community era at the other end, American policing might be described as making some progress away from the bureaucratic style toward the community policing style. Movement in such a direction does not mean, however, that community policing has been fully institutionalized.

Considering the positive, negative, and uncertain forces affecting the institutionalization of community policing, the authors predict that in the next five years community policing will neither be institutionalized in all American police departments nor abandoned. Probably, it will continue to be somewhere in the middle. The following suggests what students of policing might expect to see over the next few years:

Community policing innovations will continue to expand in police departments across the United States. Police departments will continue to explore new ways of doing things as long as the external environment remains dynamic, which is likely. More demands concerning crime, social disorder, and quality of life will force police departments and their leaders to respond and change. Community policing innovations are a good way to demonstrate that police departments are responsive to the needs of the community. There is little to risk for a local chief of police to implement outreach programs such as citizen academy, block watch, and storefront stations. These programs have been around for several years, and the public seems to like them. Programs that target crime reduction, such as weed and seed programs, also are well received. *Weed and seed* is a federally funded program that is divided into two parts. The *weed* part is strong law enforcement. Police target high-crime areas and officers intensify their law enforcement activities. The *seed* part focuses on community rebuilding, crime prevention, etc. The popularity of two types of program—crime-focused or prevention-focused—may depend on local crime trends. If the crime rate in a community has increased significantly, the crime-focused program will be given a high priority and vice versa. Either way, the police stand to lose little and gain the support of the public by trying innovative solutions.

I also expect that *change in the organizational structure of police departments will occur at a very slow pace.* Structural changes involve greater risks than programmatic changes because of the high investment of personnel in the current way of doing things. For example, to reduce the rank structure by eliminating the rank of lieutenant would take some time to get through city politics, rewrite job descriptions for sergeants and captains, develop new policies, and relocate the lieutenants. Modifying the span of organizational control and chain of command is always perceived as risky. Throughout police history, the structural arrangements in police departments have been relatively stable. Consequently, there is little reason to believe that substantial structural change will take place at a rapid pace any time in the near future.

Nevertheless, it is important to acknowledge the necessity of change. American society is changing and so are public-service agencies. Seen in this perspective, community policing is a part of broader social change. The current round of change in public-service agencies began in the late 1980s. The National Commission on the Public Service highlights the need for organizational change in public service by calling for a return to a public service ethic:

> The central message of this report of the Commission on the Public Service is both simple and profound, both urgent and timeless. In essence, we call for a *renewed* sense of commitment by all Americans to the highest traditions of the public service—to a public service responsive to the political will of the people and also protective of our constitutional values.[36]

Some scholars emphasize the need to change public-service practices—a theme commonly referred to as "reinventing government." In their book, David Osborne and Ted Gaebler provide a forceful argument that American public service is in crisis and that a fundamental change is essential for its survival:

> And then, in 1990, the bottom fell out. It was as if all our government had hit the wall, at the same time. Our states struggled with multibillion-dollar deficits. Our cities laid off thousands of employees. Our federal deficit ballooned toward $350 billion.[37]

The economic turnaround in the 1990s has changed much of the political landscape in America. Municipal governments have enjoyed a considerable economic surplus, and the economy remains strong across the country. Change is continuous and will surely affect police departments.

Crises like social turmoil and rising crime rates breed change in policing. This was the case for American policing during the late 1960s and 1970s when crime rates rose to an astonishing level, and the professional-style means of controlling crime proved to be ineffective. Today, police departments across the nation are in a much better position than they were 25 years ago. Seen from this perspective, there really is no compelling reason why police departments should make broad and sweeping organizational changes, as long as external sources are not beckoning their leadership to do so.

Unless police executives and employees share the same vision for how organizational change can serve both police personnel and the public, the future of substantial organizational change in American policing is likely to be slow. The future of community policing remains uncertain, at least in terms of the important dimension of organizational change. I think that although police departments will continue to make programmatic responses to the need for change that the external environment demands, community policing still has a way to go before it is institutionalized. But I do think it is headed in a forward direction.

Notes

1. Samuel Walker, *Sense and Nonsense About Crime* (Monterey, CA: Brooks/Cole, 1985).
2. Robert Trojanowicz and Bonnie Bucqueroux, *Community Policing: A Contemporary Perspective* (Cincinnati: Anderson, 1990). For a discussion of theoretical framework, see Harman Goldstein, *Policing a Free Society* (Cambridge, MA: Ballinger, 1977); John Angell, "Toward an Alternative to the Classic Police Organizational Arrangement: A Democratic Model," *Criminology* 8 (1971): 185–206.
3. Robert Yin, *Changing Urban Bureaucracies* (Lexington, MA: Lexington Books, 1979).
4. James Thompson, *Organizations in Action* (New York: McGraw-Hill, 1967).
5. There is very little research on the relationship between a change in organizational structure and COP innovations. To a large extent, there has been limited effort to change the structural arrangements of a police department in order to make COP programs permanent. Please also see Jack Greene, William Bergman, and Edward McLaughlin, "Implementing Community Policing: Cultural and Structural Change in Police Organizations," in *The Challenge of Community Policing: Testing the Promises,* ed. Dennis Rosenbaum (Thousand Oaks, CA: Sage, 1994), pp. 92–109.
6. Please see two books on this topic: Dennis Rosenbaum, *The Challenge of Community Policing: Testing the Promises* (Thousand Oaks, CA: Sage, 1994); and Quint Thurman and Edmund McGarrell, *Community Policing in a Rural Setting* (Cincinnati, OH: Anderson, 1997).
7. Mary Ann Wycoff, "The Benefits of Community Policing: Evidence and Conjecture," in *Community Policing: Rhetoric or Reality?* eds. Jack Greene and Stephen Mastrofski (New York: Praeger, 1988), pp. 103–120.
8. Please see the discussion in Jack Greene and Stephen Mastrofski, *Community Policing: Rhetoric or Reality?* (New York: Praeger, 1988). The programs were the early phase of implementation of community policing.
9. Please see Chapter 10 in Quint C. Thurman, Jihong Zhao, and Andrew Giacomazzi, *Community Policing in a Community Era: An Introduction and Exploration* (Los Angeles: Roxbury Publishing Company, 2000), which focuses on the implementation of community policing.
10. William DeJong, *Building the Peace: The Resolving Conflict Creatively Program (RCCP)* (Washington, DC: National Institute of Justice, 1994).
11. National Institute of Justice, *Criminal Justice Research Under the Crime Act—1995 to 1996* (Washington, DC: U.S. Department of Justice, 1997), p. 2.
12. Office of Community Oriented Policing Services, *Community Caps* (Washington, DC: U.S. Department of Justice, February/March, 1997).
13. William Bratton, *Turnaround: How America's Top Cop Reversed the Crime Epidemic* (New York: Random House, 1998), p. 239.
14. The above information was obtained on the website of the New York Police Department at *http://www.ci.nyc.ny.us/html/nypd/html/.*
15. New York Police Department News Release 268-97 (May 13, 1997). "Mayor Giuliani De-

livers Keynote Address at the International CompStat Conference."

16. The discussion about the ICAM program is adapted from Thomas Rich, "The Chicago Police Department's Information Collection for Automated Mapping (ICAM) Program," *Program Focus* (Washington, DC: National Institute of Justice, 1996).
17. Bureau of Justice Statistics, *Crime and Victims Statistics* (1998). The above data were obtained from the Bureau of Justice Statistics website at *http://www.ojp.usdoj.gov/bjs/cvict.htm.*
18. The Office of Community Oriented Policing Services, "Americans' Law Enforcement to Receive Community Policing Boost," Press Release (Wednesday, November 25, 1998).
19. Please see Chapter 5 in Quint C. Thurman, Jihong Zhao, and Andrew Giacomazzi, *Community Policing in a Community Era: An Introduction and Exploration* (Los Angeles: Roxbury Publishing Company, 2000) for a discussion. Also see Alfred Blumstein and Richard Rosenfeld, "Assessing the Recent Ups and Downs in U.S. Homicide Rates," National Institute of Justice Journal (Washington, DC: U.S. Department of Justice, October, 1998).
20. "Mayor Giuliani Delivers Keynote Address at the International CompStat Conference."
21. John Eck and Dennis Rosenbaum, "The New Police Order: Effectiveness, Equity, and Efficiency in Community Policing," in *The Challenge of Community Policing,* ed. Dennis Rosenbaum (Thousand Oaks, CA: Sage, 1994), pp. 3–26.
22. Mark Moore, "Research Synthesis and Policy Implications," in *The Challenge of Community Policing,* ed. Dennis Rosenbaum (Thousand Oaks, CA: Sage, 1994), pp. 285–299.
23. Jayne Seagrave, "Defining Community Policing," *American Journal of Police* 15 (1996): 1–22.
24. Frederick Winslow Taylor, *Scientific Management* (New York: Harper & Row, 1947).
25. Max Weber, in *From Max Weber: Essays in Sociology,* ed. C. Wright Mills and trans. Hans H. Gerth (New York: Oxford University Press, 1977).
26. Luther Gulick, "Notes on the Theory of Organization," in *Papers on the Science of Administration,* ed. Luther Gulick and L. Urwick (New York: Institute of Public Administration, 1937).
27. Lawrence James and Allan Jones, "Organizational Structure: A Review of Structural Dimension and Their Conceptual Relationships With Individual Attitudes and Behavior," *Organizational Behavior and Human Performance* 16 (1976): 74–113.
28. Peter Blau, "A Formal Theory of Differentiation in Organizations," *American Sociological Review* 35 (1970): 201–218.
29. The three books are Dennis Rosenbaum, *The Challenge of Community Policing: Testing the Promises* (Thousand Oaks, CA: Sage, 1994); Peter Kratcoski and D. Dukes, *Issues in Community Policing* (Cincinnati: Anderson, 1995); and Geoffrey Alpert and Alex Piquero, *Community Policing: Contemporary Readings* (Prospect Heights, IL: Waveland, 1998).
30. For a discussion see: Farimorz Damanpour, "Organizational Innovation: A Meta-Analysis of Effects of Determinants and Moderators," *Academy of Management Journal* 34 (1991): 555–590.
31. Egon Bittner, *The Functions of Police in Modern Society* (Washington, DC: National Institute of Mental Health, 1970).
32. Peter Kraska and Louis Cubellis, "Militarizing Mayberry and Beyond: Making Sense of American Paramilitary Policing," *Justice Quarterly* 14 (1997): 607–629.
33. Samuel Walker, *A Critical History of Police Reform* (Lexington, MA: D. C. Heath, 1977).
34. T. Chandler and R. Gely, "Union and Management Organizational Structure for Bargaining in the Public Sector," in *Handbook of Public Sector Labor Relations,* eds. Jack Rabin, Thomas Vocino, W. Bartley Hildreth, and Gerald Miller (New York: Marcel Dekker, 1994).
35. For a discussion on the history of police unions and management relations please see International Association of Chiefs of Police, *Critical Issues in Police Labor Relations* (Gaithersburg, MD: IACP, 1974); Steven Rynecki and Michael Morse, *Police Collective Bargaining Agreements: A National Management Survey* (Washington, DC: Police Executive Research Forum, 1981); and David Carter and Allen Sapp, "A Comparative Analysis of Clauses in Police Collective Bargaining Agreements as Indicators of Change in

Labor Relations," *American Journal of Policing 12* (1992): 17–46.

36. Volcker Commission, "Leadership for America: Rebuilding the Public Service," cited in *Classics of Public Personnel Policy,* ed. Frank Thompson, (Pacific Grove, CA: Brooks/Cole, 1991), pp. 386–390.
37. David Osborne and Ted Gaebler, *Reinventing Government: How the Entrepreneurial Spirit Is Transforming the Public Sector, From Schoolhouse to City Hall to the Pentagon* (Reading, MA: Addison-Wesley, 1992), p. 1.

Jihong Zhao, "The Future of Policing in a Community Era." Adapted from Quint C. Thurman, Jihong Zhao, and Andrew Giacomazzi (Eds.), *Community Policing in a Community Era: An Introduction and Exploration,* pp. 296–310. Copyright © 2000 by Roxbury Publishing Company. All rights reserved. ✦

Chapter 30
Future Issues in Policing
Challenges for Leaders

Sheldon Greenberg

Using the list of issues published in the Encyclopedia of the Future, *Sheldon Greenberg identifies a number of challenging issues for American policing. For example, reducing public fear of crime remains a major challenge. It was not until the 1970s that police administrators realized that the fear of crime can lead to instability and insecurity in a community.*

The publication of Wilson and Kelling's "Broken Windows" thesis in 1982 highlighted the intimate relationship between public fear and neighborhood decay and disorganization. However, the exact relationship between fear and criminal victimization remains tenuous. For example, fear can be irrational. Seniors tend to have a greater fear of crime than younger people, although their rate of actual victimization is much lower. Can the police reduce public fear? The answer is yes, but the cost may prove staggering.

> The future never just happened. It was created.
>
> —Will Durant

Defining future issues facing American police service is not easy. Just as the future is different for individuals, it varies significantly for law enforcement agencies. Factors such as locale, political environment, economics, and others determine how an agency and its employees will view and react to the future.

Definition of the term *future* also comes into play when discussing key issues. For some police leaders, the future is the next fiscal year. For others, it is a three- to five-year span of time toward which they have set into motion a strategic planning process. Yet, for others, the future is next Friday and surviving without a crisis until their next day off. Any discussion of future issues in policing must consider the short term as well as the long term and must give attention to operational issues, administrative issues, the community, and the basic philosophy of policing.

The *Encyclopedia of the Future* (Kurian and Molitor, 1995) identified numerous important issues facing the police, political leaders, and the community. This analysis drew upon a wide spectrum of information, ranging from reviewing current research and discussions with police executives to studies conducted on policing agencies. Listed below are 36 of the issues identified as important (not ranked by priority):

- Reducing citizen fear
- Reducing violence and sustaining the reduction
- Maintaining and demonstrating integrity and ethics
- Community policing
- Accountability for 100,000 additional police officers
- Declining federal funding for local police
- Federal agencies dictating local police strategies
- Viability of crime control models (such as the NYPD model, CompStat)
- Police infringement on individual rights as a byproduct of zero tolerance
- Independent civilian review boards
- The value of the police agencies to communities

- The role of the police in economic development
- Infusing new technology into police service—over-reliance on technology to cure all ills
- Technology-related crime
- Changing nature of narcotics use and trafficking
- The loss of experience in police agencies
- Patrol officers as leaders in identifying and handling crime patterns
- Crimes against children (pornography, child abuse, drugs, alcohol)
- Changing community demographics
- Competition for highly qualified police recruits
- Changing nature of suburbia
- Mandating higher education for police (the national Police Corps experiment)
- Proliferation of small criminal factions (independent gangs, pseudo gangs)
- Urban terrorism in United States
- Modifying police academy curricula (adult education, maximizing time)
- Accreditation of police agencies
- Resource allocation—improving efficiency and productivity
- Political influence on local police
- Changing police work schedules
- Reliance on early warning systems to identify potentially troubled officers
- Reducing ranks—flattening the structure
- Changing role of first-line supervisor
- Developing police leaders
- Labor/management relations
- Marketing the police
- Need for research, experimentation, innovation at the local level

Police leaders need to consider these and other issues relevant to their agencies and communities. Occasionally, command meetings and discussion groups with supervisors, officers, and civilian employees should center on an issue of importance. Personnel matters, policy matters, internal affairs cases, and budget concerns should be put aside during the meetings to allow open dialogue on how the agency copes with the issue. Such sessions are invaluable in formulating new approaches and assessing existing activities. The following pages address some of the key issues that police leaders will face. Many of the discussions pose questions rather than suggest answers.

Accountability to the Public for 100,000 Police Officers

One of the most pressing near-term issues that will be shared by large and small police agencies is the anticipated demand by the public for accountability for the millions of dollars spent to place 100,000 more police officers on the streets of the nation's cities, counties, and towns. The current downturn in violent crime has afforded police agencies, particularly those in large urban centers, with a temporary reprieve. The newness of community policing and problem solving to the public provides an additional reprieve.

Several factors may change the public's attitude and place increased and significant pressure on police agencies and executives to "make good" on their commitment to the public for the additional officers. The most significant will be any sustained increase in violent and other serious crime. It will be a relatively short period of time before the media and politicians, especially those out to replace their chiefs of police or sheriffs, begin to probe to determine if COPS (Office of Community Oriented Policing Services, U.S. Department of Justice) grant objectives have been met. Regardless of size, those agencies that failed to commit adequately to community policing, or used COPS officers to supplant hiring, may suffer politically, legally, and within the community.

Reducing Citizen Fear

Serious crime is down. Violent crime is down. Many of the nation's large and small jurisdictions have been publicizing the reduction of crime for five or more years. Yet, the reduction in crime has had minimal, if any, effect on reducing citizens' fear of crime. Reducing fear—not simply crime statistics—will be a major challenge facing police leaders in the future.

For generations, police officials have espoused that policing to the public's perception or fear of crime is as important as policing to the reality of crime. However, few police leaders and officers know anything about fear. What is it? How does it work? What is the cycle of fear? How can a police officer or deputy intervene to break the cycle? Why is fear contagious? What do the police do as a matter of routine to spark fear? Do problem solving, partnering, and the implementation of crime control strategies and tactics reduce fear?

An exploratory survey of 28 police academies revealed that not one offered recruits or in-service personnel a course of instruction on fear. Several police academy officials noted that *fear of crime* was addressed in courses on patrol techniques, victim assistance, and community policing. These academies presented information on the goal of the police to reduce fear of crime. None addressed the social and physical disorder [which are] the primary determinants of fear. Addressing fear of crime is not, necessarily, related to fear.

Recently, a police officer handling a theft from an auto call told the victim that he would have arrived sooner if the dispatcher had not made a mistake in broadcasting the address. He went on to talk about the police department being short of personnel and the lack of sufficient officers to handle the community's demands. In another recent situation, a deputy sheriff responding to a routine vandalism call told the victim that such calls were not a high priority and that the agency had to focus its resources on more serious crimes. What effect did this officer and deputy have on citizens' fear? What effect did they have in building public confidence in the police?

There is a need for every officer, regardless of rank or position, to be trained in the practical aspects of fear. They should be taught to assess causes and levels of individual, neighborhood, and community fear. They should be taught intervention techniques so that, during a simple conversation, they may alleviate rather than exacerbate the victim's or witness's apprehension.

Fear is a disease, and if untreated it fosters and slowly infects and takes over its host, the community. It inhibits normal functioning and paralyzes the citizens. It has several causes, most related to a person's environment, experience, and values. Fear is a complex phenomenon that has many causes, including those involving the environment and personal experiences and values.

Police have long thought that fear and crime were directly related. That is, a reduction in criminal behavior, as evidenced by crime statistics, would be followed by a reduction of fear. Unfortunately, this is not the case. Simple reductions in criminal behavior may not lead to reductions in fear. To cure the disease, the police first need to understand the underlying causes.

Changing Drug Trade

United Nations and other intelligence reports have indicated that the South American drug cartel has moved heavily into growing poppy for the purpose of producing heroin. Further evidence suggests that the cartel has a price-fixing strategy to convert cocaine users to the longer-lived addiction to heroin.

Heroin is quickly reclaiming its place as a "common" commodity—a leading drug of choice. In addition to being reasonably priced, new forms of heroin allow users to ingest [it] through smoking and other means. These new methods of use create a new market among users who may have feared the pain, scarring and disease associated with the more traditional "shooting up" with needles. As a result of new ways to use heroin, a rapidly increasing number of young women are turning to the drug, increasing the likelihood of adversely affecting children. In the past, heroin was a drug used predominantly by men.

In explaining the reduction in drug related violence over the past several years, many police and government leaders make reference to successful enforcement, problem solving, and educational efforts that reduced the use of crack and other forms of cocaine. Few, however, pose questions about where the former cocaine users have gone.

Most police agencies remain reactive to the drug trade. Traditional approaches prevail. These include street corner sweeps, arresting users and low-level dealers, relying on specialists (narcotics units) to assume primary responsibility for enforcement, and participating in regional task forces (generally when funded by the federal government).

Police leaders will have to "think out of the box" in the future in response to a changing drug market. A well-planned, strategic approach to the drug trade and problem solving related to drugs will be needed in every sized agency. More agencies must become involved in teaching employees about drug market analysis and forecasting. Police leaders will have to embrace and lobby for rehabilitation of offenders. While it brings few awards to politicians who support it, rehabilitation on a larger scale will be a primary tool in reducing crime caused by the drug market.

Two factors set apart the coming heroin epidemic from problems caused by heroin trafficking in years past. First, as stated, new forms of heroin use have emerged. Others will evolve that make it easier and cheaper to use. People—particularly young people—will be provided with an array of alternatives for consuming heroin. Second, while property crimes will increase, those committing the crimes will have grown up in an environment more prone to violence. It is feasible that a confrontation with police that may have caused a burglar or other perpetrator of property crime to run may now result in aggression or injury.

Should a police agency change its procedures and tactics? What are police agencies doing to prepare officers—particularly patrol officers—for the heroin "epidemic?" How will heroin users react when confronted by a police officer? What medical dilemmas does the heroin user pose? How will the drug affect women? These are but a few of the questions the changing drug trade poses for the foreseeable future.

Violence

In both the immediate and distant future, police will continue to deal with "the new violence" that has emerged over the past five to ten years. Far too many police executives have relished in and taken credit for the reduction in violent crime that has been realized in most jurisdictions. On the other hand, few are focusing on the nature of the violence that has been occurring.

In the past, violence was an end to a means. Revenge, robbery, and jealousy were among the many reasons that people resorted to violence. Today, an entire culture has emerged that sees the use of violence as an end unto itself. The people who make up this culture—gangs, pseudo gangs, well-armed young people, and others—are not going to change their way of thinking or relax their hostility and aggression simply because there is a fluctuation in drug usage or a switch from cocaine to heroin.

For many, violence has become a way of life, just as for others peace has become a way of life. For these people, the wanton use of violence—aggression for the sake of aggression—is not considered abhorrent behavior. Taken in combination, these factors present challenges for police leaders. Police will have to be trained and educated to understand violent behavior far beyond what they are given today.

Community Policing

"Community policing has changed the way police do business," stated a chief of police during a conference sponsored by a regional community policing institute. At the same conference, another chief said, "Community policing is a patient in critical condition whose survival looks bleak."

Determining whether community policing is a philosophy that forges the foundation of quality police service or simply a "flavor of the month" to be referenced in the history books is one of the most challenging and important significant issues facing executives in police service. Since passage of the Crime Bill, much of the growth and progress in law enforcement has been connected to community policing. The President's commitment to placing 100,000 more police officers on the nation's streets is tied directly to community policing. Extensive technical assistance, training, and research have been funded by federal agencies to support community policing. Thousands of police agencies have publicly embraced community policing.

Yet, many questions remain. For example, how many police agencies have made a commitment to community policing? How many agencies have demonstrated the link between community policing and the quality of the embraced community policing to gain a share of available federal dollars? Will community policing endure without federal funding?

The Office of Community Oriented Policing Services of the U.S. Department of Justice has been a primary source of funds and support to police agencies. Federal legislation mandates that the Office of Community Oriented Policing Services be dismantled in the year 2000. Will the legacy of the COPS office be sustained? Will community policing prevail as a philosophy and road map for the future? Or will it fade and become yet another failed policing innovation?[1]

Hard questions must be asked as police leaders look to the future. What expectations have police and political leaders set for community policing? Are they realistic? What are the motives? How is community policing being entrenched within the organization? Do supervisors and officers embrace community policing? Do they simply manipulate the system or go through the motions to meet community policing mandates?

Partnerships

As part of community policing and doing good business, police agencies have turned to creating partnerships with neighborhoods, community organizations, businesses, and others. Partnerships have been emphasized in literature, policy, education and training programs, and news and popular media. Much of society has come to realize that the police cannot function independently to address crime and disorder and are willing to create partnerships. In many jurisdictions, beat officers have been mandated to "partner" as part of their regular duties.

There is, however, more to creating and sustaining effective partnerships. As they currently exist in most jurisdictions, many partnerships are ineffective. In fact, they may be more detrimental than helpful in effecting long-term positive change. The challenge to leaders, now and in the future, is to develop meaningful and lasting partnerships rather than the superficial relationships that exist in most communities. Far too many agencies have entered into partnerships because they seemed right. Others have entered into partnerships with neighborhood groups and community organizations because they provide short-term public relations benefits or meet the requirement of federal grants. Few have entered long-term partnerships oriented toward the alleviation of crime and fear of crime.

Community policing calls for police officers to be "empowered" and many police executives contend that empowerment has been bestowed. Yet, few officers and deputies feel comfortable exhibiting authority on behalf of their agency or making significant decisions when attending neighborhood or community meetings.

For many police officers, the concept of partnership means simply attending occasional neighborhood association meetings or occasionally visiting neighborhood leaders who live on their beat. Other officers feel frustrated because they know that partnerships are important but believe their role to be one of public relations hype rather than substance.

Neighborhood residents and business people who attend community meetings and get to know officers tend to have their expectations raised toward some additional or extraordinary performance by the police. They believe their needs are going to be met in a better way.

Partnerships for the sake of partnership do not endure. Partnerships only work when the mutual benefits to the parties involved are well defined, well understood, and attainable. In fact, superficial partnerships backfire. For example, at a community meeting, residents expressed their concern about several thefts from garages and sheds that occurred over a brief period of time. Little had been stolen. They asked if patrols could be increased in the area. The police officer in attendance responded by telling the audience about the police department being shorthanded. The officer went on to tell the people that there was little chance of their crimes being solved and that the police department was targeting violence reduction as its priority. While the officer achieved his goal of attending and participating in the meeting, little good came from the encounter. The officer believed he was being candid. He gave little thought to the frustration he caused or fear he reinforced.

This scenario is repeated with far too much frequency. As police leaders look to change the nature of partnerships, emphasis must be placed on quality. Endurance, too, is important, but only if the goals of the partnership require a long-term commitment. Executives must grasp that not all partnerships should be everlasting. There are ways to achieve quality and endurance. Toward this end, several important questions must be asked before any partnership is forged:

- What is the purpose of the partnership and what are the projected outcomes?
- Who are the key players in the partnership?
- What is the experience of the key players in working with partners?
- What do the partners stand to gain or lose by participating?
- Are both partners worthy of participating in the partnership?
- Are the right players involved in the partnership (neighborhood leaders, residents, local business people, police officers, police supervisors)?
- Are officers comfortable with their position and authority to make the decisions necessary, support the outcomes of the partnership?
- Are the outcomes of the partnership well stated?
- How will the success of the partnership be measured?
- Are employees trained and well versed in the nature of partnerships?
- How much time will be allowed before the assessment occurs and a determination is made to continue or disband the partnership?

Resource Allocation

If the quality of policing is to progress, a greater number of police leaders will need to know more about resource allocation than currently exists. At a conference involving 125 police executives, questions were posed about knowledge and experience in allocating resources. The questions focused on workload analysis, scheduling, and beat alignment. Only 25 of the executives acknowledged that they had hands-on experience allocating resources through analysis. Only 15 of the 25 believed that the process adequately placed officers where they were needed most.

With the decline in federal funding for additional police officers, combined with local, state, and federal belt-tightening, greater emphasis will be placed on using available resources as efficiently as possible. Yet, few police executives and supervisors receive education and training in resource management and personnel allocation.

Some executives have grown in agencies in which resource allocation is handled by computer. Others have functioned in environments in which the number of officers provided to the agency is dictated by fiscal or political authorities. Many officials have committed simply to placing all available resources in patrol, often to the detriment of specialty units.

All police leaders, regardless of rank, should be versed in resource allocation skills. Analysis of workload and resources should be part of every supervisor's and executive's routine functioning. Justifying resources should be based on more than perception, statistics such as increased calls for service, and a simple belief that more is better. Once learned, resource allocation is neither overwhelmingly time consuming nor difficult. It becomes second nature. With the predicted reduction in federal funds for local police and a tightening of local budgets, a commitment to quality allocation of resources is essential.

Closing Comment

This is an exciting and challenging time in the history of police service. No matter what issues lie ahead, the public will continue to expect a high degree of service from its police. And this expectation will be met as it has always been met. Any time of day or night, citizens will receive quality response from professional police officers. Officers and deputies will continue to care, perform their tasks diligently, and meet whatever challenges are presented to them. Exceptions will continue be rare.

Today's leaders and those who follow will determine whether police agencies embrace their communities or return to being distant and aloof. They will look at the value of police service in new ways and demonstrate the positive effect a police or sheriff's department has on the overall quality and economic viability of neighborhoods. They will deal with unforeseen problems caused by new drugs, small but hostile groups of extremists, young people who were raised in an environment of violence, and more. They have the opportunity to deal with these issues supported by advanced technology, highly evolved information resources, better-trained officers and deputies, and a heightened commitment to interjurisdictional cooperation.

> The best preparation for good work tomorrow is to do good work today.
>
> —Elbert Hubbard

Editors' Note

1. The COPS office still exists today, although in recent years its funding has been dramatically reduced.

References

Kurian, G. T. and Molitor, G. T. T., eds. (1995). *Encyclopedia of the Future.* New York: Macmillan Library Reference USA.

Wilson, J. Q., and Kelling, G. L. (1982, March). "Broken Windows: The Police and Neighborhood Safety." *Atlantic Monthly, 249,* 29–38.

Sheldon Greenberg, "Future Issues in Policing: Challenges for Leaders." Reprinted from Ron Glensor, Mark Correia, and Ken Peak (Eds.), *Policing Communities: Understanding Crime and Solving Problems,* pp. 315–321. Copyright © 2000 by Roxbury Publishing Company. All rights reserved. ✦